International Sociological Association/ISA
CURRENT SOCIOLOGY
Association Internationale de Sociologie/La sociologie contemporaine

Volume 35
Number 1
Spring 1987

Economic Sociology: Past and Present

PART I
The Tradition of Economic Sociology, 1800s–1960s

PART II
Towards a New Economic Sociology

Richard Swedberg

SAGE Publications

Editor
James A. Beckford
Department of Sociology, University of Durham,
Durham DH1 3JT

Published three times a year by
SAGE Publications
London, Newbury Park, Beverly Hills, New Delhi
under the auspices of the International Sociological Association/ISA.
Subscription and advertising details available from
SAGE Publications Ltd, 28 Banner Street, London EC1Y 8QE, UK.
Institutions £47/$70.50; Individuals £22/$33
Second class postage paid at Westwood, NJ 07675 (or application to mail at second class postage rate is pending at Westwood, NJ 07675). Air freight and mailing in the USA by PSCA, 40 Carver Avenue, Westwood, NJ 07675.

ISSN 0011-3921
Printed by J.W. Arrowsmith Ltd, Bristol, UK

Current Sociology is regularly listed in *Current Contents* and abstracted in *Sociological Abstracts*.

CURRENT SOCIOLOGY
La sociologie contemporaine

The Journal of the International Sociological Association/
Association Internationale de Sociologie

Volume 35 Number 1 Spring 1987

Economic Sociology: Past and Present

PART I
The Tradition of Economic Sociology, 1800s–1960s

PART II
Towards a New Economic Sociology

Richard Swedberg

SAGE Publications

Contents

About the Author, v
Acknowledgements, vii
Foreword by Ulf Himmelstrand, ix

ECONOMIC SOCIOLOGY:
PAST AND PRESENT

Richard Swedberg

Introduction, 1

PART I
THE TRADITION OF ECONOMIC SOCIOLOGY,
1800s–1960s

1
Economics and Sociology – Early Clashes, 11

2
The Launching of Economic Sociology,
1890–1920, 25

3
European Economic Sociology, 1920s–1960s, 42

4
The 'Economy and Society' Perspective in
US Sociology, 53

PART II
TOWARDS A NEW ECONOMIC SOCIOLOGY, 1960s–?
Introduction, 63

5
Women in the Economy, 65

6
The Neo-Marxist Contribution, 78

7
The International Dimension, 91

8
The Sociology of Markets, 105

9
The New Relationship between
Economics and Sociology, 119

Notes, 135

Résumé, 145

Bibliography, 155

Author Index, 216

About the Author

Richard Swedberg is Assistant Professor ('forskarassistent') in the University of Stockholm's Department of Sociology. He is the author of *Sociology as Disenchantment* (1982) and several articles on economic sociology. He has a PhD in sociology from Boston College in Boston, Mass. and a LLB from the University of Stockholm. Dr Swedberg was born in 1948 and is presently working on a study of economic power.

Acknowledgements

I would first of all like to thank Ulf Himmelstrand of Uppsala University, who has been extremely helpful and let me work on this report within the framework of Project IDEA (Interdisciplinary Dimensions of Economic Analysis). A special thanks should also be directed to James Beckford, Editor of *Current Sociology*.

There are, in addition, a huge number of people who have kindly answered my and Ulf Himmelstrand's questions or otherwise been helpful: Samir Amin (UNITAR), Bo Anderson (State University of Michigan), Kenneth Arrow (Stanford University), Ivar Berg (Vanderbilt University), Fred Block (University of Pennsylvania), Rae Lesser Blumberg (University of California at San Diego), Göran Brulin (Uppsala University), Severyn Bruyn (Boston College), Tom Burns (Uppsala University), Peter Ekegren (Uppsala University), Amitai Etzioni (George Washington University), Helena Flam (University of Lund), Matz Franzén (University of Uppsala), Jonathan I. Gershuny (University of Bath), John Goldthorpe (Nuffield College, Oxford), Mark Granovetter (State University of New York at Stony Brook), Peter Hedström (Harvard University and the Institute for Social Research in Stockholm), Björn Hettne (University of Göthenburg), Paul Hirst (Birkbeck College, London), Morris Janowitz (University of Chicago), Rosabeth Moss Kanter (Yale University), Franz-Xaver Kaufmann (Universität Bielefeld, Germany), Raimo Korpela (University Library of Stockholm), Tarmo Koskinen (University of Vaasa, Finland), David Samuel Krusé (Boston College), Eric M. Leifer (University of North Carolina at Chapel Hill), Hakon Leiulfsrud (Uppsala University), Donald Levine (University of Chicago), Siegwart Lindenberg (University of Groningen, Holland), Harry Makler (University of Toronto), Alberto Martinelli (Universita degli Studi di Milano), Lee Mintz (Harvard University), K.P. Moseley (University of Port Harcourt, Nigeria), Karl-Dieter Opp (Universität Hamburg), Alejandro Portes (Johns Hopkins University), Michael Rose (University of Bath), Günther Roth (University of Washington), Arnaud Sales (Université de Montréal), Paul Samuelson (M.I.T.), Michael Schwartz (State University of New York at Stony Brook), Endre Sik (University of Economics in Budapest), Neil Smelser (University of California at Berkeley), Aage Sorensen (Harvard

University), Rudi Supek (Yugoslavia), Hans Swedberg (S-E-Banken), Göran Therborn (Katholieke Universiteit Nijmegen, Holland), Steve Turner (Harvard University), Lars Udéhn (Uppsala University), Hildur Ve (Sociological Institute, Bergen, Norway), Immanuel Wallerstein (State University of New York at Binghamton), Harrison C. White (Harvard University), Norbert Wiley (University of Illinois at Urbana-Champaign), Johannes Winkelmann (Kommission für Sozial- und Wirtschaftsgeschichte bei der Bayerischen Akademie der Wissenschaften), Nanzy Zapheris (Widener Library, Harvard University), Maurice Zeitlin (University of California at Los Angeles) and Lynne G. Zucker (University of California at Los Angeles).

Stockholm,
July 1986

Foreword to Economic Sociology: Past and Present

Ulf Himmelstrand
University of Uppsala, Sweden

In his thorough exploration and tentative mapping out of the territory of economic sociology, Richard Swedberg often quotes Joseph Schumpeter. When reflecting on the habit of economists of invading the sociological field whenever they are in need of institutional or broadly 'exogenous' explanations of economic behaviour, Schumpeter identifies this field as 'a no-man's land or everyman's land — that might conveniently be called economic sociology'. However, when some nineteenth-century sociologists like Auguste Comte and Franklin H. Giddings not only attempted to claim this territory for sociology, but also to use it as a base for attacks on the 'unscientific' nature of economics, then the more established discipline of economics struck back and succeeded in relegating sociologists to a domain of 'left overs'.

Today we often hear references to a 'garbage can' of factors which no other established discipline has cared to elaborate systematically, but which they feel free to invade whenever they find it necessary to refer to the possible but rarely documented effects of 'exogenous factors'. This is the soil where economic sociology grew its first seedlings.

With its extended historical perspective on the development of economics and economic sociology, the opening chapters of Swedberg's Trend Report on economic sociology clarify how the development of economics itself — from the broad-ranging social science of Adam Smith to the precisely and narrowly delimited area of neoclassical doctrine — has helped to set the stage for the emergence and development of sociology, and economic sociology in particular. The area of 'left overs', the 'garbage can' of exogenous factors, has steadily increased in volume as a result of the self-imposed limitations of modern economic theory, and thereby made more territory available for the development of economic sociology.

But why would a powerful member of the social science community give up territory and withdraw into a more narrowly defined domain, leaving a sizable remainder to its less powerful and less established siblings to explore?

These kinds of questions have often been answered in terms of the need to develop some kind of division of labour among the social sciences, in view of the growing complexity of society generated by the advent and development of capitalism. Economists maintain that they are simply in a better position to do a decent and scientifically laudable job if they can concentrate on the strictly economic while leaving the remainder to the rest of us. However, I believe that there is an ideological element involved as well.

Again, Schumpeter has formulated one of the crucial questions on this point, even if not everyone would agree with his answers. He asserted that 'the deepest problem of the economic sociology of our epoch' has been to find out whether modern imperialist tendencies 'grew out of the very logic of capitalist evolution, or were distortions of it, traceable to extracapitalist influences'.

Obviously it is more palatable, from a certain ideological standpoint, to explain distasteful aspects of life in contemporary society in terms of 'extracapitalist influences'. By externalizing what is distasteful, and by attributing it to other processes and factors than those accountable in the terms of economic theory, other social science disciplines are left not only with what is exogenous in some purely neutral 'scientific' sense, but also with what is considered ideologically distasteful by a true believer in the system of free enterprise and market economy.

To the extent that such an ideological element has been involved in drawing lines of distinction between sociology and economics, it certainly has not been a constant element. Keynesian theory and the Stockholm school of economics have included, rather than excluded, the 'distasteful' political factor in the economy.

The question that emerges from this thumbnail sketch of the history of frontier problems and disputes between sociology and economics, is whether sociology, and economic sociology in particular, has been able to evolve and develop any identity of its own reasonably independent from what is simply 'left over' from economics. What does such an independently raised breed of sociology look like, and what is its relationship to the economics of today? These are questions which occupy a great deal of attention in Swedberg's Trend Report.

One of the several virtues of Swedberg's learned exposition of the meandering development of economic sociology is his talent for finding thought-provoking and witty quotations in the works of major and minor classics. It seems as if I have been particularly taken by quotations from Schumpeter, and so the last quotation in this Foreword will again be from him when he discusses more superficial forms of co-operation between economists and sociologists: 'Cross-fertilization might easily result in cross-sterilization', he says.

Perhaps, but under what conditions? Under what conditions will a cross-fertilization of sociology and economics really fertilize, not sterilize? On this point it is significant that the earlier tendency of economists to give up territory, and withdraw into a more limited field, is nowadays being transformed into the opposite tendency — which even the contenders of this approach unashamedly label 'scientific imperialism'. This means that the basic tenets of economic theory are supposed to be valid also in other social science fields such as government, love affairs and family life, education, etc. One of the main proponents of this approach, Gary Becker, has been made Professor of Sociology at the University of Chicago. Now again, where is economic sociology in all this? Swedberg addresses this question, too, of course.

Rational expectations and rational choice are key concepts in this new 'imperialistic' brand of economics which is trying to invade the traditional lands of sociology. Attempts to expand the reach of these concepts beyond the traditional domains of economics will succeed in accomplishing only one thing, I believe. It will convincingly demonstrate perhaps not the limited reach, but the limited potency, of these concepts.

There is no question about the applicability, and in that sense the reach, of the concepts of rationality in various social science disciplines. But whenever you apply these concepts you encounter numerous cases where you must refer to 'disturbing' or 'missing' factors in order to be able to explain particular results which would seem rather difficult to explain within established models of rational behaviour. It looks as if the 'disturbing' or 'missing', seemingly non-rational factors in rational behaviour are the really determining and significant factors. Rationality then turns out to be only the medium through which a number of extra-rational factors operate.

The concept of rationality remains empty until you specify the social, normative and cognitive premises of rational decision-making, and the social and psychological options and constraints operating in the course of rational implementation. Therefore you can never separate what is social and what is rational in man. The social is involved in the rational; and the rational in the social. This is the domain where the paradigm of economic sociology is emerging.

Economic Sociology: Past and Present

Richard Swedberg

INTRODUCTION

> The Econ tribe occupies a vast territory in the far North. Their land appears bleak and dismal to the outsider, and travelling through it makes for rough sledding; but the Econ, through a long period of adaptation, have learned to wrest a living of sorts from it. They are not without some genuine and sometimes even fierce attachment to their ancestral grounds, and their young are brought up to feel contempt for the softer living in the warmer lands of their neighbours, such as the Polscis and the Sociogs. Despite a common genetic heritage, relations with these tribes are strained — the distrust and contempt that the average Econ feels for these neighbours being heartily reciprocated by the latter — and social intercourse with them is inhibited by numerous taboos. The extreme clannishness, not to say xenophobia, of the Econ makes life among them difficult and perhaps even somewhat dangerous to the outsider . . . More research on this interesting tribe is badly needed.
>
> Axel Leijonhufvud, 'Life among the Econ' (1973)

From the quotation above, which is taken from Axel Leijonhufvud's delightful satire of the economic profession (31), it is clear that the relationship between economists and sociologists is filled with tension. We have nevertheless decided to try to account for the contribution that sociology can make to the study of economics in this issue of *Current Sociology*, well aware of the 'taboos' against such an undertaking.

Our focus in this issue will be on the history of economic sociology and its recent development. Our first theme is that economic sociology needs to be re-established as a distinct field of sociological inquiry. We say 're-established' because the project of economic sociology — as well as the term 'economic sociology' — is to be found in the works of the classical sociologists, such as Max Weber and Emile Durkheim.[1] Our second theme is that economic sociology, roughly since the early 1970s, has entered a new and very exciting stage. Sociologists, who for most of the twentieth century have shied away from the topic of economics, are thus today becoming increasingly interested in the whole area of economics. A number of interesting works in economic sociology have been produced, which are discussed below.

In addition, there exists quite a number of fascinating sociological studies of the economy, which are hidden away in the various subfields of sociology. One of our tasks in this issue of *Current Sociology* has been to draw attention to some of these works and to show that they can be given a new and interesting meaning by being looked at from the perspective of economic sociology.

As just mentioned, 'economic sociology' is the term used by the classical sociologists. In itself this hardly constitutes a compelling reason for claiming that economic sociology deserves a place as a distinct subfield in sociology. The main point has to be that economic sociology has its own, distinct perspective and that this is a scientifically productive one. The attempt to show that this is the case has informed each chapter of this Trend Report. It is also the reason for having included a comparison in this introduction between the premises of economic sociology and mainstream economics as well as a brief account of the present state of economic sociology.

A Comparison of the Premises of Economic Sociology and Neoclassical Theory

An important reason for being optimistic about the project of economic sociology is that sociology today has a number of theories and methodologies at its disposal, which have proven very fruitful when analysing other social phenomena than the economy. If one adds to this that the basic assumptions of economic sociology are quite different from those of mainstream economic theory, it is easy to see why economic sociology today is in a position to produce novel and worthwhile contributions to the scientific understanding of economic phenomena.

Our comparison of the premises of neoclassical theory and economic sociology is summarized in Figure 1. There are at least seven points of principled importance on which economic sociology and neoclassical theory differ: (1) the concept of the actor, (2) the arena of action, (3) the types of economic action, (4) the result of economic actions, (5) the view of the analyst, (6) the concept of time, and (7) the general scientific method. Elsewhere (46) we have outlined in detail each of these seven points, so here we shall be rather brief.

FIGURE 1
The Paradigms of Neoclassical Theory and Economic Sociology: A Comparison

	NEOCLASSICAL THEORY	ECONOMIC SOCIOLOGY
CONCEPT OF THE ACTOR	*separate actor* (individuals, households and firms)	*social actor* (type: individual, group, institution)
ARENA OF ACTION	any situation where choice and scarcity are present; by preference the market (*separate economy*)	economic system as part of society (*social economy*)
TYPES OF ECONOMIC ACTION	exclusively rational actions with emphasis on choice and maximization (*formalistic rationality*)	rational actions as well as other forms of economic actions (*social rationality and social economic actions in general*)
RESULT OF ECONOMIC ACTION	tendency to equilibrium (*equalibrated harmony*)	tendency to controlled and tension-filled interest struggle (*tension-filled interest struggle*)
VIEW OF THE ANALYST	producer of scientific results (*objective outsider*)	producer of scientific results and member of society (*objective insider*)
CONCEPT OF TIME	stylized and stationary time concept; identical to action that is analysed (*stationary and adaptive time concept*)	extended and variable time concept; goes beyond the action that is the focus of the analysis (*socio-historical time concept*)
SCIENTIFIC METHOD	predictions based on radical abstractions (*abstract predictions*)	descriptions-explanations based on empirically adjusted abstractions (*empirical descriptions and explanations*)

Source: 46, p. 7.

In neoclassical theory the economy is seen as basically autonomous and separate from the rest of society. In economic sociology, on the other hand, the economy is seen as part of and subordinate to the social system (e.g. 36). Attention has thus to be paid to the relations between the economy and the other 'sub-systems' of society. Also the concept of the economic actor is different. In neoclassical theory one works with a very limited number of different actors — basically with individuals, households and firms. These are seen as separate from each other, and they are basically defined as maximizers of utility. The sociological concept of the economic actor is, in contrast, a social one. This means that the individual actor is seen as connected to other actors in a variety of ways as well as 'embedded' (Polanyi) in society in general. Further, in contrast to the mainstream economist, who focuses exclusively on economic action as rational action, the sociologist's concept of social-economic action covers a variety of behaviour. Weber's work is particularly instructive on this point when it comes to showing, for example, that rational behaviour is not something that exists a priori but is a product of a distinct historical development.

A further difference between neoclassical economics and economic sociology can be found in their attitude to the cumulative result of separate economic actions. According to the mainstream version, individual actions tend automatically to produce an equilibrium. According to the sociologist, however, they will lead to interest struggles. Whichever way these are resolved, the sociologist would argue that tensions will always remain. Consequently, sociologists feel, echoing especially the critique of Galbraith (19), that the notion of *power* has to be brought in when one looks at how the economy works. This is true also for the concept of *time*. Economic sociology thus looks at the *history* of economic phenomena and is not content, like many neoclassical authors, simply to take a kind of snapshot, which is then manipulated in the darkroom. The ways that the past as well as the future influence economic decision-making are thus crucial to economic sociology.

In general, economic sociology and neoclassical economics also differ when it comes to the conception of the scientist and how one should go about problem-solving in general. Sociologists have expended much energy on trying to deal with the fact that the social scientist is also a member of the society that he or she is studying. Mainstream economists, however, have shown little interest in this whole problematique. This is because neoclassical economics sees the scientist as basically separate from the object of study.

Another difference between the philosophy of science of mainstream economics and that of economic sociology concerns the attitude to the use of abstractions. In neoclassical economics, there is a tendency to think that there is a positive value in drastically reducing the multiplicity of facts through radical abstractions. This tendency is, among other things, connected to the high value that economists place on prediction as a scientific tool. Sociologists, in contrast, are more interested in empirical facts and people's 'definition of the situation' (W.I. Thomas). If an abstraction deviates too much from reality, the instinct of the sociologist tells him or her that it must be adjusted. Sociologists, it should also be noted, tend not to be very interested in predictions; what they basically want to produce are good descriptions and explanations.

The Present State of Economic Sociology

The comparison between the premises of economic sociology and neoclassical theory is necessarily quite abstract and does not give much of an indication of the kind of topics that economic sociology deals with and how it proposes to solve them. To remedy this, Figure 2 has been designed to show the present state of economic sociology.

FIGURE 2
The Present State of Economic Sociology

I. What is analysed?
Consumption, productivity, technological innovations, markets (labour, financial, industrial, consumer), impact of gender and ethnic factors on the economy, economic organizations (banks, insurance companies, corporations, industries, etc.), relationship between the economy and non-economic organizations (the state, unions, etc.), economic classes, life in the workplace, stratification, occupational segregation, economic theories and ideologies, attitudes towards the economy, economic professions (e.g. entrepreneurs), the welfare state, the international economy, inflation, contract, money, formal vs. informal economy.

II. How is it analysed?
a. General theories
Middle-range theories, historical sociology, dependency theory, systems theory, neo-marxist theory, feminist theory, network theory, mathematical sociology, ethnomethodology, action research, political economy, institutionalism, game theory, neoclassical theory (certain aspects of), organization theory.
b. Specific concepts
Embeddedness, network, social-economic actions (rational, traditional, etc.), economic actors, institutions, cumulative change, economic sub-system, mode of production, world system, economic classes, ideology, exploitation, imperialism, economic classes, commodification/decommodification, trust, economic institutions, profession, labour markets (internal, segmented, etc.).

Note: Some of the recent works in economic sociology are 2; 5; 6; 9; 10; 13; 15; 16; 20; 21; 22; 24; 25; 26; 29; 30; 33; 35; 42; 44; 45; 46; 47; 48; 49; 54; 55.

From this figure it is possible to get an impression of the kind of topics that economic sociology has been interested in, such as inflation, markets and banks. The extent to which different topics have been analysed, it should be noted, varies quite a bit. While the field of labour markets, for example, is expanding very fast, much less substantive work has been done on financial markets. It is also probably true that there exist many interesting studies that have eluded us. Since Figure 2 was put together, we have found studies on the prevalence of child labour (53), on mergers of banks in Norway (23), on 'the second economy' in Hungary (18), and on the Hunt brothers' attempt to corner the silver market in 1979–80 (1).

A more important flaw in the Figure may be that it gives no hint of perhaps the most exciting trait of the 'new economic sociology' that now seems to be emerging, namely, that *it attempts directly to deal with the very core of economic phenomena.* This is definitely something new, especially in relation to the economic sociology that existed during the years from the demise of classical economic sociology until roughly the early 1970s. During this period, economic sociology tended to regard one of its basic tasks as being *to complement analyses already made by the economists.*

During recent years economic sociology has approached its topics from several general perspectives: middle-range theory, neo-marxist sociology, historical sociology, and so on. Some of these general theories, such as neo-marxism and feminist theory, became popular in sociology as a result of the social movements of the 1960s and early 1970s. Others, such as systems theory and historical sociology, have a more conventional background even if their intellectual history is just as complicated. To economists, who are used to working with only one theoretical perspective, it might seem that the existence of several general theories in sociology reflects poorly on its scientific status. To some extent this is correct. It is also true, however, that the predominance of a single perspective in economics over the last fifty years should make one suspicious of how well it can handle its subject matter. Social reality is by constitution extremely complex and needs to be analysed on quite a few levels and from various theoretical perspectives. Be that as it may; in this issue of *Current Sociology* we shall make room for the present pluralism in sociology, and our main criterion for discussing a certain theory is that it attempts to explain economic phenomena on *sociological* grounds. This means, for example, that less attention will be paid to economists such as Gary Becker, who uses a fairly undiluted version of neoclassical theory to explain the most diverse non-economic phenomena (e.g. 7; 8). Economic sociology, on the other hand, is fairly close to the work of economists like Amartya Sen, George Akerlof and Albert O. Hirschman, all of whom often operate somewhere on the borderline between economics and sociology (e.g. 3; 27; 28; 41).

As to the goal of developing a new overarching science of 'socio-economics' (e.g. 16), we are in agreement that such a theory is much needed. Like Weber, we thus feel that a 'social economy' (*Sozialökonomie*), which would include not only economic theory and economic sociology but also economic history, is a goal ultimately to aim for (see e.g. 50, pp. 63-6; 52, pp. 311-12, 336, 635). Before such a science can develop, however, economic sociology must learn to stand on its own legs. As the situation stands today, mainstream economics and economic history are well defined disciplines; in economic sociology much work still needs to be done.[2]

A variety of specific concepts have also been developed by sociologists to deal directly with economic phenomena or some aspects of them. Some of these, such as 'exploitation' (Marx) or 'social-economic action' (Weber), go far back in the history of sociology, while others are the result of more recent work. The concept in the new economic sociology that has met with the greatest success and/or popularity, is probably 'network'. Polanyi's idea of 'embeddedness' and Wallerstein's notion of 'world system' are also used by many sociologists. In general, it must be said, however, that much work remains to be done on the conceptual level. What is probably most needed today is a kind of *middle-range economic sociology* in which specific economic problems are solved through theoretically imaginative and empirically solid analyses.

The Organization of This Issue

After the Introduction there follows Part I of the report, entitled 'The Tradition of Economic Sociology, 1800s–1960s'. The first chapter, 'Economics and Sociology — Early Clashes', deals with the interaction between economists and sociologists during the nineteenth century. The emphasis is on what made economics and sociology part company so decisively and become near-enemies in academia. We suggest that there were three main reasons for this: methodological, political and institutional. From early on, sociologists and economists developed very different notions about what kind of methodology to use. They also had quite diverging opinions about the role that the state should play in the economy and the need for social reforms. A further obstacle to co-operation came about when economics and sociology were institutionalized. Economists more or less made a bargain with the sociologists: if sociologists were to have their own area in the academy, they had to keep away from the field of the economists.

The next chapter is called 'The Launching of Economic Sociology, 1890–1920', and here we attempt to outline the efforts around the turn of the century by the classical sociologists (Weber, Durkheim, Simmel, Pareto and Veblen) to develop a distinctively sociological analysis of economic phenomena. Since the history of this effort has not yet been written, we have tried to make this section as complete as possible and also to point to those ideas in 'classical economic sociology' which we think could be worth following up.

In chapters 3 and 4 we try to explain why economic sociology did not 'take off' during the period between the 1920s and the 1960s despite its promising beginnings. We first analyse the situation in Europe, paying special attention to the work of Joseph Schumpeter and the French economic sociologists. We then switch over to the United States, where the European version of economic sociology never became popular but where a similar perspective — called 'economy and society' — eventually appeared. Economic sociology basically went through *a process of fragmentation* during the 1920–60 period and split up into topics like 'stratification studies', 'industrial sociology', 'consumer sociology', and so on. Despite this, many valuable insights into the economy were produced by sociologists during these years, and we stress the need for today's sociologists to learn from them.

Part II of the report is entitled 'Towards a New Economic Sociology, 1960s–?' and consists of five chapters, each of which deals with one central aspect of the new development in economic sociology since the mid-1960s. Chapter 5 is thus focused on the role that women play in the economy. Our argument is that during the last ten to fifteen years there has emerged a series of sophisticated works that analyse the position of women in the economy from a sociological perspective. Chapter 6 is entitled 'The Neo-Marxist Contribution' and contains a discussion of certain works in marxist sociology which are particularly relevant to economic sociology. The discussion covers works by 'early' neo-marxists like Harry

Braverman and also more recent ones like those by Adam Przeworski and John Roemer. Chapter 7, 'The International Dimension', argues that today's economic sociology is in the process of becoming more international in character. The importance that Third World sociologists and economists have played in this process is stressed. The emergence of new topics — from Euromarkets to transnational corporations — is also touched upon. Chapter 8, 'The Sociology of Markets', brings us to a quite recent effort in sociology to analyse a topic which by tradition has belonged to the economists. Recent research on labour markets, financial markets and industrial markets is presented and discussed.

We close with a chapter of which the new relationship between economics and sociology forms the core. The work of economists such as George Akerlof is discussed, and the need for economic sociologists to develop new concepts and theories is stressed. The reader is again reminded that economic sociology constitutes one of sociology's most dynamic areas today and that an effort should be made to have it established as a distinct subfield in the universities.

Part I
Trend Report
The Tradition of Economic Sociology 1800s–1960s
Richard Swedberg

1
ECONOMICS AND SOCIOLOGY — EARLY CLASHES

In gathering material for this Trend Report we have been struck both by the desire among today's sociologists to cooperate with economists and by the strength of the tensions that exist between sociologists and economists. In describing the attitude he finds characteristic of British sociologists to economics, John Goldthorpe, for example, writes:

> The basic approach of the subject is disliked, but its practitioners are feared. British sociologists would like to 'take on' the economists directly but hesitate to do so because they know little about economics, are reluctant to learn any and generally lose out to economists when it comes to rigour of analysis and argument. (78)

This statement, we have come to realize, could equally well have been made by a sociologist in Sweden, the US or many other countries. The preponderance of irrational factors — fear, aggression, ignorance — in the attitude of the sociologists should be noted. Economists, for their part, do not seem to base their opinion of sociology on any more scientific grounds. If one asks economists what they think of sociology, one usually gets answers of the type that economists have 'contempt' for sociologists, that they resent sociology's ambition to be 'the queen of the social sciences', and that sociology is a 'soft' science (e.g. 107, p. 911). If one keeps prodding, it soon becomes clear that most economists have read practically no sociology.

What are the reasons for this solid estrangement between economists and sociologists? And why have only economists and sociologists developed these hostile feelings for each other while, for instance, psychologists and sociologists get along quite well, as the existence of 'social psychology' testifies? Part of the answer might be that sociology and psychology developed at about the same time, while economics has a much longer intellectual history than sociology. Economics thus developed its basic principles and general mode of analysis well before sociology. Difficulties between 'old sciences' and 'newcomers' are to be expected.[3]

The early birth of economics in relation to sociology, however, explains neither the depth nor the irrational overtones of the existing hostility between economists and sociologists. And besides, do not political science, law and philosophy all have an earlier origin *and* better relations with sociology than economics? The main answer to the question must consequently be sought elsewhere.

We suggest that the reasons for much of the hostility between economists and sociologists can be sought in the clashes that took place between nineteenth-century economics and the early, rather unscientific kind of sociology. The economists and sociologists of those days, we would argue, came to blows on three specific types of issues: methodological, political and institutional. The relationship between economists and sociologists, in short, got off to a bad start.

To show this, we have picked three distinct episodes, each of which illustrates one of these points with special poignancy. In the first of these, which is centred on the debate about Comte in British political economy, the difference in methodological approach between economics and early sociology comes out with great clarity. Our second example, which has been chosen to show the importance of the institutionalization process for souring the relations between economics and sociology, depicts the fierce battle over academic turf that took place between economists and sociologists in the US in the early 1890s. In our third example we use Marx's work to highlight the political differences between economists and sociologists. We have also included a brief introductory section on Adam Smith in order to make the point that, despite their later clashes, early sociology and economics were in no way incompatible.

Adam Smith — Economist and Sociologist?

The work of Adam Smith was conceived during the dawn of modern social science, well before there were separate and well-defined social science disciplines. This, no doubt, is the reason why Smith could move with such ease between economic, political, sociological and ethical aspects of a phenomenon. It also helps to explain why his work met with such approval among the early sociologists, who conceived of sociology as a science which united all the special social sciences. Auguste Comte (70, pp. 195, 197), who heartily detested economists, thus made an explicit exception for the 'immortal master' Adam Smith and his 'illuminating analyses'. Marx was also positive towards, and deeply influenced by, Smith especially in his earlier works (see e.g. 89; 74, pp. 261-2). The most ardent Smith fan among nineteenth-century sociologists, however, was Albion Small. In *Adam Smith and Modern Sociology* (1907), which is filled with the most admiring comments, Small (104, p. 1) says that if one did not know any economics but had read some sociology, one would definitely think that *The Wealth of Nations* had been written by a sociologist. According to Small (104, p. 4), sociologists as distinct from economists were the true successors to Smith. The reason for this, we read, is that 'the sociologists have kept alive the vital spark of Smith's moral philosophy' (104, p. 4).

What mainly attracted the early sociologists to Adam Smith's work was not so much his analyses of concrete economic phenomena as his alleged attempt to construct a general social science, which was moral and very broad in scope in contrast to nineteenth-century political economy. The subtitle Small chose for his book on Smith — *A Study in the Methodology of the Social Sciences* — is indicative of this. It is to be doubted, however, that the attempt by people like Small to recast Smith exclusively as a sociologist is of much interest today (see also 99; 101). Modern sociology has no ambitions whatsoever to become 'the queen of the social sciences' and to claim every good work in some other social science as its own. Besides, Smith is about as far away from being a sociologist in the proper sense of the word as he is from being a neoclassical economist. His concern in *The Wealth of Nations* was first and foremost to contribute to the thought of his time, or more precisely to 'political economy . . . as a branch of the science of a statesman or a legislator'. To reinterpret Smith's ideas exclusively in terms of today's social sciences, such as modern sociology or neoclassical economics, would obscure their meaning and reduce their subtlety (see e.g. 68; 69).

A renewed study of *The Wealth of Nations* is, however, needed among today's economic sociologists who have pretty much ignored the contributions by Smith (for an exception, see 64). What is especially needed is an attempt to look at and further develop his concrete analysis of free trade and protectionism (see e.g. 92). A very fine example of what modern sociology can do by following Smith's lead can be found in Emile Durkheim's *Division of Labor in Society*, written nearly a century ago (72). Economic sociologists would also do well to puncture the popular image of Smith as a one-dimensional advocate of the virtues of the market. Smith does indeed speak of 'the invisible hand' and of how the individual, by pursuing his or her own interests, may also further those of society in general. He did not think it would be wise, however, to let business interests rule supreme. In *The Wealth of Nations*, he lashes out against 'the mean rapacity, the monopolizing spirit of merchants and manufacturers, who neither are nor ought to be the rulers of mankind' (106, p. 493). He also warned that when businessmen meet, it often ends with a conspiracy against the proper workings of the market. The central theme in Smith's thinking is rather an effort to determine the institutional arrangements — including those of classes (see e.g. 64, pp. 30–3) — under which the self-interest of the individual and the interest of society actually do coincide (e.g. 100). The market, in other words, does not, according to Smith, operate automatically in an efficient manner for both the individual and society except under certain well defined conditions. To pursue Smith's thinking on this point would constitute an interesting task for economic sociology, which is currently struggling to develop a sociological theory of the structure of markets (see chapter 8 below).

Which Methods Should be Used?

When one looks at Adam Smith's work from the perspective of the twentieth century, it is possible to argue that it shows how well 'economics' and 'sociology' could co-exist. Whatever the merits of this argument, it should nevertheless be emphasized that from its very beginnings sociology was involved in fights with economists. This can be exemplified by the first work in which the term 'sociology' was used, Auguste Comte's *Cours de Philosophie Positive*, which appeared in 1830–42 and which contained a vitriolic attack on political economy. Economics, the author insisted, was metaphysical nonsense and lacked any scientific value whatsoever. If one wanted to study economic phenomena in a scientific way, one should turn to 'sociology'.

Comte's attack on political economy, which can be found in Lecture 47 in Volume Four of *Cours de Philosophie Positive* (70, pp. 193–204), was of very poor quality and deserves to remain in the oblivion into which it has fallen. The reason why we shall take it up here, however, is that it came to influence quite decisively the attitudes of economists to sociology.

The setting for the debate was the following. When Comte published his critique in 1839, it met with little if any reaction in England. John Stuart Mill, who corresponded with Comte between 1841 and 1847, was probably the first British economist of any stature to become aware of its existence. He was filled with admiration for Comte's positivist philosophy and chose for a long time to ignore the sharp differences which existed between himself and Comte when it came to political economy (cf. 60). As time went on. Mill became increasingly disenchanted with Comte's authoritarianism and finally felt a need to confront his ideas publicly. This was done in *Auguste Comte and Positivism*, which appeared in 1865 and which also contains a rebuttal of Comte's critique of political economy (94, pp. 80–3). From the 1870s onwards several other economists — such as John Elliot Cairnes, Alfred Marshall, and John Neville Keynes — also started to discuss Comte's critique in the *Cours de Philosophie Positive*. The reason for this was not so much that positivism had become popular in intellectual circles in England, which was true enough (e.g. 59); it was rather that the *Methodenstreit* had now reached England and had opened up a debate about the very foundations of political economy (e.g. 66). Comte was thus drawn into this giant battle about methodology, which had started in Germany and Austria and then spread to England, France and the US.

The role that Comte came to play in the British version of the *Methodenstreit* is of special interest to sociology since it represents the only case where sociology as such emerged as one of the contenders. The main figures in the *Methodenstreit* were otherwise representatives from legal science, history and various schools of economic thought. (See in this context also the section on Max Weber in chapter 2 below.) With Comte, in brief, sociology was to have its very own *mini-Methodenstreit* with political economy.

We shall now take a closer look at Comte's ideas in the *Cours de Philosophie Positive*, which the British economists were to discuss very carefully and then reject — but not before they had developed the opinion that sociology had little or nothing of value to contribute to economic theory. Comte's main contention, to repeat, was that political economy did not constitute a true science but was merely a kind of 'metaphysics', a term which, as Cairnes put it, 'represents the strongest form of reprobation known to the Comtean terminology' (63, p. 283). Comte had very little on which to base this opinion except his own intuitions about political economy. This is clear from Roger Mauduit's thesis *Auguste Comte et la Science Economique*, in which the author has painstakingly identified the works in economics with which Comte was familiar (91, pp. 48–70). Smith, a little Malthus, and a few French economists was all that Comte had read. What Comte did not know, however, he invented. We are thus told that economists are unable to think in scientific terms since they usually start their careers as lawyers and literary authors; that each economist invents his own scholastic system of unscientific terms; and that de Tracy is an example for all economists to follow since he had the good taste to classify his own work on political economy as 'ideology' (70, pp. 194–7).

Mixed with these idiosyncratic opinions about political economy, however, were also some more substantial charges. Comte thus argued that the method used in political economy was too abstract and deductive in character; that the economy could not be studied in isolation from other parts of society; and that economists displayed an unreasonable amount of hostility to state interventions in the economy. The last of these charges will be left aside for the moment and discussed later in this chapter. The other two, as Comte saw it, were closely connected (70, pp. 198–9). It was thus only possible to analyse the economy in 'isolation' from the rest of society, if one placed oneself at the level of metaphysical abstractions. When one leaves the world of abstract concepts and starts to look at reality, he stressed, it soon becomes apparent that one must include 'moral', 'intellectual' and 'political' phenomena in the analysis. Any study of society must focus on the totality and be based on the observation of facts. The deductive method — as distinct from the inductive method — should be used only sparingly in the scientific study of the economy (cf. 73).

Quite a few people took part in the British debate about Comte's ideas on political economy, and some of these were positive towards his arguments (see e.g. 65; 71; 79; 80; 83; 84). Those who won the debate, however, felt that Comte was wrong on all the important issues, and these included the best minds among the economists: John Stuart Mill, John Elliot Cairnes, Alfred Marshall and John Neville Keynes (63; 85, pp. 112–41; 87, pp. 18, 33–9; 88, pp. 70–3; 94, pp. 80–3).

In a sense it was easy for the economists to win against an opponent like Comte, who was ignorant in economics and had not elaborated his theoretical positions very carefully. It was thus quickly established by Cairnes that 'it is . . . quite evident that M. Comte had no effective knowledge of the branch of science which he denounced' and that 'it would seem, indeed, as if M. Comte's mind lost its proper balance and edge on coming into contact with political economy' (63, pp. 283–4). Cairnes et al. also had little difficulty in showing that Comte was wrong in denying that economics could constitute a science of its own. Division of labour, it was pointed out, was needed in all branches of science, and there was no reason to exempt economics from this rule. Comte's opponents also noted that deductive thinking was useful, and that empty empiricism would lead nowhere.

The victory of Cairnes et al. was celebrated in polite but devastating phrases about the present and future uselessness of sociology. Alfred Marshall thus wrote: 'it is vain to speak of the higher authority of a unified social science [i.e. sociology] . . . it does not exist; it shows no signs of coming into existence' (87, p. 35). And in *The Scope and Method of Political Economy*, a work which was to be used as a textbook by several generations of economists, John Neville Keynes asked the rhetorical question: 'Comte charged political economy with being radically sterile as regards results. But what results has sociology, conceived as a master-science dealing with man's social life as a whole, yet to show?' (85, p. 139). In brief, the British economists had come to the conclusion that sociology was useless as a science and could teach the economists nothing.

Which Science Should Study the Economy?

It was no doubt implicit in the conclusion that Cairnes and the other leading British economists drew from the debate with Comte that sociologists should leave the study of economics to the economists; the sociologists' task — to the extent that they now had one — was to make broad, general overviews of society. This meant that sociologists, as far as the economists were concerned, could study whatever they wanted — minus the economy.

Sociology's tendency to become a 'science of leftovers', as the sociologists themselves were later to call it, was of course influenced by factors other than the unhappy debate between Comte and the British economists. By the expression 'leftover science', it should be noted, it is implied that sociology tended to shy away not only from the economists' area of study but also from political science and those other social sciences which were already in existence when sociology emerged.

The division of intellectual labour between the various social sciences was considerably strengthened when they became institutionalized. The rule quickly developed that in order to get a place in the university, a science had to be able to show that it had its own distinct topic which had not already been claimed by some other science. In the struggles at the turn of the century to get a foothold in the university, sociology was handicapped in relation to economics because the latter had a much longer and more distinguished scientific tradition on which to draw. The result, as we shall soon see, was that sociology backed off from the area of economics and settled for a rather strange assortment of 'leftover' topics, such as the family, poverty, sex, education, and so on.

That this could happen so easily was no doubt facilitated by the fact that early nineteenth-century sociology was of such low scientific quality. In Europe sociology did not have its scientific breakthrough till the 1890s with scholars like Durkheim and Weber. In the US, where sociology's character as a 'leftover science' was to become much more pronounced than in Europe, the breakthrough was not as sudden. It also started a few years later, roughly around the turn of the century when the first original works in US sociology began to appear: E.A. Ross' *Social Control* (1901), Charles H. Cooley's *Human Nature and the Social Order* (1902), and William Graham Sumner's *Folkways* (1906) (see e.g. 75, pp. 305–6). With the publication of Thomas and Znaniecki's *The Polish Peasant* (1918–20) and Park and Burgess' *Introduction to the Science of Sociology* (1921), North American sociology was finally to come into its own.

The example we have chosen to illustrate the impact that the process of institutionalization was to have on sociology's relationship to economics is from the US in the 1890s. There are two main reasons for this. First, it is in the US that twentieth-century sociology was to develop most forcefully. The relationship to economics developed by American sociologists was thus later to influence sociologists in many other countries. And second, in the US sociologists and economists were to fight so bitterly over a place in the university that the question of 'who should study economics' appears there with near exemplary clarity.

The background to the debate, which is best described in Mary O. Furner's *Advocacy and Objectivity: A Study in the Professionalization of American Social Science, 1865–1905* (1975), was as follows. The social sciences, which since 1865 had been united in the American Social Science Association, had by the 1880s started to split up into separate, professional organizations. The economists were especially eager to have their own organization and to get rid of the label 'amateur social scientist'. In 1885 the American Economic Association came into existence. In the 1890s signs started to appear that sociology also was in the process of becoming accepted as a distinct science in the universities. An observer, who understood that much more was involved than intellectual arguments, noted in 1894: 'Just now sociology is being examined by a board of trustees. Has it a field of its own which would warrant the creation of a separate chair? *Other scientists are watching for poachers*' (98, p. 714; emphasis added).

The economists in particular were worried by this development, since they were well familiar with sociology's ambition to be an encyclopaedic science which covered everything, including economics. They responded with an attack on sociology, the main purpose being to get sociologists out of the area of economics. This led to a series of heated arguments in the mid-1890s between sociologists and economists, until the sociologists finally gave up (see 96, pp. 220–l). In December 1894 the economists even summoned the sociologists to a meeting of the American Economic Association, where they were asked to explain what they thought they were doing (e.g. 103).

The sociologists were in a very weak position in the early 1890s to withstand attacks from the economists. A survey undertaken at the time thus shows that there was no consensus whatsoever among sociologists as to what 'sociology' really meant (82). According to the same survey, the opinions diverged even more when it came to the relationship between sociology and economics.

Three principally different versions of sociology's relationship with economics quickly emerged as a response to the economists' attack. According to the first, which was advocated by Lester F. Ward and Albion Small, it was sociology's task to coordinate all the social sciences, including that of economics. This was Comte's old project and it met with a devastating criticism from the economists, who were led by the aggressive Simon N. Patten (see 97).

The second line of reasoning was advocated by Franklin H. Giddings, who was very interested in applying the sociological perspective to political economy (see e.g. 76). Giddings' idea that economic problems could also be analysed in a sociological manner was thus close to the position of those sociologists who, in response to Ira Howerth's (82, p. 116) question about the relationship between sociology and political economy, had answered that 'sociology studies the same phenomena [as political economy] but from a different point of view'. It is however unlikely that Patten et al. would have been willing to accept this position, not least since no-one could explain exactly what 'sociology' was. There were also fresh memories among the economists of the battle in the 1880s between the 'historical school' and the 'British school' over issues such as what method to use, state intervention vs. *laissez-faire*, and so on (see e.g. 67; 75, pp. 59–80). Giddings (77) also opened himself up to easy attack when he claimed that political economy as a science should be secondary to sociology. Patten quickly jumped on this and claimed that, if anything, it is economics and not sociology which is the fundamental social science (e.g. 97). Behind this and other arguments that Patten et al. brought up was always the fact that the economists basically wanted the area of economics exclusively for themselves. A good sociologist was one who stayed out of economics. Patten thus ended up siding with those sociologists who — to cite the standard work on this debate — 'contented themselves with topics that their critics did indeed consider leftovers: marriage, the family, poverty, crime, education, religion, and sex' (75, p. 289).

The position that won among the sociologists was the 'leftover strategy'. The main reason was that it facilitated the institutionalization of sociology, something which most sociologists considered desirable. In the heat of the debate Lester F. Ward emphasized that 'there should be no confusion or overlapping in speaking of these [two] sciences or in teaching them, so that nothing that clearly belongs to economics should be treated as sociology' (109, pp. 23–4). Franklin H. Giddings added soberly that 'the university cannot afford duplication' and that 'if a subject is already taught under one name, nothing is to be gained by creating a new department for no other purpose than to teach the same subject under a different name' (77, p. 146). The *Realpolitik* of the leading sociologists was summed up by the flexible Albion Small, when he said that sociology has to 'gain ground by playing the academic game under the existing rules' (105, p. 228).

The strategy of Small and the others worked well, and in 1905 the American Sociological Society came into existence with Patten's help. A price had to be paid, however, and it was that the sociologists stayed out of the economists' area. In 1908 Small complained in his private correspondence, 'that sociology is merely a convenient label for left-overs within the range of human knowledge that cannot be classified under any other head' (75, p. 292). Sociology, in other words, had lost its second fight with the economists in the nineteenth century.

What Role Should Politics Play?

A third point on which sociologists and economists differed and came to blows during the nineteenth century concerned the question of politics. In the *Cours de Philosophie Positive* Comte attacked the economists for ignoring the sufferings of the working classes and for being hostile to any form of government regulation of the existing industrial 'anarchy' (70, pp. 200–3). The needy, he said, are promised by the economists that they will ultimately be better off if the state does not intervene in the economy. It is *now*, however, Comte emphasized, that these people are suffering and need assistance. Cairnes et al. had little difficulty in countering Comte's argument. In principle, Cairnes said, a science should be judged on scientific grounds and not acording to moral and political criteria (63, pp. 297–300). 'Political economy . . . has no panacea to offer for the cure of social evils, but it has that to offer which it is in the nature of science to furnish — light as to the causes on which those evils, so far as they proceed from economic agencies, depend.' Alfred Marshall also noted *à propos* of Comte that an economist *as a scientist* can never give advice about how to solve a concrete problem (87, p. 38). If he does, 'he does not speak with the voice of his science'. Marshall stressed: '. . . the economist has to be specially careful to make this clear; because there is much misunderstanding as to the scope of [economics]; and undue claims to authority or practical matters have often been put forward on its behalf' (87, p. 38).

The economists thus turned the critique of their political beliefs into a question of whether social science should be value-neutral or not, an issue on which the economists were far ahead of the early sociologists. The sociology that existed before Weber was very confused when it came to separating the 'is' from the 'ought'. In a majority of cases it was actually the mixture of values and facts which was the hallmark of sociology as a 'science'; the sociologists explicitly wanted sociology to be a moral and practical science. In the US, Oberschall tells us, 'early sociology was more a 'movement' than an intellectual discipline' (96, p. 189). All the departments of sociology in North America thus originated in connection with philanthropy, charities or social work. The only exception was at Yale where the Divinity School, instead, had its own Department of Christian Sociology (96, p. 212). Also in Europe, sociology was closely associated, from Saint-Simon onwards, with various moral and political causes, be it in the form of optimistic evolutionary doctrines or various Christian or Socialist doctrines. Comte's casual statement that positivism is 'equally valuable from the moral, scientific, or political aspect' as well as being 'the sole means of bringing this most formidable crisis in the history of humanity to a real termination', gives a hint of the atmosphere in which European sociology developed (86, p. 324).

The British economists, on the other hand, had since the 1840s developed a concept of science in which facts and values were strictly separated in a Weberian manner. This was mainly accomplished through the distinction between political economy as a 'science' and as an 'art'. In *A System of Logic* John Stuart Mill thus writes:

> A scientific observer or reasoner, merely as such, is not an adviser for practice. His part is only to show that certain consequences follow from certain causes and that, to obtain certain ends, certain means are most effectual. Whether the ends themselves are such as ought to be pursued, and if so, in what cases and to how great a length, is no part of his business as a cultivator of science to decide, and science alone will never qualify him for the decision. (93, p. 356)

Similar statements can be found throughout the works of the British economists after Ricardo (see e.g. 95, pp. 15–16).

Despite their own confused philosophy of science, the early sociologists were nevertheless correct in noting that the British economists had an affinity for the status quo, that they rigidly opposed state intervention in the market, and in general sided with the bourgeoisie rather than with the working class (e.g. 108, pp. 87–98). In the debates with the economists during the nineteenth century the sociologists were, however, unable to turn this point to their advantage, mainly because they lacked the sophistication to understand exactly where political economy stopped being a 'science' and became more of an 'art' or ideology. Exactly how this comes about constitutes a distinct and difficult theoretical problem, which cannot be solved simply by introducing the moral values that the sociologists themselves prefer.[4] The dispute over politics was also won by the economists — mainly because they had developed the distinction between 'values' and 'facts' much earlier than had the sociologists.

In discussing the sociologists' critique of the British economists, it is impossible not to mention Marx, who was by far the most knowledgeable among the early sociologists when it came to economics. It can, of course, be doubted whether the term 'early sociology' adequately captures Marx's work. Marx basically tried to construct a new type of social science and was, for instance, contemptuous of Comte's writings. Still, Marx's work was close to the paradigm of early sociology in that he saw an organic connection between the scientific and practical aspects of social science. With his emphasis on the importance of historical facts he also came closer to the methodological stance of the early sociologists than to the deductively oriented school in economic theory.

The difference between Marx and the other early sociologists is nevertheless enormous. While the works of nineteenth-century US sociologists and pre-1890 European sociologists are today regarded as being of little interest and generally unscientific, there is an increasing awareness in contemporary sociology that Marx's writings — despite their political flavouring — contain a host of valuable sociological insights (See also chapter 6 below on the neo-marxist contribution to economic sociology.)

How is Marx, then, to be situated in relation to economic sociology? It should first be noted that whatever value one ascribes to retrospective readings of Marx, the honour of having 'invented' economic sociology — both in the sense of using the precise term and, more importantly, in having made a conscious effort to develop it — belongs to Weber and not to Marx. A clue as to how one might view Marx's contribution to *economics as a social science* can actually be found in Weber's work, where Marx is mentioned as one of the key figures in the science of 'social economy' ('die sozialökonomische Wissenschaft'; 50, p. 65). By this term Weber meant an overarching kind of science, which included several different approaches to the study of economics (roughly economic theory, economic history and economic sociology). Weber's statement about Marx as a 'social economist' constitutes in our opinion a fairly reasonable summing up of Marx's contribution to economics.

Weber's remark that Marx can be seen as a 'social economist' probably also constitutes a better point of departure for evaluating Marx's multifaceted contribution to economics than Schumpeter's suggestion that one can see Marx as an 'economist', a 'sociologist', and — of less interest here — as a 'prophet' (102, pp. 1-58). The problem with this division is that it erects unnecessary barriers between 'sociology' and 'economy' in Marx's work, something which Schumpeter himself undoubtedly was aware of, since he also noted that 'all the major concepts and propositions [in Marx] are . . . both economic and sociological and carry the same meaning on both planes' (102, p. 45).

If we accept Weber's implicit suggestion that there is an 'economic sociology' — as well as 'economic history' and 'economic theory' — in Marx's work, of what exactly does it consist? This is a question for today's economic sociologists to answer in detail, and it is hoped that a discussion along these lines will develop. Marx's oeuvre is so rich that novel aspects of his thought are also likely to emerge when looked at from the perspective of economic sociology. This is especially true since today's marxist-inspired sociologists have had a tendency to hand over Marx's economic analysis to marxist economists. Economic sociology might thus help to restore some of the original balance of Marx's work.

In this chapter we shall point out only some of the more self-evident contributions of Marx to economic sociology. The first concerns Marx's insight that the economy is extremely important to society in general. 'A society', Marx says, 'can no more cease to produce than cease to consume', and he adds that the way work is organized constitutes a decisive factor for understanding the social structure (90, pp. 619-20). Freed from economic determinism and philosophy of history, this focus on the economy constitutes a much needed corrective in sociology to the tendency to set psychological and/or linguistic factors in the centre of the analysis ('Verstehen', 'conscience collective', 'symbolic interaction', and so on). Marx's suggestion that the economy consists of three huge areas — 'the process of production', 'the sphere of circulation' and 'consumption' — is also useful in countering the tendency in 'industrial sociology', 'consumer sociology', and similar areas to exaggerate the importance of one aspect of the economic process.

In addition to these more general strengths of the marxist perspective, economic sociology is also in debt to Marx for having helped to open up and conceptualize a series of important topics such as alienation, imperialism and the class struggle. Contemporary sociology, despite its adherence to a strict separation between 'values' and 'facts', has neglected problems of this type for ideological reasons. Leaving aside Marx's political values, he showed that these and similar topics constitute extremely important aspects of modern capitalist society.

2
THE LAUNCHING OF ECONOMIC SOCIOLOGY 1890–1920

From the turn of the twentieth century sociology came into its own as a science through the highly sophisticated works of Weber, Durkheim, Simmel and Pareto. This is well established in the literature that has grown up around the history of sociology during the last few decades. Not at all discussed in this literature, however, is the fact that simultaneously with the establishment of sociology as a general science, an effort was made — especially by Weber and Durkheim — to create a distinct subfield in sociology, which they called 'economic sociology'. The reasons for this gap in the literature are complicated and will not be discussed here. In this chapter we shall first of all try to describe exactly what the 'economic sociology' that the classical sociologists tried to establish, looked like.

The key figure in the attempt to launch economic sociology as a distinct project was without doubt Max Weber. Apart from using the term 'economic sociology', he specifically tried to outline a programme for what the field should look like (52, pp. 63–211). Durkheim, who also used the concept of 'economic sociology', gave the topic its blessing by regularly devoting a section to it in *L'Année Sociologique*. Throughout Durkheim's own work, there is also a constant attempt to distinguish clearly the sociological viewpoint of economic phenomena from that of economic theory. Concrete examples of what a sociological analysis should look like can also be found in several of his studies. Finally, very interesting ideas on economic sociology, as we shall see, can be found in the works of three other key figures in sociology from this period: Georg Simmel, Vilfredo Pareto and Thorstein Veblen.

Before taking a closer look at the relevant writings of these five thinkers, a few words need to be said about the climate in economic science towards the end of the nineteenth century. The most important event in economic theory was undoubtedly the marginal revolution, which roughly began in the 1870s with Jevons, Menger and Walras, and which then grew in popularity and intensity. The neoclassical theory that was then born differed on several crucial points from the earlier 'political economy'. In particular, it displayed less interest in institutional factors and was mainly preoccupied with the problem of how prices were formed. Other significant changes were also introduced, as can be seen from the comparison between the 'classical paradigm' and the 'neoclassical paradigm' in Figure 3.

FIGURE 3
A Comparison of the Classical and Neoclassical Paradigms

	CLASSICAL PARADIGM	NEOCLASSICAL PARADIGM
THE OBJECT OF ECONOMICS	accumulation and distribution	efficiency
THE AIM FOR ENGAGING IN ECONOMIC RESEARCH	to assist policy makers	the discovery of universal laws
INSTITUTIONAL FRAMEWORK AND UNIT OF ANALYSIS	specification of the institutional framework, especially in terms of the division of society between social classes; behaviour expresses class belonging	no classes, but a 'general public' making decisions through votes (individually) in the market; the idea of choice is central
CORE OF THE THEORETICAL STRUCTURE	capital, defined in a comprehensive way, is at the centre of the theoretical structure	prices form the central concept
CONCEPTION OF VALUE	a production theory of value, in which value is viewed as the expression of the social division of labour	value flows from the subjective mental evaluation of the indiv-dual agents
CONCEPTION OF PROFIT	profits result from the unequal distribution of wealth between classes; it is the source of growth	profit is the reward for abstinence

Source: 115, p. 430.

Simultaneously with the marginal revolution, another important development was going on in economic science. This was the emergence since the mid-nineteenth century of the 'historical school' with Roscher, Knies and Schmoller as some of the leading figures (e.g. 40, pp. 807–20; 122). Here the emphasis was mainly on analysing unique, historical constellations in economic life. The approaches of the marginalists and the historical economists were obviously diametrically opposed and led in the 1880s to a debate, which has become known as the *Methodenstreit*. Similar battles between theoretically and empirically oriented economists also took place in several other countries. The neoclassical economists were to emerge victorious from all these fights, while the more historically oriented economists had to retreat into 'economic history'. To some of them, however, this was not a very satisfactory solution since they saw themselves not only as historians but also as economic theorists. People like Werner Sombart were thus looking around for theoretical alternatives to abstract economic theory and toyed with the notion of adopting the term 'economic sociology' for his scholarship.[5] Max Weber, whom Schumpeter (40, p. 815) placed with Sombart in 'the youngest historical school', brought considerably more thought to the idea of an 'economic sociology'.

Max Weber

That Weber produced socio-historical studies of the economy, which are central to the sociological tradition, is of course well known. The enormous sociological literature that has been devoted to *The Protestant Ethic* is, if anything else, proof of this (for a recent overview, see 140). Little attention has, however, been paid — either by economists or by sociologists (167, p. 35) — to the fact that Weber also made an attempt to develop what he explicitly called 'economic sociology' ('Wirtschaftssoziologie'; 51, pp. 34, 41). This effort can mainly be found in chapter 2 of *Wirtschaft und Gesellschaft*, which Talcott Parsons — one of the few sociologists who has grasped its importance — describes in the following manner:

> This chapter constitutes what is in many ways the framework of a unique kind of analysis of the modern economic order. It is unique in that it starts from all the main definitions of the facts which have been current in economic science, but brings to bear upon them a totally different perspective and a quite new institutional kind of analysis. The result is a kind of orientation to a great many of the most crucial empirical problems very different from almost any other to be found in the literature. *It is probably, especially when taken in connexion with the other relevant parts of Weber's works, the most comprehensive and all things considered the most successful essay in the field of 'economic sociology' which has yet been attempted.* (138, pp. 53–4; emphasis added)

Before we take a closer look at chapter 2 of *Wirtschaft und Gesellschaft* the question must be raised about the relationship of

Weber's whole work in economics to his project of 'economic sociology'. When one attempts to answer this question, one is immediately struck by the difficulty in placing much of Weber's work in a specific academic field. This, no doubt, is due both to the fact that German economics before World War I was fairly interdisciplinary in nature and to the fact that Weber himself did work in legal science, economic history and sociology during different phases of his life.

Some of the confusion can, however, be eliminated if one looks at Weber's work in terms of a distinction between two of the terms he used, 'social economics' ('Sozialökonomie') and 'economic sociology' ('Wirtschaftssoziologie'). 'Social economics' was not an uncommon term around the turn of the century in Germany. It was also the term that was picked for the series that Weber was appointed to edit in 1909 and in which *Wirtschaft und Gesellschaft* was eventually published.[6] Weber himself used 'social economics' in several of his writings but maybe most extensively in '"Objectivity" in Social Science', an essay written in 1904 when Weber assumed, together with Werner Sombart and Edgar Jaffe, the editorship of the *Archiv für Sozialwissenschaft und Sozialpolitik*. In discussing, as he put it, 'the science of social economics' ('die sozialökonomische Wissenschaft') Weber notes that its range is 'almost overwhelming'. Three major areas can however be distinguished: (1) '"economic" events', (2) '"economically relevant" phenomena', and (3) 'economically conditioned phenomena' (50, pp. 64–6). The first of these mainly covers economic institutions; the second concerns phenomena which are not economic but which have important economic consequences; and the third concerns non-economic phenomena which are influenced by economic factors. In the essay about objectivity, Weber also discusses how a phenomenon in 'social economics' is to be studied (e.g. 50, p. 77). One starts with 'the general aspects' of an economic phenomenon; one then goes to the 'concrete historical facts'; and finally one ascertains its 'cultural significance'. It is consequently through a mixture of economic theory, economic history and sociology that an analysis in 'the science of social economics' is to be carried out.

It should be stressed that this interpretation of how Weber viewed 'social economics' (which admittedly is a reconstruction based on a few scattered remarks by Weber) has been mainly made to show that 'sociology' tended to blend with economic theory and economic history in the 'social economic' analysis. In chapter 2 of *Wirtschaft und Gesellschaft* there is, by contrast, a conscious effort to outline the specific perspective of sociology and to develop a distinct 'economic sociology' — a term which now appears in Weber's scholarship for the first time.[7]

Figure 4 gives a visual representation of the argument at this point. In most of his analyses of economic phenomena Weber operated mainly along the vertical axis of 'social economics', which led to an analysis which was a mixture of sociology, economic theory and economic history. In part one of *Wirtschaft und Gesellschaft*, on the other hand, his interest was first and foremost along the horizontal axis of 'interpretive sociology', which helps to explain how Weber came to develop a specific 'economic sociology'.

This means among other things that if one wants to locate Weber's early contributions to economic sociology one has to look in several places, such as in his legal writings, his economic-historical writings, and so on. Two examples of interesting studies in this context are 'Die Börse' and Weber's contribution to the survey of industrial workers, which was carried out from 1909 to 1911 by the *Verein für Sozialpolitik* (161; 164; see also 147, pp. 85–6; 132, pp. 111–36). In the former work Weber makes sharp sociological observations about the general function that stock exchanges play in the modern economy, and he also discusses the conditions under which speculative behaviour is apt to arise. In the study for the *Verein*, Weber touches on such topics as the sociological dimension of productivity and the life cycle of industrial workers.

It is in chapter 2 of *Wirtschaft und Gesellschaft*, however, that Weber's most sustained effort to develop an 'economic sociology' is to be found. From the very beginning of this chapter Weber emphasizes that 'what follows is not intended in any sense to be "economic theory"' (52, p. 63); the purpose is to develop a 'sociological theory of the economy' (51, p. 34). Weber goes about this task by first defining economic action exclusively from a sociological perspective ('social economic action'). It should be noted in this context that Weber was careful to stress that to analyse topics from the viewpoint of 'interpretive sociology' does not mean to reduce them to 'psychic phenomena'; economic sociology, he says, 'must start out on the one hand from the fact that there is a *desire* (demand) for utilities ... and on the other hand from the fact that *provision* is being made to furnish the supplies to meet this demand' (52, p. 64). From the concept of social-economic action Weber then goes on to construct a series of more complex 'sociological categories'. That his project of economic sociology was ambitious and

FIGURE 4
'Social Economics' and 'Economic Sociology' in the Work of Max Weber

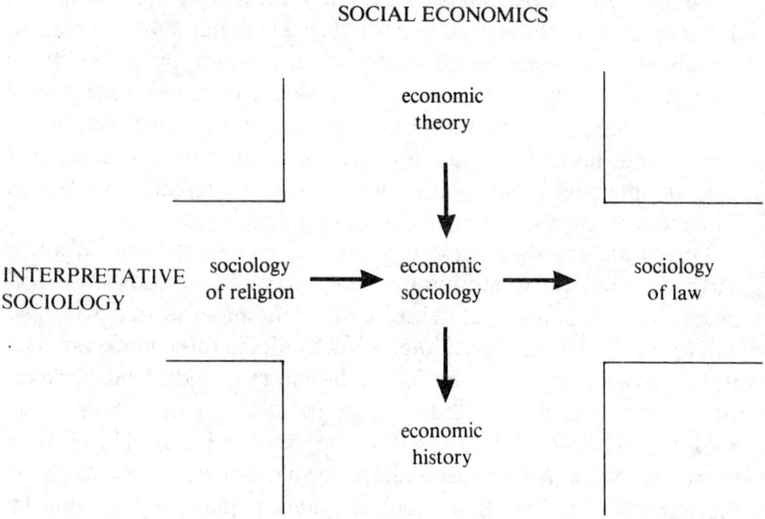

covered the core as well as the periphery of the economy, can be seen from the topics he discussed: 'the market', 'trade', 'money', 'occupation', 'the financing of political bodies', 'the expropriation of the workers from the means of production', and so on.

Throughout the second chapter in *Wirtschaft und Gesellschaft* Weber makes an effort to discern the points on which the perspectives of economic sociology and economic theory differ from each other as well as converge. In general, Weber was positive towards economic theory and felt — as noted in the discussion of Weber's 'social economics' — that the main function of economic sociology was to 'supplement' economic theory (163; 138, p. 31). His statement in chapter 2 that 'the theoretical insights of [economic theory] provide the basis for economic sociology' should not, however, blind one to the fact that economic sociology in its Weberian version differs on crucial accounts from marginal theory (52, p. 68; for a different interpretation, see e.g. 64, pp. 204–12; 108, pp. 290–5). Sociological phenomena, Weber makes clear, 'follow their own laws' (52, p. 341).

Two examples of the sharp differences that exist between the perspectives of economic sociology and neoclassical theory concern the element of *power* in economic life and the concept of *rationality*.

'It is essential', we thus read, 'to include the criterion of power of control and disposal (*Verfügungsgewalt*) in the sociological concept of economic action' (52, p. 67). As to the rationality concept, Weber splits it up into two categories, which are linked to each other in contradictory and complex ways: 'formal rationality of economic action' and 'substantive rationality of economic action' (52, pp. 85–6). The former displays many similarities with the concept of rationality that is used in economics. 'Substantive rationality', however, is linked to 'criteria of ultimate ends' and thereby goes far beyond the concerns of traditional economic theory.

Weber himself regrets at one point in *Wirtschaft und Gesellschaft* that his typology in economic sociology lacks 'the flesh and blood [of] a genuine explanation' (52, p. 116). His death in 1920 prevented him from working out his categories in a full manner. For those economic sociologists who are interested in picking up Weber's project on this point, he has, however, left good clues as to how to proceed. Several examples could be mentioned, but we shall limit ourselves to one, namely, his attempt to develop a 'sociology of the market' (52, pp. 81–3, 635). Weber suggests that one should concentrate on the conflict between 'market freedom' and 'regulation of the market'. The hypothesis is advanced that 'substantive regulation' in a formally free market 'tends to develop when certain participants in the market are, by virtue of . . . their monopolistic powers, . . . in a position to influence the market situation in such a way as actually to abolish the market freedom of others' (52, p. 83).

Emile Durkheim

At about the same time as Weber was developing 'economic sociology', Durkheim independently conceived of the same idea. In the first issue of *L'Année Sociologique*, which was published in 1896–97, we thus find a substantial section on 'sociologie économique'. This topic was from now on to be included in every issue of the journal, a fact which indicates the importance that Durkheim attached to it. When Durkheim himself first started to use the term 'sociologie économique' is unclear; in any event it can be found in his review from 1901 of Georg Simmel's *The Philosophy of Money* (14, p. 141).

Little systematic attention has been paid to Durkheim's economic sociology, and he has often been classed as a moral thinker. Raymond

Aron writes for example that 'the social problem for Durkheim is not so much economic as moral' (112, p. 85). This attitude to Durkheim's work, however, hides more than it reveals. The Durkheimian analysis of economic phenomena is in actuality very profound and deserves to be understood in its own terms. If this is done, it will soon become apparent that Durkheim's work includes substantial contributions to economic sociology as well as to the sociology of moral life.

An introduction to Durkheim's work in economic sociology would have to cover at least three topics. First, there is the critique of the economists, which recurs regularly throughout Durkheim's work. Second, the problems that the de-regulation of the economy entails is a theme to which Durkheim constantly returned. And third, there exist in Durkheim's work a few very interesting studies of the evolution of specific economic institutions, such as the contract and private property.

Durkheim's critique of the economists is interesting, not the least because it gives an indication of the knowledge that Durkheim had of economics (see e.g. 116, pp. 22–7; 117; 119; 121, pp. 468-93). Durkheim thus seems to have been fairly conversant with French, British and German economics. He knew a bit of economic history but was ignorant — like Weber — of the technical side of economic theory.[8] His main criticism of the economists was that they approached the study of economic phenomena in a fundamentally wrong manner. Instead of starting out by looking at the way 'facts are really interconnected', they took as their departure an arbitrary and 'purely individual factor, the desire for wealth' (116, pp. 26, 101). As a result, the enterprise of the economists was turned into 'a simple, logical analysis' of 'pure intellect' (116, p. 24). Durkheim points out that 'the famous law of supply and demand, for example, has never been inductively established, as should be the case with a law referring to economic reality. No experiment or systematic comparison has ever been undertaken for the purpose of establishing that, *in fact*, economic relations *do* conform to this law' (116, p. 26).

How then should a proper study in economic sociology be carried out according to Durkheim? The answer to this question can first of all be found in *The Rules of Sociological Method*, which is exemplary in the stringency with which it outlines the sociological perspective. Further hints as to how to proceed when analysing economic phenomena can be found throughout Durkheim's work.[9] In 'Sociology and the Social Sciences' (1903), an article co-authored with Paul Fauconnet, one can for instance read:

> Classical political economy has created an economic world which does not exist, a *Güterwelt*, an isolated world, which is always identical to itself and in which conflicts between purely individual forces are solved according to unchangeable economic laws. In reality it is within collectivities, which are quite different from each other, that the individuals try to enrich themselves, and the nature as well as the success of these efforts changes with the nature of the collectivity within which they appear. (121, pp. 487–8)

Given his harsh criticism of the economists, Durkheim has been accused of adopting an 'imperialist' attitude towards economic science and of wanting to absorb 'political economy' into 'economic sociology' (e.g. 131, p. 6). Economists have also criticized Durkheim severely for reducing economics to the study of mere 'opinions' (e.g. 119, pp. 117, 129). Both charges have an element of truth in them, especially the former. Durkheim thus basically approved of Comte's charge in *Cours de Philosophie Positive* that political economy was unscientific and ideological (116, p. 25; 121, pp. 468–9). The difference between Comte and Durkheim is nevertheless significant. As opposed to Comte, Durkheim did not want to absorb 'political economy' into 'general sociology'. He felt that economic phenomena could be treated as separate from other social phenomena; room was thus made in Durkheim's vision of sociology — as opposed to Comte's — for a distinct 'economic sociology'.[10]

The great theme in Durkheim's economic sociology is without doubt the de-regulation of the economy. The trend towards 'anomie', as Durkheim called it, is inherent in the *economic* development of Western society.[11] In *The Division of Labor in Society* Durkheim writes:

> In so far as the segmental type [of division of labor] is strongly marked, there are nearly as many markets as there are different segments. Consequently, each of them is very limited. Producers, being near consumers, can easily reckon the extent of the needs to be satisfied. Equilibrium is established without any trouble and production regulates itself. On the contrary, as the organized type [of division of labor] develops, the fusion of different segments draws the markets together into one which embraces almost all society ... The result is that each industry produces for consumers spread over the whole surface of the country or even of the entire world. Contact is then no longer sufficient. The producer can no longer embrace the market in a glance, nor even in thought. He can no longer see its limits, since it is, so to speak, limitless. Accordingly, production becomes unbridled and unregulated. (72, pp. 369–70)

Much of the vehemence in Durkheim's critique of the economists comes from the fact that they tended to advocate *laissez-faire* as a cure for the economy's ills, something which — in Durkheim's eyes — only meant more de-regulation. The market, as Durkheim saw it, is unable by itself to create a stable society. 'If interests relate men,' we read in *The Division of Labor*, 'it is never for more that some few moments' (72, p. 203).

Durkheim's celebrated analysis of the 'non-contractual elements of the contract' also belongs in this context (see especially 72, pp. 200–19; 128). A contract, Durkheim makes clear, involves a series of complicated and unspoken assumptions; the simple act of exchange between two people would not by itself suffice to tie the contracting parties together. Herbert Spencer's idea of an industrial society, where formal contracts would constitute the main links between people, is thus fundamentally wrong. One should try to strengthen the social element in the economy, not weaken it. An effective way of giving some cohesion to the economy, Durkheim suggested, would be to create 'professional organizations' which through their everyday activities were in contact with people as well as production (e.g. 118).

Durkheim's analysis of the social ills that the de-regulation of the economy entails has been widely discussed in the sociological literature. Less attention has been paid to his attempts in *Professional Ethics and Civic Morals* to explain the evolution of private property and the contract (118, pp. 121–200). Part of the reason for this is probably that these two studies are to be found in a lecture course. It is, however, time to make clear that they are of very high quality and deserve a prominent place in any discussion of Durkheim's economic sociology.

The analysis of private property starts by emphasizing the importance of 'the respect that property . . . inspires' (118, p. 121). Durkheim's argument, which is a real *tour de force* of theoretical brilliance, then takes a historical turn. At the beginning of time, Durkheim says, all land was regarded as sacred and owned by the gods. For privately owned property to emerge, the gods had to be driven out of the land and appeased with sacrifices at the boundaries. Durkheim writes: 'Around the thing appropriated, as around the sacred thing, a vacuum formed. All individuals had to keep at a distance, as it were, except those who had the required qualifications to approach it and make use of it' (118, p. 153).

Private property thus came into existence because individuals turned to their own benefit the respect that collective beliefs inspired. Durkheim firmly rejects the idea, however, that religion was simply used as an ideological pretext for satisfying individual greed. The situation is more complex, and Durkheim notes that landed property could originally not be sold nor could its boundaries be changed (118, p. 153). The religious conception was 'an obligation [which the owner] was under, rather than an expedient invented by himself in his own interest' (118, p. 153).

The analysis of the evolution of the contract in *Professional Ethics* has been overshadowed by the celebrated passages about the 'non-contractual elements of the contract' in *The Division of Labor in Society*. The discussion in the iecture series from 1898–1900 should, however, be seen as a complement to the ideas expressed a few years earlier in Durkheim's doctoral thesis. The starting point for Durkheim in *Professional Ethics* is the remarkable fact that in a contract two different people, by 'mere inclinations of the will', can enter into a brief relationship that is binding on both of them (118, p. 178). As in the analysis of private property, Durkheim goes far back in history for an explanation. The earliest form of contract ('ritual contract') consists of *two* binding links: those who enter the contract are tied to each other as well as to the gods invoked. The ritual element, Durkheim says, eventually fell away under the impact of trade and business ('consensual contract'), and finally the modern contract between two equal parties emerged ('contract of equity').

Durkheim's studies of private property and the contract definitely need to be discussed, so that one can see how they stand up to criticism. Whatever the outcome of such a debate, it should nevertheless be granted that Durkheim — just like Weber — has shown how powerful economic sociology can be when good theorizing and well-chosen historical facts are brought together.

Georg Simmel, Vilfredo Pareto and Thorstein Veblen

If it can be said that the 'economic sociology' of Weber and Durkheim has not been properly mapped out in the sociological literature, it is even more true of the contributions to this field of the three other key figures that helped to turn sociology into a distinct social science around the turn of the century: Simmel, Pareto and Veblen. These three thinkers, it can be noted, did not speak of 'economic sociology' as a special subfield of sociology. Nevertheless, they each made interesting sociological analyses of economic phenomena and should therefore be included in an overview of 'classical economic sociology'.

The fact that economic sociology has been allowed to fall into a certain oblivion during the twentieth century means, among other things, that the literature which tries to trace the contributions to economic sociology of Simmel, Pareto and Veblen is very meagre or non-existent. In this short overview of classical economic sociology, we shall therefore attempt to indicate only their most general contributions. Further research is needed, and it is our belief that if the works of these three thinkers were scrutinized from the perspective of economic sociology, they would show themselves to contain quite a few interesting sociological observations on the economy, which it has not been possible to include here.

Georg Simmel

In Georg Simmel's work one can find many references to economic matters since he often drew on material from different areas of social life to illustrate a point (see e.g. 150, pp. 263–4; 151, pp. 57–85). Nevertheless, it is in *The Philosophy of Money* (and in the articles that preceded this work; see 149, pp. 1, 37) that his most important contributions to economic sociology are to be found. This work is clearly not as substantial as Marx's *Capital* or Weber's *Economy and Society*, the two great classics in economic sociology, but it is still a very fine work in its own right.

Neither economists nor sociologists have paid much attention to *The Philosophy of Money* (e.g. 113, p. 216; 127, p. 97; 169, p. 646; see also 155). There are several reasons for this, the main one probably being that it is hard to fit Simmel's work into any one discipline. Just after the book was published, it was noted in *The American Journal of Sociology* that 'Simmel's *Philosophy of Money* does not belong to any special branch of science, and therefore to all; for this the competent representatives of the sciences in question will never pardon him' (111, p. 67). Durkheim, for example, felt that Simmel's book belonged to a 'genre of illegitimate [bâtard] speculation' (14, p. 145), and Weber was sure that any 'professional economist' would 'bitterly throw the book in the corner' after a few pages of reading (162, pp. 160–1).

Weber was probably more correct than Durkheim, since Simmel makes very clear that his analysis of money has nothing in common with economic theory (see however 127). *The Philosophy of Money* actually starts out with a polemic against the economists, and Simmel particularly wanted to make clear that the conventional economic analysis in no way 'exhausted' the richness of economic phenomena (149, pp. 54–6). It is actually under 'the surface level of economic affairs', he says, that the 'more profound' aspects of economic phenomena are to be found. Simmel consequently disapproved of the idea that there exist specific 'economic facts'. He noted:

> It is merely the fact that the aspect of [economic] phenomena closest to economics is the most interesting in practical terms, is the most thoroughly investigated and can be represented in the most exact manner which has given rise to the apparent justification for regarding them simply as 'economic facts'. (149, pp. 54–5)

The alternative to the economists' type of analysis that Simmel presents is a mixture of philosophical, sociological, aesthetic and historical reflections. Among these, the sociological element is relatively prominent, and Weber felt that *The Philosophy of Money* should be regarded as one of Simmel's 'major sociological writings' (162, pp. 159, 161). At times the emphasis of the sociological aspect is indeed very strong; in one place we thus read that 'money is entirely a sociological phenomenon, a form of human interaction' (149, p. 172).

To summarize the contribution of *The Philosophy of Money* to economic sociology is difficult because it is a very rich work which contains sociological observations on a multitude of economic topics, such as inflation, bribery, jewelry, credit, forged coins, lottery tickets, debasement of coins, and so on. Many of these analyses, it can be noted, are variations on the theme of 'exchange', which is central to Simmel's whole analysis. A special mention should also be made of the fact that Simmel was the first sociologist to realize the important role that 'trust' plays in economic life (e.g. 149, pp. 178–9, 480; see also 124). The following quotation from *The Philosophy of Money* gives an indication of Simmel's analysis on this point as well as the offhand way in which he presented his ingenious ideas:

> Viewed from the sociological perspective, there is no doubt that metallic money is . . . a promise and that it differs from the cheque only with respect to the size of the group which vouches for its being accepted. The common relationship that the owner of money and the seller have to a social group — the claim of the former to a service and the trust of the latter that this claim will be honoured — provides the sociological constellation in which money transactions, as distinct from barter, are accomplished. (149, p. 178)

Vilfredo Pareto

Since Vilfredo Pareto was a first-class economist as well as a prominent sociologist, the way he viewed the relationship between economics and sociology has attracted much attention. According to one interpretation, exemplified most typically by Paul Samuelson in *Foundations of Economic Analysis*, it is thus possible to 'separate economics from sociology upon the basis of rational or irrational behavior' (143, p. 90).[12] Sociologists who have looked more closely at Pareto do not necessarily disagree with this interpretation but usually point out that Pareto also saw sociology as a much needed 'complement' to economics (e.g. 123, p. 5; 137, p. 577; 139, p. 91; 141, p. 59).

Support for the idea that Pareto basically saw sociology as a complement to economics is easy to find in his writings. In 1917, for example, Pareto explicitly stated that sociology is 'an indispensable complement to the study of political economy' (Pareto as cited in 139, p. 91). And in *Trattato di sociologia generale* (according to 139, p. 94) one can read that 'the study of many so-called economic facts cannot be carried out without the help of sociology'. It should also be noted in this context that Pareto drew a sharp line between 'pure economics' and 'applied economics'. In the former, one studied 'abstract economic phenomena' and in the latter 'concrete economic phenomena', which entailed a look at many more factors (e.g. 134, pp. 337–89). 'Pure economics' and 'applied economics' were in their turn separated from 'sociology': 'economics is a small part of sociology, and pure economics is a small part of economics' (Pareto as cited in 139, p. 92).

A quite different viewpoint of the relationship between economics and sociology in Pareto can be found in Schumpeter's work. In a 1949 article on Pareto, Schumpeter argues that despite his attempt radically to separate economics and sociology, Pareto often mixed the two in the form of 'economic sociology'. That Pareto would do this was quite natural to Schumpeter, as the following quoation makes clear:

> There is nothing surprising in the habit of economists to invade the sociological field. A large part of their work — practically the whole of what they have to say on institutions and on the forces that shape economic behavior — inevitably overlaps the sociologist's preserves. In consequence, a no-man's land or everyman's land has developed that might conveniently be called economic sociology. (145, p. 134)

Guy Perrin, the leading French interpreter of Pareto's sociology, has denied that one can find any trace of 'economic sociology' in Pareto's work (139, p. 105). This is true, as we have seen, if one accepts Pareto's own distinctions between 'pure economics', 'applied economics', and 'sociology'. In the *Trattato* Pareto also makes very clear that sociology should only '*supplement*, not replace' economics (135, p. 34). Still, when one looks at the sections in Pareto's writings where economic phenomena are analysed from other viewpoints than that of 'pure economics', it is hard not to agree with Schumpeter's assessment that what we have here is a form of 'economic sociology'. To show this we shall look at the three most famous examples of 'economic sociology' in Pareto: the discussion of protectionism in the *Manual of Political Economy*, and the analyses of cyclical change and speculators/rentiers in the *Trattato*.[13]

The study of protectionism in the *Manual* is presented as an analysis in 'applied economics' as opposed to 'pure economics' (134, pp. 368–87). If one looks at Pareto's analysis more closely, it becomes clear, however, that the stance Pareto takes here is clearly *sociological*. We are told under which conditions 'the bourgeoisie' and other social classes are for or against protectionism, what consequences this will have for them as well as their country, and which role 'social movements' play in disseminating the idea of protectionism.

The analysis of economic phenomena that can be found in the *Trattato* is very similar to the study of protectionism in the *Manual*. Quick sociological sketches are made of 'speculators' and 'rentiers', and it is then suggested that their attitudes to property will make them behave quite differently from each other in times of prosperity and crisis (e.g. 135, pp. 1563–5, 1644–7). In his discussion of cyclical change — 'the *pièce de résistance* of Pareto's empirical sociological theories', according to Parsons (137, p. 288) — there is finally an attempt to see how economic factors ('speculators' vs. 'rentiers'), political factors ('foxes' vs. 'lions'), and ideological factors ('faith' vs. 'scepticism') interact and produce a typical and recurrent rhythm in society (cf. 141). We thus conclude with Schumpeter, that Pareto — despite his attempt to establish a rigorous line of demarcation between economics and sociology — occasionally ended up in 'the no-man's land of economic sociology'.

Thorstein Veblen

Like Pareto, Thorstein Veblen was a professional economist of high class. Unlike the former, however, he drew no sharp line between economics and sociology, but rather tried to renew economics by placing it on a sociological foundation. The 'evolutionary economics' that Veblen developed was thus advanced as a direct alternative to mainstream economic theory.

Any attempt to assess Veblen's contribution to 'economic sociology' has to confront the fact that Veblen's politics has unduly influenced the reception of his work. This is particularly true of US sociology (148; 154), and we shall illustrate this with some statements about Veblen by two well-known sociologists, Talcott Parsons and C. Wright Mills. According to Parsons, who had no sympathies whatsoever for Veblen's political stance, 'Veblen was a highly unsophisticated person who demonstrates the typical reaction of a disillusioned idealist in his scientific work' (138, p. 40). Since we have Weber's work, Parsons continues, there is really no reason to read Veblen (138, p. 40). C. Wright Mills, whose political ideals were close to Veblen's, had the opposite opinion of his work. Veblen was thus not only 'the best critic of America that America has produced' (Mills in 157, p. vi) but also 'the best social scientist America has produced' (Mills as cited in 154, p. 107).

A more balanced and less political evaluation of Veblen's scientific work is definitely needed. A good example of what such an analysis would look like can be found in the brief discussion of Veblen in Robert Merton's essay 'Manifest and Latent Functions' (129, pp. 123–4). The focus here is on Veblen's concept of 'conspicuous consumption' as developed in *The Theory of the Leisure Class*. Merton points out how Veblen starts by carefully establishing what consumption looks like from a conventional economic perspective and how he then proposes that we 'as sociologists ... must go on to consider the latent functions of acquisition, accumulation and consumption' (129, p. 123). The notion of conspicuous consumption, according to Merton's attempt to rescue the scientific side of Veblen, '*precludes the substitution of naive moral judgments for sociological analysis*' (129, p. 124).

A careful re-evaluation of Veblen's work would have to include an assessment of his general theoretical contribution as well as his analyses of various concrete economic phenomena. The first of these tasks could be centred on Veblen's major programmatic statement, 'Why is Economics not an Evolutionary Science?', where 'evolutionary economics' is contrasted to British political economy and the historical school in economics (156). Concepts such as 'cumulative causation' and 'habits of thought' will have to be discussed as well as Veblen's heuristic use of 'hypothetical historical reconstruction' (e.g. 166). That Veblen, as Merton has stressed, 'is given to loose terminology' will not make this task any easier (129, p. 124).

The task of going through Veblen's work and trying to establish what is valuable in it from the viewpoint of economic sociology will no doubt be laborious but also exciting. To show that interesting sociological discussions of contemporary relevance can indeed be found even in the more obscure of Veblen's writings, we shall here quickly review two articles which are rarely cited in the sociological literature: 'The Barbarian Status of Women' from 1899 and 'The Opportunity of Japan' from 1915 (see however 125; 133). In the former, Veblen (158) uses the method of 'hypothetical historical reconstruction' to explain the inferior status of women; the general idea being that 'predatory elements' are still part of the culture (e.g. in the form of the male's 'ceremonial capture' of the woman before the 'ownership-marriage'). The economic element is introduced into the analysis through Veblen's hypothesis that women were originally taken as trophies from war raids and treated as a form of private property. He writes: 'The purpose of the argument is to point out that there is a close connection, particularly in point of psychological derivation, between individual ownership, the system of status, and the paternal household' (158, p. 63). Veblen's emphasis on the role that illegal seizures — here of women — have played in the development of private property can finally be contrasted with Durkheim's focus on 'the respect for property'.

In 'The Opportunity of Japan' Veblen tries to analyse Japan's 'unique combination of a high-wrought spirit of feudalistic fealty and chivalric honor with the material efficiency given by the modern technology' (160, p. 251). He rejects the argument that this situation is due to any 'innate and irreducible specific character peculiar to this people' and tries instead to explain it in sociological terms (160, p. 256). Like England, Veblen says, Japan is basically 'a nation of borrowers'. In contrast to England, however, Japan has not been exposed to technological change in a gradual way. It has rather — somewhat like Germany — adopted a novel technological civilization in a single blow. The social habits, which accompany the technological innovations have consequently not had the time to develop; hence Japan's 'unique combination' of feudalism and industrialization.

3
EUROPEAN ECONOMIC SOCIOLOGY, 1920s–1960s

Following the launch of economic sociology, there was a fairly long period during which progress in analysing economic phenomena from a sociological viewpoint was considerably slow. The main trend in sociology after World War I was to develop various subfields (e.g. 230), and somehow economic sociology got lost in this process. A series of specialized areas appeared which were concerned with some aspect of the economy: 'industrial sociology', 'consumer sociology', 'sociology of professions', and 'stratification studies'. No subfield, however, was developed for dealing with the economy as a whole.

The knowledge that sociologists had of economics also seems to have diminished during these years. It is absolutely essential for a sophisticated economic sociology, to follow what is happening in the economics profession, and this was simply not donc during the 1920–60 period. Parsons and Smelser's verdict in *Economy and Society* can stand as an epitaph over the period in question: 'few persons competent in sociological theory have any working knowledge of economics and conversely . . . few economists have much knowledge of sociology' (36, p. xviii).[14]

One can speculate about the reason why economic sociology failed to develop after 1920 into a dynamic area along the lines that had been suggested by the classical sociologists. Part of the explanation is probably that in the US, where sociology was to progress most effectively during the twentieth century, the resistance of the economists to the sociologists was also the strongest (see chapter 1). In 1948 Louis Wirth, looking back on the decades since the beginnings of American sociology, noted:

> The attempt to legitimize sociology in academic circles on the ground that it had a subject matter of its own left to sociology, as Small put it, the unenviable role of studying the trivial and neglected aspects of the social world which were regarded as too insignificant to merit the attention of political scientists and economists. It meant, essentially, that the sociologists would have to feed on the crumbs that dropped off the table of these better-established academic disciplines. The almost exclusive initial preoccupation of sociologists with such topics as poverty, delinquency and crime, insanity, marriage and divorce, slums, and other pathologies, together with such subjects as the community, voluntary groups, classes and races, which did not fit so readily into the frames of reference of the state or the market, attests to the correctness of this view. (243, p. 277)

It will of course not do to blame just the economists. In Europe, where the economists were less hostile — if not precisely welcoming to other social scientists — the sociologists failed just as much as in the US to develop a firm knowledge of economics. Maybe it was simply too much for the sociologists, who after all were still involved in developing their own science, to follow what was going on in the economics profession at the same time. Finally, there was the fact that during the years of depression, when classical economics seemed to have lost contact with reality, the economists very quickly produced new and sophisticated theories to account for what was going on. From one point of view, one can say that Keynes and the Stockholm School pre-empted the need for economic sociology.

Even if one is justified in characterizing the years between 1920 and 1960 as a period of fragmentation as far as economic sociology is concerned, this does not mean that no progress was made. On the contrary, some very fine works in economic sociology were produced during precisely these years by people like Joseph Schumpeter, Talcott Parsons, Everett C. Hughes and Karl Polanyi. Towards the end of the period, it should also be noted, the functionalist school in US sociology (especially Talcott Parsons, Neil Smelser and Wilbert E. Moore) made an interesting effort to restore the study of the economy to its proper place in sociology.

We will be discussing the 1920–60 period in two chapters — in this one, and in another called 'The "Economy and Society" Perspective in US Sociology'. The present chapter is intended, among other things, to serve as a reminder that, despite the dynamic development of American sociology during the period after World War I, European sociology also merits some attention. This is particularly true for economic sociology, since the effort to launch a field with this name was mainly continued after 1920 by European sociologists.

It should also be noted that, just as all attempts to put intellectual developments into various categories have something artificial about them, this is also true for our division of the 1920–60 period into 'European Economic Sociology' and 'The "Economy and Society" Perspective in US Sociology'. Schumpeter has thus been placed in the section on European sociology while Polanyi has ended up in the one on US sociology, despite the fact that both were European intellectuals who moved to the US. The division of European vs. American economic sociology is still useful, however, in that it draws attention to the fact that the sociological study of the economy developed in different directions on the two continents between 1920 and 1960.

The two places where economic sociology was most entrenched by the end of World War I were Germany and France. It was also here that the attempt to promote economic sociology was undertaken the most energetically. The best works during these years were, in our opinion, produced by Joseph Schumpeter and the group around *l'Année Sociologique*, and we shall therefore present them in some detail. A few words will also be said about other European contributions to economic sociology and about the trend after World War II towards a certain fragmentation of the field.

Joseph Schumpeter

Joseph Schumpeter was probably the most talented of the young scholars who developed an interest in economic sociology after World War I. Like Veblen and Pareto he was an economist of high calibre as well as being well-read in sociology (e.g. 170, p. 111). His works are conventionally divided into those that are economic and those that are sociological (e.g. 182; 195; 204; 239). *Capitalism, Socialism and Democracy* is regarded as an interdisciplinary work with something of interest for everybody (e.g. 193).

In general, sociologists have ignored Schumpeter and one will look in vain for a discussion of his work in the standard works on the history of sociology. He has, however, achieved a certain underground reputation in political sociology through *Capitalism, Socialism and Democracy*. The best-known article on Schumpeter's sociology — Herbert von Beckerath's 'Joseph Schumpeter as a Sociologist' — is typical in this aspect in that it focuses mainly on 'Schumpeter the political sociologist' (170, p. 117).

In our overview here, it is 'Schumpeter the economic sociologist', however, who is of interest. We shall look first at Schumpeter's opinion about the general relationship between economics and sociology and how 'economic sociology' fits into this scheme. We shall then turn to Schumpeter's more specialized studies in order to determine his concrete contribution to economic sociology.

In Schumpeter's very first major work, *Das Wesen und Hauptinhalt der theoretischen Nationalökonomie* of 1908, there is a brief section on the relationship between economics and sociology (214, pp. 539–41). He emphasized that economics and sociology are close to each other and that economists should welcome the development of sociology. One reason for this is that certain 'important themes' in economic theory cannot be adequately treated in a purely economic type of analysis. This is especially true for the way in which economic actors are 'organized'. Economic theory and sociology do, however, have distinctly different approaches to social reality and should therefore not be mixed. This, Schumpeter repeats, does not mean that sociologists should refrain from analysing economic phenomena. 'It is not correct to say, as one can sometimes hear, that economic theory deals with economic phenomena and sociology with the remaining forms of human activity' (214, p. 540). The important thing is that each science keeps to its own methodology. A sociology that realizes this, Schumpeter concludes, can be of 'the greatest service' to the economist.

In his later statements about the relationship between economics and sociology Schumpeter would pretty much stick to his position from 1908: sociology is useful for the understanding of economic phenomena, and economic theory should be kept separate from sociology. He gradually elaborated on the role of 'economic sociology', however, in analysing economic phenomena (e.g. 39), and for his final statement on this point one can consult his *History of Economic Analysis*. Schumpeter wrote that '[scientific] economics' — or *Sozialökonomie*, to use Weber's term — consists of 'four fundamental fields': 'economic theory', 'economic history', 'statistics and statistical method' and 'economic sociology' (40, pp. 20–1). Together with economic history, economic sociology studies the institutional framework within which the various economic theorems are applicable. What distinguishes economic sociology from economic history is that it looks at behaviour in a more 'generalized or typified or stylized' way.

The field of economic sociology, we read in the *History of Economic Analysis*, encourages close co-operation between economists and sociologists. Today, however, little of this exists: 'it is the fact that ever since the eighteenth century both groups [that is, economists and sociologists] have grown steadily apart until by now the modal economist and the modal sociologist know little and care less about what the other does, each preferring to use, respectively, a primitive sociology and a primitive economics of his own to accepting one another's professional results' (40, p. 26). Schumpeter also makes it quite clear that a sophisticated economic sociology will not be furthered by superficial forms of co-operation between economists and sociologists. 'Cross-fertilization might easily result in cross-sterilization', the reader is warned (40, p. 27).[15]

Schumpeter's contribution to economic sociology in terms of concrete analyses can be found in his sociological as well as in his economic writings. Among his purely sociological writings one should highlight 'The Sociology of Imperialisms' and 'The Crisis of the Tax State' (218; 217). Others also exist, however, such as his essay from 1927 on classes (219; see also 222).

Schumpeter's essay on imperialism has been severely criticized on the ground that it holds that capitalism is essentially anti-imperialist and that its definition of imperialism (' "objectless" tendencies toward forcible expansion') is too narrow (e.g. 187).[16] This critique is correct as far as it goes, but it does not do justice to the skilful way in which Schumpeter actually weaves together social and economic analysis of what he maybe too ambitiously calls 'imperialisms' and 'capitalism'. Older forms of imperialism are, for instance, cleverly explained as the outgrowth of a social situation where important groups are unable to live off their own labour and therefore develop an interest in wars and conquests (e.g. 218, p. 46). And side by side with the idea that *the pure or perfectly competitive capitalist economy* is incompatible with imperialism, there is also a theory of 'modern imperialism' (218). Schumpeter here suggests that 'export-dependent monopoly capitalism' is likely to result in protectionist measures, which in their turn encourage imperialist tendencies (218, pp. 75 ff.).

In a famous footnote in *Business Cycles* Schumpeter criticizes his earlier analysis of imperialism and says that he prefers 'Karl Renner's concept of Social Imperialism' (221, p. 696). What exactly Schumpeter means by this statement has caused some consternation (see especially 232, pp. 122–3). The most likely interpretation is that he had come to question his earlier theory that pure capitalism was anti-imperialist. That he still felt that his *formulation* of the problem was essentially correct is, however, clear from another place in *Business Cycles* where Schumpeter says that 'the deepest problem of the economic sociology of our epoch' is to decide whether modern imperialist tendencies 'grew out of the very logic of capitalist evolution, or were distortions of it traceable to extracapitalist influences' (221, p. 399).

While Schumpeter's study of imperialism has been somewhat misunderstood, his essay 'The Crisis of the Tax State' (1918) has been mostly ignored. This is a pity because Schumpeter here makes an interesting effort to develop what Rudolf Goldscheid in his pioneer work *Staatssozialismus und Staatskapitalismus* (1917) had called 'fiscal sociology' (185; see also 186). Sociologists, Schumpeter says, should pay attention to this 'special field' because 'the public finances are one of the best starting points for an investigation of society, especially though not exclusively of its political life' (217, p. 7).

Schumpeter's essay on the tax state falls into two parts, one which is general in nature and one which addresses the fiscal problems of Austria after World War I. The second part is fascinating enough — especially since Schumpeter was soon to become Finance Minister of Austria — even if today's sociologists are likely to find more of interest in the first and more general part. Schumpeter gives a brilliant historical sketch of how the modern state has come into being in Germany and Austria, which is centred around the emergence of taxes in the late feudal era. Schumpeter also discusses a range of questions surrounding a state's 'fiscal potential'; and he considers the possibility of a special kind of tax on 'entrepreneurial profit' in order to safeguard creativity in economic matters. Goldscheid and Schumpeter's work in fiscal sociology, it can be added, was continued in the 1930s and 1940s by Fritz Karl Mann in particular (e.g. 201; 202; see also e.g. 231).

In his economic writings Schumpeter always made it clear that his intention was exclusively to contribute to the development of economic theory. Despite this, his works in economic theory contain observations on how the economy works, and they point just as much in the direction of economic sociology. This can be illustrated by the analysis in his most important work in economic theory, *The Theory of Economic Development* (220; see also 215, pp. 463–548). Schumpeter here attempts to transform the traditional, static type of neoclassical theory into a dynamic one by incorporating into it his theory of the entrepreneur. When Schumpeter discusses the role of the entrepreneur, his analysis often takes a distinctly sociological turn. In one place Schumpeter the economist writes like this:

> any deviating conduct by a member of a social group is condemned, though in greatly varying degrees according as the social group is used to such conduct or not . . . Surmounting this opposition is always a special kind of task which does not exist in the customary course of life, a task which also requires a special kind of conduct. In matters economic this resistance manifests itself first of all in the groups threatened by the innovation, then in the difficulty in finding the necessary cooperation, finally in winning over consumers. (220, pp. 86–7)

The Theory of Economic Development contains the germs of several important themes in economic sociology: the entrepreneur, innovations, and so on (e.g. 176; 212). How far one can take the 'economic' observations in this work in a sociological direction can best be exemplified by *Capitalism, Socialism and Democracy* (102). This work contains a broad theory of the decline of capitalism, which is centred on the difficulties that entrepreneurial activity encounters in mature capitalism, as well as a host of other observations of value to economic sociology.

The French School of Economic Sociology

Even if Schumpeter was something of a one-man orchestra, there was only so much that a single person could accomplish (who, in addition, viewed himself more as an economist than as an economic sociologist). It is, therefore, of interest to note that in France between roughly 1920 and 1940 a team effort was made to develop 'economic sociology' (see e.g. 175; 194). Those involved in this project — the key figures were François Simiand, Célestin Bouglé, and Maurice Halbwachs — had all been members of the original group around Durkheim, and their work is therefore to be found mainly in the *Année Sociologique* and *Annales Sociologiques*. Besides the sections on 'sociologie économique' in these two journals, some book-length studies were also produced.

If one were to enumerate the more important contributions by the *Année*-group to economic sociology, the list would have to include at least Maurice Halbwach's studies on the hierarchy of needs in the working class (188; 189), Célestin Bouglé's overview of economic sociology in France (175), Marcel Mauss' essay on the gift (205), and François Simiand's studies of wages and long-term fluctuations in the economy (224; 225; 226). What united these studies was a common analytical perspective, which Bouglé summarized in the following way:

> social facts, independently of which category they belong to — economics, politics, religion or morality — follow certain laws; it is possible to get to these constant elements by comparative research; if one is to understand the intricacies of social facts, institutions, customs and collective representations, one has methodically to apply the perspective of social wholes and also take into consideration the way the structure of groups, their needs and influence, keep society going. (175, p. 221)

Of the works by the *Année*-group the two most outstanding are, in our opinion, Marcel Mauss' essay 'The Gift' and François Simiand's *Le Salaire, l'évolution sociale et la monnaie*. These two studies are in many ways each other's opposites and therefore give an indication of the range of French economic sociology from this period. Mauss' study is a short essay, whose main value for economic sociology resides in its bold theorizing about various economic institutions. Simiand's work is, in contrast, a massive three-volume study with a focus on mainly empirical facts.

'The Gift' is not a work which falls into one specific field of sociology; instead, it is preoccupied with the exchange of gifts in archaic cultures viewed as a 'total social phenomenon'. In spite of this, certain aspects of Mauss' essay can be said to belong to economic sociology, and the author conducts a polemic at several points against the individualistic and utilitarian tradition in economic theory (205, pp. 69, 73–5). One of the major points in the essay obviously concerns the social structure of gifts. The author rejects the idea that the gift is simply a sign of generosity and says that what characterizes it are 'three obligations': 'the obligation to give', 'the obligation to receive', and 'the obligation to repay' (205, pp. 11, 16, 37–41).

Mauss' essay is an excellent theoretical work which contains ingenious hypotheses about several economic phenomena other than gifts. Generosity, credit, interest, alms giving, social welfare, consumption and contracts are all touched upon. To give a flavour of Mauss' brief but insightful comments on these institutions, we shall take a quick look at his analysis of credit. Mauss' main point here is that the notion of credit is centred on *an obligation to repay in the future* and that this phenomenon is present in many different forms in archaic societies, especially in the gift (205, pp. 34–5). It is consequently wrong to insist that credit as an institution represents a stage later than barter in the evolution of society: 'On this point, legal and economic theory is greatly at fault. Imbued with modern ideas, current theory tends towards a priori notions of evolution, and claims to follow a so-called necessary logic; in fact, however, it remains based on old traditions' (205, p. 34).

Simiand's *Le salaire, l'évolution sociale et la monnaie* uses as its source material workers' salaries in France from the eighteenth century until 1930. The primary aim of the study is to see how these salaries have varied over time and how this can be explained. Simiand finds five distinct phases in the fluctuations of salaries: an upturn during the period from the beginning of the French Revolution to the beginning of the nineteenth century; a downturn during the next decades until 1850; then an upturn until 1880; a downturn to about 1900; and finally an upturn until 1930. Simiand reaches this result on the basis of a very careful, statistical analysis.

To find what has caused these cyclical variations Simiand examines various demographic, legal and technological factors. He finds, however, that none of them can adequately account for the long-term fluctuations in salaries. Instead, the real cause, according to Simiand, is to be found in price movements. They, in their turn, are explained by the amount of money in circulation. We read:

> What is behind the rise in salaries during the nineteenth and twentieth centuries and, more generally, the predominantly favourable economic development in its entirety, is not the constitution of the economic system, the development of economic liberty, changes in technology, capitalism or socialism; it is the discovery and exploitation of the gold mines in California, then in Transvaal and Klondike. Also involved is the so-called 'fiduciary inflation' at the beginning of the nineteenth century and even more so during the second and third decades of the twentieth century. (226, p. iv)

Simiand's fairly surprising explanation should not be interpreted as a case of straightforward monetarism. Money, Simiand says, is a 'social reality' (227). Simiand's study can perhaps be better described as a form of 'social monetarism', to borrow an expression from Bouglé (175, p. 147). However this may be, it should be stressed that Simiand's empirical results (as distinct from his explanation) have been judged very highly by French historians. Pierre Vilar has also pointed out that Simiand's fluctuations coincide roughly with Kondratieff's cycles (237, pp. 320–1).

Mauss' and Simiand's studies give an indication of the interesting kind of economic sociology that was produced by the group around the *Année Sociologique*. It should be pointed out, however, that the impact of its work in economic sociology was to be extremely weak. The reason for this is not clear. In our opinion the main factor was probably the appearance of several new and vigorous subfields in French sociology after World War II. But there might also have been some 'internal' factors involved. The Durkheimian school of economic sociology has, for instance, been accused of being too 'social psychological' in nature (e.g. 194, pp. 25–6). The appreciation of Simiand's work has also been marred by his unsuccessful attempt to develop a totally new methodology in economics.[17] Finally, the French sociologists might have been a bit too quick in rejecting Marx's work, thereby closing themselves off from some of the great themes in economic sociology.

Other Contributions from the Period

During the period when the *Année*-group and Schumpeter were at the height of their activity, other contributions to economic sociology were also being made in Europe. They often consisted of fairly general discussions of sociology versus economic theory (see e.g. 213). Leopold von Wiese's article 'Economic Theory and Economic Sociology' (56) belongs to this category as well as Adolf Löwe's lecture series in the 1930s at the London School of Economics, *Economics and Sociology: A Plea for Co-operation in the Social Sciences* (200). There was also an emerging interest in analysing the history of economic thought from a sociological perspective (see e.g. 180; 228). Mention should finally be made of the works in economic sociology during this period by Karl Mannheim and some other German sociologists (see e.g. 198; 233; 234; 235; 240 for Tönnies and Sombart; for Oppenheimer, see 126, pp. 108–219). Mannheim's 1930 article on 'economic ambition' contains, for example, an interesting analysis of different forms of 'success' (34). His most substantial contribution to economic sociology is, however, to be found in *Man and Society in an Age of Reconstruction* with its discussion of *laissez-faire* and economic planning (203). Mannheim's general thesis, which was a result of his experience with the rise of fascism, was that *laissez-faire* had played out its role in Western society and that some form of planning was needed if further disasters like Nazism were to be avoided.

If economic sociology in France and Germany had begun to lose its vitality by the late 1930s, the situation changed for the worse during the years after World War II. Works in 'economic sociology' continued to appear during the 1950s and early 1960s, but the emphasis was almost exclusively on general discussions of economic theory versus sociology (e.g. 172; 178; 181; 238) and on sociological analyses of the history of economic theory (e.g. 131; 171; 184; 197; 241).[18] Some of this work is of good quality — in particular Eisermann's (122; 123; 182) and Weiller's (239) studies of Pareto, Schumpeter, and the Historical School — but much of it is simply a rehash of old ideas.

The economic sociology that existed in Europe in the 1950s and early 1960s thus showed clear signs of being exhausted. Whatever fascination the topic still held in certain circles paled in comparison with the interest that the new ideas from the United States were able to inspire in a new generation of sociologists. One observer, Franz-

Xavier Kaufmann, noted *à propos* the situation in Germany that 'the strong affinity between economics and sociology in the German historical school and the older concepts of 'Social Sciences' has waned after World War II, due to the reception of the American traditions both in economics and sociology' (196). In post-war France too, economic sociology quickly lost out to the new fields in sociology which were emerging under the impact of US sociology. 'Sociologie du travail', the French version of 'industrial sociology', quickly became the most popular area of research (211, p. 25). That people like Georges Friedmann, Alain Touraine and Michel Crozier produced excellent studies is not to be doubted; *The Anatomy of Work* (183), *L'Evolution du travail ouvrier aux usines de Renault* (236), and *The Bureaucratic Phenomenon* (177) are all minor classics.

What should be pointed out, however, is that in the new subfields which appeared too little attention was paid to questions of economic structure. In his book on the history of the group around *Sociologie du travail*, Michael Rose (211, p. 38) has pointed out that if Georges Friedmann had paid more attention to economic forces, he would have been less inclined to develop a theory that technology inevitably leads to the de-humanization of work. And behind the incapacity of the French sociologists to reject the popular thesis of the convergence of industrial societies was the fact that they lacked a 'modicum of technical economic knowledge or [a] passing interest in economic structures and events per se' (211, p. 168). While new subfields like *sociologie du travail* raised new and fascinating questions of distinct interest to economic sociology, it is also clear that the lack of sophistication in economic sociology among the European sociologists after World War II severely handicapped them in several ways. By looking at just one aspect of the economic process, they had in a sense purchased progress at the expense of the totality; *le travail en miettes*, as Friedmann put it.

If one were to sum up the development in economic sociology between 1920 and 1960 in Europe it would first of all be noted that the promise of a vigorous and dynamic economic sociology, which had been raised by the preceding generation, had not been fulfilled. This said, however, it should be stressed that some interesting works in economic sociology were indeed produced during these years. To save them from oblivion and to start discussing them should constitute a natural task for today's economic sociologists.

4
THE 'ECONOMY AND SOCIETY' PERSPECTIVE IN US SOCIOLOGY

Sociological analysis of the economy developed along quite different lines in the USA and in Europe. No effort was made in the USA to develop a specific 'economic sociology', and it seems that the European effort in this direction was ignored on the other side of the Atlantic.[19] The term 'economic sociology' has actually never been popular in the USA (see, however, 45; 331). There nonetheless exists a rough equivalent to what in Europe was called 'economic sociology', and that is the 'economy and society' approach.

Exactly when the expression 'economy and society' started to be used by American sociologists is unclear.[20] The term nevertheless captures something essential in the attitude of US sociologists to economic questions during 1920–60. As we recall from the discussion in chapter 1, US sociology had been forced to define itself as a 'left-over science' in order to gain legitimacy in the universities. The expression 'economy and society' is an outgrowth of this tradition; and the term essentially implies that 'society' and 'the economy' — as defined by the economists — are separate as well as different in nature.

After the fight over institutionalization, American sociologists tended to leave alone the study of those parts of the economy in which the economists had established themselves as experts. This meant quite a huge area which included markets, price formation, investment decisions, and so on. Instead, the sociologists concentrated their effort on those parts of the economy which had been ignored, such as life in the factories, the formation of professions, and social mobility. Good advances were indeed made in these areas. The lack of a natural centre, around which these contributions could gravitate is, however, equally obvious. Between 1920 and 1960 a series of new sub-areas appeared which all covered some aspect of the economy: 'industrial sociology', 'sociology of occupations and professions', 'stratification theory', 'consumer sociology', and 'sociology of business'. Each of these pulled in a direction of its own, and none dealt with the economy as a whole.

On a general level, the 'economy and society' perspective meant that a distorted and fragmented picture of the economy was all that was available in the sociological literature. It also made it exceedingly hard for those sociologists who were interested in economic questions to keep track of whatever advances were made. Since the economy was not acknowledged as a special area of interest per se, the relevant literature was scattered across a bewildering number of studies and journals. The picture that emerges, when one tries to piece together the US contribution to economic sociology from the 1920–60 period, is consequently similar to that of any specialized area of science which has not yet been acknowledged: ideas are lost, leads are not followed up and the wheel is periodically reinvented.

The very fact that the 'economy and society' perspective leads to a fragmentation of what naturally constitutes economic sociology makes it difficult to present an adequate picture of it in a few pages. We have tried to solve this difficulty by singling out three key topics: the attitude to economics in the Chicago School; concrete contributions to economic sociology during the 1920–60 period; and the attempt in the 1950s by the structural-functionalists to overcome the process of fragmentation.

The Chicago School and the Study of the Economy

Judging from Lester Kurtz' recent book on the critical literature about the Chicago School, no-one has taken a close look at its relationship to economics (273). This is a task which should be undertaken, however, in order to get a more rounded picture of the Chicago School as well as an understanding of the US contribution to economic sociology. In the meantime, it can be noted that the Chicago sociologists seem to have had a fairly limited interest in economics and a superficial knowledge of the literature. Morris Janowitz, in an answer to our queries, has put it like this: 'The Department of Sociology, ever since the 1920s, was informed about the main themes of economic research. The case was that the Department members, in general, rejected economic analysis, and did not spend extensive time and energies on the matter' (270).

Janowitz' opinion should be supplemented by a scrutiny of the 'bible' of the Chicago School, Park and Burgess' *Introduction to the Science of Sociology*. Economics as a science is here passed over in a few lines and no thorough attempt is made to establish its relationship to sociology (cf. e.g. 305, pp. 43, 53–4, 495–6). The work does contain a fairly long section on 'competition' (305, pp. 504–73), but the emphasis is more on competition as a universal form of interaction than as an economic phenomenon; it ends up being one of the four basic forms of 'the social process' — ('competition-conflict-accommodation-assimilation').[21]

On the whole, the Chicago sociologists followed the 'left-over' tradition in US sociology and stayed away from the topics that interested the economists (e.g. 243, p. 277). Luckily for sociology, mainstream economists had a very narrow view of what economics should deal with and this left some good topics for outsiders from the other social sciences. The two people of the Chicago School who were the most eager to seize on them, were William F. Ogburn and Everett C. Hughes. It can also be noted that several other works by Chicago sociologists contain material of interest to the economic sociologist, especially ethnographical details. This is, for example, true of Harvey W. Zorbaugh's *The Gold Coast and the Slum*, Paul G. Cressey's *The Taxi-Dance Hall*, Frances R. Donovan's two books on waitresses and saleswomen in Chicago, and Earl S. Johnson's 'The Function of the Central Business District in the Metropolitan Community' (255; 257; 258; 271; 346).

Of the Chicago sociologists, William F. Ogburn probably knew most about economics. He taught the topic early in his career, and throughout his life he seems to have maintained a lively interest in certain aspects of it. Some of his articles can be found in economic journals, such as the *American Economic Review*, and his work during World War I for the National War Labor Board and the Bureau of Labor Statistics established him as 'a pioneer in methods of analysing family budgets and constructing price indexes' (259, p. x). His writings on population, economic growth and the standard of living should be mentioned in this context as well as his interest in the effects of the business cycle on social trends and the electoral process (see 303, pp. 349–60).

It is for his studies on the social impact of technology, however, that Ogburn is more famous. His work on the 'cultural lag' has often been criticized on the ground that it constitutes 'a technological interpretation of history' (see e.g. 303, p. 90). This is not entirely untrue, but as so often happens, more needs to be said. Ogburn should be credited for being one of the first to attempt a 'sociology of invention' (e.g. 302, pp. 80–102). The thrust of his argument on this point is that inventions owe more to the social milieu than to individual genius. 'The existing culture', we read, 'is the mother of invention' (302, p. 83).[22]

One aspect of Ogburn's 'sociology of invention', which seems to have escaped notice, concerns his division of inventions into 'technological inventions' and 'social inventions' (e.g. 304, pp. 572–7). As examples of the latter, he mentions 'instalment selling', 'the holding company' and 'the investment trust'. The idea of 'social inventions', which originates with Weber, seems particularly useful for economic sociology since it introduces an interesting discontinuous element into the socio-economic process. Ogburn's notion that one should also look at the social changes caused by 'non-material inventions' is another idea worth following up.

By contrast to Ogburn, Everett C. Hughes does not seem to have been particularly interested in economics. He was not antagonistic to it, however, nor did he deny the validity of the approach. This comes out clearly in 'Mistakes at Work', which is one of the few places where Hughes directly addresses the question of the relationship between sociology and economics (267, pp. 323–5). Hughes says that 'in the historical and conventional division of academic labor, work has belonged to the economist'. This means that 'a sociologist should stay out of the factories because the economist was there first'. To let a social science be defined by the topic it studies is totally wrong, however, according to Hughes:

> To the extent that there is some logic in the academic division of labor, representatives of each discipline will be found studying not merely some one institution but any events which yield to effective analysis by their particular logic. Economics will cease to be merely — if it ever was — the science of markets; anthropology, of primitive peoples; education, of what happens in schools; sociology, of families, churches, play-grounds, settlement houses, and prisons. (267, pp. 324–5)

It is thus clear that Hughes saw his own work on occupations and professions as something of an intrusion into the economists' area. He went about his analysis in a very different way from the economists, however, whom he mildly reproached for not wanting to deal with 'the human mess' (267, p. 324). Hughes' contribution to the sociology of occupations — a field which he practically created on his own — is well known, and most sociologists are familiar with his subtle analyses in books like *French Canada in Transition* and articles like 'Good People and Dirty Work', 'Work and Self' and 'The Knitting of Racial Groups in Industry' (265; 266; 268; 269).

The emphasis in Hughes' work is basically on laying bare the sociological and social-psychological mechanisms that operate in 'the social drama of work', and in this effort the economic dimension is often missing. How powerful Hughes' type of analysis still is when confronted with economic questions can be seen from his somewhat neglected doctoral thesis 'A Study of a Secular Institution: The Chicago Real Estate Board'. Hughes makes clear that what he mainly wants to do is to look at 'institutions' in general (264, pp. 1–10). The study nevertheless contains many sociological observations of direct relevance to economic sociology. One of these has to do with the process of commodification, to use a marxist term. Competition in the real estate business, according to Hughes, first leads to a de-secularization of the relations between people — but then something else happens. Within the market, personal networks and professions begin to emerge:

> An interesting paradox appears at this point. The very organization which is bent on making land a commodity is also bent on introducing into the dealings of real estate men something approaching the control which the elder professions have attempted to establish over their practice. It is likely that there is a constant tendency in any group for objects and ideas to become sacred. (264, pp. 114)

The 'Hughes Paradox' is that commodification also entails de-commodification — here via the process of professionalization.

Another fine observation in the thesis on the real estate business in Chicago concerns stratification. Hughes' point here is that there are two kinds of occupational mobility; the first being the conventional, individual kind and the other when a whole group of people try to advance their position by turning an 'occupation' into a 'profession'. How unevenly this process can turn out for different members of an occupation is discussed in a companion article to the thesis, where Hughes (263, pp. 326–37) presents an interesting typology of people in the real estate business ('the realtor', 'the real estator', 'the foreign-language agent', 'the salesman' and 'the promoter or boomer').

Some Scattered Contributions

When the domination of the Chicago School had come to an end around the mid-1930s, the fragmentation of economic sociology was formalized into various subfields. It is not difficult to point out some of the weaknesses inherent in each of them from the viewpoint of economic sociology. Industrial sociology thus tended to over-emphasize the networks of workers and paid too little attention to the economic functioning of the factory and the industry involved;

modernization studies were far too often social psychological in nature and ignored the impact of imperialism and international trade relations; and stratification studies focused too much on individual mobility and abstracted from the general economic structure of society. Finally the theory of 'industrial society', which became popular in the 1950s and early 1960s, was too strongly influenced by a kind of technological determinism.

There was also the fact that many topics of interest to economic sociology fell between the various subfields. In 1959 Paul Lazarsfeld claimed that practically all aspects of 'business', for example, were neglected in US sociology ('business' was defined by the author as 'all the activities connected with the manufacture and distribution of goods, excluding farming and the free professions, but including banking and research development within industrial organizations' [275, pp. 1-2]). As an illustration he pointd out that a 'rough content analysis of the *American Journal of Sociology* reveals that up to 1950 there had been hardly any articles at all on business' (275, p. 1). The reason for this, Lazarsfeld suggested, was that 'a majority' of American sociologists had an 'ideological bias against business': 'Aiding the doctor, promoting justice, or supporting the agencies of the law — all these are in accord with accepted norms; helping the business man make money is not' (275, p. 1).

In summarizing his argument, Lazarsfeld suggested that 'sociologists studying economic institutions have been interested mainly in the factory worker and his immediate superior. Other social aspects have been neglected' (275, p. 1). This statement might be correct on a general level but it needs to be supplemented with the observation that industrial sociology also contains much more than 'plant sociology' (272). As Eugene V. Schneider has recently pointed out, the industrial sociologists started out with great hopes for what they wanted to accomplish:

> At the time of its appearance, industrial sociology was hailed as the discipline which would finally free sociology from its position as the 'science of left overs' or as the academic custodian of trivialities. At last, sociology would move into the mainstream. Along with individual psychology and economics (business schools were hardly in the picture those days) sociology would deal with *the* central institution of American life, an institution whose influence was felt throughout society through the occupations (and livings) it offered, the products it manufactured and distributed and the values it inculcated or supported. (326, p. 261)

Some of this enthusiasm was translated into splendid sociological works, such as Melvin Dalton's *Men Who Manage* and William Foot

Whyte et al.'s *Money and Motivation* (256, 343).[23] There have recently been hints that a re-evaluation of industrial sociology is under way in economic sociology (see e.g. 22; 339). A systematic effort in this direction is to be hoped for, since it appears that some of the most interesting observations in industrial sociology were left undeveloped due to the prevailing lack of theoretical tools in the field. As an example of this, one can mention William Foot Whyte's observations on the sexual division of labour in *Human Relations in the Restaurant Industry* (342).

An effort also needs to be made to locate other 'lost' contributions to economic sociology from this period. Lazarsfeld mentions quite a few interesting studies in his 1959 article, and a superficial look at the vast sociological literature from the period indicates that there are plenty more. Some of these are already famous for reasons other than their contribution to economic sociology (e.g. 247; 248; 252; 281, pp. xi-xiii, 138–83; 283; 284) while others are rarely discussed today (e.g. 254; 277; 278; 282; 322; 323; 324; 340). Since most of these works are scattered in a variety of places, it will take some energy to locate the material. Judging from the quality of the studies we have been able to find, it will nevertheless be well worth the effort.

The Challenge of the 1950s (Parsons, Smelser, Moore and Polanyi)

We shall now turn to the mid-1950s and look at the effort that was then made to challenge the 'left-over tradition' and to put the economy back on the research agenda of sociology. The two most important works in this context are *Economy and Society* by Talcott Parsons and Neil Smelser (36) and *Trade and Market in the Early Empires*, edited by Karl Polanyi, Conrad M. Arensberg, and Harry W. Pearson (321). It should be stressed, however, that the people involved in this enterprise have also produced many other works of interest to economic sociology. Books could be written — and need to be written — abut the contributions to economic sociology of Talcott Parsons, Neil Smelser, Wilbert E. Moore and Karl Polanyi. Limitations of space force us to indicate only their most important works in a footnote, and to refer the reader to the comment there.[24]

With *Trade and Market and Economy and Society* US social science can be said to have overtaken European economic sociology, which by the 1950s had lost most of its original vitality. Social scientists in the 1950s had been reared in a long tradition, according to which 'the economy' and 'society' belonged to two different sciences, and this was not to be undone in one stroke. As we soon shall see, the works by Parsons, Smelser and Polanyi et al. are shot through with a fundamental ambiguity towards economic sociology. On the one hand, it is argued that economics is unable to explain what is really going on in the economy. On the other hand there is, however, still a tendency to grant the economists exclusive rights to explain the central economic phenomena in contemporary society. In other words, Polanyi and Parsons rebelled against the 'economy and society' tradition, but they were not able to make a total break from it.

This ambiguity is worked out differently in *Trade and Market* and *Economy and Society*. The former work consists of a collection of essays on the most diverse topics, loosely held together by the theoretical perspective elaborated in 'The Economy as an Instituted Process' by Polanyi (321, pp. 243–70). The basic thrust in this important essay is that the economy has to be seen as an essentially *social* process. The key sentence reads: 'The human economy . . . is embedded and enmeshed in institutions, economic and noneconomic' (321, p. 250). A new concept of the economy, which could be used in 'all the social sciences', had to be worked out. Polanyi stressed that one must go beyond 'the formal meaning' of the economy, which can be found in mainstream economics and which is centred on the market, and replace it with a 'substantive' one, meaning a notion of the economy which focuses on 'man's dependence for his living upon nature and his fellows' (321, p. 243). The first step in such an effort, Polanyi says, would be to develop new theoretical concepts; and he himself suggested various ideal-types for analysing trade, money and markets. The most famous of these are 'the forms of integration' which give the economy its unity and stability ('reciprocity', 'redistribution' and 'exchange').

There is an element of hesitation, however, in Polanyi's attack on the economists. This has mainly to do with his failure to work out categories for the economy in contemporary, as distinct from pre-industrial, society. In principle, Polanyi wanted his analysis to be valid for 'the past *and* present' (321, p. 244; emphasis added). The main thrust of his analysis is directed at the impossibility of using the categories of modern economic science when analysing non-modern societies, and his essay contains statements of the type that the 'formal' concept of the economy fits the development in Western Europe and the US during 'the last two centuries' (321, p. 244). The discussion of 'formalism' versus 'substantivism' in economic anthropology has inadvertently helped to draw attention to this latter element in Polanyi's thought and to obscure the fact that his original ambition was to develop a methodology which was

FIGURE 5
The Economy as a Social System According to Parsons and Smelser (1956)

I. THE DIFFERENTIATED SUB-SYSTEMS OF SOCIETY

A	Economy	Polity	G
L	Cultural-Motivational system	Integrative sub-system	I

II. FUNCTIONAL DIFFERENTIATION OF THE ECONOMY AS A SYSTEM

A	Capitalization and investment sub-system	Production sub-system — including distribution and sales	G
L	Economic commitments: physical, cultural and motivational resources.	Organizational sub-system: entrepreneurial function	I

III. ENTREPRENEURIAL SUB-SYSTEM

A	Financing of innovation	New combinations of factors of production	G
L	Mobility, flexibility and substitutability of factors of production (flow of resources)	Opportunity for innovation	I

Note: The entrepreneurial sub-system is only one of the four sub-systems of the economy. (A = adaptation: G = goal attainment; I = integration; and L = latent pattern maintenance and tension management).
Source: 36, pp. 44, 53, 203

as applicable to contemporary as to pre-industrial society. Recent works in economic sociology, it can be added, have quite correctly emphasized the relevance of Polanyi's thought for the analysis of today's economy (e.g. 22; 250).

In *Economy and Society* the authors basically apply Parsons' theory of the social system to the economy. A society or rather a social system is thus said to consist of four sub-systems, each of which handles one of the four basic functions of society: adaptation (A), goal attainment (G), integration (I), and latent pattern maintenance and tension management (L). These sub-systems, which all interact with each other and with the overarching social system, can be further divided according to the AGIL scheme. When this is done to the economic sub-system, which handles 'the adaptive function', the result is as shown in Figure 5.

It is no doubt easy to get lost in the theoretical subtleties of *Economy and Society*, but this should not detract from the realization that two very important steps towards a full-scale economic sociology were taken in this work. First, the economy was conceived of as *a distinct social system*, which is subordinate to society as a whole (e.g. 279; 316). And second, *Economy and Society* is the first work in modern economic sociology where an effort is made to draw on the most recent literature in economic science, such as Keynes, Domar, Samuelson, and so on. Parsons seems to have been responsible for the first of these accomplishments and Smelser for the second (see 36, pp. xix-xxi; 336, pp. 145–51).

In a letter to us Smelser has summarized the critique directed at *Economy and Society* like this:

> (a) That Parsons and I were guilty of the reification of abstract categories . . . (b) That the theoretical scheme put forth in *Economy and Society* did not have empirical relevance nor did it suggest overall lines of research . . . (c) That Parsons and I ignored the fact that economic activities are embedded in the social and institutional dimensions of life. (337)

It might be added that *Economy and Society* is at times too conciliatory towards economic theory (see also 246; 253; 261, pp. 304–13; 274; 316; 325, pp. 166–95). This probably arose from the fact that Parsons felt that the economists' analyses were essentially correct. In Parsons' Marshall Lectures, which contain a first version of *Economy and Society*, this is expressed very clearly: 'the further I have gone, the more convinced I have become of the essential soundness, from a sociologist's point of view, of the main core tradition of economics' (314, p. 68).

In conclusion, it can be said that the task of Parsons and Smelser — to catch up with and further develop a tradition in sociology which had more or less ended with Weber — was tremendous. It is not surprising, therefore, that their work is riddled with hesitations as to the main task of a fully developed economic sociology: *to explain the workings of the economy from a sociological perspective.*

PART II
Towards a New Economic Sociology, 1960s–?
Richard Swedberg

INTRODUCTION

By the mid-1950s and early 1960s the 'economy and society' perspective in US sociology had spread to several countries as a result of the international boom of American sociology after World War II. As we tried to show in chapters 3 and 4, this type of economic sociology was fragmentary and had one particular weakness: it tended to shy away from those topics with which the economists were dealing. The result was, at best, that the so-called 'sociological dimension' of economic phenomena was researched — but not the phenomena in themselves.

Since the mid-1960s, however, a new and exciting development has been under way in economic sociology. During the paradigm crisis in the late 1960s and early 1970s the 'economy and society' perspective in US sociology came in for heavy criticism. Sociological works started to appear which examined class society, the economic position of women and the workings of the capitalist system on an international level (e.g. 355). Later in the 1970s, when the world economy started to go into decline for a variety of reasons, economic questions more or less replaced social questions on the agenda of the day. As a result, sociologists broadened their repertoire and began to look at phenomena like stagflation, productivity decline, and the worsening position of Third World countries. Eyes were also turned towards the economic profession, and an attempt was made to evaluate the economic literature (e.g. 347). Economists came under criticism and felt the need for new theoretical approaches; Keynesianism fell into disrepute, and a variety of new and not-so-new theories made their appearance (e.g. 356).

The result of developments since the mid-1960s has been that a wealth of sociological studies has been produced, which in one aspect or another touch on economic questions. No attempt to evaluate these studies from the perspective of economic sociology exists. An inventory needs to be made, however, and a discussion opened up about their value for economic sociology.

It is exactly these two tasks that we shall try to undertake in this and the following chapters. Our guiding idea will be that one of the underlying themes in these works since the mid-1960s is an attempt to put the economy back on the agenda of sociology, and that a reconstituted economic sociology would be a natural end-product of these efforts. The 'new economic sociology' would take up where the classical economic sociology of Marx, Weber and others left off, but would also go one step further: to attempt to explain the way in which the economy works primarily from a sociological perspective.

As we see it, this project is surrounded by several question marks. Is sociology 'strong enough' to serve as a theoretical basis for a radically new interpretation of the way the economy works, or is it rather that sociology can explain only a few, select economic phenomena? Is there enough theoretical boldness in the profession to make a full-scale attempt? Will sociologists — maybe after a short stab at economic sociology — prefer the safety of the already established subfields? Will those active in 'industrial sociology', 'stratification studies', and so on, resist when they see that their areas are intruded upon by economic sociology? And will sociologists be able to handle the inevitable attacks by mainstream economists?

But there are not only question marks and minuses attached to the project of a 'new economic sociology'. If the effort succeeds, the scientific payoff would be tremendous. Many economic topics are virgin territory as far as sociology is concerned, and sociologists would be approaching these with a theoretical and methodological sophistication which has been built up over a fairly long period. Mark Granovetter (349), who is one of the most talented of the 'new economic sociologists', said to us recently in an interview that economic sociology might very well be in a position today which is similar to that of economics at the time when Paul Samuelson sat down to write *Foundations of Economic Analysis*. In retrospect, Samuelson described the situation he faced in the 1930s like this:

> I was lucky to enter economics in 1932. Analytical economics was poised for its takeoff. I faced a lovely vacuum that young economists can hardly imagine. So much remained to be done. Everything was still in an imperfect state. *It was like fishing in a virgin lake: a whopper at every cast, but so many lovely specimens that the palate never cloyed.* (143, p. xxv; emphasis added)

'A whopper at every cast' is a scientist's dream, and if Granovetter's and our intuition about the potential of economic sociology is correct, there are many fascinating discoveries ahead.

The future, as always, will provide the answer. In the meantime we shall turn to the more prosaic task of accounting for the new developments which have taken place since the mid-1960s. As noted earlier, a huge number of works that deal with some aspect of the economy from a sociological viewpoint have been produced during this period. This makes it necessary to order the material so that the most important developments are accentuated. One way to go about this task would be to follow the development of economic sociology in individual countries. But we have rejected this alternative for practical reasons — not enough material is available[25] — and also because we feel that the task today should be to launch economic sociology as a distinct topic and draw attention to its exciting possibilities rather than to account in detail for what is going on in individual countries.

We have thus picked a number of topics, themes and theoretical perspectives, each of which represents an important part of today's development. In chapters 5-7 we look at women in the economy, the neo-marxist contribution to economic sociology, and the renewed interest in international questions among today's economic sociologists. Works discussed in these three chapters all have their roots to some extent in the social crisis of the 1960s. The next chapter is called 'The Sociology of Markets', and here we look at some attempts to create a sociological theory of markets as well as recent sociological works on financial and labour markets. Chapter 9, which is the last chapter, is centred on the general relationship between economics and sociology, which we feel is undergoing important changes today. The report ends with a plea for a middle-range type of economic sociology.

5
WOMEN IN THE ECONOMY

The topic of 'women in the economy' has played a marginal role in economic sociology. This has been to the detriment of economic sociology in several ways. Analyses of the economy, which at best are applicable to the behaviour of males, have been presented as valid for both sexes, and a wealth of information on the economic situation of women has been ignored. In this, of course, economic sociology is no different from other fields in sociology which have all developed with a distinct male bias. But it is also important to stress — and this will be our basic message in this section — that by excluding women from the scientific analysis of how the economy functions, a fine opportunity has been missed to show that the economy can indeed be understood primarily as a *social* enterprise. If there is one area where one needs a sociological as distinct from a traditional economic perspective to explain the way the economy really works, it pertains to the situation of women in the economy. One reason for this has to do with the fact that the task to 'embed' the economy has fallen largely on women. It is women who have educated the children, taken care of the old and sick who cannot work, and in general made it possible for the males to go to work the next day. Another reason for the importance of studies of women's role in the economy is that women's participation *in the official economy* cannot be understood in terms of the internal workings of the market; one also has to look at such factors as the structure of the family, demographic changes, broad economic developments, and women's behaviour over the life-cycle, if one is to get close to an adequate explanation (e.g. 47). The optical illusion of a market system, which works by itself and which is understandable exclusively in monetary terms, is thus based on the necessary assumption that women's work — in the home as well as in the workplace — remains 'invisible' or at least poorly understood. Add to this the documented prevalence of a sexual division of labour in all human societies, and the insufficiency of any approach which does not look at the role that gender plays in the economy will become obvious.

The importance of studies of women in the economy is ultimately due to the fact that women all over the world play a crucial role in the economy. To get a glimpse of the situation from a global perspective, we have included the following quote, which summarizes the contents of a publication issued in connection with the third UN Conference on Women in July 1985:

> Women carry out two thirds of all work in the world, get one tenth of the income, and own less than one percent of all wealth . . . The contribution that women make in their work is underestimated all over the world. Here [in Sweden] women take care of other people's children, do housecleaning and perform similar tasks outside the home, which do not show up in the statistics. In most African countries it is women who take care of food production through unpaid, agricultural work. Women all over the world are in addition responsible for the children and perform labour in the home. The urbanization process, which is going on in most countries, has as a consequence that women also must increasingly assume responsibility for everyday life while the males continue to hold economic and political power. Around 30 percent of all households in the world — in certain parts of Africa the figure is close to 70 percent — are today headed by women. (418)

The picture of women in the economy has also changed during the post-World War II period in other ways: birth rates have fallen, divorces are more common, married women are increasingly joining the official labour force, and poverty has been 'feminized'. All of these phenomena have been extensively researched, although there has been no attempt, as far as we know, to single out those aspects of the literature that are of particular relevance to economic sociology. A major aim of this chapter is to point out that this can be done — and that it needs to be done. We shall attempt to do it in the following manner. First we shall look at the critique that has been directed at the 'economy and society' paradigm in studies of women in the economy. This is followed by an account of the dialogue between economists and sociologists which has opened up in women's studies. A brief discussion of some recent sociological studies of women in the economy concludes the chapter.

The Critique of the 'Economy and Society' Perspective

Very little work was done on women's economic position in mainstream American sociology, which occupied a dominant position in many countries between World War II and the early 1970s. The tendency was to exclude women from economic sociology and to study them only within the context of the sociology of the family. This is, for example, true for the more general works in economic sociology. In Wilbert E. Moore's well-known pamphlet *Economy and Society* (290) the word 'women' is not once mentioned. In Parsons and Smelser's work with the same title, there are a few stray references to women from which it is clear that women are not of much interest when one analyses the economic 'sub-system' (e.g. 36, pp. 79–80, 150, 221–32). Some attention has to be paid to them, however, when one discusses the interaction between the economy and the family. Neil Smelser's popular textbook *The Sociology of Economic Life* has a similar approach. Its fullest discussion of women is to be found in the sections on 'kinship groupings' and 'differentiation of family activities' (329, pp. 58–61, 108).[26]

It is to the sociology of the family and not to the works which deal directly with 'the economy' that one has to turn in order to find out how mainstream sociology before the 1970s perceived the economic role of women (see e.g. 376). The picture that emerges from these studies is the following. An important characteristic of the contemporary family is that its original economic activities have been taken over by industry. Women are primarily in contact with the economy through the mediation of men — through their husbands who work in the economy and through their male children who will one day be doing the same. The reason for the 'role differentiation' within the family is that it comes naturally to men to play the 'instrumental' role and for women to play the 'expressive' one. Being sharply separated, these two roles help the family to fulfil its most important social function: to help integrate society. The exigencies of 'the social system' thus explain why there is one 'occupational' role and one 'domestic' role within the family. The following famous quote, which is from Talcott Parsons' article 'Age and Sex in the Social Structure of the United States', summarizes much of the attitude of mainstream sociology: 'The woman's fundamental status is that of her husband's wife, the mother of his children, and traditionally the person responsible for a complex of activities in connection with the management of the household, care of children, etc.' (405, p. 95).

In the late-1960s and 1970s the idea that women could only be studied within the context of the family was widely criticized, and Parsons' work was especially singled out for criticism (e.g. 362; 401). The main argument was that in order to understand the position of women, it was necessary to go beyond the family and look at larger, structural forces, such as the economy. In articles that provoked discussion in feminist social science circles Margaret Benston, for instance, claimed that 'the roots of the secondary status of women are in fact economic' (364, p. 13); Heidi Hartmann argued that 'the roots of women's present social status lie in [the] sex-ordered division of labour' (388, p. 206); and Gayle Rubin suggested that to get a grip on the 'sex/gender system' one has to 'recognize the mutual interdependence of sexuality, economics, and politics' (408, p. 210).

When efforts were made to look at the way in which these larger structures affect the lives of women, it soon became apparent that mainstream sociology had ignored the role of women in stratification studies, modernization theory, and industrial sociology. Jessie Bernard noted that in Blau and Duncan's famous study *The American Occupational Structure* (1967) 'the two-fifths of the labour force constituted by women are excluded. Women only appear (in chapter 10) as contributors to husbands' careers' (366, p. 782). Joan Acker took an inventory of stratification studies, and the conclusion she reached is clear from the subtitle to her famous article from 1973, 'A

Case of Intellectual Sexism' (357; 358; for a critique, see 385). The situation within modernization theory was not very different. In an often-quoted review of the award-winning *Becoming Modern* (1974) by Alex Inkeles and David Horton Smith, Hanna Papanek observed that 'the authors deal only with the process of making *men* modern' and emphasized that this 'raises questions about many . . . aspects [of their study]' (404, pp. 1507–8). Reviewing research by mainstream sociologists on Latin America from the 1950s to the early-1970s, June Nash concluded that 'the differential impact of modernization has not been noted until recently because women have not been part of the interviewing sample, nor have they been senior investigators of the problem' (397, p. 5). An examination of industrial sociology gave a similar result. Ann Oakley thus found that 'women are conspicuous for their absence as data in the sociology of industry and work' and cited Robert Blauner's *Alienation and Freedom* (1964) as an example (400, pp. 19–20; see also 380; 383). According to Oakley:

> the conventional sociological approach to housework could be termed 'sexist': it has treated housework merely as an aspect of the feminine role in the family — as a part of women's role in marriage, or as a dimension of child-rearing — not as a work role. The study of housework as *work* is entirely missing from sociology. (400, p. 2)

The Dialogue in Women's Studies between Economists and Sociologists

The new interest in women's role in the economy meant that many female sociologists started to take a closer look at the literature in economics. In Latin America most interest has been concentrated on the structuralist school in economics, which departs on essential points from the neoclassical paradigm. Women's studies from this continent are often, in the words of a review article, accompanied by 'a persistent critique of such concepts as occupation, informal and formal labor market, labor force, unemployment, and underemployment' (399, p. 115). In the Anglo-American world, where the neoclassical approach dominates the economic profession, the picture is different. Here one can find studies inspired by a variety of theoretical approaches such as Marxist economics, neoclassical economics and labour economics. Of these it seems that labour economics — especially the theory of internal labour markets as popularized by Doeringer and Piore (375) — has been found to be the most congenial (e.g. 371).

In the Anglo-American literature there are also neoclassical studies, however, which have contributed to our understanding of women's position in economic life (e.g. 394). An interesting consequence of this fact is that something of a dialogue has opened up in women's studies between those inspired by neoclassical approaches and those who are critical of them. This dialogue, which is fuelled by the tendency in women's studies to attach importance to all perspectives which can contribute to knowledge about women, goes beyond the nearly automatic rejection of neoclassical economics that can be found in the sociological profession, and is therefore worth noting. Efforts are, for instance, made in journals in women's studies to be very specific about where neoclassical theory goes wrong and where the critique of the neoclassical position is superficial.

As an example of the former one can mention Francine D. Blau and Carol L. Jusenius' 'Economists' Approaches to Sex Segregation in the Labor Market', which appeared in 1976 in an issue of *Signs* devoted to the implications of occupational segregation (370; see also, e.g., the critiques in 379; 382). The authors carefully examine three versions of neoclassical economics which have been used to explain sex segregation — the overcrowding approach, the human capital approach, and the monopsony model — and point out that each shows that 'the neoclassical approach has generated a number of plausible explanations for the male-female pay differential' (370, p. 189). In all three of them, however, the neoclassical argument has to be widely stretched in order to account for sex segregation. In the authors' opinion this makes it preferable to choose a different theoretical approach. They conclude:

> . . . sex segregation is far from a necessary outcome in these models, and the factors which are identified as causes of pay differentials are not persuasive as causes of sex segregation *within* the neoclassical model. A major problem is that the smooth marginal adjustment inherent in neoclassical models, particularly with respect to wage rates, makes the extreme outcome of segregation highly unlikely. This also implies that segregation would be an unlikely outcome in a world for which the neoclassical models are a reasonably accurate description. (370, pp. 189–90)

Kenneth Arrow (360, pp. 233–7) expresses some misgivings in the same issue about this argument and also about Blau-Jusenius' preference for the internal labour market perspective. According to Arrow, 'economic arguments of *all* schools deal with anonymous individuals. The characteristics of sex, race and nation are not incorporated. It may not be totally surprising that economic theories have nothing to say about the causes of sexual, racial, or national differences' (360, p. 236; emphasis added).

As an example of the attempt to show that mainstream economics is not as one-dimensional as it is sometimes depicted, one can cite Carolyn Shaw Bell's 'Women and Work: An Economic Appraisal') (363; see also e.g. 384). She discusses such issues as why the GNP excludes household work; the difficulty involved in imputing a price to women's work in the home; and she also notes that many economists have been aware of these problems for a long time. As a further example of the dialogue in women's studies about economics, one can point to the recent articles by Marianne Ferber and Elaine McCrate in *Signs* about the usefulness of various theoretical approaches to studies of women and work (381; 395). Ferber stresses that the neoclassical approach of New Home Economics 'has made and continues to make significant contributions to our understanding of household behavior' (381, p. 275; see also 365). As an example she mentions Reuben Gronau's work on time allocation within the family, which recognizes work in the home as well as in the market (386). McCrate also stresses the similarities as well as the differences between the feminist and the neoclassical approaches and calls for a 'careful and thorough feminist response' to the neoclassical theory of the family (395, p. 327). She emphasizes that Gary Becker's argument in *A Treatise on the Family* about women's economic position can be rejected, however, on the ground that it is rooted in biological and not in economic reasoning (see also 409).

By the end of the 1970s and the early-1980s the absence of studies of women in industrial sociology, stratification studies, and modernization theory was on its way to being corrected. It had by this time been established in stratification studies that a high and stable degree of sex segregation existed in many societies. A series of sophisticated measures had also been devised for studying this phenomenon (see especially 367; 368; 378). In the sociology of work, the methods of industrial sociology had been extended to housework (e.g. 400). A number of studies were also made of women in male-dominated jobs, including that of the economic profession (for an overview, see 387; see also 373).

Work on women's economic position in a variety of countries which are in the process of being industrialized has become more common. A good introduction to some of this work can be found in the two thematic issues that *Signs* devoted to women and development in 1977 and 1981 (410; see also e.g., 369; 396; 398; 415). These two volumes contain general reflections on recent developments in the field by the two pioneers Ester Boserup (372) and Hanna Papanek (402; 403) as well as representative samples of recent scholarship, such as Norma Chinchilla's (374) work on the impact of monopoly capitalism on women in Guatemala and Deniz Kandiyoti's (391; 392) studies of how socio-economic changes in Turkey have affected the female population.

There has also been rapid and interesting development in theoretical contributions to the study of women in the economy. The two most popular concepts are probably 'patriarchy' and 'reproduction'. The former, which can be defined in a variety of ways, basically denotes male domination (e.g. 361, pp. 11–9). Its value for economic sociology resides, among many things, in the fact that it can be used to correct theoretical perspectives with a sexist bias. Examples of this include some feminist-marxist studies such as those in Zillah Eisenstein's collection *Capitalist Patriarchy and the Case for Socialist Feminism* (377). In general, as is indicated in Table 1, patriarchy is a key concept in explaining women's position in the labour market for marxist-feminist theory (see e.g. 412; 413; see also 406; 416).

According to Michèle Barrett the concept of 'reproduction' has 'in

TABLE 1

Different Sociological Perspectives on Women in the Labour Market

Explanatory Variables Underlying Analysis of Women in American Labour Market	Mainstream (1) Status Attainment	(2) Dual Labour Market	Radical (3) Marxist Theories of Monopoly Capitalism	(4) Marxist Feminist Theories of the Home	(5) Marxist Feminist Theories of Patriarchal Capitalism
Sex roles	•				
Labour market structure		•	X		X
Capitalism			•	•	•
Homemaking structure				X	X
Patriarchy					•

Notes:
• = refers to most important causal factor in this theoretical perspective explaining women's participation in the labour market.
X = refers to explanatory factors deriving from the most important causal factor in this theoretical perspective. These derivative factors are particularly emphasized in this theoretical approach.
Source: 413, p. 154.

recent years been used as a crucial mechanism for relating women's oppression to the organization of production' and is as such of great relevance to economic sociology (361, p. 19). One definition of 'reproduction' that seems particularly fruitful is that of Harriet Holter, who defines it as 'the production, care and maintenance of human beings' (390, p. 11). In this version 'reproduction' can be tied to the notion that the official market economy is unable to function without the work that by tradition is carried out by women. Holter's definition, it should be noted, is also connected to the concept of 'care-giving work', which Norwegian sociologists in particular have developed (e.g. 417). The general idea is that many forms of female work have a dynamic which is different from that of male work (e.g. 407; see in this context also 393). It is less instrumental and more geared towards the needs of the other, be it a child, a handicapped person or someone who is sick. An interesting discussion of the specific kind of *rationality* that is characteristic of female social action has also started in Norway. In her widely discussed article 'The Responsibility of Women: On Goals and Means in the Thoughts of Women', Bjorg Aase Sorensen attempts to explain the resistance of female workers in a factory to the introduction of fixed wages (414). Her explanation is centred on the differences and conflicts that she finds between the 'two systems of rationality' that exist in society: one is characteristic of males and is a form of 'technical, narrow rationality', whereas the other is common among women. According to the latter system, it is rational to feel responsible for 'the way resources or needs are administered' (414, pp. 398–401).

Three Sociological Studies of Women in the Economy

To cover a huge field like women in the economy in a limited number of pages is an exercise which is not easy for the writer and probably not too enjoyable for the reader. We shall therefore end with a fuller presentation of three especially fine studies: Rosabeth Moss Kanter's *Men and Women of the Corporation* (1977), Louise A. Tilly and Joan W. Scott's *Women, Work, and Family* (1978), and Paula England and George Farkas' *Households, Employment, and Gender* (1986). Our intention in doing this, it should be added, is really more to give an idea of the high quality of research that characterizes many contemporary studies of women in the economy than to imply that other, equally interesting and sophisticated studies, do not exist.

Men and Women of the Corporation is an ethnographical study of a US multinational corporation ('Indsco'), executed in the manner of the Chicago School. The main thrust of the analysis is to show that differences in the work behaviour of men and women can, to a much larger extent than is commonly realized, be explained through the way jobs are structured in the workplace. The author explains:

> Differences based on sex retreat into the background as the people-creating, behavior-shaping properties of organizational locations become clear. Findings about the 'typical' behavior of women in organizations that have been assumed to reflect either biologically based psychological attributes or characteristics developed through a long socialization to a 'female sex role' turn out to reflect very reasonable — and very universal — responses to current organizational situations. Even discrimination itself emerges as a consequence of organizational pressures as much as individual prejudice. *Thus, specific attention to women as well as men is one way to demonstrate the utility of the perspective that 'the job makes the person'*. (29, p. 9; emphasis added)

Kanter then proceeds to analyse a series of different roles in or around 'Indsco' — managers, secretaries, and wives — with the help of three key variables: 'opportunity', 'power', and 'relative number'. How each of these affects people in the organization is summarized in chapter 9 where the author suggests, for example, that people with few opportunities 'limit their aspirations', 'have lower self-esteem', 'seek satisfaction in activities outside of work', and so on.

Of special interest from the viewpoint of women in the economy is naturally Kanter's handling of the way women behave in 'Indsco', although the sociological ingenuity that she displays also goes a long way to explain the work behaviour of males. As an example of this, one can take Kanter's analysis of why there is such resistance in huge corporations to women in managerial positions (29, pp. 47–68). This is explained with the help of two concepts which are very useful to economic sociology, 'uncertainty' and 'trust'. Kanter suggests that in the development of the modern corporation there have been periods of high uncertainty, and that they have been countered by owners and managers through a series of measures which reduce the uncertainty with the help of 'trust'. People are picked for managerial positions only if they have homogenous backgrounds, show conformity in dress and speech, and so on. People who are 'different' are weeded out. Women, Kanter suggests, have been seen as unpredictable and incomprehensible by males and have therefore been excluded from management.

The single, most famous analysis in *Men and Women of the*

Corporation concerns the case where women constitute a very small proportion of a work group ('tokens'). This situation obtains when women constitute 15 percent or less of a job category, and this leads to women being treated as representatives of a social category — as stand-ins for other women — rather than as individuals. 'Tokens', the author argues, are very easy to stereotype; they have to live in the limelight, and are under constant pressure to perform, Kanter's analysis has led to several studies where some of her hypotheses are statistically tested (see e.g. p. 387, p. 498; 359).

Women, Work, and Family by Louise A. Tilly and Joan W. Scott is very different in character from *Men and Women of the Corporation*. Its topic is the way work has changed for working class women in England and France between 1700 and 1950. The study draws on works in economics, demography and history, but the authors also did archival research and mainly use aggregate description and statistics.

Tilly and Scott's study makes two major contributions to the understanding of women's role in the economy. First, they show that the industrial revolution did not bring about as drastic a change in women's work as is commonly thought. There is, instead, a distinct continuity between the work women have done before, during and after the industrial revolution:

> The aggregate view indicates that industrialization did not change the type of work women did, nor did it greatly increase the amount of time that women in the aggregate devoted to productive work for market exchange. Indeed over the course of the nineteenth century, women's work-force participation varied very little. Early industrialization did concentrate some women in factories, but the majority of working women remained in household settings, as family farm workers, shopkeepers, and servants in France, as servants in Britain, as garment workers and casual laborers in both countries. Indeed, throughout the nineteenth century in England and in France, the majority of working women performed jobs with low levels of skill and low productivity similar to those that had characterized women's work for centuries. (47, p. 77)

The second major contribution of *Women, Work, and Family* consists of the model that the authors construct for analysing the changes that women's work has gone through since the early 1700s. The basic idea is that to understand women's work, one has to situate it in relation to the economic development, demographic change and the structure of the family. When this is done, Tilly and Scott suggest, women's work during the 1700–1950 period can be divided into the following three periods: 'the family economy' (pre-industrial society), 'the family wage economy' (early industrialization), and 'the family consumer economy' (roughly in the twentieth century). In the 'family economy'; women basically worked at home, took care of the children and produced for the market as well as for the household. In the 'family wage economy' one of the tasks of women was to bring home as much cash as possible, and this created a difficult conflict between taking care of the home and earning money. In today's economy, the 'family consumer economy', household management has become very specialized, something which has increased the division of labour in the family. During each of the three periods, Tilly and Scott stress, women's work in towns has been different from that in the countryside. It has also varied considerably over the lifecycle; and it is crucial to distinguish between the work of female children, single women, married women, mothers, and widows.

Tilly and Scott's work is meticulously researched and contains a host of interesting historical observations on the range of jobs that working class women have had since the 1700s (see especially 47, pp. 48–9, 139, 209). It also contains some sections on the role of dowries and marriage settlements (c.g. 47, pp. 24–5, 94–5; cf. 389 for a crosscultural perspective). From the viewpoint of the need to reconstitute economic sociology, one thesis in *Women, Work, and Family* should be highlighted, that is, that women's behaviour in the marketplace cannot be adequately analysed without taking into account 'the family and household setting in which women were embedded as daughters, wives and mothers' (47, pp. 3–4). Tilly and Scott, like so many other scholars in the women's studies tradition, thus give support for the idea that a sociological perspective is essential for understanding how the economy actually works.

Households, Employment, and Gender by Paula England and George Farkas (15) looks at the development of women's situation at home and in the workplace between 1950 and 1980 in the US. According to the authors, this period has been one of profound change. Women's participation in the labour force has increased, the sexual double standard has more or less disappeared, and the amount of housework has decreased. Some things, however, remain the same: the sex segregation of jobs, the amount of housework done by males, and female responsibility for the children. The changes, as well as the resistance to change, England and Farkas argue, can best be understood if one attempts an 'integration' on three levels (15, p. 4). First, one should try to see the links and interdependencies that exist between households and employment. Second, an attempt must be made to develop a perspective which emphasizes the choice of the individual as well as the importance of social structure. And third, one should try to unite the insights of economics, sociology and demography. The authors summarize their perspective like this:

> Our framework aims to escape the characteristic failings of each of the two disciplines — sociologists' lack of powerful and coherent theory and economists' predeliction for making questionable assumptions and ignoring empirical findings that do not fit comfortably within their paradigm. (15, p. 5)

Throughout *Households, Employment, and Gender* the authors oppose economic to sociological theories. When they discuss inequality in paid employment, for instance, they go through four theories in economics which try to explain discrimination in the hiring, placement and promotion of women: those of 'taste' (Becker), 'statistical discrimination' (Arrow), 'error', and 'group monopoly'. Looking at the supply side, they stress that the length of work experience explains a huge part of the sex gap in pay according to recent sociological studies.

The key theoretical part of England and Farkas' study and the one which shows how they envision the 'integration' between economics and sociology is centred on the notion of 'implicit contract'. This concept, which they have borrowed from labour economics, can be applied to marriage as well as to employment according to their interpretation. They note that getting a job usually starts with a 'search' for information. The employment itself can best be understood as an implicit contract, in contrast to both a contingency-claim contract, where everything is spelled out, and a quick deal in the spot market. The reason for this is that a job is often long-term and governed more by implicit than by explicit rules. But marriage also has to start with a 'search' for a suitable partner. And just as training in a job can be seen as firm-specific investment, so can interaction in a marriage be viewed as 'relationship-specific investment'. Even if interactions between the sexes are reminiscent of contingency-claim contracts or deals in the spot market, most marriages are similar to implicit contracts: the profit to be had in the long run outweighs the losses in the short run, and therefore the relationship lasts for some time.

Paula England and George Farkas' book comes out of the women's studies tradition and contains a forceful argument for equality between women and men. It is also a study which gives a hint of the new and interesting type of analysis which can come from juxtaposing sociology and economics when looking at women in the economy.

6
THE NEO-MARXIST CONTRIBUTION

Like feminism, neo-marxism swept like a breath of fresh air into the rather stale economic sociology of the 1960s (see e.g. 425). About twenty years later it was clear that marxism had more or less regained the position that it had once had in economic sociology, and it is today rightfully considered as one of its richest intellectual traditions. The taboo against citing the older generation of marxists (e.g. 461; 462; 475; 476; 477; 478; 509) has been lifted, and a series of new, interesting works have been produced (e.g. 421; 422; 423; 480; 482; 492; 501; 512; 514; 515). A sign that the times have indeed changed is that when Arthur Stinchcombe published in 1983 the first book in English to have the title 'economic sociology', he stated that his primary purpose was to 'complete and unify the Neo-Marxist tradition' (45, p. 20). Another sign that marxism is taken seriously again can be found in a survey of economic sociologists that Harry Makler, Arnaud Sales, and Neil Smelser carried out in 1979. The authors found that 'practically all or 90 percent of our respondents indicated that marxist or neo-marxist approaches are most often used in the study of economy and society' (479, p. 163). Even if one grants that the survey was somewhat impressionistic in nature, it is clear that marxism is back on the agenda of economic sociology.

In this chapter we shall first look at the subordinate role that marxism played in the economic sociology of the post-war period and at the marxist critique of the structural-functionalist version of economic sociology. This will be followed by a select presentation of attempts since the late 1960s to renew marxist thought. Since marxism as a whole is much broader than economic sociology, it should be made clear from the beginning that the theme we have decided to focus on — and which in our opinion represents the closest equivalent in marxism to economic sociology — is the attempt by marxist social scientists to answer the following question: *How does the control of the means of production by a minority of people affect the functioning of the economy and the rest of society?* Some of the major themes in marxist economic sociology thus include the ownership and control of the means of production, and the effect of this ownership/control on the workplace, on the economic system, and on society in general via the economic system. In passing, it can be noted that, according to Schumpeter, marxism does not acknowledge the existence of an 'economic sociology' (502, p. 203).[27] We shall only point out that according to *our* definition of economic sociology — the explanation of economic phenomena through social concepts — marxism belongs very clearly to the field of economic sociology.

Marxism and the Critique of the 'Economy and Society' Perspective

In the economic sociology that developed after World War II in Europe as well as in the US, marxism played an extremely minor role. To exaggerate a bit, one can say that it was only taken seriously by one economic sociologist of stature — Schumpeter (e.g. 102; 502; 503). Other economic sociologists, especially the Americans, were either hostile to Marx and/or felt that he had very little to contribute to the field. This becomes quite clear if one looks at the more programmatic attempts from that time: Parsons and Smelser's *Economy and Society*, Wilbert E. Moore's pamphlet and Neil Smelser's article in the *International Encyclopaedia of the Social Sciences* with the same title, and Smelser's *The Sociology of Economic Life* (36; 290; 329; 334). In Parsons-Smelser's *Economy and Society*, which is a work of more than 300 pages, there are three minor references to Marx (36; pp. 39, 96, 161). The ideas expressed here are not without interest. There is the observation, for example, that Marx's idea of a capitalist system was a predecessor to the concept of 'the economy as a social system'. It is also noted that Marx, as opposed to Marshall, failed to see that 'organization' can be regarded as a distinct force of production. It must nevertheless be stressed that Marx deserves a more substantial place in a theoretical discussion of economic sociology than Parsons and Smelser accord to him. This impression is confirmed when one looks at the annotated bibliography at the end of *Economy and Society*. Out of the nearly one hundred references to important works in 'economics' and 'sociology', there is only one reference to a work by Marx. This is to *Capital*, 'the classic text of socialistic economic theory'.

According to Gouldner's well-known analysis, Wilbert E. Moore and Neil Smelser belonged to 'left Parsonianism' and were on the verge of 'a convergence with Marxism' (261, pp. 368–70). If this is true, it certainly has left few traces in their more general works in economic sociology. In Moore's pamphlet *Economy and Society*, one can find a few scattered references to Marx (290, pp. 10, 20–1, 27–8, 34–6, 40). The gist of most of them is that Marx was wrong. In Moore's vision,

Marx was an economic determinist, and his type of analysis is simply 'not very helpful' (290, pp. 34–5). In the list of 'selected readings' that Moore had compiled for the benefit of the student, there are references to Kuznets, Weber, Caplow, and so on — but none to Marx.

In Smelser's famous textbook *The Sociology of Economic Life* and in his article on 'economy and society' in the *International Encyclopaedia of the Social Sciences*, there are a few rather nondescript references to Marx (329, pp. 7-8, 12, 41, 70, 100; 334, pp. 501, 504). In the textbook one can at least find a fairly correct presentation of Marx's general position. The general thrust of the argument is, however, that Marx was an interesting thinker whose ideas are mainly of historical interest for the economic sociologist. This impression is confirmed when one reads the text on 'economy and society' in the *International Encyclopaedia*. According to the appended bibliography, economic sociologists can profit from studying the works of people such as James S. Duesenberry, George Katona and David M. Landes (450; 468; 473). Marx is not mentioned. So much, in other words, for Moore and Smelser's 'convergence with marxism' in economic sociology.

When marxists started to criticize mainstream sociology, in the late 1960s and early 1970s, one of their major charges was that sociology ignored economics. In 'A Brief Guide to Bourgeois Culture' Robin Blackburn typically noted sociology's 'rejection of most political economy' and claimed that sociology 'assumes on principle a harmonious economic system' (430, pp. 170–1). Terms like 'exploitation', Blackburn added, are taboo in bourgeois economics as well as in sociology (430, pp. 169–70).

A particularly well executed critique along the lines of Blackburn can be found in Alvin W. Gouldner's *The Coming Crisis of Western Sociology* (1970). In a section entitled 'The Extrusion of the Economic from the Social' he argues that sociology has become a 'residual discipline', studying only 'what was left over by other disciplines' (261, pp. 92–4). These are not exactly original thoughts, but Gouldner has more to say. He thus makes the interesting observation that *since sociologists were unable to analyse economic facts, they simply rationalized them away*. This, Gouldner says, is especially clear when it comes to analyses of the social order:

> This means that Academic Sociology traditionally assumes that social order may be analysed and understood without making the concerns of economics focal and problematic. It implies that the problem of social order may be solved, practically and intellectually, without clarifying and focusing on the problem of scarcity, with

> which economics is so centrally concerned. Although aspects of sociological analysis make *tacit* assumptions about scarcity, sociology is an intellectual discipline that takes economics and economic assumptions as givens, and that wishes or expects to solve the problem of social order under any set of economic assumptions or conditions. Sociology focuses upon the noneconomic sources of social order. Academic Sociology polemically denies that economic change is a sufficient or necessary condition for maintaining or increasing social order. (261, p. 94)

Gouldner also felt that when the structural-functionalists did look at economic phenomena, their analyses were strangely inept and marred by a tendency to treat economic phenomena as if they were subcategories of sociological concepts. Gouldner illustrates this idea by a careful examination of the way property has been analysed in mainstream sociology (261, pp. 304–19). He notes that in Smelser's *Sociology of Economic Life* the author 'finds no occasion to present any sustained discussion of the nature of property' (261, p. 305). Other works in economic sociology by the structural-functionalists were not much better in Gouldner's opinion: 'When Smelser and Parsons collaborate in their *Economy and Society* or when Parsons considers the issue by himself, the problem of property is presented only in the most cursory manner' (261, p. 305).

Gouldner's critique of Parsons and Smelser can be found in a section entitled 'Towards a Sociology of Property' where the author also advances his own version of how property should be analysed from a sociological perspective. Gouldner says that Parsons and Smelser view property in a very naïve way (the example they use in *Economy and Society* is ownership of a hat), and he points out that they basically do not see any difference between property and other forms of social relationships. To Gouldner this is to miss the main point about property, namely, that it can only be enforced by the state and not by social control as is the case for most social relationships. An owner of private property can actually withdraw from various 'social systems' and construct new ones whenever he or she wants; he or she can thus avoid the normal, regulating mechanisms as long as there exists a state with a coercive apparatus. Property, Gouldner concludes, is a social relationship of a very special type; it can bypass the roles and values that make up Parsons' 'social system':

> A 'social system' is therefore a residual organization of social relationships, in that it may deal with only those things that are 'left over' after property rights have been established . . . Property constitutes the 'givens' or the limiting conditions for the construction and development of social systems in the Parsonian sense . . . Property is thus the infrastructure of social systems. (261, p. 309)

The Renewal in Marxist Economic Sociology

Gouldner's critique in *The Coming Crisis* is unusual in that it was directed at *Economy and Society* by Parsons and Smelser, which is the major work in mainstream economic sociology. Much more common were marxist critiques of specific aspects of the 'economy and society' approach, such as industrial sociology, stratification studies, modernization theory, and so on. We shall now proceed to look at a few of these critiques, presenting both their arguments against mainstream sociology and their proposals for how a proper analysis should be carried out. The first work we have chosen is Maurice Zeitlin's 'Corporate Ownership and Control: The Large Corporation and the Capitalist Class' (528), which contains a sharp critique of the previously widespread idea that the separation of ownership and control had fundamentally changed the nature of large corporations and, with them, of capitalism. (For other critiques of 'managerialism', see e.g. 456; 465; 530; for a discussion of Zeitlin's article, see 420; 529).

Zeitlin starts by pointing out that there exists an 'astonishing consensus' among social scientists, including sociologists, that a separation has taken place between ownership and control of the large corporation and that this has led to the demise of the capitalist class. It is the managers and not the old capitalist families who rule the big companies today, and they do it in a novel manner. The managers do not maximize profits but rather their own power. Ideas of this type, Zeitlin says, can be found in a variety of well-known sociological works such as Dahrendorf's *Class and Class Conflicts in Industrial Society*, Bell's 'The Breakup of Family Capitalism', and Parsons-Smelser's *Economy and Society* (36; 427; 433).

There is a problem with this type of analysis, Zeitlin says, and that is its lack of solid empirical backing. Zeitlin points out that the figures in Berle and Means' classic work *The Modern Corporation and Private Property* (429) show at most that only one out of five large corporations was controlled by the managers. Later works in the same genre are no more convincing. There is also the crucial fact, according to Zeitlin, that no-one has shown why the policies of managers should differ in any significant way from those of the owners; the fact that the owners do not personally lead their corporations does not mean that they have given up the power to make the key decisions. Zeitlin concludes that 'news of the demise of the capitalist classes ... is ... somewhat premature' (528,

p. 1107). What is needed to settle the issues involved, he says, is new and more sophisticated research:

> The methods and procedures, and the basic concepts and units of analysis, in such research will have to be quite different than those which have been commonly employed in the past. Most important, such research must focus at the outset on the complex relationships in which the single corporation is itself involved: the particular pattern of holdings and their evolution within the corporation; and the relationships between it and other corporations; the forms of personal union or interlocking between the officers and directors and principal shareholding families; the connections with banks both as 'financial institutions' and the agents of specified propertied interests, including those who control the banks themselves; the network of intercorporate and principal common shareholdings. In a word, it will be necessary to explore in detail the institutional and class structure in which the individual large corporations are situated. (528, p. 1107–8)

Zeitlin's call for new concepts and methods in the study of the capitalist class has been heeded by quite a few researchers. Three of the more recent and interesting among them are Michael Useem (517; 518), who has done work on 'the inner circle' of the capitalist class, and Beth Mintz and Michael Schwartz (e.g. 483; 484), who have launched the theory of 'financial hegemony'. Mintz and Schwartz' theory of 'financial hegemony' is most fully elaborated in *The Power Structure of American Business* (1985), and the basic idea is that it is the financial institutions — mainly banks but also insurance companies — which control the capital flow and thereby set structural constraints for all other corporations. 'The biography of American capitalism can, in a sense, be written as a chronicle of the flow of capital into certain sectors and away from others' (483, p. 47).

The theory of financial hegemony differs from traditional 'bank control theory', according to which banks control the industrial corporations in a direct manner by appointing their leadership, acquiring controlling stock, establishing capital dependency, and so on (see e.g. 462; 476). Mintz and Schwartz do not deny that show-downs occur between banks and corporations; they do, and it is usually the banks that win (see also 484). The emphasis in their analysis is, however, on 'hegemony' as a form of rather loose and indirect control by the banks over the environment in which the corporations operate. As a rule, industrial corporations cannot make major decisions without approval from the financial community. The banks themselves usually present a united front since they are connected to one another through interbank borrowings and through loan consortia.

The Power Structure of American Business uses empirical evidence of various types. A list of bank interventions in major US corporations during a five-year period has, for instance, been compiled with the help of the business press (483, pp. 76–82). The authors also use the huge and increasingly sophisticated literature on interlocking directorates to support their theory of 'financial hegemony' (see e.g. 444; 485). Mintz and Schwartz show that commercial banks send out and receive interlocks more often than other types of corporations. The authors interpret this as meaning that interlocks are needed by the banks both to determine the direction of capital flows and to get information about what is going on in the economy.

While Mintz and Schwartz have followed up on Zeitlin's suggestion that one should look into the link between the corporations and the banks, Useem has focused on the idea that there exists an 'inner group' in capitalist society which is responsible for 'the cohesiveness of the capitalist class and its capacity for common action and unified policies' (528, p. 1112). In *The Inner Circle* Useem presents evidence that businessmen are not necessarily disorganized and differentiated by heterogeneous interests, as Berg and Zald have suggested (428, p. 137) some of them do constitute a class conscious elite (for the considerably broader claim that there exists a socially cohesive upper class in the US, see especially 445; 446; 447; 448; 449). Useem's main thesis is that businessmen who are simultaneously represented on several boards of directors will develop a sense of the general interest of the business class and not only perceive what is good for their own firms. He also postulates that these businessmen will be more active in government, in non-profit organizations and in trade organizations than are businessmen in general. These hypotheses are confirmed through interviews with a large number of US and British businessmen and through an analysis of interlocks. Useem concludes: 'the members of the inner circle constitute a distinct, semi-autonomous network, one that transcends company, regional, sectoral, and other politically divisive fault lines within the corporate community' (518, p. 3).

Of special interest is Useem's finding that businessmen from large corporations basically sit on many boards in order to get information about what is going on in the economy and to find out what other large corporations are up to ('the business scan'). The 'inner circle' has consequently, according to Useem, not come into being through some conspiratorial design but as an unintended consequence of 'the unpredictability of circumstances facing all large corporations in industrial democracies' (518, p. 7). The author's speculations that the rise of an 'inner circle' of businessmen heralds a new stage of capitalism — 'institutional capitalism' — is, however, less convincing. One reason for this is that too little historical evidence is presented to substantiate such a broad claim.

According to marxist theory, the fact that a minority is in control over the means of production leads to a society which is divided into antagonistic classes. There is thus a direct and clear link in marxism between ownership and the constitution of the major groups in society, which is absent in stratification theory. Neo-marxists thus attacked mainstream stratification studies in the 1970s for ignoring the role of 'class' or social divisions based on control over property (e.g. 510; 520).

By the early 1980s a series of attempts to map out the class structure of various countries had also been made (see e.g. 511 for relevant references). The analysis which has attracted the most attention, is probably that of Erik Olin Wright (e.g. 523; 524; 527). There are two general strengths to Wright's work: his theoretical classification of certain middle class groups ('contradictory locations within class relations') and his vigorous attempt to operationalize marxist categories. It should also be mentioned that Wright has been directing a huge empirical project since 1978 involving comparisons of the class structure in at least eight countries (see e.g. 419; 442).

From the viewpoint of economic sociology it is clear that class analysis represents an advance over the kind of stratification studies which were popular in the 1950s. The reason for this is that it pays more attention to fundamental economic facts. In this context it should also be mentioned that Erik Olin Wright's most recent studies seem to be heading in a direction directly relevant to economic sociology (525; 526). Inspired by the work of John Roemer (497), Wright has decided to reconceptualize his class analysis in terms of 'exploitation'. This latter concept, which replaces 'domination' in Wright's conceptual scheme, is directly connected to the notion of 'material interests':

> ...the exploitation-centered concept is more systematically *materialist* than domination concepts. Classes are derived from the patterns of effective ownership over aspects of the forces of production. The different kinds of exploitation that define different kinds of classes are all linked to the qualitative properties of these different aspects of forces of production. (525, p. 416)

It is to be hoped that Wright, as part of his new research on classes, will examine different forms of property to see how they have evolved historically, and then determine the effect they may have on the social structure. These kinds of questions are definitely central to economic sociology and have not been extensively studied.

The neo-marxists' idea that control over the means of production is of decisive importance for what is happening in the economy brought them into a head-on clash with the mainstream version of industrial sociology. The result was a series of interesting marxist analyses of what is sometimes referred to today as the 'sociology of the labour process'.

According to the early industrial sociologists, what goes on in the workplace depends mainly on the interaction within and between local groups. From a marxist viewpoint, this is an excessively narrow perspective and a sign that 'bourgeois social science' and its 'questionnaire-sociology' are unable to deal with the objective dimension of the labour process (437, pp. 27–30; see also 430, pp. 199–201; 451, p. 185). Harry Braverman has thus argued that most industrial sociologists feel that 'their task is not the study of objective conditions of work but only of the subjective phenomena to which these give rise: the degrees of "satisfaction" and "dissatisfaction" elicited by their questionnaires' (437, p. 141). Michael Burawoy says basically the same thing when he points out that industrial sociology looked at what happens inside the factory but then 'stopped at the factory gate' (438, p. 34). Burawoy is more appreciative than Braverman, however, of industrial sociology; it is thus possible, he says, to integrate sociology's 'partial truths within a Marxist framework' (438, p. 6).

In the concrete studies that have been produced in industrial sociology by the neo-marxists, the idea that control over the means of production shapes work inside factories and offices is worked out in different ways. The general thesis of Harry Braverman's *Labor and Monopoly Capital* (1974) is that the capitalists are increasingly eliminating the element of thought in work and thereby degrading it. Human work, which Marx had characterized as a mixture of action and conceptualization, is 'deskilled' and reduced to the level of animal activity. Under capitalism thinking is monopolized by management, and Braverman writes: 'The verb *to manage*, from *manus*, the Latin for hand, originally meant to train a horse in his paces, to cause him to do exercises of the *manège*. . . Like a rider who uses reins, bridle, spurs, carrot, whip, and training from birth to impose his will, the capitalist strives, through management, to *control*' (437, pp. 67–8).

The claim that the element of thought in ordinary work is increasingly transferred to the sphere of management is elevated by Braverman to 'the general law of the capitalist division of labour' (437, p. 83).

The argument in Richard Edwards' *Contested Terrain* (1979) is somewhat different from Braverman's even though the basic idea is similar, namely, that capitalist control over the means of production determines the way in which the labour process is organized. Edward's main thesis is that workplaces are organized in a hierarchical way 'because it is profitable' (451, p. vii). The historical development of US capitalism has produced three different types of hierarchical control: 'simple control' (petty tyranny in the small workplace), 'technical control' (the labour process is directed by the machine), and 'bureaucratic control' (control via the social structure of the company). Edwards then connects his three forms of control to different labour markets. 'The working poor' thus tend to work in 'the secondary market', where 'simple control' is common. 'The traditional proletariat' can mainly be found in 'the subordinate primary market' with 'technical control'. And 'the middle layers' operate in the 'independent primary market', where 'bureaucratic control' is predominant.

The notion that the capitalist must impose control on the worker in order to get a profit is basic to the works of the 'Amherst economists' (see e.g. 434; 435). Another of their basic ideas is that the evolution of segmented labour markets has been crucial to the evolution of the US working class (see e.g. 452; 459). In this context it should also be mentioned that the Amherst economists have made an interesting attempt to use their theories of control and segmented labour markets to analyse productivity. In 'Hearts and Minds: A Social Model of Productivity Growth' Thomas Weisskopf, Samuel Bowles and David Gordon try to explain productivity through 'social' as opposed to 'economic' variables (519; see also 436). The authors especially note that 'work intensity' (defined as workers' motivation to work and the effectiveness of control) has been an important reason for the decline in US productivity between 1966–79.

Michael Burawoy's *Manufacturing Consent* is also constructed around the importance of capitalist ownership of the means of production for the way in which the labour process is structured. Work inside the factory is thus analysed from the perspective that it is absolutely necessary in capitalism to 'simultaneously obscure and secure surplus value' (e.g. 438, p. 73). What reconciles the worker to the task of producing a profit for someone else, the author says, is that his or her work is organized as a game ('making out'). The goal of 'making out' is ostensibly to earn incentive pay, but what really makes the worker play the game is that it breaks the monotony and makes it easier to become absorbed in one's work. 'Making out' also existed at the stage of 'competetive capitalism' according to Burawoy, who on this point of his study refers to Donald Roy's famous research in the very same factory thirty years earlier (500). At this earlier stage of capitalism, however, coercion was more common than consent ('the despotic organization of work'). In today's monopoly capitalism the situation is the reverse ('the hegemonic organization of work'). In his later research Burawoy has continued to focus on the notion that what happens at the point of production is crucial to the maintenance of the whole capitalist system (439).

One of the most popular topics among neo-marxist writers in the 1970s was the capitalist state. The key question here was the way in which control over the means of production by the capitalist class influenced the actions of the state. The answers that the neo-marxists gave to this question are usually labelled 'instrumentalist' and 'structuralist' (e.g. 441; 446; 467). A third possibility — that of 'class-struggle' — is sometimes added (455; see also 487). According to the instrumentalists, the state is basically used as a tool by the capitalist class. The structuralists strongly disagreed with this formulation, and they argued that the state has a certain autonomy from direct control by the ruling class ('relative autonomy'). According to the class struggle perspective, power over the capitalist state is determined by ongoing confrontations between the classes in society.

Today it seems as if the neo-marxist debate about the state is more or less over. In the recently published *Bringing the State Back In* Theda Skocpol (1985) even pronounces a post-mortem on it. The neo-marxist analyses from the 1970s, she says, had two fundamental deficiencies. First, they did not acknowledge the state as a distinct actor in its own right; they were 'society-centered' rather than 'state-centered' (506, p. 5). And second, the analyses by Poulantzas et al. were overly theoretical in nature and often made extravagant claims about being applicable to all capitalist states.[28]

Nevertheless, it is clear that neo-marxist writings on the state in the 1970s made some interesting contributions to economic sociology. Many of the works in the instrumentalist tradition thus contain excellent analyses of the interaction between businessmen and the state in specific situations. This is especially true of the works that came out of the school of 'corporate liberalism' (see e.g. 431). In the 'power structure research' by scholars like William Domhoff one can also find very fine and detailed studies of the power elite. A good example is his book on the Bohemian Grove in California, which is a social club for the upper class (447). Even if the instrumentalists failed to develop a sophisticated marxist theory of the capitalist state, they have still contributed to that underdeveloped part of sociology which can be called 'the sociology of the capitalist class' (457, pp. 32, 34).

Other neo-marxist studies of the state are also of relevance to today's economic sociology. This is especially the case with Fred Block's brilliant article 'The Ruling Class Does Not Rule: Notes on the Marxist Theory of the State' (432). The main argument here is that 'state managers' are likely to try to maintain 'business confidence' and, inadvertently, the capitalist system as well. Another study of interest in this context is Ulf Himmelstrand et al.'s *Beyond Welfare Capitalism*, where the authors, with the help of survey research, show how Swedish entrepreneurs basically ignore the negative side-effects of their businesses in the expectation that the state will handle them (463).

James O'Connor must finally be credited with having rediscovered and further developed the 'fiscal sociology' of Rudolf Goldscheid and Joseph Schumpeter (486; see chapter 3). His *The Fiscal Crisis of the State* draws attention to the cross pressures to which the contemporary capitalist state is exposed; on the one hand, there is a demand for lower taxes and, on the other, a demand for more state services. Since O'Connor's work was published, a few sociological works — marxist as well as non-marxist — have appeared which deal with the growing public sector and the problems that this entails (e.g. 427; 460; 521; 522). Surveying the literature on the fiscal crisis in 1981 Fred Block concluded that 'much research remains to be done in developing a fiscal sociology and in providing additional evidence for the existence of fiscal crisis as a widespread tendency in advanced capitalism' (433, p. 14). As neglected areas of research Block singles out state expenditures across nations and sociological investigations of tax resistance and of the sources of inflation. Some studies of these topics have appeared since Block's overview was published in 1981 (see e.g. 440; see in this context also 458; 507). State expenditures in various OECD countries, it should also be mentioned, are presently being investigated in a research project directed by Walter Korpi and Gösta Esping-Andersen. According to a report from this project, it is clear that those economists who automatically view the existence of a huge public sector as a threat to good economic performance are mistaken (470).

A New Attitude to Economics?

We are now approaching the end of our discussion of the neo-marxist contribution to economic sociology. Our theme has been that this contribution is primarily to be found in works that focus the analysis on capitalist control over the means of production and on the consequences that this has for the economy. We shall end with a discussion of some recent neo-marxist works which highlight this problematic. The reader who is interested in further aspects of the neo-marxist contribution to economic sociology is referred to chapters 5 and 7. The feminist-marxist debate was touched upon in the chapter on women in the economy, and the marxist contribution to studies of imperialism will be discussed in the following chapter on the international dimension of economic sociology.

The recent development of marxist thought, which is of special interest to economic sociology, has been called 'the new marxism of collective action' by Scott Lash and John Urry (474; but for a very negative appraisal, see 464). These authors mainly discuss Jon Elster's (453; 454) 'game-theoretic marxism' and Claus Offe and Helmut Wiesenthal's (488) article 'Two Logics of Collective Action', but they also touch on the works of John Roemer and Adam Przeworski. Why Scott and Lash decided to highlight the Offe-Wiesenthal article in this context is somewhat mysterious; it contains a fine analysis of the differences between trade unions and employers' organizations but it is very different in tone from Elster-Roemer-Przeworski, who all represent a very novel *rapprochement* between economics and sociology on a theoretical as well as on a methodological level.[29] Since the attempt to use rational choice-models in marxism is part of a much broader tendency to introduce economic methodology and thinking into the social sciences, we shall not discuss the general implications of this *rapprochement* in this chapter on neo-marxism (see chapter 9). Instead we shall draw attention to another way in which the works of John Roemer and Adam Przeworski are relevant for economic sociology, namely, through their emphasis on the importance in marxist analysis of the fact that *the capitalists own the means of production*.

This emphasis is expressed in the work of John Roemer in the form of an analysis of *exploitation* through a 'property relations approach' (497; 498; 499; see also 490; 491). By a very sophisticated use of mathematical models, Roemer concludes that 'it is the *ownership relations* that are primary' in explaining exploitation; what happens in the labour process at the point of production is 'secondary' (499, pp. 198, 210). The notion of surplus-value is of no help in the theory of exploitations, according to Roemer.

Roemer constructs his own 'general theory of exploitation and class' by combining the property relations approach with game theory. The basic idea is that members of a class are exploited in a mode of production if they would be better off by *withdrawing* with their share of the resources. This idea of withdrawal is a fascinating notion, which is so artificial and ahistorical, however, that it is unlikely to be of much value in sociology. Roemer's focus on property relations, on the other hand, seems very promising since it raises some very difficult questions.

Adam Przeworski is a political scientist who has tried to analyse the social democratic labour movement in terms of class compromise and hegemony (493; 494; 495; 496). His work is especially interesting to economic sociology because of its emphasis on the importance of investment decisions, and Przeworski should be credited with having made a substantial contribution to 'the sociology of investments' (cf. also 432). Przeworski's point of departure is Kelvin Lancaster's famous article on the dynamic inefficiency of capitalism, in which Keynes' analysis of investments and Marx's idea of two opposed classes in capitalism are combined in a game theoretical analysis (472). The main idea in Lancaster, as well as in Przeworski, is that a choice must be made by the capitalists and the workers alike whether to consume now or in the future. Przeworski, however, is much more specific than Lancaster, and he skilfully analyses what consequences different investment decisions will have under different conditions; how the threat of disinvestment works; and so on (see especially 493). Unlike Roemer, Przeworski is also involved in empirical research on the issues that he models, and this makes it easier for sociologists to acknowledge the importance of his models.

7
THE INTERNATIONAL DIMENSION

The economic sociology of Marx as well as of Weber was characterized by a profound interest in the international economy per se as well as in the economic situation of countries outside Europe. During the 1920s and 1930s, however, economic sociology became quite parochial in nature. It was rare for countries other than the US and the major European nations to be analysed, and there was little interest in what was going on in the international economy. This is especially true of the Chicago sociologists but it is also true of European economic sociologists. The situation changed during the 1950s, something which had to do with the fact that several colonized nations gained their independence after World War II. Studies of 'modernization' now started to appear, and some of them were written by economic sociologists or included analyses by sociologists of the economy in developing countries.

A few advances towards a more internationally minded economic sociology were made during the 1950s and early-1960s, but they must be considered minor in comparison to developments during the last fifteen years. From the late-1960s onwards, economic sociologists have begun — for the first time since Marx and Weber — to take a serious interest in what is happening in the international economy. As a sign of this new trend, the first sociological work about the international economy, *The New International Economy*, edited by Harry Makler, Alberto Martinelli and Neil Smelser (33), appeared in 1982. In this collection, one can find studies of such topics as Euromarkets, transnational corporations, and international trade. Among the authors are some of the people who are today at the forefront of the sociological study of the international economy: Peter B. Evans, Fernando Cardoso, Harry Makler and Barbara Stallings.

It would nevertheless be an exaggeration to say that there exists today a fully developed sociology of the international economy. Many important topics are, significantly enough, not covered in *The New International Economy*. Some of the essays in this collection are also vaguely interdisciplinary rather than distinctly sociological in nature. Much work thus remains to be done, but it is true that a movement towards the creation of a 'new sociology of the international economy' can be clearly discerned during the last ten or fifteen years. Impulses to this movement have come from many different directions: the birth of an indigenous sociology in many Third World countries, the neo-marxist analysis of imperialism, various studies in comparative sociology, and the activities of ISA's group 'Economy and Society'. Each of these will be discussed in this chapter. We shall also touch on some sociological studies that have analysed the international economy since World War II, and the critique of modernization studies that was made in the late-1960s and early-1970s.

Recent developments in economic sociology mean, among other things, that the various institutions of the international economy are increasingly being studied. Sociological works which analyse trade between nations, foreign aid, organizations like the International Monetary Fund and the World Bank, and so on, are becoming more common. But the main intellectual innovation since the 1960s — and the main theme in this chapter — has to do with a growing realization that *the social and political situation in single countries is deeply affected by the system of the international economy*. Individual nations, in brief, are less and less studied in isolation, and changes in their economies are not exclusively explained in terms of internal causes. It can also be noted in this context that the interest in the interactions between the international system and nation states is part of a broad intellectual reorientation in the social sciences, which involves several areas of sociology as well as of political science. In a recent report on the present trend in comparative and international social science research, which had been commissioned by a committee of the National Research Council and the Committee on Basic Research in the Behavioral and Social Sciences of the National Academy of Sciences, it was stressed that there is '*a general movement toward new ways of conceptualizing the relations between structures and systems that operate at the global or international level and those which operate at the domestic or national level*' (558, pp. 2–3; emphasis added).

Modernization Theory and the Economy

If we now return to the 1950s and to modernization theory, it is clear that this theory was very popular with the major economic sociologists of the period such as Talcott Parsons, Neil Smelser and Wilbert E. Moore. Today, on the other hand, it is difficult to find anyone in sociology who has a positive word to say about modernization theory, and a different approach to development in Third World countries has emerged. This virtually universal rejection of modernization theory is easy enough to understand if one looks at some of its major propositions. It was assumed that all non-industrialized countries could be meaningfully lumped together under the heading of 'traditional societies'. It was further believed that all these 'new nations' would converge in their development and become 'modern'. For this to happen, it was argued, a new mentality had to be developed, and the developing countries must break out of their 'traditionalism' with the help of some enterprising, native elite.

According to an interesting essay by Daniel Chirot, modernization theory constituted 'a veritable social movement', which was started in 1950 when Simon Kuznets created the Commission on Economic Growth of the Social Science Research Council; and it was fully institutionalized in 1952 by the founding of the journal *Economic Development and Cultural Change*, edited by Bert F. Hoselitz (550, p. 261). Its popularity seems to have lasted for about fifteen years. In 1966 André Gunder Frank published a criticism of modernization theory which was soon to be followed by many others (e.g. 539; 560; 588; for an early critique, see 569). By the mid-1970s it seems that most sociologists felt that what needed to be said, had been said. When the ASA held a debate in 1975 about modernization theory, Immanuel Wallerstein characterized it as a 'funeral service' (606, p. 131). His own contribution was entitled 'Modernization: Requiescat in Pace', and its message was that little was to be gained from flogging a dead horse.

Wallerstein may have been a bit too quick in wanting to close off the debate, at least as far as economic sociology is concerned. There are two reasons for this. First, the critiques of modernization theory have mainly come from political and comparative sociologists; a good critique from the perspective of economic sociology does not yet exist. And second, the present rejection of modernization theory is probably too radical; many works in this tradition contain contributions to economic sociology which it would be unwise to ignore.

A critique of modernization theory from the viewpoint of economic sociology would first of all have to include a discussion of the division of labour that it entailed between economists and sociologists. The former were assigned responsibility for analysing key economic phenomena while the sociologists, as usual, could do whatever they wanted with the rest. In an article in the *International Encyclopaedia of the Social Sciences*, fittingly entitled 'The Noneconomic Aspects of Economic Growth', Bert F. Hoselitz emphasized that 'the description of underdevelopment and the identification of processes and policies which will lead out of it to higher levels of performance is primarily undertaken by economists' (576, p. 423). The fact that 'traditional' economies were still embedded in a variety of social institutions was, however, to the sociologist's advantage. At least until the economies in the 'new nations' had been fully rationalized, the sociologist had a task to perform. The same argument about the division of labour between economists and sociologists was popularized by Hoselitz in *Sociological Aspects of Economic Growth* (577), which was read in many countries since the US State Department had it translated into twenty five languages (604, p. 553; for more information on the political dimension of modernization theory, see e.g. 550; 584).

Another criticism that can be made of modernization theory from the perspective of economic sociology is that it ignored the existence of the international economy. No observations on the need to take the international economy into account can be found in the more general statements on 'economy and society' at that time (e.g. 36; 290; 329; 334). International trade and the fact that the US had constructed a huge, free trade area after World War II were simply not analysed.

A further drawback to the works on modernization was their exclusive focus on the unit of the individual nation. Explanations of why something happened in a country's economy in principle involved the workings of the economic institutions inside that country alone. In an article on the social aspects of modernization by Daniel Lerner, one can find the following statement, which testifies to this tendency as well as to the conventional wisdom of many modernization theorists: '... poor lands have a built-in tendency to stay poor. This tendency is built in by the persistence of traditional lifeways among the peoples of the poor' (582, p. 392). By focusing exclusively on the internal workings of a country's economy, sociologists were also following the general trend in economics. In a well-known article from 1951 Simon Kuznets had proclaimed the nation-state to be the appropriate unit of analysis in economics. 'To the extent that the sovereign state satisfies the criteria of specificity, external independence, and internal interdependence', he said, 'it seems a natural unit in the study of economic growth' (581, p. 28).

Despite these and other criticisms that need to be made of modernization theory from the perspective of economic sociology, it should also be noted that several works from this period are of definite interest to economic sociology. The literature on modernization needs, in brief, to be re-evaluated by economic sociologists. If this is done, one will find that Clifford Geertz's superb analysis of two Indonesian towns in *Peddlers and Princes*, for example, contains a very good critique of modernization theory (566). Geertz's study is also a reminder that the modernization theorists produced a very interesting literature on entrepreneurs, a topic which has been somewhat neglected by today's economic sociologists. Besides *Peddlers and Princes* there are very fine studies on this topic from the 1960s by, e.g., Fredrik Barth (535), Fernando Cardoso (e.g. 545; 546), Seymour Martin Lipset (278), and Reinhard Bendix (248). Today's economic sociologists can also find inspiration and information in a variety of other 'modernist' writings (e.g. 536; 537; 538; 565; 567; 568).

The Latin American Contribution

One of the reasons why today's economic sociology is more international and less eurocentric in character than it was in the 1950s, is undoubtedly that many Third World nations have started to produce their own sociological studies (see e.g. 573). To sort out which works from developing countries are of specific relevance to economic sociology is definitely an important task. It is also a difficult one since the sociological tradition in many African, Asian and Latin American countries is little known in the US and Europe.[30] We shall therefore restrict ourselves in this section to a discussion of two contributions by Third World social science which are of particular interest to economic sociology: the development in the 1950s by the ECLA economists (United Nations Economic Commission for Latin America) of an internationally oriented kind of institutionalism, and the transformation of this school of thought about ten years later into a general sociological theory of development ('dependency theory').

The similarities between institutionalism in its original US version and Latin American structuralism has often been noted (e.g. 602). It is true that the concepts of 'institution' and 'structure' are roughly equivalent, for example, and that they were both developed in reaction to the neoclassical vision of the economy in terms of markets where demand and supply invariably proceed to an equilibrium (e.g. 534). There are naturally differences between the ECLA economists and the early US institutionalists; they did not examine the same countries, and they often studied different topics. There is, for example, no equivalent in the works by Veblen et al. to the extensive analysis of inflation that the ECLA people developed (see e.g. 594). And when people from the two schools did look at the same topic — technology is an example — their attitudes differed on one crucial point: the importance attributed to the role of the international economy.

The key idea of the ECLA economists was that the underdevelopment of the Latin American countries had been caused not merely by internal factors but also by their insertion into the international economy (e.g. 548; 553; 574). The one person who, more than anyone else, was responsible for developing this idea ('unleashing it' might be a better expression), was the Argentinian economist and banker Raul Prebisch (e.g. 551; 579). In a couple of writings from 1950–51, which were to influence a whole generation of Latin American social scientists, Prebisch proposed that the world economy could be conceptualized in terms of a 'centre' and a 'periphery' (590; 591; 603). If the world economy had indeed worked according to the neoclassical vision, the terms of trade should have become more favourable to the periphery, since the increased use of technology in the centre would have lowered the prices of industrial products in relation to the agricultural products from the developing countries. In reality, however, just the opposite had happened. Prebisch suggested that the failure of the prices of industrial products to fall, in relative terms, was due to two causes. First, unions in the industrialized countries had prevented wages from falling. And, second, oligopolies in the centre had kept prices of industrial products artificially high rather than let them decline in proportion to the rise in productivity.

A similar thesis about the worsening terms of trade for the developing countries was advanced at about the same time by another UN economist, Hans Singer (597), and the so-called 'Singer-Prebisch thesis' was heavily criticized on empirical grounds in the 1950s (see especially 572; 605; see however 599). Prebisch's main intuition — that one should look at the way developing countries were hooked into the world economy — was to prove itself extremely fruitful, however.

What has become known as 'dependency theory' was a direct outgrowth of the ECLA approach. It was developed in the 1960s by scholars like Fernando Cardoso, Theotonio Dos Santos and André Gunder Frank, who radicalized and fleshed out the main ideas of Prebisch et al. with the help of sociology and history (e.g. 540; 547; 580, pp. 192–94). In what was to become the 'classic' of dependency theory, Fernando Cardoso and Enzo Faletto's *Dependency and Development* (1969), the main ambition of the new approach was expressed as follows: '*the purpose of this essay is to explain the economic processes as social processes*' (13, p. 15; emphasis added). The way to go about this, according to Cardoso and Faletto, was through a revival of 'political economy' in the form of a historical and interdisciplinary type of analysis (13, p. ix; see also 547).

The attempt to make the ECLA-analysis more social was mainly directed at macroeconomic phenomena such as the economic development of individual Latin American countries or of the whole continent. Latin America's history was often divided into three major periods, each characterized by a different form of dependency and relationship to the world economy. Summarizing his research in *The American Economic Review*, Theotonio Dos Santos spoke of Latin America's history in terms of 'colonial dependence', 'financial-industrial dependence', and 'the new dependence' (552). The last of these three forms of dependency had developed after World War II and was characterized by the growing role of multinational corporations in Latin American countries.

There was considerable diversity, however, in the work of the *dependentistas*. According to André Gunder Frank, the strong capitalist countries had exploited the developing countries and stunted their development (561; 562). They had, in other words, caused 'the development of underdevelopment', and it was quite logical that the Latin American economies had made most progress at times such as World War II when the links to 'the metropolis' were especially weak. Cardoso and Faletto, on the other hand, advanced a more sophisticated version of dependency theory and argued that there can be simultaneously — to cite the title of their book — dependency *and* development (13).

In contrast to Frank, Cardoso and Faletto were also very interested in the problem of the linkage between the international economy and the situation of individual countries. 'The real question [about dependency]', they noted, 'is what the *relationship* between these two dimensions is' (13, p. xviii). They themselves saw the relationship as very complex and felt that it could not be explained by referring exclusively to 'exploitation' and 'coercion'. One also had to look at the role played by the state, class alliances and ideology:

> The very existence of an economic 'periphery' cannot be understood without reference to the economic drive of advanced capitalist countries, which were responsible for the formation of a capitalist periphery and for the integration of traditional noncapitalist economies into the world market. Yet, the expansion of capitalism in Bolivia and Venezuela, in Mexico or Peru, in Brazil and Argentina, in spite of having been submitted to the same global dynamic of international capitalism, did not have the same history or consequences. The differences are rooted not only in the diversity of natural resources, nor just in the different periods in which these economies have been incorporated into the international system

> (although these factors also have played some role). Their explanation must also lie in the different moments at which sectors of local classes allied or clashed with foreign interests, organized different forms of state, sustained distinct ideologies, or tried to implement various policies or defined alternative strategies to cope with imperialist challenges in diverse moments of history. (13, p. xvii)

Imperialism and Comparative Research

A further impulse to making economic sociology more international in character has come from neo-marxist sociologists. One of their contributions in this context has been to raise the issue of imperialism and thereby to end a silence of about fifty years on this topic in sociology (see chapter 3). They have also helped to deepen and popularize the dependency analysis from Latin America.

If we begin by looking at the neo-marxist analysis of imperialism, it is immediately clear that it differs from the classical marxism of Hilferding and Lenin in the sense that analytical attention is paid to the effects of imperialism in the exploited countries and not only to what caused imperialism in the first place (see e.g. 544). There is also a resistance among today's marxists to accepting Lenin and Hilferding's theories of imperialism. A recent overview of radical analyses of imperialism in *The Journal of Economic Literature*, suggests that three general theories have been advanced by the neo-marxists to explain why today's capitalism is imperialistic: (1) the rate of profit is declining; (2) there is a need in the advanced capitalist countries for relatively scarce raw materials; and (3) these latter countries want to be able to control development in the exploited nations (571, p. 1099).

The neo-marxists have also contributed to the theoretical development of dependency analysis. There is, for example, Samir Amin's research on Africa and on the capitalist development process in general (e.g. 531; 532). Amin, whose main theoretical contribution has been to contrast the logic of capitalism in the centre to that of 'peripheral capitalism', has also — in his capacity of key researcher at various UN organizations — helped to spread the dependency analysis in Africa (see 540, pp. 149–53; 544, pp. 233–57). Amin is presently working on a project entitled 'Strategies for the Future of Africa' at the United Nations Institute for Training and Research in Dakar.

Immanuel Wallerstein has also intensified dependency analysis with the help of a marxist perspective, especially in the two first instalments of his projected four-volume study *The Modern World-System* (48; 49). When we asked Wallerstein about his attitude to 'economic sociology', he answered — like Amin — that his approach was basically holistic and interdisciplinary in nature.[31] There can be no doubt, however, that Wallerstein's work contains important and long-lasting contributions to economic sociology. The most important of them, we feel, is his attempt to analyse economic change in economic systems in the long-term. Wallerstein's general erudition in economic history is also a very welcome addition to economic sociology.

The first volume of *The Modern World-System* has been criticized by some marxists such as Robert Brenner for paying too much attention to the market — that is, to the trade between the 'core', the 'semi-periphery' and the 'periphery' — and not enough to the class struggle and production (543). A similar critique has also been directed at the theory of 'unequal exchange' by Arghiri Emmanuel (554). What marxists of Brenner's type do not seem to realize, however, is that efforts like those by Wallerstein and Emmanuel represent attempts to come to terms with the fact that marxism lacks a theory of foreign trade, that is, a way of conceptualizing the links between individual countries through the international economy. The confusion of the neo-marxists on this point has resulted in what must be the low-point in their intellectual production: Bill Warren's decision to ignore the whole issue and to revive the idea that Third World countries must go through the same stages in their development as the countries in the West (608).

Confronted with Warren's 'economistic' argument Dudley Seers wrote a thoughtful and witty essay entitled 'The Congruence of Marxism and Other Neo-Classical Theories' (595). In this paper, which deserves to be more widely known, Seers points out some of the basic weaknesses in marxism from the perspective of economic sociology. If one looks carefully at marxism, Seers argues, one will find some disturbing similarities between marxist economic theory and the Chicago School in the sense that both ignore the role of social factors in economic actions:

> When one comes to think about it, they each [that is, marxism and the Chicago School] take perfect competition as a working hypothesis in both product and factor markets (the Marxist 'law of value'), imperfections being considered not severe enough to deprive prices of meaning, or of their functions in organizing the economy

> on a national or world scale and stimulating change. More basically, human beings are assumed to be driven — at least in their capacities as producers and consumers — by only economic motives. Consequently, material incentives are assumed to be the only ones that matter. (595, p. 3)

Even if some of the neo-marxist analysis of development failed to rise to the challenge of creating a sociological analysis of what is happening in the international economy — 'the modes of production controversy' (559) is another example akin to that of Warren — this project has been stimulated by discussions elsewhere. This is especially true of a debate which has been going on since the mid-1970s in comparative sociology and political science, and in which Theda Skocpol and Peter Gourevitch, among others, have been particularly active. Their major achievement has been to stress the importance of connecting the national and the international levels to each other; and the reader is strongly referred to the discussion of the first volume of Wallerstein's *The Modern World-System* (e.g. 570; 598; see also 564). An especially interesting attempt by a comparative sociologist to absorb and go beyond Wallerstein's insights into the role of the international economy can finally be found in Stein Rokkan's last works (e.g. 592; 593). Rokkan's writings, which have not received the attention that they deserve in either comparative sociology or economic sociology, are centered on what he saw as 'the great paradox of Western European development', namely the tensions since the seventeenth century between the capitalist system, which is international in character, and the political system of strong nation states, where territoriality and citizenship are the key features (593, p. 25) Rokkan's work was interrupted by his premature death in 1979 and therefore exists in an unfinished state, but its primary quality — to generate a multitude of testable, middle-range hypotheses — is clearly visible in his models, one of which is reproduced on the next page.

ISA's 'Economy and Society' Group

An important role in making economic sociology more international in character has also been played by the Research Committee on economic sociology of the International Sociological Association, which goes by the name 'Economy and Society' (e.g. 33, pp. 1–2; 411). This group was constituted in 1978 at the World Congress of Sociology at Uppsala. In the early and mid-1970s, economic sociology

FIGURE 6
Stein Rokkan's Model of Economy, Culture and Administration in Large-scale Territorial Systems

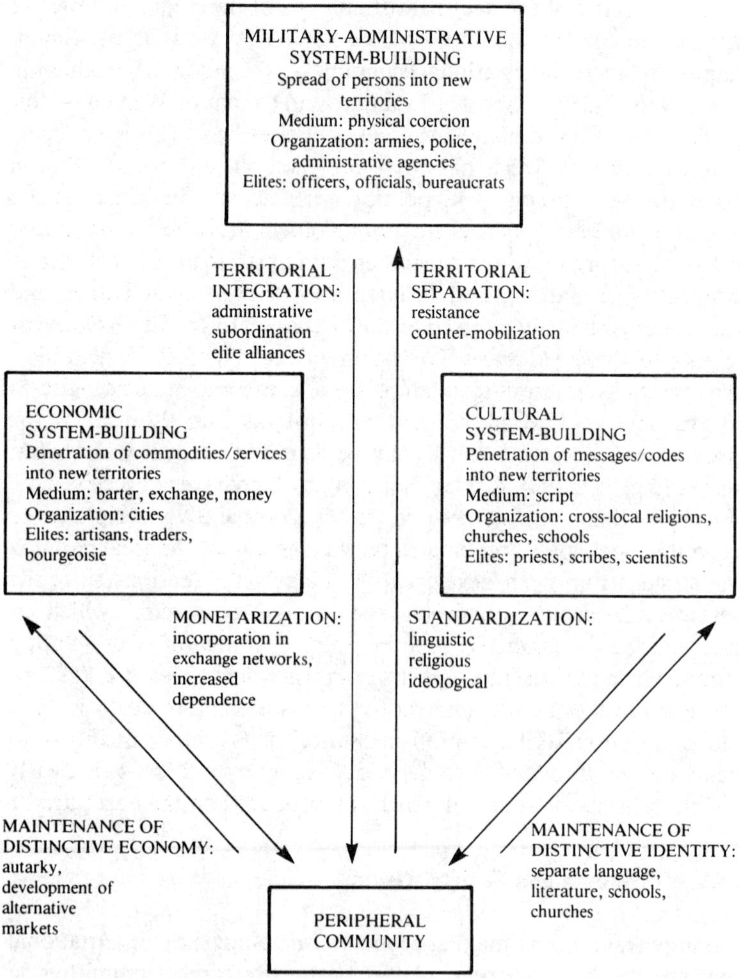

Source: 593, p. 15.

had also been studied in two other groups of the ISA — in an ad hoc group on 'Economy and Society' (led by Alberto Martinelli and Neil Smelser) and in a group on 'Entrepreneurship, Industrial Leadership and Development' (led by Fernando Cardoso and Harry Makler).

In 1979 a survey was made of the members and other people who were interested in the work of the newly constituted group on 'Economy and Society'. One of the findings was that there was great interest among economic sociologists in what happens in the international economy, and that the world-systems approach of Wallerstein was very popular (479). The recent activities of the ISA group also indicate an interest in the international economy. In 1985, for example, several members of the Economy and Society committee held a workshop on the debt crisis, and the papers from this meeting are about to be published in a volume entitled *The Debt, Its Social Impact and Alternative Development Strategies*. At the XI World Congress in New Delhi in August 1986, the committee sponsored sessions on such topics as 'Origins and Consequences of Development Strategies', 'Transnational Corporations and Technology Transfers' and 'International and National Financial Institutions and Socio-Economic Policy'. It should also be mentioned that the ISA group is thoroughly international in composition, at least to judge from the 1986 *Economy and Society Directory* (578). About half of its more than two hundred members come from outside the US and Western Europe. The three countries with the most members are the US (30%), Canada (10%) and Brazil (7.6%). The African countries are, however, severely underrepresented (only one member).

The Sociology of the International Economy

It has been argued that development theory has been in a state of serious crisis for several years (see e.g. 541; 609). Whether this is correct or not does not concern us here. The point we want to make, instead, is that a new field, which can be called *the sociology of the international economy*, has emerged and expanded. Apart from some of the works already mentioned, this field also covers a huge number of other studies of the new institutional structure of the post-war international economy. Laurence H. Shoup and William Minter's *Imperial Brain Trust* (596), for example, analyses the planning during World War II for a US-dominated 'grand area' of free trade. Fred Block's *The Origins of International Economic Disorder* picks up the story of US international economic policy where Shoup and Minter leave off and takes it to the 1970s, when the Bretton Woods institutions started to crumble (10). The role of the International Monetary Fund and the World Bank, especially in relation to Third World countries, has been analysed by Cheryl Payer (586; 587; see also 563; 600). Robert Wood (e.g. 610; 611) is about to publish a long-awaited work on foreign aid entitled *From Marshall Fund to Debt Crisis*, and it is hoped that Barbara Stallings' (e.g. 600; 601) book on the politics of the Euromarkets — *Latin America and US Capital Markets, 1915–1980* — will soon appear.

Latin American sociologists also continue to publish highly provocative and interesting research. One example is Guillermo O'Donnell's essay on the national and international context of investment decisions in the 'bureaucratic-authoritarian state' (585; for an evaluation, see 575). Another is Alejandro Portes' research on immigration and the internationalization of labour (e.g. 589). The literature on the transnational corporations is also growing fast — Peter Evans' *Dependent Development* (555) is a good example — even if it was claimed in a review article on TNCs in 1981 that the sociological contribution was still 'relatively marginal' (556, pp. 199–200). An interesting debate about the advantages and disadvantages of doing high-powered quantitative research on the TNCs, such as that of Volker Bornschier and Christopher Chase-Dunn in *Transnational Corporations and Underdevelopment* (542), has also developed (e.g. 547; 549).

Finally, a tremendous amount of literature on the world-system has appeared since 1976 when the Fernand Braudel Center was founded at the State University of Binghamton. Much of this material is historical in nature — and of this we especially want to highlight the work of the Center on economic cycles and long waves (see e.g. the 1979 and 1984 Spring issues of *The Review*) — but much of it is also contemporary. The latest of the world-system annuals — *States and Markets in the World-System* — contains excellent articles on the economies in Nicaragua, Cuba and Jamaica and their relationship to the international economy (see 557). Important work has also been done at the Center on South Africa and its place in the world economy (see e.g. the 1979 and 1984 Fall issues of *The Review*). It would consequently be no exaggeration if we, in conclusion, stated that the sociology of the international economy constitutes a very dynamic area in contemporary economic sociology.

8

THE SOCIOLOGY OF MARKETS

One of the more important achievements of 'the new economic sociology' is to have opened up the sociological study of markets. Weber (52, p. 81) had stressed the need for a 'sociology of "the market" but his call for studies of this type went unheeded for more than half a century (e.g. 640, p. 50). Parsons and Smelser and Polanyi had made interesting efforts to initiate the social study of markets but did not get very far, as we shall see soon. From the mid-1970s, however, a number of sociological works have appeared which try to delineate the concrete social structure of various types of markets. As a result a new topic, which for convenience can be called 'the sociology of markets', has come into being. For the past few years, sessions with this name have appeared at the annual meeting of the American Socological Association.

What characterizes the new economic sociology in relation to markets is basically that it attempts to look at markets as concrete social structures and to figure out the specific sociological mechanisms through which they work. The single market — or 'the hypothetical market', as John Neville Keynes (85, pp. 247–8) put it — is thus broken down into several different types and components and is thereby brought closer to reality. As distinct from the economic sociology of the 1950s, there is no artificial separation between 'the pure (economic) elements' and 'the impure (social) elements' in the new economic sociology. And contrary to neoclassical theory, the emphasis is on the concrete interaction between real actors and not on the hypothetical intersection of the demand and supply of fictitious actors. Harrison White, who is the leading sociologist in this field, captures some of the essential elements in the new departure in the following statement:

> Neoclassical microeconomics does not look directly at markets. Instead, decisions by typical actors (firms and consumers) are modelled. The theory is unable to specify analytically the boundaries of a market, or to discriminate a production market as such from an entire industrial economy . . . I argue that the need instead is to focus on markets as such, as social structures built jointly by interlocking perceptions and decisions of actors who can be modelled individually by orthodox archetypes. (668, pp. 1–2)

To give the reader an opportunity to appreciate the distance travelled by economic sociology since the 1950s, we shall quickly review the way the 'old' economic sociologists looked at markets. After that we shall look at the discussion of politics vs. markets from the 1960s onwards which, among other things, helped to set off the present interest among sociologists in markets. This will be followed by three brief sections — one on recent sociological works on markets in general, one on financial markets and one on labour markets. The chapter closes with some observations on two interesting sociological studies of the relationship between markets and human values.

The 'Old Economic Sociology' and Markets

The most important texts on markets in economic sociology after World War II are the following: the section in Parsons and Smelser's *Economy and Society* called 'The Institutional Structure of Markets' (36, pp. 143–75), Karl Polanyi's *The Great Transformation* (317) and his essay from *Trade and Market in the Early Empires* entitled 'The Economy as Instituted Process' (in particular the section on 'Market Elements', see Polanyi 321, pp. 266–70; see also e.g. 291; 329, pp. 88-93). Important advances were made in these works, and one of these was to challenge the economists' monopoly of the topic of markets. Polanyi in particular fought hard to dispell the illusion that all economic behaviour can be seen in terms of markets ('*the economistic fallacy*'), and Parsons-Smelser called for a 'systematic development of a sociology of markets' (36, p. 175). Polanyi, Parsons and Smelser also tried their hands at developing a sociological alternative to the neoclassical theory of the market. For Polanyi this meant analysing markets in terms of 'market elements' such as 'demand crowd', 'supply crowd' and 'the element of equivalency' (321, p. 267). Parsons and Smelser suggested that a market could be conceptualized as a 'social system', centered around the idea of boundary interchanges according to the AGIL-scheme.

It is our opinion that neither Polanyi's nor Parsons-Smelser's alternative conceptualizations are particularly fruitful when it comes to analysing markets. One reason for this is that Polanyi is characteristically unclear in his theoretical statements (see e.g. 637, p. 160), while Parsons-Smelser's application of the AGIL-scheme is too abstract and artificial. These deficiencies are common, however, to most analyses of economic phenomena by Polanyi and Parsons-Smelser; more to the point in this specific case is that neither Polanyi nor Parsons-Smelser succeeded in making a clean break with the idea that markets are something that basically belong to the economists' domain. In the section on markets in *Economy and Society* everything that is social is thus conceptualized in terms of 'imperfections of the market' and basically seen as 'non-economic elements' (see also 329, p. 88). The key to the price system is still the conventional demand-supply curve. Polanyi also had difficulty in taking the radical step towards showing that everything 'economic' is indeed social. This can be inferred from his vacillations when confronted with the economies of contemporary capitalism and his preference for analysing pre-industrial societies. It also finds expression in the fundamental ambiguity of his major metaphor of 'embeddedness'. The idea that an economy must be embedded in social and cultural norms in order for society to function implies that the economy in itself is something non-social.[32] Bernard Barber has criticized Polanyi in a similar manner:

> Calling market exchange [in industrial societies] *disembedded* leads attention away from analyzing just how it is interdependent with the other parts of its societal system; it gives it a false kind of analytical, as well as concrete, independence. (617, p. 27)

The Politics vs. Market Debate

After Polanyi, Parsons and Smelser had published their analyses of the market in the 1950s there was a long gap when sociologists showed little interest in the topic. It was at that time, however, that an interesting debate about politics vs. markets was launched by people like Charles E. Lindblom and Albert O. Hirschman (see also 625). In an article from 1966 entitled 'The Rediscovery of the Market' Lindblom presented an analysis which would lead to *Politics and Markets: The World's Political-Economic Systems* (651; 652). Lindblom's first point was that the political system and the market can both be conceptualized as 'politico-economic instruments' and that a comparison between them is therefore natural. His second point was that the market is not synonymous with capitalism; it is simply a way of signalling to producers what and how much they should produce. The market can consequently be used just as well in socialist as in capitalist society, as is made clear by the existence of 'market socialism' in Yugoslavia (see 653 for the same argument applied to international trade).

In *Exit, Voice and Loyalty* (1970) Albert O. Hirschman showed the fruitfulness of comparing the way markets and politics operate from a different and quite ingenious angle (27). The main idea here was that expressions of discontent — and thereby also signals that the situation needs to be improved — are structured in very different ways in the areas of economics and politics. In the former, one typically stops buying a product and one leaves the market (*exit*), while in politics one stays on and expresses discontent (*voice*). Hirschman subsequently added to the debate about markets with his analysis of 'rival interpretations of market society' (28, 642). A major message in these writings is to warn against simplistic interpretations of the capitalist system. Since the birth of capitalism, Hirschman points out, at least four fundamentally different interpretations of market society have been advanced, all with dogmatic conviction. The time has come, he says, for social scientists to start 'embracing complexity' in their analyses of the market (642, p. 1483).

The increasing role of the state in the economy since World War II has also influenced the debate on politics vs. markets. The work by the Norwegian sociologist Gudmund Hernes is especially relevant here. Hernes, who essentially works in the tradition of Lindblom, pays special attention to the interaction between what he calls the three 'steering systems' in society: the market, the political system, and the administrative system (25; 641). In today's West European society, Hernes has noted, a businessman's skill in arranging subsidies from the state can be more instrumental to his company's success than any other talent he might have (641, p. 142). In economic matters, Hernes feels, the trend is increasingly to negotiate prices rather than let the market determine them. As a result, something Hernes calls '*the bargaining economy*' ('*forhandlingsokonomi*') has come into being. The distance between Hernes' type of analysis and neo-corporatism, it can be added, is not far (see e.g. 24). Most neo-corporatist works, however, pay little attention to concrete economic matters and are therefore of marginal interest to economic sociology (but for an exception, see 635).

The resurgence of conservatism since the 1970s, with a US president slashing social services and lecturing Third World countries on 'the magic of the market', has also fuelled the politics vs. market debate. Social scientists with sympathies for the labour movement have reasserted the importance of using politics as a way to offset the negative effects of the market. In Gösta Esping-Andersen's *Politics against Markets* (627), which is a comparative study of the

Scandinavian social democracies, analysis is centered on the need for reforms which make it possible to treat people according to principles other than those of the market ('decommodification policies'; see also 626). In *Markets or Politics?* by Walter Korpi and Rune Aberg, also published in 1985, statistics are presented from a comparative study of eighteen OECD countries to show that the welfare state has not had the negative effects on economic growth and productivity that are claimed by many conservatives and neoclassical economists (647; see 470 for a version in English of the same argument). In general, it seems that several political sociologists have become interested in economic questions as a result of the economic difficulties beginning in the 1970s. According to Leon Lindberg, the situation is similar in political science, and he notes optimistically that 'the economic performance problems of the American economy in the 1970s and into the 1980s may have set the stage for a promising intellectual marriage between political science and institutional economics' (650, p. 15; for the situation in political sociology, see e.g. 638).

General Sociological Theories of Markets

We shall now turn to the problem of what a general sociological theory of markets might look like. Since the most ambitious effort in this direction has been made by Harrison C. White, we shall devote most of the space to a presentation of his work. We shall also comment briefly on Ronald S. Burt's studies of market constraint and the analysis of markets that is in the process of being produced by Amitai Etzioni and others within the context of 'socio-economics'.

Harrison White's model of markets, the so-called W(y) model, was worked out between 1976 and 1979 in three technical memoranda and presented to the profession in 1981 (55; 664; 665; 666; 667; 668). Little attention was paid to White's writings at first, and they are generally considered difficult to penetrate because of their sophisticated mathematics and somewhat short-hand language. Two articles appeared in 1985 and 1986, however, which present White's ideas in a simple and straightforward manner, and it is more likely that a discussion of White's ideas will now take place (see 30; 649).

Such a discussion is definitely needed because White's ideas represent a new and important stage in the sociological study of markets. They are novel in two main ways. First, there is an attempt to explain the functioning of markets *in exclusively sociological terms.*

And second, there is White's ingenious model for how markets operate. In 'Production Markets as Induced Role Structures' White has summarized his project in the following way:

> What I propose is embedding economists' neoclassical theory of the firm within a sociological view of markets. This is almost the inverse of longstanding preconceptions of how sociology relates to economics (Smelser, *The Sociology of Economic Life*, 1963, chap. 4). Sociology's main concern, I argue, should not be urging a richer view of individual character and of culture upon economics conceived as providing the skeleton of theory. My view, rather, is that a market is a role structure of differentiated firms linked together through an equilibrated set, W(y), of interacting observations. Producers see each other's volume/revenue decisions, and whether or not these observations congeal determines whether or not a market is maintained. (668, p. 44)

In his model of market operation, White has been greatly influenced by Edward Chamberlin and a few young economists — especially Michael Spence, Michael Rothschild and Joseph Stiglitz — who have updated Chamberlin's theories in various ways (see e.g. 623; 624; 657; 658; 661). Chamberlin's main contribution, in White's mind, was his realization that the neoclassical assumption of homogeneous products in a market must be replaced with a theory which acknowledges that each producer's product is distinct and is valued differently by the consumers. To move from here to a new theory of markets, however, one needs a *sociological* perspective.

The advantage of the sociological perspective, according to White, is that it allows one to go from an individual level to a structural level. In relation to markets this means that one can tie together the individual decisions that businessmen make with the fact that markets have distinct and stable structures. Businessmen act *as if* the market had a stable structure and consequently it gets one, White says.

During the ten or so years that White has been working on his model, he has dealt with and suggested solutions for a variety of special problems such as the conditions under which markets emerge, how consumers and producers can connect, and so on. The key feature of the W(y) model is, however, the theory of how firms produce a market by observing each other's behaviour, and we shall therefore take time to outline White's reasoning on this point.

We shall examine White's reasoning by taking an example which can be found in Leifer and White's article 'A Structural Approach to Markets' (649). Tony is a frozen pizza producer with a product that is different from that of other pizza makers. Like other pizzas, it has a distinct reputation and Tony's pizza can therefore be said to occupy a specific niche in the market. Tony occasionally checks on his market situation and is then aware that there exists a specific relationship ('terms of trade') between the quantity of pizzas sold and the revenue received; an expensive and high quality pizza will sell less well than a cheap and low quality pizza. Quality, however, is nothing that Tony can observe directly — unlike volume (y) and revenue (W). Information about W and y can be found in trade publications and the like. Since Tony is a maximizing individual, he will base his decision on these *ex ante* figures and try to make as much money as possible. Other pizza makers will do the same, and together their decisions will — under certain, specified conditions — form a self-fulfilling prophecy: there now *is* a market. See Figure 7 on the next page for a visual representation of the argument.

As noted earlier, there has not been any general discussion of the W(y) model. It is clear, however, that the model has to be tested empirically before a final verdict can be reached. Until this has been done, White must nevertheless be commended for having shattered the illusion that the conventional demand-supply model is indispensable. In hindsight, it may turn out that this was the most difficult thing to do. White should also be credited with having asked several challenging and basic questions, such as 'where do markets come from?' and 'under what conditions can they exist?'

The attempts by Ronald Burt and the socio-economists to analyse markets are interesting but definitely less bold than that of White. Though these authors seem committed to analysing markets from a sociological perspective, they base their theories on fairly conventional economics. This said, however, it should be stressed that Ronald Burt has made an especially important contribution to the sociology of markets in *Corporate Profits and Cooptation* (621; see also 620; 622). Through a sophisticated network analysis of data on US manufacturing industries Burt convincingly shows that 'market constraint' affects the level of profit. Thus when an industry sells its products to a small number of consumer industries or purchases supplies from just a few supplier industries, there is a fall in the profit level. Another of Burt's interesting findings is that consumer/supplier constraint is about twice as important as constraint due to intra-industrial competition. The common notion that vigorous competition in an industry is all that is needed for the market to work efficiently, is thus incorrect. Burt's hypothesis that overlapping directorships are used to offset the consequences of

FIGURE 7
A Self-reproducing Market according to the W(y) Model

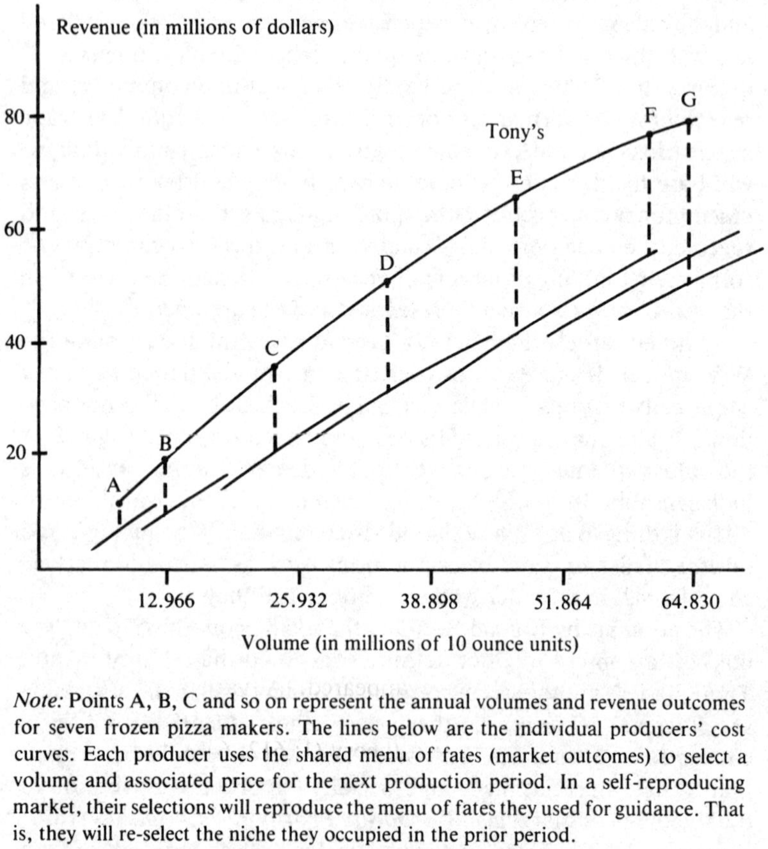

Note: Points A, B, C and so on represent the annual volumes and revenue outcomes for seven frozen pizza makers. The lines below are the individual producers' cost curves. Each producer uses the shared menu of fates (market outcomes) to select a volume and associated price for the next production period. In a self-reproducing market, their selections will reproduce the menu of fates they used for guidance. That is, they will re-select the niche they occupied in the prior period.
Source: 649, p. 21A.

market constraint, on the other hand turns out to have a more shaky empirical foundation.

The socio-economists tend to use a mixture of policy analysis and systems theory in their approach to markets (see also the section on socio-economics in chapter 9). Etzioni has written mainly on competition, and his contribution is centred on the concepts of 'encapsulated competition' and 'interventionist power' (628; 629). For competition to exist, Etzioni argues, it has to be 'encapsulated' by 'ethical', 'social', and 'governmental' rules — an idea which is quite similar to that of 'embeddedness' in Polanyi. 'Interventionist power' — defined as 'the use of governmental power by economic actors for their (own) ends' — is more refreshing since it tries to introduce the notion of political power into that of economic power (629, p. 173; see 630). Etzioni points out that analyses of industrial organizations usually look only at economic factors such as, for example, the number and nature of economic actors in a study of oligopoly. Oligopolies are also shaped, however, by *political* factors, and this has to be taken into consideration for the analysis to be realistic. The most ambitious effort yet by the socio-economists to analyse markets can be found in Tom Burns and Helena Flam's 'A Theory of Markets: Their Social Structure and Performance Properties' (619). The strength of this essay, which is an attempt to develop a theory of social rule system, lies mainly in the emphasis that it puts on the fact that every market has specific rules which regulate entry ('market exclusion rules').

The Sociological Structure of Financial Markets

Until quite recently there were practically no sociological works on financial markets (for two exceptions, see 322; 323). In 1984, however, an anthology appeared which was entitled *The Social Dynamics of Financial Markets* (2), and since then a series of interesting sociological analyses of markets that deal in securities, bonds and commodities have appeared. A variety of different sociological approaches have by now been tried out, such as network analysis (615; 616), organization theory (1; 612; 648), the theory of collective behaviour (613), and neo-marxist theory (666). Of interest to the economic sociologist is also the fact that these studies often contain a sharp critique of neoclassical theory (e.g. 1; 616). The reason for this is that financial markets are often portrayed in neoclassical textbooks as the prototype of the perfectly competitive market.

The three key figures in the sociology of financial markets are presently Mitchel Y. Abolafia, Wayne E. Baker and Susan S. Shapiro, all of whom presented their doctoral theses in 1980 or 1981 (see also 662). Shapiro's *Wayward Capitalists* (42) is a study of the Securities and Exchange Commission in Washington, D.C. and looks at financial markets from the perspective of *trust* in economic life (see p. 134 below and note 35). Mitchel Abolafia's most fascinating work is 'Market Crisis and Organizational Intervention', which is a study of the 1979–80 crisis in the silver market when the Hunt brothers tried to make a billion dollar killing (1). The author presents this crisis from three different perspectives which he labels 'The Efficiency Model', 'The Market Politics Model' and 'The Market Sector Model'. According to the first model, which summarizes the neoclassical position, a market will always clear, and there is basically no room for a crisis. If a crisis takes place anyway, it will be due to an exogenous event along the lines that Kindleberger (646) suggests. The other two models are similar in that they view the market in terms of power struggles between various groups. Conflicts are endogenous and hence to be expected. 'The Market Sector Model', however, takes many more factors into account than 'The Market Politics Model', such as regulatory agencies and actors outside the market. The historical context is also taken into consideration, and the market is seen as a kind of system of interlocking organizations. Abolafia shows in a convincing way that 'The Market Sector Model' is best suited for explaining the 1979–80 silver crisis, and he summarizes his position in the following way: 'market crises are fundamentally interorganizational phenomena' (1, p. 1).

Wayne Baker's 'The Social Structure of a National Securities Market' is an exceptionally fine study, which contains a sharp sociological analysis of trading in stock options on a securities exchange as well as a critique of neoclassical theory from a new and interesting angle (616). Baker shows that buyers and sellers of stock options form distinct networks at the exchange, with different social structures. This may not be surprising to a sociologist, but Baker succeeds in showing that these structures have a direct effect on the determination of prices. Small cohesive networks thus dampen price volatility, while large ones with a more differentiated structure have the opposite effect. Neoclassical theory, Baker concludes, is consequently incorrect when it claims that markets will operate more efficiently, the more buyers and sellers there are. He also shows that the larger a market is, the more differentiated it will probably be — also contrary to standard neoclassical theory. Whereas Abolafia considers the market to be a kind of interorganizational phenomenon, for Baker it is primarily a set of networks.

Labour Market Sociology

Since the mid-1970s a new sub-area, called the sociology of labour markets (see e.g. 644), has developed within stratification studies and until 1980 the idea that labour market studies could improve stratification studies and replace attainment research was enthusiastically and uncritically received. Since 1980, however, several critical voices have been raised in the demand for a new theoretical approach. A few studies have been produced in response to this critique even if a powerful theory is still awaited. For the reader who wants a good introduction to the issues in today's labour market sociology, Ivar Berg's anthology *Sociological Perspectives on Labor Markets* is especially recommended (9).

The novelty in labour market sociology is basically that the emphasis has been shifted from the individual person to the macrostructures of the labour market. In the early studies it was also common to include a critique of the attainment tradition in sociology and to emphasize how similar it is to the human capital approach in neoclassical economics.

Early labour market sociology consisted of studies from a variety of theoretical perspectives that were held together by little more than opposition to the neoclassical assumption of market homogeneity (e.g. 643). The two most popular approaches were to divide the national labour market into 'segments' and to focus on the 'internal' as opposed to the 'external' labour market. The theory of dual labour markets was developed in the late 1960s primarily by institutional and neo-marxist economists. Some of the more important people involved were Michael Piore (e.g. 655; 656), David Gordon (e.g. 633) and Barry Bluestone (e.g. 618). They portrayed the national labour market as having two or more sectors with little mobility between them. In the primary sector the pay is fairly high, there is job security and chances for advancement are good; in the secondary sector, the situation is more or less the opposite. Workers who are discriminated against on racial grounds, as well as women, tend to accumulate in the secondary sector, and this benefits the capitalist class (e.g. 459).

The notion of internal versus external labour markets goes back to the institutional economics of the 1950s, and reference is often made to Clark Kerr's article on 'the balkanization of labor markets' (645). The work that popularized the approach, however, was Peter B. Doeringer and Michael J. Piore's *Internal Labor Markets and*

Manpower Analysis from 1971 (375). Its basic idea is that there are 'markets' inside firms and that they have a structure which differs from the ordinary labour market, where market forces decide who gets ahead. Internal labour market studies typically focus on job ladders, seniority entitlements and the like. The idea of internal labour markets can easily be combined with the notion of dual labour markets, for most jobs in the primary sector, according to Doeringer and Piore, come via internal labour markets. In the secondary sector, on the other hand, one has to go outside the firm to find a better job.

Several critiques of labour market studies have appeared since 1980. The most interesting critiques have been authored by Aage B. Sorensen (44; 660), Mark Granovetter (634), and James N. Baron and William T. Bielby (5). Sorensen argues that labour market sociology is actually quite similar to attainment research. Both use individual level regression analysis on large cross-sectional samples in order to explain as much variance as possible. Neither has much of a notion of what causes the difference in earnings. In labour market studies one simply adds a measure for market structure to the measures used in conventional attainment research:

> This model provides a conception of the attainment process where, at any moment in time of the individual's career, he receives some part of his earnings as payment for his individual qualifications and another part (which may be negative) as a bonus for working in a particular firm, industry, or labour market segment. The model does partition the variance in earnings according to these variables and thus informs about whether or not something makes a difference, assuming things add up in the manner suggested by the linear equation used to estimate the effects of the variables. However, it is unlikely to capture what goes on in the labour market, since it is unlikely that the mechanisms that actually govern the attainment of people are those proposed by the model. (660, pp. 25–6)

To improve the situation, Sorensen feels that stratification analysts must reassess their general relationship to sociological theory. The effort should be directed at finding 'the mechanisms' that underlie the mobility, the difference in earnings, and so on. These mechanisms should preferably be modelled mathematically and then tested empirically. Mathematics should in other words be used not so much as a statistical tool as a way of doing theory. Sorensen also feels that longitudinal data are needed if one is to find out whether market barriers are temporary (the neoclassical position) or not (the segmented labour market position). He suggests that areas to focus on for theoretical renewal are the roles of firms and unions in the wage formation process and he also calls for 'a sociology of pay scales' (44, pp. 278, 284–5).

Like Sorensen, Granovetter is very critical of most labour market sociology and feels that what is needed first of all is 'deeper and broader theoretical development' (634, p. 11). His own suggestion for how to improve the situation is linked to the idea that there are three main factors which contribute to earned income: '(a) the characteristics of the job and the employer; (b) the characteristics of the individual who occupies the job; and (c) how (a) and (b) get linked together' (634, p. 12). Granovetter believes that one of these three factors, has been especially neglected in sociological and economic theory, and that is how demand and supply get linked up in the labour market ('*the matching problem*'). As an illustration of what can be done on this point, Granovetter refers to one of his earlier studies, *Getting a Job* (21). In this fine analysis of job changers in a Boston suburb, Granovetter shows that when workers look for a job they have a preference for information derived from *personal* contacts. The reason for this is that personal information is much more relevant to what the worker needs to know about a job than what he or she can get from an agency or an advertisement. According to Granovetter's study, jobs which are found through personal contacts also pay more than those found through agencies, advertisements, or direct application.

The by-now-familiar charge that studies in labour market sociology do not rest on much of a theoretical foundation can also be found in a famous article by James Baron and William Bielby, 'Bringing the Firms Back In: Stratification, Segmentation, and the Organization of Work' (5). The authors stress that, despite an outpouring of descriptive studies, there is no coherent theory of what is going on in the labour market. To overcome this shortcoming, Baron and Bielby suggest that sociologists should examine the firm, which they claim to be '[the] missing link in contemporary structural stratification research' (5, p. 738). Stratification analysts have to stop treating the firm as a 'black box' and to start examining organization studies, in particular.

Although Baron and Bielby's article was received very favourably when it appeared it did not inspire much research (44, p. 277), but interesting attempts to analyse the wage formation process by focusing on the firm have recently been undertaken. In a 1986 paper Trond Petersen, for example, analyses the role that incentives play in income earned (654). Petersen, who bases his study on a huge sample of sales people in department stores in the US, deserves praise for having opened up an area for discussion which by tradition only economists have looked at: the importance for wages of individual performance within positions. In another interesting study Peter Hedström suggests that the number of authority levels in a corporation is of crucial inportance for generating income differences (639). Using data from Sweden, Hedström makes a good case for his argument; his next step, he informs us, will be to look at the process behind the formation of authority levels. A difficulty with doing stratification research on the level of the firm, it should finally be noted, is that few data of this type are presently available. In Norway, Western Germany and the US, however, the first steps are being taken towards the collection of data on individuals in corporations. Once these data are available, there will be an opportunity to test new theories and to 'bring the economy back in' in stratification research.

The Market and Human Values

There are quite a few topics which are important to the sociology of markets but which unfortunately cannot be covered in this brief overview. One of them would be the existence of various forms of black market, and another the tendency to use reciprocal exchange of labour. For the reader who is interested in the 'informal economy' in post-industrial society, we especially recommend Jonathan Gershuny's very enjoyable analyses (e.g. 631; 632). According to Gershuny, the informal economy consists of three sectors — 'the household economy', 'the communal economy' and 'the underground economy' — which all interact with each other as well as with the official economy. Empirical research on the reciprocal exchange of labour between households has also recently been conducted by the Hungarian sociologist Endre Sik (659).

Another topic which is of much interest to the sociology of markets is that of human values and the market. An early and important work in this genre is Richard M. Titmuss' *The Gift Relationship: From Human Blood to Social Policy* (1971), which is a study of blood donors and transfusion services primarily in Great Britain and the US. The main point that Titmuss wants to make is that certain problems in human societies are best handled outside the market. The British way of supplying blood for transfusions on a voluntary basis is actually more efficient than the mixed system of commercial and non-commercial blood banks in the US. *The Gift Relationship* is a sociological work which raises important questions for the economist as well, as is clear from the fact that Kenneth Arrow has devoted an article to it (614).

A study which is very much in the tradition of Titmuss' book is Viviana A. Zelizer's 'Human Values and the Market: The Case of Life Insurance and Death in Nineteenth-Century America' (669; see also 670; 671). Her topic is the attempt during the nineteenth century to introduce life insurance in the US, which met with fierce resistance for several decades before it finally succeeded. Zelizer describes the reason for the failure as follows:

> Putting death on the market offended a system of values that upheld the sanctity of human life and its incommensurability. It defied a powerful normative pattern: the division between the nonmarketable and the marketable, or between the sacred and the profane. (669, p. 594)

Zelizer's article also contains interesting sociological observations on the changing function of wills and the symbolic relationship between money and death in funerals. 'Human Values and the Market' is highly recommended as an introduction to the more profound questions that can be asked within the context of a sociology of markets.

9
THE NEW RELATIONSHIP BETWEEN ECONOMICS AND SOCIOLOGY

> POLITICAL ECONOMY or ECONOMICS is a study of mankind in the ordinary business of life; it examines that part of individual and social action which is most closely connected with the attainment and with the use of the material requisites of wellbeing.
>
> —Alfred Marshall, *Principles of Economics*

If ever there was a time when economists and sociologists had their own specific subject area and research methods, it was in the past. We are now in the middle of a chaotic and creative period when nobody is exactly sure where to draw the line betwen the two sciences. Several suggestions have recently been made — by economists as well as by sociologists — as to how to relate the study of economics and society to each other, and they will be commented upon in this chapter. We shall then present what we consider to be the most adequate response by sociologists to the present situation of fluidity, that is, the creation of a flexible and non-dogmatic economic sociology (*middle-range economic sociology*). The emphasis here should be on explaining economic phenomena on primarily sociological grounds. Special attention should in our opinion be given to empirical research of the various 'social mechanisms' that can be found in the economy; and economic behaviour should be seen as part of the human experience or '*the business of life*', as Marshall put it.

In itself it is undoubtedly a positive development that the old ideas about which topics 'belong' to sociology and which 'belong' to economics are breaking down. It is also important, however, to develop new and sensible guidelines for the future relationship between economics and sociology. If the wrong strategy is followed by today's sociologists, many years of work might easily be lost — and maybe even the chance itself to have a say in the redefinition of the relationship between economics and sociology. A discussion of the various alternatives that are presently available is therefore needed.

The four approaches we have chosen to discuss are: (1) *economic imperialism*, (2) *the structural-individualistic research programme*, (3) *the new political economy*, and (4) *socio-economics*. There are a few other perspectives as well but they are not likely to be among the contenders.[33] From the outset it should be said that while we think there are positive and creative qualities to each of these four approaches, none seems suitable as a candidate for how sociology should be related to economics in general.

Why these approaches have developed to challenge the old relationship between economics and sociology just now is a complicated question. Roughly speaking, it seems that sociologists have become interested in economics mainly as a result of social and economic events since the mid-1960s, while economists have started to look at society for reasons which are more connected with developments within their profession. Quite a few sociological works on economic topics can thus be traced directly to the social movements of the 1960s or to the economic difficulties since the 1970s. Such works as *The Calculus of Consent* (1962) by James Buchanan and Gordon Tullock or *The Economic Approach to Human Behavior* (1976) by Gary Becker are more difficult, however, to connect to specific social events. On the other hand, there are also examples which do not fit into these general trends. The work by Harrison White and his students seems to have been immune to the radicalism of the 1960s as well as to the conservatism of the 1970s. And the recent re-examination of economic theory has been directly influenced by some socio-economic events of which the breakdown of keynesian economics is the most obvious example (see e.g. 347; 356).

The term 'economic imperialism' was first used in 1969 by Kenneth Boulding, who defined it as 'an attempt on the part of economics to take over all the other social sciences' (689, p. 131). Since then it has been accepted in the economic profession (e.g. 732; 766; 775; 780). The general programme of the economic imperialists consists of a belief that the economic type of analysis can also be used outside the traditional fields of economics; and that, when this is done, it will prove superior to what the non-economic social sciences can accomplish. If one were to single out a programme in 'economic imperialism', it would be the introductory chapter to Gary Becker's *The Economic Approach to Human Behavior*. Becker states that '. . . I have come to the conclusion that the economic approach is a comprehensive one that is applicable to all human behavior' (7, p. 8). The 'economic approach' is defined as 'the combined assumptions of maximizing behavior, market equilibrium, and stable preferences, *used relentlessly and unflinchingly*' (7, p. 5; emphasis added).

There are already quite a few works in the tradition of economic imperialism. According to many observers, they can basically be grouped into the following four areas *law* (see especially 764; 765), *economic history* (see especially 755), *sociology* (see especially 7; 8; 682; 683), and *politics* (see especially 692; 703; 754; 756; see also 681). How should sociology look on these 'imperialistic' works, especially since Becker has become a member of the department of sociology at the University of Chicago? On the positive side, it can be noted that there is a very elegant use of models in, e.g., Becker's work. It must also be said that a few analyses have been produced — especially that of the free rider in Mancur Olson's work — which constitute creative and important contributions to social science in general (see 756; 757; 758). On the negative side, much can be said. Space prohibits us from giving a detailed criticism of the imperialists' advocacy of sociobiology, their sexual stereotyping, and the profoundly anti-sociological character of most of their writings. Their ambition of superseding all the other social sciences must also be characterized as little more than a fantasy. According to the latest survey of the field —

filled incidentally with that bombastic jargon which befits a movement which calls itself 'imperialistic' — the first stage of 'easy successes' is now over and 'difficulties' have begun to arise (732, p. 54). There will no doubt be more of them before the imperialists scale down their ambitions and settle for making a small — and valuable — contribution.

Very few sociologists have shown an interest in the ideas of the economic imperialists. Since the early 1970s, however, a group of European sociologists calling themselves 'structural-individualists' has been trying to apply the economic model to sociological analysis. Most of these people come from Germany and Holland but there are signs that the approach is also becoming popular in the US (see e.g. 725; 788; 789). Karl-Dieter Opp (e.g. 759; 760; 761) is a leading proponent of the 'structural-individualistic research programme' as well as Siegwart Lindenberg (e.g. 745; 746; 747) and Reinhard Wippler (e.g. 788; 789). Hans Albert (e.g. 672; 673) and Bruno Frey (e.g. 717; 718; 719; 720) share many of the same ideas. On the periphery are Raymond Boudon (e.g. 687; 688), Jon Elster (e.g. 706; 707; 708; 709; 710) and Philippe van Parijs (e.g. 489; 762) who are all outstanding scholars (see also 740).

Karl-Dieter Opp has described the structural-individualists as a group of sociologists who are 'committed to methodological individualism [and who] apply the rational choice model or similar theories to solve sociological problems' (761, p. 213). The necessity to use models in theory construction and to increase the explanatory capacity of sociology is also heavily emphasized. Structural-individualism started out as a programme for a theoretical renewal of sociology and has not, as of yet, resulted in many empirical studies. The existing studies mainly focus on social movements, which is probably a reflection of the impact that James Coleman's (e.g. 699) work has had on the structural-individualists.

The structural-individualists should be credited with having instigated discussion among sociologists about the economic approach. Their emphasis on the need for models in sociological theory and on the belief that the explanatory power of sociology should be increased is also useful. A drawback to the structural-individualistic perspective is that its proponents have tended to follow the economists a bit too uncritically. In our opinion, it is a mistake, for example, to accept the idea that maximization of utility can account for the rise of non-market institutions (see e.g. 701). The concept of rationality, about which Jon Elster has written so well, also tends to get lost in the works of Opp et al. Methodological individualism, finally, is not without serious problems as a philosophy of science (see especially 781).

There are signs, however, that the structural-individualists are increasingly feeling that as sociologists they also have something to teach the economists, especially when it comes to the formation of preferences (see e.g. 747; 761, p. 230–7). From the viewpoint of economic sociology it is to be hoped that the structural-individualists will devote more empirical research to economic topics; one occasionally gets a feeling that they think it is unnecessary for sociologists to study the economy since the economists are already doing such a good job in that area.

Another contender for deciding how the new line between economics and sociology is to be drawn is the perspective of 'the new political economy'. This term has been used by a variety of people, but the group we have in mind here mainly consists of people like John Goldthorpe, Fred Hirsch, Leon Lindberg and Charles Maier. Their most relevant works in this context are Hirsch and Goldthorpe (eds), *The Political Economy of Inflation* (1978); Goldthorpe (ed.), *Order and Conflict in Contemporary Capitalism* (1984); and Lindberg and Maier (eds), *The Politics of Inflation and Economic Stagnation* (1985) (20; 26; 744). Hirsch's *Social Limits to Growth* (728), which is an interesting work in its own right for economic sociologists, might also be included. It should also be noted that Lindberg has recently written a couple of fine essays on the role of economists as policy advisers (650; 742; 743).

The basic approach of the 'new political economists' has been most concisely outlined by John Goldthorpe in the introduction to *Order and Conflict in Contemporary Capitalism* (20, pp. 1–14). The main idea is that the capitalist market has a tendency to destabilize society and must therefore be politically regulated through the state. By omitting a proper analysis of the political dimension, it is argued, conventional economists usually go wrong. Economics, in brief, is not something that only takes place in the market; it is also a question of the struggle for power between various groups in society. This analysis of the interaction between political and economic actors is then typically applied to the economies of the Western nations since the early 1970s.

The main strength of the 'new political economy' is its focus on politics and the role of power in economics, which is usually neglected in mainstream economics. In relation to economic sociology,

Goldthorpe defines the new political economy like this:

> I would say that 'political economy' is somewhat narrower than 'economic sociology' in having a particular concern with the political processes involved in the formation and implementation of (chiefly) national economic policy and in economic management generally, but broader in that it seeks to incorporate in this respect the perspectives of the political scientist as well as the sociologist. (78)

The basic weakness of the approach by Goldthorpe et al. is a tendency to turn economic questions into political ones and to disregard the impact that the social structure of the economy is bound to have. This comes out very clearly in the analysis of inflation, which tends to be explained as if it was exclusively, in Goldthorpe's words, 'the monetary expression of distributional conflict' (26, p. 195). Albert O. Hirschman, who has developed a considerably more sophisticated analysis of inflation, goes as far as saying that 'the explanation of inflation in terms of social conflict between groups, each aspiring to a greater share of the social product, has become the sociologist's monotonous equivalent of the economist's untiring stress on the undue expansion of the money supply' (734, pp. 57–8).

A fourth way of looking at the new relationship between economics and sociology is that of 'socio-economics'. The key figure in this approach is Amitai Etzioni, who is director of a project on socio-economics at George Washington University and who has organized a campaign for a section on socio-economics in the American Sociological Association. After serving at the White House in 1979–80, it appears that Etzioni began to do work on re-industrialization and that this led him to suggest the creation of 'socio-economics' (see e.g. 712; 713; 714). The best introduction to this new field so far (Etzioni is working on a book tentatively entitled *The Bi-Utility of Socio-Economics*) is an article called 'Making Policy for Complex Systems: A Medical Model for Economics' (16). The argument is that a new 'policy science' should be formed, which would be similar to medicine in that it would draw on several different disciplines when confronted with a problem: 'The policy science that would emerge . . . could be called "socioeconomics" to distinguish it from economics as an analytic science. Socioeconomics would combine contributions from other disciplines whose subjects are political, cultural, and psychic' (16, p. 392). Socio-economics has also been defined by Etzioni as 'part economics and part sociology' (714, p. 178). According to the first issue of *Socio-Economic Notes*, published at George Washington University, 'socio-economic propositions contain at least one independent variable of economics and one of another science' (772, p. 1).

Etzioni should definitely be commended for trying to form a section on socio-economics at the ASA, and his proposal for socio-economics *as a policy science* sounds interesting. If there is a problem with socio-economics, it has more to do with its additional quality as an 'analytic science', to use Etzioni's terminology. Etzioni, for instance, talks of socio-economics as an 'interstitial discipline', which would bridge economics and the other social sciences in a manner that is similar to the way in which biochemistry 'bridges' biology and chemistry (714, p. 178). This sounds good enough, but few original ideas have yet been presented by the socio-economists to back up this ambitious scheme (see in this context also the discussion of the socio-economists in chapter 8 above). Since socio-economics is only just beginning, this criticism might very well be premature. In 1986–87, it should be noted, both Etzioni and Tom Burns are scheduled to publish programmatic books on 'socio-economics'; and the final verdict will have to wait until these books are available.

Economic Theory and Economic Sociology

We have been examining perspectives which all try to stake out a new position somewhere in between economics and sociology. In our opinion, there are problems with each of them. The economic imperialists do not want to reform sociology; they want to get rid of it. The socio-economists are basically interested in policy science and the idea of a scientific mutation between economics and sociology has not advanced very far. The new political economists have a focus which is too narrow, being limited as it is to the interaction between the political and the economic system. Finally, the structural-individualists' ambition is too broad for they want to make a clean sweep of *all* sociology and to place it on a totally new foundation.

In our opinion the best strategy for sociologists would be to use the present fluidity in the relationship between economic theory and sociology as a basis for firmly establishing *economic sociology*, that is *the sociological study of the economy*. Since a 'new economic sociology' would definitely have to define itself in relation to economic theory, we shall try in the next few pages to show where economic sociology can benefit from the economists' ideas and where this is not possible. Throughout the discussion, we have tried to use a

TABLE 2
Different Types of Articles Published in the *American Economic Review* 1972–81

Type of Article	March 1972 to December 1976 (in percentage)	March 1977 to December 1981 (in percentage)
Mathematical models without any data	50.1	54.0
Analysis without mathematical formulation and data	21.2	11.6
Statistical methodology	0.6	0.5
Empirical analysis based on data generated by the author's initiative	0.8	1.4
Empirical analysis using indirect statistical inference published or generated elsewhere	21.4	22.7
Empirical analysis not using indirect statistical inference based on data generated by author	0.0	0.5
Empirical analysis not using indirect statistical inference based on data generated or published elsewhere	5.4	7.4
Empirical analysis based on artificial simulations and experiments	0.5	1.9

Source: 739, p. 49.

broad concept of economic sociology, as is proper in a study which is more concerned with helping to establish a subfield than with advocating a specific theoretical position. Our opinion about the general thrust that economic sociology needs if it is to prosper is quite precise, however, and should for the purpose of discussion be made explicit. The economic sociology we have in mind can probably best be summarized as a kind of *middle-range economic sociology* which broadly follows the programmatic statement in Merton's classical essay 'On Sociological Theories of the Middle Range' (see also 776; 779, pp. 107–13). It differs on a few points from Merton's position, however, as will soon become clear. The concept of 'social mechanism', for instance, is used instead of 'function', and so on.

Sociologists can learn a lot from economists in terms of theory, but the situation is different when it comes to the role that facts should play in an analysis. Mainstream economists are often reluctant to test their theories against facts. Leontief, to take one example, made a content analysis a few years ago of articles published in the *American*

Economic Review between 1972 and 1981 and found that more than half of them presented mathematical models with no data whatsoever (739; see Table 2). He also pointed out that there is actually a tremendous amount of empirical material which the neoclassical economists simply ignore: 'masses of concrete, detailed information contained in technical journals, reports of engineering firms, and private marketing organizations are neglected' (739, p. 107).

In general, it is clear that economists are more advanced than sociologists when it comes to theory construction. The idea that 'theory' is something that one eventually obtains by generalizing from data is still common among sociologists. There are also some real pitfalls in mainstream economic theory, however, one of them being its strong social darwinism. This sometimes achieves rather ludicrous expressions, as in Andrew Schotter's *The Economic Theory of Social Institutions* from 1981. The main idea of this work is that one can explain the emergence of all social institutions through a mixture of microeconomic theory and game theory. The author asserts that every institution emerges as an adaptive response to a 'problem':

> Economic and social institutions evolve the way species do. To ensure their survival and growth, they must solve a whole set of problems that arise as the system evolves. Each problem creates the need for some adaptive feature, that is, a social institution. Analogously, then, the problem facing social scientists is to infer the evolutionary problem that must have existed for the institution as we see it to have developed. (769, pp. 1–2)

It is understandable that Schotter's book with its darwinian argument is not a favourite among sociologists, but it is more difficult to grasp why Oliver Williamson's transaction cost-approach is so popular since it rests on basically the same argument, namely, that any institution exists because it is economically efficient. In *Markets and Hierarchies* and later articles, Williamson suggests that economic functions will be performed in a market or in an organization ('hierarchy') depending on the transaction costs involved. If it is more efficient to make the transaction within a corporation, it will be done that way and not through the market (784; 785; 786; 787). Mark Granovetter (22, pp. 493-504) and Charles Perrow (37) have both criticized Williamson on the ground that he is too functionalistic/darwinian and that his findings run counter to some pertinent literature, especially Robert Eccles' work on transfer pricing (705; see in this context also 738). They also point out that markets and corporations are not the clear-cut alternatives that Williamson seems to think (for a similar argument, see 777; 783).

A certain scepticism about the application of the insights of economic theory to sociology is therefore recommended. A good rule of thumb when one needs to make a quick distinction between what is acceptable from a sociological viewpoint and what is not, is Max Weber's dictum that every 'economic action' is not necessarily a 'social action'. 'The economic activity of an individual', we read in *Economy and Society* 'is social only if it takes account of the behaviour of someone else' (52, pp. 22, 63).

There are other elements in economic theory, however, which can be very useful for theory construction in economic sociology. This is especially true of (1) the concept of rationality and (2) the use of sophisticated mathematical models. The concept of rationality has been widely neglected in sociology in general. As a consequence, *homo sociologicus* has tended to become a person who reacts to his surroundings rather than makes a conscious choice about the course of action to take. According to a famous line by James Duesenberry, 'economics is all about how people make choices; sociology is all about how they don't have any choices to make' (704, p. 233). Recently, however, Jon Elster (e.g. 706; 709; 710) has tried to develop a concept of rationality which is sociological in nature. He calls this 'strategic rationality' (as opposed to 'parametric rationality'), and it combines the insights of microeconomic theory with those of game theory:

> Game theory enables us to look at the individual as a person, who is strategically rational. In other theories of decision, the individual is exclusively parametrically rational; that is, the choice is made under circumstances which cannot be affected by the actor himself. Parametric rationality does not allow, in other words, that the surroundings consist of other actors who can also act strategically. Game theory, to put it another way, means that the interaction between individuals can be analysed strategically or intentionally and not only causally. (711, p. 214; *our translation*)

To carry out a whole analysis one has, according to Elster, to proceed in two steps. First one must decide which actions are structurally possible, and then one can use game theory to see which of the possible actions will actually be undertaken ('the two-step model'; 707, p. 113).

Elster has helped to make the rationality concept popular in circles outside economics and he has also, following Herbert Simon and others, tried to make it more useful by increasing its complexity. He has not, however, confronted his 'two-step model' and the concept of 'strategic rationality' with concrete data. The claim that a more sociological concept of rationality can be very useful in an empirical analysis has, however, been demonstrated in a very convincing manner by Samuel L. Popkin in *The Rational Peasant*. This 1979 work, which is a study of the economy of rural society in Vietnam, deserves close attention by economic sociologists, and to give the reader a sense of how Popkin handles the concept of rationality, we shall briefly summarize its contents.

The Rational Peasant is intended as a critique of the 'moral economy' approach of writers like James C. Scott, Joel Migdal and Eric Wolf. The tendency of the 'moral economists' is to depict the pre-capitalist village as a community where the peasants and the landlords have found a certain *modus vivendi*. The peasants, according to this perspective, are traditional in economic matters; they help each other in times of trouble; and they resist innovations. When capitalism emerges, the village is penetrated by market forces from the outside and the peasants may very well rebel to restore the original balance.

According to Popkin, this picture of the peasant is not correct. The peasant has his own interests which frequently fail to coincide with those of the village. The idea that capitalism introduces selfish principles into a resistant peasant community is also shown to be false by Popkin in a series of brilliant sociological sketches of the attitudes of the peasants to innovation, investment, taxation, and the like. Popkin points out that the strategy of having scattered fields, for instance, is an expression of the peasant's suspicion that the village will not take care of him and his family if his crop is lost as a result of bad weather or some other catastrophe (763, pp. 48–50). Popkin stresses that historical evidence shows that if the peasants helped each other, the collective crop of the village would be larger than if each peasant had land in several different places. Being a rational and practical person, the peasant realizes, however, that in the absence of this ideal situation, he has to rely on his own resources.

In addition to the concept of rationality, it has been claimed that sociology can learn much more from economic theory in terms of model building. Aage Sorensen has repeatedly stressed that labour market sociology, for example, needs a new approach to theory in which mathematics can be used as a language of theory and not only as a statistical tool (44; 660). According to Sorensen, the focus should be on the various 'mechanisms' that generate income inequality, mobility, and so on, and not on general theories about class and stratification (660, pp. 11–2). Through sophisticated mathematical modelling, sociology will then be able to go from 'story telling' to science (cf. 782, pp. 179–90).

Mathematical models have been used in economic sociology with success especially by Harrison White and his students (see e.g. 21; 54; 667; 723; 737). White's concept of 'vacancy chains' is, among other things, a way 'to link sociology to institutional economics' (54, pp. vii, 193–215). Since Mark Granovetter, according to a recent overview of mathematical sociology, has developed a 'style [which] achieves a near-to-optimal mix of mathematics and sociological theory for the present epoch' (715, p. 156), his work can serve as an illustration of what can be accomplished in economic sociology with the help of mathematical models.

Many readers are probably already familiar with Granovetter's (721; 724) early studies of 'threshold models', and we have therefore chosen the most recent one — 'Threshold Models of Interpersonal Effects in Consumer Demand' as our example (723). This article constitutes among other things an attempt to see what happens to standard economic theory when sociological elements are introduced. Granovetter looks at a situation of simple product demand, where there is perfect information, utility maximizing individuals and profit maximizing firms. The only departure from conventional theory is that the individuals are influenced by each other in their decisions either to purchase a product or to stop purchasing it. If something is bought because others already have it, there is a 'forward bandwagon effect'; when somebody stops buying something because 'too many' already have it, there is a 'reverse bandwagon effect'. Demand schedules are then modelled, and their interaction with supply curves analysed. The result, according to the author is a series of 'unstable, oscillatory and even completely indeterminate market situations' (723, pp. 21–2). In his concluding comment Granovetter points out that industrial organizations, which can handle uncertainties of this type, must have 'peculiar features' (723, p. 22).

When one discusses the topic of economic sociology and mathematical modelling, it is hard not to mention the extremely interesting work by George Akerlof and in particular his collection of essays entitled *An Economic Theorist's Book of Tales* (1984). Akerlof's project in this volume is actually quite similar to that of Granovetter in the article on threshold models of consumer demands, namely, to introduce elements of sociological reasoning directly into conventional economic models. Akerlof calls the area he is working in 'psycho- socio- anthropo-economics' and hints that this awkward-sounding field has a great future; 'thirty years ago mathematical economics was probably at a similar stage of development' (3, p. 6). It is difficult to say whether Akerlof's assessment of the great future of PSA-economics is correct or not. Granovetter's essay can be read as an indication that standard economic models will go wild when a sociological dimension is introduced. Akerlof's essays, on the other hand, show that 'customs', 'loyalty changes', 'castes' and the like can be incorporated into a conventional economic analysis without too much difficulty (see e.g. 736, p. 3).

It should also be pointed out that whether PSA-economics is on the right track or not, Akerlof's essays are worth reading for their fine *sociological* insights. An essay like 'The Economics of Caste and of the Rat Race', for example, contains many sharp sociological observations of the middle-range type. In discussing Kenneth Arrow's theory of 'statistical discrimination', Akerlof notes:

> In this (that is, Arrow's) example . . . employers use the average quality of a given race to predict the quality of individuals of that race. It is easy to see that if such an *indicator* is used, it will destroy all incentive for self-improvement for that race, since all individuals of the race are judged the same and therefore paid the same wage irrespective of individual merit. In this way prejudice may produce a lower level equilibrium trap: if a race is deemed by prejudice to be unqualified, no incentive is given to become qualified, and the prophecy is self-fulfilling. (3, pp. 31–2)

The mention of Kenneth Arrow's name gives us an opportunity to touch on a pet idea of ours, namely that the best works in sociology and economics often have much in common.[34] This is especially true today for some of the works by Kenneth Arrow (e.g. 614; 675; 676; 677; 678), George Akerlof (e.g. 3), Albert O. Hirschman (e.g. 27; 28; 733), Thomas C. Schelling (767; 768), and Amartya Sen (e.g. 41; 770; 771). It is possible to find evocative themes for the sociologist as well as for the economist in this type of economic theory. As a sign of convergence in interest between economists and sociologists, one can also point to the concept of *trust*. This is a topic which has attracted comments by some of the best economists as well as by several sociologists.[35] Many more of these topics of converging interest are apt to develop during the next few years, since economists and sociologists have started to stray into each others' areas on a permanent basis. To cite George Akerlof again:

> ... the recent extensions of the model of supply and demand to discrimination, household organization, crime and marriage show that the boundaries between sociology and economics are by no means clear; if economic models can explain sociological phenomena, so also *the process can work in reverse with sociological models describing economic phenomena*. (3, p. 36; emphasis added)

Some Tasks for Today's Economic Sociologists

In these concluding pages we would like to draw attention to a few questions to which we feel that today's economic sociologists should address themselves. One of these has to do with the relationship between economic sociology and social science disciplines other than economics. Our point here is that economic sociology is becoming fairly familiar with economic theory but that attention should also be paid to *economic history* and *industrial economics*. A second task for today's economic sociologists, we feel, is to start planning for how the field can be securely established and institutionalized. There is a chance to put the topic on the academic map today, and it should not be missed. A third task would be to initiate a general discussion about economic sociology. New concepts and theories are needed, if economic sociology is to prosper intellectually.

Today's economic sociologists are definitely becoming more familiar with economic theory, and some articles by sociologists have actually started to appear in economic journals (e.g. 628; 723). Much remains to be done, no doubt, but at least the first steps have been taken. The situation is very different when it comes to economic history. This is deplorable since topics like inheritance, property, banking, and so on are impossible to handle without a proper historical grounding. Economic history has a rich tradition upon which few sociologists have drawn. Given the high quality of recent works in historical sociology by people such as the Tillys and Skocpol, one can assume that the payoff would be high if economic sociologists started to pay serious attention to economic history.

Economic sociologists would also do well to look more closely at the field which has been known since the early 1950s as 'industrial economics'. This part of economics, which goes back at least to Marshall's *Industry and Trade* (751), has the general goal of studying the way economic forces operate within the industrial sector (see e.g. 702). The characteristics of various industries are analysed, such as degree of concentration, size, decisions to invest, rates of exchange, and so on. Some sociological works on different industries do exist but much remains to be done.[36] Since neoclassical economists have tended to avoid material of this kind, it can also be used to bolster the position of economic sociologists in relation to neoclassical economics. Studies of industries would in addition increase the chance for economic sociologists to get a foothold in the business schools, which has already started to happen in the United States.

Another task for today's economic sociologists has to do with putting economic sociology back on the map and having it properly institutionalized. The field of economic sociology is indeed fairly wideranging in nature and covers several areas in sociology. It nevertheless needs a natural centre to which it can gravitate; a few chairs in the universities and a high-quality journal would be of help. It is definitely not a question of increasing the balkanization of sociology but of getting a subfield accepted which should be as fundamental to the profession as political sociology or sociology of the family. It should also be pointed out that several attempts were made in the past to have 'economic sociology' accepted as a subfield, and that they all failed. In other words there are good reasons for playing it safe this time and for trying to anchor the topic as much as possible in various institutions.

From an intellectual point of view, there is a need for discussions about economic sociology *as such*. It is true that a few European textbooks in economic sociology have been published in the last ten or so years as well as Arthur Stinchcombe's *Economic Sociology* (see 45 and e.g. 4; 11; 12; 38). None of these works, however, properly addresses the question of what a new, hardhitting economic sociology would be like. The European textbooks are somewhat oldfashioned in conception and can perhaps be characterized more as survivors in the field than as innovators. Stinchcombe's study — despite its title — has astonishingly little to say about economic sociology (for a critical appraisal, see e.g. 684).

The most substantial effort so far to present a general theory of economic sociology is Mark Granovetter's article from 1985 in the *American Journal of Sociology* on 'the embeddedness approach to economic life' (22; see also 46). The general idea in 'Economic Action and Social Structure: the Problem of Embeddedness' is taken from Polanyi, who coined and popularized the concept of 'embeddedness'. As we noted in an earlier chapter, there is a certain ambivalence towards Polanyi's notion since 'embedded' basically means to be grounded in *pre-capitalist* social relations; capitalist economic relations are 'disembedded' more or less by definition and can therefore in principle be analysed with the tools of neoclassical economics. Granovetter avoids this trap by emphasizing that for him 'embedded' means being 'embedded in concrete, ongoing systems of social relations' (22, p. 487). For Granovetter 'social relations' mean first of all networks of interpersonal relationships. These exist on a microlevel and also link up to the macrolevel; Granovetter, like many network people, thus defines his general approach as one of 'structural sociology' (22, p. 508).

Even if Granovetter's approach to economic sociology is very interesting — especially his attempt to stake out 'a middle ground between undersocialized and oversocialized views [in sociology and in economics]' (22, p. 487) — there is room for plenty of more theoretical approaches in economic sociology. A good debate about Parsons and Smelser's *Economy and Society*, for instance, is long overdue (but see 279; 749; 752 for a beginning). Several other topics are conceivable; it is about time for sociologists to start to analyse economic theories from a sociological perspective.[37] It would also seem that economic sociologists should try to start developing *new concepts*. We have earlier mentioned the concept of 'trust', which is becoming popular with economists as well as sociologists. Another candidate might be the concept of 'economic inventions', that is 'social inventions' in the area of economics (cf. 698; 753). This concept, which originally comes from Weber (52, p. 200), emphasizes the discontinuous and singular nature of economic life. It also allows the researcher in a natural way to bring up the question of the various 'social mechanisms' through which the economy works. A social mechanism could, for instance, be defined as the if-then-relationship that sociologists should try to establish between two or several sociological facts and which optimally is elegant, powerful and surprising.

Three rules of thumb for how to produce good middle-range economic sociology would therefore be:

—*economic phenomena should be analysed primarily on sociological grounds*;

—*the analysis should keep close to 'the business of life' (Marshall)*;

—*the analysis should centre on a social mechanism which optimally aims at elegance, power and surprise.*

Notes

1. A note on the term 'economic sociology' is in order. This concept is to be found not only in the works of Max Weber (51, pp. 34, 41) and Emile Durkheim (e.g. 14, p. 141) but also in those of Joseph Schumpeter (e.g. 39, pp. 34–5; 40, pp. 20–1; 537), Karl Mannheim (e.g. 34), Werner Sombart (e.g. 43, p. 12), Leopold von Wiese (e.g. 56) and several post-war European sociologists (e.g. 4; 11; 12; 17; 38; 57; 58). In the US the term 'economy and society' seems to be the accepted one, and 'economic sociology' is more sparingly used (see note 20). Our own preference for the term 'economic sociology' comes first and foremost from the fact that it clearly indicates that economic phenomena are here analysed from the viewpoint of *sociology*.

2. On this point we refer to Wassily Leontief's article from 1948 on interdisciplinary research, 'Note on the Pluralistic Interpretation of History and the Problem of Interdisciplinary Co-operation' (32). It is here argued that the best strategy for solving a specific scientific problem is not necessarily to have representatives from the various social sciences working together and then to 'add up' the individual analyses. One should rather so-to-speak impose the single interpretations on top of each other in order to find which one represents 'the best possible solution of the problem at hand' (32, pp. 8–9). There exists no particular reason to believe that neoclassical economics (or economic sociology for that matter) will always be the one that comes up with 'the best solution'.

3. Exactly how far back one should go to trace the history of economics as a distinct science, is a disputed question (see, e.g., 61, pp. 29–35). That there is a considerable historical gap between the emergence of economics and that of sociology, is however clear. While the first solid work in economics — Adam Smith's *Wealth of Nations* — appeared in 1776, high quality works in sociology did not see the light of day until the 1890s, when Weber, Durkheim and Simmel appeared on the scene. This means that the economists were roughly a hundred years ahead of the sociologists. In actuality, the gap is probably larger. Mark Blaug, the author of one of today's standard works on the history of economic theory, sets the beginning of economic science ('pre-Adamite economics') to the end of the sixteenth century (61, p. 10). Also, sociology has its 'pre-1890 history'. It would be hard, however, to date the emergence of sociology much earlier than the 1830s (Auguste Comte) or the 1840s (Karl Marx). The term 'political economy', it can finally be mentioned, was introduced in 1615 by Monthchrétien (81, p. 508) and that of 'sociology' by Comte in the late 1830s (e.g. 62).

4. Here too the economists have been way ahead of the sociologists as *Vetenskap och Politik i Nationalekonomien (The Political Element in the Development of Economic Theory)* by Gunnar Myrdal (95) was later to show. Myrdal points to the contradiction between 'the framework of principles' in economics (which is value-neutral) and 'the results of its research' (which are value-laden) and stresses that one needs 'a theoretical framework just to locate this problem properly' (95, pp. 17–19). Those sociologists who complacently regard Myrdal's study as an indictment of economics as a science, might ponder what a similarly well-executed work entitled *The Political Element in the Development of Sociology* would do for sociology's stature as a science.

5. See especially Sombart's pamphlet *Nationalökonomie und Soziologie*, in which the author argues that the theoretical part of economic science really should be called 'economic sociology' ('Wirtschaftssoziologie') while its empirical part belongs to 'economic history' (43). Sombart's most important work is generally considered to be *Der moderne Kapitalismus* (152), which Schumpeter calls a 'peak achievement of the historical school' (as well as an example of 'often unsubstantiated brilliance'; 40, pp. 816–7). Since Sombart has fallen into something of an oblivion in contemporary sociology, we want to take this opportunity to draw attention to some interesting interpretations of his work, such as those by Parsons (136), Sutton (153), Kraft (126, pp. 319–56), and Mitzman (130, pp. 135–264). That Sombart's work still has much to offer the sophisticated scholar can, for instance, be seen from the use that Fernand Braudel makes of Sombart's scholarship in *The Wheels of Commerce* (114).

6. According to a communication from the late Johannes Winkelmann, 'in a letter from Le Lavandeou in 1912 Max Weber wrote to his publisher and friend Paul Siebeck that ('Sozialökonomik') was not only the most modern but also the most suitable term to use (in the work intended to replace *Handbuch der politischen Okonomie*)' (168). Günther Roth has written us that 'Weber and his publisher Paul Siebeck chose *Sozialökonomik* in order to avoid a law suit with the Schönberg heirs (that is, with the heirs to the editor of *Handbuch der politischen Ökonomie*)'; for details, he refers to Marianne Weber's biography (142).

7. As far as we have been able to reconstruct the matter, Weber only uses the term 'Wirtschaftssoziologie' in part one of *Wirtschaft und Gesellschaft* (see however 165, p. 45 for the similar expression 'Soziologie der Wirtschaft'). 'Sozialökonomik', as noted above, appears at least in Weber's writings from 1904 and probably earlier. (For an interpretation of Weber's work as 'social economics', see 146, 147). It is generally considered that Weber by around 1910 had accepted the term 'sociology' for his interpretive study of social action and for his comparative approach.

8. Durkheim's relationship to economics needs to be further researched. In Guy Aimard's *Durkheim et la science économique* it says:

> Even though it is practically impossible to determine which economic works Durkheim had in his library since it was destroyed during the occupation, one can conjecture that he had a very good knowledge of the classics — Smith, Ricardo and Say — at the time when he was preparing his doctoral thesis on the division of labour in society. (110, pp. 5–6)

9. Durkheim was not particularly interested in defining what exactly constitutes 'the economy'. In a lecture course he thus said:

> We speak of 'economic' things or functions, without having previously said what they consist of, or by what external sign one may recognize them. The fault is due to the science of economics, which has not clarified its own fundamental concepts better, so that we must borrow it in the same condition in which it is presented to us. However, this is no great inconvenience, for if one does not know the precise limits of the economic domain, one understands generally the nature of the essential things it embraces — and that suffices for the moment. (117, p. 57)

10. Is it not, however, possible to find an 'economic sociology' in Comte's work as well? Roger Mauduit says 'no' for the following reasons:

> Auguste Comte wanted to construct a general social science, in which the economic aspect was studied just as much as other aspects of society. But he paid no special attention to the phenomena of wealth. 'Economic sociology', as some conceive of it today, cannot be found in Auguste Comte's work. As a matter of

> fact, he regarded sociology as a general science of society and not as the systematic philosophy of the 'corpus of the social sciences'. The point of view of Auguste Comte, as opposed to that of certain contemporary sociologists, stopped him from looking at the phenomena to which the science of wealth is exclusively devoted. That is why one will not find exclusively economic considerations in Auguste Comte's work of the kind that exist in the specialized studies of political economy. (91, p. 81)

11. Durkheim was of course far from being an economic determinist. He did, however, feel that 'economic social facts' played a key role in society. In a debate that took place at the *Société d'Economie politique* in April 1908, Durkheim spoke as follows:

> Political economy can claim primacy from a certain point of view . . . It thus appears that some economic factors profoundly affect the way populations are distributed, their density, and the form of human groups. They thereby exert an often deep influence on the state of opinions. It is mainly in this indirect way . . . that economic facts act on moral ideas. (119, p. 115)

In this context Durkheim's ideas on the relationship between economics and religion should also be consulted in 120, pp. 165, 282, 326, 335.

12. That Samuelson had Pareto in mind when he wrote this famous line about the relationship between economics and sociology, has been confirmed by Samuelson in a letter to the author (144). *Foundations of Economic Analysis*, it can be added, was written during the 1930s at Harvard, where Pareto was popular.

13. Schumpeter notes that Pareto's economic sociology is 'not easy to characterize and to appraise'. This, he says, is especially so since 'several minor works and a large number of newspaper articles would have to be considered' (145, p. 35).

14. There exist some exceptions, and one of these is undoubtedly Gunnar Myrdal who, at the time when he wrote *An American Dilemma* (1944), was fully conversant with sociology as well as economics. Myrdal, who after World War II was to produce some excellent works on developmental economics, defined himself as an institutionalist and seems after the 1940s to have stopped following what was happening in sociology. For an analysis of the generation of economists who responded to the depression of the 1930s with a more socially oriented form of economic analysis, see Shackle (223) and to an extent Hansson (192). Few articles unfortunately exist which emphasize the sociological aspects of Keynes' thought (see however 36; 191; 199; 242).

15. Schumpeter's attempt at a sociology of knowledge in the *History of Economic Analysis* should naturally be included in a discussion of his economic sociology. The central section is chapter 4, entitled 'The Sociology of Economics', where Schumpeter singles out 'the problem of ideology' as 'by far the most important one' (40, p. 33). He warns against 'the dangers of ideological bias', and it is clear from the unfinished chapter 4 that he had originally hoped to develop 'a set of rules by which to locate, diagnose, and eliminate ideological delusion' (40, pp. 41, 43-4). Schumpeter's interest in the ideological aspects of economic theory, it should be noted, did not imply that he lacked faith in the possibility of developing 'ideologically neutral' theorems in economics or 'stainless-steel concepts', as he also called them (40, p. 44). For a discussion of Schumpeter's attempt at a sociology of knowledge in *History of Economic Analysis*, see e.g. 210, 229.

16. Another criticism can be found in Wolfgang Mommsen's assessment of various theories of modern imperialism, where it is argued that Schumpeter basically

took all his ideas on imperialism from Weber but 'developed them in a very one-sided fashion' (208, p. 21). (For a discussion of Weber's theory of imperialism, see 208, pp. 19–21, 29-30. Basically, Mommsen feels that 'Weber . . . although he did not develop a consistent theory of imperialism . . . did assemble important elements of such a theory from the sociological point of view').

17. Simiand's attempt to develop a new methodology for economics has been widely discussed by French sociologists and historians (see e.g. 173; 174; 179, pp. 185-207, 268–70; 190; 209). Marc Bloch, who like many historians was very impressed by Simiand's work, felt that his methodology was too narrow-minded: 'to exclusively take into account what can be seen as 'objective' would not only lead to a wholesale rejection of many aspects of sociology and history . . . it would also bring economic sociology itself to a total stop' (173, p. 30). Charles Morazé, another historian, gave his essay on Simiand's methodology the telling subtitle 'The History of a Failure' (209). Schumpeter, who liked the work by the *Année*-group very much, found Simiand's critique of conventional economic theory totally useless and blasted the incompetence of the author (216; but for his appreciation of Simiand's empirical work, see 40, pp, 820–1).

Sociologists have also had problems with Simiand's methodology. Marcel Mauss thus said that 'even if Simiand knew and said that the economic world is part of the social, his reasoning always takes as its departure that most economic facts are caused by other economic facts' (206, p. 36; see also 141, p. 7).

18. See also the magazine *Cahiers de Sociologie Economique*, which was published by the Centre havrais de recherche et d'étude des Peuples et de Sociologie Economique from 1959 to 1966 and from 1971 to 1972. The three major topics analysed in this magazine were the economy of new cities, developing countries and seaports (207, pp. 3–4). This magazine is somewhat reminiscent of *The American Journal of Economics and Sociology* (1941/42 –) in the sense that both were marginal to the academic communities in their respective countries.

19. When Wilbert E. Moore began his work in economic sociology in the 1940s, he quickly noted: 'Although for the most part of the present century some European scholars have been analyzing certain phenomena in economic activity in terms of genuinely sociological conceptual schemes, a comparable development in American scholarship is very recent'. (285, p. 440; emphasis added).

20. We have been unable to trace the intellectual history of the concept 'economy and society'. That it is central to US sociology is nevertheless clear from the fact that it is the term preferred by the American Sociological Association and that about one out of four graduate departments of sociology teaches a course with this designation (e.g. 245). 'Economy and Society' is of course also the title of the works by Talcott Parsons and Neil Smelser (36) and Wilbert E. Moore (290). For a general introduction to the history of the various sub-areas in US sociology, see e.g. 230; 280.

21. In his recent essay on 'the current interregnum in American sociology', Norbert Wiley says that 'Park and Burgess made unabashed use of classical and neoclassical economics in the thirties' (344, p. 202). As a support for this rather surprising opinion, the author refers the reader to pages 544–50 in the 1921 edition of Park and Burgess, *Introduction to the Science of Sociology*. In a letter to the author Wiley clarifies his statement in the following manner:

> What I meant by saying that Park and Burgess made 'unabashed' use of classical economics was merely that they included such selections in their famous reader (three editions), without any attempt to distance, disagree, add or 'socially

> embed'. What I was implying was that they *based* sociology on economics. The way I think they did this was with their notion of an ecological order, which comes as half biological and half economic. On that they superimposed, in a clashing eclecticism, a moral order . . . I agree that they didn't go substantively into economics, though the eventual development of ecology does get closer to that field. (345)

When one discusses the relationship of the Chicago School to economic sociology, it can also be noted that even though a very brief excerpt from Simmel's *Philosophy of Money* can be found in Park and Burgess, this work was basically ignored by US sociologists according to Donald N. Levine (276).

22. At the time when Ogburn was publishing his ideas on inventions, economists had done little work in this field (e.g. 212, pp. 599–600). In this context, S.C. Gilfillan's *The Sociology of Invention* should also be mentioned (260). This work is very similar to Obgurn's in the sense that Gilfillan also emphasizes the central role of the social milieu for the emergence of inventions. For a critique of Gilfillan and Ogburn on the ground that they fail to account for the element of creativity, see e.g. 212, pp. 600–1.

23. For several of the ideas on industrial sociology expressed here, we are grateful to Mark Granovetter's luncheon roundtable discussion on 'The New Sociology of Economic Life' at the meeting of the American Sociological Association on 2 September 1985 in Washington, D.C.

24. Talcott Parsons' extremely interesting analysis of economics goes back to the late 1920s, and he should be credited in particular with having introduced Weber and Marshall — and partly also Pareto and Sombart — into US economic sociology (see e.g. 36; 136; 137; 138; 306; 307; 308; 309; 310; 311; 312; 313; 314; 341). For Parsons' own comments on the role that economics played in his life, see 36, xvii–xxi; 315. Parsons, it seems, had good relations with economists such as Duesenberry, Dunlop and Schumpeter. With Gershenkron, who was directing Harvard's Research Center in Entrepreneurial History, Parsons became involved in a conflict which can be followed in the pages of *Explorations in Entrepreneurial History* from 1953 to 1954.

Karl Polanyi, a basically interdisciplinary scholar, lacked the systematic spirit of Parsons and has left behind a series of brilliant but uneven studies on pre-industrial societies as well as on the industrial revolution in England (see e.g. 317; 318; 319; 320; 321).

Neil Smelser, apart from his neglected role in the writing of *Economy and Society*, wrote the first modern textbook on economic sociology, helped to establish the ISA's 'Economy and Society' section, and is the author of a steady stream of insightful articles and books on the sociology of economic life (see e.g. 327; 328; 329; 330; 331; 332; 333; 334; 335; 338). Smelser's finest work is probably *Social Change in the Industrial Revolution* which unites theorizing with profound historical knowledge. (See also note 26.)

Wilbert E. Moore's scholarship must also be mentioned when one discusses the economic sociology of the 1950s. His major work is probably *The Conduct of the Corporation*, and during the 1940s and early 1950s he was the only scholar who kept economic sociology alive in the US (see e.g. Moore 285; 286; 287; 288; 289; 290; 291; 292; 293; 294; 295; 296; 297; 298; 300; 301). In an autobiographical article Moore described his work in this way: 'For more than twenty years most of my research and writing had a common underlying focus, although it was scarcely detectable to those identified with one or another of the specialties with which my work was identified:

labour and property systems, industrial sociology, and theory of complex organizations, social stratification, modernization ... The unifying thread was simple but clearly not very restrictive; the intersection of the economy and society, "everywhere"' (299, p. 123). Like Neil Smelser, Wilbert E. Moore belongs to the small group of really experienced economic sociologists who exist today.

'Exchange theory', it might be added, also has its roots in the 1950s, more precisely in George C. Homans' article 'Social Behavior as Exchange' (262). (For an overview of the relevant literature here see, e.g., 251.) It can also be noted that one successful interaction between economists and sociologists took place during this period; this concerns the transmission of research methods from econometrics to sociology (we thank Prof. Bo Anderson of the State University of Michigan for having emphasized this to us).

25. Some exceptions naturally exist. For Finland, Sweden and Italy, see 350; 351; 355. For some recent French economic sociology, see Michael Rose's article on the work by the Laboratoire de Sociologie et d'Economie du Travail (LEST) in Aix-en-Provence (352). The work on 'social economics' by the Technology and Social Change (TASC) group at the University of Sussex is presented in 348. In the US there seem to be four places where particularly interesting work in economic sociology is being done: around Harrison C. White at Harvard University; at Stony Brook, where Mark Granovetter and Michael Schwartz are active; at George Washington University, from where Amitai Etzioni is directing his project on 'socio-economics'; and at the University of Texas at Dallas, where Paula England and George Farkas work.

The difficulty of writing the history of economic sociology can be illustrated by our attempt to find out what is happening in India. When we finally located N.R. Sheth and P.J. Patel's standard work *Industrial Sociology*, we found that the original report by Patel had covered 'economic as well as industrial sociology' but that the former part had been eliminated (354, p. vii). (See also note 30 for economic sociology in Africa.)

The reader who is interested in making contact with economic sociologists in a specific country is recommended to contact the 'Economy and Society' section of the International Sociological Association via Prof. Arnaud Sales, Département de Sociologie, Université de Montréal, Case Postale 6128, Succ. 'A', Montréal, Québec H3C 3J7, Canada. (Arnaud Sales, it should be added, is one of the most interesting Canadian economic sociologists; see e.g. 353).

26. The emphasis in Smelser's *Social Change in the Industrial Revolution* is different; see especially chs. 8–11. Smelser says in a recent letter:

> My work in economic sociology in recent years has not been really extensive ... I am currently working a on a very long-term project on the development of education in nineteenth-century Britain and the United States, and I will be making much reference to the economic influences in that period. *In particular, I will be interested in the family economy, and the way it shaped educational demand (or lack of demand) in that period.* (411, p. 3; emphasis added)

27. Schumpeter's argument, which can be found in his article from 1949 on the Communist Manifesto, is that marxism views the social process as an 'indivisible whole' and 'uses only one conceptual schema in all its parts' (502, p. 203; see also Schumpeter's very similar discussion of marxism in *Capitalism, Socialism, and Democracy*). The concept of class that is used in marxism — as opposed to non-marxist social science — is the same regardless of whether one is analysing a topic

from an economic or from a sociological point of view. The distinction between 'economics' and 'economic sociology' is consequently 'entirely non-Marxist' (502, p. 203). According to Schumpeter, 'economic sociology deals with the problem of how people came to behave as they do at any time and place; and economics with the problem of how they do behave and what economic results they produce by behaving as they do'. (502, p. 204)

Göran Therborn, a leading neo-marxist scholar, commented as follows when he had read the first version of this chapter:

> From a logical and historical point of view I feel that Schumpeter was correct [about marxism and economic sociology being incompatible] ... Given the situation today, I feel on the other hand that there are practical, pragmatic and concrete reasons for speaking about a marxist economic sociology since marxism today exists and lives within already established disciplines. More than that, I feel that the development of such an economic sociology would be very valuable ... (513)

The comments by Michael Schwartz were similar to those of Therborn. He notes that,

> ... in the modern context the notion of economic sociology is less alienating for people who consider themselves to be Marxist scholars. I doubt whether we would have coined the term, since Marxists are so attached to the notion of political economy which is in no sense incompatible with the concept of economic sociology. But I don't know anyone who finds it objectionable because the term economic sociology has come to be a rather loose umbrella under which certain subject matters of analytical usefulness are grouped for a good purpose. (504)

It can finally be mentioned that the *Wörterbuch der marxistisch-leninistischen Soziologie (A Dictionary of Marxist-Leninist Sociology)* has no entry under 'Wirtschaftssoziologie'. The reason for this, it appears, is that topics which might be seen as belonging to economic sociology are studied in 'political economy' (see 424, pp. 292–4; 490–5, 599–615).

28. Skocpol herself advocates a 'Weberian-Hintzean' perspective in political sociology as opposed to the neo-marxist approach. Some of the studies she mentions as outstanding examples of the 'state-centered' type of analysis are also of interest to economic sociology because of the sophisticated way in which the interaction between economic and political forces is handled. This is obviously true of Skocpol's own *States and Social Revolutions* in which the French, the Russian and the Chinese revolutions are analysed (505). Another work in the Weberian-Hintzean tradition is Ellen Kay Trimberger's *Revolutions from Above*, which contains an analysis of four historical situations where strategic elites have taken control over the state apparatus and then used it in an effort to restructure the economy (516). Also Alfred Stepan's *The State and Society: Peru in Comparative Perspective* discusses what can be seen as an extreme instance of autonomous state action with its emphasis on attempts by state elites in Latin America to institute various forms of corporatist regimes (508). Two other studies in the 'state-centered' tradition, which are probably less familiar to sociologists, are Peter J. Katzenstein's *Between Power and Plenty* (469) and Stephen Krasner's *Defending the National Interest* (471). The former of these works focuses on the foreign economic policies of advanced industrial nations and the latter on the continuity of US foreign policy in relation to foreign investments in raw material.

29. Other scholars who are close to these 'neoclassical marxists' or 'deductive marxists', as they are sometimes called, include e.g. Erik Olin Wright (e.g. 526) and

Philippe van Parijs (e.g. 489). Another marxist, who is working on the border between economics and sociology is Stephen Marglin. In *Growth, Distribution, and Prices*, a work which has not received the attention it deserves, Marglin confronts marxism, keynesianism, and neoclassical economics in a technically very sophisticated way (481). His conclusions are (1) that these three theories are roughly equal in terms of logical consistency and completeness; (2) that they differ mainly when it comes to making different assumptions about the determinants of employment and accumulation; (3) that the assumptions of all three theories are very difficult to test empirically; and (4) the greatest promise resides in a synthetic model that integrates the assumptions of keynesian and marxist economics (481, pp. 524–7).

30. To give an indication of what the situation is like in Africa, we reproduce here excerpts from a letter, written by K.P. Moseley of the University of Port Harcourt in Nigeria in response to our queries:

> The revival [in Africa] of sociological interest in economic questions . . . has been, if anything, even more intense than in the West . . . In Nigeria, 'economic sociology' as such, as a specific area of research or as a course offering, seems hardly to exist. Sociologists, however, do of course work on economic phenomena. This is particularly the case with work in such substantive areas as rural, urban, industrial, occupational, and development sociology. Thus, for instance, the analyses of peasantry and rural economy figures in the work of Nzimiro, Anikpo, Ekpenyong, and Eteng (all now at Uniport); Ekpenyong, Ayenoye, and Dike have worked on the urban informal sector (as has Ayo Fowler in Sierra Leone); Akeredolu-Ale (Ibadan) has written on entrepreneurship and industrial growth, and Ukaegbu (Nsukka) has begun publishing in the area of work and occupations within industry. Economic aspects of ethnicity, a burgeoning area elsewhere, has received some attention from Anikpo and Otite (Ibadan).
>
> Two new research areas have also directed attention to economic factors and dimensions. One, spearheaded elsewhere in the world, is the area of feminism, gender, and women's studies (cf. e.g. C. Oppong, *Male and Females in Africa*), much of which relates to women's economic roles and 'women in development'. At Uniport, Badru has a particular interest in this area, which has become part of the curriculum; in addition to C. Oppong (Ghana), Philomena Steady and J. Beoku-Betts (both Sierra Leoneans currently in the US) might be mentioned as African women working in this domain. A second academic growth area, one which is strongly interdisciplinary, is petroleum and energy studies . . . An Energy and Social Development Research Group has been established within the Faculty of Social Sciences at Uniport, where sociological research on the 'political economy of oil' and 'oil communities' is now underway, and where courses on 'energy and society' have been introduced. (583)

31. Wallerstein wrote: 'The term I use to describe my work is "historical social science"'. I personally do not believe that there are valid *intellectual* grounds to distinguish among anthropology, economics, geography, history, political science, and sociology. They comprise for me a single discipline' (607). Similarly Amin wrote in answer to a question of his relationship to 'economic sociology': 'I have never accepted the split of the social sciences into its academic disciplines. This artificial division of tasks has made quite difficult the main point i.e. precisely the relations between economic and social behaviours' (533).

32. It was probably Polanyi's tremendous aversion to the market which made him

see it as fundamentally 'anti-social'. See, for example, the following apocalyptic passage from *The Great Transformation*:

> To allow the market mechanism to be sole director of the fate of human beings and their natural environment, indeed, even of the amount and use of purchasing power, would result in the demolition of society ... Robbed of the protective covering of cultural institutions, human beings would perish from the effects of social exposure; they would die as the victims of acute dislocation through vice, perversion, crime and starvation. Nature would be reduced to its element, neighborhoods and landscapes defiled, rivers polluted, military safety jeopardized, the power to produce food and raw materials destroyed. (317, p. 73)

33. One of these would be the tradition of 'social economy' which is probably best represented in sociology by the work of Severyn Bruyn (690; 691). Bruyn's analysis, which is profoundly humanistic and activistic in nature, has developed over the last few years within the framework of the programme in social economy and social policy at Boston College in Massachusetts. Another perspective on economy and society, which is called 'social economics', has been developed by the TASC (Technology and Social Change) group at the Science Policy Research Unit at the University of Sussex. A couple of participants have described the work at Sussex in the following manner:

> We are pursuing a number of related lines of research in the area that may broadly be described as 'social economics'; we seek to relate technological innovation, ways of life and social relations (in the household as well as in the wider political arena) to such 'economic' affairs as labour markets, industrial structure and long-term development processes. (348, p. 24)

34. The following statement by Kenneth Arrow in response to our question about the role that sociology should play in economics, is relevant in this context:

> It is difficult to answer 'in a line or two' what I think the role of sociology in economic analysis is. One must draw a distinction between an ideal analysis of social factors in economics and a realistic account of what sociology as it is now constituted can contribute. Let me confine myself to what I think the most promising lines of study are likely to be.
>
> Modern economic theory has emphasized the role of information and communication. It has also begun to recognize that when markets are incomplete, there are many possible equilibria, which depend on alternative sets of beliefs. It seems to me that the conveying of information is to a large extent a property of the social context, of culture. Signals which have economic significance can take very different forms, some of which are more economical than others. Both the role of networks in job search and the internal culture of the factory which has been so much discussed in United States-Japanese comparisons seem to me to fall into this category.
>
> A second area is equally apparent at the surface but even harder to make into a useful theory. It is the role of social motives in modifying economic ones. Alleged examples are the unwillingness of workers to compete with each other by reducing wages or the resistance to price increases in situations of unanticipated scarcity. The problem is to state these apparent facts in a way that does not simply empty theoretical statements of any content. (679)

35. For observations by economists on the importance of 'trust' in economic life, see e.g. 3, pp. 21–2; 124; 614, p. 357; 676, p. 949, 965–6; 678, pp. 23–6. Sociologists have recently become increasingly interested in the role of trust in society in general (e.g. 680, 741, 750) as well as in its role in the economy (e.g. 700). Granovetter in

particular has called for a more differentiated concept of trust in economic life than that used by the economists (722, p. 28ff.; 22, pp. 491–3). A few studies exist, where the focus is on a specific type of trust. For people's trust in businessmen, see e.g. 748; for the necessity of the state to maintain the confidence of businessmen in the economy, see e.g. 432; for the need of banks to maintain trust among depositors so that a run on the bank is avoided, see e.g. 778. Susan Shapiro's interesting study of the Securities and Exchange Commission in *Wayward Capitalists* looks at the way 'trust' is policed and maintained by a specific agency in the stock market (42). Shapiro's study, it should be added, is based on unique data from the Securities and Exchange Commission in Washington D.C. — Since the notion of 'uncertainty' is related to that of 'trust', we would also like to draw the reader's attention to Carol Heimer's excellent studies of uncertainty in the context of insurance (e.g. 726; 727).

36. Mitchel Abolafia notes — and gives exact references to — sociological studies of industry systems in publishing, recording and broadcasting, health-care, defense, grain export, art and petroleum production (1, p. 24). Some of the recent sociological studies of various industries are extremely good, and we would like to draw the attention of the reader to especially those of Robert Faulkner (716), Paul M. Hirsch (e.g. 729; 730; 731) and Glenn R. Carroll (e.g. 693; 694; 695; 696).

37. Very few studies of economic theories exist in the area of the sociology of knowledge (see however e.g. 228; 774, pp. 213–44), but in economics a few relevant studies have recently appeared (see e.g. 697; 719; 720; for earlier works, see e.g. 40, pp. 33–47; 61, pp. 8–9; 735; 773). The articles by Leon Lindberg on the role of economists as policy intellectuals should also be mentioned (742; 743). Lindberg notes for instance that 'a comparative sociology of knowledge of economics remains to be written' (742, p. 5). Another study which should be highlighted is Fred Block's recent article 'Postindustrial Development and the Obsolescence of Economic Categories' (685). He argues, among other things, that the productivity decline in the US economy has been exaggerated due to the use of outmoded and distorting economic categories. Block wrote to the author that,

> the way forward for all economic sociology is through the 'deconstruction' of accepted economic categories and concepts and reconstruction of models of how an economy actually works when understood as an embedded entity. (686)

Block, it can be added, is currently working on a book on productivity in the US economy.

Résumé
La sociologique économique: au temps passé et présent

Notre propos dans le présent numéro porte sur la sociologie économique et son développement récent. *Notre premier thème est la nécessité de 'rétablir' la sociologie économique en tant que champ particulier de la recherche sociologique.* Nous disons 'rétablir', car l'on trouve déjà un projet de sociologie économique — ainsi que l'expression de 'sociologie économique' — dans les oeuvres de sociologues classiques tels que Max Weber et Emile Durkheim.[1] *Notre second thème est que la sociologie économique est entrée, depuis 'grosso modo' le début des années 1970, dans une phase nouvelle et excitante.* Les sociologues, qui durant la majeure partie du XXe siècle ont gardé leurs distances vis à vis de l'économie, s'intéressent de plus en plus aujourd'hui au domaine économique. Un certain nombre d'ouvrages de sociologie économique d'un très haut intérêt ont déjà été publiés et sont discutés dans ce rapport.

Par ailleurs, toute une série de passionnantes études sociologiques de l'économie se cachent dans les différents sous-champs de la sociologie. Une de nos tâches dans ce numéro de *Current Sociology* a donc été d'attirer l'attention sur quelques unes d'entre elles et de montrer que, replacées dans la perspective de la sociologie économique, elles prennent une signification nouvelle et intéressante.

Le fait que l'expression 'sociologie économique' ait été employée par les sociologues classiques n'est pas en soi une raison d'affirmer que la sociologie économique mérite d'être considérée comme un sous-champ particulier de la sociologie. Mais, ce qu'il faut bien voir est que la sociologie économique a une perspective propre et distincte et que cette perspective est scientifiquement productive. C'est ce que nous nous efforçons de démontrer dans chacun des chapitres de ce rapport. Et c'est aussi pourquoi nous avons inclus dans ce résumé un tableau comparatif des prémisses de la sociologie économique et de la théorie néoclassique, ainsi qu'un bref compte-rendu de l'état actuel de la sociologie économique.

Comparaison des prémisses de la sociologie économique et de la théorie néoclassique

Une importante raison d'être optimiste en ce qui concerne le projet de sociologie économique est que la sociologie dispose aujourd'hui d'un certain nombre de théories et de méthodologies qui se sont révélées fécondes dans l'analyse de phénomènes sociaux autres que l'économie. Si l'on ajoute à cela que les hypothèses de base de la sociologie économique sont tout à fait différentes de celles de la théorie économique au sens courant du terme, l'on voit aisément pourquoi la sociologie économique est aujourd'hui en mesure d'apporter de nouvelles et précieuses contributions à la compréhension scientifique des phénomènes économiques.

Notre comparaison des prémisses de la théorie néoclassique et de la sociologie économique est présentée succinctement au tableau 1. Comme on peut le voir, la sociologie économique et la théorie néoclassique diffèrent sur au moins sept points d'importance fondamentale : 1) la notion d'acteur; 2) le champ d'action; 3) les types d'action économique; 4) le résultat des actions économiques; 5) le point de vue auquel se place l'analyste; 6) la notion de temps; et 7) la méthode scientifique générale.

Nous avons dans un autre article précisé chacun de ces sept points, aussi serons-nous ici relativement brefs (Cf. 46).

Dans la théorie néoclassique, l'économie est considérée comme essentiellement autonome et distincte des autres aspects de la société. Dans la sociologie économique, au contraire, l'économie est considérée comme faisant partie du système social et comme subordonnée à ce système (Cf. 36). D'où la nécessité de s'intéresser aux rapports entre l'économie et les autres 'sous-systèmes' de la société. Le concept d'acteur économique est également différent. Dans la théorie néoclassique, on travaille avec un nombre très limité d'acteurs — en gros, les individus, les foyers, les entreprises. Ils sont envisagés séparément et sont définis essentiellement en fonction de l'utilité maximale de leur action. La notion sociologique d'acteur économique est, par contre, un concept social. Ce qui signifie que l'acteur individuel est envisagé comme lié de toutes sortes de manières aux autres acteurs et aussi 'intégré' (Polanyi) dans la société en général. De plus, contrairement à l'économiste ordinaire, qui ne s'intéresse qu'à l'action rationnelle — ce qui sous-entend un certain choix dans une situation de ressources limitées — pour le sociologue la notion d'action économique recouvre toute une variété

Tableau 1
Paradigmes de la théorie néoclassique et de la sociologie économique: une comparaison

	Théorie néoclassique	Sociologie économique
CONCEPT D'ACTEUR	*Acteur séparé* (individus, foyers, entreprises)	*Acteur social* (type individuel, groupe, institution)
CHAMP D'ACTION	Toute situation où l'on retrouve le choix et la rareté des ressources; de préférence le marché (*économie séparée du reste*)	Système économique en tant que composante de la société (*économie sociale*)
TYPES D'ACTION ECONOMIQUE	Actions exclusivement rationnelles, accent sur le choix et la maximalisation (*rationalité formalistique*)	Actions rationnelles et tout autres formes d'actions (*rationalité sociale*)
RESULTAT DES ACTIONS ECONOMIQUES	Tendance à l'équilibre (*harmonie d'équilibre*)	Tendance aux conflits d'intérêts contrôlés et aux tensions (*Conflits d'intérêts et tensions*)
VUE DE L'ANALYSTE	Produit des résultats scientifiques (*sujet extérieur objectif*)	Produit des résultats scientifiques et membre de la société (*sujet intérieur objectif*)
CONCEPT DE TEMPS	Temps stylisé et stationnaire identique à l'action analysée (*Temps stationnaire et adaptable*)	Temps étendu et variable, va au-delà de l'action analysée (*notion socio-historique du temps*)
METHODE SCIENTIFIQUE	Prédications fondées sur des abstractions radicales (*prédictions abstraites*)	Descriptions-explications fondées sur des abstractions empiriquement ajustées (*descriptions et explications empiriques*)

Source: 46, p. 7.

de comportements. Les travaux de Weber sont particulièrement instructifs sous ce rapport, notamment lorsqu'ils démontrent qu'il n'existe pas de comportement rationnel *a priori*, mais que le comportement rationnel est le produit d'un développement socio-historique spécifique.

L'économie néoclassique et la sociologie économique diffèrent également quant à leur attitude vis à vis du résultat cumulatif des actions économiques séparées. Selon la version généralement admise par les économistes, les actions individuelles tendent automatiquement à un équilibre. Alors que pour le sociologue, elles conduisent plutôt à des conflits d'intérêts. Et, dira le sociologue, de quelque manière qu'elles se résolvent, les tensions demeureront toujours. Faisant écho, en particulier, à la critique de Galbraith (19), les sociologues considèrent que la notion de pouvoir doit nécessairement intervenir lorsqu'on étudie le fonctionnement de l'économie. Ceci vaut également pour la notion de *temps*. Et donc la sociologie économique s'intéresse à l'*histoire* des phénomènes économiques et ne se contente pas, comme de nombreux auteurs néoclassiques, d'une sorte d'instantané photographique, manipulé ensuite dans la chambre noire. L'influence du passé, tout comme celle de l'avenir, sur les décisions économiques font donc partie intégrante de la sociologie économique.

Dans l'ensemble, la sociologie économique et l'économie néoclassique diffèrent aussi dans leur conception du scientifique et dans leur approche de la résolution des problèmes en général. Les sociologues ont dépensé beaucoup d'énergie sur la problématique liée au fait que le scientifique qui étudie la société est en même temps membre de la société qu'il étudie. Les économistes ordinaires, par contre, ne s'en sont guère préoccupés, car dans l'économie néoclassique le scientifique est perçu comme essentiellement distinct de l'objet étudié.

L'économie ordinaire et la sociologie économique accusent encore une autre différence en ce qui concerne leur philosophie de la science, à savoir leur attitude respective vis à vis de l'utilisation des abstractions. Dans l'économie néoclassique, il existe une tendance à accorder une valeur positive à la pratique consistant à réduire de façon draconienne la multiplicité des faits par l'emploi d'abstractions radicales. Cette tendance est liée, entre autres choses, à la grande valeur attachée par les économistes à la prédiction comme instrument scientifique. Par contre, les sociologues sont plus intéressés par les faits empiriques et par la 'définition de la situation' telle qu'elle est donnée par les individus (W.I. Thomas). Quand une abstraction s'écarte par trop de la réalité, l'instinct du sociologue lui dit que l'abstraction en question doit être rajustée. En outre, il faut reconnaître que les sociologues ne sont pas tellement intéressés par la prédiction: leur principal objectif est de fournir de bonnes descriptions et de bonnes explications.

Tableau 2
Etat actuel de la sociologie économique

---

1. Ce qui est analysé?
Consommation, productivité, innovations technologiques, marchés (du travail, financiers, industriels, de la consommation), impact des facteurs de genre et ethniques sur l'économie, organisations économiques (banques, sociétés, etc.), rapports de l'économie et des organisations non-économiques (Etat, syndicats, etc.), classes économiques, vie sur le lieu de travail, stratification, ségrégation professionnelle, théories et idéologies économiques, attitudes vis à vis de l'économie, professions économiques (p.ex., entrepreneurs), Etat providence, économie internationale, inflation, contrats, monnaie, économie formelle et économie informelle.

2. Analysé comment?
a. Théories générales
Théorie à moyenne portée, sociologie historique, théorie de la dépendance, théorie des systèmes, théorie néomarxiste, théorie féministe, théorie des réseaux, sociologie mathématique, ethnométhodologie, recherche active (action research), économie politique, institutionalisme, théorie des jeux, théorie néoclassique (certains aspects).

b. Concepts spécifiques
Intégration, réseau, actions économiques (rationnelle, traditionnelle, etc.), acteurs économiques, institutions, changement cumulatif, sous-système économique, mode de production, système mondial, classes économiques, marchandisation/démarchandisation, trust, institutions économiques, profession, marchés du travail (interne, fractionné, etc.).

Note: Quelques travaux récents en sociologie économique: 2; 5; 6; 9; 10; 13; 15; 16; 20; 21; 22; 24; 25; 26; 29; 30; 33; 35; 37; 42; 44; 45; 46; 47; 48; 49; 54; 55.

L'état actuel de la sociologie économique

La comparaison entre les prémisses de la sociologie économique et celles de la théorie néoclassique est fatalement assez abstraite et ne renseigne pas beaucoup sur le genre de problèmes que traite la sociologie économique et sur les solutions qu'elle propose. Pour remédier à cet inconvénient, nous avons dressé le tableau 2, qui résume l'état actuel de la sociologie économique. D'après ce tableau, l'on pourra se faire une idée du genre de problèmes auxquels la sociologie économique s'est intéressée jusqu'ici, tels que l'inflation, les marchés, les banques, etc. Il faut noter, toutefois, que la mesure dans laquelle ces différents problèmes ont été analysés varie assez considérablement. Alors que l'étude des marchés du travail s'est rapidement développée, les recherches qui ont été faites sur les marchés financiers sont beaucoup plus modestes. De plus, il est probable qu'un certain nombre d'études intéressantes nous ont échappé. Nous avons découvert, par exemple, depuis que nous avons établi le tableau 2, un certain nombre d'études sur la fréquence du travail des enfants (53), sur les fusions de banques en Norvège (23), sur 'la seconde économie' en Hongrie (18) et sur la tentative des Frères Hunt d'accaparer le marché du métal-argent, en 1979–80 (1).

Un autre défaut de notre tableau, encore plus grave sans doute, est qu'il ne suggère en aucune manière un trait de la 'nouvelle sociologie économique' qui semble maintenant se dessiner et qui est peut-être le plus intéressant, à savoir la *tendance de la sociologie économique à vouloir traiter le fond des problèmes économiques*. C'est là quelque chose de vraiment nouveau, surtout si l'on songe à la sociologie telle qu'elle a existé dans les années allant de l'abandon de la sociologie économique classique jusqu'au début de la décennie 1970, à peu près. Durant toute cette période, la sociologie économique considérait qu'une de ses principales tâches était de *compléter les analyses déjà faites par les économistes*.

Ces dernières années, la sociologie économique a adopté une approche multiple de ses sujets en se plaçant dans différentes perspectives générales : les théories à moyenne portée, la sociologie néomarxiste, la sociologie historique, etc. Certaines de ces théories générales, telles que le néomarxisme et la théorie féministe, sont devenues populaires en sociologie à la suite des mouvements sociaux des années 1960 et du début des années 1970. D'autres, telles que la théorie des systèmes et la sociologie historique, ont un arrière-plan plus conventionnel, même si leur histoire intellectuelle est tout aussi compliquée. Pour les économistes, habitués à travailler avec une seule perspective théorique, le fait que la sociologie ait recours à plusieurs théories générales peut paraître révélateur d'un statut scientifique laissant à désirer. Ce qui est vrai dans une certaine mesure. Néanmoins, il est également vrai que la prédominance d'une perspective unique en économie depuis un demi-siècle devrait conduire à se demander si vraiment l'économie est en mesure de bien traiter son sujet. La réalité sociale est par nature extrêmement complexe et doit être analysée à différents niveaux et dans diverses perspectives théoriques. Quoi qu'il en soit, dans le présent numéro de *Current Sociology* nous ferons place à l'actuelle pluralité en sociologie et nos critères pour discuter d'une théorie consisteront essentiellement à se demander si oui ou non elle tente d'expliquer les phénomènes économiques en se basant sur des arguments *sociologiques*. Ce qui implique, par exemple, que nous accorderons moins d'attention à des économistes tels que Gary Becker (7; 8), qui se fondent sur une version parfaitement concentrée de la théorie néoclassique pour expliquer toutes sortes de phénomènes non-économiques. En revanche, la sociologie économique est passablement proche de la manière de travailler d'économistes tels qu'Amartya Sen (41), George Akerlof (3) et Albert O. Hirschman (27; 28), qui opèrent quelque part à la frontière entre économie et sociologie.

Quant à l'objectif visant à développer une nouvelle science enjambant tout le 'socio-économique', nous convenons qu'une théorie de ce genre serait nécessaire. Comme Weber, nous pensons qu'une 'économie sociale' (*Sozialökonomie*), qui engloberait non seulement la théorie économique et la sociologie économique, mais également l'histoire économique, est un objectif qu'il faut s'efforcer d'atteindre, finalement (voir Weber 50, pp. 63-6; 52, pp. 311-2, 336, 635). Mais avant qu'une science comme celle-là puisse se développer, il faut que la sociologie économique apprenne à se tenir sur ses pieds. Telle que se présente la situation aujourd'hui, l'économie ordinaire et l'histoire économique sont des disciplines bien définies; et en sociologie économique, il reste encore beaucoup à faire.[2]

Toute une variété de concepts spécifiques ont aussi été développés par les sociologues pour traiter directement les phénomènes économiques, ou certains aspects de ces phénomènes. Certains de ces concepts, tels que 'l'exploitation', ou 'l'action économique (socialc)', remontent loin dans l'histoire de la sociologie, tandis que d'autres découlent de travaux plus récents. Le concept de la nouvelle sociologie économique qui a connu le plus de succès et/ou de popularité est probablement celui de 'réseau' ('network'). L'idée d''intégration' ('embeddedness'), que l'on doit à Polanyi, et la notion de 'système mondial', que l'on doit à Wallerstein, sont également utilisées par de nombreux sociologues. Mais, il faut bien le reconnaître, il reste encore beaucoup à faire au niveau conceptuel. Ce dont on a sans doute le plus besoin aujourd'hui est une sorte de *sociologie économique de moyenne portée ('middle-range economic sociology*') dans laquelle les problèmes économiques spécifiques soient résolus grâce à des analyses imaginatives sur le plan de la théorie et solides sur le plan des faits empiriques.

Plan général du présent numéro

Après l'introduction, vient la première partie du rapport, intitulée 'La tradition de la sociologie économique, 1800–1960'. Le premier chapitre, 'Economie et sociologie - premiers conflits', couvre, en gros, l'interaction entre économistes et sociologues durant le XIXe siècle. L'accent est mis sur ce qui a conduit l'économie et la sociologie à se séparer de façon aussi décisive et devenir presque ennemies au sein de l'académie. Nous suggérons qu'il y a eu à cela trois raisons : la première *méthodologique*, la seconde *politique* et la troisième *institutionnelle*. Dès le début, les sociologues et les économistes ont développé des idées très différentes sur le genre de méthodologie à appliquer. Leurs opinions divergeaient également sur le rôle que devrait jouer l'Etat dans l'économie et sur la nécessité de réformes sociales. Enfin, un autre obstacle à la coopération surgit quand l'économie et la sociologie furent institutionalisées. Les économistes ont plus ou moins conclu un marché avec les sociologues — si les sociologues veulent une place à l'université, qu'ils se tiennent à l'écart du champ des économistes.

Dans le chapitre suivant, intitulé 'Le lancement de la sociologie économique, 1890–1920', nous essayons de retracer les efforts des sociologues classiques au tournant du siècle — en particulier de Weber, Durkheim, Simmel, Pareto et Veblen — pour développer une analyse sociologique propre des phénomènes économiques. Comme l'histoire de cette tentative n'a pas encore été écrite, nous nous sommes efforcés dans cette partie d'être aussi complets que possible et également d'indiquer les idées de la 'sociologie économique classique', qui à notre avis mériteraient d'être développées.

Dans les chapitres III et IV, nous nous efforçons d'expliquer pourquoi la sociologie économique n'a pas 'décollé' durant la période allant des années 1920 aux années 1960, en dépit de ses débuts prometteurs. Nous analysons pour commencer la situation en Europe, en prêtant une attention particulière aux travaux de Schumpeter et des économo-sociologues français. Après quoi nous passons aux Etats Unis, où la version européenne de la sociologie économique n'a jamais été largement admise, mais où est finalement apparue une perspective similaire présentée sous l'appellation d''économie et société'. Au cours des années 1920–60, la sociologie économique est passée par un *processus de fragmentation* et s'est sub-divisée en un certain nombre de sous-champs thématiques, tels que les 'études de stratification', la 'sociologie industrielle', la 'sociologie de la consommation', etc. Malgré cela, de nombreuses idées pénétrantes sur l'économie ont été dégagés et les économo-sociologues feraient bien, à notre avis, de s'en inspirer.

La deuxième partie du rapport est intitulée 'Vers une nouvelle sociologie économique, 1960– ?' et comporte cinq chapitres, traitant chacun d'un aspect capital du nouveau développement qui s'est produit en sociologie économique depuis le milieu des années 1960. Le chapitre V est centré sur le rôle des femmes dans l'économie. Nous y examinons toute une série de travaux très élaborés, parus au cours des dix ou quinze dernières années, travaux dans lesquels la position des femmes dans l'économie est analysée d'un point de vue sociologique. Dans le chapitre VI, intitulé 'La contribution néomarxiste', nous discutons certains travaux de sociologie marxiste présentant un intérêt particulier pour la sociologie économique. Notre discussion couvre à la fois certains travaux de néomarxistes 'des débuts', tels qu'Harry Braverman, et de néomarxistes plus récents, tels qu'Adam Przeworski et John Roemer. Le chapitre VII, intitulé 'La dimension internationale', démontre que la sociologie économique d'aujourd'hui acquiert un caractère de plus en plus international. Nous y soulignons l'importance que les sociologues et les économistes du Tiers Monde ont joué dans cette évolution. Nous y indiquons aussi l'apparition de thèmes nouveaux en sociologie économique — des euromarchés aux sociétés transnationales. Avec le chapitre VIII, "La sociologie des marchés', nous en venons à un effort tout à fait récent de la sociologie, qui n'hésite pas aujourd'hui à analyser une question relevant traditionnellement du champ des économistes : nous présentons et discutons les recherches qui ont été faites dernièrement sur les marchés du travail, les marchés financiers et les marchés industriels.

Nous terminons par un chapitre essentiellement consacré aux rapports de l'économie et de la sociologie. Nous y examinons les travaux d'économistes tels que George Akerlof et nous insistons sur la nécessité pour les économo-sociologues de développer de nouvelles théories. Nous rappelons encore une fois au lecteur que la sociologie économique constitue un des domaines les plus dynamiques de la sociologie d'aujourd'hui et qu'un effort devrait être fait pour l'admettre en tant que branche distincte dans les universités.

Notes

1. Une note sur l'expression 'sociologie économique' s'impose. On peut retrouver ce concept non seulement dans les oeuvres de Max Weber (51, pp. 34, 41) et d'Emile Durkheim (14, p. 141), mais également dans celles de Joseph Schumpeter (39, pp. 34–5; 40, pp. 20–1, 537), de Karl Mannheim (34), de Werner Sombart (43, p. 12), de Léopold von Wiese (56) et de plusieurs sociologues européens d'après la guerre (11; 17; 38; 57). Aux Etats Unis, l'expression 'économie et société' semble être la plus largement employée, tandis que l'expression 'sociologie économique' n'est utilisée que plus rarement (voir, cependant, 45). Un département universitaire de sociologie sur quatre, environ, propose donc des cours d''économie et société', et cette expression est aussi celle que préfère l'*American Sociological Association* (Association américaine de sociologie) (voir 245). Notre propre préférence pour l'expression 'sociologie économique' tient principalement au fait qu'elle indique clairement que les phénomènes économiques y sont analysés exclusivement du point de vue de la *sociologie*. Tous les travaux auxquels il est fait référence dans ce résumé sont cités par ailleurs dans le rapport. Nous renvoyons donc le lecteur à l'index des auteurs cités.

2. Sur ce point, nous nous référons à l'article de Léontief (32) sur la recherche interdisciplinaire, 'Note on the Pluralistic Interpretation of History and the Problem of Interdisciplinary Co-operation', écrit en 1948. L'auteur y soutient que 'la meilleure stratégie pour résoudre un problème scientifique spécifique n'est pas nécessairement de faire travailler ensemble sur un problème des représentants des diverses sciences sociales et d' ''additionner'' leurs analyses individuelles, mais plutôt d'appliquer les interprétations individuelles les unes après les autres, pour voir quelle est celle qui offre la meilleure solution possible du problème qui se pose' (32, pp. 8–9). Il n'existe aucune raison particulière de croire que l'économie néoclassique (ni d'ailleurs la sociologie économique) sera toujours celle qui proposera 'la meilleure solution'.

traduit par Nina Godneff

Bibliography

Items are grouped in the bibliography according to the chapter of the Trend Report in which they first occur.

Introduction

1 ABOLAFIA, Mitchel Y., 'Market crisis and organizational intervention', paper presented at the annual meeting of the American Sociological Association, Washington, D.C., August 1985.

2 ADLER, Patricia A. and Peter ADLER (eds), *The social dynamics of financial markets*, Greenwich, Conn., JAI Press, 1984. x, 212 pp.

3 AKERLOF, George A., *An economic theorist's book of tales: essays that entertain the consequences of new assumptions in economic theory*, Cambridge, Cambridge University Press, 1984. viii, 196 pp.

4 BANCAL, Jean, *L'économie des sociologues: objet et projet de la sociologie économique*, Paris, Presses Universitaires de France, 1974. 329 pp.

5 BARON, James N. and William T. BIELBY, 'Bringing the firms back in: stratification, segmentation, and the organization of work', *American Sociological Review*, 45, 1980: 737-65.

6 BAUMGARTNER, Thomas, Tom R. BURNS and Philippe DEVILLE, *The shaping of socio-economic systems: the application of the theory of actor-system dynamics to conflict, social power, and institutional innovation in economic life*, New York, Gordon and Breach Science Publishers, 1985. 369 pp.

7 BECKER, Gary S., *The economic approach to human behavior*, Chicago, University of Chicago Press, 1976. 314 pp.

8 BECKER, Gary S., *A treatise on the family*, Cambridge, Mass., Harvard University Press, 1981. xii, 288 pp.

9 BERG, Ivar (ed.), *Sociological perspectives on labor markets*, New York, Academic Press, 1981. 374 pp.

10 BLOCK, Fred, *The origins of international economic disorder: a study of United States international monetary policy from World War II to the present*, Berkeley, Ca., University of California Press, 1977. xii, 282 pp.

11 BURGHARDT, Anton, *Allgemeine Wirtschaftssoziologie. Eine Einführung (An introduction to general economic sociology)*, Munich, Verlag Dokumentation, 1974. 227 pp.

12 BUSS, Eugen, *Lehrbuch der Wirtschaftssoziologie (A textbook in economic sociology)*, New York, Walter de Gruyter, 1985. ix, 272 pp.

13 CARDOSO, Fernando H., Enzo FALETTO, *Dependency and development in Latin America*, Berkeley, Ca., University of California Press, 1979. xxv, 227 pp. [Originally appeared in 1971.]

14 DURKHEIM, Emile, 'Review of Georg Simmel, *The Philosophy of Money*', *L'Année Sociologique*, 1900/1901: 140-5.

15 ENGLAND, Paula and George FARKAS, *Households, employment, and gender: a social, economic, and demographic view*. New York, Aldine Publishing Company, 1986. vii, 237 pp.

16 ETZIONI, Amitai, 'Making policy for complex systems: a medical model for economics', *Journal of Policy Analysis and Management*, 4, 3, 1985: 383-95.

17 FÜRSTENBERG, Friedrich, *Wirtschaftssoziologie (Economic sociology)*, Berlin, Walter de Gruyter & Co, 1970. 141 pp. [2nd rev. ed.]

18 GALASI, Péter and György SZIRACZKI (eds), *Labor market and second economy in Hungary*, Frankfurt, Campus Verlag, 1985. 339 pp.

19 GALBRAITH, Kenneth J., 'Power and the useful economist', *American Economic Review*, 63, March 1973: 1-11.

20 GOLDTHORPE, John (ed.), *Order and conflict in contemporary capitalism: studies in the political economy of Western European nations*, Oxford, Clarendon Press, 1984. xii, 373 pp.

21 GRANOVETTER, Mark, *Getting a job: a study of contacts and careers*, Cambridge, Mass., Harvard University Press, 1974. 179 pp.

22 GRANOVETTER, Mark, 'Economic action and social structure: the problem of embeddedness', *American Journal of Sociology*, 91, 3, 1985: 481-510.

23 HALVORSEN, Knut, 'Foretaksfusjon som ulikhetsskapende prosess' (Merger of companies as creator of inequality), *Tidsskrift for samfunnsforskning*, 25, 1984: 389-414.

24 HEDSTRÖM, Peter, 'The bargaining society: political-economic dependencies — an introductory theoretical analysis', *European Sociological Review*, 1986 (forthcoming).

25 HERNES, Gudmund, *Forhandlingsokonomi og blandings-administrasjon (The bargaining economy and mixed administration)*, Bergen, Universitetsforlaget, 1978. 248 pp.

26 HIRSCH, Fred and John H. GOLDTHORPE (eds), *The political economy of inflation*, Cambridge, Mass., Harvard University Press, 1978. 307 pp.

27 HIRSCHMAN, Albert O., *Exit, voice and loyalty: responses to decline in firms, organizations, and states*, Cambridge, Mass., Harvard University Press, 1970. x, 162 pp.

28 HIRSCHMAN, Albert O., *The passions and the interests: political arguments for capitalism before its triumph*, Princeton, Princeton University Press, 1977. ix, 152 pp.

29 KANTER, Rosabeth Moss, *Men and women of the corporation*, New York, Basic Books, 1977. xv, 348 pp.

30 LEIFER, Eric M., 'Markets as mechanisms: using a role structure', *Social Forces*, 64, 2, 1985: 442-72.

31 LEIJONHUFVUD, Axel, 'Life among the Econ', *Western Economic Journal*, 11, 3, 1973: 327-37.

32 LEONTIEF, Wassily, 'Note on the pluralistic interpretation of history and the problem of interdisciplinary co-operation' in: W. Leontief, *Essays in economics: theories and theorizing*, New York, Oxford University Press, 1966. [Originally appeared in 1948.]

33 MAKLER, Harry, Alberto MARTINELLI and Neil J. SMELSER (eds), *The new international economy*, Beverly Hills, Ca., SAGE Publications, 1982. 336 pp.

34 MANNHEIM, Karl, 'On the nature of economic ambition and its significance for the social education of man' in: K. Mannheim, *Essays on the sociology of knowledge*, London, Routledge & Kegan Paul, 1952: 230-75. [This essay had as its subtitle when it first appeared in 1930, 'Ein Beitrag zur Wirtschaftssoziologie' (A contribution to economic sociology).]

35 MINTZ, Beth and Michael SCHWARTZ, *The power structure of American business*, Chicago, University of Chicago Press, 1985. xix, 327 pp.

36 PARSONS, Talcott and Neil J. SMELSER, *Economy and society: a study in the integration of economic and social*

theory, London, Routledge and Kegan Paul, 1956. xxi, 322 pp.

37 PERROW, Charles, 'Economic theories of organization', *Theory and Society*, 1986 (forthcoming).

38 PIERENKEMPER, Toni, *Wirtschaftssoziologie. Eine problemorientierte Einführung mit einem Kompendium wirtschaftssoziologischer Fachbegriffe (Economic sociology: a problem oriented introduction with a list of economic sociological terms)*, Köln, Bund-Verlag, 1980. 328 pp.

39 SCHUMPETER, Joseph A., 'Gustav v. Schmoller und die Probleme von heute' (Gustav v. Schmoller and the problems of today), *Schmollers Jahrbuch*, 50, 1926: 337-88.

40 SCHUMPETER, Joseph A., *History of economic analysis*, London, George Allen & Unwin, 1954. xxv, 1260 pp.

41 SEN, Amartya, *Poverty and famines: an essay on entitlement and deprivation*, Oxford, Clarendon Press, 1981. ix, 257 pp.

42 SHAPIRO, Susan P., *Wayward capitalists: target of the Securities and Exchange Commission*, New Haven, Yale University Press, 1984. ix, 227 pp.

43 SOMBART, Werner, *Nationalökonomie und Soziologie (Economic theory and sociology)*, Kiel, Gustav Fischer (Kieler Vorträge), 1930. 15 pp.

44 SORENSEN, Aage, 'Sociological research on the labor market', *Work and Occupations*, 10, 3, 1983: 261-87.

45 STINCHCOMBE, Arthur, *Economic sociology*, New York, Academic Press, 1983. ix, 269.

46 SWEDBERG, Richard, Ulf HIMMELSTRAND and Göran BRULIN, 'The paradigm of economic sociology: premises and promises', Research Report Series of the Department of Sociology at Uppsala University, 1985, 1. 62 pp. [Forthcoming during 1987 in *Theory and Society*.]

47 TILLY, Louise A. and Joan W. SCOTT, *Women, work, and family*, New York, Holt, Rinehart and Winston, 1978. xiv, 274 pp.

48 WALLERSTEIN, Immanuel, *The modern world-system: capitalist agriculture and the origins of the European world-economy in the sixteenth century*, New York, Academic Press, 1974. xiv, 410 pp.

49 WALLERSTEIN, Immanuel, *The modern world-system II: mercantilism and the consolidation of the European world-economy, 1600–1750*, New York, Academic Press, 1980. xi, 370 pp.

50 WEBER, Max '"Objectivity" in social science and social policy' in: M. Weber, *The methodology of the social sciences*, New York, The Free Press, 1949: 49-112. [Originally appeared in 1904.]
51 WEBER, Max, *Wirtschaft und Gesellschaft. Grundriss der verstehenden Soziologie*, fünfte revidierte Auflage mit textkritischen Erläuteringen, 3 vols, Tübingen, J.C.B. Mohr, 1976. [Originally appeared in 1922.]
52 WEBER, Max, *Economy and society: an outline of interpretive sociology*, 2 vols, Berkeley, Ca., University of California Press, 1978. cx, 1469, lxiv pp. [Originally appeared in 1922.]
53 WHITE, Benjamin (ed.), 'Child workers', *Development and Change*, 13, 4, 1982: 465-652.
54 WHITE, Harrison C., *Chains of opportunity: system models of mobility in organizations*, Cambridge, Mass., Harvard University Press, 1970. xv, 418 pp.
55 WHITE, Harrison C., 'Where do markets come from?', *American Journal of Sociology*, 87, 3, 1981: 517-47.
56 WIESE, Leopold von, 'Wirtschaftstheorie und Wirtschaftssoziologie' (Economic theory and economic sociology), *Schmollers Jahrbuch*, 6, 2, 1936: 7-35,
57 ZAHN, E., *Nieuwe terreinen der economische sociologie (New areas in economic sociology)*, Amsterdam, N.V. de Arbeiderspers, 1963. 31 pp.
58 VAN ZUTHEM, H.J., *Inleiding in de economische sociologie (Introduction to economic sociology)*, Amsterdam, J.H. de Bussy, 1973. 250 pp.

PART I: THE TRADITION OF ECONOMIC SOCIOLOGY, 1800s–1960s

(1) Economics and Sociology — Early Clashes

59 ADELMAN, Paul 'Frederic Harrison and the "positivist"attack on orthodox political economy', *History of Political Economy*, 3, 1, 1971: 170-89.
60 ASHLEY, William, 'Introduction' in: J.S. Mill, *Principles of political economy*, New York, Augustus M. Kelley Publishers, 1969. v-xxxvi. [Originally published in 1909.]

61 BLAUG, Mark, *Economic theory in retrospect*, 3rd ed. Cambridge, Cambridge University Press, 1983. xxiv, 756 pp.

62 BRANFORD, Victor V., 'On the origin and use of the word 'sociology'', *American Journal of Sociology*, 9, 2, 1903: 145-62.

63 CAIRNES, John Eliot, 'M. Comte and political economy' in: J. Cairnes, *Essays in political economy*, London, Macmillan, 1873: 265-311. [Originally appeared in 1870.]

64 CLARKE, Simon, *Marx, marginalism and modern sociology: from Adam Smith to Max Weber*, London, Macmillan, 1982. 250 pp.

65 CLIFFE LESLIE, T.E., 'Political economy and sociology', *Fortnightly Review*, 25 (January-June 1879): 25-46.

66 COATS, A.W., 'The historist reaction in English political economy', *Economica*, 21, 81-84, 1954: 143-53.

67 COATS, A.W., 'The first two decades of the American Economic Association', *American Economic Review*, 50, 4, 1960: 555-74.

68 COATS, A.W., 'Adam Smith: the modern re-appraisal', *Renaissance and Modern Studies*, 6, 1962: 25-48.

69 COATS, A.W., 'Adam Smith: reflections on the bicentennial reappraisal', *Studies in Economic Analysis*, 3, 2, 1979: 3-21.

70 COMTE, Auguste, *Cours de philosophie positive*, tome quatrième, troisième édition, Paris, J.B. Ballière et Fils, 1869. 520 pp. [Originally appeared in 1839.]

71 CUNNINGHAM, W., 'The comtist criticism of economic science' in: R.L. Smyth (ed.), *Essays in economic method*, New York, McGraw-Hill Book Company, 1963: 98-111.

72 DURKHEIM, Emile, *The division of labor in society*, New York, The Free Press, 1964. xxiv, 439 pp. [Originally appeared in 1902.]

73 EKELUND, Robert B. Jr. and Emile S. OLSEN, 'Comte, Mill, and Cairnes: the positivist-empiricist interlude in late classical economics', *Journal of Economic Issues*, 7, 3, 1973: 383-416.

74 FOUCAULT, Michel, *The order of things: an archaeology of the human sciences*, New York, Vintage Books, 1973. xxiv, 387 pp. [See especially Ch. 6.]

75 FURNER, Mary O., *Advocacy & objectivity: a crisis in the professionalization of American social science, 1865–1905*, Kentucky, University of Kentucky Press, 1975. 357 pp.

76 GIDDINGS, Franklin H., 'The sociological character of political economy', *Publications of the American Economic Association*, 3, 1, March 1888: 29-47.

77 GIDDINGS, Franklin H., 'The relation of sociology to other scientific studies', *Journal of Social Science*, 32, 1894 (November): 144-50.

78 GOLDTHORPE, John, Letter to Ulf Himmelstrand dated 20 November 1985.

79 HARRISON, Frederic, 'The limits of political economy', *Fortnightly Review*, 1, 1865: 356-76.

80 HARRISON, Frederic, 'Professor Cairnes on M. Comte and political economy', *Fortnightly Review*, 8, (1 July–1 December) 1870: 39-58.

81 HECKSCHER, Eli, 'Nationalekonomi' (Economic theory), *Nordisk familjebok*, vol. 19. Stockholm, Nordisk Familjeboks Förlags Aktiebolag, 1913: 507-18.

82 HOWERTH, Ira H., 'Present condition of sociology in the United States', *Annals of the American Academy*, 5, 1894: 260-69.

83 INGRAM, J.L., 'The present position and prospects of political economy' in: R.L. Smyth (ed.), *Essays in economic method*, New York, McGraw-Hill Book Company, 1963: 41-72. [Originally appeared in 1878.]

84 INGRAM J.L., 'Political economy' in: *Encyclopaedia Britannica*, vol. 19, 9th ed., Edinburgh, Adam and Charles Black, 1885: 346-401.

85 KEYNES, John Neville, *The scope and method of political economy*, New York, Kelley & Macmillan, 1955. 382 pp. [Originally appeared in 1891.]

86 LENZER, Gertrud, *Auguste Comte and positivism*, New York, Harper and Row, 1975. lxviii, 505 pp.

87 MARSHALL, Alfred, *The present condition of economics*, London, Macmillan and Co, 1885. 57 pp.

88 MARSHALL, Alfred, *Principles of economics*, Vol. 1, 2nd ed., London, Macmillan and Company, 1891. 770 pp. [Originally appeared in 1890.]

89 MARX, Karl, *Economic and philosophic manuscripts of 1844*, New York, International Publishers, 1967. 255 pp.

90 MARX, Karl, *Capital: a critique of political economy*, New York, The Modern Library, 1906. 869 pp. [Originally appeared in 1867.]

91 MAUDUIT, Roger, *Auguste Comte et la science économique*, Paris, Félix Alcan, 1928. 292 pp.

92 MICHALET, Charles-Albert, 'From international trade to world economy: a new paradigm' in: H. Makler, A. Martinelli and N. Smelser (eds), *The new international economy*, Beverly Hills, Ca., SAGE Publications, 1982: 37-58.

93 MILL, John Stuart, 'A system of logic' in: J.S. Mill, *Philosophy of scientific method*, New York, Harper Publishing Company, 1950: 3-358. [Originally appeared in 1843.]

94 MILL, John Stuart, *Auguste Comte and positivism*, Michigan, University of Michigan Press, 1961. 200 pp. [Originally appeared in 1865.]

95 MYRDAL, Gunnar, *Vetenskap och politik i national-ekonomien (The political element in the development of economic theory)*, Stockholm P.A. Nordstedt & Söners Förlag, 1930. 308 pp.

96 OBERSCHALL, Anthony. 'The institutionalization of American sociology' in: A. Oberschall (ed.), *The establishment of empirical sociology*, New York, Harper & Row, 1972: 187-251.

97 PATTEN, Simon N., 'The relation of economics to sociology', *Annals of the American Academy*, 5, July 1894–June 1895: 577-83.

98 POWERS, H.H., 'Terminology and the sociological conference', *Annals of the American Academy*, 5, 1894/1895: 705-17.

99 REISMAN, D.A., *Adam Smith's sociological economics*, London, Croom Helm, 1976. 274 pp.

100 ROSENBERG, Nathan, 'Some institutional aspects of *The wealth of nations*', *Journal of Political Economy*, 68, 1960: 557-70.

101 SALOMON, Albert, 'Adam Smith as sociologist', *Social Research*, 12, 1, 1945: 22-42.

102 SCHUMPETER, Joseph A., *Capitalism, socialism, and democracy*, New York, Harper & Row, 1975. xiv, 437 pp. [Originally appeared in 1942.]

103 SMALL, Albion W. 'The relation of sociology to economics', *Publications of the American Economic Association*, 10, 3, Supplement, March 1895: 106-7. [Followed by a discussion in which Patten, Giddings, Ward and Ashley took part.]

104 SMALL, Albion W., *Adam Smith and modern sociology: a study in the methodology of the social sciences*, Chicago, The University of Chicago Press, 1907. 247 pp.
105 SMALL, Albion W., 'Fifty years of sociology in the United States (1865-1915)' in: *American Journal of Sociology: Index to Volumes I-LII*, Chicago, University of Chicago Press, 1948: 177-269. [Originally appeared in 1916.]
106 SMITH, Adam, *An inquiry into the nature and causes of the wealth of nations*, Oxford, Clarendon Press, 1976. 1080 pp.
107 SWEDBERG, Richard, 'Economic sociology and exogenous factors', *Social Science Information*, 24, 4, 1985: 905-20.
108 THERBORN, Göran, *Science, class and society: on the formation of sociology and historical materialism*, London, New Left Books, 1976. 461 pp.
109 WARD, Lester F., 'The place of sociology among the sciences', *American Journal of Sociology*, 1, 1, July 1895: 16-27.

(2) The Launching of Economic Sociology, 1890–1920

110 AIMARD, Guy, *Durkheim et la science économique: l'apport de sa sociologie à la théorie économique*, Paris, Presses Universitaires de France, 1962. 317 pp.
111 ALTMANN, S.P., 'Simmel's philosophy of money', *American Journal of Sociology*, 9, 1, 1903: 46-68.
112 ARON, Raymond, *Main currents in sociological theory*, vol. 2, New York, Anchor Books, 1970. 346 pp. [Originally appeared in 1967.]
113 BECKER, Howard, 'On Simmel's *Philosophy of money*' in: K. Wolff (ed.), *Georg Simmel, 1858–1918*, Columbus, Ohio State University Press: 216-32.
114 BRAUDEL, Fernand, *The wheels of commerce*, London, Fontana Press, 1982. 670 pp. [Originally appeared in 1979.]
115 DE VROEY, Michel, 'The transition from classical to neoclassical economics: a scientific revolution', *Journal of Economic Issues*, 9, 3, 1975: 415-39.
116 DURKHEIM, Emile, *The rules of sociological method*, New York, The Free Press, 1964. xxxvi, 146 pp. [Originally appeared in 1895.]
117 DURKHEIM, Emile, *Socialism*, New York, Collier Books, 1962. 287 pp. [This course was originally given in 1895-96.]

118 DURKHEIM, Emile *Professional ethics and civic morals*, London, Routledge and Kegan Paul, 1957. xi, 228 pp. [This course was originally given in 1898–1900.]

119 DURKHEIM, Emile, 'Discussion at the Société d'Economie Politique', *Journal des Economistes*, 18, 1908 (avril à juin): 108-21.

120 DURKHEIM, Emile, *Durkheim on religion*, edited by W.S.F. Pickering, London, Routledge & Kegan Paul, 1975. x, 376 pp.

121 DURKHEIM, Emile and Paul FAUCONNET, 'Sociologie et sciences sociales', *Revue Philosophique*, 55, 1903 (janvier à juin): 465-97.

122 EISERMANN, Gottfried, *Die Grundlagen des Historismus in der deutschen Nationalökonomie (The fundamentals of historicism in German economic theory)*, Stuttgart, Ferdinand Enke Verlag, 1956. xv, 249 pp.

123 EISERMANN, Gottfried, *Vilfredo Pareto als Nationalökonom und Soziologe (Vilfredo Pareto as an economist and sociologist)*, Tübingen, J.C.B. Mohr, 1961. 76 pp.

124 FRANKEL, S. Herbert, *Two philosophies of money: the conflict of trust and authority*, New York, St. Martin's Press, 1977. x, 163 pp.

125 GREENWOOD, Daphne, 'The economic significance of "women's place" in society: a new-institutionalist view', *Journal of Economic Issues*, 18, 3, 1984: 663-80.

126 KRAFT, Jürgen, *Das Verhältnis von Nationalökonomie und Soziologie bei Franz Oppenheimer, Werner Sombart, Max Weber in der sozialwissenschaftlichen Systembildung des 19. Jahrhunderts (The relationship between economic theory and sociology in 20th-century social science systems by Franz Oppenheimer, Werner Sombart and Max Weber)*, Göttingen, unpublished thesis, 1961. 357 pp.

127 LAIDLER, David and Nicholas ROWE, 'Georg Simmel's *Philosophy of money*', *Journal of Economic Literature*, 18, March 1980: 97-105.

128 MACAULEY, Stewart, 'Non-contractual relations in business: a preliminary study', *American Sociological Review*, 28, 1, 1963: 55-67.

129 MERTON, Robert K., *Social theory and social structure*, enlarged ed., New York, The Free Press, 1968. xxiii, 702 pp.

130 MITZMAN, Arthur, *Sociology and estrangement: three sociologists of imperial Germany*, New York, Alfred A.

Knopf, 1973. 375 pp. [See especially part III on Werner Sombart.]

131 NATANSON, Jacques, 'Pour situer la sociologie économique', *Cahiers de Sociologie Economique*, 1, 1959: 6-18.

132 OBERSCHALL, Anthony, *Empirical social research in Germany 1848–1914*, Paris, Mouton & Co. 1965. viii, 153 pp. [See especially ch.6, 'Max Weber and the problem of industrial work'.]

133 OSHIMA, H.T., 'Veblen on Japan', *Social Research*, 10, 1943: 487-94.

134 PARETO, Vilfredo, *Manual of political economy*, London, Macmillan, 1972. xii, 504 pp. [Originally appeared in 1906; see especially ch. 5 for Pareto's 'economic sociology'.]

135 PARETO, Vilfredo, *The mind and society (Trattato di sociologia)*, 4 vols, New York, Harcourt, Brace and Company, 1935. 2032 pp. [Originally appeared in 1916.]

136 PARSONS, Talcott, '"Capitalism" in recent German literature, Sombart and Weber, I-II', *Journal of Political Economy*, 36, 1928: 641-61; 37, 1929: 31-51.

137 PARSONS, Talcott, *The structure of social action: a study in social theory with special reference to a group of recent European writers*, 2 vols, New York, The Free Press, 1968. xxxvii, 775, lxi pp. [Originally appeared in 1937.]

138 PARSONS, Talcott, 'Weber's "economic sociology" in: T. Parsons, 'Introduction' to Max Weber's *The theory of social and economic organization*, New York, The Free Press, 1964: 30-55. [Originally appeared in 1947.]

139 PERRIN, Guy, 'Economie et sociologie dans l'oeuvre de Pareto', *Cahiers Internationaux de Sociologie*, 20, 1956: 90-108.

140 POGGI, Gianfranco, *Calvinism and the capitalist spirit: Max Weber's Protestant ethic*, Amherst, University of Massachusetts Press, 1983. xii, 121 pp.

141 POWERS, Charles H. and Robert A. HANNEMAN, 'Pareto's theory of social and economic cycles: a formal model and simulation' in: R. Collins (ed.), *Sociological theory 1983*, San Francisco, Jossey-Bass Publishers, 1983: 59-89.

142 ROTH, Günther, Letter to Richard Swedberg dated 12 March 1985.

143 SAMUELSON, Paul, *Foundations of economic analysis*,

enlarged ed., Cambridge, Mass., Harvard University Press, 1983. xxvi, 604 pp. [Originally appeared in 1947.]
144 SAMUELSON, Paul, Letter to Richard Swedberg dated 23 January 1986.
145 SCHUMPETER, Joseph A., 'Vilfredo Pareto 1848–1923' in: J.A. Schumpeter, *Ten great economists: from Marx to Keynes*, New York, Oxford University Press, 1951: 110-42. [Originally appeared in 1949.]
146 SCHWEITZER, Arthur, 'Review of Max Weber, *Economy and society*', *Journal of Economic Literature*, 8, 1970: 1203-9.
147 SCHWEITZER, Arthur, 'Typological method in economics: Max Weber's contribution', *History of Political Economy*, 2, 1970: 66-96.
148 SIMICH, J.L. and Rick TILMAN, 'On the use and abuse of Thorstein Veblen in modern American sociology, I', *American Journal of Economics and Sociology*, 42, 4, 1983: 417-29.
149 SIMMEL, Georg, *The philosophy of money*, Boston, Routledge and Kegan Paul, 1978. xiii, 512 pp. [Originally appeared in 1907.]
150 SIMMEL, Georg, *The sociology of Georg Simmel*, edited by Kurt Wolff, New York, The Free Press, 1950. lxiv, 445 pp.
151 SIMMEL, Georg, 'Competition' in: G. Simmel, *Conflict & the web of group-affiliations*, New York, The Free Press, 1955: 57-85.
152 SOMBART, Werner, *Der moderne Kapitalismus (Modern capitalism)*. 3 vols, Leipzig, Duncker und Humblot, 1902–27.
153 SUTTON, Francis X., 'The social and economic philosophy of Werner Sombart: the sociology of capitalism' in H.E. Barnes (ed.), *An introduction to the history of sociology*, Chicago, University of Chicago Press, 1966: 314-29. [Originally appeared in 1948.]
154 TILMAN, Rick and J.L. SIMICH, 'On the use and abuse of Thorstein Veblen in modern American sociology, II', *American Journal of Economics and Sociology*, 43, 1, 1984: 103-14.
155 TURNER, Bryan S., 'Simmel, rationalization and the sociology of money', *Sociological Review*, 34, 1, 1986: 93-114.
156 VEBLEN, Thorstein, 'Why is economics not an evolutionary science?' in M. Lerner (ed.), *The portable Veblen*, New York, The Viking Press, 1948: 215-40. [Originally appeared in 1898.]

157 VEBLEN, Thorstein, *The theory of the leisure class: an economic study of institutions*, with an introduction by C. Wright Mills, New York, Mentor Books, 1953. 259 pp. [Originally appeared in 1899.]

158 VEBLEN, Thorstein, 'The barbarian status of women': in T. Veblen (ed.), *Essays in our changing order*, New York, The Viking Press, 1945: 50-60. [Originally appeared in 1899.]

159 VEBLEN, Thorstein, *Imperial Germany and the industrial revolution*, Ann Arbor, University of Michigan Press, 1966. xxi, 343 pp. [Originally appeared in 1915.]

160 VEBLEN, Thorstein, 'The opportunity of Japan' in: T. Veblen (ed.), *Essays in our changing order*, New York, The Viking Press, 1945: 248-66. [Originally appeared in 1915.]

161 WEBER, Max, 'Die Börse' (The stock exchange) in: M. Weber, *Gesammelte Aufsätze zur Soziologie und Sozialpolitik*, Tübingen, J.C.B. Mohr, 1924: 256-322. [Originally appeared in 1894.]

162 WEBER, Max, 'Georg Simmel as sociologist', *Social Research*, 39, 1, 1972: 155-63. [Probably written in 1908.]

163 WEBER, Max, 'Marginal utility and the fundamental law of psychophysics', *Social Science Quarterly*, 56, 1, 1975: 21-36. [Originally appeared in 1908.]

164 WEBER, Max, 'Psychophysik der industriellen Arbeit' (Psychophysics of industrial work) in: M. Weber, *Gesammelte Aufsätze zur Soziologie und Sozialpolitik*, Tübingen, J.C.B. Mohr, 1924: 61-255. [Originally appeared in 1908–9.]

165 WEBER, Max, 'The meaning of "ethical neutrality" in sociology and economics' in: M. Weber, *The methodology of the social sciences*, New York, The Free Press, 1949: 1-47. [Originally appeared in 1917–18.]

166 WEED, Frank J., 'Interpreting "institutions" in Veblen's evolutionary theory', *American Journal of Economics and Sociology*, 40, 1, 1981: 67-78.

167 WINKELMANN, Johannes, *Erläuterungsband* in: M. Weber, *Wirtschaft und Gesellschaft. Grundriss der verstehenden Soziologie (Economy and society: an outline of interpretive sociology)*, Tübingen, J.C.B. Mohr, 1976. 303 pp.

168 WINKELMANN, Johannes, Letter to Richard Swedberg dated 29 May 1985.

169 WOLFF, Kurt H., 'Review of Simmel, *The philosophy of money*', *Contemporary Sociology*, 8, 4, 1979: 646-49.

(3) European Economic Sociology, 1920s–1960s

170 BECKERATH Herbert von, 'Joseph A. Schumpeter as a sociologist', in: S.E. Harris (ed.), *Schumpeter — social scientist*, Cambridge, Harvard University Press, 1951: 110-18.

171 BETTELHEIM, Charles, 'Economie politique et sociologie économique', *Annales - Economies - Sociétés - Civilisations*, 3, 3, 1948: 267-78.

172 BETTELHEIM, Charles, 'Idéologie économique et réalité sociale', *Cahiers Internationaux de Sociologie*, 4, 1948: 119-34.

173 BLOCH, Marc, 'Le Salaire et ses fluctuations économiques à longue période', *Revue Historique*, 173, janvier-juin 1934: 1-31.

174 BOUGLE, Célestin, 'La Méthodologie de François Simiand et la sociologie', *Annales Sociologiques (Série A)*, 2, 1936: 5-28.

175 BOUGLE, Célestin, 'Sociologie économique': in C. Bouglé, *Bilan de la sociologie français contemporaine*, Paris, Librairie Félix Alcan, 1938: 121-57. [This essay is more or less identical to Bouglé's 'La sociologie économique en France', which appeared in 1934 in *Zeitschrift für Sozialforschung*.]

176 CARLIN, Edward A., 'Schumpeter's constructed type — the entrepreneur', *Kyklos*, 9, 1956: 27-42.

177 CROZIER, Michel, *The bureaucratic phenomenon*, London, Tavistock, 1964. x, 320 pp. [Originally appeared in 1963.]

178 CUVILLIER, Armand, 'Sociologie de la connaissance et idéologie économique', *Cahiers Internationaux de Sociologie*, 11, 1951: 80-111.

179 DAMALAS, Basile, *L'Oeuvre scientifique de François Simiand*, Paris, Presses Universitaires de France, 1943. 276 pp.

180 DOBRETSBERGER, Josef, 'Zur Soziologie des ökonomischen Denkens' (On the sociology of economic thought), *Archiv für angewandte Soziologie*, 4, 1, 1931: 21-55.

181 EISERMANN, Gottfried, 'La Sociologie de la connaissance et la théorie économique', *Cahiers Internationaux de Sociologie*, 18, janvier-juin 1955: 17-34.

182 EISERMANN, Gottfried, 'Joseph Schumpeter als Soziologe' (Joseph Schumpeter as a sociologist), *Kyklos*, 17, 1965: 288-315.

183 FRIEDMANN, Georges, *The anatomy of work: the implications of automation*, New York, The Free Press, 1961.

203 pp. [Originally appeared in 1956.]
184 FÜRSTENBERG, Friedrich, 'Die soziologische Dimension wirtschaftstheoretischer Aussagen' (The sociological dimension of statements in economic theory)', *Zeitschrift für die gesamte Staatswissenschaft*, 112, 1, 1956: 398-409.
185 GOLDSCHEID, Rudolf, *Staatssozialismus oder Staatskapitalismus. Ein finanzsoziologischer Beitrag zur Lösung des Staatsschulden-Problems (State socialism or state capitalism: a contribution in fiscal sociology to the problem of state debts)*, Wien, Anzengruber-Verlag Brüder Suschitsky, 1917. xviii, 186 pp.
186 GOLDSCHEID, Rudolf, 'A sociological approach to problems of public finance' in: R.A. Musgrave and A.T. Peacock (eds), *Classics in the theory of public finance*, London, Macmillan & Co., 1958: 202-13. [Originally appeared in 1925.]
187 GREENE, Murray, 'Schumpeter's imperialism — a critical note', *Social Research*, 19, 1952: 453-63.
188 HALBWACHS, Maurice, *La classe ouvrière et les niveaux de vie: recherches sur la hiérarchie des besoins dans les sociétés industrielles contemporaines*, Paris, Librairie Félix Alcan, 1913. xvii, 495 pp.
189 HALBWACHS, Maurice *L'évolution des besoins dans les classes ouvrières*, Paris, Librairie Félix Alcan, 1933. xii, 173 pp.
190 HALBWACHS, Maurice, 'La méthodologie de François Simiand — un empirisme rationaliste', *Revue Philosophique*, 121, janvier-juin 1936: 281-319.
191 HALBWACHS, Maurice, 'La 'Théorie générale' de John-Maynard Keynes', *Annales Sociologiques (Série D)*, 4, 1940: 25-41.
192 HANSSON, Björn A., *The Stockholm school and the development of dynamic method*, London, Croom Helm, 1982. 286 pp.
193 HEERTJE, Arnold (ed.), *Schumpeter's vision: capitalism, socialism, and democracy after 40 years*, New York, Praeger, 1981. xvi, 208 pp.
194 ISHBOLDIN, Boris, 'Die Hauptrichtungen der gegenwärtigen französischer Soziologie' (Main trends in contemporary French sociology), *Schmollers Jahrbuch*, 61, 2, 1937: 23-37.

195 KARRER, Hans, 'Schumpeters Beitrag zur Soziologie' (Schumpeter's contribution to sociology), *Kyklos*, 5, 1951/52: 197-211.

196 KAUFMANN, Franz-Xavier, Letter to Ulf Himmelstrand dated 7 January 1986.

197 KOCH, Woldemar, *Die Bedeutung der theoretischen Ökonomik für die allgemeine Soziologie (The importance of economic theory for general sociology)*, Tübingen, J.C.B. Mohr, 1955. 21 pp.

198 LEBOVICS, Herman, *Social conservatism and the middle classes in Germany, 1914–1933*, Princeton, Princeton University Press, 1968. xi, 248 pp. [See especially chapter 2, 'Werner Sombart: The Age of Late Capitalism'.]

199 LEKACHMAN, Robert, 'The non-economic assumptions of John Maynard Keynes' in: M. Komarovsky (ed.), *Common frontiers of the social sciences*, Glencoe, Ill., The Free Press, 1957: 338-57.

200 LÖWE, Adolf, *Economics and sociology: a plea for co-operation in the social sciences*, London, George Allen & Unwin Ltd, 1935. 156 pp.

201 MANN, Fritz Karl, 'The sociology of taxation', *The Review of Politics*, 5, 1943: 225-35.

202 MANN, Fritz Karl, 'The fiscal component of revolution: an essay in fiscal sociology', *The Review of Politics*, 9, 1947: 331-49.

203 MANNHEIM, Karl, *Man and society in an age of reconstruction: studies in modern social structure*, New York, Harcourt, Brace and Company, 1940. xxii, 469 pp.

204 MARTINELLI, Alberto, 'Analisis económico y analisis sociológico en el sistema teórico de Schumpeter' (Economic and sociological analysis in Schumpeter's theoretical system), *Revista Española de Investigaciones Sociológicas*, 30, abril-junio 1985: 41-68.

205 MAUSS, Marcel, *The gift: forms and functions of exchange in archaic societies*, London, Cohen & West Ltd, 1969. xiv, 130 pp. [Originally appeared in 1925.]

206 MAUSS, Marcel, 'Discussion', *Annales Sociologiques (Série D)*, 3, 1938: 36-38.

207 MIROGLIO, Abel, 'Avertissement du directeur honoraire', *Cahiers de Sociologie Economique*, 1 (seconde série), juin 1971: 3-4.

208 MOMMSEN, Wolfgang, *Theories of imperialism: a critical assessment of the various interpretations of modern imperialism*, New York, Random House, 1980. x, 180 pp. [Originally appeared in 1977.]

209 MORAZE, Charles, 'Essai sur la méthode de F. Simiand — le leçon d'un échec (I-II)', *Mélanges d'histoire sociale*, 1, 1942: 5-24; 2, 1942: 22-42.

210 PERMAN, David, 'Schumpeter's sociology of economics: the role of the competent economist', *Economy and Society*, 14, 4, 1985: 429-49.

211 ROSE, Michael, *Servants of post-industrial power? Sociologie du travail in modern France*, London, Macmillan, 1979. xviii, 226 pp.

212 RUTTAN, W., 'Usher and Schumpeter on invention, innovation, and technological change', *Quarterly Journal of Economics*, 73, 4, 1959: 596-606.

213 SAUERMANN, Heinz, 'Die soziologische Fragestellung in der ökonomischen Theorie' (The sociological viewpoint in economic theory), *Archiv für angewandte Soziologie*, 4, 1, 1931: 185-97.

214 SCHUMPETER, Joseph A., *Das Wesen und Hauptinhalt der theoretischen Nationalökonomie (The nature and content of theoretical economics)*, Leipzig, Duncker & Humblot, 1908. xxxii, 626 pp.

215 SCHUMPETER, Joseph A., *Theorie der wirtschaftlichen Entwicklung (Theory of economic development)*, Leipzig, Duncker & Humblot, 1912. viii, 548 pp. [See especially chapter 7 for economic sociology.]

216 SCHUMPETER, Joseph A., 'Die 'positive' Methode in der Nationalökonomie' (The 'positive' method in economic theory) in: J. Schumpeter, *Aufsätze zur ökonomischen Theorie*, Tübingen, J.C.B. Mohr, 1952: 549-52. [This review of François Simiand's *La méthode positive en science économique* originally appeared in 1914.]

217 SCHUMPETER, Joseph A., 'The crisis of the tax state', *International Economic Papers*, 4, 1954: 5-38. [Originally appeared in 1918.]

218 SCHUMPETER, Joseph A., 'The sociology of imperialisms' in: J.A. Schumpeter, *Imperialism, social classes*, New York, World Publishing Company, 1971: 3-98. [Originally appeared in 1919.]

219 SCHUMPETER, Joseph A., 'Social classes in an ethnically homogenous environment' in: J.A. Schumpeter, *Imperialism, social classes*, New York, World Publishing Company, 1971: 101-68. [Originally appeared in 1927.]

220 SCHUMPETER, Joseph A., *The theory of economic development: an inquiry into profits, capital, credit, interest, and the business cycle*, New York, Oxford University Press, 1961. xii, 255 pp. [Originally appeared in 1934.]

221 SCHUMPETER, Joseph A., *Business cycles: a theoretical, historical, and statistical analysis of the capitalist process*, New York, McGraw-Hill Book Co., 1939. 2 vols, 1095 pp.

222 SCHUMPETER, Joseph A., *Aufsätze zur Soziologie (Essays in sociology)*, Tübingen, J.C.B. Mohr, 1953. 232 pp.

223 SHACKLE, G.S., *The years of high theory: invention & tradition in economic thought 1926–1939*, Cambridge, Cambridge University Press, 1983. viii, 328 pp. [Originally appeared in 1967.]

224 SIMIAND, François, *Le salaire des ouvriers des mines de charbon en France*, Paris, Société Nouvelle, 1907. 520 pp.

225 SIMIAND, François, *Les fluctuations économiques à longue période et la crise mondiale*, Paris, Librairie Félix Alcan, 1932. vi, 1932.

226 SIMIAND, François, *Le salaire, l'évolution sociale et la monnaie — essai de théorie expérimentale du salaire*, Paris, Librairie Félix Alcan, 1932. 620 pp; xxix, 586 pp; xliv, 147 pp.

227 SIMIAND, François, 'La monnaie, réalité sociale', *Annales Sociologiques (Série D)*, 1, 1934: 1-58.

228 STARK, Werner, *The history of economics in its relation to social development*, London, Kegan Paul, Trench, Trubner & Co., 1944. viii, 80 pp.

229 STARK, Werner, 'Joseph Schumpeters Umwertung der Werte' (Joseph Schumpeter's re-evaluation of values), *Kyklos* 8, 1955: 225-51.

230 STARR, Jerold M., 'Specialization and the development of sociology: differentiation or fragmentation?', *Qualitative Sociology*, 6, 1, 1983: 66-86.

231 SULTAN, Herbert, 'Finanzwissenschaft und Soziologie' (Monetary theory and sociology) in: W. Gerloff and F. Neumark (eds), *Handbuch der Finanzwissenschaft*, 2nd ed., Tübingen, J.C.B. Mohr, 1952: 66-98.

232 SWEEZY, Paul M., 'Schumpeter on 'Imperialism and Social Classes'' in: S.E. Harris (ed.), *Schumpeter social scientist.* Cambridge, Mass., Harvard University Press, 1951: 119-24.

233 TOENNIES, Ferdinand, *Das Eigentum (Property)*, Vienna, V. Braumüller, 1926. 50 pp.

234 TOENNIES, Ferdinand, *Soziologische Studien und Kritiken (Studies and criticisms in sociology)*, vol. 2, Jena, Gustav Fischer, 1926. [Toennies discusses economic philosophy, economic theory and insurance on pp. 104-9, 183-89, and 243-65.]

235 TOENNIES, Ferdinand, 'Eigentum' (Property) in: A. Vierkandt (ed.), *Handwörterbuch der Soziologie*, Stuttgart, Ferdinand Enke Verlag, 1931: 106-12.

236 TOURAINE, Alain, *L'évolution du travail ouvrier aux usines Renault*, Paris, Centre National de la Recherche Scientifique, 1955. 200 pp.

237 VILAR, Pierre, *Gold and money 1450–1920*, London, Verso, 1984. 360 pp. [Originally appeared in 1969.]

238 WEILLER, Jean, 'Introduction à une critique sociologique de l'étude des grandes doctrines économiques du XIXe siècle et de l'histoire de la pensée économique du XXe siècle', *l'Année Sociologique*, 1957–58: 19-28.

239 WEILLER, Jean, 'L'économie sociologique de Schumpeter', *Cahiers Internationaux de Sociologie*, 11, 1951: 112-30.

240 WEIPPERT, Georg, 'Sombart, Werner' in: E. v. Beckerath et al. (eds), *Handwörterbuch der Sozialwissenschaften*, vol. 9, Stuttgart, Gustav Fischer 1956: 298-305.

241 VON WIESE, Leopold, 'Wirtschaftssoziologie' (Economic sociology): in E. von Beckerath (ed.), *Handwörterbuch der Sozialwissenschaften*, Stuttgart, Gustav Fischer, vol. 12, 1962: 247-54.

242 WILEY, Norbert, 'The congruence of Weber and Keynes' in: R. Collins (ed.), *Sociological theory 1983*, San Francisco, Jossey-Bass Publishers, 1983: 30-58.

243 WIRTH, Louis, 'American sociology, 1915–47', *American Journal of Sociology: Index to Volumes I-LII*, 1948: 273-81.

244 ZIEGENFUSS, Werner, 'Wirtschaftssoziologie und Wirtschaftstheorie' (Economic sociology and economic theory), *Schmollers Jahrbuch*, 70, 1, 1950: 1-18.

(4) The 'Economy and Society' Perspective in US Sociology

245 AMERICAN SOCIOLOGICAL ASSOCIATION (ASA), *Guide to graduate departments of sociology*, Washington, D.C., ASA, 1984.

246 AYRES, C.E., 'Review of Parsons-Smelser, *Economy and society*', *American Economic Review*, 47, 1957: 686-88.

247 BARNARD, Chester, *The functions of the executive*, Cambridge, Mass., Harvard University Press, 1938. xvi, 334 pp.

248 BENDIX, Reinhart, *Work and authority in industry: ideologies of management in the course of industrialization*, New York, Wiley, 1956. 466 pp.

249 BLOCH, Herbert A., 'The sociology of gambling', *American Journal of Sociology*, 57, 3, 1951: 215-21.

250 BLOCK, Fred and Margaret R. SOMERS, 'Beyond the economistic fallacy: the holistic social science of Karl Polanyi' in: T. Skocpol (ed.), *Visions and method in historical sociology*, Cambridge, Cambridge University Press, 1984: 47-84.

251 BREDEMEIER, H.C., 'Exchange theory': in T. Bottomore and R. Nisbet (eds), *A history of sociological analysis*, London, Heinemann, 1979: 418-56.

252 CAPLOWITZ, David, *The poor pay more: consumer practice of low-income families*, New York, The Free Press, 1963. 220 pp.

253 CASANOVA Jean-Claude, *Essai sur quelques tentatives d'intégration de l'économie et de la sociologie*, Paris, thesis, 1964. cxxx, 854 pp.

254 COTTRELL, W.F., 'Death by dieselization: a case study in the reaction to technological change' *American Sociological Review*, 16, 3, 1951: 358-65.

255 CRESSEY, Paul G., *The taxi-dance hall: a sociological study in commercialized recreation and city life*, Chicago, University of Chicago Press, 1932. xxi, 300 pp.

256 DALTON, Melville, *Men who manage: fusions of feeling and theory in administration*, New York, John Wiley & Sons, 1959. 318 pp.

257 DONOVAN, Frances R., *The woman who waits*, Boston, R.G. Badger, 1920. 228 pp.

258 DONOVAN, Frances R., *The sales lady*, Chicago, University of Chicago Press, 1929. 267 pp.

259 DUNCAN, Otis Dudley, 'Introduction': in William F. Ogburn, *On culture and social change: selected papers*, Chicago, University of Chicago Press, 1964: vii-xxii.

260 GILFILLAN, S.C., *The sociology of invention*, Chicago: Follet Publishing Company, 1935. 185 pp.

261 GOULDNER, Alwin W., *The coming crisis of Western sociology*, New York, Avon Books, 1971. xv, 528 pp. [Originally appeared in 1970. See especially 'Toward a sociology of property', pp. 304-13.]

262 HOMANS, George, 'Social behavior as exchange', *American Journal of Sociology*, 62, 1958: 597-606.

263 HUGHES, Everett C., 'Personality types and the division of labor' in: E.C. Hughes (ed.), *The sociological eye*, Chicago, Aldine- Atherton, 1971: 326-37. [Originally appeared in 1928.]

264 HUGHES, Everett C., *The growth of an institution: the Chicago Real Estate Board*, New York, Arno Press, 1979. 124 pp. [Hughes' thesis was originally published in 1931 as 'A Study of a secular institution: the Chicago Real Estate Board'.]

265 HUGHES, Everett C., *French Canada in transition*, Chicago, University of Chicago Press, 1971. xx, 227 pp. [Originally appeared in 1943.]

266 HUGHES, Everett C., 'The knitting of racial groups in industry' in: E.C. Hughes, (ed.), *The sociological eye*, Chicago, Aldine-Atherton, 1971: 265-75. [Originally appeared in 1946.]

267 HUGHES, Everett C., 'Mistakes at work' in: E.C. Hughes (ed.), *The sociological eye*, Chicago, Aldine-Atherton, 1971: 316-25. [Originally appeared in 1951.]

268 HUGHES, Everett C., 'Work and self' in: E.C. Hughes (ed.), *The sociological eye*, Chicago, Aldine-Atherton, 1971: 338-47. [Originally appeared in 1951.]

269 HUGHES, Everett C., 'Good people and dirty work': in E.C. Hughes (ed.), *The sociological eye*, Chicago, Aldine-Atherton, 1971: 87-97. [This article originally appeared in 1962.]

270 JANOWITZ, Morris, Letter to Richard Swedberg dated 26 November 1985.

271 JOHNSON, Earl S., 'The function of the central business district in the metropolitan community': in J.F. Short, Jr. (ed.), *The social fabric of the metropolis: contributions of the Chicago School of Urban Sociology*, Chicago, University of Chicago Press, 1971: 87-102.

272 KERR, Clark and Lloyd H. FISCHER, 'Plant sociology: the elite and the aborigines': in M. Komarovsky (ed.), *Common frontiers of the social sciences*, Glencoe, Ill., The Free Press, 1957: 281-309.

273 KURTZ, Lester R., *Evaluating Chicago sociology: a guide to the literature, with an annotated bibliography*, Chicago, University of Chicago Press, 1984. x, 303 pp.

274 KUZNETS, Simon, 'Review of T. Parsons and N. Smelser, *Economy and Society*', *Annals of the American Academy of Political and Social Science*, 312, 1957: 175-76.

275 LAZARSFELD, Paul F., 'Reflections on business', *American Journal of Sociology*, 65, 1, 1959: 1-31. [This article also appears in Robert A. Dahl, Maison Haire and Paul F. Lazarsfeld, *Social science research on business: product and potential*. New York, Columbia University Press, 1959. 185 pp.]

276 LEVINE, Donald N., Letter to Richard Swedberg dated 21 November 1985.

277 LIPSET, Seymour M. and Martin TROW, 'Reference group theory and trade union wage policy' in: M. Komarovsky (ed.), *Common frontiers of the social sciences*, Glencoe, Ill., The Free Press, 1957: 391-439.

278 LIPSET, Seymour Martin, 'Values, education, and entrepreneurship' in: S.M. Lipset and A. Solari (eds), *Elites in Latin America*, New York, Oxford University Press, 1967: 3-60.

279 LUHMANN, Niklas, 'The economy as a social system' in: N. Luhmann, *The differentiation of society*, New York, Columbia University Press, 1982: 190-225. [Originally appeared in 1970.]

280 LUNDBERG, George A., 'The interests of the members of the American Sociological Society', *American Journal of Sociology*, 37, 3, 1931: 458-60.

281 MERTON, Robert K., *Science, technology & society in seventeenth century England*, New York, Fertig, 1970, xxxii, 279 pp. [Originally appeared in 1938.]

282 MERTON, Robert K., *Mass persuasion: the social psychology of a war bond drive*, Westport, Conn., Greenwood Press, 1971. xiii, 210 pp. [Originally published in 1946.]

283 MILLS, C. Wright, *White collar: the American middle*

classes, London, Oxford University Press, 1956. xx, 378 pp. [Originally appeared in 1951.]

284 MILLS, C. Wright, *The power elite*, New York, Oxford University Press, 1971. 423 pp. [Originally published in 1956.]

285 MOORE, Wilbert E., 'Sociology of economic organizations': in G. Gurvitch and W.E. Moore (eds), *Twentieth century sociology*, New York, Philosophical Library, 1945: 438-65.

286 MOORE, Wilbert E., *Industrial relations and the social order*, New York, Macmillan, 1946. 660 pp.

287 MOORE, Wilbert E., 'Theoretical aspects of industrialization', *Social Research*, 15, 1948: 277-303.

288 MOORE, Wilbert E., *Industrialization and labor: social aspects of economic development*, Ithaca, Cornell University Press, 1951. xx, 410 pp.

289 MOORE, Wilbert E., 'The exportability of the ''labor force'' concept', *American Sociological Review*, 18, 1953: 68-72.

290 MOORE, Wilbert E., *Economy and society*, New York, Doubleday & Company, 1955. ix, 48 pp.

291 MOORE, Wilbert E., 'The market' in: W.E. Moore and A.S. Feldman (eds), *Labor commitment and social change in developing areas*, New York, Social Science Research Council, 1960: 41-61.

292 MOORE, Wilbert E., *The conduct of the corporation*, New York, Random House, 1962. xxi, 292 pp.

293 MOORE, Wilbert E., 'Social aspects of economic development' in: R.E.L. Faris (ed.), *Handbook of modern sociology*, Chicago, Rand McNally, 1964: 882-911.

294 MOORE, Wilbert E., *The impact of industry*, Englewood Cliffs, New Jersey, Prentice-Hall, 1965. x, 117 pp.

295 MOORE, Wilbert E., 'Industrialization: social aspects' in: D.L. Sills (ed.), *International encyclopaedia of the social sciences*, New York, Macmillan, 1968, 7: 263-70.

296 MOORE, Wilbert E., *The professions: roles and rules*, New York, Russel Sage Foundation, 1970. xi, 303 pp.

297 MOORE, Wilbert E. (ed.), *Technology and social change*, Chicago, Quadrangle Books, 1972. vii, 236 pp.

298 MOORE, Wilbert E., 'Economic and professional institutions' in: N.J. Smelser (ed.), *Sociology: an introduction*, New York, Wiley, 1973: 347-97.

299 MOORE, Wilbert E., 'An interim report on the calling and career of an American sociologist', *International Social Science Journal*, 25, 1973: 117-28.
300 MOORE, Wilbert E., 'Modernization as rationalization: processes and restraints' in: M. Nash (ed.), *Essays on economic development and cultural change in honor of Bert F. Hoselitz*, Supplement to vol. 25 of *Economic Development and Cultural Change*, 1977: 29-42.
301 MOORE, Wilbert E. and Bert F. HOSELITZ (eds), *Industrialization and society*, Paris, UNESCO and Mouton, 1963. 437 pp.
302 OGBURN, William F., *Social change with respect to culture and original nature*, New York, The Viking Press, 1950. viii, 393 pp. [Originally appeared in 1922.]
303 OGBURN, William F., *On culture and social change: selected papers*, Chicago, University of Chicago Press, 1964. xxii, 360 pp.
304 OGBURN, William F. and Meyer F. NIMKOFF, *A handbook of sociology*, London, Routledge & Kegan Paul, 1956. xi, 644 pp. [A reprint of the third ed. from 1953.]
305 PARK, Robert E. and Ernest W. BURGESS, *Introduction to the science of sociology*, Chicago, University of Chicago Press, 1921. xxi, 1040 pp.
306 PARSONS, Talcott, 'Wants and activities in Marshall', *Quarterly Journal of Economics*, 46, 1931: 101-40.
307 PARSONS, Talcott, 'Economics and sociology: Marshall in relation to the thought of his time', *Quarterly Journal of Economics*, 46, 1932: 316-47.
308 PARSONS, Talcott, 'Some reflections on "The nature and significance of economics"', *Quarterly Journal of Economics*, 48, 1934: 511-45.
309 PARSONS, Talcott, 'Sociological elements in economic thought, I-II', *Quarterly Journal of Economics*, 49, 1934: 414-53; 49, 1935: 645-67.
310 PARSONS, Talcott, 'H.M. Robertson on Max Weber and his school', *Journal of Political Economy*, 43 (1935): 688-96.
311 PARSONS, Talcott, 'On certain sociological elements in Professor Taussig's thought' in: J. Viner (ed.), *Explorations in economics: notes and essays in honor of F.M. Taussig*, New York, McGraw-Hill, 1936: 359-79.

312 PARSONS, Talcott, 'Motivation of economic activities', *Canadian Journal of Economics and Political Science*, 6, 1940: 187-203.
313 PARSONS, Talcott, 'The rise and decline of economic man', *Journal of General Education*, 4, 1949: 47-53.
314 PARSONS, Talcott, *The integration of economic and sociological theory ('the Marshall lectures').* Unpublished manuscript, Pusey Library at Harvard University, 1953. 69 pp. [Permission has been granted by the Harvard University Archives to publish a facsimile of the original manuscript in the Report Series of the Sociology Department at Uppsala University during 1986.]
315 PARSONS, Talcott, 'On building social system theory: a personal history', *Daedalus*, Fall 1970: 826-81.
316 PEARSON, Harry W., 'Parsons and Smelser on the economy' in: K. Polanyi, C.M. Arensberg and H.W. Pearson (eds), *Trade and market in the early empires*, Chicago, Henry Regnery, 1971: 307-19. [Originally appeared in 1957.]
317 POLANYI, Karl, *The great transformation*, Boston, Beacon Press, 1957. xii, 315 pp. [Originally appeared in 1944.]
318 POLANYI, Karl, *Dahomey and the slave trade: an analysis of an archaic economy*, Seattle, University of Washington Press, 1966. xxvi, 204 pp.
319 POLANYI, Karl, *Primitive, archaic and modern economies: essays of Karl Polanyi*, Boston, Beacon Press, 1971. liv, 346 pp. [Edited by George Dalton; originally appeared in 1968.]
320 POLANYI, Karl, *The livelihood of man*, New York, Academic Press, 1977. lv, 280 pp.
321 POLANYI, Karl, Conrad M. ARENSBERG, and Harry W. PEARSON (eds), *Trade and market in the early empires: economies in history and theory*, Chicago, Henry Regnery, 1971. 382 pp. [Originally appeared in 1957.]
322 ROSE, Arnold, 'Rumor in the stock market', *Public Opinion Quarterly*, 15, 1951: 461-86.
323 ROSE, Arnold, 'A social psychological approach to the study of the stock market', *Kyklos*, 19, 2, 1966: 267-88.
324 ROSE, Arnold, 'Confidence and the corporation', *American Journal of Economics and Sociology*, 26, 3, 1967: 231-36.
325 SAVAGE, Stephen P., *The theories of Talcott Parsons: the*

social relations of action, London, Macmillan, 1981. xiii, 279 pp. [See especially chapter 5, 'The economy and the social system'.]

326 SCHNEIDER, Eugene V., 'A note on Delbert C. Miller, "Whatever will happen to industrial sociology"', *Sociological Quarterly*, 25, Spring 1984: 261-65.

327 SMELSER, Neil J., *Social change in the industrial revolution: an application of theory to the British cotton industry*, Chicago, University of Chicago Press, 1959. xii, 440 pp.

328 SMELSER, Neil J., 'A comparative view of exchange systems', *Economic Development and Cultural Change*, 7, 2, 1959: 173-82.

329 SMELSER, Neil J., *Sociology of economic life*, Englewood Cliffs, New Jersey, Prentice-Hall, 1963. 120 pp. [A second revised version appeared in 1976.]

330 SMELSER, Neil J., 'Mechanisms of change and adjustment to change in economic development' in: W.E. Moore and B.F. Hoselitz (eds), *Industrialization and society*, The Hague, Mouton, 1963: 32-54.

331 SMELSER, Neil J. (ed.), *Readings on economic sociology*, Englewood Cliffs, New Jersey, Prentice-Hall, 1965. ix, 303 pp.

332 SMELSER, Neil J., 'The sociology of economic life' in: T. Parsons (ed.), *American sociology*, New York, Basic Books, 1967: 143-55.

333 SMELSER, Neil J., 'Notes on the methodology of the comparative analysis of economic activity' in: *Transactions of the Sixth World Congress of Sociology*, The Hague, Edition Neuwelarts, 1968, II: 101-17.

334 SMELSER, Neil J., 'Economy and society' in: D.L. Sills (ed.), *International encyclopaedia of the social sciences*, New York, Macmillan, 1968, IV: 500-6.

335 SMELSER, Neil J., 'Re-examining the parameters of economic activity' in: E.M. Epstein and D. Votaw (eds), *Rationality, legitimacy, and responsibility*, Santa Monica, Goodyear Publishing Company, 1978: 19-51.

336 SMELSER, Neil J., 'On collaborating with Talcott Parsons: some intellectual and personal notes', *Sociological Inquiry*, 51, 3/4, 1981: 143-54. [See especially pp. 145-51 on the background to Parsons-Smelser, *Economy and society*.]

337 SMELSER, Neil J., Letter to Richard Swedberg dated 28 November 1984.
338 SMELSER, Neil J. and Seymour Martin LIPSET (eds), *Social structure and mobility, and economic development*, Chicago, Aldine Press, 1966. ix, 399 pp.
339 STINCHCOMBE, Arthur, 'Rationality and subjectivity in economic sociology': in U. Himmelstrand (ed.), *Sociology: from crisis to science*, Beverly Hills, Ca., SAGE Publications, 1986 (forthcoming).
340 SUTTON, Francis X. et al., *The American business creed*, Cambridge, Mass., Harvard University Press, 1956. 414 pp.
341 WEBER, Max, *The protestant ethic and the spirit of capitalism*, New York, Charles Scribner's Sons, 1958. xvii, 292 pp. [This translation by Talcott Parsons of Weber's 1904–05 essay was originally published in 1930.]
342 WHYTE, William Foote, *Human relations in the restaurant business*, New York, McGraw-Hill Book Company, 1948. 378 pp.
343 WHYTE, William Foote et al., *Money and motivation: an analysis of incentives in industry*, New York, Harper & Row, 1955. xii, 268 pp.
344 WILEY, Norbert F., 'The current interregnum in American sociology', *Social Research*, 52, 1, 1985: 179-207.
345 WILEY, Norbert, Letter to Richard Swedberg dated 12 November 1985.
346 ZORBAUGH, Harvey Warren, *The gold coast and the slum: a sociological study of Chicago's near North side*, Chicago, University of Chicago Press, 1929. 287 pp.

PART II: TOWARDS A NEW ECONOMIC SOCIOLOGY, 1960s– ?

Introduction

347 BELL, Daniel, 'Models and reality in economic discourse' in: D. Bell and I. Kristol (eds), *The crisis in economic theory*, New York, Basic Books, 1981: 46-80.
348 GERSHUNY, J.J. and I.D. MILES, 'Towards a new social economics' in: B. Roberts et al. (eds), *New approaches to economic life*, Manchester, Manchester University Press, 1985: 24-47.

349 GRANOVETTER, Mark, Interview with Richard Swedberg, Stony Brook, 27 December 1985.
350 KOSKINEN, Tarmo and Kari LILJA, *Työ, talous ja suomalainen yhteiskunta: arvioita tutkimuksen tilasta (Work, economy and the Finnish society: three papers on the state of the research).* Vaasa, Vaasan Korkeakoulun Julkaisuja, Tutkimuksia No 92, Sosiologia 7, 1983.84 pp.
351 MARTINELLI, Alberto, 'Lo sviluppo ineguale della sociologia economica italiana' (The uneven development of economic sociology in Italy), *Quaderni di Sociologia*, 4-5, 1985: 259-86.
352 ROSE, Michael, 'Universalism, culturalism and the Aix group: promise and problems of a societal approach to economic institutions', *European Sociological Review*, 1, 1, 1985: 65-83.
353 SALES, Arnaud and Noël BELANGER, *Decideurs et questionnaires: étude sur la direction et l'encadrement des secteurs privé et public*, Québec, Conseil de la langue française, 1985. 421 pp.
354 SHETH, N.R. and P.J. PATEL, *Industrial sociology in India*, Jaipur, Rawat Publications, 1979. 134 pp.
355 SWEDBERG, Richard, 'The critique of the "economy and society" perspective during the paradigm crisis: from the United States to Sweden', *Acta Sociologica*, 29, 2, 1986: 91-112.
356 THUROW, Lester, *Dangerous currents: the state of economics*, New York, Vintage Books, 1984. xix, 259 pp. [Originally appeared in 1983.]

(5) Women in the Economy

357 ACKER, Joan 'Women and social stratification: a case of intellectual sexism', *American Journal of Sociology*, 78, 4, 1973: 936-45.
358 ACKER, Joan, 'Issues in the sociological study of women's work' in: A.H. Stromberg and S. Harkess (eds), *Women working: theories and facts in perspective*, Palo Alto, California, Mayfield Publishing Company, 1978: 134-61.
359 ALEXANDER, Victoria and Peggy A. THOITS, 'Token

achievement: an examination of proportional representation and performance outcomes', *Social Forces*, 64, 2, 1985: 332-40.

360 ARROW, Kenneth, 'Comment I' in: M. Blaxall and B. Reagan (eds), *Women and the workplace: the implications of occupational segregation*, Chicago, University of Chicago Press, 1976: 233-37.

361 BARRETT, Michèle, *Women's oppression today: problems in marxist feminist analysis*, London, Verso, 1980. 269 pp.

362 BEECHEY, Veronica, 'Women and production: a critical analysis of some sociological theories of women's work' in: A. Kuhn and A. Wolpe (eds), *Feminism and materialism: women and modes of production*, London, Routledge and Kegan Paul, 1978: 155-97.

363 BELL, Carolyn Shaw, 'Women and work: an economic appraisal' in: A.H. Stromberg and S. Harkess (eds), *Women working: theories and facts in perspective*, Palo Alto, California, Mayfield Publishing Company, 1978: 10-28.

364 BENSTON, Margaret, 'The political economy of women's liberation', *Monthly Review*, 21, 2, 1969: 13-27.

365 BERK, Richard A. and Sarah Fenstermaker BERK, 'Supply-side sociology of the family: the challenge of the new home economics', *Annual Review of Sociology*, 9, 1983: 375-95.

366 BERNARD, Jessie, 'My four revolutions: an autobiographical history of the ASA', *American Journal of Sociology*, 78, 4, 1972: 873-91.

367 BIELBY, William T. and James N. BARON, 'A woman's place is with other women: sex segregation within organizations' in: B.F. Reskin (ed.), *Sex segregation in the workplace: trends, explanations, remedies*, Washington, D.C., National Academy Press, 1984: 27-53.

368 BIELBY, William T. and James N. BARON, 'Men and women at work: sex segregation and statistical discrimination', *American Journal of Sociology*, 91, 1986: 759-99.

369 BLACK, Naomi and Ann Baker COTTRELL, (eds), *Women and world change: issues in development*, Beverly Hills, SAGE Publications, 1981. 288 pp.

370 BLAU, Francine D. and Carol L. JUSENIUS, 'Economists' approaches to sex segregation in the labor market', in: M. Blaxall and B. Reagan (eds), *Women and the workplace: the*

implications of occupational segregation, Chicago, University of Chicago Press, 1976: 181-200.
371 BLAXALL, Martha and Barbara REAGAN, (eds), *Women and the workplace: the implications of occupational segregation*, Chicago, University of Chicago Press, 1976. x, 326 pp. [Originally issued as a supplement to *Signs*, 1, 3, pt.2.]
372 BOSERUP, Ester, *Women's role in economic development*, London, Allen & Unwin, 1970. 283 pp.
373 CHAPMAN, Jane Roberts, 'Review essay: economics', *Signs*, 1, 1, 1975: 139-46.
374 CHINCHILLA, Norma S., 'Industrialization, monopoly capitalism, and women's work in Guatemala', *Signs*, 3, 1, 1977: 38-56.
375 DOERINGER, Peter B. and Michael J. PIORE, *Internal labor markets and manpower analysis*, Lexington, Mass., D.C. Heath Company, 1971. viii, 214 pp.
376 EHRLICH, Carol, 'The male sociologist's burden: the place of women in marriage and family texts', *Journal of Marriage and the Family*, 33, 3, 1971: 421-30.
377 EISENSTEIN, Zillah R. (ed.), *Capitalist patriarchy and the case for socialist feminism*, New York, Monthly Review Press, 1979. ix, 394 pp.
378 ENGLAND, Paula, 'Assessing trends in occupational sex segregation, 1900–1976' in: I. Berg (ed.), *Sociological perspectives on labor markets*, New York, Academic Press, 1981: 273-95.
379 ENGLAND, Paula, 'The failure of human capital theory to explain occupational sex segregation', *Journal of Human Resources*, 17, 3, 1982: 358-70.
380 FELDBERG, Roslyn L. and Evelyn Nakana GLENN, 'Male and female: job versus gender models in the sociology of work', *Social Problems*, 26, 5, 1979: 524-38.
381 FERBER, Marianne, 'Review essay: women and work — issues of the 1980s', *Signs*, 8, 2, 1982: 273-95.
382 FOLBRE, Nancy, 'Household production in the Philippines: a non-neoclassical approach', *Economic Development and Cultural Change*, 32, 2, 1984: 303-30.
383 GLAZER-MALBIN, Nona, 'Review essay: housework', *Signs*, 1, 4, 1976: 905-22.
384 GOLDSCHMIDT-CLERMONT, Luisella, 'Does house-

work pay? A product-related microeconomic perspective', *Signs*, 9, 1, 1983: 108-19.

385 GOLDTHORPE, John H., 'Women and class analysis: in defence of the conventional view', *Sociology*, 17, 4, 1983: 465-88.

386 GRONAU, Reuben, 'Leisure, home production, and work', *Journal of Political Economy*, 85, 6, 1977: 1099-123.

387 HARKESS, Shirley, 'Women's occupational experiences in the 1970s: sociology and economics', *Signs*, 10, 3, 1985: 495-516.

388 HARTMANN, Heidi, 'Capitalism, patriarchy, and job segregation by sex' in: Z.R. Eisenstein (ed.), *Capitalist patriarchy and the case for socialist feminism*, New York, Monthly Review Press, 1979: 206-47.

389 HIRSCHON, Renée (ed.), *Women and property — women as property*, London, Croom Helm, 1984. 222 pp.

390 HOLTER, Harriet (ed.), *Patriarchy in a welfare society*, Oslo, Universitetsforlaget, 1984. 234 pp.

391 KANDIYOTI, Deniz, 'Sex roles and social change: a comparative appraisal of Turkey's women', *Signs*, 3, 1, 1977: 57-73.

392 KANDIYOTI, Deniz, 'Economie monétaire et rôles des sexes: le cas de la Turquie', *Current Sociology*, 31, 1, 1983: 214-28.

393 LILJESTRÖM, Rita and Edmund DAHLSTRÖM, *Arbetarkvinnor i hem-, arbets- och samhällsliv (Working-class women at home, at work and in society)*, Stockholm, Tidens förlag, 1981. 366 pp.

394 LLOYD, Cynthia B. and Beth T. NIEMI, *The economics of sex differentials*, New York, Columbia University Press, 1979. 355 pp.

395 McCRATE, Elaine, 'Comment on Ferber's "Women and work: issues of the 1980s"', *Signs*, 9, 2, 1983: 326-30.

396 MICHEL, Andrée, 'Multinationales et inégalités de classe et de sexe', *Current Sociology*, 31, 1, 1983: 1-208.

397 NASH, June, 'A critique of social science roles in Latin America' in: J. Nash and H.I. Safa (eds), *Sex and class in Latin America*, New York, Praeger, 1976: 1-21.

398 NASH, June and Helen SAFA (eds), *Sex and class in Latin America*, New York, Praeger, 1976. 330 pp.

399 NAVARRO, Marysa, 'Review essay: research on Latin

American women', *Signs*, 5, 1, 1979: 111-20.
400 OAKLEY, Ann, *The sociology of housework*, Bath, Martin Robertson, 1974. viii, 242 pp.
401 OPPENHEIMER, Valerie Kincade, 'The sociology of women's economic role in the family', *American Sociological Review*, 42, 3, 1977: 387-406.
402 PAPANEK, Hanna, 'Purdah in Pakistan: seclusion and modern occupations for women', *Journal of Marriage and the Family*, 33, 1971: 517-30.
403 PAPANEK, Hanna, 'Purdah: separate worlds and symbolic shelter', *Comparative Studies in Society and History*, 15, 3, 1973: 289-325.
404 PAPANEK, Hanna, 'Comment on Gusfield's review essay on *Becoming modern', American Journal of Sociology*, 83, 1978: 1507-11.
405 PARSONS, Talcott, 'Age and sex in the social structure of the United States' in: T. Parsons, *Essays in sociological theory*, New York, The Free Press, 1964: 89-103. [Originally appeared in 1942.]
406 POWER, Marilyn, 'From home production to wage labor: women as a reserve army of labor', *Review of Radical Political Economics*, Spring 1983: 71-92.
407 RESSNER, Ulla, *Vordarbetarkollektiv och facket inom omsorgsvarden (Collectives and unions among workers in the caretaking professions)*, Stockholm, Arbetslivscentrum, 1982. 75 pp.
408 RUBIN, Gayle, 'The traffic in women: notes on the "political economy" of sex' in: R.R. Reiter (ed), *Toward an anthropology of women*, New York, Monthly Review Press, 1975: 157-210.
409 SAWHILL, Isabel V., 'Economic perspectives on the family', *Daedalus*, 106, 2, 1977: 115-25.
410 SIGNS, 'Special issue: women and national development', 3, 1, 1977; 'Special issue: development and the sexual division of labor', 7, 2, 1981.
411 SMELSER, Neil J., Letter to Ulf Himmelstrand dated 29 January 1986.
412 SOKOLOFF, Natalie J., *Between money and love: the dialectics of women's home and market work*, New York, Praeger, 1980. 299 pp.
413 SOKOLOFF, Natalie J., 'Theories of women's labor force

status: a review and critique', *Current Perspectives in Social Theory*, 2, 1981: 153-86.

414 SORENSEN, Bjorg Aase, 'Ansvarsrasjonalitet: om mal-middeltenkning blant kvinner' (The rationality of responsibility: about women's thinking the rationality of ends and means), in: H. Holter (ed.), *Kvinner i felleskap (Women together)*, Oslo, Universitetsforlaget, 1982: 392-402.

415 STROBEL, Margaret, 'Review article: African women', *Signs*, 8, 1, 1982: 109-31. [See especially the section on 'Women's productive and reproductive behavior'.]

416 VOGEL, Lise, 'Marxism and socialist-feminist theory: a decade of debate', *Current Perspectives in Social Theory*, 2, 1981: 209-31.

417 WAERNESS, Kari, 'Caring as women's work' in: H. Holter (ed.), *Patriarchy in welfare society*, Oslo, Universitets-forlaget, 1984: 67-87.

418 ZAAR, Christina, 'Kvinnokonferensen — mot jämnlikhet ar 2000' (The conference on women — towards equality in the year 2000), *Dagens Nyheter*, 13 July 1985. p. 22.

(6) The Neo-Marxist Contribution

419 AHRNE, Göran and Erik Olin WRIGHT, 'Classes in the United States and Sweden: a comparison', *Acta Sociologica*, 22, 3/4, 1983: 211-35.

420 ALLEN, Michael Patrick, 'Management control in the large corporation: comment on Zeitlin', *American Journal of Sociology*, 81, 4, 1976: 885-94.

421 ALTHUSSER, Louis, *For Marx*, New York, Vintage Books, 1970. 272 pp. [Originally appeared in 1965.]

422 ANDERSON, Perry, *Lineages of the absolutist state*, London, NLB, 1974. 573 pp.

423 ANDERSON, Perry, *Passages from antiquity to feudalism*, London, NLB, 1974. 304 pp.

424 ASSMAN, Georg et al. (eds), *Wörterbuch der marxistisch-leninistischen Soziologie (Handbook of marxist-leninist sociology)*, Berlin, Dietz Verlag, 1977. 738 pp.

425 ATTEWELL, Paul A., *Radical political economy since the sixties: a sociology of knowledge analysis*, New Brunswick, N.J., Rutgers University Press, 1984. x, 306 pp.

426 BELL, Daniel, 'The breakup of family capitalism: on changes in class in America' in: D. Bell, *The end of ideology: on the exhaustion of political ideas in the fifties*, Glencoe, Ill., The Free Press, 1962: 39-46. [Rev. ed.].
427 BELL, Daniel, 'The public household: on "fiscal sociology" and the liberal society' in: D. Bell, *The cultural contradictions of capitalism*, New York, Basic Books, 1978. [Originally appeared in 1976.]
428 BERG, Ivar and Mayer N. ZALD, 'Business and society', *Annual Review of Sociology*, 4, 1978: 115-43.
429 BERLE, Adolf A. and Gardiner C. MEANS, *The modern corporation and private property*, New York, Macmillan Co., 1932. xiii, 396 pp.
430 BLACKBURN, Robin, 'A brief guide to bourgeois culture' in: A. Cockburn and R. Blackburn (eds), *Student power: problems, diagnosis, action*, Harmondsworth, Penguin Books, 1969: 164-284.
431 BLOCK, Fred, 'Beyond corporate liberalism', *Social Problems*, 24, 13, 1977: 352-61.
432 BLOCK, Fred, 'The ruling class does not rule: notes on the marxist theory of the state', *Socialist Revolution*, 7, 3, 1977: 6-28.
433 BLOCK, Fred, 'The fiscal crisis of the capitalist state', *Annual Review of Sociology*, 7, 1981: 1-27.
434 BOWLES, Samuel, 'The production process in a competitive economy: Walrasian, neo-Hobbesian, and Marxian models', *American Economic Review*, 75, 1, 1985: 16-36.
435 BOWLES, Samuel and Richard EDWARDS, *Understanding capitalism: competition, command, and change in the US economy*, New York, Harper & Row, 1985. xi, 419 pp.
436 BOWLES, Samuel, David M. GORDON and Thomas E. WEISSKOPF, *Beyond the waste land: A democratic alternative to economic decline*, New York, Anchor Press, 1984. xii, 465 pp.
437 BRAVERMAN, Harry, *Labor and monopoly capital: The degradation of work in the twentieth century*, New York, Monthly Review Press, 1974. xiii, 465 pp.
438 BURAWOY, Michael, *Manufacturing consent: Changes in the labor process under monopoly capitalism*, Chicago, University of Chicago Press, 1979. xvii, 267 pp.
439 BURAWOY, Michael, *The politics of production: factory*

regimes under capitalism and socialism, London, Verso, 1985. 272 pp.

440 BURNS, Tom, Thomas BAUMGARTNER and Philippe DEVILLE, 'Inflation, politics, and social change: institutional and theoretical crisis in contemporary economy-and-society', *International Journal of Contemporary Sociology*, 25, 1-2, 1984: 73-90.

441 CARNOY, Martin, *The state and political theory*, Princeton, New Jersey, Princeton University Press, 1984. 282 pp.

442 COLBJÖRNSEN, Tom et al., *Klassestruktur og klasseskiller (Class structure and class differences)*, Bergen, Universitetsforlaget, 1982. 161 pp.

443 DAHRENDORF, Ralf, *Class and class conflict in industrial society*, Stanford, Stanford University Press, 1959. 336 pp.

444 DIDONATO, Donna et al., 'Theories of corporate interlocks: a social history' in: S. Bacharach (ed.), *Perspectives in organizational sociology*, Greenwich, Conn., JAI Press, 1986 (vol. 3; forthcoming).

445 DOMHOFF, G. William, *Who rules America?* Englewood Cliffs, N.J., Prentice-Hall, 1967. 184 pp.

446 DOMHOFF, G. William, *The higher circles: the governing class in America*, New York, Random House, 1970. xii, 367 pp.

447 DOMHOFF, G. William, *The Bohemian Grove and other retreats: a study in ruling-class cohesiveness*, New York, Harper & Row, 1974. xvi, 250 pp.

448 DOMHOFF, G. William, *The powers that be: processes of ruling-class domination in America*, New York, Random House, 1979. xv, 206 pp.

449 DOMHOFF, G. William, *Who rules America now? A view for the eighties*, Englewood Cliffs, N.J., Prentice-Hall, 1983. 230 pp.

450 DUESENBERRY, James S., *Income, saving, and the theory of consumer behavior*, Cambridge, Mass., Harvard University Press, 1949. 128 pp.

451 EDWARDS, Richard, *Contested terrain: the transformation of the workplace in the twentieth century*, New York, Basic Books, 1979. ix, 261 pp.

452 EDWARDS, Richard, Michael REICH and David M. GORDON (eds), *Labor market segmentation*, Lexington, Mass., Lexington Books, 1975. 297 pp.

453 ELSTER, Jon, 'Marxism, functionalism, and game theory', *Theory and Society*, 11, 1982: 453-82.

454 ELSTER, Jon, *Making sense of Marx*, Cambridge, Cambridge University Press, 1985. xv, 556 pp.

455 ESPING-ANDERSEN, Gösta, Roger FRIEDLAND and Erik Olin WRIGHT, 'Modes of class struggle and the capitalist state', *Kapitalistate*, 4-5, 1976: 186-220.

456 GLASBERG, Davita Silfen and Michael SCHWARTZ, 'Ownership and control of corporations', *Annual Review of Sociology*, 9, 1983: 311-32.

457 GOLD, David A., Clarence Y.H. LO and Erik Olin WRIGHT, 'Recent developments in marxist theories of the capitalist state (I)', *Monthly Review*, 27, 5, 1975: 29-43.

458 GOLDTHORPE, John H., 'The current inflation: towards a sociological account' in: F. Hirsch and J.H. Goldthorpe (eds), *The political economy of inflation*, Cambridge, Mass., Harvard University Press, 1978: 186-214.

459 GORDON, David M., Richard EDWARDS and Michael REICH, *Segmented work, divided workers: The historical transformation of labor in the United States*, Cambridge, Cambridge University Press, 1982. xii, 288 pp.

460 GOUGH, Ian, *The political economy of the welfare state*, London, Macmillan, 1979. xii, 196 pp.

461 GRAMSCI, Antonio, *Selections from the prison notebooks*, New York, International Publishers, 1971. xcvi, 482 pp. [Originally written in 1929–35; see especially 'Americanism and fordism'.]

462 HILFERDING, Rudolf, *Finance capital: A study of the latest phase of capitalist development*, London, Routledge and Kegan Paul, 1985. vi, 466 pp. [Originally appeared in 1910.]

463 HIMMELSTRAND, Ulf et al., *Beyond welfare capitalism: issues, actors and forces in societal change*, London, Heinemann, 1981. xviii, 370 pp. [A second edition is to appear in 1987.]

464 HINDESS, Barry, 'Rational choice theory and the analysis of political action', *Economy and Society*, 13, 3, 1984: 255-77.

465 JAMES, David R. and Michael SOREF, 'Profit constraints on managerial autonomy: managerial theory and the unmaking of the corporation president', *American Socio-*

logical Review, 46, 1981: 1-18.
466 JESSOP, Bob, *The capitalist state*, Oxford, Martin Robertson, 1982. xvi, 296 pp.
467 KASINITZ, Philip, 'Neo-marxist views of the state', *Dissent*, Summer 1983: 337-46.
468 KATONA, George, *Psychological analysis of economic behavior*, New York, McGraw-Hill, 1951. ix, 347 pp.
469 KATZENSTEIN, Peter (ed.), *Between power and plenty: Foreign economic policies of advanced industrial states*, Madison, University of Wisconsin Press, 1978. vii, 344 pp.
470 KORPI, Walter, 'Economic growth and the welfare state: leaky bucket or irrigation system?', *European Sociological Review*, 1, 1985: 97-118.
471 KRASNER, Stephen D., *Defending the national interest: Raw material investments and US foreign policy*, Princeton, N.J., Princeton University Press, 1978. xiii, 404 pp.
472 LANCASTER, Kelvin, 'The dynamic inefficiency of capitalism', *Journal of Political Economy*, 81, 1973: 1092-109.
473 LANDES, David M., 'French business and the businessman: a social and cultural analysis' in: E.M. Earle (ed.), *Modern France: Problems of the third and fourth republic*, Princeton, Princeton University Press, 1951: 334-53.
474 LASH, Scott and John URRY, 'The new marxism of collective action: a critical analysis', *Sociology*, 18, 1, 1984: 33-50.
475 LENIN, V.I., *The development of capitalism in Russia: The process of the formation of a home-market for large-scale industry*, Moscow: Foreign Languages Publishing House, 1956. xvi, 751 pp. [Originally appeared in 1899.]
476 LENIN, V.I., *Imperialism, the highest stage of capitalism: A popular outlook*, New York: International Publishers, 1939. v, 138 pp. [Originally appeared in 1917.]
477 LUKACS, Georg, *History and class consciousness: Studies in marxist dialectics*, Cambridge, MIT Press, 1971. xlvi, 356 pp. [Originally appeared in 1923; see especially 'Reification and the consciousness of the proletariat'.]
478 LUXEMBURG, Rosa, *The accumulation of capital*, London, Routledge and Kegan Paul, 1951. 475 pp. [Originally appeared in 1913.]
479 MAKLER, Harry, Arnaud SALES and Neil J. SMELSER,

'Recent trends in theory and methodology in the study of economy and society' in: T. Bottomore, S. Nowak and M. Sokolowska (eds), *Sociology: the state of the art*, Beverly Hills, Ca., SAGE Publications, 1982: 147-71.

480 MARGLIN, Stephen A., 'What do bosses do? The origins and functions of hierarchy in capitalist production' in: A. Giddens and D. Held (eds), *Classes, power, and conflict: classical and contemporary debates*, London, Macmillan, 1982. [Originally appeared in 1974–75.]

481 MARGLIN, Stephen A., *Growth, distribution, prices*, Cambridge, Mass., Harvard University Press, 1984. 573 pp.

482 MILIBAND, Ralph, *The state in capitalist society: The analysis of the Western system of power*, London, Quartet Books, 1978. 262 pp. [Originally appeared in 1969.]

483 MINTZ, Beth and Michael SCHWARTZ, *The power structure of American business*, Chicago, University of Chicago Press, 1985. xix, 327 pp.

484 MINTZ, Beth and Michael SCHWARTZ, 'Capital flows and the process of financial hegemony', *Theory and Society*, 1986 (forthcoming).

485 MIZRUCHI, Mark S., *The American corporate network*, Beverly Hills, Ca., SAGE Publications, 1982. 216 pp.

486 O'CONNOR, James, *The fiscal crisis of the state*, New York, St. Martin's Press, 1973. 276 pp.

487 OFFE, Claus and Volker RONGE, 'Theses on the theory of the state', *New German Critique*, 6, 1975: 137-47.

488 OFFE, Claus and Helmut WIESENTHAL, 'Two logics of collective action: theoretical notes on social class and organizational form' in: M. Zeitlin (ed.), *Political Power and Social Class*, 1, 1980: 67-115.

489 VAN PARIJS, Philippe, 'Sociology as general economics', *Archives Européennes de Sociologie*, 2, 1981: 299-324.

490 PETERSEN, Trond, 'Class and exploitation: description and ethics — notes on John Roemer's *General theory of Exploitation and Class*', *Acta Sociologica*, 27, 4, 1984: 323-37.

491 POLITICS AND SOCIETY, 'Symposium on John Roemer', 11, 3, 1982: 251-394.

492 POULANTZAS, Nicos, *Political power and social classes*, London, NLB, 1973. 367 pp. [Originally appeared in 1968.]

493 PRZEWORSKI, Adam, 'Material bases of consent:

economics and politics in a hegemonic system', *Political Power and Social Theory*, 1, 1980: 21-66.

494 PRZEWORSKI, Adam, 'Material interests, class compromise, and the transition to socialism', *Politics and Society*, 10, 2, 1980: 125-53.

495 PRZEWORSKI, Adam, *Capitalism and social democracy*, Cambridge, Cambridge University Press, 1985. viii, 269 pp.

496 PRZEWORSKI, Adam and Michael WALLERSTEIN, 'The structure of class conflict in democratic capitalist societies', *American Political Science Review*, 76, 1, 1982: 215-38.

497 ROEMER, John E., *A general theory of exploitation and class*, Cambridge, Harvard University Press, 1982. ix, 298 pp.

498 ROEMER, John E., 'New directions in the marxian theory of exploitation and class', *Politics and Society*, 11, 3, 1982: 253-87.

499 ROEMER, John E., 'Exploitation, class, and property relations' in: T. Ball and J. Farr (eds), *After Marx*, Cambridge, Cambridge University Press, 1984: 184-211.

500 ROY, Donald, *Restriction of output in a piecework machine shop*, Ph.D. dissertation, University of Chicago, 1952.

501 SARFATTI LARSON, Magali, *The rise of professionalism: a sociological analysis*, Berkeley, Ca., University of California Press, 1977. xviii, 309 pp.

502 SCHUMPETER, Joseph A., 'The *communist manifesto* in sociology and economics', *Journal of Political Economy*, 57, 1949: 199-212.

503 SCHUMPETER, Joseph A., 'March into socialism', *American Economic Review*, 40, 1950: 446-56.

504 SCHWARTZ, Michael, Letter to Richard Swedberg dated 18 April 1986.

505 SKOCPOL, Theda, *States and social revolutions: A comparative analysis of France, Russia, and China*, Cambridge, Cambridge University Press, 1979. xvii, 406 pp.

506 SKOCPOL, Theda, 'Bringing the state back in: strategies of analysis in current research' in: P.E. Evans, D. Rueschemeyer and T. Skocpol (eds), *Bringing the state back in*, Cambridge, Cambridge University Press, 1985: 3-37.

507 SMITH, Michael R., 'Accounting for inflation in Britain', *British Journal of Sociology*, 33, 3, 1982: 301-30.

508 STEPAN, Alfred, *The state and society: Peru in comparative*

perspective, Princeton, N.J., Princeton University Press, 1978. xix, 348 pp.

509 SWEEZY, Paul M., *The theory of capitalist development*, New York, Monthly Review Press, 1970. ix, 398 pp. [Originally appeared in 1942.]

510 THERBORN, Göran, *Klasser och ekonomiska system (Classes and economic systems)*, Kristianstad, Zenit, 1971. 334 pp.

511 THERBORN, Göran, 'Class analysis: history and defense' in: U. Himmelstrand (ed.), *Sociology: from crisis to science*, Beverly Hills, Ca., SAGE Publications, 1986 (forthcoming).

512 THERBORN, Göran, *Why some people are more unemployed than others*, London, Verso, 1986. 160 pp.

513 THERBORN, Göran, Letter to Richard Swedberg dated 27 March 1986.

514 THOMPSON E.P., *The making of the English working class*, New York, Pantheon, 1963. 848 pp.

515 THOMPSON, E.P., 'The moral economy of the English crowd in the eighteenth century', *Past & Present*, 50, 1971: 76-136.

516 TRIMBERGER, Ellen Kay, *Revolutions from above: Military bureaucrats and developments in Japan, Turkey, Egypt and Peru*, New Brunswick, N.J., Transaction Books, 1978. viii, 196 pp.

517 USEEM, Michael, 'The social organization of the American business elite and participation of corporate directors in the governance of American institutions', *American Sociological Review*, 44, 4, 1979: 553-71.

518 USEEM, Michael, *The inner circle: large corporations and the rise of business political activity in the US and UK*, New York, Oxford University Press, 1984. xii, 246 pp.

519 WEISSKOPF, Thomas E., Samuel BOWLES and David M. GORDON, 'Hearts and minds: a social model of US productivity growth', *Brookings Papers on Economic Activities*, 2, 1983: 381-450.

520 WESTERGAARD, John, 'Sociology: the myth of classlessness' in: R. Blackburn (ed.), *Ideology in social science: readings in critical social theory*, New York, Vintage Books, 1973: 119-63.

521 WILENSKY, Harold L., *The welfare state and equality: Structural and ideological roots of public expenditures*,

Berkeley, Ca., University of California Press, 1975. xvii, 151 pp.

522 WILENSKY, Harold L., *The 'new corporatism', centralization and the welfare state*, Beverly Hills, Ca., SAGE Publications, 1976. 73 pp.

523 WRIGHT, Erik Olin, *Class, crisis and the state*, London, NLB, 1978. 266 pp.

524 WRIGHT, Erik Olin, *Class structure and income determination*, New York, Academic Press, 1979. xxvi, 271 pp.

525 WRIGHT, Erik Olin, 'A general framework for the analysis of class structure', *Politics and Society*, 13, 4, 1984: 383-423.

526 WRIGHT, Erik Olin, *Classes*, London, Verso, 1985. 291 pp.

527 WRIGHT, Erik Olin et al., 'The American class structure', *American Sociological Review*, 47, 1982: 709-22.

528 ZEITLIN, Maurice, 'Corporate ownership and control: the large corporation and the capitalist class', *American Journal of Sociology*, 79, 5, 1974: 1073-119.

529 ZEITLIN, Maurice, 'On class theory and the large corporation: Response to Allen', *American Journal of Sociology*, 81, 4, 1976: 894-903.

530 ZEITLIN, Maurice and Samuel NORICH, 'Management control, exploitation, and profit maximization in the large corporation: an empirical confrontation of managerialism and class theory', *Research in Political Economy*, 2, 1979: 33-62.

(7) The International Dimension

531 AMIN, Samir, *Accumulation on a world scale*, New York, Monthly Review Press, 1974. 2 vols, 666 pp. [Originally published in 1970.]

532 AMIN, Samir, *L'Afrique de l'ouest bloquée: l'économie politique de la colonisation, 1880–1970*, Paris, Editions de Minuit, 1971. 324 pp.

533 AMIN, Samir, Letter to Ulf Himmelstrand dated 30 December 1985.

534 ARNDT, H.W., 'The origins of structuralism', *World Development*, 13, 2, 1985: 151-59.

535 BARTH, Fredrik, 'Introduktion till "Entreprenörens roll i social förändring i norra Norge"' (Introduction to 'The role of the entrepreneur in Northern Norway') in: F. Barth, *Socialantropologiska problem*, Stockholm, Prisma, 1971: 174-92. [Originally appeared in 1963.]

536 BARTH, Fredrik, 'Kapital, investeringar och social struktur hos en pastoral nomadgrupp i södra Persien' (Capital, investments and social structure in a pastoral group of nomads in Southern Persia) in: F. Barth, *Socialantropologiska problem*, Prisma, Stockholm, 1971: 193-208. [Originally appeared in 1964.]

537 BARTH, Fredrik, 'Economic spheres in Darfur' in: R. Firth (ed.), *Themes in economic anthropology*, London, Tavistock Publications, 1970: 149-74. [Originally appeared in 1967.]

538 BELSHAW, Cyril S., *Traditional exchange and modern markets*, Englewood Cliffs, Prentice-Hall, 1965. viii, 149 pp.

539 BENDIX, Reinhard, 'Tradition and modernity reconsidered', *Comparative Studies in Society and History*, 9, 1967: 292-346.

540 BLOMSTRÖM, Magnus and Björn HETTNE, *Beroende och underutveckling. Den latinamerikanska beroendeskolans bidrag till utvecklingsteorin (Dependency and underdevelopment: The contribution by the Latin American school of dependency to the theory of development)*, Stockholm, Prisma, 1981. 289 pp.

541 BOOTH, David, 'Marxism and development sociology: interpreting the impasse', *World Development*, 13, 7, 1985: 761-87.

542 BORNSCHIER, Volker and Christopher CHASE-DUNN, *Transnational corporations and underdevelopment*, New York, Praeger, 1985. xii, 179 pp.

543 BRENNER, Robert, 'The origin of capitalist development: a critique of neo-smithian marxism', *New Left Review*, 104, 1977: 25-92.

544 BREWER, Anthony, *Marxist theories of imperialism: a critical survey*, London, Routledge & Kegan Paul, 1980. xi, 308 pp.

545 CARDOSO, Fernando H., *Empresario industrial e desenvolvimento economico no Brasil (Industrial entrepreneurs and economic development in Brazil)*, Sao Paulo, Difusao Europeia do Livro, 1964. 196 pp.

546 CARDOSO, Fernando H., 'The industrial elite' in S.M. Lipset and A. Solari (eds), *Elites in Latin America*, New York, Oxford University Press, 1967: 94-114.

547 CARDOSO, Fernando H., 'The consumption of dependency theory in the United States', *Latin America Research Review*, 12, 3, 1977: 7-24.

548 CARDOSO, Fernando H., 'The originality of a copy: CEPAL and the idea of development', *CEPAL review*, 2nd half, 1977: 7-40.

549 CHASE-DUNN, Christopher, 'The uses of formal comparative research in dependency theory and the world-system perspective' in: H. Makler, A. Martinelli and N.J. Smelser (eds), *The new international economy*, Beverly Hills, Ca., SAGE Publications, 1982: 117-37.

550 CHIROT, Daniel, 'Changing fashions in the study of the social causes of economic and political change' in: J.F. Short (ed.), *The state of sociology: Problems and prospects*, Beverly Hills, Ca., SAGE Publications, 1981: 259-82.

551 DI MARCO, Luis Eugenio (ed.), *International economics and development: Essays in honor of Raul Prebisch*, New York, Academic Press, 1972. 515 pp.

552 DOS SANTOS, Theotonio, 'The structure of dependence', *American Economic Review*, 60, 2, 1970: 231-36.

553 ECLA (UNITED NATIONS. ECONOMIC COMMISSION FOR LATIN AMERICA), *Development problems in Latin America*, Austin, Texas, University of Texas Press, 1970. xlviii, 318 pp. [A collection of the major ECLA texts.]

554 EMMANUAL, Arghiri, *Unequal exchange: a study of the imperialism of trade*, New York, Monthly Review, 1972. [Originally published in 1969.]

555 EVANS, Peter, *Dependent development: The alliance of multinational, state and local capital in Brazil*, Princeton, Princeton University Press, 1979. xviii, 362 pp.

556 EVANS, Peter, 'Recent research on multinational corporations', *Annual Review of Sociology*, 7, 1981: 199-213.

557 EVANS, Peter, Dietrich RUESCHEMEYER and Evelyne Huber STEPHENS (eds), *States versus markets in the world-system*, Beverly Hills, Ca., SAGE Publications, 1975. 295 pp.

558 EVANS, Peter, et al., *Report of the working group on the*

internationalization of social, political and economic life, 31 July 1985. 32 pp.

559 FOSTER-CARTER, Aidan, 'The modes of production controversy', *New Left Review*, 107, 1978: 47-77.

560 FRANK, André Gunder, 'Sociology of development and underdevelopment of sociology' in: A.G. Frank, *Latin America: underdevelopment or revolution*, New York, Monthly Review Press, 1970: 21-94. [Originally appeared in 1966.]

561 FRANK, André Gunder, *Capitalism and underdevelopment in Latin America: historical studies of Chile and Brazil*, New York, Monthly Review Press, 1967. xx, 298 pp.

562 FRANK, André Gunder, *Latin America: Underdevelopment or revolution*, New York, Monthly Review Press, 1969. xviii, 409 pp.

563 FRENKEL, Roberto and Guillermo O'DONNELL, 'The "stabilization programs" of the International Monetary Fund and their internal impacts' in: R.R. Fagen (ed.), *Capitalism and the state in US-Latin American relations*, Stanford, Stanford University Press, 1979: 171-216.

564 GARST, Daniel, 'Wallerstein and his critics', *Theory and Society*, 14, 4, 1985: 469-95.

565 GEERTZ, Clifford, *Agricultural involution: The processes of ecological change in Indonesia*, Chicago, University of Chicago Press, 1963. xx, 176 pp.

566 GEERTZ, Clifford, *Peddlers and princes: social change and economic modernization in two Indonesian towns*, Chicago, University of Chicago Press, 1963. viii, 162 pp.

567 GEERTZ, Clifford, 'The bazaar economy: information and search in peasant marketing', *American Economic Review*, 68, 2, 1978: 28-32.

568 GEERTZ, Clifford, 'Suq: the bazaar economy in Sefrou' in L. Rosen et al. (eds), *Meaning and order in Moroccan society: three essays in cultural analysis*, New York, Cambridge University Press, 1979: 123-314.

569 GERSCHENKRON, Alexander, *Economic backwardness in historical perspective: a book of essays*, Cambridge, Mass., Harvard University Press, 1962. 456 pp.

570 GOUREVITCH, Peter, 'The international system and regime formation', *Comparative Politics*, 10, 3, 1978: 419-38.

571 GRIFFIN, Keith and John GURLEY, 'Radical analyses of imperialism, the third world, and the transition to socialism', *Journal of Economic Literature*, 23, 1985: 1089-143.

572 HABERLER, Gottfried, 'International trade and economic development', in: G.W. Betz and N.K. Choudhry (eds), *Readings in economic development*, Belmont, Ca., Wadsworth Publishing Co., 1963: 240-49.

573 HETTNE, Björn, *Development theory and the third world*, Stockholm, SAREC (R 2:1982), 1982. 168 pp.

574 HIRSCHMAN, Albert O., 'Ideologies of economic development in Latin America' in: A.O. Hirschman, *A bias for hope: essays on development and Latin America*, New Haven, Yale University Press, 1971: 260-311. [Originally appeared in 1961.]

575 HIRSCHMAN, Albert O., 'The turn to authoritarianism in Latin America and the search for its economic determinants' in: D. Collier (ed.), *The new authoritarianism in Latin America*, Princeton University Press, 1979: 61-98.

576 HOSELITZ, Bert F., 'Economic growth, noneconomic aspects' in *International Encyclopaedia of the Social Sciences*, New York, Macmillan, 1968, vol. 4: 422-29.

577 HOSELITZ, Bert F., *Sociological aspects of economic growth*, Glencoe, Ill., The Free Press, 1960. 250 pp.

578 INTERNATIONAL SOCIOLOGICAL ASSOCIATION (ISA), *Economy and society directory*. 1986. 73 pp.

579 JAMESON, Kenneth P., 'Latin American structuralism: a methodological perspective', *World Development*, 14, 2, 1986: 223-32.

580 KAHL, Joseph A., *Modernization, exploitation and dependency in Latin America: Germani, Gonzales Casanova and Cardoso*, New Brunswick, Transaction Books, 1976. 215 pp.

581 KUZNETS, Simon, 'The state as a unit in the study of economic growth', *Journal of Economic History*, 2, 1951: 25-41.

582 LERNER, Daniel, 'Modernization, social aspects' in: *International Encyclopaedia of the Social Sciences*. New York, Macmillan, 1968, vol. 10: 386-95.

583 MOSELEY, K.P., Letter to Ulf Himmelstrand dated 24 January 1986.

584 NORTH AMERICAN CONGRESS ON LATIN AMERICA

(NACLA), *Subliminal warfare: The role of Latin American studies*, New York, NACLA, 1970. 63 pp.

585 O'DONNELL, Guillermo, 'Reflections on the pattern of change in the bureaucratic-authoritarian state', *Latin American Research Review*, 13, 1, 1978: 3-38. [Originally appeared in 1975.]

586 PAYER, Cheryl, *The debt trap: the International Monetary Fund and the third world*, New York, Monthly Review Press, 1974. xiii, 251.

587 PAYER, Cheryl, *The World Bank: a critical analysis*, New York, Monthly Review Press, 1982. 414 pp.

588 PORTES, Alejandro, 'Modernity and development: a critique', *Studies in Comparative International Development*, 7, 3, 1973: 247-79.

589 PORTES, Alejandro, 'International labor migration and national development' in: M.M. Kritz (ed.), *US immigration and refugee policy*, Lexington, Lexington Books, 1982: 71-91.

590 PREBISCH, Raul, 'The economic development of Latin America and its principal problems', *Economic Bulletin for Latin America*, 7, 1, 1962: 1-22. .[Originally appeared in 1950.]

591 PREBISCH, Raul, 'Cinco etapas de mi pensamiento sobre el desarollo' (The five stages of my thinking on development), *El Trimestre Económico*, April-June 1983: 1077-96.

592 ROKKAN, Stein, 'Eine Familie von Modellen für die vergleichende Geschichte Europas' (A group of models for the comparative history of Europe), *Zeitschrift für Soziologie*, 9, 2, 1980: 118-28.

593 ROKKAN, Stein and Derek W. URWIN, (eds) *Economy, territory, identity: politics of West European peripheries*, Beverly Hills, Ca., SAGE Publications, 1983. 217 pp.

594 SEERS, Dudley, 'A theory of inflation and growth in underdeveloped economies based on the experience of Latin America', *Oxford Economic Papers*, 14, 2, 1962: 173-95.

595 SEERS, Dudley, *The congruence of marxism and other neoclassical doctrines*, Brighton, Institute of Development Studies at the University of Sussex Discussion Paper (DP 136), 1978. 20 pp.

596 SHOUP, Laurence H. and William MINTER, *Imperial brain trust: the Council on Foreign Relations and United States*

foreign policy, New York, Monthly Review Press, 1977. x, 334 pp.

597 SINGER, Hans, 'The distribution of gains between investing and borrowing countries', *American Economic Review*, 40, 2, 1950: 472-85.

598 SKOCPOL, Theda, 'Wallerstein's world capitalist system: a theoretical and historical critique', *American Journal of Sociology*, 82, 5, 1977: 1075-90.

599 SPRAOS, John, *Inequalizing trade?*, Oxford, Oxford University Press, 1983. ix, 169 pp.

600 STALLINGS, Barbara, 'Peru and US banks: privatization of financial relations' in: R.R. Fagen (ed.), *Capitalism and the state in US-Latin American relations*, Stanford, Stanford University Press, 1979: 171-216.

601 STALLINGS, Barbara, 'Euromarkets, third world countries and the international political economy' in: H. Makler, A. Martinelli and N.J. Smelser (eds), *The new international economy*, Beverly Hills, Ca., SAGE Publications, 1982: 193-230.

602 STREET, James H., 'The Latin American "structuralists" and the institutionalists: convergence in development theory' in: W.J. Samuels (ed.), *The economy as a system of power: papers from the Journal of Economic Issues*, New Brunswick, Transaction Books, 1979, vol. 1: 34-52.

603 UNITED NATIONS, *Economic survey of Latin America 1949*, New York, United Nations, 1951.

604 VALENZUELA, J. Samuel and Arturo VALENZUELA, 'Modernization and dependency: alternative perspectives in the study of Latin American underdevelopment', *Comparative Politics*, 10, 4, 1978: 535-57.

605 VINER, Jacob, *International trade and economic development*, New York, The Free Press, 1952. 154 pp.

606 WALLERSTEIN, Immanuel, 'Modernization: requiescat in pace' in: L.A. Coser and O.N. Larsen (eds), *The uses of controversy in sociology*, New York, The Free Press, 1976: 131-35.

607 WALLERSTEIN, Immanuel, Letter to Richard Swedberg dated 30 December 1985.

608 WARREN, Bill, 'Imperialism and capitalist industrialization', *New Left Review*, 81, 1973: 3-44.

609 WERKER, Scott, 'Beyond the dependency paradigm',

Journal of Contemporary Asia, 15, 1, 1985: 79-95.
610 WOOD, Robert E., 'Foreign aid and the capitalist state in underdeveloped countries', *Politics and Society*, 10, 1, 1980: 1-34.
611 WOOD, Robert E., 'The aid regime and international debt: crisis and structural adjustment', *Development and Change*, 16, 2, 1985: 179-212.

(8) The Sociology of Markets

612 ABOLAFIA, Mitchel Y., 'Structured anarchy: formal organization in the commodities futures market' in: P.A. Adler and P. Adler (eds), *The social dynamics of financial markets*, Greenwich, Conn., JAI Press, 1984: 129-50.
613 ADLER Patricia A. and Peter ADLER, 'The market as collective behavior' in: P.A. Adler and P. Adler (eds), *The social dynamics of financial markets*, Greenwich, Conn., JAI Press, 1984: 85-105.
614 ARROW, Kenneth J., 'Gifts and exchanges', *Philosophy and Public Affairs*, 1, 4, 1972: 343-62.
615 BAKER, Wayne E., 'Floor trading and crowd dynamic' in: P.A. Adler and P. Adler (eds), *The social dynamics of financial markets*, Greenwich, Conn., JAI Press, 1984: 107-28.
616 BAKER, Wayne E., 'The social structure of a national securities market', *American Journal of Sociology*, 89, 4, 1984: 775-811.
617 BARBER, Bernard, 'Absolutization of the market: some notes on how we got from there to here' in: G. Dworkin (ed.), *Markets and morals*, New York, John Wiley & Sons, 1977: 15-31.
618 BLUESTONE, Barry, 'The tripartite economy: labor markets and the working poor' *Poverty and Human Resources Abstract*, 5, 1970: 15-35.
619 BURNS, Tom and Helena FLAM, 'A theory of markets: their social structure and performance properties', Unpublished paper, Department of Sociology, Uppsala University, 1986. [A similar version will be published in 1986 in Tom Burns, *The shaping of social organization*.]
620 BURT, Ronald S., *Toward a structural theory of action:*

network models of social structure, perception, and action, New York, Academic Press, 1982. 381 pp. [See especially chs. 4 and 8 on 'Stratification in American Manufacturing' and 'Market Constraints and Directorate Ties with respect to Manufacturing Industries'.]

621 BURT, Ronald S., *Corporate profits and cooptation: networks of market constraints and directorate ties in the American economy*, New York, Academic Press, 1983. xv, 331 pp.

622 BURT, Ronald S., 'The stability of American markets', Paper presented at the meeting of the American Sociological Association, Washington D.C., August 1985.

623 CHAMBERLIN, Edward H., *The theory of monopolistic competition*, Cambridge, Mass., Harvard University Press, 1933. x, 213 pp.

624 CHAMBERLIN, Edward H., 'The origin and early development of monopolistic competition theory', *Quarterly Journal of Economics*, 75, 4, 1961: 515-43.

625 DAHRENDORF, Ralf, 'Market and plan: two types of rationality', in: R. Dahrendorf, *Essays in the theory of society*, Stanford, Stanford University Press, 1968: 214-31.

626 ESPING-ANDERSEN, Gösta, 'Politics against markets: decommodification in social policy', Paper presented at the Arne Rude Symposium, Lund, 1981.

627 ESPING-ANDERSEN, Gösta, *Politics against markets: the social democratic road to power*, Princeton, Princeton University Press, 1985. xix, 366 pp.

628 ETZIONI, Amitai, 'Encapsulated competition', *Journal of Post Keynesian Studies*, 7, 3, 1985: 287-302.

629 ETZIONI, Amitai, 'The political economy of imperfect competition' *Journal of Public Policy*, 5, 2, 1985: 169-86.

630 FLAM, Helena, 'Toward a framework for socio-economic studies', Paper presented at the Social Science Theory-Methodology Workshop in Amsterdam, 29–30 November 1985.

631 GERSHUNY, Jonathan, *After industrial society? — the emerging self-service economy*, London, Macmillan, 1978. 181 pp.

632 GERSHUNY, Jonathan, 'The informal economy: its role in post- industrial society', *Futures*, 11, 1, 1979: 3-15.

633 GORDON, David M., *Theories of poverty and*

underemployment, Lexington, Mass., Heath, 1972. 177 pp.
634 GRANOVETTER, Mark, 'Towards a sociological theory of income differences', in: I. Berg (ed.), *Sociological perspectives on labor markets*, New York, Academic Press, 1981: 11-47.
635 GRANT, Wyn (ed.), *The political economy of corporatism*, London, Macmillan, 1985. xiv, 274 pp.
636 HAWLEY, James P., 'Protecting capital from itself: US attempts to regulate the eurocurrency system', *International Organization*, 38, 5, 1984: 131-65.
637 HECHTER, Michael, 'Karl Polanyi's social theory: a critique' in: M. Hechter (ed.), *The microfoundations of macrosociology*, Philadelphia, Temple University Press, 1983: 158-89.
638 HEDSTRÖM, Peter, 'From political sociology to political economy: the sociology of politics and the paradigm crisis', in: U. Himmelstrand (ed.), *Sociology — from crisis to science*, Beverly Hills, SAGE Publications, 1986 (forthcoming).
639 HEDSTRÖM, Peter 'Organisationsstruktur och lönebildning: en ekonomisk-sociologisk analys' (Organizational structure and wage formation: a study in economic sociology), *Sociologisk Forskning*, 23, 1, 1986: 6-17.
640 HEINEMANN, Klaus, 'Elemente einer Soziologie des Marktes' (Elements of a sociology of the market), *Kölner Zeitschrift für Soziologie und Sozialpsychologie*, 28, 1, 1976: 48-69.
641 HERNES, Gudmund, *Okonomisk organisering (Economic organization)*, Bergen, Universitetsforlaget, 1982. 217 pp.
642 HIRSCHMAN, Albert O., 'Rival interpretations of market society: civilizing, destructive, or feeble?', *Journal of Economic Literature*, 20, 1982: 1463-84.
643 HORAN, Patrick M., E.M. BECK and Charles M. TOLBERT II, 'The market homogeneity assumption: on the theoretical foundations of empirical knowledge', *Social Science Quarterly*, 61, 2, 1980: 278-92.
644 KALLEBERG, Arne L. and Aage B. SORENSEN, 'The sociology of labor markets', *Annual Review of Sociology*, 5, 1979: 351-79.
645 KERR, Clark, 'The balkanization of labor markets' in: E.W. Bakke et al. (eds), *Labor mobility and economic*

opportunity, Cambridge, Mass., The MIT Press, 1954: 94-110.

646 KINDLEBERGER, Charles P., *Manias, panics, and crashes: a history of financial crisis*, New York, Basic Books, 1978. 271 pp.

647 KORPI, Walter and Rune ABERG, *Marknad eller politik? — Om de politiska alternativen i 80-talets Sverige (Market or politics? — On the political alternatives in Sweden during the 80s),* Stockholm, LO, 1985. 80 pp.

648 LEBLEBICI, Huseyin, and Gerald R. SALANCIK, 'Stability in interorganizational exchanges: rulemaking processes of the Chicago Board of Trade', *Administrative Science Quarterly*, 27, 1982: 227-42.

649 LEIFER, Eric M., and Harrison C. WHITE, 'A structural approach to markets' in: M. Schwartz and M. Mizruchi (eds), *Structural analysis of business*, New York, Academic Press, 1987 (forthcoming).

650 LINDBERG, Leon N., 'The problems of economic theory in explaining economic performance', *Annals*, 459, 1982: 14-27.

651 LINDBLOM, Charles E., 'The rediscovery of the market', *Public Interest*, 4, Winter 1966: 89-101.

652 LINDBLOM, Charles E., *Politics and markets: the world's political-economic systems*, New York, Basic Books, 1977. xi, 401 pp.

653 LINDBLOM, Charles E., 'Epilogue' in: H. Makler, A. Martinelli and N.J. Smelser (eds), *The new international economy*, Beverly Hills, SAGE Publications, 1982: 323-33.

654 PETERSEN, Trond, 'Incentives and wage inequality: the case of selling employees in department stores', Unpublished paper, Harvard University, Cambridge, Mass., December 1985.

655 PIORE, Michael J., 'Fragments of a "sociological" theory of wages', *American Economic Review*, 63, 1973: 377-84.

656 PIORE, Michael J., 'Notes for a theory of labor market stratification' in: R.C. Edwards, M. Reich and D.M. Gordon, *Labor market segmentation*, Lexington, Mass., Heath, 1975: 125-50.

657 ROBINSON, Joan, *The economics of imperfect competition*, London, Macmillan, 1933. xii, 352 pp.

658 ROTSCHILD, Michael and Joseph STIGLITZ,

'Equilibrium in competitive insurance markets: an essay on the economics of imperfect competition' *Quarterly Journal of Economics*, 1976, 40: 629-49.

659 SIK, Endre '"Small is useful" or the reciprocal exchange of labour' in: P. Galasi and G. Sziraczki (eds), *Labour market and second economy in Hungary*, Frankfurt, Campus Verlag, 1985: 179-214.

660 SORENSEN, Aage B., 'Theory and methodology in stratification research' in: U. Himmelstrand (ed.), *Sociology — from crisis to science*, Beverly Hills, Ca., SAGE Publications, 1986 (forthcoming).

661 SPENCE, A. Michael, *Market signalling: informational transfer in hiring and related screening processes*, Cambridge, Mass., Harvard University Press, 1974. viii, 221 pp.

662 STEARNS, Linda, *Corporate dependency and the structure of the capital market, 1880–1980*, Ph.D. dissertation, State University of New York at Stony Brook, 1982.

663 TITMUSS, Richard M., *The gift relationship: from human blood to social policy*, New York, Vintage Books, 1972. 339 pp. [Originally appeared in 1971.]

664 WHITE, Harrison C., 'Subcontracting with an oligopoly: Spence revisited'. Harvard University (RIAS Program Working paper No. 1), 1976.

665 WHITE, Harrison C., 'Markets and hierarchies revisited', Unpublished paper, Harvard University, Department of Sociology, 1978.

666 WHITE, Harrison C., 'Markets as social structures', Talk at the annual meeting of the American Sociological Association, Boston, 28 August 1979.

667 WHITE, Harrison C., 'On markets', Cambridge, Harvard University (RIAS Program Working Paper No. 16), 1979.

668 WHITE, Harrison C., 'Production markets as induced role structures' in: Samuel Leinhardt (ed.), *Sociological methodology 1981*, San Francisco, Jossey-Bass Publishers, 1981: 1-59.

669 ZELIZER, Viviana A. Rotman, 'Human values and the market: the case of life insurance and death in 19th century America', *American Journal of Sociology*, 84, 3, 1978: 591-610.

670 ZELIZER, Viviana A. Rotman, *Morals and markets: the*

development of life insurance in the United States, New York, Columbia University Press, 1979. 208 pp.

671 ZELIZER, Viviana A. Rotman, *Pricing the priceless child: the changing social value of children*, New York, Basic Books, 1985. 277 pp.

(9) The New Relationship between Economics and Sociology

672 ALBERT, Hans, *Marktsoziologie und Entscheidungslogik: ökonomische Probleme in soziologischer Perspektive (The sociology of the market and the logic of decisions: economic problems from a sociological perspective)*, Neuwied am Rhein, Luchterhand, 1967. 531 pp.

673 ALBERT, Hans, 'The economic tradition: economics as a research programme for theoretical social science' in: K. Brunner (ed.), *Economics & social institutions*, Boston, Martinus Nijhoff, 1979: 1-27.

674 ALLEN, Sheila and Brian BURLKITT (eds), *The sociology of economic life*, Brighton, Wheatsheaf Publishers, 1987 (forthcoming).

675 ARROW, Kenneth J., 'The economic implications of learning by doing', *Review of Economic Studies*, 29, 1962: 155-73.

676 ARROW, Kenneth J., 'Uncertainty and the welfare economics of medical care', *American Economic Review*, 53, 5, 1963: 941-73.

677 ARROW, Kenneth J., 'Models of job discrimination' in: A.H. Pascal (ed.), *Racial discrimination in economic life*, Lexington, Lexington Books, 1972: 83-102.

678 ARROW, Kenneth J., *The limits of organization*, New York, W.W. Norton & Co., 1974. 86 pp.

679 ARROW, Kenneth J., Letter to Richard Swedberg dated 22 July 1986.

680 BARBER, Bernard, *The logic and limits of trust*, New Brunswick, Rutgers University Press, 1983. 190 pp.

681 BARRY, Brian, *Sociologists, economists and democracy*, London, Collier-Macmillian Limited, 1970. vi, 201 pp.

682 BECKER, Gary S., *The economics of discrimination: a theoretical and empirical analysis with special reference to education*, Chicago, Chicago University Press, 1957. x, 137 pp.

683 BECKER, Gary S., *Human capital*, New York, Columbia University Press, 1964. xvi, 187 pp.
684 BIELBY, William T., 'Review essay: imperatives of the enterprise — Stinchcombe's techno-marxism', *American Journal of Sociology*, 90, 1, 1984: 192-96.
685 BLOCK, Fred L., 'Postindustrial development and the obsolescence of economic categories', *Politics & Society*, 14, 1, 1985: 71-104.
686 BLOCK, Fred L., Letter to Richard Swedberg dated 7 April 1986.
687 BOUDON, Raymond, *Education, opportunity and social inequality: changing perspectives in Western society*, New York, Wiley, 1974. 220 pp.
688 BOUDON, Raymond, *The unintended consequences of social action*, London, Macmillan, 1982. 232 pp.
689 BOULDING, Kenneth, 'Economics as a moral science' in: K. Boulding, *Economics as a science*, New York, McGraw-Hill, 1970: 117-57 [Originally appeared in 1969.]
690 BRUYN, Severyn, *The social economy: people transforming modern business*, New York, Wiley, 1977. xxii, 392 pp.
691 BRUYN, Severyn, *The field of social investment*, Cambridge, Cambridge University Press, 1986 (forthcoming).
692 BUCHANAN, James M. and Gordon TULLOCK, *The calculus of consent*, Ann Arbor, University of Michigan Press, 1972. 361 pp.
693 CARROLL, Glenn R., 'A stochastic model of organizational mortality: review and reanalysis', *Social Science Research*, 12, 1983: 303-29.
694 CARROLL, Glenn R., 'Organizational ecology', *Annual Review of Sociology*, 10, 1984: 71-93.
695 CARROLL, Glenn R. and Yangchung Paul HUO, 'Organizational task and institutional environment in ecological perspective: findings from the local newspaper industry', *American Journal of Sociology*, 91, 4, 1986: 838-73.
696 CARROLL, Glenn R., *Publish and perish: a dynamic analysis of organizational mortality in the newspaper industries of Argentine, Ireland and the United States*, Greenwich, Conn., JAI Press, 1986 (forthcoming).
697 COATS, A.W., 'The sociology of knowledge and the history

of economics', *Research in the History of Economic Thought*, 2, 1984: 211-34.
698 COLEMAN, James S., 'Social inventions', *Social Forces*, 49, 2, 1970: 163-73.
699 COLEMAN, James S., *The mathematics of collective action*, Chicago, Aldine, 1973. 191 pp.
700 COLEMAN, James S., 'Introducing social structure into economic analysis', *American Economic Review*, 74, 2, 1984: 84-88.
701 COSER, Lewis, 'Review of Karl-Dieter Opp, *Die Entstehung sozialer Normen*', *Contemporary Sociology*, 14, 3, 1985: 407-08.
702 DEVINE, P.J. et al., *An introduction to industrial economics*, London, George Allen & Unwin, 1979. xi, 502 pp.
703 DOWNS, Anthony, *An economic theory of democracy*, New York, Harper & Row, 1957. 310 pp.
704 DUESENBERRY, James, 'Comments on "an economic analysis of fertility" by Gary Becker' in: Universities-National Bureau Committee for Economic research (ed.), *Demographic and change in developed countries*, Princeton, Princeton University Press, 1960: 231-40.
705 ECCLES, Robert, 'Transfer pricing, fairness and control'. Working Paper no. HBS 83-167, Cambridge, Mass., Harvard Business School, 1983.
706 ELSTER, Jon, *Logic and society: contradictions and possible worlds*, Chichester, Wiley, 1978. 235 pp.
707 ELSTER, Jon, *Ulysses and the sirens: studies in rationality and irrationality*, Cambridge, Cambridge University Press, 1979. ix, 193 pp.
708 ELSTER, Jon, 'Marxism, functionalism and game theory', *Theory and Society* 11, 1982: 453-82.
709 ELSTER, Jon, *Sour grapes: studies in the subversion of rationality*, Cambridge, Cambridge University Press, 1983. viii, 177 pp.
710 ELSTER, Jon, *Explaining technical change: a case study in the philosophy of science*, Cambridge, Cambridge University Press, 1983. 273 pp.
711 ELSTER, Jon, 'Marxismen har framtiden för sig' (Marxism has a great future), *Tiden*, 4, 1985: 211-21.
712 ETZIONI, Amitai, 'Reindustrialization of America', *Policy*

Studies Review, 2, 4, 1983: 677-94.
713 ETZIONI, Amitai, *An immodest agenda: rebuilding America before the 21st century*, New York, McGraw-Hill, 1983. xiv, 418 pp.
714 ETZIONI, Amitai, 'Toward socio-economics (Review of Lester Thurow, *Dangerous Currents)*', *Contemporary Sociology*, 14, 2, 1985: 178-79.
715 FARARO, Thomas J., 'Neoclassical theorizing and formalization in sociology', *Journal of Mathematical Sociology*, 10, 1984: 361-93.
716 FAULKNER, Robert, *Music on demand; composers and careers in the Hollywood film industry*, New Brunswick, Transaction Books, 1983. ix, 281 pp.
717 FREY, Bruno S., 'Ökonomie als Verhaltenswissenschaft' (Economics as a science of behavior), *Jahrbuch für Sozialwissenschaft*, 31, 1, 1980: 21-35.
718 FREY, Bruno S., 'A new view of economics: comparative analysis of institutions', *Economia delle scelte pubbliche*, 1, 1984: 3-16.
719 FREY, Bruno S. et al., 'Are we all monetarists now? an empirical inquiry', *Journal of Post Keynesian Economics*, 6, 1, 1983: 89-96.
720 FREY, Bruno S. et al., 'Consensus and dissension among economists: an empirical inquiry', *American Economic Review*, 74, 5, 1984: 986-94.
721 GRANOVETTER, Mark, 'Threshold models of collective behavior', *American Journal of Sociology*, 83, 6, 1978: 1420-43.
722 GRANOVETTER, Mark, 'Labor mobility, internal markets and job-matching: a comparison of the sociological and economic approaches', Unpublished paper, State University of New York at Stony Brook, April 1983.
723 GRANOVETTER, Mark, 'Threshold models of interpersonal effects in consumer demand', Paper presented at the annual meeting of the American Sociological Association, 26-30 August 1985 in Washington, D.C. [Forthcoming in *Journal of Economic Behavior and Organization*.]
724 GRANOVETTER, Mark and Roland SOONG, 'Threshold models of diffusion and collective behavior', *Journal of*

Mathematical Sociology, 9, 1983: 165-79.
725 HECHTER, Michael, *The microfoundations of macro-sociology*, Philadelphia, Temple University Press, 1983. 289 pp.
726 HEIMER, C.A., 'Substitutes for experience-based information: the case of offshore oil insurance in the North Sea' in: A. L. Stinchcombe, C.A. Heimer, *Organization theory and project management*, Bergen (Norway), Universitetsforlaget, 1985: 172-224.
727 HEIMER, C.A., *Reactive risk and rational action: managing moral hazard in insurance contracts*, Berkeley, California University Press, 1985, x, 273 pp.
728 HIRSCH, Fred, *Social limits to growth*, Cambridge, Mass., Harvard University Press, 1976. x, 208 pp.
729 HIRSCH, Paul M., 'Processing fads and fashions: an organization-set analysis of cultural industry systems', *American Journal of Sociology*, 77, 4, 1972: 639-59.
730 HIRSCH, Paul M., 'Organizational effectiveness and the institutional environment', *Administrative Science Quarterly*, 20, 1975: 327-44.
731 HIRSCH, Paul M., 'The study of industries' in: S. Bachrach and S. Mitchell (eds), *Research in the Sociology of Organizations*, vol. 4, Greenwich, Conn., JAI Press, 1985: 269-307.
732 HIRSCHLEIFER, Jack, 'The expanding domain of economics', *American Economic Review*, 75, 6, 1985: 53-68.
733 HIRSCHMAN, Albert O., 'Against parsimony: three easy ways of complicating some categories of economic discourse', *Bulletin of the American Academy of Arts and Sciences*, 37, 8, 1984: 11-28.
734 HIRSCHMAN, Albert O., 'Reflections on the Latin American experience' in: L.N. Lindberg and C.S. Maier (eds), *The politics of inflation and economic stagnation*, Washington, D.C., The Brookings Institution, 1985: 53-77.
735 JOHNSON, Harry G., 'National styles in economic research: the United States, the United Kingdom, Canada, and various European countries', *Daedalus*, 102, 2, 1973: 65-74.
736 JONES, Stephen R.G., *The economics of conformism*, Oxford, Basil Blackwell, 1984. x, 123 pp.

737 LEIFER, Eric M., 'Equality through involvement and ambiguity', Unpublished paper, April 1986, University of North Carolina.

738 LEIFER, Eric M. and Anthony OBERSCHALL, 'Efficiency and social institutions: uses and misuses of economic reasoning in sociology', *Annual Review of Sociology*, 12, 1986: 233-53.

739 LEONTIEF, Wassily, 'Academic economics', *Science*, 217, 4555, 9 July 1982: 106-07.

740 LEVY-GARBOUA, Louis (ed.), *Sociological economics*, London, SAGE Publications, 1979. 306 pp.

741 LEWIS, J. David and Andrew WEIGERT, 'Trust as a social reality', *Social Forces*, 63, 4, 1985: 967-85.

742 LINDBERG, Leon N., 'Economists as policy intellectuals and economics as a policy profession: reflections on the retreat from keynesianism and from the interventionist state', Paper presented at the XIIth World Congress of the International Political Science Association, Rio de Janeiro, August 1982.

743 LINDBERG, Leon N., 'The production and selection of economic knowledge: economic theory, economic advice, and the societal rules of economists', Unpublished paper, University of Wisconsin-Madison, 1985.

744 LINDBERG, Leon N. and Charles S. MAIER (eds), *The politics of inflation and economic stagnation: theoretical approaches and international case studies*, Washington, D.C., The Brookings Institution, 1985. xviii, 621 pp.

745 LINDENBERG, Siegwart, 'Utility and morality', *Kyklos*, 36, 1983: 450-68.

746 LINDENBERG, Siegwart, 'The new political economy: its potential for the social sciences and for sociology in particular', *Sociological Theory*, 3, 1, 1985: 99-114.

747 LINDENBERG, Siegwart, 'Rational choice and sociological theory: new pressures on economics as a social science', *Zeitschrift für die gesamte Staatswissenschaft*, 141, 1985: 244-55.

748 LIPSET, Seymour Martin and William SCHNEIDER, *The confidence gap: business, labor, and government in the public mind*, New York, The Free Press, 1983. xxii, 434 pp.

749 LUHMANN, Niklas, 'Knappheit, Geld und die bürgerliche Gesellschaft' (Scarcity, gold and bourgeois society),

Jahrbuch für Sozialwissenschaft, 23, 1972: 186-210.

750 LUHMANN, Niklas, 'Trust' in: N. Luhmann, *Trust and power*, New York, John Wiley & Sons, 1979: 1-103. [Originally appeared in 1973.]

751 MARSHALL, Alfred, *Industry and trade: a study of industrial technique and business organization; and of their influences on the conditions of various classes and nations*, London, Macmillan and Company, 1919. xxiv, 875 pp.

752 MATTFELDT, Harald, 'Einige Bemerkungen zur Bedeutung des systemtheoretischen Ansatzes von Luhmann für die Nationalökonomie' (Some observations on the use to economic theory of Niklas Luhmann's efforts in systems theory), *Jahrbuch für Sozialwissenschaft*$ 25, 1974: 158-69.

753 MILLER, S.M., 'Economic inventions: the prelude to theory', *Challenge*, 20, 2, 1977: 53-55.

754 MUELLER, Dennis, C., *Public choice*, Cambridge, Cambridge University Press, 1979. xiii, 297 pp.

755 NORTH, Douglas C., *Structure and change in economic history*, New York, Norton, 1981. 228 pp.

756 OLSON, Mancur, *The logic of collective action: public goods and the theory of groups*, Cambridge, Mass., Harvard University Press, 1965. x, 186 pp.

757 OLSON, Mancur, 'Economics, sociology, and the best of all possible worlds', *Public Interest*, 12, Summer 1968: 96-118.

758 OLSON, Mancur, *The rise and decline of nations: economic growth, stagflation, and social rigidities*, New Haven, Yale University Press, 1982. xi, 273 pp.

759 OPP, Karl-Dieter, 'Das "ökonomische Programm" in der Soziologie' (The 'economic program' in sociology), *Soziale Welt*, 29, 2, 1978: 129-54.

760 OPP, Karl-Dieter, *Die Entstehung sozialer Normen. Ein Integrationsversuch soziologischer, sozialpsychologischer und ökonomischer Erklärungen (The emergence of social norms: an attempt to integrate intergrations in sociology, social psychology and economics)*, Tübingen, Mohr Siebeck, 1983. 240 pp.

761 OPP, Karl-Dieter, 'Sociology and economic man' *Zeitschrift für die gesamte Staatswissenschaft*, 141, 2, 1985: 213-43.

762 VAN PARIJS, Philippe, *Evolutionary explanation in the social sciences*, Totawa, New Jersey, Rowman and Littlefield, 1981. xv, 255 pp.

763 POPKIN, Samuel L., *The rational peasant: the political economy of rural Vietnam*, Berkeley, Ca., University of California Press, 1979. xiii, 287 pp.

764 POSNER, Richard A., *The economic analysis of law*, Boston, Little Brown and Co. 1972. 415 pp.

765 POSNER. Richard A., *The economics of justice*, Cambridge, Mass., Harvard University Press, 1981. ix, 415 pp.

766 RADNITZKY, Gerard and Peter BERNHOLZ (eds), *Economic imperialism: the economic approach applied outside the traditional areas of economics*, New York, Paragon House, 1986 (forthcoming).

767 SCHELLING, T.C., *Micromotives and macrobehavior*, New York, W.W. Norton, 1978. 252 pp.

768 SCHELLING,T.C., *Choice and consequence*, Cambridge, Harvard University Press, 1984. xi, 363 pp.

769 SCHOTTER, Andrew, *The economic theory of social institutions*, Cambridge, Cambridge University Press, 1981. xiii, 177 pp.

770 SEN, Amartya, 'Rational fools: a critique of the behavioural foundations of economic theory', *Philosophy and Public Affairs*, 6, 1977: 317-44.

771 SEN, Amartya, *Choice, welfare and measurement*, Oxford, Basil Blackwell, 1982. viii, 460 pp.

772 SOCIO-ECONOMIC NOTES, No. 1, November 1985.

773 SPENGLER, Joseph J., 'Exogenous and endogenous influences in the formation of post-1870 economic thought', in: R.V. Eagly (ed.), *Events, ideology and economic theory*, Detroit, Wayne State University Press, 1968: 159-205.

774 STARK, Werner, *The sociology of knowledge: an essay in aid of a deeper understanding of the history of ideas*, London, Routledge and Kegan Paul, 1958. xi, 356. [See especially chapter 5.]

775 STIGLER, George J., 'Economics — the imperial science', *Scandinavian Journal of Economics*, 86, 3, 1984: 301-13.

776 STINCHCOMBE, Arthur L., 'Merton's theory of social structure' in: L.A. Coser (ed.), *The idea of social structure*, New York, Harcourt, Brace, Jovanovich, 1975: 11-33.

777 STINCHCOMBE, Arthur L., *Contracts as hierarchical documents*, Bergen, The Institute of Industrial Economics (Work report No. 65), 1984. 52 pp.

778 SWEDBERG, Richard, 'Prudence versus profit: the role of the private banks in the origin of the debt crisis, 1974–1982', Paper presented at the XI World Congress in Sociology, New Delhi, 18–22 August 1986.

779 SZTOMPKA, Piotr, *Robert K. Merton: an intellectual profile*, London, Macmillan, 1986. 324 pp.

780 TULLOCK, Gordon, 'Economic imperialism' in: J.M. Buchanan and R.D. Tollison (eds), *Theory of public choice: political applications of economics*, Ann Arbor, The University of Michigan Press, 1972: 317-29.

781 UDEHN, Lars, *Methodological individualism: a critical inquiry*, London, Routledge and Kegan Paul, 1987 (forthcoming).

782 WARD, Benjamin, *What's wrong with economics*?, New York, Basic Books, 1972. x, 273 pp.

783 WHITE, Harrison C. and Robert G. ECCLES, 'Control via concentration: political and business evidence', Unpublished paper, Harvard University, 1985.

784 WILLIAMSON, Oliver E., *Markets and hierarchies: analysis and impact of antitrust implications*, New York, The Free Press, 1975. xvii, 286 pp.

785 WILLIAMSON, Oliver E., 'Transaction-cost economics: the governance of contractual relations', *Journal of Law and Economics*, 22, 2, 1979: 233-61.

786 WILLIAMSON, Oliver E., 'The economics of organization: the transaction cost approach', *American Journal of Sociology*, 87, 3, 1981: 548-77.

787 WILLIAMSON Oliver E., *The economic institutions of capitalism: firms, markets, relational contracting*, New York, The Free Press, 1985. xiv, 450 pp.

788 WIPPLER, Reinhard, 'The structural-individualistic approach in Dutch sociology', *The Netherlands' Journal of Sociology*, 14, 1978: 135-55.

789 WIPPLER, Reinhard, 'Explanatory sociology: the development of a theoretically oriented research programme', *The Netherlands' Journal of Sociology*, 21, 1985: 63-74.

Author Index

Aberg, R. 647
Abolafia, M.Y. 1, 612
Acker, J. 357, 358
Adelman, P. 59
Adler, P. 2, 613
Adler, P.A. 2, 613
Ahrne, G. 419
Aimard, G. 110
Akerlof, G. 3
Albert, H. 672, 673
Alexander, V. 359
Allen, M.P. 420
Allen, S. 674
Althusser, L. 421
Altmann, S.P. 111
American Sociological Association (ASA) 245
Amin, S. 531, 532, 533
Anderson, P. 422, 423
Arensberg, C.M. 321
Arndt, H.W. 534
Aron, R. 112
Arrow, K.J. 360, 614, 675, 676, 677, 678, 679
Ashley, W. 60
Assman, G. 424
Attewell, P.A. 425
Ayres, C.E. 246
Baker, W.E. 615, 616
Bancal, J. 4
Barber, B. 617, 680
Barnard, C. 247
Baron, J.N. 5, 367, 368
Barrett, M. 361
Barry, B. 681
Barth, F. 535, 536, 537
Baumgartner, T. 6, 440
Beck, E.M. 643
Becker, G.S. 7, 8, 682, 683
Becker, H. 113
von Beckerath, H. 170
Beechey, V. 362
Belanger, N. 353
Bell, C.S. 363
Bell, D. 347, 426, 427
Belshaw, C.S. 538
Bendix, R. 248, 539
Benston, M. 364
Berg, I. 9, 428
Berk, R.A. 365
Berk, S.F. 365
Berle, A.A. 429
Bernard, J. 366
Bernholz, P. 766
Bettelheim, C. 171, 172
Bielby, W.T. 5, 367, 368, 684
Black, N. 369
Blackburn, R. 430
Blau, F.D. 370
Blaug, M. 61
Blaxall, M. 371
Bloch, H.A. 249
Bloch, M. 173
Block, F.L. 10, 250, 431, 432, 433, 685, 686
Blomström, M. 540
Bluestone, B. 618
Booth, D. 541
Bornschier, V. 542
Boserup, E. 372
Boudon, R. 687, 688
Bouglé, C. 174, 175
Boulding, K. 689
Bowles, S. 434, 435, 519
Branford, V. 62
Braudel, F. 114
Braverman, H. 437
Bredemeier, H.C. 251
Brenner, R. 543
Brewer, A. 544
Brulin, G. 46
Bruyn, S. 690, 691
Buchanan, J.M. 692
Burawoy, M. 438, 439
Burgess, E.W. 305
Burghardt, A. 11
Burlkitt, B. 674
Burns, T.R. 6, 440, 619
Burt, R.S. 620, 621, 622
Buss, E. 12

Cairnes, J.E. 63
Caplowitz, D. 252
Cardoso, F.H. 13, 545, 546, 547, 548
Carlin, E.A. 176
Carnoy, M. 441
Carroll, G.R. 693, 694, 695, 696
Casanova, J-C. 253
Chamberlin, E.H. 623, 624
Chapman, J.R. 373
Chase-Dunn, C. 542, 549
Chinchilla, N.S. 374
Chirot, D. 550
Clarke, S. 64
Cliffe Leslie, T.E. 65
Coats, A.W. 66, 67, 68, 69, 697
Colbjörnsen, T. 442
Coleman, J.S. 698, 699, 700
Comte, A. 70
Coser, L. 701
Cottrell, A.B. 369
Cottrell, W.F. 254
Cressey, P.G. 255
Crozier, M. 177
Cunningham, W. 71
Cuvillier, A. 178

Dahlström, E. 393
Dahrendorf, R. 443, 625
Dalton, M. 256
Damalas, B. 179
Deville, P. 6, 440
Devine, P.J. 702
De Vroey, M. 115
DiDonato, D. 444
Di Marco, L.E. 551
Dobretsberger, J. 180
Doeringer, P.B. 375
Domhoff, G.W. 445, 446, 447, 448, 449
Donovan, F.R. 257, 258
Dos Santos, T. 552
Downs, A. 703
Duesenberry, J.S. 450, 704
Duncan, O.D. 259
Durkheim, E. 14, 72, 116, 117, 118, 119, 120, 121

Eccles, R.G. 705, 783
Economic Commission for Latin America (ECLA) 553
Edwards, R. 435, 451, 452, 459
Ehrlich, C. 376
Eisenstein, Z.R. 377
Eisermann, G. 122, 123, 181, 182
Ekelund, Jr., R.B. 73
Elster, J. 453, 454, 706, 707, 708, 709, 710, 711
Emmanuel, A. 554
England, P. 15, 378, 379
Esping-Andersen, G. 455, 626, 627
Etzioni, A. 16, 628, 629, 712, 713, 714
Evans, P.B. 555, 556, 557, 558

Faletto, E. 13
Fararo, T.J. 715
Farkas, G. 15
Fauconnet, P. 121
Faulkner, R. 716
Feldberg, R.L. 380
Ferber, M. 381
Fischer, L.H. 272
Flam, H. 619, 630
Folbre, N. 382
Foster-Carter, A. 559
Foucault, M. 74
Frank, A.G. 560, 561, 562
Frankel, S.H. 124
Frenkel, R. 563
Frey, B.S. 717, 718, 719, 720
Friedland, R. 455
Friedmann, G. 183
Furner, M.O. 75
Fürstenberg, F. 17, 184

Galasi, P. 18
Galbraith, K.J. 19
Garst, D. 564
Geertz, C. 565, 566, 567, 568
Gerschenkron, A. 569
Gershuny, J. 348, 631, 632
Giddings, F.H. 76, 77
Gilfillan, S.C. 260
Glasberg, D.F. 456
Glazer-Malbin, N. 383
Glenn, E.N. 380
Gold, D.A. 457
Goldscheid, R. 185, 186
Goldschmidt-Clermont, L. 384
Goldthorpe, J.H. 20, 26, 78, 385, 458

Gordon, D.M. 436, 452, 459, 519, 633
Gough, I. 460
Gouldner, A.W. 261
Gourevitch, P. 570
Gramsci, A. 461
Granovetter, M. 21, 22, 349, 634, 721, 722, 723, 724
Grant, W. 635
Greene, M. 187
Greenwood, D. 125
Griffin, K. 571
Gronau, R. 386
Gurley, J. 571

Haberler, G. 572
Halbwachs, M. 188, 189, 190, 191
Halvorsen, K. 23
Hanneman, R.A. 141
Hansson, B.A. 192
Harkess, S. 387
Harrison, F. 79, 80
Hartmann, H. 388
Hawley, J.P. 636
Hechter, M. 637, 725
Heckscher, E. 81
Hedström, P. 24, 638, 639
Heertje, A. 193
Heimer, C.A. 726, 727
Heinemann, K. 640
Hernes, G. 25, 641
Hettne, B. 540, 573
Hilferding, R. 462
Himmelstrand, U. 46, 463
Hindess, B. 464
Hirsch, F. 26, 728
Hirsch, P.M. 729, 730, 731
Hirschleifer, J. 732
Hirschman, A.O. 27, 28, 574, 575, 642, 733, 734
Hirschon, R. 389
Holter, H. 390
Homans, G. 262
Horan, P.M. 643
Hoselitz, B.F. 301, 576, 577
Howerth, I.H. 82
Hughes, E.C. 263, 264, 265, 266, 267, 268, 269
Huo, Y.P. 695

Ingram, J.L. 83, 84
International Sociological Association (ISA) 578
Ishboldin, B. 194

James, D.R. 465
Jameson, K.P. 579
Janowitz, M. 270
Jessop, B. 466
Johnson, E.S. 271
Johnson, H.G. 735
Jones, S.R.G. 736
Jusenius, C.L. 370

Kahl, J.A. 580
Kalleberg, A.L. 644
Kandiyoti, D. 391, 392
Kanter, R.M. 29
Karrer, H. 195
Kasinitz, P. 467
Katona, G. 468
Katzenstein, P. 469
Kaufmann, F-X. 196
Kerr, C. 272, 645
Keynes, J.N. 85
Kindleberger, C.P. 646
Koch, W. 197
Korpi, W. 470, 647
Koskinen, T. 350
Kraft, J. 126
Krasner, S.D. 471
Kurtz, L.R. 273
Kuznets, S. 274, 581

Laidler, D. 127
Lancaster, K. 472
Landes, D.M. 473
Lash, S. 474
Lazarsfeld, P.F. 275
Leblebici, H. 648
Lebovics, H. 198
Leifer, E.M. 30, 649, 737, 738
Leijonhufvud, A. 31
Lekachman, R. 199
Lenin, V.I. 475, 476
Lenzer, G. 86
Leontief, W. 32, 739
Lerner, D. 582
Levine, D.N. 276

Levy-Garboua, L. 740
Lewis, J.D. 741
Lilja, K. 350
Liljeström, R. 393
Lindberg, L.N. 650, 742, 743, 744
Lindblom, C.E. 651, 652, 653
Lindenberg, S. 745, 746, 747
Lipset, S.M. 277, 278, 338, 748
Lloyd, C.B. 394
Lo, C.Y.H. 457
Löwe, A. 200
Luhmann, N. 279, 749, 750
Lukacs, G. 477
Lundberg, G.A. 280
Luxemburg, R. 478

Macauley, S. 128
Maier, C.M. 744
Makler, H. 33, 479
Mann, F.K. 201, 202
Mannheim, K. 34, 203
Marglin, S.A. 480, 481
Marshall, A. 87, 88, 751
Martinelli, A. 33, 204, 351
Marx, K. 89, 90
Mattfeldt, H. 752
Mauduit, R. 91
Mauss, M. 205, 206
McCrate, E. 395
Means, G.C. 429
Merton, R.K. 129, 281, 282
Michalet, C-A. 92
Michel, A. 396
Miles, I.D. 348
Miliband, R. 482
Mill, J.S. 93, 94
Miller, S.M. 753
Mills, C. Wright, 283, 284
Minter, W. 596
Mintz, B. 35, 483, 484
Miroglio, A. 207
Mitzman, A. 130
Mizruchi, M.S. 485
Mommsen, W. 208
Moore, W.E. 285, 286, 287, 288, 289, 290, 291, 292, 293, 294, 295 296, 297, 298, 299, 300, 301
Moraze, C. 209
Moseley, K.P. 583
Mueller, D. 754
Myrdal, G. 95

Nash, J. 397, 398
Natanson, J. 131
Navarro, M. 399
Niemi, B.T. 394
Nimkoff, M.F. 304
Norich, S. 530
North, D.C. 755
North American Congress on Latin America (NACLA) 584

Oakley, A. 400
Oberschall, A. 96, 132, 738
O'Connor, J. 486
O'Donnell, G. 563, 585
Offe, C. 487, 488
Ogburn, W.F. 302, 303, 304
Olsen, E.S. 73
Olson, M. 756, 757, 758
Opp, K-D, 759, 760, 761
Oppenheimer, V.K. 401
Oshima, H.T. 133

Papanek, H. 402, 403, 404
Pareto, V. 134, 135
van Parijs, P. 489, 762
Park, R.E. 305
Parsons, T. 36, 136, 137, 138, 306, 307, 308, 309, 310, 311, 312, 313, 314, 315, 405
Patel, P.J. 354
Patten, S.N. 97
Payer, C. 586, 587
Pearson, H.W. 316, 321
Perman, D. 210
Perrin, G. 139
Perrow, C. 37
Petersen, T. 490, 654
Pierenkemper, T. 38
Piore, M.J. 375, 655, 656
Poggi, G. 140
Polanyi, K. 317, 318, 319, 320, 321
Politics and Society, 491
Popkin, S.L. 763
Portes, A. 588, 589
Posner, R.A. 764, 765
Poulantzas, N. 492

Power, M. 406
Powers, C.H. 141
Powers, H.H. 98
Prebisch, R. 590, 591
Przeworski, A. 493, 494, 495, 496

Radnitzky, G. 766
Reagan, B. 371
Reich, M. 452, 459
Reisman, D.A. 99
Ressner, U. 407
Robinson, J. 657
Roemer, J.E. 497, 498, 499
Rokkan, S. 592, 593
Ronge, V. 487
Rose, A. 322, 323, 324
Rose, M. 211, 352
Rosenberg, N. 100
Roth, G. 142
Rotschild, M. 658
Roy, D. 500
Rubin, G. 408
Rueschemeyer, D. 557
Ruttan, W. 212

Safa, H.J. 398
Salancik, G.R. 648
Sales, A. 353, 479
Salomon, A. 101
Samuelson, P. 143, 144
Sarfatti Larson, M. 501
Sauermann, H. 213
Savage, S.P. 325
Sawhill, I.V. 409
Schelling, T.C. 767, 768
Schneider, E.V. 326
Schneider, W. 748
Schotter, A. 769
Schumpeter, J.A. 39, 40, 102, 145, 214, 215, 216, 217, 218, 219, 220, 221, 222, 502, 503
Schwartz, M. 35, 456, 483, 484, 504
Schweitzer, A. 146, 147
Scott, J.W. 47
Seers, D. 594, 595
Sen, A. 41, 770, 771
Shackle, G.S. 223
Shapiro, S.P. 42
Sheth, N.R. 354
Shoup, L.H. 596
Signs 410
Sik, E. 659
Simiand, F. 224, 225, 226, 227
Simich, J.L. 148, 154
Simmel, G. 149, 150, 151
Singer, H. 597
Skocpol, T. 505, 506, 598
Small, A.W. 103, 104, 105
Smelser, N.J. 33, 36, 327, 328, 329, 330, 331, 332, 333, 334, 335, 336, 337, 338, 411, 479
Smith, A. 106
Smith, M.R. 507
Socio-Economic Notes 772
Sokoloff, N.J. 412, 413
Sombart, W. 43, 152
Somers, M.R. 250
Soong, R. 724
Soref, M. 465
Sorensen, A.B. 44, 644, 660
Sorensen, B.A. 414
Spence, A.M. 661
Spengler, J.J. 773
Spraos, J. 599
Stallings, B. 600, 601
Stark, W. 228, 229, 774
Starr, J.M. 230
Stearns, L. 662
Stepan, A. 508
Stephens, E.H. 557
Stigler, G.J. 775
Stiglitz, J. 658
Stinchcombe, A.L. 45, 339, 776, 777
Street, J.H. 602
Strobel, M. 415
Sultan, H. 231
Sutton, F.X. 153, 340
Swedberg, R. 46, 107, 355, 778
Sweezy, P.M. 232, 509
Sziraczki, G. 18
Sztompka, P. 779

Therborn, G. 108, 510, 511, 512, 513
Thoits, P.A. 359
Thompson, E.P. 514, 515
Thurow, L. 356
Tilly, L.A. 47
Tilman, R. 148, 154

Titmuss, R.M. 663
Toennies, F. 233, 234, 235
Tolbert II, C.M. 643
Touraine, A. 236
Trimberger, E.K. 516
Trow, M. 277
Tullock, G. 692, 780
Turner, B.S. 155

Udéhn, L. 781
United Nations 603
Urry, J. 474
Urwin, D.W. 593
Useem, M. 517, 518

Valenzuela, A. 604
Valenzuela, J.S. 604
Veblen, T. 156, 157, 158, 159, 160
Vilar, P. 237
Viner, J. 605
Vogel, L. 416

Waerness, K. 417
Wallerstein, I. 48, 49, 606, 607
Wallerstein, M. 496
Ward, B. 782
Ward, L.F. 109
Warren, B. 608
Weber, M. 50, 51, 52, 161, 162, 163, 164, 165, 341
Weed, F.J. 166
Weigert, A. 741
Weiller, J. 238, 239
Weippert, G. 240
Weisskopf, T.E. 436, 519
Werker, S. 609
Westergaard, J. 520
White, B. 53
White, H.C. 54, 55, 649, 664, 665, 666, 667, 668, 783
Whyte, W.F. 342, 343
von Wiese, L. 56, 241
Wiesenthal, H. 488
Wilensky, H.L. 521, 522
Wiley, N.F. 242, 344, 345
Williamson, O.E. 784, 785, 786, 787
Winkelmann, J. 167, 168
Wippler, R. 788, 789
Wirth, L. 243
Wolff, K.H. 169
Wood, R.E. 610, 611
Wright, E.O. 419, 455, 457, 523, 524, 525, 526, 527

Zaar, C. 418
Zahn, E. 57
Zald, M.N. 428
Zeitlin, M. 528, 529, 530
Zelizer, V.A.R. 669, 670, 671
Ziegenfuss, W. 244
Zorbaugh, H.W. 346
van Zuthem, H.J. 58

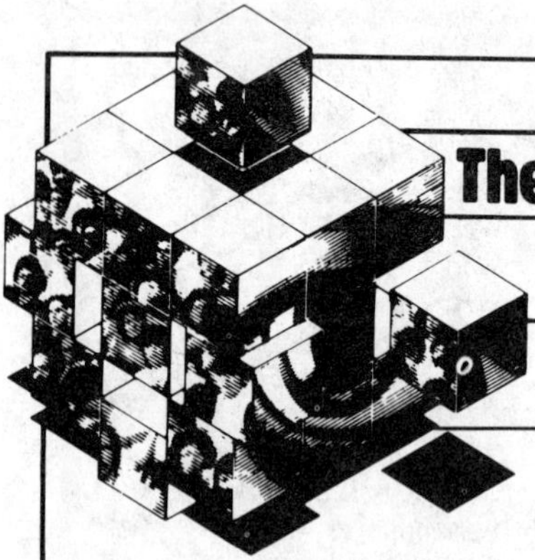

Revue française de sociologie

publiée avec le concours de
L'INSTITUT DE RECHERCHE SUR LES SOCIÉTÉS CONTEMPORAINES
CENTRE NATIONAL DE LA RECHERCHE SCIENTIFIQUE

59-61, rue Pouchet, 75849 Paris Cedex 17 — Tél. : 42 63 27 00

JANVIER-MARS 1987, XXVIII-1

Facteurs institutionnels de la diversité des carrières scolaires	Marie DURU et Alain MINGAT
La construction sociale du risque face aux dangers industriels	Denis DUCLOS

SUR DURKHEIM

Durkheim et la mobilité sociale	Charles-Henry CUIN
L'institution démotivée Fustel de Coulanges et Durkheim	François HÉRAN
Le statut de la sociologie chez Simmel et Durkheim	Marc SAGNOL

DÉBAT

Durkheim et le suicide des femmes	Claude DUBAR et Philippe BESNARD

LES LIVRES

Abonnements : L'ordre et le paiement sont à adresser **directement** à :
Centrale des Revues, CDR
11, rue Gossin, 92543 Montrouge Cedex — Tél. : (1) 46.56.52.66
CCP La Source 33-368-61 CDR-Gauthier-Villars
Les abonnements sont annuels et partent du premier numéro de l'année en cours.

Tarif 1987 : L'abonnement (4 numéros) France .... 255 F
Etranger .... 300 F

Vente au numéro : Par correspondance : Presses du CNRS, 20-22, rue Saint-Amand, 75015 Paris. Tél. : (1) 45.33.16.00 — Télex : 200 356 F.

A la librairie du CNRS, 295, rue Saint-Jacques, 75005 Paris.
Tél. : (1) 43.26.56.11

Tarif 1987 : Le numéro .... 81 F

Editor
James A. Beckford
Department of Sociology, University of Durham,
Durham DH1 3JT

Published three times a year by
SAGE Publications
London, Newbury Park, Beverly Hills, New Delhi
under the auspices of the International Sociological Association/ISA.
Subscription and advertising details available from
SAGE Publications Ltd, 28 Banner Street, London EC1Y 8QE, UK.
Institutions £47/$70.50; Individuals £22/$33
Second class postage paid at Westwood, NJ 07675 (or application to mail at second class postage rate is pending at Westwood, NJ 07675). Air freight and mailing in the USA by PSCA, 40 Carver Avenue, Westwood, NJ 07675.

ISSN 0011-3921
Printed by J.W. Arrowsmith Ltd, Bristol, UK

Current Sociology is regularly listed in *Current Contents* and abstracted in *Sociological Abstracts*.

International Sociological Association/ISA

CURRENT SOCIOLOGY

Association Internationale de Sociologie/**La sociologie contemporaine**

Volume 35
Number 2
Summer 1987

THE SOCIOLOGY OF LEGITIMATION

Issue co-ordinator: Roberto Cipriani

PART I
Theories of Legitimation
PART II
Forms and Contents of Legitimation
PART III
Hypotheses on Legitimation
PART IV
Remarks on Legitimation

SAGE Publications

CURRENT SOCIOLOGY
La sociologie contemporaine

Information for Contributors

Each issue of this unique journal is devoted to a comprehensive Trend Report on a topic of interest to the international community of sociologists. Authors review current trends and tendencies in all areas of sociological work — theories, methods, concepts, substantive research and national or regional developments. The aim is to review new developments, to discuss controversies, and to provide extensive bibliographies. From time to time, Commentaries on Trend Reports are published in subsequent issues of the journal.

If you would like to propose a Trend Report, please send the Editor an outline or prospectus of the proposed issue and a brief *curriculum vitae*. A style sheet and detailed notes for the guidance of authors are available. Contributions may be written in English or French.

Correspondence concerning Trend Reports should be addressed to the Editor: James A. Beckford, Department of Sociology & Social Policy, University of Durham, Durham DH1 3JT, England.

All subscription enquiries should be addressed to the Publisher:

SAGE Publications
28 Banner Street, London EC1Y 8QE

NEW RELIGIOUS MOVEMENTS AND RAPID SOCIAL CHANGE

Edited by
James A Beckford

The twentieth century has seen a considerable and unexpected proliferation of new religious movements in many parts of the world, often associated with periods of rapid social change. **New Religious Movements and Rapid Social Change** explains the development and characteristics of these movements comparatively and analyses their outstanding features.

The book shows how rapid social change gives rise to novel religious interpretations and how new religious movements, in turn, try to influence the process of change. This analysis is illustrated by studies of the advanced societies of North America and Europe, of Japan during the first phase of industrialization and of countries and regions in the developing world.

New religious movements are revealed as a normal aspect of social life and as critical indicators of social change. This is reflected in each movement's social composition, teachings, values, religious practices and organizational structures as well as their engagement in politics, business and their structuring of social relationships.

November 1986 • 272 pages
Cloth (8039-8003-5) £19.50

SAGE Publications Ltd, 28 Banner Street, London EC1Y 8QE

SAGE Publications Ltd, 2111 West Hillcrest Drive, Newbury Park, CA 91320, USA

CURRENT SOCIOLOGY
La sociologie contemporaine

The Journal of the International Sociological Association
Association Internationale de Sociologie

Volume 35 Number 2 Summer 1987

THE SOCIOLOGY OF LEGITIMATION

PART I
Theories of Legitimation

PART II
Forms and Contents of Legitimation

PART III
Hypotheses on Legitimation

PART IV
Remarks on Legitimation

SAGE Publications

Contents

Editorial Note, v
About the Authors, vi

The Sociology of Legitimation: an Introduction, 1
Roberto Cipriani

PART I
THEORIES OF LEGITIMATION

Legitimation, Representation and Power, 21
Franco Ferrarotti

The Moral Question and Legitimation, 29
Achille Ardigò

Legitimation and Society: a Critical Review, 41
Alberto Izzo

PART II
FORMS AND CONTENTS OF LEGITIMATION

Legitimacy and Legitimization, 57
François Bourricaud

Sociality as Legitimation of Sociological Method, 69
Michel Maffesoli

PART III
HYPOTHESES ON LEGITIMATION

Legitimation Processes in Politics and Religion, 89
Robert N. Bellah

The Representation of Society within Society, 101
Niklas Luhmann

PART IV
REMARKS ON LEGITIMATION

Comments on Legitimation, 109
Thomas Luckmann

Legitimacy and Political Processes, 119
John Fraser

A Different Historical Perspective
on Legitimation, 127
Srdjan Vrcan

Résumés, 135

Bibliography, 147

Editorial Note

Nearly all the contributions to this issue were prepared for the International Conference on Legitimation and Society (Legittimazione e Società), held in Rome at the National Research Council (CNR) between 2nd and 5th November 1983, and organized by the 'Cultural Processes' section of the Department of Sociology at the University of Rome — La Sapienza. Thanks are due to Dr Vittorio Cotesta and Dr Alessandro Ferrara for guidance with the Introduction; to Professor John Fraser for the English version of some chapters; and to Dr Consuelo Corradi, Dr Marco Marroni and Dr Enrico Pozzi for their invaluable support. The chapters by F. Bourricaud and M.Maffesoli were translated from the French by Millie Kerkham. Thanks also go to James Beckford whose suggestions have proved invaluable in preparing this issue.

Roberto Cipriani is Professor of the Sociology of Knowledge at the University of Rome and Secretary of the ISA Research Committee for the Sociology of Religion. Born in 1945, he received a doctorate in Literature (1968) and in Philosophy (1971), and he took post-graduate degrees in Sociology (1970) and in Social Sciences (1973). He was Visiting Scholar at the University of California, Berkeley, in 1982. His main publications include books on legitimation, popular culture, politics and religion, qualitative methodology, religious phenomena, the Frankfurt School, youth, life histories, and symbolism.

He is a member of the Executive Committee of the CISR (International Conference for the Sociology of Religion) and AISLF (Association Internationale des Sociologues de Langue Française).
Address: via della Chimica 8, 00144 Roma, Italy.

Franco Ferrarotti is Professor of Sociology at the University of Rome and editor of the journal *La Critica Sociologica.* He was an independent member of the Italian Parliament from 1958 to 1963 and then returned to full-time scholarly activity in 1964 as a Fellow at the Center for Advanced Studies in the Behavioral Sciences in Palo Alto, California. He has held guest appointments at Columbia University, Boston University, City University of New York, and a directorship of studies at the Ecole des Hautes Etudes en Sciences Sociales in Paris. His publications include: *Toward the Social Production of the Sacred* (1977); *An Alternative Sociology* (1979); *Histoire et histoires de vie* (1983); *The Myth of Inevitable Progress* (1985); *Five Scenarios for the Year 2000* (1986); *A Theology for Non-believers* (1986); *Le Paradoxe du Sacré* (1987).
Address: via Appennini 42, 00198 Roma, Italy.

Achille Ardigò was the first President of the Italian Association of Sociology. He is Professor of Sociology and Chairman of the Department of Sociology at the University of Bologna. He is a member of the National Council for Economics and Work (CNEL). Main publications: *Crisi di governabilità e mondi vitali* (Crisis of governability and life worlds), 1982; *Informazione, partecipazione e mondi vitali* (Mass media, participation and life worlds), with G. Chiari, C. Cipolla, 1982; *Per Milano, una rifondazione del Welfare State* (For Milan, a re-establishment of Welfare State), ed., 1984; *Le bancarie. Lavoro, strategie emancipative, partecipazione e qualità della*

vita delle impiegate (Female bank clerks. Work, emancipatory strategies, participation and life quality of female clerks), with C. Cipolla, 1985. He is editor of the journal *La Ricerca Sociale*.
Address: via Bellinzona 5, 40135 Bologna, Italy.

Alberto Izzo, born in Venice (1933), has studied at the University of Ferrara (Law), where he graduated in 1957, and at Brandeis University, USA (Graduate School in Sociology). From 1963 to 1969 he was Assistant Professor in Sociology at the University of Trento. PhD (*Libero Docente*) in Sociology (1969), was Associate Professor (*Professore Incaricato*) in the History of Sociological Thought at the University of Trento from 1969 to 1975, and in the History of Sociology at the University of Rome since 1970. He has been Full Professor for the same subject matter in the latter University from 1975. Main interests: sociological theory, sociology of knowledge. Main publications: *Sociologia della conoscenza* (The sociology of knowledge), 1966; *Alienazione e sociologia* (Alienation and sociology) ed., 1973; *Storia del pensiero sociologico* (History of sociological thought), ed., 3 vols, 1974–5–7; *Ricerca di una sociologia critica* (The search for a critical sociology), 1975; *Il concetto di ideologia* (The concept of ideology), 1977. He has translated several books from English into Italian. He is the Representative of Italy on the ISA Research Committee for the Sociology of Knowledge.
Address: via Giacinto Gallina 41, 00123 Roma, Italy.

Michel Maffesoli is Full Professor of Sociology at the Sorbonne, University of Paris 5. Main publications: *Logique de la domination* (1976); *La violence fondatrice*, with A. Pessin (1978); *Violence et transgression*, with A. Bruston (1978); *La violence totalitaire. Essai d'anthropologie politique* (1979); *La conquête du présent. Pour une sociologie de la vie quotidienne* (1979); *La galaxie de l'imaginaire. Dérive autour de l'oeuvre de Gilbert Durand* (1980); *L'ombre de Dionysos. Contribution à une sociologie de l'orgie* (1982); *Essais sur la violence banale et fondatrice* (1984); *Une anthropologie des turbulences. Hommage à Georges Balandier*, with C. Rivière (1985); *La connaissance ordinaire. Précis de sociologie compréhensive* (1985). He is editor of the journal *Sociétés*.
Address: 32, rue des Archives, 75004 Paris, France.

François Bourricaud, born in 1922, has been Full Professor of Sociology at the Sorbonne, University of Paris 4 since 1979. He has

been Rockefeller Fellow at Harvard University (1950–2), Fellow at the Center for Advanced Studies in the Behavioral Sciences (1964–5), Professor of Sociology at the University of Paris 10—Nanterre (1966–7), at the Sorbonne (1968), at the University of Paris 5 (1969–79). His main publications include: *Esquisse d'une théorie de l'autorité* (1961, 1970); L'individualisme institutionnel. Essai sur la sociologie de Talcott Parsons (1977), translated as *The sociology of Talcott Parsons* (1981); *Le bricolage idéologique. Essai sur les intellectuels et les passions démocratiques* (1980); *Dictionnaire critique de la sociologie*, with R. Boudon (1982); *Le retour de la droite* (1986).
Address: 41, rue des Martyrs, 75009 Paris, France.

Robert N. Bellah is Ford Professor of Sociology and Comparative Studies at the University of California, Berkeley, where he has been Chairman of the Department of Sociology. He published his first book, *Apache Kinship Systems*, in 1952. He received the PhD from Harvard in 1955, and his doctoral research was the basis of his second book, *Tokugawa Religion* (1957), a study of Japanese religion and society. He edited *Religion and Progress in Modern Asia* (1965). In 1964–5 he held a fellowship at the Center for Advanced Studies in the Behavioral Sciences at Stanford University. He has published *Beyond Belief. Essays on Religion in a Post-traditional World* (1970); *Emile Durkheim: On Morality and Society* (1973); *The Broken Covenant: American Civil Religion in Time of Trial* (1975); *Varieties of Civil Religion*, with P.E. Hammond (1980); *Habits of the Heart* (1985).
Address: Department of Sociology, University of California, Berkeley, CA 94720, USA.

Niklas Luhmann is Full Professor of Sociology at the University of Bielefeld, West Germany. He has studied in the USA where he collaborated with Talcott Parsons. He is a prolific sociologist. Main publications: *Grundrechte als Institution* (1965); *Studien über Recht und Verwaltung* (1967); *Theorie der Gesellschaft oder Sozialtechnologie*, with J. Habermas (1971); *Politische Planung. Aufsätze zur Soziologie von Politik und Verwaltung* (1971); *Soziologische Aufklärung* (1972); *Legitimation durch Verfahren* (1976); *Funktion der Religion* (1977); *Theorietechnik und Moral*, ed., with S. Pfürtner (1978); *Trust and Power: Two Works by N. Luhmann* (1979); *Gesellschaftstruktur und Semantik*, 2 vols. (1980–1); *Politische Theorie im Wohlfahrtstaat* (1981); *The Differentiation of Society* (1982); *Soziale Systeme: Grundrisse einer allgemeinen Theorie* (1984); *A Sociological Theory of Law* (1985).

Address: Marianne Weber Str. 13, 4811 Oerlinghausen, West Germany.

Thomas Luckmann was born in Yugoslavia. He studied at the Universities of Innsbruck and Vienna, 1945–9, and as a post-graduate at the New School for Social Research, New York (1950–6). He taught in USA, Germany and Australia. Since 1970 he has been Professor of Sociology at the University of Konstanz, West Germany. Luckmann has written numerous journal articles and several books including: *The Invisible Religion*; *The Sociology of Language*; *The Social Construction of Reality*, with P.L. Berger; *The Structures of the Life-World*, with A. Schutz; *Life-World and Social Realities.*
Address: Sozialwissenschaftliche Fakultät — Fachgruppe Soziologie, Universität Konstanz, Postfach 5560, 7750 Konstanz, 1, West Germany.

John Fraser studied at Cambridge and Leicester Universities. He taught Politics at Leicester, at Laurentian University and Waterloo University, both in Canada. Since 1984 he has taught Sociology at Rome and Ferrara Universities, and is currently a Visiting Research Fellow in Politics at the University of Reading. Among his publications are studies of left-wing Italian intellectuals in politics, of Marxist theory of crisis, and he is currently engaged on research on the theoretical implications of 'community'.
Address: via Ignazio Jacometti 2, 00061 Anguillara Sabazia (RM), Italy.

Srdjan Vrcan has been Professor of Sociology at the Law School of the University of Split, Yugoslavia, since its foundation. He received his PhD in Sociology at the School of Philosophy of Zagreb University with the thesis 'The Notion of Ideology in Marx and Mannheim'. He is President of the Yugoslav Sociological Association and first Editor of the journal for social problems *Pogledi.* His main publications include: *Radničko samoupravljanje u nekim industrijskim organizacijama u Dalmaciji* (Workers' self-management in some industrial organizations in Dalmatia); *Društvene nejednakosti i moderno društvo* (Social inequalities and modern society); *Raspeto katoličanstvo* (Catholicism at a crossroad); *Od krize religije do religije krize* (From the crisis of religion to the religion of the crisis); *Klasno-socijalna struktura SKI (1968–1980)* (Class and social composition of the LCY 1968–1980).
Address: Mrduljaševa 38, 58000 Split, Yugoslavia.

The Sociology of Legitimation: an Introduction

Roberto Cipriani

Among the various possible meanings of what has been defined as legitimation (see the article by Izzo), two should be borne in mind as more pertinent to sociological analysis: the attribution of validity to a given situation, action, function or authority (from below); and (from above) the more or less motivated justification of what by itself would not be lawful or valid. Independently of the subject or object in question in one or other case, or in both together, the legitimating intervention involves at all events substantial departure from the initial situation. In fact, claim, demand, recognition, ratification, acceptance — all are social and individual actions which presuppose endowing what is going to be done with meaning. This especially concerns the fact that denial–rejection (delegitimation) or confirmation–approval (legitimation) derive from a principal decision, on the conditioning of which — as an object of study — sociology has staked a good deal of its scientific credibility (Izzo, 1970, 1978).

By way of further distinction, legitimation in reality is said to be based on two 'couples' of behaviour: from above, as a claim of validity only for what one is convinced of, or, instead, as a cynical claim of validity for what one knows is not justifiable; and from below, as a well-founded recognition of the legitimacy of something or, contrarily, as a de facto acceptance, though without foundation, of the legitimacy of something.

The attribution of a 'foundation' simply means that this does not exist and so must be 'constructed', and on this depends the whole scaffolding of a complex of guiding ideas which orient attitudes and behaviour. And since, in general, a foundation is something in common, to be shared, its own particular character represents its potential for diffusion and ability to provide the sense of belonging to a group as to a party, a community or a whole nation.

To this should be added the specific case of a supposedly charismatic personality which can, through the fascination of its individual character, guarantee and justify otherwise unacceptable solutions and choices. However, such an occurrence also signals an essential lack of legitimation, scarcely concealed by the 'fascinating' skill of the leader, whose function as safety curtain helps to put off reactions of rebellion or revolution. We should note here Levi's distinction between revolt and revolution, when he says:

> The attitude of revolt restricts itself to simple negation, the abstract rejection of social reality, without historically causing its real negation and rejection. Consequently, it is incapable of recognizing the historical movement of society, or identifying concrete objectives of struggle, and ends up being a prisoner of the reality it cannot manage to change. The revolutionary attitude, on the other hand, carries out an historically determinate negation of social reality. Its problem is always that of uncovering the concrete struggle brought to light by real historical movement, which permits the realization of the potential transformations of society. This means revolutionary action never has the objective of radically changing society, but of overthrowing the political institutions which hinder its development, and creating new ones capable of liberating the tendencies which have matured in society, towards higher forms of coexistence. (Levi, 1976: 521–2)

In fact, the interruption of leadership for whatever reason always produces effects of readjustment within the existing system, with the compelling need to do something about it, through solutions which guarantee an appearance of continuity and with the intention of harvesting the legacy of existing legitimacy, and possibly constructing others. An exemplary case is provided by Edmund Leach, discussing the biblical story of the succession of Solomon to the throne of Israel, where he defines it as a myth intended to mediate quite different contradictions (Leach, 1966). Thus we may have the case not only of the rise ex novo of a party or social class to the management of power but also of a return, a restoration, which has already undergone its historical test (for example, the legitimism of the last century in Europe, with the occasionally successful attempt to give authority back to sovereigns who have already been dethroned).

In the course of socio-political history, the justificatory appeals have been numerous and often mutually overlapping: from tradition to divine investiture, from patri- and matri-linear succession to the law of nature, and to the sovereignty of the people. Even the Mazzinian 'realm of moral law' has found a raison d'être to rationalize legitimacy and illegitimacy at the level of political authority. Nor is a similar ethical invocation wholly alien to the contemporary reality of societies in a crisis of governability. However, one must ask what morality one is dealing with, and whether this contradicts the social pact of solidarity, and the hypothesis of real democracy.

Before starting an examination of current positions regarding legitimation, however, it is not out of place to return to the distant historico-linguistic origins of the term under discussion, and to stress that its formation and use are relatively recent — even though in classical Latin there was certainly mention of *legitimus*, whereas *legitimatio* arrived first in specialist language and then in common speech only a few centuries ago, as established scholars have fully documented. This clearly does not mean that processes of legitimation were lacking in the middle ages or in biblical times. The fact is that full awareness of, and the need to have recourse to, a defining term are born when the usual self-sufficient and taken-for-granted formulas of the conformity or validity of an action, especially of succession to power, begin to waver. It is at this point, long before the Weberian sociological notion, that the claims of legitimation (that is, of *Legitimitätanspruchen*), begin to emerge. Appeal to an acceptable argument is adopted in support of a request for recognition, intended to obtain, if not total consent, at least non-conflictuality, with responses diverging from the destructive hypothesis in the proposal actually carried out.

However, it is clear that the components of a society do not refer to the same principles which inspire social action. This is why forms of consent and dissent can change in intensity and intentionality, and therefore have meanings which are differently articulated. In this perspective, the possibility of a different solution has already been indicated, beyond the prison or the trap of the dilemma of choosing between compliance–habituation (consent) and aggressivity–contestation (dissent). Thus there has been mention of *assent* (Cipriani et al., 1983: 16–19), as an intermediate position of passive consent. Bobbio discusses abstention as being close to this effect of 'assent':

> Consent and dissent are two opposite forms of behaviour: when faced with two opposing forms of behaviour and a *tertium non datur*, the prohibition of one undoubtedly implies the compulsoriness of the other. Things are complicated a little if we admit that between consensus and dissent a third form of behaviour is possible: that is, abstention, with the result that prohibition of dissent implies the obligatoriness either of consensus or of abstention. (Bobbio, 1981: 36–7)

In reality, however, the path of abstention is not linked to absolutist contexts where, once dissent has been prevented, distancing oneself from the regime is the only possibility. Really, abstention finds its concrete expression, on the contrary, in a matrix of democratic openness, and it then takes the form of indifference, a kind of stoical unconcern, possibly watchful and far-sighted but with no concessions to any form of involvement. (In fascist Italy this was the criterion preferred by those who refused to join Mussolini's party and who never wore the black shirt despite the regulations.) Even enforced obedience can retain the character either of dissent or of consent, and of indifference as well, but never that of free acceptance.

Legitimation, on the other hand, is to be regarded as a perpetual but historically concrete process which involves not only politics and law but also other realms in which reference to values is involved. It goes without saying that possible gaps in sociological discussion of the current phenomena of legitimation do not call their implementation in question and, rather, can make implementation still more effective precisely through lack of critical analysis in its regard. One must therefore assume that the emergence of this problematic, first with Weber, then with Schmitt, and latterly with Luhmann, Habermas and Offe (with some legitimate descent between the first two and among the last three), is connected to contingent factors such as, firstly, the absence of warfare which is also disruptive in various ways for the circulation of ideas and freedom of expression of thought. In times of relative freedom from armed hostilities, it should be possible to return to a discussion which is not affected by additional variables. However, one cannot finally remain silent on the fact that it is precisely the outbreak of war which unleashes a series of processes of legitimation, starting with the first skirmishes, preparatory for the explosion of the conflict, and later arriving at the justification of mobilization, as well as the acceptance of the strategic choices made by the leaders. Final victory is undoubtedly a triumph of legitimation: but even defeat can give rise to an 'explanation' which avoids the invalidation of a regime or political formula.

From this we conclude that we see no break, at least in the contemporary age, in the processual nature of legitimation at every level. However, no legitimation remains static (even if this used to be the case when, for example, the inheritance of a throne was still by divine right and/or descent). It is always dynamic and therefore involves the delegitimating modalities themselves. The latter are already legitimate within their own frame of reference, but they remain so in a wider and obvious form when the objective of the management of power has been achieved. Every expedient is used to secure widespread acceptance of the resultant status quo.

Cynicism as a Constant in Legitimation

Reading the various contributions which have been made to the discussion of legitimation, one is struck by a remarkable agreement which, certainly unintentionally, distinguishes many passages from classical and not yet classical authors. This involves the frequent use of the category of cynicism to explain, qualify and describe many aspects of legitimating processes. Sorokin also uses this category when he says, à propos of the 'fluctuations of the systems of social relationships':

> The political ideologies reflect this situation. Hypocrisy, lying, cynicism, partiality, factionalism, carelessness about the truth and the lasting values — these are the conspicuous traits of the present-day political ideologies, no matter whether they are communistic, socialistic, fascist, Nazistic, conservative, liberal, or democratic. All claim 'open-mindedness', 'impartiality', 'scientific validity', and of course, 'justice'; and all break these claims on the first pretext. Other ideologies are '*cynical*'. They openly admit that their ideologies are but a mere means — 'derivations' and 'rationalizations' — to help the respective practices of their creators. (Sorokin, 1957: 482, emphasis added)

In the last part of this quotation there is a clear echo of Pareto in the assimilation of 'derivations' to ideologies. But the same evidence is provided for the instrumental and non-communicative function of ideologies which serve ends justifying any means. Thus, wherever the presumption of truth is flaunted, it is easy to find falsehood erected into a system. Where the need for equality is proclaimed, faction prevails. Where external rigour is manifest, special interests are concealed. Everything is carried through with a cynical attitude, looking only to the final result, the final reckoning. The claim of neutrality is thus already a choice of terrain, a legitimation of one's own opinion, however expressed. The rule is then cynical indeed, as it lies in the failure to observe those norms which are supposedly intended to be enforced for reasons of social control. Often it is not even felt necessary to try to explain the choices adopted: whoever 'constructed' a particular ideology knew well enough what to aim at, without many problems.

The ambivalence pervading every form of legitimation, in its double version as transformation-conservation (or legitimation first ascending in its constructive phase, and then descending into its conservative phase), also directly touches the basic cynicism which is its foundation. In fact, the cynical constant of modern forms of legitimation is found in the lack of concern with common norms, in contempt for the rules of the game, in the non-problematic nature of interpersonal relations, in the unconditional rejection of others' perspectives, in apparent and essential impunity attaching to the actions to be performed, in the banal defence of 'what is lawful is not legitimate'. One thus has the reverse of what could be initial ideals, even based on shared values, a common ethic, socially relevant principles, conventions established through long practice.

At first sight all this may appear to be the result of a further legitimating attempt on the part of an analyst using sociology on a phenomenon which seems rather to have the characteristics of a political ethic (see the chapter by Ardigò). In reality, rather than value judgements (although there is plainly no lack of them, and due warning should be clearly given that they can be discerned in this as in other perspectives), the investigation proposed here is a distillation of many ideas which are based on theoretical foundations as well as on empirical studies.

Not to recognize and not to admit the real nature of the dynamics of legitimation means falling into the hypocrisy of premeditated censorship and conscious reticence. And, again, hypocrisy and cynicism would be coupled in an attempt at manipulation, though a refined one. On the other hand, the very lack of discussion is an indication of an intentionality which is well aware of what is involved, and thus refrains from commitment by intervening. The accusation of easy moralism against a position of this kind is a risk to be run exactly in order to identify the real scope of formally unexceptionable viewpoints, which, however, are deeply imbued with ideologism and trappings linked to interests of various kinds.

The cynicism of legitimation (see the article by Bourricaud) is certainly quite close to the French concept of 'cynique', which has been translated as impudent, shameless, brazen. We are thus close to the peculiarities of an exercise of power which is insensitive and impartial, even scornful and contemptuous, as one can afford to be, knowing one is sufficiently protected by the untouchability of one's job, the formal recognition of the 'legitimate' right to decide for others. These are the elements adumbrated whenever the description appears in connection with the analysis of themes which touch on democracy, popular participation, education, socialism, the domination of world views imposed rather than proposed.

Further, cynicism is part of the norms, the praxis of the socio-political game. It becomes an essential part of it, with the difference that the cynics of today are very unlike the followers of Antistenes who for eight centuries, a little before and a little after the beginning of the Christian era, preached principles of equality but, most importantly, practised them plainly through a daily existence indifferent to privilege. Quite different too is the mode of dealing with values. In the past, from the Cynics, this involved basically contesting existing principles. Contemporary legitimators also manage to show respect for the norms, only to violate them cynically, perhaps to attain as status symbol a level on which further effective legitimating procedures can be engendered.

This is not, thus, the cynicism of freedom as a reaction to an unjust regime, nor yet that of a constantly alert critical spirit, ready to rage against peculation and fraud. If a vein of cynicism is at work, it is scarcely that which considers other people as individuals incapable of reacting, and so destined to the sequence of legitimation and cowering. If this were not so, it would be impossible to explain the numerous appearances of the term 'cynical' in relation to power and democracy, before and after Sorokin, in authors on the most conservative side as well as those more inclined to a perpetually dissenting sociology.

Apart from being 'muted power', cynicism is also at times a display of power itself, a clear exhibition of muscles and strength. At bottom, authoritative decision-making contains much cynicism: it is something arbitrary, binding from above, for the formal leadership. The echo in Schmitt of a similar meaning of 'classical' authoritative decision-making is clearly defined and critically re-considered by Gian Enrico Rusconi, who discusses the legitimacy of the majority in using its position of strength to justify its functioning (Rusconi, 1984: 108).

Cynical behaviour can also enter into a strategy intended to take advantage of a specific situation. Rather than concerning himself directly and from the beginning with the so-called 'prisoner's dilemma' and the 'chicken' problem, Rusconi deals with role structure and its results (Rusconi, 1984: 183–5, 240–44; Boudon, 1979: Chapter 2 para 2). But the tendency is often to consider the other person as a 'chicken', that is, quite ready to give in, to say nothing of the numerous, complex variations which are potentially inherent in feasible choices. However, this kind of analysis would involve a rather precise and speculatively problematic treatment, which implies a specific investigation.

Within the scenario of cynical action there is also the dilemma of the double option which is enforced, and not mediated, between the government of the law and the government of men. In the one case, primacy is given to the laws in force; in the other, primacy lies with the rulers. If preference is given to the first type of legitimation it might at the same time hide a rejection of individuals' innovatory demands, although their equality could be guaranteed. But something quite different is also true: the abstractness of the norms necessarily carries a strong charge of cynicism, to the extent of not taking the characteristics of individuals into account.

At all events, a government of men which resolved itself into forms of monarchy or dictatorship would increase still more the rate of cynicism, through the obvious connection with the individual interests of the potentate who is called on to exercise his right to rule in many different areas and is never neutral in his personal reckonings. Bobbio has referred to another term, the game, which from game theory to the rules of social action makes legitimation a question of prior calculations, with the intention in most cases of making trouble for someone, under the guise of the defence of what is held necessary simply because it exists in codified form. He says: 'It is useless to ask Weber if the government of men or the government of laws is better. . . . Considered objectively, the government of the charismatic leader and that of the laws are neither good nor bad. One cannot substitute the one for the other at a whim. They are different manifestations of different historical conditions' (Bobbio, 1984: 169). However, one knows which, to Weber, was the most opportune solution (Cavalli, 1981). In reality, the process of know-how confers legitimacy and adds charisma where it is lacking, so that legitimation appears as a juxtaposition, with no pre-existing consistency. Thus, a character of secondary rank at the historical level then becomes one of the first magnitude. Alone, he manages to legitimate what a whole parliament had failed to legitimize. This may occur as a result of fortuitous historical circumstances, but they certainly converge with elements already active in the protagonist involved.

It is not by chance that Claus Offe asks about the nature of the action of the majority, involving legitimation within a nation. He suggests that we use the heuristically fruitful distinction between constituted and constituting power. The important thing is to understand how the greater possibilities of legitimation are achieved (Offe, 1983). In general, the legitimating procedure begins with a principle of special importance. In this, religious ideologies have almost always played a role of the first order, sacralizing-legitimating the institutions of the status quo or the demands of a revolution. That type of intervention has become more difficult with the spread of democractic principles. With this, every legitimating solution has become precarious, provisional and contingent. Thus the elitist perspectives of the law of oligarchy so dear to Michels have been contradicted. Above all, the new legitimations seem to cut through the (weakened) social class and family structures, given that science and economics do not seem to have primary functions, at least in this aspect (Mol, 1976: 109–28, 129–41). In more concrete terms, Gellner insists on the cognitive dimension of legitimation, which would thus embrace sectors usually neglected by classical political sociology (Gellner, 1974: 25) (see too the article by Maffesoli).

From being juridically relevant, the dynamics of legitimation have become a topic for the sociology of knowledge, as G. Kateb pertinently reminds us: legitimation is the process whereby social knowledge explains and justifies prevailing social reality. Typically, legitimation is both cognitive and normative: that is, it is oriented towards not only what is but also what ought to be (Kateb, 1979). Except that, when we enter the field of practical imperatives, the trend to cynicism begins to show through in the drive to achieve desired objectives.

Power and Legitimation

Some scholars have discussed whether the exercise of force, violence, threats and terror always accompanies the legitimating process. It is easy to hypothesize that at any rate, even in less traumatic situations, change itself implies force against the existing situation or a violation of what is given. Thus, the very counterposing of the one who legitimates himself and the other who is considered illegitimate involves a conflict, in so far as the other side is also involved in a similar process, with the roles reversed. This cannot but create motives for conflict and tendencies towards definitive solutions. From a sociological viewpoint, typically value-free, it should not be possible to distinguish between legitimation and delegitimation, or, in the same way, between legitimate and illegitimate. Otherwise one would take sides for one or the other. At least the warning should be given that this double qualification occurs only for the purpose of analysis, with the understanding that a reversed reading of the two perspectives discussed is permissible.

However, the problem of legitimation is not reducible to the mere *game* of majority and minority. This would be a very narrow view, played out along the axis of solely political exchange, where, from Berger and Luckmann onwards (but going well beyond their interpretation), the phenomenon of legitimation should be located between wider co-ordinates, without which one could not even achieve an adequate scientific clarification of the mechanisms at work within state structures.

The hypostasis of power and its consequent sacralization have not, even today, lost much ground despite the collapse of many legitimations on the basis of divine or hereditary right. Only the modalities have changed, but in fact the characteristics of superiority that are acknowledged and power that is feared remain almost unaltered, despite the change of context and its protagonists. The observation that 'a large part of the possibilities that pluralistic-competitive society has for not further dissolving are probably tied to the vitality of national sentiment and the persistence of religious faith' (Pellicani, 1983: 129), can be understood in this light, aside from its divergent conclusions. The old legitimations come back into the limelight and make themselves known to the new realities as they emerge. Amongst these realities, sport, for instance, brings to light the same, now typical, problematics of socio-political and institutional management: a lack of democratic legitimation and the need for integration (Winkler, 1984). Winkler stressed the different dynamics of legitimation in the assemblies and in the procedures in acquiring competence and the power of expertise. Another emerging dimension, that of new radio and TV media, creates new divinities; the idols (no longer the actors of the past) are legitimated as national myths by the academic citadel on the scientific level, and this in turn avails itself of the new intermediaries to get across its own *creed*, and above all prestige and *credibility*. Such a process is the perfect terrain for investigation by the sociology of knowledge, with the aim of understanding how one reaches the situation where 'a dimension of epistemological prestige is not distinguished from that of social prestige' (Namer, 1982: 170; 1980: 197–201).

Science thus becomes a basis of social legitimation, but by virtue of passing through the media of advanced technologies which supersede the obsolete characters of type founts. That, in turn, is possible thanks also to a 'spirit of the whole' as Comte might say, capable of launching messages into radio waves, instead of via the slower, more elaborate approach of printed paper and reading in snatches, gradually and ponderously. With the new reality of massified communications, one old, habitual demand should be satisfied — 'The tendency accords with a corresponding system, inherent in us as individuals, of special dispositions towards command in some, and towards obedience in others' (Comte, 1848, Vol. 2: 147). On this basis, the Positivist philosopher-sociologist added

> and it is certain that we are all more or less disposed to respect any superiority, especially any moral or intellectual elevation, in our neighbour, independently of any view to our own advantage; . . . there can be no one who, in his secret mind, has not often felt, more or less vividly, how sweet it is to obey when he can have the rare privilege of consigning the burdensome responsibility of his general self-conduct to wise and trustworthy guidance. . . . (Comte, 1848, Vol. 2:148)

Such a *sweet* obedience (not to forget, on the other hand, Tocqueville's hypothesis of a 'softened' despotism) is the substratum of assent which is a solution freeing people from the travails of dangerous and difficult conflictuality in the face of power. This, further, represents the other face of cynicism, originating from below and manifesting itself in forms of instrumental service, with the prospect of personal benefits in the long term. Thus subordination to the centre, to the leader, to the institution, goes on. A similar occurrence can be found above all in critical situations, when choices have to be made quickly, as in the case of war. This therefore reinforces the pressure towards legitimation thanks to the fear of total collapse. In periods of peace, on the other hand, justifications are subjected to more critical and delegitimating analyses.

Further, 'persistent militancy, maintaining adapted institutions, must inevitably prevent, or else neutralize, changes in the direction of more equitable institutions and laws; while permanent peace will of necessity be followed by social ameliorations of every kind' (Spencer, 1902, 2: 663–4). Conditions of tranquillity, theoretically at least, favour the development of innovative demands and implementation which are obviated by the contingent necessities of *defending* the homeland (or, better, a certain type of social structure). However, on close examination, the differences are not so marked. Gaetano Mosca was right to criticize Spencer:

> For example, when he asserts that organization of the military type is coercive and that of the industrial type spontaneous, he forgets that any political organization is at one and the same time spontaneous, because it is a consequence of the sociable nature of men, and coercive, because man is not able to live without belonging to some, even primitive, political organization. (Mosca, 1972: 207)

Spontaneity (though its forms must be investigated) and coerciveness are the principal coordinates provided for the legitimation of power. In particular, there does not seem to be a clear dichotomy between their legitimating forms.

In Rousseau, the problem was to some extent resolved by the ethical justification of the social contract for maintaining political order through coercion. In fact, if called on to assist social stability, so-called de facto authority also needs to be made legitimate by, for example, ethical principles. It has rightly been observed that no moral value can be imposed under the pressure of violence, as consent would then be inspired by the prospect of defence. An *essential* trust in one who presents himself primarily as an oppressor rather than as defender is not thus to be expected. So, 'the legitimacy of a government rests not merely on consent of the governed, as Locke had maintained, but on *the freedom of the will* which makes such consent possible, whether it is ever explicitly given or not' (Adams et al., 1938: 288).

Social actions, catalysed by power as an element which is simultaneously receptor and regulator, are not wholly homogeneous, in so far as they follow different phases and achieve different results. Vilfredo Pareto recalled this explicitly in a penetrating article in the newspaper *Il Resto del Carlino* of 29 September 1920, well in advance of the arrival of fascism, and, of course, even further ahead of its collapse:

> In general, we observe various periods in the conflict which always, latent or open, exists between the select part which rules and the other which, while still ruled, aims at dethroning the former. In the first period, the ruling part simply resists innovations: in the second, it gives way, though keeping its power: in the third, it tries to go ahead of its adversaries, to deprive them of popular favour, to give even more than what is asked; but in this period, as in the preceding one, it ends up sacrificing principally its form, the more to save the substance. Finally, there comes a fourth period, in which these tricks are foiled and the chosen ruling class must give way to another. Then there begins a new cycle, partly similar to the last one.

This passage seems like a prophecy of the trajectory of fascism in Italy. First, an arrogant power (the Matteotti murder), then accommodating (the incomplete application of the race laws, for example), later, a power prepared even to sacrifice the figure of the leader himself (the night of the Grand Council), and finally a headlong rout, but with obvious infiltrations into the new leadership which was not wholly 'purged' of members of the preceding administration. Beneath this striking historical development, however, there runs the constant thread of the attitude of the mass. A *Massenloyalität*, not Habermasian but sui generis, not definable in terms of pure consensus (after De Felice) but rather of obedience (according to Bobbio's suggestion). Finally, it is symptomatic that the results of Pareto's foresights should have escaped the probing enquiries of his contemporary Weber who was supremely sensitive to the question, even more so than the Italian scholar (Weber, 1922).

Detailed analyses of the historical vicissitudes of fascism, as well as of nazism and Francoism, are offered respectively by Paolo Farneti, M. Rainer Lepsius, and Juan J. Linz (Linz and Stepan, 1978). The problem they deal with is that of the reasons for the crisis and collapse of democratic systems. The hypothesis, and the eventual proof, is based on the fact that 'political violence is both an important indicator, and a contributing cause of breakdown, but the line between cause and effect is blurred' (Linz and Stepan, 1978: 14). Indeed, if it is clear that the overthrow of democratic governments is principally due to forces of the right, it is equally clearly shown by Linz and his colleagues that the formations of the left are not wholly incapable of producing an anti-democratic conclusion either, especially if they fail to contribute to the legitimation of the existing scenario. The factors governing the degree of support for freely elected government are multiple, but it is above all this type of political regime which makes a popular contribution necessary, and not that of the administration or the police. To some extent, legitimation is also required of 'loyal' oppositions. Thus: 'legitimacy is the belief that in spite of shortcomings and failings, the existing political institutions are better than any others that might be established, and that they therefore can demand obedience' (Linz and Stepan, 1978: 16). On the other hand, the survival capacity of a democratic order is guaranteed by its *effectiveness*, that is, its achievement of a pre-established and desired goal, as well as by its *efficiency* — the satisfaction of intentions related to the pre-established goal. Clearly, a defect in the first or the second does not create problems of legitimacy, but an accumulation of negative results leads to alternatives which threaten the existing situation. By contrast, positive results in terms of effectiveness or efficiency will reinforce democracy, demonstrating, first, skill in realizing projects on the part of the political 'class' in power and, second, farsightedness in finding satisfactory solutions for emerging problems. The latter satisfaction affects above all those categories of people who are most knowledgeable in the political field and thus most active in the promotion of legitimation (or delegitimation). In this context, Ferrarotti's conception of power as both relation or interdependency, and as a structural element, is important (Ferrarotti, 1980; 1977. See also his article on page 21).

Very different in kind is legitimation through socialization, to which Rousseau refers to some extent. But, in the last analysis, this seems fairly close to the necessities of political order. It is no accident that the use of popular folklore has long gratified the nationalist spirit, justifying it completely and from earliest infancy. Geiger (who thus argues against Spencer) comments on this phenomenon in an illuminating way:

> The stratum of teachers is actually the undisputed bearer of an idyllic nationalism, permeated with romantic folklore and native lyricism, which bears its fruits in school texts and during teaching. A state of mind and a mentality are thus prepared amongst the broad strata of the population, making them sensitive to political propaganda flavoured with national slogans. The holders of political power need this faith of the population in its own unity and greatness as a cultural nation, with the aim of being able to call on it at the right moment to defend (always and only 'defend') these, its dearest possessions. (Geiger, 1970: 441)

The phenomenon is by no means new. Sorokin analysed it in the history of Christianity as a new idea with the power to transform Roman sensate culture: 'After that time the Ideational source and sanction of secular power became necessary' (Sorokin, 1957: 479). From St Ambrose to Leo the Great and Gregory the Great, the teaching of the Church pervaded education and politics with a theocratic influence which delegated every spiritual (and other) controversy to the Papacy. For the conservation of power, submission to pontifical power was necessary.

> The doctrine that God is the only source of any government and the prevailing doctrine of explicit or implicit supremacy of the spiritual power over the secular one are the manifestation of this change. . . . The objective historical reality and then the ideologies begin to show the first signs of the coming turn from the theocratic constitution to the secular. (Sorokin, 1957: 480)

In more concrete terms, Sorokin identified and listed the behaviour that was typically required for obtaining legitimation at any price:

> (1) eliminate all the *laws* that are inconvenient to it . . . ; (2) to prohibit any *religious* or *moral* or *scientific* beliefs, theories, opinions, convictions that contradict it; (3) to try to create their own 'ideologies' . . . ; (4) to forcibly teach the young, in the schools

> and outside them, mainly — and only — their hurriedly tailored doctrines . . . ; (5) to silence all opponents . . . ; (6) to seize all the means of communication. . . . (Sorokin, 1957: 481)

These procedures were launched by whoever obtained power. And once more, cynicism rules unchallenged: 'any theory, however silly it may be, is elevated to the rank of the eternal truth when it glorifies government' (Sorokin, 1957: 481). In this perspective, knowledge of the constituted social order has a legitimating function in itself; what is taken for granted becomes knowledge *tout court*. The only form of cognitive approach available becomes the only 'true' reality, and the social construction of one's own reality depends essentially on this. So, 'integration in the institutional order is the property of legitimation, whose first aim is to make the individual's life in the social world objectively meaningful' (Hamilton, 1974: 141). This statement also clearly springs from Berger and Luckmann's famous analysis (Berger and Luckmann, 1967; Cipriani et al., 1983: 33–56) (see also Luckmann's article on page 109).

Manfred Stanley is also associated with Sorokin in examining that logico-meaningful integration whose common denominator is the central meaning or idea which orders the various fragments into a unitary cosmos (Sorokin, 1957: 107–18). More original, on the contrary, is his attempt to distinguish between the three formulas of legitimation: as intellectual product, as conformity, and as coherence. (Stanley, 1973: 411–18). After distinguishing between legitimacy as adaptation to the world, and legitimation as a hermeneutic process in search of the ethical meaning of reality, Stanley develops the first distinction primarily in relation to institutions, rules and procedures. A first form of legitimacy is the product of systematic reflection, with an intellectual type of justification. The second mode is represented by a complex of habitual, conventional actions, as in common law, if not precisely of actions taken for granted and natural. The third strategy of legitimacy is found in the logico-meaningful integration already referred to which is intended to unify cognitive systems, values, norms and even institutions in a coherent model. Stanley's approach essentially suggests an intersection between the classical Weberian interpretation (traditional power is clearly recalled by legitimation as conformity), and some Schutzian (phenomenological) suggestions. The final result is stimulating: the constant striving towards the delegitimation of every pre-established routine comes from society itself (Stanley, 1973: 440).

Legitimation as an Unresolved Sociological Problem

The pressure to destabilize the legitimate, pre-constituted universe is countered by forces which are contrary not simply in the opposi-tional–conservative sense but also in the oppositional-dialectical one. (In accordance with the usual logic of cynicism, however, they are more or less masked.) That is, delegitimating action clashes with the will of others to preserve what they already have, but at the same time it faces an adversary which is much more difficult when it presents itself in its dual, as it were, double-headed, nature. In his examination of the problems of democracy and socialism Tawney is highly aware of this:

> Complete candour on such subjects, therefore, is rarely desired, and more rarely practised. In some countries, the open discussion of them is forbidden under legal penalties, for fear that the foundations of the social pyramid will be eroded or undermined. In others, they become the subject of decorous equivocation. A half-conscious hypocrisy with regard to them is a powerful vested interest. (Tawney, 1964: 190)

This hypocrisy is a close relation of cynicism and indeed logically accompanies it. At all events, there remains a strong drive at the level of the popular base towards knowledge of the truth. Tawney continued:

> That attitude does not, indeed, prevent the facts from being known, for the practical necessities of a complex society require them to be available. Its action is more subtle, but not less effective. It interposes a veil between men's minds and the realities, which, though not too opaque to allow the latter to be seen, changes their colour and proportions, and, while revealing their existence, conceals their significance. Thus shielded against too violent an impact of disturbing truths, the rulers of mankind are able to maintain side by side two standards of social ethics without the risk of their colliding. Keeping one set of values for use, and another for display, they combine, without conscious insincerity, the moral satisfaction of idealistic principles with the material advantages of realistic practise. (Tawney, 1964: 190)

In this mix of convenience and necessity, truth-knowledge-legitima-tion are the three obligatory steps of a process without legitimate issue, but also without a problematic character. The more emphatic and extended is legitimation, the less truth is attainable, at least in this overall picture, halfway between closure-masking-facade on one side and opening-unveiling-reality on the others. In any event, an ethical realism whose basic component is an inability to be frank, prevails together with an intention to deceive, with a Machiavellian flavour. Faced with such a scenario, sociology itself is sometimes forced to take on almost moralistic attitudes when its discussions are made futile or sacrificed on the altar of interests, at times directed towards legitimation, or to delegitimation (legitimating the alternative).

Clearly, not many scholars choose to build scepticism into a specific research methodology. Indeed, it seems that those champions who have taken a vow of virginity regarding the basic question of *cui prodest*, of the interests at stake in each perspective, are in the majority. The question may be asked as a matter of secondary importance, but the answer often seems to take the same form of a single line of explanation (either conspiratorial or reassuring).

On the two fronts of the debate some of the heavy guns among contemporary sociologists are entrenched as regards sharpness of observation, fecundity in articles, and academic charisma. The contribution of Habermas and Luhmann to the discussion of legitimating processes has now become a set piece for anyone undertaking a treatment of the subject. As is well known, Luhmann's argument is based on legitimation through procedure (or *by* procedure, as others prefer to translate the German term *durch*) (Luhmann, 1983). The Bielefeld sociologist starts from the observation that it is the system which produces legitimacy, to which the person is called to adapt himself through the cognitive process. The laws themselves presuppose such adaptation. Briefly, every decision of the system derives its legitimation from the fact that one takes this acceptance for granted. However, at the individual level this may not happen, which is why legitimation must be acquired either with pure and simple coercion of a physical kind, or thanks to the procedure (or proceeding) which foresees four solutions: elections, legislation, judicial activity and administration. Each of these procedures is set up to achieve its goal, that is, decision, but also to give meaning, a sense, to social action.

Thus Luhmann (see his article p. 101) goes beyond Weber in investing legitimation with a systemic-institutional character. But he agrees with Weber on the analysis of social action whilst arguing that it is so complex that it requires a *reduction* (of complexity). All these stratagems ought, in the perspective of legitimation through procedures, to bridge the gap between political system and society. In fact, however, the questions left open at the level of voting, legislative planning, judicial and administrative process restore meaning to the perennial question: is not legitimation basically self-legitimation?

Again, is real and non-discriminatory co-ordination between all the projects of political intervention really practicable? Can the expressive nature of an electoral consultation really converge with the instrumental nature of administrative acts? What is not convincing in Luhmann is above all the ethereal, indefinable, common ceiling of *value-programmes* which are supposed to guarantee a propitious outcome of the many operational difficulties. On the concrete level, then, all consideration of the feelings, the basic expectations of individuals, is set aside (Gozzi, 1980: 46–60). Moreover, the result of value-programmes could not be otherwise; they are too much like functional requisites and they minimize the weight of opinions to the point of cancelling them out. Everything is assessed in the light of the legal system.

These and other objections (see Fraser's article p. 119) to Luhmann's theorization have had ample resonance among students of the crisis of legitimacy (see also Vrcan's article p. 127) and of the ungovernability of the system. It is not worth repeating them in this Introduction, but see Poggi, 1978; Tulumello, 1984; Scamuzzi, 1982; Febbrajo, 1975. But it is useful to take up, however briefly, Habermas's alternative argument which counterposes his theory of society to Luhmann's social technology (Habermas and Luhmann, 1971) and 'clearly rejects any explanation of legitimacy as an effect or by-product of the management of the administrative political system and thus of legitimacy as a *grundlos* acceptance, without reasons and motivations, of the existing order' (Rusconi, 1982: 77). The Frankfurt sociologist starts from an analysis of the concept of crisis and establishes a differentiation between crisis linked to the system and crisis related to identity, the first with the characteristic of rationality, the second that of legitimation (Habermas, 1976a). Within these parameters, Habermas's argument moves forward with a crucial superimposition of wishful thinking, his scholar's dreams and desires which at times make his analysis awkward and even imprecise (also linguistically). This consequently affects the very description of the political system under discussion (the German, obviously) which does not facilitate its applicability in other contexts. Even later capitalism's ability to resist seems to disappoint Habermas's expectations: 'contrary to the predictions . . . social values and, above all, possessive individualism are still capable of supporting late capitalism' (Hall, 1981: 84).

Instead of ending at this point, the question gives rise to the theory of communicative action (Habermas, 1985) in order to overcome the hiatus between the formation of consensus and the exercise of power. The underlying hypothesis is that of a consensual theory of truth (Cotesta, 1984) which resists any attempt to impose a constrictive formula and is not subject to the cynicism of the old modes of legitimation. In fact, in 'Wahrheitstheorien' Habermas (1973a) had already pointed to non-discrimination, equality, reciprocity of roles and so on as elements of the ideal situation. However, not even in this new formula is respect for something 'binding' lacking, even though this is expressed as legitimate rule. It has been rightly observed that

> there is a significant distinction between levels, of which Habermas does not seem fully aware. On one level there are the individual decisions whose legitimacy is tested one by one, and on the other the almost transcendental problem of deciding in favour of a specific conception of legitimacy (the decision about discursive rationality). On both levels the criterion is reference to the ideal lingusitic situation. But how is this approximation measured? (Rusconi, 1982: 63–4)

In practice one is faced with two legitimating forms: a *micro*-legitimation, referring to routine in the interventions of the ordinary administration of power, and a *macro*-legitimation which involves choice of *the* basic orienting criterion for defining and measuring the quality and quantity of approximation to the ideal goal of discursive action (Brena et al., 1984).

Finally, Alan Wolfe's long chapter on capitalism has more of a cutting edge to it. His horizon is typically North American, but the perspective ranges more widely to France, Germany, Great Britain and Italy. He discusses, among other things, the crisis of the parties, which are themselves transformed into objects of conflict, in so far as the history of capitalism necessarily produces a progressive shift of the areas of legitimating intervention from families to parties and finally to the State itself. 'The fact that the State assumes responsibility as legitimator of last resort means that all other institutions have failed in this regard . . . The nationalization of the legitimation function is a symptom of, not a solution to, the legitimacy crisis of late capitalism' (Wolfe, 1977: 311–12). The conclusion is more ideological than properly reasoned sociologically: 'it is capitalism that should be under attack, for democracy is working' (Wolfe, 1977: 334).

The theme of democracy indeed remains the key to the dynamics of legitimation. To recognize it as such, its philosophical and social matrices should be acknowledged:

> Democracy can be defined in many ways . . . it can be defined as the political system which is characterized by the transferral of dissent, if one can call it such, from outside the system to the inside. The passage from the autocratic to the democratic State has occurred, technically speaking, through the process of constitutionalization of the right of resistance, which has transformed the purely natural right of resistance to oppression, whose legitimation has always been only posthumous, depending on its result, into a positive right to opposition, whose legitimacy is pre-constituted and which is thus lawful whatever its result may be. (Bobbio, 1981: 42–3. See also Mongardini, 1969; Ardigò, 1980; Fisichella, 1982)

In essence, legitimacy should not need heroes, nor have recourse to the exercise of benevolent tolerance. Dissent remains a right to be expressed without fear of coercion. However, this is perhaps an already obsolete, exhortatory formula. The driving force of new, refined, effective legitimatory mediations seems ever more evident (see the conclusion to Bellah's article), and it requires scientific alertness and informed preparation. This is why the problem of the sociological understanding of legitimation is very far from being resolved and remains immediate, perhaps even more so than in the past.

PART I
THEORIES OF LEGITIMATION

Legitimation, Representation and Power

Franco Ferrarotti

In an historic moment like the present one, where in the East as in the West all ideologico-political systems seem to be shaken to their foundations in different ways, and in the aftermath of a crisis of their function and direction, the theme of legitimation has emerged in its broader significance. It is forcing itself both on the attention of the specialists and on the median awareness of the broad masses. We live in a nuclear condition where the question is not just that of escaping the inconveniences of endemic social disorder, widespread criminality and potential anarchy, as it was in Hobbes's time. The very physical survival of humanity is daily and immediately put in jeopardy today.

All-embracing ideological formulas seem to have lost their captivating *pathos*. Their promises can no longer capture the loyalty of human beings. They are no longer capablc of justifying sacrifices made for them today in the prospect of a better tomorrow. Rarely in history has there been such *a pronounced break between institutional services and popular expectations* as in the current state. The rhythm of development of the major public organisms and their ability to respond to the demands of society are in a state of serious, chronic backwardness as regards the periods of existence in which people actually experience their problems. The basic everydayness of society is acknowledged less and less in the rites of officialdom. The social is richer and more interconnected than the institutional in its formal sense. Between the experience of individual citizens and the organisms supposedly delegated to represent them, a process of mutual estrangement is under way. The suspicion that *political representation is no longer representative* is gaining ground.

In these circumstances, the political systems and their elites, which today are in a position of leadership that is nearly untouchable in their respective societies, cannot delude themselves that they can continue indefinitely to live on accumulated capital. *Today, on a world scale we are witnessing the transition from political power as a personal, absentee or passive domain to a rational collective function.* This means legitimacy can no longer be considered as beyond discussion, like a metaphysical premise, or as belonging to a purely speculative or juridico-formal order, secured once and for all. Today, legitimacy refers us to a laborious process of legitimation, with historical roots, and therefore in constant, problematic development. Consequently, inert power, formerly the most certain kind in that it was by definition removed from the challenges of the present, runs the risk of becoming simply irrelevant. Today, power has to translate itself into initiative and control. However, *one can only control what one knows*, and then not in general or abstract terms, but rather in functional, specific ones. On the other hand, knowledge itself does not obey a purely internal logic, but *seems linked to the cluster of material interests in life, directly or indirectly*, interests which the beings who make up real society necessarily enter into among themselves.

In this perspective, one can state at the outset that the theme of 'legitimation and society' has been presented so that, while appreciating its modesty, reasonable doubts arise about its rigour. It laudably precludes too pronounced a guiding emphasis, restricting itself to indictating broadly and very generally *opening up the problems*. The conjunction connecting 'legitimation' with 'society' is certainly a weak, elided one, putting 'legitimation' and 'society' on the same plane, perhaps mindful of Weber's famous title 'Economy and Society'. However, whether this be understood as a post-historical postulate of a metaphysical kind, an historically produced and evolving process, or again as a voluntaristic result ahistorically determined and conceived of as 'geometrically' demonstrable, the fact remains that legitimation is fundamental for the constitution of society. Legitimation constitutes the social in the sense that there is no society which does not rest on the original agreement. This not only guarantees its temporal duration, but puts it in being from the start. In other words, *between 'legitimation' and 'society' there lies a relation not of chance circumstance, but rather of necessity*.

However, it is true that amongst contemporary sociologists and politologists and in addition the great majority of observers of social phenomena, a rather 'weak' notion of legitimation is widespread. Thus, on the one hand, there is diligently and primarily an emphasis on psychologico-behavioural aspects, whilst on the other there is stress on its formal characteristics, or at least those open to complete, probing translation into formally codified institutions. This proceeds to the point where the concept, the very term, of 'society' is absorbed into the more structured and manageable one of 'State'. Yet it should scarcely be necessary to observe that *legitimacy thereby runs the risk of becoming confused with legality*, and that one thus loses sight of the living essence of the problem: the fact that *the basis and taproot of legitimacy lie in what has usually, perhaps too hastily, been called the subject population.* It is here and nowhere else that the summits of society and the power they exercise find, or may hope to find, their legitimation.

In its true meaning, legitimation goes beyond its reductively politico-institutional sense, what neo-Marxists speak of as the 'autonomy of the political', as though this could leave the 'social' out of discussion. Alternatively, there is discussion of the 'concept of the political', impoverished and reduced to the schematic antithesis between 'enemy' and 'friend', according to the theory of the 'political concept' (*politische Begriff*) lately popularized by Carl Schmitt. In reality, *legitimation involves the origins of obligation, which are the source of the social and the original formation of the political community*.

On the basis of the reductive conception of legitimacy it is all too easy to equate the problem posed by legitimation with that of governability, to be guaranteed by the patching-up job of 'social engineering', or purely internal modifications of the existing institutional fabric. This would make it the equivalent of psychological consensus, obtained with the procedures offered today by mass psychology and its manipulative techniques. Much wider is the range of the legitimating matrix of power in its different forms: social, economic, and political.

Popular sovereignty cannot be said to be either absorbed or satisfied in the institutional forms to which it gives rise, unless we fall into the procedural conception of democracy whereby wanting democracy means being content with it. *Undoubtedly democracy is a whole made up of norms and procedures, but it is also a whole composed of 'ideal' contents, transcendental values and futuristic impulses*, for which pressure from below and agreement from the summit seem equally indispensable. This, it seems clear, involves a conception of legitimacy which is not purely legalistic: an open conception, which does not eliminate possibilities not yet normatively defined, and yet not reducible to the letter of existing norms. Perhaps here one should repeat an important Aristotelian lesson, that which discusses the *politéia*, the polity, a term almost always translated as 'political system' or still more as 'constitution'. However, the constitution is precisely the written law, in that it concerns the basic law to which the ordinary laws must refer as to their original framework and source of obligation. The Aristotelian polity, on the other hand, probably indicates a term, and a source, which go beyond the written laws. Rather than of written laws and the constitution, they make us think of the 'regime', or what emerges from, or lies behind, the written laws: that harmony in the community which no written law could create if it did not already exist which gives the various written laws and the constitution itself their binding form. The latter is linked to that everydayness of historical life in the broad sense, and the internal disposition which ante-date written laws, and which in a similar context Montesquieu termed the 'spirit of the laws'.

In this strong sense, legitimacy includes and also goes beyond, and precedes, legality. The process of legitimation itself could not be exhausted in a formal production of norms were it not coherently underpinned by the *common sentiments of the community*. Furthermore, legitimacy is a fundamentally historical concept. That is, it is not established once and for all, but rather, in a Weberian sense, it is open as 'chance', the possibility–probability of guaranteed effectiveness; understanding 'guarantee' always problematically, never as a dogmatic possession. In this regard we might perhaps recall an especially penetrating passage from Heidegger, rather than Lukàcs's concept of 'possible consciousness':

> All legitimation is necessarily located in a certain circle of the *possible*. In effect, it is a purposeful relation with the existing, and thus with regard to its possibility, already subject to an ontological motivation, explicit or not. By virtue of its being, this motivation always by necessity provides certain spheres for the flowering of the possible, by way of the self-modification of the nature of the possibility: according to the constitution of the Being of the existing, which is to be revealed. In fact, the Being, or rather the motivating constitution of Being, is to be found there, in the form of the transcendental necessity for human reality, rooted in the special *freedom* of the latter. By essentially deriving its ground or 'reason', its origin, from the fact that what 'grounds' is a finite liberty, it is the reflection of *this* origin which manifests itself in the 'rather than' (*potius quam*) of the propositions of the principles of reason. However, in its turn, bringing out the concrete transcendental connections between the 'reason' and the 'rather than' leads to clarifying the Idea and Being as such (essence and existence, 'something', nothing, negativity). (M. Heidegger, 'What is the essential being of a ground or "reason".' Emphasis in original)

Maybe this text sounds too 'philosophical', and thus unduly abstract in the ears of the students of systems theories, and of the brisk engineers and menders of constitutions in trouble. However, 'possible consciousness' has already had its tests on the historical level, and perhaps Robespierre's statement, the day before his arrest on 26 July 1794, sounds relevant here:

> I swear it exists . . . that tender, impetuous and irresistible passion, torment and delight of magnanimous souls, that deep horror of tyranny, that compassionate zeal for the oppressed, that sacred love of one's country, that still *more sublime and sacred love of humanity* without which a great revolution is merely one dazzling crime that destroys another; it exists, that generous ambition to establish on earth the first Republic in the world. (Hampson, 1974: 293. Emphasis added)

It is in these words, to be taken as a spiritual testament, given the occasion on which it was delivered by the protagonist of the 'longest year of the Revolution', 1793, that the specific, unique contribution of the French Revolution must be grasped. Here too one should seek the not merely polemical and politically contingent motive for the critical questions posed of the Revolution by the greatest English conservative, Edmund Burke. In his *Reflections* (Burke, 1982), he remarked that the French Revolution, unlike the 1776 American Revolution, was not pervaded by a pragmatic political orientation, as was expressed clearly and forcefully in the American motto 'no taxation without representation'. Rather, it appeared as a radical overthrowing of the existing situation and its legitimating tradition, as social re-birth justified by a dogmatic rationalist scheme. It was justified by a timeless and absolute schema indifferent to traditions and the peculiarities of time and place. It took place according to the abstract-ideological logic of those Jacobin ardours which tended to liquidate traditions as a whole, en bloc, recognizing in them neither psychologically reassuring functions nor cognitive values as a technique of survival (Ferrarotti, 1961).

I have remarked elsewhere that Burke's undoubted merit lay in being the only eighteenth-century politician to have understood the new, historically unheard-of nature of the French Revolution. Burke grasped that a revolutionary movement whose leading ideas are presented as a systematic body of doctrines, instead of originating in specific problems based on the concrete experience of everyday coexistence (in his words, a matter of 'local grievance or of local accommodation'), involves the whole person, achieves universal importance, and must ultimately show itself to be necessarily exclusive and dogmatic.

This is essentially the reason Burke first rather warmly welcomed the American Revolution, which seemed to him pragmatic and shot through with that prudent good sense he regarded as the politician's most important virtue, following Aristotle's teaching. In contrast, he was later to oppose and criticize the French Revolution with decisiveness, as 'revolution of principles'. For us, the difference between the two revolutions, with the benefit of two centuries of critical hindsight, seems evident. This was not the case for contemporaries, or rather more recent commentators. Thomas Jefferson's harshly negative judgement is well known. He saw in Burke's behaviour the most sickening opportunism, as in the letter to B. Vaughan of 1791.

> The Revolution of France does not astonish me so much as the revolution of Mr Burke. I wish I could believe the latter proceeded from as pure motives as the former. . . . How mortifying that this evidence of the rottenness of his mind must oblige us now to ascribe to wicked motives those actions of his life which wore the mark of virtue and patriotism.

This is a judgement that Marx, decades later, was to follow to the letter:

> This sycophant . . . was an out and out vulgar bourgeois. . . . The laws of commerce are the laws of Nature, and therefore the laws of God . . . No wonder that, true to the laws of God and of Nature, he always sold himself in the best market. (Marx, 1946; 786)

In the failure to perceive the difference between the two great revolutionary phenomena there is clearly a serious limitation which still marks contemporary politology. There is an analytical inability to make a *conceptual, operational distinction between power and authority*. At the same time this must avoid the formal simplification of the phenomenon of power, which is both *relation* and *structure*, and thus not reducible to a pure semiological sign (N. Luhmann), a biological metaphor (T. Parsons), simple communicative competence (J. Habermas), nor yet a pure psychological drive suspended between legitimacy and 'fear' (G. Ferrero) (Ferrarotti, 1981). Such reduction can be effected only at the cost of a process of elimination which amounts to radical de-realization.

Neither the understanding–justification of a neo-systemic or technocratic kind (typical of neo-structural-functionalism in its radical version), nor a more or less sophisticated theorization of a psychological or socio-linguistic variety, seems adequate to take full measure of the process of legitimation. This is essentially an historical process with an uncertain outcome. This makes it dramatic in the true sense, not to be confined to a closed system with timeless validity. This in fact would require basing legitimacy on normative formalism, and repressing the permanent tension between civil society and State to the point of disregarding it. It requires cancelling legitimacy's basic function as a stimulus open to the possible, and as transcendent parameter against which the effective performance of existing institutions can be measured.

As an historical process, legitimation cannot be allowed to exhaust itself in an existing, formally codified legality, nor in popular, psychologically conceived, expectations. It appeals and is linked to interests as they are experienced and perceived by basic groups and social classes. Linked to the partition of society, legitimation is directly connected with the power which dominates society in every specific phase of its development. Thus one cannot rightly discuss legitimation in a general sense. For this reason, it would still be useful to refer to the 'Discourses on the Decades of Livy' by Niccolò Machiavelli (rather than to the recent reflections of René Girard), where Machiavelli makes us recognize that beneath any formal legitimacy there lies an act of violence and basic illegitimacy, necessary for the foundation of the city. That is, a Romulus who kills Remus *prevents any ambiguity or uncertainty in attributing power to either one of the twins.* The problem, raised here with clarity, is that of the particular viewpoint of the discussant, which determined his historical and political self-location. Furthermore, for this reason, *legitimation is not a question of self-legitimation.* From this perspective, it seems clear that elitism (Mosca) and radical neo-structural-functionalism (Luhmann) are contrary and symmetrical. As a conceptual orientation and as regards their explanatory capacity, they are equivalent. The threat which hangs over legitimation is its adequacy from the ethical standpoint, insofar as this is expressed in the average social awareness of a given historical phase (Ferrarotti, 1979; 1983).

The Moral Question and Legitimation

Achille Ardigò

Immanuel Kant concluded his *Critique of Practical Reason* (1788) with a remark that has become famous: 'two things fill the mind with every new and increasing admiration and awe . . . *the starry heavens above*, and the moral law within' (Kant, 1959: 260). As we know, Kant deduced from the common character of his feelings of admiration for these two objects the common nature of the rational method in research. The success of astronomical research and of the natural sciences in general suggested entering 'on the same path in treating of the moral capacities of our nature' which 'may give us hope of a like good result' (Kant, 1959: 261). Kant's conclusion comes to my mind as I begin this discussion of the relation between morality and legitimation. The connection between the two objects — 'the starry heavens above and the moral law within' — established by his admiration, reminded me that it has also, as it were analogously, prompted other scholarly reflections. In the 1950s and 1960s, Talcott Parsons, with an effectiveness which has no subsequent rivals, led us sociologists to grasp the basis of every concrete society at a given time as lying in the correspondence between the constellation of culture and societal norms composed of values and symbols (the cultural-normative cluster), and the moral law, internalized in every citizen through family, school and social education.

If I still believed in this approach for my own sociological analysis, and wanted to understand the most significant connections between social change and the 'moral question' which is so clearly at the centre of the crisis of democracy in my country (but not only in mine), I should direct myself towards totally macro-sociological types of analysis. I should want to look for the impact which changes in social organization have had on the cultural heaven of values, and above all on which particular values. Taking a less 'objectifying' attitude, I should investigate the impact which reciprocal alterations occurring between the cultural system and its agencies of control and reinforcement, and social structures in general, have had on the collective, and also the motivational, aspects of institutional and private behaviour. I should ask myself how much the urgent immediacy of today's 'moral question' in Italy, at the root of its political democracy, results from crises of social integration in the ruling classes, and how much from the current discovery of a long-standing contradiction: that between traditional private and public morality, and the objective structural dynamics which create contradictions between the ends and norms of the political system. In short, I should ask if the 'moral question' reflects crisis in the agencies socializing, selecting and controlling the ruling class, or if it is for the most part a result of the current transition from one social system, whose cultural-normative and control apparatus is now inadequate, to another still being born.

I do not in fact believe it possible to apply the approach of the natural sciences to considerations of relations between morality, social transformation and problems of democracy. Moreover, I am not even convinced that the current condition of moral malaise in our democracy, and its remedy, mainly depend either on the collapse or on the restoration of particular ethico-cultural values existing, in the first instance, at the societal level. Nor do they depend on the crisis in the controlling agencies which enforce conformity to these values. As a sociologist, I do not propose primarily a reading of the current moral crisis of democracy in terms of a 'metaphysics of values'. This does not mean that the approach is not valid, but it is valid in other systems of thought.

Certainly, to select the metaphysics of value and the primacy of education as a way of examining the connection between morality and society has the advantage of avoiding the dangers of relativism and situationism. However, transformations in the social organization of life and work in the past few decades have deeply affected both the heaven of values, the nature of societies and the human phenomenon itself, as well as our thinking about them. As examples, I would point to the time of the economic miracle and mass consumption, then the following years of the long stagflation crisis after 1971, with the collapse of the Bretton Woods monetary system: after this, the oil crises, and finally the current transformations connected with the new scientific-technical revolution.

Thus, the re-discovery of the moral problem, not just of the 'moral question', has been accompanied by a search for new epistemological approaches, especially in the social sciences. One such approach refuses to follow Kant in separating the empirical and the rational in questions of morality. It seeks the moral system through a study of concrete communication between persons, in the direct interactions and relations between the Ego and the Other (the others). It sees this as the origin and process of change-adaptation of political structures as well as of economic, civil and cultural ones. This is the social communications approach, applicable to morality as well, which has brought together such disparate theorists as N. Luhmann and J. Habermas.

For the former, as a systems theorist, morality springs from successful communication exchanges which involve relations between individuals, real people. In complex societies, for Luhmann at least, there is in all moral questions only a 'confrontation between persons' (Luhmann, 1984c: 12; 1977b; 1978). Like any other human expression, morality for Jürgen Habermas may also be generated for societal norms by way of linguistic intersubjectivities, which result from communication between individualities. The discursive formation of the norm, in Habermas's schema, also includes language (Habermas, 1980: 301).

As he says, 'the intersubjectivity of the world in which subjects live together only by reason of their current linguistic communication is not a universal to which individuals may be subordinated in the same way as elements are subordinated to their classes' (Habermas, 1980: 301).

Analysis of the moral norm in communications terms, rather than those of the metaphysics of values, is further exposed to the risk of indeterminacy regarding the ultimate basis of morality itself, as I mentioned. In this approach, as Mario G. Lombardo rightly observed, 'the horizontal axis of communication takes the upper hand over the vertical one of decision, and the finiteness of the subject must presuppose that its decision itself is contingent' (Lombardo, 1984: 23).

I believe, therefore, that one should at least integrate the communications analysis of ethics with the following assumption. Behind understanding, which is always partial, both during and then after interpersonal, doubly contingent and morally selective communication, there lies the transcendental mystery of man, which cannot be reduced to a psychic system. One may see in this mystery, as St Paul says, the person with new life in Christ, who is thereby 'free from the (moral) law', as law which reverts into a prescriptive, sanctionary commandment whenever the newly-born in Christ falls back into sin (*Romans* 7). The genesis of moral knowledge cannot, in short, be entirely reduced to communication.

It is not fortuitous that Habermas, in *Legitimation Crisis* (Habermas, 1976a: 95) should follow Piaget's authority in entrusting the genesis of moral consciousness to the individual's own ontogenetic development. Moral consciousness in the normal child should thus grow simultaneously with his cognitive development. However, this empirical grounding of the moral sense also has its limits. Moreover, the communications approach also has every limitation in terms of moral self-reference. It corresponds to a social situation where no one can any longer honestly say there is a normative value centre in the Western, or indeed the global, social system so powerful that it can integrate all subjectivities. This is precisely because of the excess of functional differentiation in organized society. Nor, still less, can it be said that such a centre reduces people's freedom to the point of determinism in strategic areas.

No Galbraith can tell us today what he wrote in Chapter 19 of *The Industrial State*, in 1967, that the technostructure was so prescient and powerful as to eliminate the freedom of the consumer and to base the market on the supply of commodities designed years before.

It is true that new technostructures, today based on computers and tomorrow on mass bio-engineering, produce unsettling shock-waves in production and the division of labour. However, a mammoth like IBM, even in its biggest research and development investments and joint projects like the recent one with the Italian IRI (Institute for Industrial Reconstruction), is not assured of the outcomes. It must always be afraid that new enterprises are being formed from nothing, which will capture segments of the market because they are better interpreters of the demand that the great colossus had been planning to create for years.

Many analysts followed Daniel Bell in arguing that the cultural-motivational and the scientific-technological-economic systems each proceeded by different paths which never met. Thus, the contradictions of capitalism were seen as essentially cultural, and so ultimately as moral, especially where they involved the conduct of the broad mass of citizens and the conduct professed or prescribed by technocratic-political-economic-military elites. Not by chance, it is precisely in this period of moral crisis in the democracies that at every social level the demand for greater moral, personal and collective selectivity is growing. This is despite the growth in some areas of diachronic planning for enterprises and ruling elites. (However, totalitarianisms too are suffering from widespread phenomena of demoralization without growth in productivity and innovation.)

Others have interpreted this demand for an increase of morality in democracy and a revival of interest in ethical themes as the result, primarily, of a perceived, widespread loss of overall meaning in national and international social systems as well as in individuals. The current transformations produce a maximum of functional differentiation in the adaptive responses to an environment laden with danger and imbalances, and a future which is rich with potential and promise, but as a whole threatening.

We possess ever broader, more up-to-date capabilities for information, documentation and sectoral analyses, increasingly with instant access. However, apart from immediate circumstances and some extrapolations regarding the socio-technological future, no one really knows anything about the compatibility between parts of the whole, nor whether the various, separate trends under way are compatible. This naturally encourages ambivalent judgements. In a recent work, Armando Peccei has remarked:

> Even by those who have the highest political or social functions, or whose opinion has considerable moral influence, an overall judgement on the total situation is never made. . . . Indeed, in practice, individual sectors or fields are considered separately, as though we were dealing with discrete entities on which others had no influence. (Peccei, 1984: 6,8)

Thus, he continues, one passes off as a projection of the future 'the indelible illusion that scientific-technical developments are the decisive element of human progress, despite their anarchic character and the thoroughly bad use made of them . . .' (Peccei, 1984: 8).

Moreover, as enunciated in the well known book by M. Crozier, S.P. Huntington and J. Watanuki, the criticism of participatory and corporate democracy that was elaborated in the late 1960s and throughout the 1970s also moves in this direction. Democracy is consolidated in its formal practices, but consensus is aimless, and democracy is anomic. Democracy which is no longer underpinned by goals such as, formerly, religion, nationalism and ideology, loses its force (Crozier et al., 1975).

New demands for morality arise unexpectedly as a *lucus a non lucendo* (light from a place without light) precisely from the growing observation of a 'global lack of modern moral and political leadership, which shakes the confidence of people'. The new moral demands are thus different from the utilitarian motivation, theorized, for example, in Hume's *Enquiry Concerning the Principles of Morals*, which was open to the sense of humanity. After decades of pan-economism and pan-politicism not only confined to the field of politics, today's demand for morality is not just inspired, as Hume maintained, by the pleasant sensation of esteem and approval for any action considered to be useful by the lights of reason. The civilization of the mass media and of political spectacle has made increasingly broad strata of the public distrustful of the manipulatory procedures for acquiring or bestowing consensus through spectacularized images and sentiments. As Luhmann has also recognized, it is precisely because of this that, especially today, morality implies *reference to the person in his uniqueness and identity* which is 'ineffable' in the language of science. It implies personal example, the moral responsibility of leadership, or the confidence born of interpersonal communication, confronted with brief face-to-face solidarity. These solidarities exist, without the screening effect of representation, in everyday experience, but in the light of the overall control of compatibilities for the individual, the small group and the social system.

In Hume's analysis of morality, the leap of civilization means that morality no longer stops at the frontiers of the nation. An elementary solidarity with all those who dwell on earth, especially in the Third and Fourth worlds, thus grows among active minorities, despite or perhaps because of the old nationalistic disputes which still hold back Western European politics.

A new moral system which has recovered its autonomy from economics, politics and aesthetics, if in fact it cannot avoid internally differentiating itself, will have to confront the remaining systemic logic which consists of differentiation, fragmentation and selectivity in communications of self-referential, specialist, and other kinds.

I distance myself from Luhmann's 'theoretics of ethics' because of the difference in their nature between the moral system, which cannot avoid being based on the personal and the interpersonal, and the collective system, which on the contrary can be analysed entirely in terms of the evolution of forms and the differentiation of functions and organisms. A communications analysis of ethics with an empirical base (heuristically valid as regards the increasing differentiation and fragmentation of behaviour and codes of self-reference) should at least be integrated with the presumption that there exists a possibility of encounter in the fullness of the term, interpersonal empathy (Husserl), or at least of effective processes of reciprocal interaction lying behind that always uncertain grasp of anyone committed to successful communication with others. As I have said, there is above all a conception of the human person which is not merely systemic-empirical.

When applied to democratic societies, this fundamental argument means that there is no room for morality where the practice and to some extent active respect for the rules of the democratic game are merely put at the service of goals of utility, for interest-aggregating groups, or for sentiments.

And yet, in these years of adaptation to the great stagflation crisis, democracy in several Western countries has also often celebrated its rites through greater participation from workers and clients in schools, public health and cities. Their motivations are obvious and Pareto would have classified them, with due exceptions, simply as instincts of combination or the persistence of aggregates. It is not fortuitous that in the 1960s the ideology of development, measured in terms of gross national product, was dominant. In the 1970s, it was the ideology of political exchange, including social and union policy, even when the deeper and unacknowledged inspiration of some union action was of a moral, universalistic kind, i.e. that of distributive justice.

Democracy in this period, especially in Western Europe, had been adapted in a neo-corporativist direction by central political exchange. But by good fortune a vast, diffuse movement of communication and action arose to restore the moral dimension as an independent variable of solidarity. It was also inspired by the urging of fear and need, but it existed despite its inevitable, illegitimate agglomeration with other motives and inspirations.

I refer to the deep inspiration of peace and to the 'desire for friendship and neighbourliness among men which we can recognize — phenomenologically — as present and operational . . . at the civil level' (*La forza*, 1984: 42). I refer to the growth of conscientious objection to compulsory military service, to movements for ecological morality, for peace and disarmament, for the struggle against world hunger, for alternative health care, a religious defence of life, and a non-manipulatory use of the mass media. I refer to the growth of questions, if not of ethical judgements, about the traditional divisions between the sexes as well as about the most varied pioneering exploits of scientific research in biology.

Ecological ethics, peace, biological and therapeutic ethics and so on, are perhaps the chapter headings of the new differentiation, albeit emerging uncertainly, of the moral system. It is significant that much of the — also mass — communication whereby these ethical demands are broadcast has a character contrary to that of differentiating specificity. It implies small groups for mutual assistance, local and universalistic at the same time, which are virtually inseparable from the human environment as opposed to the political system.

Thus the ongoing social transformations seem to have paradoxical effects in terms of morality: On the one hand, they emphasize the fragmentation and specialist differentiation within the media of communication, the fragmentation of roles and communication with only partial commitment. They thereby increase the 'difficulty of creating unity within the person' and the subsequent fear at the personal and collective level of starting non-resolvable processes which are thus not controllable in their negative effects. On the other hand, they stimulate the demand for a synthetic, moral selection of behaviour which is capable of overcoming the crisis of personal identity, and at the collective level of controlling overall compatibilities in the interaction between persons and collectivities.

In the contemporary societies of the advanced West, it is especially in the delegated moral sphere of the family that we can observe the growth in demand for interpersonal morality. It comes just when the success of communication in the desired sense is most unlikely.

> On the one hand it seems there is some indication of increased demand for genuine family relations. Often the family is seen as the reality which can and must revive and set to rights situations of existential suffering and loneliness . . . On the other, the fragility of family ties is growing . . . Little is needed to send considerable numbers of families into crisis . . .
>
> In general, one notes a worrying lack of communication, of welcome and dialogue within families. . . . We may discern in the background of this circle of social relations the unsatisfying and really conflictual way in which the man–woman relation is generally experienced. (*La forza*, 1984: 46)

It is also significant that the 'moral question' constantly involves the political life of Italy's democracy just as public morality is experiencing one of its periods of greatest crisis, despite the great efforts expended in promoting it, and the revolt of the corporate interests of the tax-evaders attains unprecedented levels of collective expression in the country.

One asks why these apparently paradoxical aspects exist. Does the lack of mutual acceptance and common consensus in the system of guiding values of life explain this simultaneous moral demand and the maximum fragility of personal identities and genuinely moral communication? The 'metaphysicians of values', the theorists of morality as product of education, reply affirmatively. Or did perhaps pan-economism, together with political exchange, and the subsequent pan-ideologism replace with money and consumption the importance of personal recognition of esteem and disfavour, on which many, after Hume, say morality in society depends?

Those, like Luhmann, who reject the explanations of the 'metaphysicians of values' tend towards the second variety. For Luhmann, if there is to be communication specifically oriented by morality, or morally relevant communication, two prerequisites are needed. First, communication must be expressed as an encounter *between real persons* and not merely between players of roles. In this sense, as noted, the moral system, unlike the social one, must be 'fully personalized'. Second, interpersonal communication must be regulated by marks of esteem and be corrected 'as though it were a cybernetic process of esteem and disfavour' (Luhmann, 1984c: 12, 14). (In this, as I remarked, Luhmann takes up Hume's thought.)

Both prerequisites are, for Luhmann, liable to influence, and really are influenced, by variations in the socio-structural conditions of the social context where communication occurs. Thus: 'the solid blocks of morality float on a soft base' (Luhmann, 1984c: 13).

Moreover, as functional differentiation proceeds, replacing the society of orders and strata, and destroying the dominant form of inclusion in extended families and ethnic groups, the less easy communication becomes. This is because the reflexive autonomy of the moral choices of individuals increases. One could say that for Luhmann the evolution of morality undergoes a process contrary to that described by Max Weber. That is, there is a passage from the ethic of responsibility to that of conviction or intention, and not vice versa. In this way, by the personalization of morality, one arrives at another paradox. More moral authority means more personal self-direction, but also more impediments to communication. As Luhmann notes, not by chance is '[personalized] morality a reality which generates conflicts. The moralists are polemical people. . . . morality distances itself from communication' (Luhmann, 1984: 16).

Conflicting normative and moral group codes actually multiply. However, this is only part of contemporary social phenomenology. There is also a synchronic and at times contradictory calling to account of the 'moral question' in politics. There is also a need for synthetic human selectivity. After many decades of discharging every responsibility on to the anonymous collectivity or social structures, we are thrown back on to the Weberian ethic of (personal) responsibility.

In fact, once again the limitations of the purely empiricist approach are revealed in the multi-paradoxical conclusion of Luhmann's thematization of ethics.

Unless we recognize the capacity of people to attain that transcendental 'something' which lies in each of us as a human being communicating with 'alter egos', the utmost of individualization (the product of evolution) can only lead to the utter improbability of moral communication. We can adapt two systemic recipes to system–environment relations which have been applied in the sphere of social relations, and use them in the above crisis of communication. Thus one might work out a more adequate theory capable of effecting more distant encounters. Or, one might attempt a reduction of the room for systemic normativeness whereby the system accepts the demand for morality originating in the human environment. However, in both cases this involves only a partial, unsatisfactory adaptation. In the first instance, a more adequate theory capable of judging at greater distances is ill-adapted to a sphere of relations, such as the moral one, which is conceived of as eminently interpersonal and thus linked to proximity.

Logically, there only remains open the reductionist road for moral crisis: a social system which refuses to use an overly-fragmented moral pluralism, which is also a source of conflicts, as a basis for its collective morality. This way, the 'moral question' is resolved by institutionally reducing the claims of public morality in a series of areas of the political system and systems connected with it. The political system internally acknowledges a narrower moral sense, establishing procedures for a 'lower moral threshold' as well as reducing the fields of its activity to which one can formally apply the self-referential nature of moral judgement. The profits of lobbies, financial contributions paid by interest groups to candidates, the spoils system, *raison d'état*, greed in the political 'market', would thus be explicitly recognized in areas of the political system where they have until now been classified as immoral, though with widespread tolerance, compromise and hypocrisy. In that event, morally neutral restrictions on procedures and quantitatively very high thresholds would be imposed.

However, this means that the evolution of morality towards personal self-reference is lost in paradoxes. The ultimate of these is that the more morality evolves and is personalized, the less it can bear on social structures to effect a higher collective moralization. Then, according to the logic of system–environment relations, the amoral selective processes of the social system will, like so many new Leviathans, struggle all the more strongly against the riotous, fragmented pluralism of the excess of individual ethics of conviction.

The abstract argument I have followed may seem to have taken me away from the third referent of our subject: social transformations and legitimation. On the contrary, it has prepared us to confront the kernel of their common theme.

Hard though it is to anticipate the future in the present, we can say that the future appears to favour both the further differentiation, specialization and fragmentation of communication, and at the same time the maximum of information and knowledge, instantly shared, but through *machines and programmes.* In metropolitan areas, factories, offices, public places and thoroughfares we can foresee less territorial concentration of persons, along with more decentralization in housing and for other purposes, work, learning and collective communication. We can above all forecast the decline of that great pragmatic-normative fabric, the 'society of dependent labour' (cf. the latest Dahrendorf, 1979).

Save in the imperial nations, we shall also have, for several years at least, a transformation, unfavourable to communication, of dependent labour power: fewer employed in industry, more polarization between many de-skilled roles linked to computer-based and highly programmed machines, smaller technico-managerial elites, and more irregular and flexible jobs.

We shall have increases in social distances and thus larger 'communications improbabilities' of a moral kind, whilst information and the possibility of multiple telematic contacts increase. How can social systemics still be thought of as merely putting in order an increasingly heterogeneous system, when introducing order to overall compatibilities means inserting both systemic selectivity and moral guidances?

It is at this point that even the rich theoretico-ideological debate on the subject of legitimation and legality runs the risk of obsolescence. The thematization excellently synthesized from Habermas's viewpoint in the third chapter of his *Legitimation Crisis* supposes that a given social system of advanced material and technological development can master circumstances and the challenges of the competitive human environment in various ways. It can do this authoritatively or contractually, by political exchange mixed with manipulation from above, or through processes of a highly contingent kind of systemic selection. It might do this by paying out lavish general welfare benefits, providing better services and welfare state guarantees, or by persuasive methods, along with threats, linked to the danger of unemployment or the expansion of employment (if in fact the transformations of class structure latent in mature capitalism are really not possible).

The discussion concerns how to obtain consensus: by prior legitimation, or mere rewarded legality?

However, this question loses its consistency when the problem is that of the very *loss of substance* of the consensus obtained. Legitimation which is vitiated by entropy and which loses significance at every test may be produced through merely cognitive communication, or communication established through mediations of interest. In contrast, a demand for morality emerges as 'something more' regarding a legitimation obtained through even unconstrained discursive formation, processes of a Habermasian type derived from the pragmatic interplay of interests.

It is not just because of growing unemployment and informal adaptation (through a mass of inter-subjective communications from the life-world, increasingly distant from the culture of the 1960s) that the requirements and restraints on political legitimation postulated by the great workers' unions are losing their hold on the new entrepreneurial and managerial leaderships as well as on political public opinion.

The basic prerequisite for the legitimation of political power, posited by Habermas in *Legitimation Crisis*, is that 'a system of authority . . . must be legitimized as a whole if pure legality is to be able to count *as an indication* of legitimacy' (Habermas, 1976a: 100). This is very limited if taken in the primarily procedural sense of a discursive formation, as it was then expressed by Habermas, without constraints and also unconnected to the promptings of interests. Beneath the legitimation of the norm and of power, there opens up the problem of meaning.

In a recent seminar in Italy, it was significant that Habermas himself had to recognize that the discursive formation of the norm, the real *discourse* 'becomes necessary for legitimation only when it replaces a challenge or a request for judgement on the very criteria on which the validity of the norm . . . is based.' He concluded, in 1983, 'A formal ethic, a theory of action, a self-correcting political praxis: all these we have. But we do not have a method of theoretically confronting totality, or the problem of a total meaning' (Brena et al., 1984: 15).

This, however, is a much broader theme than legitimation itself.

Legitimation and Society: a Critical Review

Alberto Izzo

Perhaps it is safer to introduce the subject 'legitimation and society' not so much as attempted definitions destined to failure but rather as a critical review of some different positions. This should serve to pose problems which have not yet found, and perhaps never will find, a universally accepted solution. However, even a simple, necessarily partial, selection involves some initial clarifications. Only recently in sociology has the discussion of legitimation begun to take place more regularly than sporadically. The literature indicates that this subject has been approached, as it must be, in relation to the specifically sociological problem of anomie. This too has returned to the limelight in recent years, along with the more specifically political problem of 'governability' which has also received so much attention of late.

However, the concept of legitimation is, of course, very old even in its sociological sense, perhaps *avant la lettre*. Political and religious power has always sought some form of justification, has always proclaimed itself legitimate in opposition to possibly usurped power. Paradoxically, this has been true even when it has been argued that successful usurpation was the basis of the legitimation of power.

In very general terms, and not only in reference to political power but to any form of institutionalization of social action crystallized in forms endowed with a certain stability, Berger and Luckmann wrote that 'Legitimation "explains" the institutional order by ascribing cognitive validity to its objectivated meanings. Legitimation justifies the institutional order by giving a normative dignity to its practical imperatives' (Berger and Luckmann, 1967: 93).

This statement on the nature of legitimation throws some light on the problem of the usefulness of this sociological category in comparison with other more basic ones. It draws attention to the problem of consensus. Indeed, as A.W. Gouldner has shown, all official sociology, that which opposes either the individualist thought of the classical economists or socialist and Marxist thought, consists of the search for consensual factors. These are the factors which hold a society together notwithstanding all the forces, the individual egoisms, which tend to break it up. In Gouldner's view, sociology is

> an N + 1 science. In other words, it was a theory of the *complementary* structures needed to make whole the new utilitarian society. . . . Saint-Simon, Comte, and later, Durkheim contributed to a sociological tradition that stressed the importance of developing shared belief systems, common interests and wants, and stable social groupings. It was expected that they would have a moral authority strong enough to restrict the striving of competitive individualists and provide them with anxiety-reducing group memberships. (Gouldner, 1970: 91–2)

If Gouldner's statement is correct, as I think it is, and if by legitimation we simply understand the internalization of common principles, we should reach the conclusion that the problem of legitimation is neither more nor less than the centre of the whole sociological tradition, or at least that which has made integration the linchpin of its thought.

These observations have no polemical intention. They merely tend to stress that in Berger and Luckmann's definition, as has been said, the meaning of legitimation is narrower, and this will be seen more clearly when I deal with these authors later. But difficulties, at least terminological ones, arise at this point. If we mean legitimation as a principle of justification, and limit discussion to the more specifically political context, we must then at least pose the problem of the possible difference between 'legitimation' and 'political formula'. Gaetano Mosca defined the political formula as:

> . . . the observation that in all countries to have achieved even a limited level of culture the political class justifies its power by leaning on some better belief or sentiment generally accepted in that epoch and in that nation. These beliefs could be, according to the situation, the presumed will of the people or of God, a consciousness of forming a distinct nationality or chosen people, traditional fidelity to a dynasty, or trust in an individual endowed with exceptional qualities. (Mosca, 1972: 249)

One might object that whilst legitimation logically follows the 'practical imperative', the political formula only favours certain principles in the social environment which are already shared.

However, this objection seems rather fragile because it is not sociologically plausible that the creation of legitimation should not refer to a principle that is already shared. Mosca said:

> Naturally, every political formula must be in harmony with the degree of intellectual and moral maturity of the people and the period in which it is adopted. Thus it must closely correspond to the particular conception of the world that a people has at a given moment, and it should constitute the moral cement among all the individuals who are part of that society. (Mosca, 1972: 249)

It is hard to imagine an argument on legitimation as justification of constituted power which could refute Mosca's assertion. It does no harm to repeat that Pareto's distinction between residues and derivatives does no more than widen and systematize Mosca's ideas.

As for Weber, his argument is certainly more complex and would require a fuller analysis. It should, however, be noted at once that when he confronts the subject in general terms, he refers to a 'generally observable need of any power . . . to justify itself' (Weber, 1968, 2: 953). But then the argument becomes more problematic. If indeed it is true that constituted power always invents some 'legend' to justify itself, it is also true, Weber added, that its credibility cannot be taken for granted in every social situation.

> Under conditions of stable distribution of power . . . that myth is accepted by the negatively privileged strata. Such a situation exists as long as the masses continue in that natural state of theirs in which thought about the order of domination remains but little developed, which means, as long as no urgent needs render the state of affairs 'problematical'. But at times in which the class situation has become unambiguously and openly visible to everyone as the factor determining every man's individual fate, that very myth of the highly privileged about everyone having deserved his particular lot has often become one of the most passionately hated objects of attack; one ought only to think of certain struggles . . . in which such myths and the claim of legitimate domination based upon it have been the target of the most powerful and most effective attacks. Indeed, the continued exercise of every domination (in our technical sense of the word) always has the strongest need of self-justification through appealing to the principles of its legitimation. (Weber, 1968, 2: 953–4)

Legitimation does not thus automatically follow constituted power, and, as we should say today, using a fashionable word of the moment, that can create problems of governability. In any case, whilst asserting that 'every such system attempts to establish and to cultivate the belief in its legitimacy' (Weber, 1968, 1: 213), Weber also feels the need to add that legitimacy is only one possibility, and that power can also exist without it, as when one obeys 'for reasons of material self-interest' (Weber, 1968, 1: 213). Again, 'a system of domination may . . . be so completely protected, on the one hand by the obvious community of interests between the chief and his administrative staff (. . .) as opposed to his subjects, on the other hand by the defencelessness of the latter, that it can afford to drop even the pretence of a claim to legitimacy' (Weber, 1968, 1: 214). He then proceeds to analyse the legitimacy of power on a rational, a traditional, and a charismatic basis, so constructing possibly the most famous typology of all sociological thought. He also distinguished between legitimacy and legitimation, assigning to the latter a more restricted meaning, as regards charismatic power. When transformed into constituted power, it becomes the source from which those who find themselves in a position of economic or social power derive *legitimation* (Weber, 1968, 2: 1111).

Weber deals with the problem of legitimacy and legitimation in mainly political terms. In sociological terms, however, as has been mentioned, the question seems to have a wider significance. Indeed, it does not seem an exaggeration to maintain that for the other great sociological classic, Emile Durkheim, society itself is a normative system which is more or less cohesive. On the other hand, this means that there is no society without a system of reference which can guide the individual by giving a sense of legitimacy to his activity, and on the other, more specifically, that in society there are special organs for the formation and diffusion of normative and justificatory principles of specific social behaviour. The importance that Durkheim attributes to pedagogy should leave few doubts in this regard. Certainly, it has the function of creating consensus, which, as has been remarked, should take us to the general problematic of traditional sociology itself. However, one must also add that, at least according to one common criticism, this formation of consensus is a function of pre-constituted practical interests, defended by the status quo, or in Berger and Luckmann's words, a conferral of the 'dignity of the norm' on 'practical imperatives'. The theme of legitimation also comes down to us from Durkheim. This is confirmed, too, by the latest developments in this debate, as when Dahrendorf, as we shall see, tends to interpret the current crisis of legitimation in contemporary societies in terms of anomie.

Much of classical sociological literature, therefore, seems in some way linked to the theme of legitimation, especially if this is understood in the broad sense. The task to be confronted here thus lies in grasping the possible connections between the problem as posed by classical sociology and the current debate. However, it is impossible to move on to these connections without first referring to Marxism, both for its intrinsic importance and its influence on a part of the current literature on legitimation. One might even argue that Marx's argument in this regard has a special importance in that it opens up the possibility of posing the problem in a double sense: indeed, in referring to him one may grasp a clear division between two approaches to dealing with the problem of legitimation. To clarify the argument, one can point out that what has already been said is located rather uncritically in a *relativistic* conception of legitimation.

In other words, it has not been thought important to take the *content* of social norms into consideration because they change radically from one society to another. Rather, it has been observed that there is a normative system, of various kinds, an organ or organs of a particular type which perform the specific function of justifying, *legitimating*, this system. There is no doubt that Marx, with his theory of ideology, also poses the question in these terms. In fact, Marx took ideology as a conceptual system (juridical, religious, ethical, philosophical, literary, etc.) which has the precise, if latent, function of legitimating the existing economic order, the fabric of the modes and relations of production in the current system, on which the political fabric and the whole social organization is constructed.

However, Marx's sociologico-relativist argument about the relation between the economic structure and the ideological superstructure being a force for legitimation is accompanied by a *critical* argument, a radical denunciation of this form of legitimation. One might say that Marx invites us to consider the current ideological system of justification non-legitimate. There is not only a denunciation of an ethical kind, though it would be ingenuous to deny that there is an ethical impulse in Marx. The argument goes deeper. For Marx, the intrinsic contradictions in capitalist society make the systems of legitimation that are generated within it ever less valid, ever less able to keep the society really united. Marx posed the problem of the *crisis of the systems of legitimation*.

I have felt it appropriate to refer to these classical themes because the contemporary discussion cannot be properly understood without such references. Even today, there is an opposition between a sociologico-relativistic conception of the theme under consideration and a conception which could be described as critical.

As regards the first, one must start with the treatment accorded by Berger and Luckmann to legitimation. They maintain that although social life is a human construct arising through interaction, it takes on the appearance of objective reality for the subjects of society themselves. Through routine, social activity is crystallized into forms which appear independent of the will of the individual. This is the process of objectivation. Legitimation, on the other hand, is defined as 'second-order' objectivation (Berger and Luckmann, 1967: 92). It 'produces new meanings that serve to integrate the meanings already attached to disparate institutional processes' (Berger and Luckmann, 1967: 92). In other words, the various institutional processes in a society are not necessarily interconnected. People who work in specific sectors of society still need a global institutional order. This is provided precisely through legitimation which creates a total system of integrated meanings. Again, the 'individual biography, in its several, successive, institutionally predefined phases, must be endowed with a meaning that makes the whole subjectively plausible' (Berger and Luckmann, 1967: 93). Legitimation therefore performs the function of justifying what occurs in the world of practical activity. The argument becomes more difficult, perhaps, when the authors say that it is possible to distinguish between 'different levels of legitimation' (Berger and Luckmann, 1967: 94) which are necessarily intermingled in the concreteness of life. They state that 'Incipient legitimation is present as soon as a system of linguistic objectifications is transmitted. For example, the transmission of a kinship vocabularly ipso facto legitimates the kinship structure' (Berger and Luckmann, 1967: 94). Here, it seems justifiable to ask in what sense legitimation is a second-order objectivation. In what sense is it distinguished from that very formation of meanings which makes social life possible? A second level of legitimation lies in very rudimentary theoretical statements which obviously have the function of justifying the existing norms of society. One reaches the third level with a body of individuals specialized in such theoretical activity.

Berger and Luckmann write: 'Symbolic universes constitute the fourth level of legitimation. These are bodies of theoretical tradition that integrate different provinces of meaning and encompass the institutional order in a symbolic totality' (Berger and Luckmann, 1967: 95). The symbolic process is distinguished from that of the formation of meanings of the objects of social life in that they are 'processes of signification that refer to realities other than those of everyday experience' (Berger and Luckmann, 1967: 95). Naturally, this does not mean that this symbolic totality has no relation with the social order in daily life; in fact, it has the precise function of legitimating it. 'The symbolic universe provides the ultimate legitimation of the institutional order by bestowing upon it the primacy in the hierarchy of human experience' (Berger and Luckmann, 1967: 98). This concerns the world of religion, or mythology because 'theological thought may be distinguished from its mythological predecessor simply in terms of its greater degree of theoretical systematization' (Berger and Luckmann, 1967: 111). It also concerns worlds which might be defined as para-religious, in that they involve an absolute faith in values which give meaning to the whole society.

This method of posing the problem has produced a particular reaction in the subsequent sociological debate. This involves the subject of identity in relation to legitimation. Berger and Luckmann maintained the existence of such a relation in so far as legitimation, as they understood it, helped to create a feeling of security and belonging. Only the symbolic totality of legitimation could give an individual the certainty of his own social identity. The world of everyday life was itself unstable and subject to change despite the processes of objectivation and institutionalization. A man can know who he is by 'anchoring his identity in a cosmic reality protected from both the contingencies of socialization and the malevolent self-transformations of marginal experience' (Berger and Luckmann, 1967: 100). Or, in much more dramatic terms which foretell the concerns of later books: '*All* societies are constructions in the face of chaos. The constant possibility of anomic terror is actualized whenever the legitimations that obscure the precariousness are threatened or collapse' (Berger and Luckmann, 1967: 103).

This terrifying possibility seems to be regarded as a present reality in *The Homeless Mind: Modernization and Consciousness* (Berger, Berger and Kellner, 1974). Their view is that, whereas in historical periods preceding the current industrial and urban society, men lived in relatively unified life-worlds, today they live on the contrary in a situation characterized by the plurality of such worlds. This did not occur in the past because there was a general order which integrated individuals into society. This was the religious order which permeated the whole of the public and private spheres of the life of an individual who was always 'in the same "world" ' (Berger, Berger and Kellner, 1973: 64). Now, if we recall what Berger and his previous collaborator had argued about legitimation as symbolic totality, we can immediately see that this totality seems to be breaking up or at least to be endangered. Pluralization takes place not only between different spheres but also within the same sphere. In the world of work, for example, there are really many different spheres in either technological production or bureaucracy. In private life as well one encounters individuals with different outlooks which reflect differing earlier experiences. This pluralization of both public and private spheres is closely related to the experience of urban life and modern means of mass communication. In the metropolis, indeed, different cultural worlds coexist, and through mass communications the 'individual, wherever he may be, is bombarded with a multiplicity of information and communication' (Berger, Berger and Kellner, 1973: 67).

The multiplicity of the worlds concerns, clearly, secondary socialization, education and work in its various manifestations. But not even primary socialization is exempt.

> Very probably this is the case with an increasing number of individuals in modern societies. The important implication of this is that such individuals not only experience the multiplication of worlds in adult life but do so from the very beginning of their social experience. Indeed it may be said that such individuals have never possessed an integrated and unchallenged 'home world'. (Berger, Berger and Kellner, 1974: 67–8)

One can certainly say that this plurality of worlds broadens individual consciousness and makes it more problematic and open. The authors of this book maintain that there are intellectual means of legitimating this situation in the name of democratic ideals themselves. However, it should at once be added that this legitimation is very different from that previously dealt with. In fact, instead of creating a 'symbolic totality' it justifies the fragmentation of this totality in the name of the freedom and independence of the individual.

It is plain to see that there is a transition from the work of Berger and Luckmann of 1966 to that of Berger, Berger and Kellner in 1974. The argument of the first book was mainly in abstract and ahistorical terms. But the second book takes into consideration the historical specificity of modern industrial societies. Yet, one might hazard the opinion that the convergences between the two works are more significant than the divergences. This is not only due to the hints in *The Social Construction of Reality* about the pluralization of life-worlds in modern societies, but above all because the orientation in both books is relativistic. In other words, the authors do not seem concerned with judging the contents of the norms which legitimate activities in a society — the problem, indeed, does not even seem to be posed — but rather with the idea that there should exist in some sense a 'symbolic totality' which performs the legitimating function in society. Thus, they were not concerned with the possible iniquity in the normative system of modern industrial societies but merely with its fragility, presumed or real. The theme, albeit in a new guise, is that of anomie.

In other words, Peter Berger and his collaborators display no specifically political concern with the problem of legitimation. Others, by contrast, start from precisely this concern. Indeed, without fear of contradiction one may say that the current debate on legitimation is posed in political terms and, more precisely, those of the relation between juridico-political institutions and the members of societies where those institutions should function and be seen as valid, for they are interconnected, at least within certain limits.

This problem also has quite remote origins. It may be better however, to renounce the searching for its older sources and confine ourselves to looking at Carl Schmitt's position, before moving on to our own time. In 1932, a crucial year for Germany, he wrote an article on *Legality and Legitimacy*. Schmitt stated that 'a legislative state is a state system dominated by norms with a measurable, ascertainable content, impersonal and thereby general, pre-established, and so devised to last' (Schmitt, 1972: 212). This should not, however, conjure up a purely formalistic or official conception of legality. Rather, Schmitt criticized the parliamentary system for being formalistic and maintained quite passionately that 'the authority and dignity of the state depend exclusively and directly, and with immediate significance and importance from the viewpoint of positive law . . . on faith in the justice and reason of the legislator . . . and all instances making up the legislative procedure' (Schmitt, 1972: 228).

Thus, legality must be based on legitimacy, on consensus. However, the modalities of this consensus and its difficulties, problems which have become central in the current debate, are not considered by Schmitt. He was eventually led into involvement in heavy responsibilities, after the catastrophe, as well as into a much more formalistic view of the problem, if not a wholly 'disenchanted' one.

In fact, it seems as though the problem was itself dismissed. The problem of legitimacy disappears in so far as it coincided with questions about the efficient functioning of the existing legal system.

> In a modern industrialized system, highly organized and specialized, based on the division of labour, legality means a specific method of working and functioning of offices. The procedures for dealing with business, the routine and habits of offices, their functioning in a manner to some degree predictable, concern for the maintenance of this type of structure, and the need for 'coverage' in relation to the need for responsibility: all this belongs to the whole range of legality conceived in functionalist-bureaucratic terms. (Schmitt, 1972: 284)

This was Schmitt's view in 1950, and he added that legal positivism lay in the 'acceptance of the normative force of the real datum' (Schmitt, 1972: 286).

Much more recent positions are not basically different from Schmitt's. The reference, possibly a polemical one, is to Niklas Luhmann who sees the very basis of legitimation in the validity of the juridical process. But, one should add at once, the analogy ends here because Luhmann works out his personal conception of legitimation. It is true that he says 'procedures are social systems of a special type which are constituted . . . to attain binding decisions' (Luhmann, 1985: 203). This clearly involved him in a series of accusations of formalism. Luhmann tries to show how the procedures themselves are at the basis of legitimation in so far as they guarantee a certain level of consensus as well as the control of deviance. However, this does not refer to procedures being shared as given, as presented, but rather as the guarantee of functional differentiation within a social system.

> Their legitimating function is based upon this role differentiation. In procedure, participants obtain particular individual roles as voters, representatives, plaintiffs, defendants, claimants, judges presiding over a hearing, etc., in procedures within which they can behave freely, but only according to the rules of the procedural system — and not just directly as husband, sociologist, trade unionist or doctor. Their behaviour is therefore detached from the natural context of their daily lives. (Luhmann, 1985: 203)

However, even with this clarification, Luhmann's formalism does not seem to be transcended in any way. To consider procedures as the basis of legitimation, he must in fact create a fictitious break between juridical life (where legitimation operates) and 'daily life'. Juridical formalism reappears in all its clarity. The current problem, as I have already remarked, is rather that of finding a link between juridico-political institutions and everyday life, an uncertain and unstable connection which Luhmann is in danger of considering in wholly non-problematical terms. He makes no distinction between the juridico-political sphere and the 'cultural system', to use the term that Jürgen Habermas employs in this context. Leaving aside the well-known *querelle* between the two, it is nonetheless useful to see how Habermas confronts the problem of legitimacy because he seems to present an alternative to Luhmann's position.

He distinguishes between crises and problems of legitimacy, in the sense that the current system of juridico-political institutions is not necessarily destined to undergo radical changes, that is, to be revolutionized. Habermas argues that state intervention in the economic sphere means that class relations and conflicts are no longer comprehensible by means of purely economic categories. The situation has become complex and confused:

> On the one hand, administrative and fiscal filtering of economically conditioned crisis tendencies make the fronts of repeatedly fragmented class oppositions less comprehensible. The class compromise weakens the organizational capacity of the latently continuing classes. On the other hand, scattered secondary conflicts also become more palpable, because they do not appear as objective systemic crises, but directly provoke questions of legitimation. (Habermas, 1976a: 69)

In other words, the State which intervenes in the economic sphere by controlling potential class conflicts must justify this intervention. In this sense it performs a specifically *ideological* function. It must try to create interests and problems in society which divert attention away from the problems which could endanger the stability of the system. At this point, Habermas expresses his — possibly most original — idea as follows: 'Manoeuvering room' on the state's part 'is . . . narrowly limited, for the cultural system is peculiarly resistant to administrative control. *There is no administrative production of meaning*' (Habermas, 1976a: 70).

The world of tradition, norms and unreflecting values has its own autonomy which at any event is not thrown into crisis by the state's attempt to intervene or to control. A cultural tradition loses its strength as 'soon as it is objectivistically prepared and strategically employed' (Habermas, 1976a: 71).

> Traditions can retain legitimizing force only so long as they are not torn out of interpretive systems that guarantee continuity and identity. The structural dissimilarity between areas of administrative action and areas of cultural tradition constitutes, then, a systematic limit to attempts to compensate for legitimation deficits through conscious manipulation. (Habermas, 1976a: 71)

This discrepancy between 'administrative action' and 'cultural tradition' does not, however, necessarily provoke crisis. 'A legitimation crisis arises as soon as the demands for such rewards rise faster than the available quantity of value, or when expectations arise that cannot be satisfied with such rewards' (Habermas, 1976a: 73). However, it may also occur that the 'claims for compensation' are to some extent satisfied by state intervention. In this case, 'legitimation needs *do not have to* culminate in crisis' (Habermas, 1976a: 74).

Other authors, such as James O'Connor and Claus Offe, are searching for factors which could produce a real crisis of legitimation in state power. The former argues that in monopoly capitalism the state is increasingly involved in the economic sphere. State intervention is necessary to protect the economy from crisis. In O'Connor's formula, 'the growth of the state sector is indispensable to the expansion of private industry' (O'Connor, 1973b: 9). It is opportune to leave this hypothesis to the economists. On the other hand, the problem of legitimation explicitly concerns the structural contradiction in which the state in advanced capitalism finds itself. O'Connor says:

> The capitalistic state must try to fulfill two basic and often contradictory functions — *accumulation* and *legitimation*. This means that the state must try to maintain or create the conditions in which profitable capital accumulation is possible. However the state also must try to maintain or create the conditions for social harmony. A capitalist state that openly uses its coercive forces to help one class accumulate capital at the expense of other classes loses its legitimacy and hence undermines the basis of its loyalty and support. But a state that ignores the necessity of assisting the process of capital accumulation risks drying up the source of its own power. (O'Connor, 1973b: 6)

The welfare state is an attempt to create legitimation, but this attempt, together with the necessary state intervention on behalf of monopoly capital, creates a ' "fiscal crisis" or "structural gap" between state expenditures and state revenues' (O'Connor, 1973b: 9). In O'Connor's view, only a socialist policy could lead to the overcoming of the current contradiction which is both an economic crisis and a crisis of legitimation.

Claus Offe also seems to be seeking structural changes which might lead to a solution of the current legitimation crisis. He openly polemizes with Luhmann, arguing that procedures by themselves can only constitute the basis of legitimation if they themselves are recognized as possessing an essential value, or if they involve questions of secondary importance: 'procedural rules apparently give the impression of possessing an autonomous capacity for legitimation only where material significance is given to them, or in the event they can be applied to relatively innocuous problematics with little conflictuality' (Offe, 1977: 105). But this is precisely where an incurable contradiction within 'mature capitalism' arises, in that the only legitimation that this economico-political system can offer is that of 'procedural rules of a formal nature' (Offe, 1977: 105).

As Marx argued, the economic sphere acquires such autonomy in the capitalist economy that it takes on the appearance of a natural reality which cannot be changed by human action, and this is why even political decisions now appear to be endowed with irremovable necessity rather than being the result of real choices. This situation involves 'the need to formulate *ex novo* the problem of legitimation, at least as regards the analysis of capitalist societies, as a conflict between criteria of values on the one hand and *power-structure extraneous to those criteria and so incapable of responsibility* on the other' (Offe, 1977: 108). Clearly, one can find a formal acknowledgment of the values of liberty or democracy, but 'the capitalist state is systematically exposed to functional imperatives of action. To respond to these imperatives, it is necessary for the state's representatives to deny themselves' (Offe, 1977: 109). According to Offe again, the difficulties increase as a result of the very search for remedies. Indeed, welfare policy in mature capitalism tends to create ever-increasing expectations; in their turn, these expectations also create the policy of intervention.

> The contradictory attempts at policy by the welfare state and the interventionist state, which tend to subordinate the productive process to a conscious social control by simultaneously defending the power of private disposal of capital, probably have the latent function of stimulating broad expectations on both sides. (Offe, 1977: 113)

The state thus tries to control the situation with ideological instruments or 'repressive violence' (Offe, 1977: 115), but these attempts at control certainly do not heal the contradictions.

Offe's penetrating analysis ends with the much less persuasive reference to some forms of action which might lead to a transcendence of the current situation. He refers to 'spontaneous strikes, occupation of factories and other forms of political "self-help" ' (Offe, 1977: 118), 'initiatives of mutual aid organized autonomously — possibly illegally' (Offe, 1977: 119), 'autonomistic movements, generally characterized by linguistic, religious or ethnic community as well as conditions of economic discrimination' (Offe, 1977: 120) and to the erosion of the credibility of political parties.

Offe's essay on legitimation dates from 1975. Certainly, leaving aside political judgement on it, his hopes do not seem historically well-founded. Indeed, the de-stabilizing factors to which he refers seem to have lost their impetus since then. His (extreme) position, however, helps us return to the more general problem. We have seen that originally the terms in which the problem was posed were basically relativistic. It was a matter of seeking factors justifying constituted norms, in the belief that what mattered most was not so much the content of these norms as their effective power of control and of social integration. Now, on the contrary, the quotations from Offe not only make legitimation appear to be in crisis but they also seek a transcendence of the current norms because they are considered inequitable as well as no longer functional. Principles of social justice are sought outside the existing normative systems. The once relativistic viewpoint becomes a critical one.

I have cited two examples of a Marxist orientation, but one can observe that the transcendence of the current crisis of the relation between institutions and people is sought from other directions too. Neo-liberal thought (for example, Dahrendorf) is not radically different in its analysis from the Marxist arguments. 'It is . . . conceivable — and indeed at times inevitable — that the potential of a society outgrows its reality. Institutions harden and do not bend to the pressures of a new potential' (Dahrendorf, 1979: 111). Or again, in terms still more like Offe's:

> Today, we can grasp the contradictions of modernity with our hands. All over they transcend the limitations of existing institutions. At the same time, the representatives of these institutions, those in power, are constitutionally unable to master the problems which result from their own assumptions. (Dahrendorf, 1979: 117–8)

Dahrendorf explicitly recognizes that 'progress creates new problems which cannot be solved with the old tools; but as yet there are no tools at our disposal' (Dahrendorf, 1979: 119). He points out that in modern industrial societies liberty is not only guaranteed by the possibilities of choice between different alternatives, but also by the 'ligatures' which give meaning to the choices themselves which would otherwise be reduced to arbitrary acts and to the roles exercised by individuals in relation with others.

Dahrendorf's position necessarily leads to the problem of anomie. The risk that modern industrial societies run is precisely that they may lack a system of shared norms. Yet Dahrendorf distances himself from the relativistic position which does not take the content of norms into consideration so much as their strength of cohesion. It is more important that there be norms than that they should have a particular content. He claims that the society towards which we should be moving is that which offers greater chances in life, made possible by the coexistence of choices and ligatures or bonds. Only that society which guarantees both elements, it seems, can call itself legitimate. Dahrendorf poses the problem convincingly, but again his efforts to formulate concrete proposals about the possibly valid bonds in contemporary society are much less convincing. In fact, after saying that 'the social construction of human life is a kind of basic ligature', after, that is, a very generic, ahistorical statement, he adds: 'One might identify a few other basic ligatures, although their selection remains somewhat arbitrary: religion, the social contract (with its *obligations*), awareness of history, patriotism, sense of family' (Dahrendorf, 1979: 73–4). In other words, the concrete examples bring us right back to the most traditional ties (the old trinity of God, country and family) which, at a time of crisis in modern societies, if one limits oneself to proposing this once more, can only leave an audience with a deep sense of disappointment.

At any rate, there is no doubt that Dahrendorf also places himself alongside those who confront the problem of legitimation as one of the relation between institutions and society. It is precisely the inadequacy of this relation which leads to anomie.

In Italy as well, some scholars have confronted the problem in terms of a crisis of governability. Achille Ardigò's view is that this crisis is due to the remote, abstract character of political structures bearing on the needs of individuals in their daily lives. Referring to phenomenology and especially to Alfred Schutz, Ardigò contrasts the life-world of intersubjectivity to the world of institutions which cannot find consensus and thus remains unlegitimated. He hopes for a 'transaction' 'between the subjective and the objective, the production of meaning in the daily life-worlds on the one hand, and the structural organization of the social system on the other' (Ardigò, 1980: 27). One can, however, object that the 'vivid present' created in the 'face-to-face' relation that Schutz mentions arises in any institutional context and is equally present even where individuals seem 'manipulated' and 'alienated' to the utmost. It thus seems hard to rely on subjectivity in this sense as a remedy for the crisis of governability, and Ardigò's critical intention seems very problematic. The 'objective' institutional context does not really seem shaken by the reference to an inter-subjectivity which is necessarily present every time there is a direct social relationship: this intersubjectivity is thus conceived in an ahistorical fashion.

I started by saying that I should restrict myself to a simple review. Perhaps even this simple critical review of some classical and contemporary positions has not avoided the danger of posing too many questions and of letting too many doubts emerge. It may be appropriate here to try to recapitulate by saying that on the one hand legitimation is seen as a 'wide acceptance of norms, values, and meanings which uphold the kind of behaviour which ultimately enacts and re-enacts the web of relationships perceived as the order in question' (Bauman, 1976: 98). On the other hand, it is precisely the crisis of this 'acceptance' which takes the problem of legitimation beyond the given order in search of historically non-realized criteria. The call to universal emancipation as the sole form of common life to which to aspire and for which it is worth struggling, according to Habermas, is possibly the extreme example of this second conception of legitimation.

One could certainly argue that only the first belongs to the field of scientific research, whereas the second belongs to the realm of utopia. Yet we also know that scientific research which wishes to stick rigidly to the given without looking at its potentialities for transformation is by no means neutral. It is as value-laden as utopia, but in the sense of acquiescence and passivity.

PART II
FORMS AND CONTENTS OF LEGITIMATION

Legitimacy and Legitimization*

François Bourricaud

Ideologists fluctuate between an obsession with legitimacy and the cynical thesis that there is no such thing as legitimacy. I stress 'ideologists' because sociologists, provided that they have a reasonable conception of *consensus*, can escape this vulgar alternative. The purpose of the few remarks which follow is to seek to determine the meaning that the requirement for legitimacy has retained in our societies. The thesis that I put forward is that the concept of legitimacy, understood as a stable and clearly defined state, must be replaced by the concept of legitimization, which does not refer to a given state but to a method, or rather to a corpus of methods which lead to, without reaching, the achievement of such a state. This substitution of terms is not simply a verbal exercise. By insisting on the plurality of the processes of legitimization, we will reach a concept of the ideal of legitimacy which is very different from the one on which various ideologies have lived. At the same time, it will become possible to understand more fully the nature of consensus.

I

Social ideologies, whatever their content, share the feature of presenting society to us as a coherent whole — a system or a structure — to which the distinction between the possible and the real is not relevant. Let us examine this in more detail.

If we consider the concepts of traditional legitimacy which developed in Europe in the first half of the nineteenth century following the great upheaval of the French Revolution, we are struck by its hierarchical and complete character. As Louis de Bonald said: 'Torrents do not create the dams that control them' (Brehier, 1926–1935: 518). For society to restrain, discipline and above all *integrate*

*Translated by Millie Kerkham.

the divergent interests and opinions of its members, the sovereignty that it claims to exercise over them must be strictly transcendental. It can only have its foundations outside these interests and opinions, in what Alain Touraine calls the 'metasocial guarantees'. The legitimate social order is essentially hierarchical; and the principle from which the social hierarchy results, only capable of existing outside of individuals and, moreover, beyond all existence, is God himself. The union of the socio-political hierarchy and the 'metasocial guarantees' takes place thanks to tradition, an 'hereditary word preserved in the family and that is indelibly written into the history of nations' (de Bonald) (Brehier, 1926–1935: 521).

Opposed to this traditional legitimacy is revolutionary legitimacy. This valorizes not the hierarchy, but rather the community, the reconciliation of men and their solidarity. So this situation does not exist in our societies which rely upon domination and exploitation: therefore they are not legitimate. They are just as illegitimate in the eyes of conservatives as in the eyes of revolutionaries. According to de Bonald, the society that arose out of the French Revolution is illegitimate because, by failing to recognize the dependence of the created on the Creator (or, more prosaically, of the individual in relation to transcendent values), it can only produce violence and anarchy. For the different branches of revolutionary ideologies (democratic, radical or socialist) 'bourgeois' or 'capitalist' society is equally illegitimate because it violates the two fundamental values: equality and liberty.

Challenged from left and right, the societies of post-revolutionary Europe, and particularly continental Europe, suffered throughout the whole of the nineteenth century and generally until the years following the Second World War from a deficiency of political and ideological legitimacy, even if elsewhere more or less effectively preserved morals maintained a way of life that conformed, if not with reason, then at least with their traditions for broad sectors of the population.

II

For Max Weber the question of legitimacy is seen in a radically different manner. According to Weber, legitimacy is not based on 'metasocial guarantees'. It is, in a manner of speaking, secularized. Moreover, it does not depend on one single criterion but on several:

legality, tradition and charisma. At least, it does not apply to society in general, but rather a certain type of social relations: authority and obedience. The question of legitimacy is discussed in the section of 'Economy and Society' devoted to domination (*Herrschaft*): 'All domination seeks to arouse and maintain the belief in its legitimacy' (Weber, 1971: 220). One can, then, define domination as the capacity to obtain obedience on condition that the claim to being obeyed can be validated by the character of the authority. Thus Weber introduced his famous distinction between the three types of 'legitimate domination' (Weber, 1971: 222). It does not concern us here, but what we retain from it is the idea that 'legitimate domination' (which he still calls authority) is only maintained on the condition of mobilizing 'the most diverse motives of obedience which range from dismal habit to, in the final instance, pure, rational considerations' (Weber, 1971: 220).

Legitimacy always has an ideological dimension, with the reservation that the term 'ideology' is taken in a strictly neutral sense. I mean that one must be wary of taking the term 'ideology' in the manner of Marxist authors, as being synonymous with mystification. It is this interpretation which Marx suggests in his texts on *The German Ideology*. By ideology, Marxists mean the ideas of the 'dominant class'. As definitions are independent, in principle one does not object to their being defined. But apart from the fact that the term 'dominant class' is vague, it seems difficult to limit the beliefs which become part of the formula of legitimacy of a society to the ideas of the only 'dominant class'. Dissident intellectuals, for example the 'philosophers' in the age of Enlightenment, contributed to the idea that cultivated Frenchmen at the end of the eighteenth century were transforming the legitimate social order, at least as much as the Jesuits or the Jansenists who were embroiled in their theological quarrels.

The ideological dimension of legitimacy is simultaneously expressed in beliefs and practices, in 'derivations' (or, as Tocqueville said, in 'dogmatic beliefs') and in residues (Tocqueville spoke of general and dominant passions). The 'derivations' are formed by theories, which are fairly capricious, about sovereignty, the rule of the majority. These 'derivations' change with the mood of the times. But they are associated with more stable elements, with the 'residues' that Pareto reunited with these roots which, through the evolution of a language or between different languages which belong to the same linguistic family, stayed the same despite the multiplicity of variants. These variants are formed by the values, preferences or general and dominant passions which enter in combination into the formula of legitimacy. In our democratic societies, equality and liberty are, as Tocqueville said, stable references in relation to which ideological promises, which make it possible to compare societies that arise from a similar tradition, can be defined.

Let us ask ourselves, for example, what the French would call legitimate or illegitimate today. If their rulers were imposed on them by an occupying power, the vast majority of Frenchmen would not consider them legitimate. What would be the outcome? Although resistance to oppression is presented in our 'declaration of rights' as 'the most sacred of duties' it is not certain that French citizens would all immediately join a state of insurrection. It is likely, however, that the authorities would experience some difficulties. Now let us suppose that a military group, or a party capable of paralysing the economy for a sustained length of time, installed itself in power either by violence or by blackmail; imagine still further that regularly elected governments get the idea that they are self-perpetuating. Such situations would be judged illegitimate.

But there is a whole range of intermediary cases between situations of pure legitimacy and pure illegitimacy. Did General de Gaulle return as head of government in 1958 in conditions of strict legitimacy? His adversaries spoke of a coup d'état and even the most illustrious of them went so far as to speak of a 'permanent coup d'état'. Twenty-five years later, time, which heals all wounds, had done its work and de Gaulle is acclaimed almost unanimously as the French Washington.

But the question of legitimacy does not simply arise in connection with the method of electing rulers. As well as the principles of government, it concerns a whole host of matters relating to everyday life. Is it legitimate to make students pay for their university education? Is it legitimate to introduce free public transport? Is it legitimate to abolish, maintain or reintroduce the death penalty? Such questions bear on the sensitive areas of what Durkheimians call the 'collective conscience'. They lead to *moral* stances. 'One does not have the right to . . .' or 'A society worthy of its name can't not . . .' The first formula allows us to discern what I will call the *restrictive* dimension of judgements of legitimacy which claim to be opposable to certain practices, alongside the *incitative* dimension of the second formula, which authorizes or requires measures which for the moment have not yet entered the repertoire of legally obligatory or simply customary practices. This dynamic dimension of legitimacy must not be lost from sight. When a right has been recognized, even if only in the shape of a doctrinal principle, it is, as it were, destined to be fulfilled.

Thus legitimacy is not only a sanction which serves as a safety net. It is also a springboard which guides and accelerates the application of certain collective values. Because we seek to characterize the regulatory function of judgements of legitimacy we must stress their integrative capacity. Should we consider the criteria of legitimacy as a system of principles which would enable people to set up judgements that would be applicable in all circumstances of life? This conception is at the source, at least implicitly, of many authors' 'world views', collective representations or value systems. Whatever their differences, some lay emphasis on the cognitive character, others on the dynamic affective, character of collective values, but they share a similar conception of the consensus.

According to Durkheim, for example, the diversity of opinions and individual interests is irreducible. Left to themselves and deprived of all collective discipline, individuals are condemned to an anomie which dissolves all attachments and exacerbates all conflicts. Durkheim sets up a strict opposition between a consensual society and an anomic society, which finally ceases to be a society. But the consequences of this process appear hard to accept. First, it arbitrarily casts a slur on large sections of social experience. The pursuit of individual interest does not always lead to confrontation. Morality — not in the Kantian but in the Hegelian sense — constitutes a part of social experience which is not devoid of all legitimacy. The martyr or person committed to religious ideals, both patriotic and political, are worthy of admiration. Are we to conclude from this that only societies that are capable of arousing such devotion are legitimate? I would not say so: the depreciation of bourgeois morality (*Sittlichkeit*), whether civil or private, even if it constitutes one of the traditional exercises of our radical intelligentsias, does not seem to me to be well founded. Common sense does not consider the morality of the man who raises his children decently and the morality of the man who abandons them as making no moral difference and being interchangeable. Too rigorous a definition of *consensus* leads to 'tarring with the same brush' types of behaviour between which public opinion insists that there are differences of nature and of worth. If one is reluctant to accept such an overview, one must reject a unitary conception of consensus and legitimacy and replace the criterion of integration with the criterion of compatibility.

In our democratic societies — according to Tocqueville's definition — there is no single conception of legitimacy. Weber speaks of three ideal types: tradition, charisma and legality. Let us temporarily leave the first two and concentrate on the third. In Weber's text, to which reference has already been made, (Weber, 1971), legality is understood as the conformity of conduct with explicit rules which bind equally those who apply them and those to whom they are applied. The result is that those who 'command' are responsible and that they can be called to account either in their own name or by way of the offices that they hold. Another result is that those who 'obey' are only obliged to do so under specific and explicit conditions. The appeal against an excess of power, classic in French administrative law, constitutes a protection against the arbitrariness of bureaucracy, not only because it safeguards the people under the administration from abuses by the State and its officials, but also because it has led the State to modify the definition of its responsibilities. In most Western countries, except during periods when power has been exercised in a dictatorial, despotic or totalitarian manner, a conception of the legal State or of the constitutional régime which defines the legitimacy of administrative and political action has taken shape in various institutional forms. The State is nobody's property. Officials, unlike the officers of pre-revolutionary France in so far as they owned their offices, only exercise their power by delegation.

In our conception of legitimacy the criteria of 'rational authority' are of very great importance. The 'rationality' in question is not merely categorical. It does not simply define legitimate procedures. It also implies valorization, the recognition that certain activities are legitimate. Everything not forbidden is allowed. There is more: no one has the right to stop anybody else from doing what is permissible, and particularly in disposing of their own property. The private domain is defined as a place where each man, as the proverb says, is king of his own castle. In the definition of private property, economic activities occupy a great place, and particularly the decisions that individuals make about consumer goods in so far as they constitute alternative uses of their incomes. A society in which even the most enlightened and benevolent officials decide for us what we eat and what we wear, on the pretext of a theory of 'social needs', for example, would not fail to arouse strong resistance. It would not be legitimate.

Liberal values (protection against transgressions by the authorities, respect for private property) are ingredients of the formula of legitimacy in our democratic societies. But these values can be combined with, and contrasted to, other values. Having stressed the individualistic component of democratic ideologies, we can stress the requirement for solidarity, which is just as significant here as the liberal requirement. The requirement for solidarity is reflected in all 'social democractically' inspired schemes for guaranteeing a 'reasonable' income for everyone, whatever their performance and productivity. It is also reflected in the transfer schemes which claim to reduce the excessively wide gaps in the distribution of incomes. In our democratic societies, liberal and socialist values contribute to the formula of legitimacy in variable and unstable proportions.

I spoke earlier of a sectoral legitimacy. What I was thinking of was the heterogeneity of criteria in the light of which we evaluate the performances and qualities of various individual and collective actors. One does not judge Victor Hugo and Napoleon, Verdi and Garibaldi according to the same criteria. The search for higher productivity can be invoked to legitimize the reforms that the leaders of an organization put forward as ways of obtaining better results. But not all activities can be optimized. Several cases exist where the optimum cannot be defined. There are also several cases where the procedures of optimization are not relevant, where their use even seems shocking. The heterogeneity of the criteria of legitimacy thus has two causes. Firstly, there are many forms of action and each one arises from a logic of its own. Moreover, for each type of action there are, or there can be, distinctive and irreconcilable criteria of action.

If there are many criteria of legitimacy, and if there should be a need to arbitrate between them, it is easier to understand our starting position. It is not legitimacy as a state of the social system which is interesting. To be more precise, we are interested in the criteria in the name of which its designation as legitimate does or does not take place. In short, what interests us is not the state of legitimacy but the process of legitimization.

III

But here we encounter another difficulty. The discussion of the criteria of legitimacy *can* remain on a purely ideological level. A theologian armed with the principle 'omnis potestas a Deo' can determine what should be the legitimate political régime. But it is much more difficult to determine the conditions in which this ideal régime could be *realized*. So the requirement of realization is present in all theories of legitimacy. A theory of this type has a starting point and a finishing point. Its starting point is in the discrepancy between a situation and its model. Its finishing point, as often as not, is in the reduction of this discrepancy.

The process of legitimization is not confined to a theory, even when the legitimation has been achieved by an implementation of projects or objectives which survive the process of theorizing. It has, it seems to me, a dimension other than the ideological, or even authentically critical, dimension. Legitimization is more than a certificate of intellectual conformity. Legitimization is not a pure and simple logical or dialectical process of dispute and consent.

This point, which is of the greatest importance, has not always received the attention that it deserves. Most social reformers, who are, if I may say, professionally tied to the restoration of consensus, take for granted that this restoration presupposes a transformation of *fundamental beliefs*. Once again, it will be necessary to clarify these two terms.

'Belief', as Littré says, 'is a persuasion determined by any motive whatever'. One could not dream up a broader definition. Persuasion refers to a subjective state of the believer. To believe something is to affirm in front of others that one believes it, or to act as if one believed it. Thus in belief there is a reduplication following on from duplication. I see no reason for minimizing the distance between the subject and the object about which the belief is stated. This is an arbitrary view which limits belief to states of fusion where the subject is absorbed and drowned in his belief. These situations can occur in what Weber calls 'unio mystica'. But not all beliefs are of the type of the 'unio mystica'. On the other hand, what is essential in the act of believing is that the persuasion is produced by quite ordinary means. After a fashion, this is what the theologians teach. I believe because, in Pascal's words, my reason has been 'dulled' by taking holy water. But I also believe because I saw God on the road to Damascus. It is possible that I believe because I have been moved by the arguments of theologians, or again because, even though I am quite incapable of understanding its power and logic, I found myself, thanks to the strict discipline in which I had been brought up, ready to follow a path with only a barely distinguishable outline. Belief is a persuasion which involves not only intellectual elements but also moral ones, in the sense of the term that we will give a little further on.

As for the epithet *fundamental*, it must be taken with as much caution as we used to define the term 'belief'. What hinders the understanding of belief is that we comprehend this term either as the evidence relating to a proven proposition, or as the unreserved adherence to an acquired practice. Equally, 'fundamental' does not designate the principles with which we qualify acts and qualities, performances and actors. In any case these principles, if they can be discovered, are far from being always explicit and they often have very limited productivity in logical terms and, even if they don't contradict each other, it is not always easy to reconcile them. I hold as a fundamental belief that it is necessary to achieve a balance between rewards and efforts. But I do not prohibit myself from affirming my denial that no one has the right to let an individual 'die like a dog', however unproductive and ineffectual he may be. It is perhaps because neither of these two notions of reward and effort is very clear that somehow or other I manage to reconcile meritocratic and philanthropic values.

It is useless to fight fundamental beliefs with evidence or intuitions which resist all challenge, or even with 'long chains of reasons' which establish a coherent and explicit order between propositions. These fundamental beliefs entail our conviction, but usually because we take them for granted. Secondly, they can be called fundamental because, without being coherent in the logical sense of the term, there is a diffuse congruence between them. In this respect, one is reminded of the famous image of dominoes. The fall or withdrawal of a single piece, which in itself is no more important than any other, can lead to the collapse of the whole structure. The questioning of a single fundamental belief can result in scepticism or a general rejection of all beliefs. On the subject of moral beliefs, Bergson used to speak about the 'totality of obligation'. Stealing is stealing, whatever the value of the theft.

The process of legitimization ends with the crystallization of several fundamental beliefs — those which, if I may say, are untouchable and which affect the total conduct of actors in a significant but diffuse manner. This is noticeable in the case of properly educated individuals, who are said to have 'good moral character'. I speak deliberately of habits and not of ethics because the latter emphasizes the importance of correct intentions. We judge what 'good' habits are from certain practices, from certain ways of acting and behaving with regard to others. Some of these ways of behaving are practically insignificant, like picking up your knife with your left or right hand. But others provide information which is not without interest: what would be thought of me if I went to dinner at the Elysée Palace without a tie? Some of them, then, testify to my qualities or moral character. Even if I am guilty of no crime, I can be judged adversely by indelicacy, vulgarity and loutishness. At the root of the relevant censure will be the feeling of other people that I take pleasure in behaving badly, that I am insensitive to the pain or pleasure of others. By contrast, the correctly socialized individual, even if he cannot say what is good and what is evil, will know how to recognize which ways of behaving are good and which are bad. In a civilized society, individuals who have received the same education will agree on how to judge certain types of behaviour. Consensus appears as the subjective dimension of the legitimacy of institutions. Plato said this: 'Pleasure and hatred must come into the soul along their proper courses, *while we are still incapable of reason*' (Plato, Laws, II, 653. Emphasis added). The function of 'good morals' is therefore twofold. When we conform to them, they assure others that we have, to use Plato's words, established a firm association between our passions and their 'proper' (or legitimate) courses. As far as we are concerned, they reinforce this association by ensuring, through the application of appropriate sanctions, that connections are made between good behaviour and other people's gratitude, between bad behaviour and their censure.

Legitimization by good habits remains incomplete. One can have a good moral character in the sense of establishing a strong link between our passions and their 'proper courses' without, however, cultivating a 'deep awareness' either of their passions, of their 'right course', or of the relation between them. Legitimization by ideas is superimposed on legitimization by habits and education. It can proceed by two mediums: philosophical legitimization and ideological legitimization.

I leave aside the question of knowing whether, as Plato affirms, there are criteria which could allow us to distinguish the one from the other. By what signs would we decide that one teaching is genuinely philosophical and another is obviously sophist or ideological, that is to say, irregular in its procedures of exposition and verification, subject to the interests and passions of the sophist or the ideologist (or those who use it), and manipulative with respect to the people at large at whom it is directed?

To finish, I will make two observations. Firstly, there is a need for legitimization or rationalization which cannot be met simply with mere conformity between conduct and norms. A nation, even when equipped with good morals, is not 'satisfied' (in the Hegelian sense) with what it is or what it does when its morals do not also seem 'reasonable'. The requirement for legitimacy will take, in this case, the form of a gap to be filled. But it must be remembered that the two Western philosophers (Plato and Hegel) who, according to Karl Popper, pushed this requirement to its furthest limit and, it could be said, to absurdity, only managed to do so with the help of dubious myths like the 'end of history' or government by philosopher-Kings or king-Philosophers.

Lastly, even if one or other of these outcomes seemed feasible, one very great difficulty would remain: how to ensure the 'conformity of behaviour' to legitimate morals if individuals do not correctly identify the 'right course' of their passions? A lot of faith can be placed in the effectiveness of pedagogy. Unfortunately its success, like its failure, is evidence against pedagogy and the likelihood of a legitimate society. If pedagogy manages to make everyone's behaviour conform to morals and laws, the very notion of legitimacy loses its meaning. With all individuals behaving as they ought to, the question of good and evil, of legitimacy and illegitimacy, no longer arises. But if recalcitrants continue to exist who conform neither to laws nor to morals, sanctions must be applied to them and, if necessary, physical ones. The limit which such a society imposes upon its attempts to render itself legitimate in the eyes of its members is the recourse to force that it must take in order to guarantee respect for laws and morals. The notion of a legitimate society thus has no meaning, nor does the notion of a society which would renounce all legitimacy. It is left to the sociologist, who means to escape from the double utopia of a society of saints or a society of cynics, to understand the processes of legitimization.

Sociality as Legitimation of Sociological Method*

Michel Maffesoli

'A little course in commonsensology.' This is how Schopenhauer (1966: 17) introduced *The World as Will and Idea*, in the face of what he considered to be the dominant lucubrations of his time. Bearing in mind the immodesty of this remark, this is what will be attempted in the course of this article. These pages, conclusions of solitary thought, passionate polemics, diatribes with students and colleagues and even, why make a secret of it, flimsy daydreams, have the aim of being a reminder of everything which, contrary to other sciences, sociology owes to life without quality, to all and sundry and to humdrum life made up of anecdotes and tragedy.

Of course, economic problems remain of great importance, nor is it any easier to forget geo-politics, or even the crucial aspect which education, bureaucracy and technical development assume. But all that is well 'covered' by sociology. Thus it is necessary that sociology acknowledges that it has a duty to root itself in an everyday which is *less a content than a putting into perspective*. More recently, a manager of a large industrial firm recognized that the conflicts which were disturbing the firm owed less to ideology than to everyday life (interview with the PDG of Renault in the newspaper *Libération*, 19 July 1983). Such lucidity must upset the 'intellectual workers' who are too often clouded by their concepts and their criticisms to pay attention to the often 'non-logical' logic of the social flow. In wanting to be too distanced, we take the risk of forgetting the thing which legitimates intellectual research. In the *Discourses*, Machiavelli makes a distinction between the thought of the palace and the thought of the public square. If we consider this distinction in its widest applications (sites of economic, political and symbolic power as well) there can be no doubt that it is right up to date. It is certainly an anthropological constant. The question that will be asked here is this: do we still know how to listen to the thought of the public square?

Indeed, there is an everyday, empirical 'understanding' with which we cannot dispense. All this *savoir-faire*, *savoir-dire*, *savoir-vivre*, with

* Translated by Milli Kerkham.

multiple and varied implications, amounts to something given, the richness of which has been correctly brought out by phenomenology. Now, if there is an essential problem, a real *experimentum crucis*, for positivisms (neo-Marxism, functionalism, conservatism) it is really how to work out the criterion which would allow us, on the one hand, to ground the distinction between fact and right in reason and, on the other hand, to justify the supremacy of the latter over the former. Perhaps even, having taken into account rationalist quasi-monovalence, it is necessary to insist upon the originality of the empirical knowledge in question. This is what I did elsewhere (Maffesoli, 1985), and we shall now see that a number of intellectuals, who are by no means irrationalists, do not fail to cherish this opinion. It has been said that in rebelling against positivist pretensions, Kuhn (1962) showed that sociology had far more in common with common sense than did geometry (cf. Brown, 1980: 72). It is necessary to draw out the full consequence of such a remark. Thus, what can be stressed in Kuhn's thought is that the transition from one scientific 'paradigm' to another is brought about by the build-up of 'anomalies' which are left aside by a dominant mode of thought. The history of science is there to verify such a constant.

With regard to social life, it is very evident that anomalies, or what are called the anomalies, amount to a large part of the everyday. Or, to be more precise, in the course of several centuries of domestication of morals and normalization, numerous attitudes and situations have been progressively classified under this rubric. This is the paradox, well known in political or even legal form, that the minority 'excludes' the majority. This can end in the type of social structuring described by Orwell in *1984*, where the real activity of such and such a minister is indicated in an antiphrastic manner by its opposite. Whether this is done in a humorous manner (Fort, 1955; Brodu, 1982) or with the scientific equipment with which we are familiar (Auclair, 1982), the 'news items', which are excellent revealers of social reality, are good at bringing out the extent and the importance of the anomaly. 'Monstrosity', in its etymological sense, is mundane, and only moralists or good souls deny it. As far as we are concerned, in this epistemological discussion, it is enough to point out that, to use an expression of Fort's science runs the risk of becoming a 'one-armed octopus' if it avoids contact with anything that is considered disturbing or monstrous by the dominant rationalism (Fort, 1955). The attention that for several years we have been focusing on the banal, the current, the everyday and the paroxystic, finds its theoretical justification here: what is rejected, like an underground centrality, very often constitutes the firm basis on which all sociology is built. In the image of the 'mundus', the cesspit which stood for the visible world in the eyes of the Romans, the sociality which concerns us is above all determined by what Pareto, naturally giving this term its various accepted meanings, called the 'residues'.

In placing too much emphasis on *society* and on the purely rational, intentional or economic elements which constitute it, we have left aside *sociality* which is, in a way, a *communalized empathy*. *Erlebnis* or *Einfühlung*, which were principally associated with the individual domain in the German tradition, can be grasped in their collective applications. Sociology can no longer ignore the fact that the values attached to vitalism are equally at work in what constitutes the social game. It is thus possible, contrary to the analyses of certain sociologists who are too Manichaean (Boudon, 1975: 88) to avoid at one and the same time the traps of disembodied scientific research without, for all that, falling into the complacent indulgences of what Boudon calls the 'Tout Paris intellectuel'. Indeed it must not be forgotten that, before the university locked itself away, in the name of the conceptual purity that is all too familiar to us, in an isolation which like all ghettos engenders either escape (in the 'publicist' outcome) or slow decrepitude, participated in its auspicious periods and, in its own way, in the elaboration of the discourse of its time. As a genuine 'collective intellectual', with organic links to the social whole, the university understood the cognitive project in all its dimensions: scientific, aesthetic, ethical and political. In short, in its etymological sense, it fulfilled the 'comprehensive' function, that is, to render an account of social existence in its entirety. Now that the positivist interlude is coming to its completion, and with it the defence of discrimination and separation, a start can be made in rethinking social life from a holistic perspective (Maffesoli; 1979a, Chaps III & IV).

Here we find a difficult task, a real mountain crest where we must advance without the guard-rails that have been progressively installed by two centuries of rationalist prudence. It really is a question of a specific method which tends primarily to follow the meanderings of social existence as closely as possible. Of course, there are many who only see repetitions, petitio principii, or unverifiable assertations in this. And yet we are sure of a procedure which is beginning to bear fruit, to stimulate research, to bring original thought to fruition and to direct social actions towards ways of being.

Without claiming exhaustiveness (note, in regard to this, the prudence of Weber who reflected on his method in the form of 'essays') we can, however, be precise about the ways in which the comprehensive outlook and experience are closely linked. I have insisted at great length (Maffesoli, 1985) on the fascination (perhaps the sideration) which the 'inhuman' sciences have exercised over the human sciences, and particularly over sociology at the time of its foundation. We can now recall, briefly, that when Popper bases the scientific value of a theory on its 'capacity to eliminate or exclude certain possible events — to defend or condemn the occurrence of these events', it is what he calls the 'problem of demarcation' (Popper, 1981: 63; 1982: 30). On this point, we can disagree strongly with Popper, or to be more exact, we can make it clear that, if it is a question here of the criterion of 'science', then sociology can only have difficulty in being scientific. Indeed, as has been said time and time again, 'everything is fit' for sociology, everything is method, everything 'sets in motion'. In this sense experience, whatever it may be, has a cognitive potentiality. Demarcation may be a concept belonging to politics, ethics or to a certain form of science, but in no circumstance can it define knowledge.

This highly allusive observation has the primary function of establishing, *a contrario*, an end-stop from which sociology, as a method, can exist. It is, indeed, striking to note that many of the most sophisticated analyses acknowledge that they are unsuited to accounting for the object of their analysis. This is a matter of an atmosphere which is widespread, although still somewhat indistinct. It makes no small contribution to the discredit in which our discipline is generally held. It will be necessary to come back to this more specifically, but it is clear that the reactivation of the method known as 'life histories' is intended, if it does not fall back into scientific ruts, to be an answer to the feeling of impotence which was formulated with great lucidity by D. Bertaux: 'The truth is that sociologists don't know much about the societies in which they live' (Bertaux, 1979: 18). This admission is really rather banal coming from an intellectual, but it becomes disturbing when it is applied to those sociologists who, with their familiar complacency and presumptuousness, claim to speak the truth about a given society! Whether this is by talking jargon or by dressing up various truisms to make the most of mathematics or statistics, research reports or works of sociological theory have not failed to complicate their analyses as it suits them, in order to mask their own impotence. Unemployed intelligence if ever there was! In this respect it is worthwhile recalling this line of Goethe's *Faust*: 'It is in vain to have a complicated key if you can't manage to open the lock' (*Faust*, I, 1. 671)

By trying too hard to be scientific, one falls into a byzantinism which is only remotely connected with the social existence that we are supposed to put into words, but which also has an 'open sesame' function in relation to the strict and sectarian intellectual conventicles with which our capital cities are swarming. Be that as it may, as far as we are concerned here, it is important to indicate an attitude of mind which is precisely intended to escape from the hallucination of exhaustiveness, but which at the same time provides some elements of a deep understanding of sociability. Because, and this is the paradox, in trying too hard to be comprehensive we lose sight of the main point; in trying too hard to make discriminations and to draw boundaries we suppress whatever makes sense, the whole, with the blind effectiveness of the bulldozer which crushes all in its path.

It must be said that the legitimization of this effectiveness lies in the great movement of rationalization or intellectualization that was analysed so well by Weber. But a close reading of his work shows that social rationalization by no means signifies a generalized rationalization of everyday existence. Contrary to my analysis in an earlier work (Maffesoli, 1979a), participant observation, the reading of various media, the wavering attention to the discussion at the Café du Commerce and the intrusion of the news item, oblige us to state that 'on the whole, individuals are increasingly turning away from the rational basis of the rational techniques and regulations which concern them on a practical level and that, in all, this basis is usually more hidden from them than is the meaning of the magician's procedures to the primitive man' (Weber, 1965: 397).

This resistance runs the risk of becoming more pronounced with the development of technological progress, without in the least challenging it, and it must force us to adjust our instrumentation and our epistemological claims at the same time. There is a clandestine side of life which could never be grasped in a macroscopic manner and which cannot be accounted for, in the main, by the quantitative documents that could be considered. Extrapolating a Weberian remark, we thought that the 'disenchantment of the world', which correlates with the development of science and techniques, could apply equally to subjective life, to mass phenomena and to political and everyday life. It is time to acknowledge that it is nothing of the kind. Gods, their myths and their rites have changed names and shapes, but they continue to operate in sociality and in the environment. This clandestinity, which I have already called 'subterranean centrality', can be expressed in perfectly anodine situations which could be compared to Freudian *lapsi* but which, unlike them, are of value in themselves. It is because they have not taken these situations seriously that in many domains politicians, heads of firms, heads of administration and top journalists are completely confused by the way that events, that they are supposed to direct or at least control, turn out.

The cognitive aspect of experience forces us to pay attention to events, to phenomena and to everything which occurs fleetingly and immediately. I have already spoken about this using several large categories: duplicity, theatricality, tragedy, ritual (Maffesoli, 1979b). I would now like to stress the whole weight of feelings, even sensual feelings, which can be associated with it. In his book on Montaigne, Starobinski declares that 'phenomenalism' and its various modulations are 'the familiar consequences of sceptical doubt' (Starobinski, 1982: 8). Certainly the latter is a societal form that is as widespread as it is possible to be and this is beyond an apparent adherence to various moral, religious or political values. 'Situationism' and popular doubt are intimately linked; one can envisage, from a theoretical point of view, an identical couple made from phenomenalism and scepticism. It is by no means a case of a universal remedy but this would not fail to slim down the intellectual paranoia which, after two centuries of good and loyal service, has dug the widest possible ditch between the social base and the representations which have been made of it.

Without being mechanistic and without falling into a simplistic materialism, it is clear that there is a process of reversibility or retro-action between the mastery of time and space, which belongs to middle-class ideology, and the rational project (*projectum*) of theory which is as much suited to functionalism as to critical thought. The optimal condition for such an approach is, to use an expression of Marx's, a *post festum* knowledge. To keep the same tone, it would be better to say that it is a question of *post mortem* knowledge. By contrast, focusing on the order of experience refers to an 'in statu nascendi' observation, with all the difficulties with which we are familiar as well as with the uncertainty and incompleteness which are inherent in such a procedure. But let us acknowledge that the multiple social experiments, the alternative ways of life, the collapse of numerous dogmatisms, a certain existential unconstraint, all things of which each of us is capable of giving a clear example, all this simultaneously urges us to be both prudent, if not sceptical in relation to established truths, and audacious in our thinking which drives us to welcome what is happening, with reservations.

Thus it is no longer a question either of an epistemological 'cut' or 'break', or of critical diversion, but much more of an understanding of the popular present (that one finds in redundancy and theatricality) by means of intellectual variations which do not 'prove' but which 'express'. Several years ago, I proposed the concept of 'monstration', complementing classical demonstration. While the latter is linked to unity, the former aims to record things in the plural (the plural is, by construction, 'monstrous'), and this is why redundancy, variation and reflexion are necessary. Reflexion is like waves beating against a rock as it keeps coming back in some kind of a shooting fashion to subjects and forms which are close but not identical. This is how the texture of everyday life is built up.

With regard to a subject which lends itself well to it (that is, the totalitarian structure of the USSR), E. Morin has taken the trouble to apply the principles of thought that are revealed in his work in progress on Method. And without thinking, like him, that the work of the intellectual is to inform the politician, I also consider that 'Cartesian reason and the reason of utilitarianism can only dissolve or refuse the monstrousness of a reality which seems totally unreasonable to them' (Morin, 1977, 1979, 1983). The nature of the USSR is an example of a paroxysm, but such a remark cannot fail to apply to the life without quality which exists in our districts and towns.

The politician means, as is only normal, to adapt this or that reality to the conception of reality that he makes for himself. His programmatic worry makes him refuse, and often fight against, everything which does not fit into his conception. The person in a position of administrative responsibility, more precisely the civil servant of authority, servant and guarantor of the public service, 'knows' what society is and what it should be; from then on, he can *deny* whatever goes beyond his scheme. There is no going back on it. On the other hand, it is dangerous for the scholar to copy his attitude from those which have just been outlined. Now, there has been a tendency for this to gain the upper hand for more than a century. The famous distinction that Weber made between the scholar and the politician is not a simple 'flatus vocis', for it underlines a necessity that one is apt to forget. Naturally, it is not a question of a moral judgement, but rather of noticing that what is legitimate for a politician or a leading civil servant is harmful to the intellectual: one can refuse or deny in order to act more effectively, at least in the short term, but it is a completely different matter as soon as it is a question of understanding. Thus, what 'is' has priority over what 'should be'. That is the irresponsibility of the intellectual: he does not have to answer on *behalf of* others and he does not have to answer *to* others: he has to listen to them. It is the eternal relation to otherness which, throughout the ages, speaks through the religious, the political and the bureaucratic; it is a relation which has always been differentiated: there are those who provide its *administration* (churches, parties, technostructure: Promethean categories), and there are those who speak of its *mystery* (mystics, poets, thinkers: Dionysiac categories). It is perhaps not very advisable to mix the genres.

We must be very vigilant on this point, for the mechanism of reduction is a natural inclination of the intellectual attitude. It has been stressed that the philosophy of consciousness brought order into the variety and confusion of the world, from the standpoint of the unity of the thinking being, but had only succeeded in substituting itself for 'objective ontological unity' which characterizes the world of medieval Christianity. In both cases we are dealing with the reduction of polysemy. It is easy to show that monotheism and monothetism share the same logic. Just as God is *U*n (One), the world becomes a *U*nity, which is explained by *U*n (A) conscious subject. This is the starting point of what I will call the *thought of suspicion*, which invalidates or makes secondary everything which exceeds the unity. Karl Mannheim has an exact formulation of this problem: 'Thenceforth, however, the experiences of everyday life are no longer accepted at face value, but are shot through by thinking in all their implications and are traced back to their presuppositions' (Mannheim, 1956: 57, 59). That is exactly right: as a consequence of monothetism, the situations, experiences, attitudes and discourses of everyday life no longer have any value in themselves, but are referred back to an exterior, of whatever order it may be, which goes beyond them. It is clearly a question of a reductive thinking which in the same movement does not want to see and is afraid of the 'everyday monster'.

Now, everyday existence is splintered, polysemic, made up of dark and light and, in a nutshell (as is becoming increasingly accepted), made by man who is simultaneously 'sapiens' and 'demens'. Without wishing to miniaturize this daily existence (Bellasi, 1983) in order to contemplate, master, channel or asepticize it (hallucinations which are constants in human history), it must be accepted that everything which goes into its construction comes down to an architectonic which can be hierarchical but which can in no instance dispense with any element whatsoever, even if this element is considered unimportant. This is where we meet up again with the mystical or poetic outlook on correspondences which were discussed above. This perspective can be of major help to us, as it can allow us, on the one hand, to make it clear that fiction does not have the attribute of situations in which people and things correspond to each other, and, on the other hand, to show that, contrary to what has prevailed in iconoclastic rationalism, the image exerts an attraction which is sure to be socialized. Causality is no longer valid; there has been a return to the cycle of repetition and ritual whose importance for everyday life is recognized. In the game of theatricality, forms fit together as so many metaphors which are worth less in their isolation than in their concatenation.[1] Of course, this series of metamorphoses must not be understood in the manner of a historical linearism, but rather as dotted, sinusoidal, made up of 'rapti' and latencies but nevertheless of a foolproof solidity, which for us is the solidity of sociality. Let us remember the words of the mystic: 'God writes straight using curved lines.'

It is this imperfect (compared with the confident direction of linearism), but for that very reason, vivid cycle which appeals to a theory that is forever calling itself into question. Indeed, it is a basic rule of scientific procedure which makes a plea to be perpetually overtaken. The hard sciences are obviously based on this attitude; it might even be said that their performance is the direct consequence of it. Curiously, it is not the same with human or social sciences which proceed by successive rigidifications. The only thing that they have retained from the requirement for truth is the spectre of excommunication. And yet, and this has often been said, if there is an area where flexibility is necessary, it is that of the social whose essential characteristic is lability. Once again, it is not a question of 'progress' here, but rather of the re-emergence of problems which had been forgotten for a while or which had been relegated to lower importance. I have already indicated that there were no 'Americas' in social science; new worlds were never discovered, but it must be understood that a specific work, and this is its principal quality, can and must give rise to new aspects that had previously been neglected. As Weber notes, 'no "finished" scientific work has any meaning other than to give rise to new "questions": it thus asks to be "surpassed" and to grow old. Anyone who wishes to serve science must resign himself to this fate' (Weber, 1959: 76).

Such a remark of good sense, that can be observed several times in the course of a scientific career and which sometimes arises in the very core of research, must make us consider claims to exhaustiveness and to the intangibility which all too often characterizes the monologues in our disciplines as childish in the very least. A comprehensive scheme is valid for a time, occasionally for a given space. It can, in other respects, serve as a point of reference and can be used in a historical perspective or in an intrinsic fashion for the perceptiveness of its considerations. But attempts to extrapolate it invariably lead to dogmatism and often to the legitimation of the harshest tyrannies. As Marx of the bourgeoisie said on the subject of history, it is a mistake, and above all futile, to say 'until now (before me), science has existed, but from now on there is no more need of it'. The *ultima verba* have been uttered.

Of course, we still have to make the connection secure, to acknowledge the correspondences and to establish points of comparison between the various thematic or historical approaches, but that can be done without giving one or another of them any pre-eminence whatsoever. One can make use of them without using them. It is an aesthetic or nominalist attitude which would de facto attribute more importance to situations and realities than to theories. To come back to a notion which is starting to gain the freedom of the sociological city (Brown, 1977), it is a case of using concepts as if they were so many metaphors which enable us to *experience* life and its facts in all their concrete manifestations. The metaphor checks, underlines and emphasizes this or that characteristic of social life without, for all that, constraining it. It is therefore the metaphors which can be preserved from the various theories which try to account for life in society. The metaphors represent 'softened' moments of their operation in which they are perhaps closest to their object. I have in mind Francis Ponge's witticism about literature, which 'does not develop from concepts but from conceptacles, by analogy with the receptacle of flowers'. The question arises of whether this could not be applied to sociology. For, in opposition to what some people consider to be the intellectual scandal of the relativization of concepts, I maintain that it is better to make use of the 'conceptacles' — something that I have analysed in the terms of notion, metaphor and category — which are capable of receiving life rather than reducing it. Now, the most memorable parts of classical or contemporary works, works of erudition or circumstance, are exactly those exceptional moments (should one say of lassitude?) when the web of concepts allows a glimpse of the social reality which gives it strength, these moments when societal fact connects with sociological fact. A nice collection could be made of these moments which would then certainly brighten up the picture that is being painted. It just so happens, besides, that this is how all analysts proceed, without even saying so: great authors have had their epigones of 'right' and 'left', a fortiori their heretics and schismatics, without forgetting their distant cousins or their vague intellectual allies. All arrange and come to terms with the concepts of the master. This goes to prove that, owing to the force of circumstance, one cannot stay faithful to a concept. 'Traduttore traditore' can also be applied to whoever wishes to implement a system.

It is important to dwell on this as it allows us to stress that, whatever one may say, revision is always necessary. The concept itself also moves. What has just been said from a diachronic point of view can also be observed synchronically. Indeed, the same situation can elicit various points of view. And whether one likes it or not, this very multiplicity is the de facto negation of everlasting concepts and of various explanations 'in the last instance'. The least amount of lucidity would compel us to admit that, in Mannheim's words: 'our definition of concepts depends on our position and our point of view which are, in turn, influenced by a good number of unconscious steps of our thinking.' It is better to acknowledge the *particularism* of a thought and hence of its products, if only to enrich them in a complementary manner by confronting them with other perspectives. But limiting definitions in this way means that one can only accede to the 'discovery of the approximate truth' (Mannheim, 1956: 85, 115). These are all things which seem to go without saying, but the inevitable conclusions are rarely drawn from them.

Amongst these consequences, and we can never return too often to this, is the primacy of societal existence. We do not have to define it as such, which is the province of a philosophical theory; however, it is important to note that, on the one hand, once the *economic* component is established and analysed, the 'residue' can be observed. The same thing can be seen concerning the *political* aspect, the *organizational* aspect, the analysis in terms of *work* or *leisure*, as well as with regard to *consumption*, and we could multiply the perspectives endlessly. It is this 'residue', in the sense that Pareto gave it, which raises questions for the sociologist of everyday life. It is less a matter of content than of aim or, in the phenomenological vocabulary, of intentionality. On the other hand, this residual existence that we can observe, as has been said by means of various social categories, is always a factor of sociality. It is therefore the simple meaning of the term 'coexistence'. Indeed, it is in the chinks of official life, moments or spaces which are re-appropriated in what I called a miniscule manner or, to use an expression of A. Moles, by 'smuggling' (Moles, 1982) that the intensity of the collective being is best expressed. It will be necessary to come back to this, but it is clear that simple sociability, the various forms of solidarity, the conflicts and the détentes, in a nutshell, the passion which is famous for its importance for social structuration, this all goes alongside what is generally thought acceptable to take into account. The 'residue', or the factor of sociality, is considered by many people to be a frivolous research topic. It is hard to quantify it, so it is unworthy of 'intellectual workers'.

And it is true that the two aspects to which I have just drawn attention: residues and collective-being, do not sit easily with conceptual rigidity. That is why it is neccssary to elaborate new procedures of investigation. I have already explained elsewhere that the social *vouloir-vivre* did not take a specific verbal form (Maffesoli, 1979b); likewise *savoir-faire* and *savoir-vivre* are not expressed through rigid and intangible laws. To take a well known categorization, the determinism and interactionism active in social life, along with their continual overlapping, resist confinement in a normative scheme. Empirical knowledge exceeds rational construction in every respect and, as it were, mocks it. Phenomenological sociology certainly makes this assertion, so for Schütz, this empirical knowledge 'is not without presenting hypotheses, inductions and predictions but they all have the character of the *approximative* and the typical. The ideal of everyday knowledge is neither certitude nor even probability in a mathematical sense, but simply likelihood' (Schütz, 1964: 73; Williame, 1973: 137). This mode of 'typical' and probable knowledge is clearly quite close to the existential *chassé-croisé*, the rhapsody of popular discourse or the mottled spectacle of our towns. How could anyone imagine that the heterogeneity of the social could be the grounding for its conceptual double?

Lest there be any misunderstanding, it is not a question of defending irrationalism here — besides, dogmatism invariably leads to it — it is simply a case of outlining a *theory of knowledge which would accept that the structural incompletion of sociality is an incitement to intellectual open-endedness.* Thus one trusts to the plurality of approaches, of whatever order, to fill out the description of a given time and space which would contain the least possible number of mistakes. This reflexive patchwork is not the worst way of understanding a specific society; and the independent minds who try to break the boundary of disciplines and definitions share the view that the fluidity of analysis, the multiplicity of references and of sources of inspiration make a good match with the flow of life that we are trying to understand. In his essay on the objectivity of knowledge, Max Weber elaborated on the opposition between 'ought' (*Seinsollende*) and the 'is' and clearly showed that it is impossible for a 'science of experience' to discover the norms and 'ideals of an imperative character from which we could deduce recipes for practice' (Weber, 1965: 123, 129). The atmosphere which emerges from his analysis — which is symptomatic in this respect of Weber's continual struggle between the rationalist and the relativist — is that it is futile and even 'naïve on the part of certain specialists' to postulate a 'univocal solution'. In the succession of meaninglessness which characterizes all life in society, the only thing to do is to adopt a low profile, determine potentialities, describe the forms taken by the many relational situations, and emphasize the missed opportunities and lost dreams; in short, to employ, in relation to this *divine being which is sociality*, the same method that apophatic theology used to employ in the Middle Ages, in relation to its God: to speak only *a contrario*, at a distance, saying as little as possible about it. This is a wise attitude which, in advance, purges the mind of the spectre of absoluteness and invalidates it in a way, knowing anyway that its natural tendency will push it a little further ahead than where it ought to go. Since the inclination to extrapolate is, as it were, a natural burden on the human mind, relativist prudence can never be exaggerated.

With his typical didactic clarity, Julien Freund, the great French specialist on Weber, corroborates this interpretation in his introduction to *The City*. His opinion is that, on the one hand, Weber never ceased to plead for the diversity of possible approaches to the same phenomenon, but that, on the other hand, no approach was superior to any other for him; in the end, it seemed to him to be beside the point to search for universal explanations on the basis of more or less arbitrary generalizations (Weber, 1982: 16).[2] This is the lesson that can be drawn from comprehensive comparativism. The approximate truth is, all things considered, potentially more 'scientific' than an approach which makes out that it is exhaustive, because it will have the tendency to take up a position of affinity with, or opposition to, other approaches. For the same reason, it will constitute, *volens nolens*, an architectonic which will be much closer to social reality than one that is produced by the superb isolation of the perfect system in which nothing is left vague. And the city, such as Weber, Simmel or their common inspiration, Machiavelli of the *Florentine Histories*, spoke of it, can be an instructive metaphor in this respect; it is a disparate and 'contradictorial' (Lupasco) whole where, however, the whole thing forms a body. Lights and shadows, places of ill repute, monumental works, and work and pleasure are all arranged in a complex edifice which cancels grotesque and grandiloquent reactions for ever, regardless of their presupposition.

Even if this seems obvious, we have to point out, if only as lines of research to be developed later on, that the characteristic of 'ought to be', which provides a basis for conceptual or systematic procedures, is above all of a *moral* order. I consider that there is a distinction to be made between the ethic which arises from the social body itself, which acts as a cement and has a coenesthesic, balancing function (I have discussed this in connection with 'ethical immoralism', in Maffesoli, 1982) and the morality which is always imposed from outside. Nothing can be more laudable than this imposition because it is a case of making the masses happy, albeit against their wishes! And that is the very thing which enables us to understand that the cleric and the intellectual very often, however they disguise it, are incorrigible moralists. Perhaps it is because these perpetual 'cuckolds' of history give the impression that they are having an effect on reality, with either triumphalism or resentment according to the favours bestowed by the prince. Now, what could be more contingent than morality? After Montaigne and Pascal, Max Weber repeats it on many occasions (Weber, 1971). On the one hand, according to place and time, the anomic and the canonic have differential values, and on the other hand, there are evolutions and changes in the moral order at the heart of the same civilization or the same age. It is banal to point this out but no less useful because it brings out the structural weakness of constructions, each one of which occurs, as such, as absolutely necessary. It goes without saying that these constructions have their validity; as was said in the plurality of approaches, each one is indispensable. And yet it is when one or several of them tends to present itself as the *nec plus ultra* of theory that there is a real danger, for in various ways they (institutions, university authorities, commissions, publishing, the media) are going to exert themselves to have their hegemony. There is no question of studying the problem here, but of noting that the logic of 'ought' by an effect of structure which goes beyond it, ends up by hypostasizing theoretical production in relation to the social substratum.

It is well captured in common sense: the road to hell is paved with good intentions. And, indeed, it is dangerous to construct a made-to-measure world: it is not without consequences. And bureaucracy, state violence, terrorism and the technostructure, to mention only a few contemporary problems, have been able to develop in the guardian shadow of critical or institutional thoughts which dreamt of a world 'which had to be' rather than observing what existed. As a result, these thoughts have certainly *legitimized* apparatuses in which the gap between the institutor and the instituted, or between society and basic sociality is widening.

Contrary to moral thought proceeding by exclusion yet remaining utilitarian, it is worth reminding ourselves that the Weberian position, which was simultaneously pluralist and aware of the contingency of social customs, refers to a tragic vision. That is to say that the situations of social life are not finalized; or again that the fact that they are dressed up as final does not prevent them from being ephemeral. Of course, Weber does not push this logic to its ultimate consequences, as does his friend, colleague and fellow admirer of Nietzsche, the sociologist Simmel. Simmel believed that, in order to judge an event, 'one will no longer orientate oneself towards a final goal situated outside this event which would provide its measure . . .' (Simmel, 1912: 6). Instead, it will be necessary to appreciate it for itself, as an abridgement or a concentrate of the whole of existence. In this perspective, whatever happens has a right to its letters-patent *because* it occurs. This does not prevent the occurrence from being subject to thought, but this thought knows how to recognize the depth of the factual. This is what constitutes the bitter grandeur of the tragical meaning of existence. Henceforth, the sociologist is going to follow a direction which will lead from what I have called 'formism' to empathy, or from experience to phenomenology. Again, we find the mark of the ideal-typical procedure. Relativism is definitely, at base, the common matrix of empiricism and of phenomenology.[3]

Knowledge through experience, which is so difficult for conceptualism to accept but which is no less difficult to refuse in the sociological order, is going to find its condition of theoretical possibility in relativism or pluralism. The renewal of ethnomethodology, the stammerings of participatory sociology, the attempts at action research, the development of life histories, all this is based, without necessarily saying so, on fatigue with various socio-theoretical finalisms and on a recognition of the pregnant nature of popular wisdom. Thus, contrary to the scholastic visions which have always existed and which still have some fine weather ahead of them, the type of research that we are developing is designed to show, in Mannheim's words, that thought 'is not confined to books alone, but gets its *chief* meaning from the experiences of daily life . . .' or from the 'shifting values of the everyday world' (Mannheim, 1956: 66). Effectively, as E. Bloch seems to regret, it is a case of a perspective which functions like double-entry book-keeping; logic and experience both have a right to be there. But there are times when normative constructions no longer suffice to move minds; there are times when the perfection of enticing tomorrows fails to wipe out the attraction of facticity and of the imperfection of what exists. And as this force of life in no way signifies the surrender of mind, we know how to find meaningful structures, which are of value in themselves, in the midst of banality. In a clumsy fashion and beyond the scope of the institutional sociologies which continue to reign, for the moment, over our universities, this desire for empirical knowledge can be found among young sociologists who take up research topics which are widely considered insignificant or frivolous. In fact, the social sciences cannot wall themselves up in deadly cosiness. They are tuned in to a social world which is simultaneously given (I will come back to this) and something that is alive. There is a great deal at stake in knowing how to account for this double perspective which has what it takes to fascinate those who are compelled by intellectual necessity to smash thoughts that are too conformist.

In a text dedicated to Augustin Thierry, Renan reflected on the different ways of elaborating history and, without denying the effort of what he calls 'the Benedictine school', i.e. the methodical and rather onerous extraction of historical materials, he shows that in order to understand the 'confusion of passions and interests' which characterizes the life of cities and peoples, it is necessary to have, in addition to erudition and alongside lucidity, originality and an inner passion. 'The wider meaning of human things can only be obtained by an understanding of the *present*, and the present only surrenders its secret in proportion to what is staked on it' (Renan, 1859: 111, 117).

It is really the understanding of the present which forces us to relativize, if not to throw overboard, the whole set of the theoretical presuppositions which corresponded to a stage when the *individual* and the *economy* (of the person and of the world) were the two great pivots of social structurations. On the basis of these pivots, various processes of reduction have been able to operate by, in particular, eliminating polysemy and the monstrosity of experience. The heterogeneity of social life, in all its dimensions, is currently making a return in full force to the field of actuality. Nothing stays quietly within the frameworks that the overarching theories had worked out, and this applies to the order of sexual identities, psychological characters, economic plans, political divisions, productive functions or social determinations. This existential disorder obviously has an influence on scientific statement and research. In my opinion, it refers us back to experience which is, lest we forget, the foundation of all scientific progress. Concerning what he calls the 'Novalis complex', Bachelard emphasizes the connection between erotic rubbing and a friction lighter; so, according to him, love could be 'the first scientific hypothesis about the objective production of fire' (Bachelard, 1938: 54). This observation from someone who is a great theoretician both of the exact sciences and of the realm of images clearly shows that production on its own, or theoretical production in general, is strictly connected with everyday life.

It is because everyday life represents wagers that it becomes an object that can be known. I pointed this out by using the emblematic image of Dionysus and it seemed to me that we are returning to a more carnal relation to the social world and to the natural environment. The separation of objectivity is in the process of giving way to the *intuition* of experience. Of course, the terms are rather abbreviated, but there is no doubt that, as G. Durand put it, we are on our way towards communication on the basis of experience. There is so much truth in the claim that, in the strong sense of the term, 'a fundamental compassion is at the root of all science that intends to be human' (Durand, 1980: 47). To take only the most striking aspects astrology, ecological movements, 'alternative' medicines, macrobiotic food, the importance of nature, an attachment to the 'countryside', various localist features, all this shows that the 'distancing' which used to be the shared attitude of epistemologies and social practices, is giving way to a more open 'participative' method. The individual and/or collective body experiences the world and makes experiments with the world. To put the change which is currently taking place into words, and whose effects will be felt in decades to come, we can refer to Alfred Schütz's notion of 'familiarity'; the world taken for granted 'just as it is', the world is 'pre-given' (Schütz, 1964, vol. I: 13, 228). Through these expressions, we can see a relation to the world becoming clear which is completely different from the one to which we have been accustomed by the criticism or the activism of bourgeoisism. In this sense, I had proposed several years ago that we should use the expression 'social given' (Maffesoli, 1979a). It was in order to emphasize that there can be a relation to the world which does not rely on mastery (conceptual, economic, political) but rather on constraint or, more precisely, on the intuition of massive and incontrovertible evidence. In the words of a good introduction to interpretive sociology: 'the pre-given world is the physical world and the social world accepted as unquestionable' (Williame, 1973: 36). This is a perfectly anodine remark, but it is certainly full of consequences, for it acknowledges that experience is the primary reality that can be illustrated, but definitely not reduced, in thought.

In order briefly to characterize this relation to the world based on intuitive experience, we can draw on a distinction proposed by the art historian Wilhelm Worringer. On the basis of a very precise analysis of pictorial and sculpted works, he notes a dichotomy which checks with the distinctions implemented in my development. His view was that some periods are dominated by what he calls *abstraction* and others are mainly the product of *Einfühlung*. There is no point in going back over this in detail, but 'abstraction' is based on the distance which is established from the phenomena of the outside world. For Worringer (1978: 52), it was even a matter of an 'enormous, spiritual anxiety in the face of space', and it is space which leads the mind to cleanse itself of everything which is natural or, it could be said, familiar. On the other hand, *Einfühlung*, or what I called 'empathy', is an 'intuitive communication with the world'; this refers to a 'cosmic feeling' (Worringer, 1978: 50; Maffesoli, 1982: 62–102, 1979b: Chap. III) and it leans towards the 'truly organic, the alive, that is to say, towards naturalism'. We are in the presence of a pantheism based on the strong thrust that exists between men and the various elements of what is 'given' in the world. Sensualism, vitalism or naturalism, are all to do with a polarity which sometimes tends to predominate in everyday life as in art. It is an organic attitude which favours participation as distinct from separation. 'This manner of feeling oneself in things' (*Sich-in-den-Dingen-Fühlen*) (Weber, 1964), is a particularly illuminating way of understanding numerous situations that can be observed nowadays. Discriminating and reductive rationalism is obviously in the worst position to account for these situations. Sociology must also be permeable to this *Einfühlung* which is spreading to the whole of the social body. Sociology must understand, in particular, that concepts are sometimes a rather childish barrier erected in front of the vital flow of social existence which is in perpetual motion.

Notes

1. I have already shown the importance of theatricality and rituals in social life (Maffesoli, 1979b); with his own typical fulgurance, J. Baudrillard (1983: 215) develops a similar idea on metamorphoses.

2. R. Boudon, for his part, also acknowledges the diversity of sociological paradigms and although certain dimensions, of which we are beginning to measure the social importance, elude him *totally*, (for example, ritual, symbolism and play) he gives some illustrations concerning the behaviour of Mrs Smith 'filling her shopping basket' (Boudon, 1979: 248). However, his research on logical coherence, actually his presuppositions, leads him to postulate a 'syntactical unity', i.e. the 'intentional behaviour of individual action' (Boudon, 1979: 252).

The remarkable fresco of social paradigms that he gives (Boudon, 1979: 187–252) clearly illustrates, in my opinion, the limits of a sociology based on individualism, at a time when the community, which I call *sociality*, is regaining a place on the agenda.

3. Compare the points of similarity that Bloch (1978: 292) makes in this sense. Of course, this is a detestable intellectual position as far as he is concerned.

PART III
HYPOTHESES ON LEGITIMATION

Legitimation Processes in Politics and Religion

Robert N. Bellah

In most traditional societies religion and politics provided the central organizing institutions of society and were the primary locus of the legitimation of social action. The relationship between these institutions, in the West what we usually call church and state (in Islamic, Indian and East Asian societies there were analogous institutions), was often conflicted. Each on occasion claimed an ultimate loyalty in defiance of the other. But the normal situation was one of compromise and a degree of collaboration. The religious institution needed political recognition, support and sometimes protection from dissident movements, from the state; and the political institution needed ideological justification and the assurance that its rule was legitimate, or at least preferable to the alternatives, from the church. At moments religious devotion and political allegiance tended to fuse, particularly during time of war. In any case both religion and politics were spheres of solemn public obligation. Both were in a sense public and sacred.

This pattern by no means disappeared in modern times, though it was challenged more or less directly in the West from at least the seventeenth century. In many parts of the world even today — one thinks of Iran — an intense fusion of religion and politics provides the major focus of social action. I will argue that in a number of contemporary societies religion and politics are no longer able to provide effective legitimation for social action and have been replaced in part by other mechanisms and in part by the cynicism that seems to accompany privatization and secularization. I would like to illustrate my argument with the examples of two societies: one, the United States, where the older pattern gradually ebbed away, and the other, Japan, where it ended abruptly in 1945.

Japan is frequently offered these days as a model for other industrial societies. Certainly many features of modern society can be seen most vividly displayed there, and we may not be wrong in taking Japan, as we once took the United States, as the most modern society and thus as illustrative of more general trends. With respect to changing patterns of legitimation, the Japanese case is certainly vivid.

The creators of modern Japan erected in the last decades of the nineteenth century a formidable system of religious and political legitimation. Out of the much older traditional materials, but using modern organization and mass media to propagate them, Japanese leaders created National Shinto and the modern Emperor System. Fusing a sense of the divine nation and mission with loyalty to the state, Japan mobilized its population for the most rapid economic and military expansion outside the West. Assailed by criticism from the intellectuals and inner doubts in the minds of educated Japanese, the system reached the heights of fervor, enforced by the heavy hand of bureaucracy, during the 1930s and the early 1940s. Many Japanese living today remember being forced as high school children in virtual military fashion to visit the Grand Shrine of the Sun Goddess at Ise, Japan's most sacred spot, and feeling the fearful presence of the brooding spirits in the dark groves of giant trees that surround the shrine. There could hardly be a starker contrast with the holiday crowds of private families that visit the shrine today, more as tourists than as pilgrims.

The change came as suddenly as such changes ever do. Shortly after the surrender and the beginning of the occupation the Japanese emperor on 1 January 1946 went on the radio to announce that it was an error to believe he was divine. State Shinto was disestablished and the shrines were left to fend for themselves with voluntary support. Patriotism went overnight from being the highest virtue to being a quasi-crime. The Japanese have experienced something of a spiritual vacuum ever since, but only a tiny minority would like to return to the former system. For most young Japanese the presence in the country of Shinto shrines and a Bronze Age imperial institution are archaeological remnants almost unintelligible and in any case without interest.

What took the place of the older system of legitimation? The Americans hoped to nurture a vital democratic culture that would provide a politics of citizen participation in place of the older military-fascist regime. Or at first they did, before geo-political considerations led to another policy. Many Japanese responded, with some initiative, to the new democratic possibilities and political struggles occurred throughout the 1950s, petering out in the at times hysterical student outbursts of the 1960s. But the strength of Japanese bureaucracy was never undermined and, in combination with a virtually unbroken one-party political rule, began to construct a new system by the middle 1960s that was neither military-Shinto nor democratic. Masao Miyoshi, my colleague at Berkeley, has recently described the new system as follows:

> [The] period that begins at the close of the unrest of the 1950s and 1960s [has been one of] unprecedented economic growth . . . [It has seen] the emergence of a new corporate Japan with features clearly marking it as distinct. The organization of this new Japan is incomparably powerful. It regulates its citizens to be well-adapted functionaries for its economic program far more efficiently than militarist Japan ever could have mobilized its subjects. It is centrally planned and painlessly enforced. Of course, Japan's economic and technological advance is spectacular, and the pride and confidence the Japanese feel about the development are genuine and justified. Yet in this national celebration of success, consumerism is pervasive, eating deeply into the fabric of traditional life. Nothing is left intact; all social and cultural institutions are quietly, noiselessly, being readjusted. Even the privatized experience [such as Zen meditation] that [was] once legitimated among the educated is now being emptied of [genuine] contemplation. Thus critical opposition [is] now nearly non-existent. Periodically, people may protest against rearmament and pollution, but such movements are both specific and sporadic. The overall sense of affluence dominates, and occasional signs of unease about the harried pace of living are put aside and unacknowledged. (Miyoshi, 1983: 18–19)

This new system is called in Japanese *kanri shakai*, administered society. It is in one sense continuous with a long history of *kanryo seido*, bureaucratic system, in government and industry. But it has reached a new level of fine-tuning and co-optation. In talking this spring to Masao Maruyama, one of Japan's leading intellectuals and most thoughtful democrats, I found him actually nostalgic for the 1930s. In the 1930s, harsh though things were, there was at least an opposition. Now, Maruyama agrees with Miyoshi, there is virtually no opposition. The holy alliance of capital, labour and bureaucracy has co-opted not only the Socialist party; even the Japan Communist Party is part of the establishment. The only anxiety that really rouses people is, will the prosperity continue?

In this new system, what has happened to religion and politics and what provides at least a semblance of legitimation? Religion and politics have become in important respects privatized and secularized, and thus incapable of providing the legitimation they once did. The 1946 Constitution in separating church and state not only disestablished State Shinto but freed all other religions from government control. What emerged in the immediate post-war period was a competing cacophony of 'new religions' vying for the private allegiance of individuals and families. In the new open competition, what Thomas Luckmann has called the 'religious cafeteria' (Luckmann, 1967), the rewards that were offered were primarily secular and material: psychological and physical wellbeing; a better job and more money. Religion by and large reinforced the new secular emphasis on material comfort rather than challenging it.

To speak of politics as privatized and secularized may seem odd, but George Armstrong Kelly has recently argued, to me convincingly, that these processes occur in contemporary society as much in the political field as in the religious (Kelly, 1983: 207–28). The secularization of politics in post-war Japan is fairly obvious. Japanese are proud of their achievements and of their unique culture, but this is not translated into hyper-patriotism or a desire for world power, militarily or even politically. Japanese international political aspirations are confined to a desire to keep a free market for Japanese goods. When we argue that Japanese politics have become privatized we mean to say that the public political process has come to have less and less meaning. The real politics is the jockeying of private interests that goes on in the factional struggles of the quasi-permanent ruling party, entirely outside the control of any public political process.

If legitimation is not provided primarily by religion or politics, where does it come from? In accordance with the logic of the administered society it comes first of all from technical expertise, which has effectively engineered the prosperity so central to Japanese society today. The bureaucrats of the Ministry of International Trade and Industry, orchestrating finance and industrial organization, have proven their mettle in international competition. In times of economic disturbance the votes of the ruling party go even higher than usual, indicating the popular reliance on expert bureaucratic management. No society in the world is more oriented to education and personal career advancement through entry into membership in the great private and public bureaucracies than Japan. If sheer economic aggrandizement seems a bit soulless, as it does in Japan as elsewhere, it can coexist remarkably easily with a widespread cynicism, especially among young people. And if there is a need for something more, the governing party tries to provide a degree of personalized charisma, so different from the public charisma of the emperor system, by running well known film and television stars for the Diet. So far a movie star has not become prime minister, but such an eventuality is probably not out of the question.

Tendencies that we see abruptly and vividly in Japan have been under way for a much longer time in the United States and are still not as complete. One must go back to the eighteenth century to find a political-religious order at all comparable to pre-war Japan. The older British pattern of an established church headed by the reigning monarch was never but partially translated to the colonies. Only in the Southern colonies was there an Anglican establishment, but it was not as effective as the Congregational establishment in New England. Only there do we see a fully operating pattern of traditional political-religious legitimation.

In colonial New England the roles of Christian and citizen, though not fused, were very closely linked. In the earliest period in Massachusetts church membership was a condition for voting. The minister was a public officer, representing not only the church members but the town. Even when dissent gradually came to be tolerated, the established Congregational Church (it is worth remembering that establishment at the state level was not abolished by the Constitution and in Massachusetts did not entirely disappear until 1833) was the focus of community life and its unifying institution. Sermons were preached on all public occasions. Particularly important was the election sermon preached annually on election day, when the minister let his views on public matters be thoroughly known. What has been called New England 'communalism' valued order, harmony and obedience to authority and these central values were centred on the figure of the 'settled minister', who usually spent most of his life in a single town. Such a minister was 'both the keeper and purveyor of the public culture, the body of fundamental precepts and values that defined the social community, and an enforcer of the personal values and decorum that sustained it' (Scott, 1978:12).

The tight linkage of religion and public life that characterized the New England standing order was challenged long before the revolution, although at least at the local level it survived with remarkable resilience all through the eighteenth century. It was undoubtedly the pressure from the dissenting sects with their large popular following on the one hand, and from that significant portion of the educated and politically effective elite influenced by Enlightenment thought on the other, that finally led to the disestablishment of religion in America. By the early decades of the nineteenth century the older communal and hierarchical society was rapidly giving way to one in which economic and political competition was the order of the day. The mid-nineteenth century town, though considerably more consensual than the suburban town today, was still very different from the colonial township. No longer united religiously and politically around a natural elite of 'the wise and the good', it was much more publicly egalitarian. For religion to have emphasized the public order in the old sense of deference and obedience to authority would no longer have made sense. Religious teaching came to emphasize self-control rather than deference. It prepared the individual to maintain self-respect and establish ethical commitments in a dangerous and competitive world, not to fit into the stable harmony of an organic community. Churches, no longer made up of the whole community but only of the like-minded who felt most comfortable together, became not so much pillars of public order as 'protected and withdrawn islands of piety' (Scott, 1978: 147). Sermons turned more 'to Christ's love than to God's command' (Scott, 1978: 139). By the middle of the nineteenth century the 'feminization' of American religion that Ann Douglas has described was fully evident (Douglas, 1977). Religion, like the family, was a private place of love and acceptance in an otherwise harsh and competitive society.

Privatization, though an important long-run trend in the history of American religion, was never the whole story. Religion continued to play a public role even when churches were not directly involved. The public language of local consensual communities and of the national community when represented 'above partisanship' by the president speaking for all the people, tended to be religious in a non-sectarian way. It is to this tradition of the use of religious symbols in American public life that I have referred in speaking of 'civil religion' (Bellah, 1970: 168–89; 1975). Another way in which religion influenced public life was through the social movement, motivated by powerful moral conviction, and frequently led by religious persons. Examples include abolitionism, populism, the early Socialist Party, and more recently the Civil Rights movement and the anti-Vietnam War movement. But while religion has never been entirely privatized in America — the religious involvement in the anti-nuclear movement at present is a counter-example — certainly religion no longer provides the central social legitimation that it did a century ago, when a dominant Protestant consensus prevailed in our public consciousness.

The secularization of American religion has gone on concomitantly with its privatization. As theological speculation has become ever more remote from the popular culture the very idea of 'salvation' has been less accessible to Americans. Instead religion offers an array of psychological and social benefits including, in our electronic church, material benefits quite as vivid as the Japanese new religions. Again, this is not the whole story and there has been a modest revival of spiritual practice in the last twenty years and an even longer-term effort to reappropriate a vital liturgy. Yet whether on the right religion is viewed as a support for 'traditional morality' or on the left it is viewed as an incentive for 'social change' the process of secularization seems strongly under way. The more religion is secularized the less able it is to supply social legitimation, for it becomes just one more element in the secular competitive scene.

The privatization and secularization of politics, as in the case of religion, has been a long slow process. Already in the late eighteenth century in the process of the institutional formation of the new republic, we see the conflict of an older public or republican conception of politics — politics as public concern for the common good — and a newer liberal conception of politics — politics as the contention of private interests under the adjudication of a neutral 'nightwatchman' state. Over the two centuries since the ratification of the Constitution 'politics' has come to mean, for many Americans, 'interest group politics', and as such more than a little illegitimate. Such a privatized and secularized politics, though celebrated by many political scientists, seems unable to stimulate not only patriotism but even respect. Being of uncertain legitimacy itself it cannot supply social legitimation and instead becomes the source of widespread cynicism and disaffection.

The progress of individualism, whose early symptoms Alexis de Tocqueville so clearly diagnosed in the 1830s (de Tocqueville, 1835), and which has taken an increasingly psychological tone in the twentieth century, has contributed to the privatization of both religion and politics. A conception of the self as the only reality and concomitantly of society as artificial and oppressive has led to a declining commitment to all formal structures, including churches and political parties. The sovereign individual is to follow his or her immediate feeling which may lead one into a meditation group or an ecology demonstration but just as easily out again. As Robert Coles has put it, 'When the self becomes our transcendence, politics becomes, along with everything else, a matter of impulse, whim, fancy, exuberance, indulgence, bored indifference, outright angry rejection. A political analogue to "doing one's own thing" is a one-issue politics' (Coles, 1980: 140). And again Coles quotes a New Mexico activist expressing his political motivation as saying, 'I am in the struggle because it means a lot to me. It's where I'm at' (Coles, 1980: 140). Even the very notion of citizenship is lost when the phrase 'private citizen' becomes widely used and no one notices that it is a contradiction in terms (Kelly, 1983: 220). If politics becomes a matter of the private feelings of private citizens and is concerned not so much with the commonweal but with the distribution of secular goods in response to interest group pressure, then it is largely deprived of legitimacy, much less the power to legitimate.

Yet as Seymour Martin Lipset and William Schneider have recently pointed out in their book, *The Confidence Gap* (Lipset and Schneider, 1983), though confidence in all our major institutions, especially business, labour and government, has declined steadily for twenty years, Americans still express confidence in the validity of the American system as a whole. Whether this confidence is the lingering remnant of older patterns of religious and political legitimation or depends on the capacity of the system to meet basic needs at least of a majority of the people, or a combination of the two is not clear. Or perhaps America, like Japan, is moving to new patterns of legitimation, beyond religion and politics altogether.

Perhaps a look at the two most recent presidencies will be instructive in this matter, for it is the role of president above all that focuses the question of legitimation. Neither the Congress nor the Supreme Court are seen as representative of the nation as a whole but rather as contending elements in the partisan struggle. Only the president can claim that representative role and he with difficulty. Let us consider the extent to which Carter and Reagan relied on older forms of religious or political legitimation before we look at the newer forms on which they also counted. Carter was the most personally religious president in recent memory but it is questionable whether this gave him religious legitimacy. From the beginning a large part of the population, even of those who voted for him, were sceptical of his Southern Baptist particularity. But it was when he attempted to formulate his religious and moral concerns as an approach to the problems of the nation as a whole, as in the 'moral malaise' speech of 15 July 1979, that he seemed to suffer the most severe rebuff. Perhaps it was the unclarity of his message or the uncertainty of his conviction, or rather the incapacity to translate personal conviction into public vision, that was the difficulty. In any case the speech gave the opportunity to those who would extrude religion from our public life to suggest that Carter had taken an entirely wrong tack.

Ronald Reagan has at moments associated himself with the so-called 'religious right' and has on occasion adopted their Manichaean terminology when speaking of the Soviet Union as 'the evil empire'.

Yet Reagan has never appeared to embrace totally the politics of the religious fundamentalists and has failed conspicuously to lend his political clout to legislation that might enforce it. Thus Reagan's appeal to his religious constituency has been seen by most Americans, and increasingly by that constituency itself, as election politicking that does not determine the course of his administration itself. Thus religion, for Reagan, is a device for getting votes not a source of fundamental legitimation.

Politically both Carter and Reagan appealed to a vaguely populist tradition in that they were both Washington outsiders and both ran in a sense 'against the government'. Yet neither of them stimulated a genuinely participatory political movement and their populist rhetoric cut two ways in legitimating their administrations. Particularly with Carter the outsider role gave rise to questions as to whether he was really a 'professional' and ultimately to doubts about his 'competence', doubts that lurk just below the surface with respect to Ronald Reagan. Both Carter and Reagan appealed to an older image of small town America, to friendly people congregating in the corner drug store, to 'work, family and neighbourhood', as Reagan put it. But since neither offered any realistic plan to regain this idyllic state the appeal to nostalgia was not so much political as anti-political, turning people away from public issues to the desire for a more satisfactory private life. Thus it is doubtful if either Carter or Reagan generated very much real political legitimation either.

On what, then, have they and other recent presidents relied? In two words, on expertise and personality. Carter came in as an exceptionally intelligent president with an engineering background and with definite programmes to reorganize the bureaucracy, create a workable energy programme, redesign the defence establishment so that it would be more efficient and less expensive, and so forth. It was when little progress in any of these areas occurred that public confidence began to drop and Carter developed his 'competence' problem. Personality was also part of Carter's difficulty. At first he seemed a likeable and modest person whose religious convictions perhaps bespoke personal integrity. But as he came to appear remote, indecisive and unable to deal with a contentious congress, here too public confidence waned. The growing focus on the personality of the president that seems to derive from the relentless personalized exposure to television, that most private of media, is yet perhaps the result of a deeper cause. Having little that we can agree on religiously or politically, what else can we rely on but the president's personality, and his expertise or ability to command it?

Reagan has based his appeal on a claim to have a new technological fix for our economic problems in 'supply side economics' and certainly there were many Americans who believed him when he claimed that 'we have tried everything else'. The early apparent failure and later uncertain success of the Reagan economic policies have largely accounted for the vicissitudes of his public popularity. Yet the fervent conviction that Reagan really had a new answer to our basic difficulties did not survive the early days of his administration. There is little doubt that he has been able to retain the degree of support that he has because he is trusted by most Americans and has, as an ex-actor, a particularly effective television personality. Indeed it is his effectiveness as 'the great communicator' that has, to the amazement of the journalists, allowed him to survive gaffes that would have finished other leaders.

If America, though much more slowly and circuitously, has, like Japan, largely abandoned its reliance on religion and political legitimation, are we, too, headed for *kanri shakai*, the administered society, toward which many are urging us with the Japanese model in mind? Certainly there are some notable differences. The American bureaucracy, both corporate and governmental, seems notably less competent than the Japanese bureaucracy and so has generated less public confidence. No political party has been able to maintain power long enough to orchestrate the competing interest-demands into a symphony of rising productivity and successful international competition, as the Japanese Liberal Democratic Party has. Giant structures of bureaucratic power exist in America but they seem much more fragmented and at odds with each other than in Japan. Under these circumstances the appeal to expertise, though continuously offered by all political aspirants, seems less convincing. Thus it may be that we rely on the other horn of modern legitimacy, personality, much more than the Japanese do. So indeed we may explain the election of a grade B movie actor to the office of Washington, Jefferson and Lincoln, sad though the decline may be. A word that is frequently used in American politics is 'charisma', and this frequently in the context of the growing importance of 'personality'. We should not confuse this 'charisma' with that attributed to the great leaders of twentieth-century totalitarianism. This is not the charisma of George Orwell's Big Brother. Rather than the harsh tyranny of *1984*, the current American preoccupation with charisma should call up the image of the soft despotism of the administered society, where, so far at least, it is the carrot that motivates and not the stick.

Finally it may be asked whether religion and politics, two central dimensions of human society in history hitherto, can permanently be banished from supplying social legitimation and replaced instead by expertise and personality. The current Japanese and American systems certainly rely on an extraordinary degree of secular success, on their ability, the Japanese more effectively than the Americans of late, to 'deliver the goods'. Yet even when successful they both seem to generate a surprising amount of public cynicism and a failure of civic commitment. If either society faced a really severe problem, for example an extended period of economic collapse, would the structures of the administered society provide a minimum of public order? Or would we not see once again a turn to religious and/or political legitimation, perhaps in new forms, but probably not discontinuous with previous historical experience?

The Representation of Society within Society

Niklas Luhmann

In the second half of the eighteenth century, all the basic concepts of the European political tradition changed their meaning. An epoch, that of *societas civilis*, of political society, was closed, and a new one began. This change had long been under way when the Bastille was stormed. It cannot be related back to the French Revolution, but through this it received a politico-ideological stamp which still today makes it difficult to approach political concepts with political impartiality. Since then, as regards political concepts — one thinks of freedom, equality, democracy, legitimacy, representation, participation — we have been assisting in the political struggle which began with the French Revolution, and this, only this, conflict makes clear where the progressive and where the conservative forces are.

If as sociologists we wish to distance ourselves from this conflict of ideologies and political trends, we must take into consideration the complex development already in progress at the level of the history of ideas, before entering into the analysis of historical realities. First, we must take account of the changes of meaning in the conceptual heritage of the ancient European tradition, which are connected with the dissolution of the concept of civil society. Words like 'legitimacy', 'representation' and 'participation' undergo a profound change of meaning, whose causes must be sought in a structural change in the societal system. And on the other hand, there is a growth of political interest in these concepts which, historical rather than accidental, is determined through Revolution and Restoration.

Given this state of things, it may be advisable to leave aside the consequences of the French Revolution for the moment, and so too the use of the term legitimacy in the context of Restoration politics, and concentrate instead on the phase shortly before the French Revolution. It seems to me that in the two or three decades preceding the French Revolution, rather than after it, one can see why the old European semantics of the social and the political lost their plausibility, and why new ways of posing the problem distorted the ancient concepts.

Let us first look at how the right to exercise power of government was justified. Essentially, there are two answers. The 'English' solution, which was also welcomed as such in Paris, lay in the separation of powers and thus in the principle of the balance of political forces. The other was supported by the Physiocrats, especially by Le Mercier de la Rivière. Governing power is set up through the formula of 'legal despotism'. Both these proposals had something in common: they no longer deduce what we would call legitimacy from the law. The concept of legitimacy generally takes a step back and in any case loses its character as a juridical concept. On the other hand, political authority was considered the solution to a problem, be it that of the control of arbitrariness or of the scientific orientation of the direction of the State. Occasionally, formulations emerged that were first to be believed only in the second half of the nineteenth century. Authority was seen as nothing more than the effective tenure of power: 'sovereigns enjoy it because they enjoy it. The very exercise of their power is their title to it', Linguet states in his *Théorie des loix civiles* (1767: 1, 73). This in no way means the ruler can do everything he wants. The old problem of tyrannical despotism has dissolved itself. In their own interest, authority is restricted through the ecological and economic assumptions of social development, and in fact even more strongly than it could be controlled by juridical regulations or moral appeals.

Economic problems of social development, those of the agrarian economy, so strongly dominate that the ruler can also be described as the proprietor of sovereignty. On the one hand, this means that 'mere caprice becomes his rule' (Linguet, 1770: 40). And on the other, the room for manoeuvre in his actions is restricted by the rules of the economic system. Authority is thus the realization of what is economically necessary, and it is legitimated through the economic result. 'The spirit of the laws is property': Marx found this statement in Linguet and noted it (Marx, 1946: 629).

It is not difficult to see that this is still true two hundred years later. Hypotheses on the economic system and the interdependence between economics and politics have been refined. One can undoubtedly relate the problem of political legitimacy to the fact that wealth, as a source of political legitimation, has collapsed. Rich politicians, such as a Rockefeller, are suspect to us. On the other hand, political legitimation has been related to economic results that the politician has not himself created and indeed cannot by any means fully control. The effects of politics on the economy, and of the economy on politics have led to new problems: for example, what can politics do about the elimination of unemployment? Or, how can the economy calculate its economic investments when the interest rates are politically manipulated? Despite such problems, with which reality has to deal, it does however seem that positive development in the economy is the single decisive factor in keeping a government in power, whilst on the contrary recessions are politically dangerous.

Despite some evidence for this connection, such a mode of judgement is superficial. We have inadvertently equated legitimacy with popularity. This is evidently quite common, with the result that opinion polls and press reports treat legitimacy like stockmarket trends or employment figures. One then finds that their tendency to accept the opinions of the government diminish, or that their distance from the judgements of the opposition lessens. But only fictitious descriptions are produced, and their socio-theoretical relevance remains obscure. I therefore propose going back to the eighteenth century and again questioning both our authorities, Linguet and Le Mercier. This time, the central questions must be: who is specially authorized to speak on behalf of society? Who really, as part of the whole, can represent the whole?

Linguet replies very clearly to this question: many, and therefore no one. 'In France, for example, the monarch calls himself the nation; the parlements call themselves the nation; the nobility calls itself the nation; the nation only can't say what it is, nor even if it is. Waiting for this point to be clarified, everything stays confused; everything serves as material for claims and disputes' (Linguet, 1778: 13).

A few years earlier, Le Mercier still had in mind the general sovereign, the legal despot. Only he was considered. He represented the unity of the system in the system, and indeed, in the old sense of representation, in the sense of the tangible presence of something that cannot appear as such, 'the majesty of the sovereign and his despotic authority ever-present, even in those parts of his empire most distant from his person' (Linguet, 1778: 180). But already the disaster is becoming clear. The parliamentarism of particular interests cannot represent unity. It would be meaningful only if politics lacked clarity, if it were thus not possible to establish what was legal (Linguet, 1778; 137–8). Indeed, this was to become clear a little later. Representation must indeed be parliamentarized, and thus the fiction of the general will must be created. The legitimacy of parliamentary representation must then be grounded in the fact that a representation of unity, a representation of the system in the system, is no longer possible. Since then, 'representation' has been a hopeless, romantic category. This emerged, not least, from the discussion of the doctrine of constitutional law in the Weimar Republic (Schmitt, 1928: 204 ff).

My argument is that the problems of the legitimacy of political power are linked with this impossibility of representation. The capacity to represent the overall system in the system, the society in the society, is the source of legitimation. Whoever can represent the society in the society is thereby legitimate. Representation gives him the right. It is his right. If it dissolves, whoever still wishes to rule legitimately must then invoke values and ultimately show results. Starting from the premise that a part of the whole can represent the whole in the whole, the right of authority is a natural right. Without being able to think of an opposition or alternatives, it is up to the *maiores partes*, who clearly stay within the law and who, in the event of its infringement, must reckon with justified resistance.

All this world has foundered, and with it its semantics of self-observation and self-description. In place of *civilitas* we have civilization; in place of the good life, the difference between values and circumstances; and in place of the representation of unity, the representation of difference. Authority has been dissolved into nothingness. How can this change be explained sociologically? And to what extent do the changes experienced in the meaning of political semantics help us in this?

I believe that the explanation lies in a modification of the primary principle of societal differentiation: in the re-organization of the social system of stratification into functional differentiation. This transformation gives modern society its character. In the eighteenth century, this development was more or less clearly grasped, and this is why the conceptual universe of old Europe lost its plausibility.

The problem which forms our point of reference, the representation of the system in the system, plays a role in both social orders. One can thereby compare the old and the new, the traditional and the modern society on the basis of the question of how they are represented in themselves. And the difference appears, on the semantic as well as on the socio-structural level, to lie in the fact that the basic acceptance of a hierarchy in one instance corresponds to the facts, and in the other does not.

From a logical viewpoint, there is a paradox in both cases, a re-fusion of logical levels or 'types' which must be produced if one wants to analyse the self-referential relations involved (Herbst, 1976; Barel, 1979). However, this is not an objection against the possibility of real systems. They do not collapse because of a logical error.

Evolution is not a 'logical construction (or de-construction) of the world'. All differentiated systems have the problem that in relation to their surroundings they function as a unity, but at the same time they are broken down internally into partial systems, none of which as partial systems can represent the unity of the total system. For, as *everything* within, be it a sub-system, or a process or operative element, is *only a part*, they lack the ability to be what they are. They exist notwithstanding their logical impossibility: as paradox. But as this is clearly possible, one can only ask in what forms does the system experience the paradox of its existence, how it can be elaborated, and how it can nevertheless reproduce itself.

The classical answer to this question is in the form of hierarchy. Hierarchy was the evolutionary achievement produced to resolve this problem. In fact, it was a discovery of genius. The unity of the system was re-introduced into the system as difference, and in fact as a difference which exactly reconstructs the problem with which we are dealing: as a difference of rank. The unity of the system is the difference of ranks, with a double significance: it gives each part a rank, and so lets the part participate by means of the difference. And it uses the same difference to represent itself in the supreme rank at the summit of the system. It is unity as difference, as difference permits the representation of the unity of the system through the *maior et sanior pars*. Hierarchy is the paradox dissolved, paradoxicalness reflected in itself, as it were, and which thereby becomes interconnectable. It was discussed precisely in this sense in the old European semantics of participation and representation, service and authority. Whoever uses these words today outside their context must be aware that he is taking on the responsibility of giving them a new meaning.

We can now only dream of this fine artistic product of social imagination. Socio-cultural evolution has gone far beyond it. It has replaced the stratification of society as the form of primary system differentiation with the re-differentiation between functional systems. This removed the plausibility of the semantic hierarchy. When we experience stratification, we do so as if it was a contingent, not necessary structure: as class structures, without legitimating power. No system of functions, not even the political, can take the place of hierarchy and its summit. We live in a society which cannot represent its unity in itself, as this would contradict the logic of functional differentiation. We live in a society without a summit and without a centre. The unity of society no longer comes out in this society. And so for us legitimacy is a question of the popularity of the current government.

However, we shall remain romantics and, what amounts to virtually the same thing, we shall remain critics if we have to be satisfied with this explanation. If our society can no longer represent itself in itself as a unity, there remains, however, the paradoxicalness of each differentiated system. And if this paradox no longer takes the form of a hierarchy, it remains for us to ask in what other form it will now be active. The basic problem in fact remains unchanged; every operational act, every structured process, every partial system participates in the society, and is society, but in none of these instances is it possible to discern the existence of the whole society. Even the criticisms of society must be carried out within the society. Even the planning of society must be carried out within the society. Even the description of society must be carried out within the society. And all this goes on as the criticism of a society which criticizes itself, as the planning of a society which plans itself and always reacts against what happens, and as the description of a society which describes itself.

With the benefit of two hundred years' hindsight we can perceive the formation and development of theories of reflection which restrict themselves to particular systems of functions and deal with their specific problems. At the beginning, in the eighteenth century, these theories still appeared almost like theories of society, as though they involved jointly providing the reflection of society. So Kant, in the theory of cognition and thus in his reflections on the conditions of the possibility of science, sought the road to moral law and systematic organizations, and by this route achieved an unparalleled influence on movements seeking profound social reform. The Physiocrats also saw in their economic theories both a political theory and a theory of law. The concept of society is more or less limited to economic relations, so that reflection on the economy can at the same time serve as a theory of society. Marx was perhaps the last to have followed this approach in grand style. The result of his work, however, was only that the theory of society has subsequently appeared in sociology as an excessive demand and as a coercive, ideological position.

Clearly, official and academic sociology is backward today in lacking a description of society in the sense of a theory of reflection, a regulated theory of the unity of the system. Many writers on sociology, or even opponents of it, are involved in this task — even people who criticize it as a presumption. And in fact, how should sociology resolve a problem of this stature? How should it as a mere science, if this is not too strong a description, be able to perform the representation of society within society? How might we obtain the ability to give form to the paradoxicalness of the self-reference of the societal system, to which society might orientate itself? Or, to refer back once more to Linguet, sociology is not the nation in the nation. It participates, at most, in the claim to be such, and, for that reason, its relations with society remain confused.

Marxism has sought with great logic to turn this problem around by proposing itself as the unity of science and ideology, a particular kind of science. In line with this, it expresses its own theory as a condition of legitimation. This can only appear dogmatic. A science is involved in issuing certificates of authenticity, and thereby becomes a science of *appellations contrôlées*. However, what is good for wine is not thereby valid for science. This may admittedly be a good way of resolving the paradoxicalness of representation of the system in the system. But it is not the only one.

We must in any case start from this to establish precisely our distance from such an approach. But then one very quickly sees that this is much more feasible as it occurs at present. I want to propose only three possibilities which lie, so to speak, on the threshold, and they are:

1. a perfecting of theoretically-oriented *historical analysis*, with the aim of clarifying the identity and difference of modern society in relation to older social formations;

2. a precise analysis of the problematic area of *self-referential systems* in connection with an interdisciplinary and persistent discussion;

3. a clarification of the logic and consequences of the *functional differentiation* of the societal system on the premise that it is possible to obtain from this a better understanding of the positive and negative characteristics of the modern one.

One would not readily expect that a theory of society would emerge from this capable of serving as a universally accepted representation of the system in the system. What might emerge, however, is a clearer recognition and foundation of the reasons why this is a very difficult problem in modern, functionally differentiated society.

However, the consequences for the problem of legitimation with which we are concerned lie at hand: legitimation under modern conditions can only be self-legitimation (Luhmann, 1981c). Every action which causes damage today gives itself a legitimation, and only criminals take the liberty of renouncing this. So, whether this concept is confined to the political system, or whether one thinks primarily of legitimation of the law through a 'higher law', or whether it should function in every system of functions so that educators or doctors should be questioned about their 'legitimation', in every case the answer can only be the same: they do it because they do it. Or to formulate this in a less provocative way: every activity in a system finds its legitimacy in the fact that it is made possible through other activities of the same system. Systems of functions can only legitimate themselves. That is, no system can legitimate another.

More than one error can be eliminated at a stroke. The health service legitimates itself not as the application of a science but rather in its capacity to make a further medical service possible. The legal sentence legitimates itself not as the result of a legitimate political decision, but rather as the transfer of a normative quality from one action to another. The structures of functional systems have long been organized around these real situations. Only the false descriptions are still irritating as regards the vain search for legitimation from outside, from above, or through basic values or consensus by means of rationally ordered discussion. For this reason our society tries to include the population in all the functional systems, e.g. as the democratization of politics, or to ensure the solvency of everyone, even the poor. We know that this has happened in only very limited cases, but the type of concern reveals something about the type of legitimation. This should be interpreted as an *endowment of the functional system with the faculty of self-legitimation*. And a *functionally differentiated society can provide nothing else to its subsystems*.

The social cladding of the legitimation problem can thus no longer be formulated 'hierarchically'. Rather, it expresses itself as the imperative to self-legitimation. So it is not enough to replace authority by relations of value, or discussion, and with this modification stick to the model of hierarchy. We must take a radical position, and the central question in this matter seems to me to concern the socio-structural importance of the functional differentiation of environmentally-dependent, but also self-referential, subsystems.

We are, to use the current terminology, in a hopeless 'legitimation crisis'. What is lacking is not, however, a real legitimation but rather a better insight into the particularity of our societal system.

PART IV
REMARKS ON LEGITIMATION

Comments on Legitimation

Thomas Luckmann

I

I was invited to offer a few comments on the preceding chapters, and this is what I will do. Although I shall not comment on them systematically I do, however, wish to take up a few of the points that were made.

There was at first much discussion of definitions of legitimacy and legitimation (Bourricaud); then there was a shift, first to an analysis of one interesting instance of legitimation (Maffesoli), then to a comparative case study (Bellah) and finally to a broad evolutionary theory explaining the impossibility of legitimacy in modern society (Luhmann). Everybody seems to be concerned with major legitimatory constructs, with ideologies, and entire symbolic universes. I cannot deny that I also find these problems of considerable significance and that I have done some work in this area myself. (Incidentally, I thank Alberto Izzo for his masterful summary of certain theoretical points formulated by Berger and myself, but I don't feel that I should repeat myself — or him — on these issues.) As my task is that of a commentator, I shall take it upon myself to try to redress the balance, that is, to draw the attention away from the grand ideological systems and down to ordinary legitimatory processes in everyday life.

Unfortunately I do not have any detailed studies on which to report. There is too little work on, for example, the legitimatory practices used by husbands vis-à-vis their wives or vice-versa; or by school children vis-à-vis their teachers and vice-versa. But such 'small time' legitimatory strategies are the kind of thing I have in mind. My own comments will try to connect the conceptual definitional issues with the more empirical ones which arise in a study of everyday legitimation practices.

It is a truism that concepts are not the same as that to which they refer; ideas are not life, if by life we mean pre-conceptual experience in the fullness of all its nuances. But once having said that, the question remains which concepts are more adequate to their subject matter than others. Even if we admit that concepts are concepts and life is life, not all concepts are equally untrue to life. In any case, an effort to define precisely what one is talking about is more necessary in scholarly, scientific discourse than in ordinary, everyday communication. There, precision of denotation is not only not absolutely necessary, but sometimes positively dangerous. That much is by way of justification for my following remarks.

It seems to me obvious that legitimation refers to a process by which some state of affairs is to be made legitimate. Of course I agree that no perfect state of legitimacy is to be found anywhere. But that should not prevent us from realizing that that is precisely what many people at many times have tried to accomplish. The aim of accomplishing a state of perfect or near-perfect legitimacy and the actions motivated by that aim are therefore an important subject matter for sociological investigation. Now, in the most general sense one could say that any procedure by which something that *is*, is made to appear as something which *should* be, is a process of legitimation. But that is evidently rather too broad a view; after all, much of human life is conscious life, and much of conscious life consists of articulating what is and what should be. And that, in turn, is a presupposition of substantial segments of collective action.

Action is a project into the future. It is based on an articulation of what is the case now and an expectation of what should be the case later. Only highly routinized action does not directly presuppose articulation of what is and of what should be. When we brush our teeth, for example, no syntactically distinct articulatory processes are going on. But all action that implies a clear choice between alternatives does presuppose articulation of two states of affairs, a present one and a desirable future one. The project thus involves a decision between more or less distinct alternatives. One of them is taken to be better or preferable to the other. Such a decision, based on an articulation of what is and a choice of an alternative, is in my view the obvious beginning and the substratum of all legitimatory processes. It is the beginning of justifying a choice, first to oneself and eventually to others; justifying a choice first prospectively and then, occasionally, retrospectively.

In my opinion, the roots of legitimating processes cannot be found in social systems; here I find myself in total disagreement with Luhmann. The roots of legitimating processes are to be found in intersubjective action. But that, of course, does not mean that legitimacy is not an attribute which is particularly important for social systems. However, I want to stress this particular difference between Luhmann's position and mine. Let me repeat: the roots of legitimating processes are to be found in human social action, by justifying what is in the terms of what should be. Legitimatory processes evidently consist of articulations, primarily linguistic, but occasionally also iconographic ones. Even gestural articulations are possible. But this is still taking in too much territory. Nonetheless it is useful, I think, to be reminded of this general interactional basis of legitimatory processes. But upon that basis the term 'legitimation' must be narrowed down so that it becomes analytically useful.

Legitimation, although based upon the process of making sense of things in general, is a very specific process of making sense. It conforms with Max Weber's position as well as with ordinary linguistic usage to say that legitimation is making sense of power. The real sociological questions — which are not definitional questions — start at this point.

Making sense to whom? Analytically we have three possibilities: to those who exercise power; to those who are subject to the exercise of power; or to both. In opposition to the conventional sociological wisdom I suspect that legitimation which makes sense to *both* is the most frequent case in human history. Legitimation and the subjects of legitimation are very often convinced of the same thing.

One important task is to identify the producers of legitimation and the consumers of legitimation as well as its beneficiaries (and victims, if any). Normally, producers and beneficiaries, on the one hand, and consumers and victims, on the other, should be the same, but there may be exceptions. The sociology of knowledge and studies in historical semantics should be able to provide a wide variety of data with which one could analyse the legitimatory 'personnel' and the results of its activities. Let me mention a few instances that come to mind.

To begin with some early instances: the debate on the permissibility of the pagan mission in the early Christian communities; the debate between the Jewish Christians and the 'Greek' Christians, its documentation in the Acts of the Apostles and later in Patristic theology.

Another religious instance, but with definite political implications: the debate in American Methodism on the slavery issue in the nineteenth century. One basic text could be used for the legitimation of two radically different positions: the legitimatory strategies are particularly fascinating.

Another religious instance that comes to mind is the systematic use of fairly complex legitimatory practices in the organization of

Catholic piety in the so-called anti-modernistic movement during the nineteenth century. One could go on for pages listing additional examples of studies — and problems for study.

Legitimation as a process of making sense of power implies its corollary, a process of making nonsense of power, or making sense of a different distribution of power. For empirical analysis, such processes of legitimation (or should we say, somewhat fashionably, delegitimation?) may be particularly interesting because they show, in stark relief, the nature of the procedures used. Thus, for example, the delegitimation of the *Ancien Régime* by the *Philosophes* and the spread of their fairly sophisticated 'theories' to broader, educated strata in society.

Another example: the delegitimation practices used by political parties (and not only by them), especially by the National Socialists (but not only by them) in the Weimar Republic. Or, to go back again in time: the delegitimating practices of the radical wing of the Franciscan movement in the Middle Ages. Although these were not 'successful', success or failure makes the study of the structure and practice of legitimation neither more nor less interesting.

Power is to be found in all social institutions; it is not only politically institutionalized. That point has been made in several previous contributions, and I need not elaborate it here. But the fact that power and its legitimation can be found almost everywhere in society has certain consequences for research strategies. In studying legitimatory processes one must study the various procedures by which people — in different societies and at different times — make sense of power in the *family*, make sense of power at *work*, in *church*, and so forth. I repeat Maffesoli's point: legitimation is a process which is located in ordinary, everyday experience as well as in ideological supersystems. We all practise legitimation and we are all subject to it.

Here I come to my second set of remarks. The highest, most inclusive level of legitimation is the level on which an entire social order is presented as something that should be *so* rather than otherwise. This level, the level of symbolic universes, of ideologies, has been investigated — if not exhaustively then certainly very adequately — by historians of ideas, by political theorists and by sociologists of knowledge and religion. We know something of the structure of the rhetoric which is used; we also know something of the social basis and of the conditions of legitimatory strategies. Some, perhaps still tentative, generalizations might already be possible about legitimatory processes on that level.

Another level, the level of intersubjective, interactional justifications has been, if not entirely overlooked, then surely neglected. Anecdotal instances are not enough. Systematic study is urgently required here. Promising beginnings have been made. Modern folklore studies, ethnography (especially the ethnography of speaking), and related theoretical developments in anthropological and sociological linguistics already provide rich materials. In my opinion, considerable promise for the systematic study of everyday legitimation processes and strategies is held by the newly emerging analyses of *oral communicative genres*, of maxims, proverbs and parables. We all use them for legitimatory purposes in everyday life. Conversational analysis, the ethnography of speaking, and a few other recent developments in linguistics and socio-linguistics, have already contributed substantial data; one can expect more in the future.

Of particular interest should be the study of an intermediate level, of the level on which the grand legitimatory constructs, produced by experts (often mainly *for* experts), are 'translated' into the 'language' used for justificatory practices in everyday life. This intermediate level of 'translation' has been studied sporadically, but I doubt whether a systematic inventory is yet possible; here we have an area for future research. The study of the pastoral transformation of 'high' theology and the study of pedagogic practices rather than theory should be particularly instructive. We do have 'content analyses' of school books, for example, as instances of texts with legitimatory functions. More of that is needed, more sophisticated interpretative techniques are needed, and comparative studies are needed. We need ethnographies of organized and semi-organized youth groups and of the influence of adults within these groups; of the structure of the rhetoric which they are using to transmit more or less successfully (and occasionally unsuccessfully) what is derived from legitimatory constructs on the upper level. The research strategies on this level, in my opinion, must be concerned with face-to-face communication in everyday life, with the study of justificatory narratives used by anyone who finds himself obliged to use justificatory narratives (and that is all of us); of literary genres, wherever they become models for justificatory rhetoric; and of institutionalized forms of justificatory narratives (e.g., in court, in parliamentary hearings, etc.). Studies of police interrogation of suspects, for example, and court proceedings are already available.

A particularly useful item might be a comparative study of 'grand' legitimatory constructs when they are 'translated' into the 'language' of biographical justification, as for example in funerary orations. A comparison between religious funerals in the Federal Republic of Germany and State funerals in the German Democratic Republic, for example, might be quite instructive. My hunch is that the structure as well as the function of the procedures are the same; but I have no material to support this assumption.

Another strategic area for the analysis of legitimatory *processes* (rather than legitimatory *constructs*) would be the study of conversions — of religious as well as political conversions. Big ideological systems tend to produce big ideological texts. Such texts can be (and have been) studied by the interpretive techniques of historical semantics comparatively, across different periods. Contemporary texts are being analysed comparatively across different societies. I have no intention to belittle the importance of such studies for a sociological understanding of legitimation. But I do think that it would be even more illuminating for us sociologists to see how such texts are *used* and 'translated', how they are *applied* in everyday life. I think so, first of all, for theoretical reasons. The basis of all complex, expert legitimatory practices is to be found in the non-expert, lay justificatory practices. The level of complexity and of systematization is of course quite different. There is another reason. If the ambitious evolutionary theories of the transformations of traditional into modern societies are correct, they are most likely to be correct in the assumption that the functional systems and subsystems of the social structure no longer receive any kind of transcendental legitimation. The comparative study presented in Bellah's contribution supports this assumption convincingly for two societies, at best. But legitimatory processes are not generally disappearing, they are not an 'evolutionary relict'. They may have waned on certain levels of the social system, but they have certainly not disappeared from social life. Legitimation is still around, and not only as a relict of bygone days, as in the political parties, for example, but also as an ongoing practice in everyday life.

II

I could never see much sense in the distinction between 'micro' and 'macro' levels. This may be a useful label for certain kinds of academic-bureaucratic-taxonomic differentiations, and I have no intention of challenging its practical applicability. In serious theoretical discourse it has no place. Of course there is a difference between a *perspective* on face-to-face interaction and a *perspective* on highly anonymous institutions. I suppose that most of us agree that complex organizational action systems have become functionally specialized and segmented in modern industrial societies to an unprecedented degree. Whether that is an evolutionary accomplishment, as Luhmann puts it, or not, is another question, but it is a shorthand formula for a complex set of facts.

One can look at much of modern life from this perspective, as life that is organized in functionally specialized action systems. This is quite evidently not all that is of interest to us. Much life, much social life, goes on outside these systems. To call this part of social life the 'micro level' is a linguistic abomination. Along with other reasonable people I prefer to talk of institutional *structures* and of social inter*action*.

So much for that. In the circumstances I thought it useful to direct attention to the interactional perspective, a perspective which I take to be elementary (as did Max Weber, among others). That is not to deny the supreme importance of the complex institutional structures of which our society is composed. One of Luhmann's points — and the one which I most definitely share — is that the particular form of the organization of complex functional systems in modern (capitalist) nation states no longer requires any transcendental legitimation. More precisely, whether it requires it or not, it does not effectively have it any longer.

Luhmann also thinks that the functionally differentiated subsystems require no other legitimation than the one that they produce themselves. Here I disagree. To be sure, it seems that the functional subsystems continue to produce certain kinds of legitimations, although that is a debatable point. The overarching transcendental symbolic justifications of the nation state (as a representative form of the organization of societal subsystems) no longer exist, as Luhmann pointed out. Attempts to reintroduce such a symbolic 'umbrella' tend to be regressive, occasionally with dangerous consequences, occasionally with remarkable triviality.

Does this necessarily mean, however, that there are no other points of articulation, of coherence, between those complex institutional systems (including the nation states) and social interaction in individual life? It is my view that it does *not* mean that. It may be, however, that the term legitimation does not provide privileged access to such points of articulation.

By the way, I have my doubts about the term 'legitimation by procedure'. I must agree, however, that if there is any legitimation on such levels it tends to be of a nature roughly suggested by that expression. Unless there are serious delegitimating movements, no special legitimating efforts are necessary to sustain the facticity of ongoing procedures. Evidently I do not refer to other than the modern industrial societies. The point clearly does not apply to any other kind of social system. As for modern industrial societies: as long as they function, they function. 'Legitimation' does not require any transcendent *point d'appui*. That is a major point made by Luhmann and others (including myself in a different context).

It should be noted that there are legitimatory practices which are not merely individual justifications in face-to-face social interaction but justifications of collective aims and motives on a *regional* level. By 'regional' I mean both the literal 'historical' regions as well as, metaphorically, the many other areas of social life between the 'grand' institutional systems and personal existence (Luckmann, 1970). For this reason I tried to draw attention to the importance of the intermediate levels.

The nation state is not falling apart although it lacks a transcendent justification. It does not need it *unless* it ceases functioning at least semi-adequately and lapses into a state of severe crisis. This is a point of considerable significance. If an extrapolation of the status quo of the major (capitalist and noncapitalist) modern industrial societies leads us to conclude that the social system will no longer function adequately within a generation, two generations, three generations, if these prophecies of ecological collapse or 'system collapse' because of over-complexity, or, for assorted other reasons, are not entirely unrealistic (and I confess that occasionally I am forced by the evidence to half believe at least *some* of the prophets of doom), then no ad hoc legitimations will suffice to point to a solution of such crises. If simple extrapolations of the socio-structural organization which characterizes modern industrial societies lead us to expect major structural crises, no end of legitimation will do any good. The crises will be on a different level of reality from that of legitimatory practices and notions of legitimacy. It is therefore entirely possible that if this point is taken *au sérieux* (and it is evidently being so taken by some groups), more serious delegitimating movements than those we have known heretofore may arise in opposition to the social order of modern nation states. Such movements may hasten the oncoming crisis or act as agents of a self-fulfilling prophecy of an otherwise unlikely crisis. I am not convinced that this will be the case; I am just saying that this is a calculable possibility. But evidently some social movements believe in this possibility wholeheartedly. They may produce a legitimatory system of new dimensions, with a profoundly religious (but not *necessarily* anti-rational) character. Such movements may have consequences for the organization of modern industrial societies or they may not. But the point that nation states nowadays are no longer transcendentally legitimated seems to me to be provisionally valid.

Legitimacy and Political Processes

John Fraser

Luhmann's design seems to trace a passage, a progression from theories of hierarchy to a self-repressive, authoritarian internalization of pure, absolute, universal power. And yet it seems that power relations are still hierarchical, no longer socioeconomic but truly political. They are still historically relativist, these relations between rulers and ruled, but obedience, 'compliance' and consensus produce an 'operational' effect at the *semantic* level. That is, the semantic level becomes a sedimentation of all the previous paleo-repressive stages. After two centuries of populist and *dirigiste* attempts, at this semantic level there has now emerged a valid language/law for the purpose of achieving a universal legitimacy. This semantics, then, is the product of a complex, hierarchically ordered legal and executive process. But in what sense is it a 'product'? It appears final and complete, but in reality it is precarious. The semantics of power resembles a further mystification, as regards its basic social and historical referents.

Any description of social processes requires the concepts of tradition and transition, and it is these terms which are not well defined in Luhmann (1979; 1980; 1981a; 1982; 1983; 1984a; 1985). In part, this is because the historico-juridical scheme underlying his position seems arbitrary and above all scarcely 'social', interactive. This combination of the jurist and the historicist sociologist becomes alarming when the account of change turns out to be a search for a pre-constituted conservative origin, an absolutism of order deeply sceptical of the rationality of the historical project in which it is born.

The goal of submission, self-legitimation, would seem to be that of avoiding violence, and not that of suppressing power itself. Thus violent reaction by or against power marks a breakdown in the system. Thus, for governors and governed this breakdown is at all costs to be avoided. If self-legitimation is the norm, then power will be non-violent, almost benevolent. Perhaps, too, threats and challenges to it will be equally non-violent and benevolent. At least semantically, the threat to order is logically annulled by its premises. But what is the motive for challenges to power, that is, to *order*? What is the order to be defended? Why does the historical project of reason in civil society become exhausted, and yet produce a new semantic order, or code, for complex society? Or again, if the code is not rational but rests on a logic of deterrence, this does not exclude alternative, rational orders. Again, if it does, what makes pragmatic power dysfunctional or violent?

In attempting to establish transition, tradition and transcendence in creating mass or subsystemic self-legitimation, Luhmann makes a typically juristic confusion between legitimacy and consensus. It is a confusion found both among theorists of legitimation and of consensus. For the former, legitimation involves internalization of an historico-juridical myth, whereas for the latter both history and real society disappear. Consensual coexistence is different from Kafka's torture-punishment-justice machine, where the law is the message, the 'judicial communication', the 'sentence'. Both theorists of legitimation–legitimacy (a process with two terms) who see the law as power, and of consensus who see the social, social relations or rules, as though compliance were a rational, functional and self-justifying process, suffer from the selectivity of their approaches. The jurists of legitimacy trace a continuity from the first attempts to 'marry' power and law which has little that is historical or social, while theorists of consensus ignore the larger dimensions of law and power. In both cases, the complexity of political mediations — parties, the judicial system, legislatures, reformers and protesters, revolutionaries — is reduced to simplistic schema. If people do not break the rules and provoke power, these mediations are not really necessary, are not — given the existence of a universal law-language, or code, legal or behavioural in the sense of cipher and codex — *functional.* Though we know that the essence of politics and social coexistence lies, for good or ill, in mediations as a continual process, not as means to a finality, Luhmann drastically curtails the social mode of politics. For him, power becomes another version of the black box, where mediation occurs mysteriously in the invisible (or concealed) process which converts inputs into outputs. However, the problem of power and its analysis as law remains inside the black box, which is far from mysterious to those who manipulate its mechanisms. In fact, as system, legal apparatus or semantic code, the black box is for him both power and society. The old 'fictions' of reason, the 'English' system, hierarchy, representation and representativeness are all 'historically' transcended, exhausted, and dismissed.

An important first step is indicated when tradition and processes of transition are discussed (processes for Luhmann more juridico-constitutional than socio-historical), and the difference between traditional and transitional legitimacy is brought out. This qualitative break implicitly challenges the static nature of the jurist's attempt to establish a continuous flow from a partial mystified legitimacy to a radical internalized self-legitimation, where deference or submission to a hierarchy of social power (with the appearance of juridical formalism) is replaced by spiritual acquiescence to a hierarchy of *absolute* power. For this is the goal, however precariously approached, and however disillusioning, to which Luhmann aspires. Total legitimation, internalized, equals total order, the aim and conclusion of the political processes. Political processes *threaten* order unless, originating from the side of power, they contribute to absolutizing order.

Where Kelsen posed the problem of the break between tradition and the dynamic of the modern in terms of the passage from partial, arbitrary absolutism to a system of flexible and also reasonable norms, Luhmann resolves the old problem of absolute power differently. The partial absolutisms lack crucial elements of submission and compliance regarding both *Macht* and *Herrschaft*. He proposes a continuity and transcendence of absolutism which accepts the elimination of reason along with them, whilst insisting on the absolute internalization of legitimacy. On this internalization depends absolute order. This power is no longer experienced as either *Macht* or *Herrschaft*, as it is no longer partial or dialectical. It lacks mediations. Yet, is it possible to say that the new absolute replaces the old, both in part absolut*ist* and rationalist? In reality, the old juridical types are not transcended. And could one say that they constitute in any case the source of the problematic of modern power? Luhmann's historical pessimism and historico-juridical pessimism underlie his analysis of the 'modern'. The Past is past. Partial responses to the problem of legitimacy-consensus (power as it creates order–submission as taken for granted) are transcended. Totality is required, even if the perspective is that of a disappointed eighteenth-century citizen.

For non-traditional societies, a non-traditional theory of legitimacy and legitimation is needed. One may agree with Luhmann that this would be 'radical', not 'English' or rational-despotic, nor hierarchical. But 'radical' for whom? With what historical context? The jurist presupposes the answer to the problem of power, and its translation into a legitimate form lies in a code, in codification, in a powerful, polysemic semantics which punishes transgressors and is 'benevolent' (indifferent) to conformists using everyday language. The theorists of legitimacy want an internal structuring, in individuals and in social subsystems, of the code; while theorists of consensus want the code deciphered through 'Anglo-Saxon' encounters, face-to-face, reasonable encounters of the 'do unto others . . .' type. After a somewhat nineteenth-century liberal attack on Reason and the 'English' solution, Luhmann sees as legitimacy the traditional, paleo-legitimate form deprived of reason and of checks and balances — recognition of the effective utility of power.

In reality, self-legitimation has no meaning unless I state norms. It is pure obedience. I, the group, the subsystem or system proper must internalize a basically arbitrary code with neither Kelsen's transparency nor Rawl's neighbourliness. For Luhmann, not only my priority for order but my ascription of what and why something is 'order' depends on my ingestion of the code as if it were language. This supposes a form of communication: but in fact, without power as its source, the code has no significance, it leaves everything as it was. The code 'means' order, but internalized may rest on hedonism, tradition, common sense or convention.

Luhmann stresses the marriage of a Eurocentric juridical discourse to the universal problem of passage to post-rational, post-hierarchical, post-representative systems, seen as 'modern' society. Even if these are ideal types, are there empirical referents? Can this become a non-European, non-historically-conditioned model? He uses a kind of Marxist-realist critique of the English model (it mystifies the subordinate classes but works for an expanded, loosely articulated ruling class), and an Hegelian one of partial representation (representation of all that is, hence of nothing, thus really representation of interests through hierarchies). Yet despite critiques, these forms — and others — persist: they cannot be made to disappear by philosophy. How then to seek the totality Luhmann sees as necessary, when totality is a function of total power, total legitimacy? This is justified because totalities are themselves precarious — as precarious as the individual, the speech act, comprehension. The Eurocentric legal tradition comes to underpin something like the proposition that legitimacy is totally legitimated power. This is premise as well as conclusion.

The real problem is that of keeping order in modern society without (excessive) violence, given that social complexity itself does not guarantee order. The viewpoint must thus be that of power. But power as problem remains. Self-legitimation requires both self-policing and the absolute functionalism of 'modern' society. Rather than resolving the problem of power, this means power is no longer problematical (Fraser, 1983). Pessimism regarding the past is transformed into a rejection of political mechanisms in favour of a learned language, a system of juridico-linguistic rules in the service of an 'absolutely relative' functionalism of self-contained, closed, encoded systems. This functionalism breaks down when violence is used.

By not discussing the State and its mediating functions, Luhmann can resolve the distinction between legitimacy and consensus. Legitimacy is the formal, institutionalized expression of power relations which may be zero-sum (either acquiescence or violence), but which have as their mediating forms the subsystems of power-society. On the other hand, consensus is based on formal and real inequality, which may be formalized, encoded, and thus for power cease to be problematic. For the Marxist critique of consensus (and for others), the formalization or routinization of consensus is essentially a mystification of real inequalities, which do not substantially alter through formalization. Yet in fact Luhmann does not seem impressed by that equality (formal) criticized by Marxists, even if he sees the process of formalization as equivalent to that of securing social consensus. Yet it is hard to discuss legitimacy and consensus without distinguishing real from formal equality, just as it is hard to conceive of a code, let alone a language, which does not entertain the same distinction. This leads to identifying symbols and conventions with purposive and intentional actions, the representation for the thing represented.

Luhmann thus wishes legitimacy to achieve the high-point of consensus. Many American theorists, on the other hand, would seek to invert the process — to express consensus formally, through reverse discrimination, or the ERA. To Luhmann, however, legal power starts off as functional power. For an 'egalitarian' American school, after Rawls, equality is a basic principle of the social, which can be expressed juridically. Both projects rest on dubious assumptions about real equality, legal or social. They have not explained their only partial effectiveness. As projects, they become static and conformist in dynamic, unequal and aggressive societies. Representative government tries to legitimate consensus; it tries, that is, to convert consensus into power. But it also tries to formulate consensus through its legitimacy expressed as power, and thus has this power conceived of as non-coercive, and, in an unequal social context, seen as reasonable, as against being seen as rational in a juridically equal context. However, the attempt to fuse equality and law, social inequality and power is no longer, if it ever was, an attempt at unity. It is a recognition, pluralistic, of inescapably asymmetrical social relations of power: 'before the *law* all men are equal', but not before consensus.

Rather, it denotes a process. Social complexity and the complexity of power are not expressed in a shared code nor a semantics, but a complexity of processes. The proponent of the existing order sees the coexistence of contradictory principles as a necessary good — and evil, the essence of a certain freedom. The Marxist sees it as a way of perpetuating and mystifying a status quo, albeit a fluid one.

The input–output model tries to reflect and convert needs, stimuli, into consensus, and no more. It often overloads (O'Connor, 1973a; 1973b). In fact, within the conversion process, the black box, there is feverish activity, even if its details, the institutional realities of judges, warders, execution squads, the penitent, are more easily left aside. Here, however, it is the function of power itself, not of consensus, to offload or carry the charge. In moral and practical terms, power bears practical responsibilities. In the absolutely egalitarian model (Rawls, 1962; 1967; Lessnoff, 1971), the criminal confesses and acts as his own judge; there is no logical motivation for crime, hence no logic for disorder. If one must accept the punishment as deterrent inflicted on oneself as victim by oneself as judge, then one is a priori deterred. There is no need for the deterrent as there is no logic of the offence. Thus there is ultimately no need for the black box, for power socially organized and mediated. Repentance-submission, a semantic act, rests on our presumed equality. So too Luhmann uses a similar argument — self-legitimation provides a real consensual basis to our inequality with regard to power. In reality, though, it is the political process, the mediations (and mystifications) which promise bridges between the reality of inequality and forms of power and equality which are not based on the fictional 'real equality' of Rawls, but rather a real social equality.

If to Luhmann absolute power does not even require Rawls's theatrical courthouse, as it is self-inflicted — a real solipsism — he is less ingenuous than Rawls. He knows that not only disorder but power punishes. Power as agent is not structured symmetrically with the victim. (Though it seems, casuistically, as though legitimate punishment must always be self-punishment.) As against Rawls, he sees that deviance, disorder, is not only a question between neighbours but one of 'legal' power itself. For him, deviance is always dysfunctional, and thus non-logical. Whereas Rawl's system seems to break down in relations between non-neighbours (between states, for example), or where actors are dead or have different systems of culture or interest, Luhmann achieves a certain Hobbesian realism. He does this by easing out discussion of reason, values and interests, finalities and alternative projects. But he cannot surmount the problem that power relations are asymmetrical, that politics recognizes this, and that recognition of inequality and acceptance of it as a changing and changeable relation are different processes. Recognizing and acceptance can be codified, but they can never be summarized in the same linguistic act. Only absolutism or natural law can get away with a statement 'I command, you must obey' as though it were self-evidently true in both parts.

Rawls sees American society as necessarily highly mobile, one where, despite real experience, social roles are interchangeable. Luhmann, on the other hand, sees power as a conventional relation: a code of expectations and meanings which maintains a *modern*, not a potentially *just*, society against disorder. Power, oddly, seems the converse of disorder. The essential myth of order is a fine net cast over a sea of violence, to contain it. It is a myth essential to the survival of both powerful and weak. Legitimacy requires no ideology of fairness, nor reciprocity, but rather that of deterrence.

It is today almost impermissible to admit to having or using power. Yet everyone, every day, uses it and/or submits to it. Luhmann is highly aware of power's 'everydayness'. But his research into it is disappointing, traditional. He suggests three research strategies: historical-comparative, subsystemic, and functional differentiation. These concern areas where power is already set up and legitimated, ongoing systems, and the transition from *Macht* to domination. Maybe power is no longer a mystery, historically, and is hard to modify and so tedious to research. But if power as legitimated process is to be studied, the process must be studied not dismissed as empirical crumbs, nor defined, in terms of its goal (maintaining order without violence), as a modern process. Luhmann's own criticism of functionalism shows that the level of juridical functionalism is not enough. Empirical referents and institutional mediations cannot be discarded as though they were but the technical vocabularies of universal power.

By leaving aside empirical referents, Luhmann seems not so much to offer grand theory as an apologetic for that functional base where rulers and ruled can retain their respective positions without violence. But why should they hate and fear each other? Why do they misunderstand the code? In either case, hatred or ignorance, it is broken. Why is hierarchy seen as an historical theory, rather than as a condition both of power and of 'dis-order'? Self-legitimation certainly protects the weak, because they become less aggressive, but it also reinforces the powerful, in a way closer to classical despotism than reciprocating consensus. This conception of power cancels out ideology, philosophy, and cultural differences, since all systems are self-sufficient with respect to their performance regarding the codification of legitimated power. This has a Hobbesian value. It is useful, but limited. It is a kind of conservative infantilism (borrowing from Lenin's strictures on the disorder of left-wing communism), the beginner's level, for good or ill, and it is hard to see how it can be pushed further.

A Different Historical Perspective on Legitimation

Srdjan Vrcan

I had originally intended to address the subject 'From the crisis of legitimation to the legitimation of the crisis'. This intention was initially derived from Alvin W. Gouldner's remarks on the functions of social theory and sociological thought in general. In *The Coming Crisis of Western Sociology* (Gouldner, 1970: 484–6) he stressed the fact that social theory and sociological thought have another important function in addition to the cognitive one, that of normalization. This function consists of locating within the realm of social normality certain social phenomena which at first sight seem highly problematical: abnormal, anomalous, and consequently disturbing. It seemed to me that it would be interesting to analyse the current debates on legitimation by way of a shift from 'legitimation crisis' to that of 'legitimation of the crisis'. For there is a suspicion that behind part of the current debate on legitimation there is an attempt to normalize, through theoretical discussion, that same serious, profound and current social crisis, with its undoubtedly disturbing aspects.

However, it might be argued that behind the discussion of the social, as against social institutions and structures, there lies not only a legitimate attempt to widen the scope of sociological research and theory, but also an attempt to leave behind these troubled waters of a contemporary society in crisis. This also means leaving behind those dominant social institutions and structures wavering under the impact of crisis, with the aim of entering the supposedly calm waters of the social *tout court*, of everyday routine. Here, everything would seem to be in good order, functioning smoothly and automatically behind the *corpus mortuum* of society and its institutions. It might be suggested that the growing fascination of the social, of everyday life and its routine, has the obvious advantage of freeing us from the nightmare of a worldwide, long-lasting crisis. Thus, it could be argued that the new social theory, centred on the social, functions in a normalizing, tranquillizing manner, reducing the importance of the mystery of the present crisis to something marginal and superficial for theory.

On reflection, however, I wanted to remove the emphasis from a discussion of legitimacy and legitimation, which has so far been based on a precise social and cultural background, and a specific historical experience. The assumptions have been those of so-called advanced industrial societies. The historical experience has been that of the recent historical vicissitudes of Western, metropolitan, late-capitalist industrial societies, even though different theoretical orientations are involved. Even the experience of the so-called Western societies at the margins of the metropolis, such as Greece, Spain, Portugal and Turkey, has not been invoked. This is why it seems interesting to explore the possibilities open to sociological theorization based on other historical backgrounds and experience, and in particular that provided by Yugoslav sociology, and the immediate personal experience of individual Yugoslav sociologists.

I should like to draw attention to some elements of this background and experience in the context of a discussion of legitimation and legitimacy.

First, Yugoslavia has experienced the collapse of a political system and order as a result of attack from outside. It has also witnessed the intensification of existing internal social contradictions and conflicts, combined with an almost complete exhaustion of the resources of purpose, values and ideas which might have produced a response from the system, satisfying the claims and needs of the mass of the population — or at least one which could guarantee the necessary minimum of mass loyalty to enable the system to persist and function in the face of strong pressure from without.

Second, Yugoslavia has had the historical experience of organizing, establishing and consolidating a new political order during this same period, employing a complex, flexible strategy of legitimation in different parts of the country. This included the maximum or minimum forms of legitimation of a dominant, victorious force. One recalls the simple formula of such legitimations in the Italian army's wartime slogan 'Rome tames' (*Roma doma*).

Third, this experience has also preserved the memory of the total defeats of all such efforts and of all their specific claims to legitimacy. This has also included defeat by autonomous popular uprising and social revolution, as well as by their powerful legitimating and delegitimating potential.

Fourth, the experience is that of establishing, almost from nothing, a radically new social system and political order, arising out of a popular revolutionary movement. However, this movement subsequently underwent important internal structural and cultural changes, initially quite unexpected and unforeseeable. They resulted in obvious shifts in legitimation and legitimacy, and the political order changed the basis of its legitimacy.

Finally, there have been several traumatic social and political crises which have shaken existing methods of legitimation and the dominant bases of legitimacy. For example, we may mention briefly the dramatic, unexpected crisis of 1948, created and driven home from outside, the political crisis in the leadership in the early 1970s, and the current social and economic crisis.

There are some important lessons in this specific, but nonetheless rich historical experience which should not be overlooked in discussing our present subject.

To begin with some preliminary clarifications, we might start by examining legitimacy and legitimation in Max Weber's (1947: 122–4) classical terms. This means that legitimation and legitimacy are essentially linked to authority and overlordship (*Herrschaft*, and *Herrschaffen*). Thus legitimation and legitimacy do not refer to the real foundation of power and domination, but to ways of justifying them (i.e., to *Rechtfertigung*). The need for, the faith in, and the claim to, legitimacy are basically related to power and domination. This is simply because there is an inherent precariousness in power and domination, which is not just the natural consequence of all human endeavour or the human condition *sub specie aeternitatis*. Obedience to power and authority has an inherent moment of precariousness, and so creates a need for legitimation and legitimacy. One should stress that there is a clear distinction between an overly generic discussion of legitimation and legitimacy which presupposes the almost universal need for legitimacy in every social contact and action, and a specific discussion focused on power and domination. Further, one should clearly distinguish between a sociological discussion of the terms starting from the premise of a *herrschaftsfrei* social context (one cleansed of any pollution by power or domination), and one involving the terms which assumed a social context permeated by power and domination. The historical experience described above is relevant only to the latter case.

What lessons may be learned from a critical sociological analysis of this experience? First, some relate to a quite abstract level of theorizing. For example, in his celebrated book *Legitimation Crisis* Habermas (1976a: 117) operates with some very general assumptions. Essentially he takes them from Peter Berger's argument in *The Sacred Canopy* (1967) which stresses the generic, anthropological need in man as such for *nomos*, meaning and order, with no historical specificity. This then appears in the form of a fundamental, universal and permanent dilemma which is faced by men and their collectivities everywhere. This is the dilemma of a choice between *nomos* and anomie, meaning and meaningless, order and disorder or chaos. In the light of the historical experience referred to, it seems that the problem has been posed in an overly generic and abstract, as well as a biased, way. In reality the dilemma is never, or hardly ever, posed to real men, of necessity living in specific historical conditions, in Berger's terms. Possibly Berger's postulation refers only to the very beginning of human life, to Adam and Eve in Eden, the earthly paradise. And perhaps they faced the dilemma of choosing between absolute, divine *nomos* or total meaning with no conceivable lacunae or voids, total unchanging and immutable order in Eden on the one hand, and total, inescapable anomie, absolute meaninglessness and disorder outside Eden, on the other. Their choice is well known and very significant, however, if only mythologically. That is, their choice could well be interpreted as evidence that it is humanly impossible to live under the rule of an absolute *nomos*, a pre-given, unchangeable meaning and total order. It shows that humans find it very hard, if not impossible, to live under the protection of an absolute, sacred canopy of *nomos*, meaning and order.

In contrast to Berger, we might argue that a critical sociological analysis permits the following conclusions:

1. The current dilemma, also faced by any historical human collectivity, is rarely posed in the extreme terms of a choice between *nomos* and anomie, meaning and meaninglessness, order and disorder. Generally, the choice is between one type of *nomos* and another, one type of meaning, of order, and another. Thus, real historical legitimation always concerns the choice of a specific historical *nomos* and order in a determinate plurality of possible alternative *nomoi* and orders, even though it may be presented as an absolute, unqualified choice between *nomos* and anomie, order and disorder. It is precisely this type of choice which increases the need for legitimation.

2. These alternatives do not appear in history and society as two diametrically opposed entities, totally and coherently excluding each other. There is always a more complex, dialectical relationship between them. There is always a degree of anomie inherent in any given *nomos*, produced by an existing *nomos*. A degree of meaninglessness and absurdity is always concealed and reproduced by a

concrete system of meaning, and there is always a degree of disorder in order, necessarily produced by the existing order itself.

3. In an argument such as Berger's there is an obvious emphasis on the risks to individual and collective identity and integrity which of necessity arise from anomie, meaninglessness and disorder. However, it seems reasonable to stress that there is also a latent risk to them *within* a certain type of *nomos*, meaning and order. Thus, as is suggested by the historical experience mentioned, it is necessary to detach oneself from this type of *nomos*, meaning and order, and to challenge them in order to protect and develop one's individual and collective identity and integrity.

4. There is a risk of slipping into an ideologically biased discourse, whereby an historically given and arbitrary order is made into order *tout court*. This is also true of meaning and *nomos* if they are identified with their pure condition and thus allow no alternative except inevitable anomie.

5. *Nomos* and anomie, meaning and non-meaning, order and disorder, are relational concepts. Hence, what from one standpoint may seem to be an ideal type of *nomos* may from another seem to be a clear case of anomie. And the same is true of meaning, and of order, as a supreme example of a stable order which may simply look like disorder when viewed from a different perspective.

At a lower level of abstraction, this historical experience may serve as a warning, for example, to distinguish between society and social system, system and political order; between social and systemic integration, and so on. A political order, for example, may dissolve and collapse without automatically implying the total disintegration of society and a complete destruction of the social fabric, or even the decay of all the important parts of the social system. In social life things often arrange themselves adequately, even when a previously legitimate, stable political order has collapsed. For instance, in such situations the role of other non-political institutions — church, family, kinship, etc. — may increase. One might then agree with the position that there is no illegitimate society, but that this does not mean there are no illegitimate political orders. Alternatively, it does not mean that all imaginable political orders are by definition legitimate, and to the same degree.

Another element emerges from the analysis of the Yugoslav experience. Weber analysed the problem of legitimation and legitimacy from the perspective of an established and uncontested *Herrschaft*. The exception was charismatic authority which erupted on the social scene unpredictably and with innovative vigour. Since Weber, a whole tradition has concentrated on the legitimation and legitimacy of an already established and functioning *Herrschaft*. This tradition takes into consideration the fact that, in this case, legitimation may empirically fail; thus a shortfall in the legitimacy of the established authority may occur and lead to a crisis of legitimation and legitimacy. However, our current historical example suggests that there is another side to the story and that, in discussing legitimacy, one must take into account that two different, conflicting processes are at work. One is well known and easily identified. It is the active process of legitimation: producing and reproducing the legitimacy of *Herrschaft*. The other is the active process of delegitimation, challenging the legitimacy of *Herrschaft*. In this sense, delegitimation and the crisis of legitimacy are not merely the negative results of a legitimation which fails to produce legitimacy at the required level. Delegitimation may be the positive result of an active process, challenging existing *Herrschaft* and questioning its legitimacy, creating new, stable conditions for refusing loyalty to *Herrschaft*. It could be argued that the essential precariousness inherent in power and domination, creating a permanent need for legitimation and faith in legitimacy, is also continually operative as delegitimation and as a permanent, if latent, denial of legitimacy.

Moreover, a critical analysis of the Yugoslav experience emphasizes the importance of the socio-cultural system, or aggregate, in producing consensus. That is, it points to the fact that, as Habermas has remarked, the stability and credibility of *Macht* and *Herrschaft* depend on the store of meanings, values and ideas that a political system can mobilize for its own purposes (Habermas, 1976a). Legitimacy rests on a kind of faith which is essentially a socio-cultural phenomenon. Thus, the shifting balance between legitimation and its opposite rests on socio-cultural dynamics, and this produces a particular type of faith, as well as on the creation and stimulation of meaning, value, and the use of tradition.

In this respect we may observe, first, that there can be no such creation and stimulation of meaning and value administratively or by decree, however powerful *Herrschaft* may be (Habermas, 1973b: 644–7). *Herrschaft* itself cannot create and stimulate the minimum of meaning, values and ideas with that minimum of credibility which serves the purposes of legitimation. Second, it is clear that the store of meanings and values available to a political system for the purposes of legitimation are never unlimited. Thus, this store can easily be exhausted. There is therefore a constant need to create and re-create meaning and values to ensure an essential level of legitimacy, but this process cannot be taken for granted. The political system may certainly stimulate or block this process, but it cannot create it to order. It may, and often does, happen that a system fails to obtain the required supply of meaning and value from the socio-cultural mass to keep legitimacy alive, and thus it must fail to maintain minimum loyalty in the population.

Third, there is no meaning or value system which can be used in processes of legitimation which are a priori credible and intrinsic by reason of their content. There is either a divergence or a convergence with the needs, interests and aspirations of different sections of the population which directly and indirectly affect the credibility of specific meanings, values and ideas employed for legitimation. Thus neither simple availability nor creativity can by themselves resolve beforehand and permanently the problem of the credibility of meanings and values for the purposes of legitimation.

Finally, the Yugoslav background to my argument suggests that legitimation is not generally a smooth and comprehensive process. As Weber pointed out (1947: 124), all effective obedience to the demands of *Herrschaft* need not necessarily be linked to faith in its legitimacy in the eyes of those who obey. Individuals, as well as social groups, may pretend that their obedience is motivated by faith in the legitimacy of the particular *Herrschaft*. They may act in conformity with it for a multitude of reasons having nothing to do with faith in its legitimacy. They may simply obey out of convenience, or for personal or collective interests, or because they find it inevitable in the light of their personal and social impotence. As Habermas adds, they may obey a superior power through lack of social imagination. Our historical example shows that this latter aspect may be quite complex. That is, a sense of individual and collective powerlessness, and a lack of social imagination, should not be seen as a necessary result of a spontaneous process or a chance conjuncture of circumstances in social life, untouched by power and authority. They may appear as the end result of premeditated action by the existing *Macht*. Established power defends its position by inducing a sense of powerlessness as well as by blocking social imagination which might exacerbate its lack of legitimacy. Thus a special form of legitimacy may be obtained, which legitimates the existing *Herrschaft*, but not because it is believed to be just or good, or represents the nation, or functions efficiently. Ultimately, loyalty and obedience are obtained, and the reverse is rejected, even when the *Herrschaft* is believed to be bad, unjust, corrupt, corrupting and inefficient. However, it is obeyed because it is felt that under the circumstances there is no feasible alternative.

Résumés

Roberto Cipriani: 'La sociologie de la légitimation: une introduction'. Il y a deux significations principales au concept de légitimation: l'attribution de validité et la justification. Si l'on considère en outre l'action sociale de la reconnaissance, de la ratification et de l'acceptation, il faut distinguer le consentement de l'assentiment. Dans le premier cas il s'agit d'une condescendance et d'une accoutumance, dans le second cas par contre l'on observe une attitude favorable mais accompagnée de nombreuses réserves et de nombreuses critiques. Cependant c'est précisément par l'assentiment que passe la légitimation la plus répandue.

Le processus de légitimation ne concerne pas seulement les milieux politico-juridiques, mais aussi les contextes au sein desquels l'on identifie des références aux valeurs.

La présence du cynisme, soulignée par divers auteurs, est un élément constant dans divers cas de légitimation.

Ce cynisme consiste essentiellement dans le non-respect de certaines *règles du jeu*, dans l'absence de problématiques dans les rapports interpersonnels, dans l'absolutisme de ses propres perspectives aux dépens de celles d'autrui.

Le cynisme est aussi une mise au tapis du pouvoir, une exhibition de muscles — si l'on peut dire. Certaines formes de prises de décision sont l'expression la plus évidente d'une légitimation fondée sur le cynisme.

L'alternative entre gouvernement des lois et gouvernement des hommes, autrement dit entre primauté des lois et primauté des gouvernants, n'élimine pas le phénomène du cynisme, dans la mesure où, dans un cas, les normes sont susceptibles de cynisme en ne tenant pas compte des exigences individuelles, et dans l'autre l'arbitraire des législateurs (ou en tous cas de ceux qui détiennent le pouvoir) peut être exercé de façon cynique aux dépens des citoyens.

Le problème de la légitimation ne se réduit pas au simple rapport entre majorité et minorité, ni au seul échange politique. Il embrasse d'autres milieux plus vastes, en premier lieu les processus de socialisation.

En définitive la légitimation reste une question sociologique non entièrement résolue. Quant au problème de la démocratie, qui y est lié, il reste lui aussi irrésolu.

Franco Ferrarotti: 'Légitimation, représentation et pouvoir'.
Il existe aujourd'hui un écart très marqué entre prestation institutionnelle et attentes populaires. En d'autres termes, la représentation politique n'apparaît plus comme représentative.

Le pouvoir politique, d'apanage personnel, est devenu une fonction rationnelle et collective.

En outre, entre la société et la légitimation, il n'existe pas un rapport fortuit de contingence mais d'étroite nécessité.

La légitimité en particulier risque d'être confondue avec la légalité, confusion qui fait perdre de vue ce qui est la racine même de la légitimité, à savoir la population, les citoyens.

La légitimation en effet concerne l'origine de l'obligation sociétaire et de la communauté politique. La souveraineté populaire n'est donc pas épuisée, n'est pas mise à l'écart par l'existence de normes et de procédures. La légitimation, par conséquent, n'est pas seulement un problème de procédures — comme l'affirme Luhmann — mais également de contenus idéaux.

En d'autres termes, la légitimité comprend la légalité, mais va aussi au-delà de celle-ci et la précède. La légitimation elle-même ne s'épuise pas en une production de normes car elle est toujours animée par le sentiment collectif de la communauté.

Il faut en outre distinguer pouvoir et autorité, et, en particulier, tenir compte du fait que le pouvoir est à la fois *relation* et *structure*. Ce n'est pas une métaphore biologique à la Parsons ou une compétence communicative à la Habermas ou une pulsion psychologique à la Ferrero.

Enfin la légitimation n'est pas une question d'autolégitimation.

Achille Ardigò: 'Demande de moralité et légitimation'.
Pourquoi la question morale émerge-t-elle aujourd'hui avec force dans notre pays? L'on examine du point de vue critique certaines réponses possibles à cette question et l'on avance ensuite une ébauche d'hypothèses. En particulier, l'on souligne l'insuffisance des explications centrées sur l'absence d'un horizon de valeurs partagées par tous, sur l'échec des institutions socialisatrices, sur la fragmentation de la morale due à la différenciation de codes normatifs de groupes, de sous-groupes et à la limite d'individus, et sur les carences de la sélection de la classe dirigeante. Parallèlement, on explique la situation actuelle de malaise dans la démocratie, dont l'émergence de la question morale dépend à son tour, sur la base de la triple

constatation: 1. d'une 'carence de *leadership* morale et politique'; 2. d'une méfiance populaire croissante envers les techniques manipulatrices des *media* et envers la spectacularisation de la politique et 3. d'une modification du concept même de morale, liée aux transformations sociales de ces dernières années.

Dans la deuxième partie de l'essai, on s'interroge sur le type de nouvelle éthique qui pourrait satisfaire la demande de moralité engendrée par les causes précitées, et sur la présence de symptômes du développement éventuel d'une telle éthique. La nouvelle éthique sera solidaire et humanitaire, indépendante de la sphère économique et de la sphère politique, et susceptible d'opposer à la logique différentiatrice du système social une poussée vers le rapprochement entre système et monde de la vie. Parmi les divers symptômes de l'émergence de cette éthique, on signale la naissance de mouvements pour la protection de l'environnement, pour la paix, contre la faim, pour une approche alternative des problèmes de la santé, pour une utilisation non manipulatrice des *media*, pour la défense religieuse de la vie et pour la rediscussion des séparations traditionnelles entre les sexes.

Enfin l'on s'attarde sur les tendances probables de l'évolution du climat moral dans le proche avenir. L'effet de ces mouvements et de ces ferments culturels se traduira d'une part par une accentuation de la fragmentation des morales de groupe, et d'autre part par une accentuation de la demande de réunification des codes de comportement moral et de consolidation de l'identité personnelle. Dans l'ensemble l'identification croissante des codes moraux réduira la possibilité qu'a la morale d'exercer son influence sur l'ensemble de la société, en favorisant ainsi indirectement la suprématie du système. Un résultat probable de ces développements pourra se traduire par la spécialisation et la fragmentation ultérieure de la communication, tandis que le système politique, de son côté, continuera d'abaisser le seuil de ce qui est considéré comme moralement acceptable.

Alberto Izzo: 'Légitimation et société: un panorama critique'.
Même un simple survol de certaines interprétations sociologiques du problème de la légitimation comporte des difficultés notables. Avant tout, si on donne au terme 'légitimation' une acception large, il n'est guère aisé ensuite de la distinguer du consentement, entendu comme l'ensemble des valeurs fondamentales qui unifient une société.

Mais ceci réduirait le thème de la légitimation au problème central de toute la théorie sociologique classique non marxiste. En termes plus strictement politiques, en outre, il est difficile de distinguer la légitimation de la formule politique de G. Mosca. On rencontre donc une certaine difficulté à distinguer le cadre problématique de la légitimation d'autres thèmes connexes de la tradition sociologique.

Malgré les diversités qui distinguent les divers auteurs, dans la théorie sociologique classique prévaut en tous cas une conception relativiste de la légitimation. Il ne semble pas important d'examiner le contenu des normes sociales, mais plutôt de veiller à ce qu'il y ait un système normatif, quel qu'il soit, et des organes particuliers qui assurent la fonction spécifique de justifier, de légitimer ce système. Dans le marxisme, par contre, le propos est inversé: les contradictions intrinsèques à la société capitaliste rendent les systèmes de légitimation établis au sein de cette société toujours moins valables, toujours moins capables d'unifier une société. Marx pose déjà le problème de la crise des systèmes de légitimation.

Il est utile de remonter aux classiques et au marxisme si l'on veut saisir la continuité historique du problème. Aujourd'hui aussi, à des conceptions formalistes (Luhmann) et relativistes s'opposent des conceptions qui semblent surtout être inspirées par le souci que suscite la crise des systèmes de légitimation dans les sociétés contemporaines économiquement plus avancées. Il en est ainsi pour Habermas de même que pour certains représentants de la pensée marxiste (Offe, O'Connor), ainsi que pour d'autres auteurs qui se attachent à une tradition pluraliste et libérale (Berger, Dahrendorf, Ardigò).

François Bourricaud: 'Légitimité et légitimation'.
Quel sens a conservé l'exigence de légitimité? Au concept de légitimité entendu comme état stable et défini il faut substituer le concept de légitimation, qui se réfère non pas à un tel état, mais à un processus ou plutôt à un ensemble de processus qui tendent sans y parvenir à la réalisation d'un tel état.

1) Les idéologies sociales nous présentent la société comme un ensemble cohérent auquel ne s'applique pas la distinction entre le possible et le réel. Les conceptions de la légitimité traditionnelle qui se développent après la Révolution française ont un caractère hiérarchique et total, transcendant. L'ordre social légitime est par essence hiérarchique. A cette légitimité traditionnelle s'oppose la légitimité

révolutionnaire. Celle-ci valorise la communauté, la réconciliation des hommes, leur solidarité. Nos sociétés reposent sur la domination et l'exploitation: elles ne sont donc pas légitimes. Illégitimes elles le sont tout autant aux yeux des conservateurs qu'aux yeux des révolutionnaires. Les sociétés de l'Europe post-révolutionnaire ont souffert d'un déficit de légitimité.

2) Chez Weber la légitimité n'est pas fondée sur des 'garants métasociaux'. D'après lui elle ne dépend pas d'un critère unique, mais de plusieurs critères: légalité, tradition, charisme. Enfin, elle qualifie non pas la société en général mais un certain type de relations sociales. La légitimité a toujours une dimension idéologique, sous réserve que le terme d'idéologie soit pris dans un sens strictement neutre. Il faut se garder de prendre le terme d'idéologie comme synonyme de mystification. La dimension idéologique de la légitimité s'exprime à la fois dans des croyances et dans des pratiques, dans des 'dérivations' et dans des 'résidus'. Mais entre des situations de pure légitimité et des situations de pure illégitimité, il y a tout un dégradé de cas intermédiaires. Il n'y a pas dans nos sociétés démocratiques une conception unique de la légitimité. Les valeurs libérales sont des ingrédients de la formule de légitimité. Mais ces valeurs entrent en combinaison et en opposition avec d'autres valeurs. L'hétérogénéité des critères de légitimité a deux causes. En premier lieu les formes d'action sont multiples et chacune relève d'une logique qui lui est propre. En outre pour chaque type d'action il y a, ou il peut y avoir, des critères d'action distincts et opposés. Ce qui nous intéresse c'est le processus de légitimation.

3) La légitimation n'est pas un pur et simple processus logique ou dialectique de contestation-approbation. Le processus de légitimation aboutit à la cristallisation de quelques croyances fondamentales, celles qui sont intouchables et qui affectent d'une manière significative mais diffuse tout le comportement des acteurs. A la légitimation par les moeurs et par l'éducation se superpose une légitimation par les idées qui peut emprunter deux véhicules. On peut évoquer une légitimation philosophique et une légitimation idéologique. Il existe une exigence de légitimation ou de rationalisation qui ne peut pas se contenter de la simple conformité entre une conduite et la norme. Si la pédagogie parvient à rendre conforme la conduite de tous aux moeurs et aux lois, c'est la notion même de légitimité qui perd son sens. L'idée d'une société légitime n'a donc pas de sens, pas plus que l'idée d'une sociéte qui renoncerait à toute légitimité.

Michel Maffesoli: 'La socialité comme légitimation de la démarche sociologique'.
Il existe une 'connaissance' empirique quotidienne dont on ne peut faire l'économie. Tout ce 'savoir faire', 'savoir dire', 'savoir vivre' constitue un donné dont la phénomènologie a fait ressortir à juste titre la richesse. Il est bien evident que l'anomalie, ou ce qui est nommé ainsi, constitue une bonne partie du quotidien. Mais en effet on a laissé de côté la *socialité*, qui est une *empathie communalisée*. A trop vouloir discriminer on supprime tout ce qui fait bon sens, avec l'efficacité du bulldozer qui écrase tout. La légitimation de cette efficacité se trouve dans le grand mouvement de rationalisation analysé par Weber. Mais la rationalisation sociale ne signifie pas une rationalisation généralisée de l'existence quotidienne.

L'aspect cognitif de l'expérience nous force à prêter attention aux événements, aux phénomènes, à tout ce qui s'inscrit dans l'instant et le présent. Il n'est plus question de 'coupure' ou de 'rupture' épistémologique, mais bien plutôt d'une compréhension du présent populaire. Or l'existence quotidienne est éclatée, polysémique, constituée d'ombres et de lumières, en un mot, ce qui est de plus admis, faite par un homme *à la fois* 'sapiens' et 'demens'.

Il y a une prétention à l'exhaustivité et à l'intangibilité qui trop souvent caractérise les monologues dans les sciences sociales. Un schéma compréhensif vaut pour un temps. Il peut servir de point de référence. Mais vouloir l'extrapoler conduit toujours au dogmatisme et souvent à la légitimation des plus rudes tyrannies.

A l'encontre du scandale intellectuel qui est aux yeux de certains la relativisation du concept, il vaut mieux mettre en oeuvre des 'conceptacles'. Par la force des choses on peut pas rester fidèle à un concept. Le concept lui aussi bouge. Il y a une multiplicité de points de vue qui est la négation du concept.

L'on n'y reviendra jamais assez: la primauté de l'existence *sociétale*. Il est important de remarquer que l'on observe du 'résidu', une fois les autres composantes (économiques, politiques, organisationnelles, etc.) posées et analysées. C'est ce 'résidu' à la Pareto qui pose question au sociologue de la vie quotidienne. Cette existence résiduelle est toujours facteur de socialité. Elle est le sens simple du terme 'co-existence'. Elle exprime au mieux l'intensité de l'être-ensemble. C'est la sociabilité simple, le 'résidu' facteur de socialité. Il n'est pas question de faire l'apologie de l'irrationalisme. Il s'agit simplement d'*une théorie de la connaissance qui admet que l'inachèvement structurel de la socialité en appelle à un inachèvement intellectuel.*

Le regain de l'ethnométhodologie, les balbutiements de la sociologie participante, les essais de recherche-action, le développement des histoires de vie, tout cela repose sur une fatigue par rapport aux divers finalismes socio-théoriques et sur une reconnaissance de la prégnance de la sagesse populaire. La recherche tire sa signification *principale* de la vie quotidienne (Mannheim).

La sociologie doit, elle aussi, être perméable à l'*Einfühlung* qui gagne l'ensemble du corps social, pour surmonter la barrière du concept dressée devant le flux vital de l'existence sociale.

N. Luhmann: 'Les représentations de la société dans la société'.
Tous les concepts relatifs au milieu politique ont vu leur signification se modifier à partir de la deuxième moitié du XVIIIe siècle. Depuis lors la société est entendue davantage dans le sens d'une domination (*Herrschaft*) qui s'exprime essentiellement dans la réalisation des besoins économiques et donc la légitimation est mesurée sur la base de l'*output* économique du système. Cette interprétation prévaut encore aujourd'hui.

Mais dans un contexte social, qui peut légitimement représenter le tout en étant seulement une partie? La réponse, déjà donnée, à l'époque, par Linguet, est la suivante: *un grand nombre*, donc *personne*. C'est aussi compte tenu de ce fait que dans les systèmes parlementaires on a adopté une catégorie comme celle de la représentation (*Repräsentation*).

Les problèmes qui assaillent le concept de légitimité du pouvoir politique sont liés à la mise en évidence de l'impossibilité de réaliser la représentation. Celui qui peut représenter la société dans la société est, de par ce fait même, légitime. La représentation lui confère le droit (*Recht*). Au cas où celle-ci s'annule, celui qui entend gouverner légitimement doit se rapporter à des valeurs et, au bout du compte, offrir des résultats tangibles.

Ce que nous avons pu observer depuis 200 ans jusqu'à aujourd'hui, c'est la formation et le développement d'une série de théories de la réflexion (*Reflexionstheorien*) qui se limitent à considérer des systèmes individuels fonctionalistes ou de fonctions (*Funktionssysteme*).

D'autre part, aujourd'hui la sociologie officielle et académique recule clairement devant l'obligation de fournir une description de la société entendue comme une théorie de la réflexion, une théorie visant à l'unité du système.

A partir de ces considérations, trois voies possibles se présentent: 1) le perfectionnement de *l'analyse historico-comparative* orientée théorétiquement; 2) une analyse précise du contexte problématique des systèmes autoréférentiels (*selbstsreferentieller Systeme*); 3) une explication de la logique et des conséquences de la différenciation fonctionnelle (*funktionaler Differenzierung*) du système social.

Dans le cadre de la société moderne, la légitimation peut être uniquement autolégitimation. Chaque activité d'un système trouve sa légitimité dans le fait que celle ci est possible grâce à d'autres activités du même système. Les systèmes fonctionnels peuvent seulement être autolégitimés, ce qui signifie qu'aucun système fonctionnel ne peut en légitimer un autre.

Robert N. Bellah: 'Le processus de légitimation dans la politique et dans la religion'.
On analyse du point de vue comparatif deux modalités différentes du déclin de la politique et de la religion comme facteurs primaires de la légitimation. Aussi bien au Japon qu'aux Etats-Unis, la légitimation des systèmes institutionnels et de l'ordre social lui-même a depuis quelque temps cessé de reposer sur le binôme de procédures politiques et de symboles religieux, et a commencé à tourner autour de la combinaison de la compétence et du charisme personnel.

Cette transformation s'est faite plus rapidement et de façon plus discontinue au Japon, tandis qu'aux Etats-Unis le processus a été plus progressif mais aussi plus lent.

Au Japon la séparation entre religion et l'Etat s'est opérée à l'improviste à la fin de la seconde guerre mondiale, comme condition de l'armistice. La politique japonaise, cependant, au cours des dernières décennies, s'est vidée de ses contenus idéaux et a fini par se limiter à être une confrontation entre les intérêts particuliers représentés par les diverses factions du parti qui a gouverné sans interruption depuis la fin de la guerre. Les lettres de créance que la classe dirigeante japonaise peut offrir à son électorat, dans ces conditions, se réduisent à sa compétence indiscutée à gérer l'organisation industrielle et financière du pays dont l'objectif est la prospérité. Dans diverses circonstances, on a associé à ces lettres de créance l'*appeal* charismatique de personnalités du spectacle opportunément insérées dans les listes électorales.

Aux Etats-Unis, c'est au moins depuis le milieu du siècle dernier que la religion a cessé d'avoir un rapport légitimant avec l'intégration de l'individu dans l'ordre social, et que les diverses Eglises, des 'piliers de l'ordre public', sont devenues simplement des 'îlots de piété'. De même, dès la fin du VIIIe siècle la politique a été de moins en moins associée à la recherche consensuelle du bien commun et de plus en plus assimilée à la lutte d'intérêts privés.

A la fin de ce processus, les deux présidences de Carter et de Reagan ont montré qu'elles dépendaient, respectivement, par suite de l'effondrement ou du maintien de leur popularité, justement de la perception de masse d'une compétence susceptible d'assurer la prospérité et d'un charisme personnel dans la prise de décisions.

Enfin on s'interroge sur la dépendance de ces versions contemporaines du despotisme doux tocquevillien, de la permanence de conditions économiques favorables: on souligne leur apport au renforcement d'un cynisme diffus.

Thomas Luckmann: 'Observations sur la légitimation'.
Au sens très large, chaque procédé grâce auquel quelque chose qui est montré comme quelque chose qui devrait être constitue un processus de légitimation. L'action est un projet tourné vers l'avenir qui comporte une décision à prendre entre diverses alternatives; une telle décision, basée sur l'articulation de ce qui est, et sur un choix alternatif, constitue le début de tout processus de légitimation. Les racines des processus de légitimation ne doivent pas être rechercheés dans les systèmes sociaux, mais dans l'action humaine intersubjective, en identifiant les producteurs et les consommateurs de légitimation, ainsi que ses bénéficiaries et ses victimes.

Alors que le niveau le plus élevé de légitimation — univers symboliques et idéologies — a été étudié comme il se doit, le niveau des justifications intersubjectives a été sans aucun doute négligé. Dans ce domaine, par exemple (analyse des genres de communication orale, maximes, proverbes, paraboles), après quelques études initiales prometteuses, c'est l'analyse systématique par contre qui s'impose. Le niveau intermédiaire présente en outre un intérêt particulier, car les grands concepts de légitimation y sont traduits dans le langage des justifications dans la vie quotidienne: on trouverait particulièrement instructives les études de la transformation pastorale de la haute théologie, des pratiques plutôt que des théories pédagogiques, de la communication face à face; ou encore l'analyse des *processus* plutôt que des *concepts* de légitimation.

La thèse selon laquelle la forme particulière de l'organisation des Etats nationaux modernes ne requiert plus aucune légitimation transcendantale est parfaitement valable, mais cela ne signifie pas qu'il n'existe pas de points d'articulation, de cohérence entre ces systèmes institutionnels complexes et l'interaction sociale individuelle. Il existe par contre des pratiques de légitimation au niveau 'régional' ou intermédiaire qui ne doivent pas être négligées.

John Fraser: 'Légitimité et processus politique'.
Luhmann semble proposer une solution au problème du pouvoir. Il élimine les médiations historiques des processus politiques et les significations collectives des idéologies pour proposer une simplification du rapport pouvoir-code (procédure). En fait, les problèmes restent inchangés. Le pouvoir est hiérarchique et, étant donné qu'il est maintenant fondé sur la précarité du *langage* (le 'code'), les structures sociales et historiques de la tradition et de la transition font défaut. Donc, il manque une dimension historico-sociale: le but est surtout d'éviter la violence, mais sans modifier l'essence mystificatrice et mystifiée du pouvoir lui-même. Pourquoi le pouvoir est-il un problème, s'il s'agit de réciprocité et non pas d'un langage particulier et d'une procédure pure et mystérieusement auto-suffisante? Eviter la violence, d'ailleurs, n'explique pas les raisons et les racines de la violence elle-même. Luhmann confond la conception juridique de la légitimité avec celle socio-historique de consentement: ainsi pour Luhmann le pouvoir (légitime) est surtout le pouvoir légal, tandis que pour les théoriciens du consentement la base de la loi réside dans la raison de la masse; pour Luhmann, la loi légitime le pouvoir, tandis qu' 'à partir du bas' le consentement, la 'raison de masse', impose des limites au pouvoir lui-même.

Luhmann décrit un pouvoir absolu et non-médiatisé qui, cependant, devient précaire et réciproque parce que fondé sur le langage, et parce que la violence représente un *échec* du pouvoir. Mais ce sont là des présupposés minimes et passifs, et quoiqu'il en soit, des présupposés. Même si nous pouvons pour le moment négliger les aspects historico-culturels d'une théorie du pouvoir et de la transition (autrement dit, quand un pouvoir devient un autre, une loi entre en conflit avec un consentement), la discussion récente de théories des droits donne lieu à penser que les rapports collectifs et éthiques ont des répercussions constantes, renforçant et affaiblissant ainsi le 'pouvoir d'en haut'.

La vision de Luhmann est une vision absolue du pouvoir 'd'en haut', modifiée par son pessimisme vis-à-vis de tout projet ou de toute norme absolue, ou *raisonnable*. Si l'on réussit à maintenir l'ordre, en effet, il n'y a plus de problème de pouvoir, selon Luhmann. Certains théoriciens du consentement voient dans le contrat, dans le pacte social, une réponse analogue à celle de Luhmann, fondée sur le code: une réponse sémantique, en un mot, même si elle est basée sur des principes différents. Ces théories sémantiques, cependant, sont non seulement fondées sur des considérations *non*-sémantiques (éviter la violence, exiger que tous les rôles sociaux soient interchangeables), mais encore ne proposent pas une recherche concrète sur le pouvoir et sur ses rapports: bien au contraire, elles proposent des recherches qui doivent confirmer les présupposés eux-mêmes, et ne les modifient pas.

Srdjan Vrcan: 'Une perspective historique diverse sur la légitimation'. Le cas de la Yougoslavie est suffisamment significatif pour analyser les processus de légitimation d'un point de vue qui ne relève pas exclusivement de la phase ultime du capitalisme. Il s'agit d'une période historique qui a connu l'effondrement d'un système politique à la suite d'interventions extérieures, qui a vu les tentatives d'instauration d'ordres divers sur son territoire, qui a conservé le souvenir de l'échec de ces tentatives, qui a instauré un système nouveau issu de la révolution.

D'où il est aisé de soutenir qu'en effet légitimité et légitimation se fondent sur le pouvoir et sur la domination, mais tout particulièrement sur leur justification.

En outre la distinction opérée par Peter Berger entre *nomos* et anomie n'est pas applicable concrètement si elle en reste à un niveau d'absolution abstraite. Dans la réalité le choix est opéré entre un *nomos* historique et un autre. Elle est toujours liée au contingent et non pas à l'immuable et au préordonné. Il y a donc une dialectique complexe et même contradictoire, qui cependant évite l'ordre par excellence, à savoir l'ordre unique.

Egalement dans l'usage de certains concepts, il est opportun d'observer une plus grande prudence: il ne faut pas confondre entre eux les termes de société, de système social, de système politique, d'ordre politique, d'intégration du système et d'intégration sociale.

Sur la lancée de Weber, l'on tend d'habitude à considérer la légitimation et la légitimité dans la perspective du pouvoir déjà constitué. Mais outre le processus de construction et de reconstruction de la légitimité, il faut aussi examiner celui de délégitimation qui invalide la légitimité elle-même. Ainsi l'on construit les bases d'un refus du pouvoir existant.

Enfin il ne faut pas négliger la donnée selon laquelle la légitimité est toujours un fait socio-culturel, qui engendre sens et valeurs à partir de la tradition disponible.

ACHINSTEIN, P. (1977) 'Function Statements', *Philosophy of Science*, September: 341–47.

ADAMS, G.P. et al. (1938) *Knowledge and Society. A Philosophical Approach to Modern Civilization.* New York: Appleton-Century.

ADLEY, G and FRISBY, D. (eds) (1976) *The Positivist Dispute in German Sociology.* London: Heinemann.

ADORNO, T.W., FRENKEL-BRUNSWICK, E., LEVINSON, D.J., SANFORD, R.N. (1950) *The Authoritarian Personality.* New York: American Jewish Committee.

AHUMADA, R.B. (1976) 'La crisi dello stato in America Latina' (The Crisis of the State in Latin America), *Centro Sociale*, 23: 127–29.

ALBERT, H. (1969) *Traktat über Kritische Vernunft* (A Treatise on Critical Reason). Tübingen: Mohr.

ALKAN, M.T. (1982) 'Maintenance of Political Legitimacy in a Post-Revolutionary Regime', *International Review of Modern Sociology*, 11: 197–208.

ALTHUSSER, L. (1970) 'Idéologie et appareils idéologiques d'état', *La Pensée*, 151: 3–38.

ALVARO, M.J. (1978) 'Clases populares y politica en Brasil (Notas para una revision teorica)' (The Popular Classes and Politics in Brazil. Notes toward a Theoretical Revision), *Revista Mexicana de Sociologia*, 4: 1429–51.

AMINZADE, R. (1977) 'Breaking the Chains of Dependency: From Patronage to Class Politics, Toulouse, France, 1830–1872', *Journal of Urban History*, 4: 485–506.

AMMASSARI, P. (1985) 'Validità e legittimità nell'analisi causale' (Validity and Legitimacy in Causal Analysis), *Annali di Sociologia*, 1: 97–117.

APEL, K.O. (1973) *Transformation der philosophie* (Transformation of Philosophy). Frankfurt: Suhrkamp.

APPLEWHITE, H.B. (1978) 'Political Legitimacy in Revolutionary France, 1788–91', *The Journal of Interdisciplinary History*, 2: 245–73.

ARCHER, M. (1982) 'Morphogenesis versus Structuration', *British Journal of Sociology*, 33: 455–83.

The Bibliography for this issue was compiled by Roberto Cipriani and Gianni Fatelli.

ARDIGO, A. (1980) *Crisi di governabilità e mondi vitali* (Crisis of Governability and Life-worlds). Bologna: Cappelli.
ARJOMAND, S.A. (1979) 'Religion, Political Action and Legitimate Domination in Shiite Iran: Fourteenth to Eighteenth Centuries A.D.', *Archives Européennes de Sociologie*, 1: 59–109.
AUCLAIR, G. (1982) *Le mana quotidien*. Paris: Anthropos, 2nd edn.
AUGE, M., (1979) *Symbole, Fonction, Histoire. Les Interrogations de l'Anthropologie*. Paris: Hachette.
AUSTIN, J.L. (1962a) *How to Do Things with Words*. Cambridge: Harvard University Press.
BACHELARD, G. (1934) *Le nouvel esprit scientifique*. Paris: PUF.
BACHELARD, G. (1938) *Psychanalyse du feu*. Paris, PUF.
BACHRACH, P. and BARATZ, M. (1962a) *Power and Poverty: Theory and Practice*. New York, Oxford University Press.
BACHRACH, P. and BARATZ, M. (1962b) 'The Two Faces of Power', *American Sociological Review*, 56: 947–52.
BADIA, J.F. (1975) 'Las dos caras del dios Jano: Potestas y auctoritas' (The Two Faces of the God Janus: Power and Authority), *Revista Española de la Opinión Publica*, 42: 7–18.
BAILEY, F.G. (1969) *Stratagems and Spoils: A Social Anthropology of Politics*. New York: Schocken Books.
BALBUS, I. (1975) 'Politics as Sports: The Political Ascendency of the Sports Metaphor in America', *Montly Review*, 10: 26–39.
BANTON, M. (ed.) (1965) *Political Systems and the Distribution of Power*. London: Tavistock.
BARATZ, S.S. and BARATZ, J.C. (1970) 'Early Childhood Intervention: The Social Science Base of Institutional Racism', *Harvard Educational Review*, 29–47.
BARBAGLI, M. (ed.) (1978) *Istruzione, legittimazione e conflitto* (Education, Legitimacy and Conflict). Bologna: Il Mulino.
BARBANO, F. (ed.) (1982) *Nuove tecnologie ed informazione quotidiana* (New Technology and Daily Press). Milano: Angeli.
BARBE C. (1984) 'Identidad e identidades colectivas en el análisis del cambio institucional' (Identity and Collective Identities in the Analysis of Institutional Change), *Revista de Estudios Políticos*, 37: 67–87.
BAREL, Y. (1979) *Le paradoxe et le système: Essai sur le fantastique social*. Grenoble: PUF.
BARNES, S.H. (1967) 'Mobilitazione e conflitto politico. Ricerca teorica sulle basi strutturali del consenso e del dissenso' (Mobilization and Political Conflict. A Theoretical Inquiry into the

Structural Bases of Consensus and Dissent), *Rassegna Italiana di Sociologia*, 4: 503–24.

BARNES, S.H. and KAASE, M. (eds) (1979) *Political Action*. London: Sage.

BARTHOLOMEW, J. (1974) 'Sustaining Hierarchy through Teaching and Research', pp. 70–85 in: Flude and Ahier (1974).

BAUDRILLARD, J. (1983) *Les stratégies fatales*. Paris: Grasset.

BAUMAN, Z. (1976) *Towards a Critical Sociology: an Essay on Commonsense and Emancipation*. London: Routledge and Kegan Paul.

BECHELLONI, G. (1974a) *Informazione e potere* (Information and Power). Roma: Officina.

BECHELLONI, G. (1974b) *La macchina culturale in Italia* (The Culture Industry in Italy). Bologna: Il Mulino.

BECK, U. and LAU, C. (1983) 'Bildungsforschung und Bildungspolitik-Öffentlichkeit als Adressat sozialwissenschaftlicher Forschung' (Educational Research and Educational Policy — The Public as Addressee of Social Science), *Zeitschrift für Sozialisationsforschung und Erziehungssoziologie*, 2: 165–73.

BEISENHERZ, H.G. (1980) *Legitimation durch Vertrauen* (Legitimation through Trust). Marburg: Lahn.

BELL, D. (1975) *The Cultural Contradictions of Capitalism*. London: Heinemann.

BELLAH, R.N. (1970) *Beyond Belief: Essays on Religion in a Post-Traditional World*. New York: Harper and Row.

BELLAH, R.N. (1975) *The Broken Convenant: American Civil Religion in Time of Trial*. New York: Seabury Press.

BELLAH, R.N. and HAMMOND, P.E. (1980) *Varieties of Civil Religion*. San Francisco: Harper and Row.

BELLASI, P. (1983) 'L'iconographie de la vie quotidienne', *Cahiers Internationaux de Sociologie*, (Paris) LXXIV: 47–56.

BEN DAVID, J. and NICHOLS CLARK, C. (1977) *Culture and its Creators*. Chicago: Chicago University Press.

BENNET, W.L. (1975) 'Political Sanctification: The Civil Religion and American Politics', *Social Science Information*, 6: 79–102.

BERGER, P. (1967) *The Sacred Canopy*. Garden City, NY: Doubleday.

BERGER, P., BERGER, B. and KELLNER, H.F. (1973) *The Homeless Mind: Modernization and Consciousness*. Harmondsworth: Penguin Books.

BERGER, P. and LUCKMANN, T. (1964) 'Elaborated and Restricted Codes: Their Social Origins and Some Consequences', *American Anthropologist*, 2: 55–69.

BERGER, P.L. and LUCKMANN, T. (1967) *The Social Construction of Reality*. New York: Anchor.

BERGESEN, A. (1981) 'Nation-Building and Constitutional Amendments: The Role of the Thirteenth, Fourteenth, and Fifteenth Amendments in the Legal Reconstitution of the American Polity following the Civil War', *Pacific Sociological Review*, 1: 3–15.

BERNSTEIN, R.J. (1976) *The Restructuring of Social and Political Theory*. New York: Harcourt Brace Jovanovich.

BERTAUX, D. (1979) 'Ecrire la Sociologie', *Information sur les Sciences Sociales*, 1.

BETTINI, R. (1983) *Il circolo vizioso legislativo* (The Vicious Circle of Legislation). Milano: Angeli.

BLAU, P.M. (1970) 'Critical Remarks on Weber's Theory of Authority', in D.H. Wrong (ed.), *Max Weber*. Englewood Cliffs, NJ: Prentice Hall.

BLOCH, E. (1978) *Héritage de ce temps*. Paris: Payot.

BOBBIO, N. (1981) *Le ideologie e il potere in crisi. Pluralismo, democrazia, socialismo, comunismo, terza via e terza forza* (Ideologies and Power in Crisis. Pluralism, Democracy, Socialism, Communism, "The Third Road to Socialism"). Firenze: Le Monnier.

BOBBIO, N. (1984) *Il futuro della democrazia. Una difesa delle regole del gioco*. (The Future of Democracy. A Defence of the Rules of the Game). Torino: Einaudi.

BOHNISCH, L. and SCHEFOLD, W. (1980) 'Auf der Suche nach einer neuen politischen Legitimation' (The Search for New Political Legitimation), *Betrift: Erziehung*, 9: 32–34.

BOHNISCH, S., BRUHNS, K., DENNELER, H., HEMMER, C. (1981) 'Die Veranderung der Wohnformen und Wohverhaltnisse im historischen Entwicklungsprozess' (Changes in the Forms and Conditions of Housing in the Historical Development Process). *Soziologenkorrespondenz*, 8: 53–83.

BORLANDI, M. (1975) 'L'efficacia della legislazione: una categoria per l'analisi sociologica del diritto' (Efficacy of Legislation: a Category for the Sociological Analysis of Law), *Sociologia*, 2: 17–48.

BORSONI, P. (1984) 'Legittimazione e scambio politico nel dibattito Habermas-Luhmann' (Legitimation and Political Exchange in the

Habermas-Luhmann Debate), *La Critica Sociologica*, 69: 48–63.

BOUDON, R. (1975) *Effets pervers et ordre social*. Paris: PUF.

BOUDON, R. (1979) *La logique du social. Introduction à l'analyse sociologique*. Paris: Hachette.

BOVERO, M. (ed.) (1982) *Ricerche politiche. Saggi su Kelsen, Horkheimer, Habermas, Luhmann, Foucault, Rawls* (Political Investigations. Essays on Kelsen, Horkheimer, Habermas, Luhmann, Foucault, Rawls). Milano: Il Saggiatore.

BREHIER, E. (1926–35) *Histoire de la philosophie*. Paris: PUF, 3 vols.

BRENA, G.L., CORTELLA, L., CUNICO, G., CRISTIN, R., PONSETTO, A., VOLPI, F., PIAZZA, G., FASSA, R. (1984) *La svolta comunicativa. Studi sul pensiero dell'ultimo Habermas* (The Communicative Turn. Studies on the Thought of the Later Habermas). Milano: Angeli.

BRIGHT, J. and BRIGHT, W. (1965) 'Semantic Structures in Northwestern California and the Sapir–Whorf Hypothesis', *American Anthropologist*, 5: 249–58.

BRODEUR, J.P. (1983) 'High Policing and Low Policing: Remarks about the Policing of Political Activities', *Social Problems*, 5: 507–20.

BRODU, J. (1982) 'Charles Fort', Thèse no. LD 4141, Paris VII, UER Charles V.

BROWN, R. (1958) *Words and Things*. New York: The Free Press.

BROWN, R.H. (1977) 'Métaphore et Méthode. De la logique et de la découverte en sociologie', *Cahiers internationaux de sociologie*, LXII: 61–73.

BROWN, R.H. (1980) 'Ordre et révolution dans les formes normales du discours et de la conduite', *Cahiers internationaux de sociologie*, LXVIII: 69–81.

BRUNER, J.B., GOODNOW, J. and AUSTIN, G. (1965) *A Study of Thinking*. New York: Wiley.

BURKE, E. (1982) *Reflections on the Revolution in France*. Harmondsworth: Penguin.

CALDEIRA, G.A. (1977) 'Children's Images of the Supreme Court: A Preliminary Mapping', *Law and Society Review*, 5: 851–71.

CAPECCHI, V. and LIVOLSI, M. (1971) *La stampa quotidiana in Italia* (The Daily Press in Italy). Milano: Bompiani.

CAPPELLETTI, M. (ed.) (1981) *Access to Justice and the Welfare State*. Firenze: European University Institute.

CARBONARO, A. (ed.) (1986) *La legittimazione del potere* (The Legitimation of Power). Milano: Angeli.
CARNAP, R. (1928) *Der logische Aufbau der Welt* (The Logical Construction of the World). Berlin: Benary.
CARNIOL, B. (1983) 'Democracy and Community Development in Canada', *Community Development Journal*, 3: 247–50.
CARROL, J.B. (1964) *Language and Thought*. Englewood Cliffs: Prentice Hall.
CARTWRIGHT, J. (1977) 'Some Constraints upon African Political Leadership', *Revue canadienne des études africaines*, 3: 435–53.
CASTIGNONE, S. (1977) 'Legalità, legittimità e legittimazione' (Legality, Legitimacy, and Legitimation), *Sociologia del Diritto*, 1: 19–38.
CASTORIADIS, C. (1975) *L'institution imaginaire de la société*. Paris: Seuil.
CAVALLI, L. (1981) *Il capo carismatico. Per una sociologia weberiana della leadership* (The Charismatic Leader. For a Weberian Sociology of Leadership). Bologna: Il Mulino.
CERVANTES, F.A. (1976) 'Chicanos within the Political Economy: Some Questions Concerning Pluralist Ideology, Representation and the Economy', *Aztlan*, 3: 337–45.
CESAREO, V. (1981) *Socializzazione e controllo sociale. Una critica alla concezione dell'uomo ultrasocializzato* (Socialization and Social Control. A Critique of the Oversocialized Conception of Man). Milano: Angeli.
CHEVALIER, G. (1986) 'Parascience et procédés de légitimation', *Revue française de sociologie*, 2: 205–19.
CHOMSKY, N. (1957) *Syntactic Structures*. The Hague: Mouton.
CHRISTENSON, J.A. and WARNER, P.D. (1982) 'An Assessment Model for the Cooperative Extension Service', *Rural Sociology*, 2: 369–90.
CIPRIANI, R., COTESTA, V., DE NARDIS, P. and LANDI, F. (1983) *Verità, conoscenza e legittimazione* (Truth, Knowledge and Legitimation). Roma: Ianua.
CIPRIANI, R. (ed.) (1986a) *La legittimazione simbolica* (Symbolic legitimation). Brescia: Morcelliana.
CIPRIANI, R. (ed.) (1986b) *Legittimazione e società* (Legitimation and Society). Roma: Armando.
COHN, T. (1981) 'Educational Knowledge Structures, Social/Political Education and the Legitimation Crisis: A Consideration of

Recent Developments in Britain, West Germany and the United States', *International Journal of Political Education*, 3: 181–94.

COLEMAN, J. (1974) *Power and the Structure of Society*. New York: W.W. Norton and Co.

COLES, R. (1980) 'Civility and Technology', *Daedalus*, 3: 133–41.

COMTE, A. (1848) *The Positive Philosophy of Auguste Comte*. London: Trubner, 2 vols.

CORRADI, J.E. (1979) 'The Avatars of Socio-Political Discourse in Latin America', *Social Science Information*, 1: 59–77.

CORSALE, M. (1979) *Certezza del diritto e crisi di legittimità* (The Certainty of Law and the Legitimation Crisis). Milano: Giuffrè.

CORTES ENCINAS, A. (1982) 'La crisis de la sociedad en Jürgen Habermas' (The Crisis of Society in Jürgen Habermas), *Cuadernos de Realidades Sociales*, 20–21: 325–33.

COTESTA, V. (1984a) *Nuove legittimazioni* (New Legitimations). Roma: Ianua.

COTESTA, V. (1984b) 'Senso, riferimento e cultura' (Meaning, Reference, and Culture), *Sociologia e Ricerca Sociale*, 13: 21–44.

CRESPI, F. (1982) *Mediazione simbolica e società* (Symbolic Exchange and Society). Milano: Angeli.

CRESPI, F. (1983) 'Identità e potere soggettivo' (Identity and Subjective Power), *Rassegna Italiana di Sociologia*, 1: 5–18.

CROZIER, M. et al. (1975) *The Crisis of Democracy*. New York: NYU Press.

D'AGOSTINO, F. (1977) *Immaginazione simbolica e struttura sociale* (Symbolic Imagination and Social Structure). Bologna: Il Mulino.

DAHL, R. (1957) 'The Concept of Power', *Behavioural Science*, 2: 201–05.

DAHL, R. (1961) *Who Governs? Democracy and Power in American City*. New Haven: Yale University Press.

DAHRENDORF, R. (1979) *Life Chances*. London: Weidenfeld and Nicolson.

DAVIDSON, D. (1967) 'Truth and Meaning', *Synthese*, 17: 304–23.

DAVIDSON, D., HARMAN, G. (eds) (1972) *Semantics of Natural Language*. Dordrecht and Boston: Reidel.

DAVIS, C.L. and COLEMAN, K.M. (1975) 'Political Symbols, Political Efficacy and Diffuse Support for the Mexican Political System', *Journal of Political and Military Sociology*, 1: 27–42.

DE GIORGI, R. (1979) *Scienza del diritto e legittimazione* (Jurisprudence and Legitimation). Bari: De Donato.

DE MONTLIBERT, C. (1982) 'La professionalization de la sociologie et ses limites', *Revue française de sociologie*, 1: 37–53.

DENITCH, B. (ed.) (1979) *Legitimation of Regimes. International Frameworks for Analysis*. London: Sage Publications.

DERBER, C. (1978) 'Unemployment and the Entitled Worker: Job-Entitlement and Radical Political Attitudes among the Youthful Unemployed', *Social Problems*, 1: 26–37.

DE RIZ, L., (1976) 'La lucha de clases en la sociedad chilena: Hipótesis para su interpretación' (Class Struggle in Chilean Society: Hypothesis for its Interpretation), *Revista Mexicana de Sociologia*, 1: 127–47.

DE SAUSSURE, F. (1916) *Cours de linguistique générale*. Lausanne: Payot.

DE TOCQUEVILLE, A. (1835, 1840) *Democracy in America* (2 vols).

DE WAAL MALEFIJT, A. (1968) *Religion and Culture*. New York: Macmillan.

DIAZ, E. (1978) *Legalidad-legitimidad en el socialismo democrático*. (Legality and Legitimation within Democratic Socialism). Madrid: Civitas.

DI PALMA, G. (1980) 'Founding Coalitions in Southern Europe: Legitimacy and Hegemony'. *Government and Opposition*, 2: 162–89.

DI TELLA, T.S. (1979) 'Edmund Burke y las precondiciones del estado de derecho' (Edmund Burke and the Preconditions of the Legal State), *Revista Paraguaya de Sociologia*, 44: 7–30.

DÖBERT, R. and NUNNER-WINKLER, G. (1975) *Adoleszenkrise und Identitätsbildung* (Adolescence Crisis and Identity-Formation). Frankfurt: Suhrkamp.

DOLBEARE, K.M. and EDELMAN, M.J. (eds) (1981) *American Politics. Policies, Power and Change*. Lexington MA and London: Heath.

DORMAN, W.A. (1979) 'Iranian People v. US News Media: A Case of Libel', *Race and Class*, 1: 57–66.

DOUGLAS, A. (1977) *The Feminization of American Culture*. New York: Avon.

DOUGLAS, J.D. (ed.) (1970) *Understanding Everyday Life. Toward the Reconstruction of Sociological Knowledge*. Chicago: Aldine.

DOUGLAS, J.W.B. (1964) *The Home and the School*. London: MacGibbon and Kee.

DOUGLAS, M. and TIPTON, S. (eds) (1983) *Religion in America: Spirituality in a Secular Age*. Boston: Beacon Press.

DOWNEY, J.E. (1978) 'A Note on Violent Crime in Northern Ireland', *The Wisconsin Sociologist*, 4: 172–75.

DOWNS, A. (1957) *An Economic Theory of Democracy*. New York: Harper and Brothers.

DRONBERGER, I. (1971) *The Political Thought of Max Weber. In Quest of Statesmanship*. New York: Appleton-Century-Crofts.

DUNCAN, H.D. (1953) *Language and Literature in Society*. Chicago: Chicago University Press.

DUNHAM, R.G. and MAUSS, A.L. (1976) 'Waves from Watergate: Evidence Concerning the Impact of the Watergate Scandal upon Political Legitimacy and Social Control', *Pacific Sociological Review*, 4: 469–90.

DURAND, G. (1980) *L'âme tigrée. Les pluriels de psyché*. Paris: Denoël/Gouthier.

DUVERGER, M. (1964) *Introduction à la politique*. Paris: Gallimard.

EDELMAN, M. (1964) *The Symbolic Uses of Politics*. Urbana, Chicago and London: University of Illinois Press.

EDELMAN, M. (1975) *Politics as Symbolic Action. Mass Arousal and Quiescence*. New York and London: Academic Press.

EDELMAN, M. (1977) *Political Language. Words that Succeed and Policies that Fail*. New York and London: Academic Press.

EDER, K. (1976) *Die Enstehung staatlich organisierter Gesellschaften* (The Rise of State-organized Societies). Frankfurt: Suhrkamp.

EGEBERG, M. (1978) 'Institusjonell pluralisme som interesseartikulerende system' (Institutional Pluralism as an Interest-Articulating System), *Tidsskrift for samfunnsforskning*, 1: 42–54.

EISENSTADT, S.N. (1980) 'Comparative Analysis of State Formation in Historical Contexts', *International Social Science Journal*, 4: 624–54.

ELIADE, M. (1952) *Images et symboles. Essais sur le symbolisme magico-religieux*. Paris: Gallimard.

EVAN, W.M. (ed.) (1962) *Law and Sociology: Exploratory Essay*. New York: Free Press.

FACH, W. (1975) 'Fach/Habermas: Kontroverse über Herrschaft und Legitimität' (Controversy about 'Power and Legitimacy'), *Soziale Welt*, 1: 110–12.

FALEIROS, V. (1982) 'Les centres sociaux urbains au Brésil', *Revue internationale d'action communautaire*, 8: 191–95.

FAVRE, P. (1983) 'La connaissance politique comme savoir légitime et comme savoir éclaté. Les enseignements à objets politiques dans les facultés françaises à la fin des années 70', *Revue française de sociologie*, 3: 467–503.

FEBBRAJO, A. (1975) *Funzionalismo strutturale e sociologia del diritto nell'opera di Niklas Luhmann* (Structural Functionalism and the Sociology of Law in the Work of Niklas Luhmann). Milano: Giuffrè.

FEHER, F. and HELLER, A. (1980) 'Hungary 1956: The Anatomy of a Political Revolution', *Radical America*, 1: 51–65.

FEIN, H. (1978) 'A Formula for Genocide: Comparison of the Turkish Genocide (1915) and the German Holocaust (1939–1945)', *Comparative Studies in Sociology*, 1: 271–94.

FERRARA, A. (1980a) 'An Extended Theory of Speech Acts: Appropriateness Conditions for Subordinate Acts in Sequence', *Journal of Pragmatics*, IV: 233–52.

FERRARA, A. (1980b) 'Appropriateness Conditions for Entire Sequences of Speech Acts', *Journal of Pragmatics*, IV: 321–40.

FERRARA, A. (1985) 'Per una sociologia critica del linguaggio' (Towards a Critical Sociology of Language), *Sociologia e Ricerca sociale*, 16: 7–41.

FERRARI-OCCHIONERO, M. (1977) 'Il ruolo della donna nella vita politica del paese' (The Woman's Role in the Italian Political Life), *Sociologia*, 2–3: 227–50.

FERRAROTTI, F. (1961) 'La ricerca della comunità in Robert A. Nisbet' in his *La sociologia come partecipazione e altri saggi*. Torino: Taylor, 62–75.

FERRAROTTI, F. (ed.) (1977) *La sociologia del potere* (The Sociology of Power). Bari: Laterza.

FERRAROTTI, F. (1979) *La società come problema e come progretto* (Society as Problem and Project). Milano: Mondadori.

FERRAROTTI, F. (1980) *Studi e ricerche sul potere*. (Studies and Investigations on Power). Roma: Ianua.

FERRAROTTI, F. (1981) *Il potere come relazione e come struttura* (Power as Relationship and Structure). Roma: Ianua.

FERRAROTTI, F. (1983) 'G. Mosca e la sociologia politica' (G. Mosca and Political Sociology) *Archivio internazionale G. Mosca per lo studio della classe politica*, vol. 2: 39–51.

FEUER, L.S. (1953) 'Sociological Aspects of the Relation Between Language and Philosophy', *Philosophy of Science*, 2: 85–100.

FEYERABEND, P.K. (1962) 'Explanation, Reduction, and Empiricism' in H. Feigl, G. Maxwell (eds), *Scientific Explanation, Space, and Time*. Minneapolis: University of Minnesota Press.

FEYERABEND, P.K. (1975) *Against Method.* London: NBL.

FIRTH, R. (1973) *Symbols: Public and Private.* London: Allen & Unwin.

FISICHELLA, D. (1982) *Elezioni e democrazia. Un'analisi comparata* (Elections and Democracy. A Comparative Analysis). Bologna: Il Mulino.

FLISFISH, A. (1984) 'Concentración de poder y desarrollo social' (Power Concentration and Social Development), *Revista Paraguaya de Sociologia*, 59: 41–53.

FLUDE, M. and AHIER, J. (eds) (1974) *Educability, Schools and Ideology.* London: Croom Helm.

FLYNN, C.P. (1983) 'Militarism, Means of Coercion, and the Sociological Construction of Reality', *Humanity and Society*, 1: 1–9.

FORT, C. (1955) *Le livre des damnés.* Paris: Editions des Deux Rives.

FRANZ, G. (1985) 'Zeitreihenanalysen zu Wirtschaftsentwicklung, Zufriedenheit und Regierungsvertrauen in der Bundesrepublik Deutschland. Entwicklung eines dynamischen Theorieansatzes zur Konstitution der Legitimität einer Regierung' (Economic Development, Satisfaction, and Trust in the Federal Republic of Germany: the Development of a Dynamic Theoretical Assessment of the Constitution of the Legitimacy of a Regime), *Zeitschrift für Soziologie*, 1: 64–88.

FRASER, A. (1978) 'The Legal Theory we Need to Know', *Socialist Review*, 4–5: 143–45.

FRASER, J. (1983) 'Dopo lo storicismo, l'organicismo e il meccanicismo: ci serve una nuova sistematica?' (After Historicism, Organicism and Mechanicism: Do We Need a New Systematics?), *La critica sociologica*, 67: 56–63.

FREEMAN, L. and WINCH, R. (1957) 'Societal Complexity', *The American Journal of Sociology*, 62: 461–69.

FREGE, G. (1892) 'Über Sinn und Bedeutung' (Meaning and Reference), *Zeitschrift für Philosophie und philosophische Kritik*, 100: 25–50.

FREUND, J. (1965) *L'essence du politique.* Paris: Sirey.

FROMM, E. (1951) *The Forgotten Language.* New York: Holt, Rinehart and Winston.

FRUDA, L. (1975) 'Leaders politici e autorità: progetto e collaudo di alcune schede a differenziale semantico' (Political Leaders and Authority: an Application of the Semantic Differential to some Polls), *La Critica Sociologica*, 33–34: 176–96.

FULLER, L. (1965) *The Morality of Law*. New Haven: Yale University Press.

FUNDERBURK, C. (1975) 'Political Legitimacy and Approval of Political Protest and Violence among Children and Adolescents', *Journal of Youth and Adolescence*, 2: 109–25.

FUSE, T. (1975) 'Japan's Economic Development: Success, Stress and Prospects for the Future', *Journal of Asian and African Studies*, 3–4: 138–54.

GADAMER, H.G. (1956) 'Che cos'é la verità?' (What's the Truth?), *Rivista di Filosofia*, 3: 251–66.

GADAMER, H.G. (1960) *Wahrheit und Methode* (Truth and Method). Tübingen: J.B.C. Mohr (P. Siebeck).

GALASKIEWICZ, J. (1985) 'Interorganizational Relations', *Annual Review of Sociology*, 11: 281–304.

GARIAZZO, A. (1981) 'Origines ideologicos de los movimientos obreros Chileno y Argentino' (Ideological Origins of Chilean and Argentine Workers' Movements), *Revista Paraguaya de Sociologia*, 51: 59–96.

GEERTZ, C. (1975) *The Interpretation of Cultures*. London: Hutchinson.

GEIGER, T. (1963) *Demokratie ohne Dogma* (Democracy without Dogma). München: Szczesny Verlag.

GEIGER, T. (1970) *Vorstudien zu einer Soziologie des Rechts* (Explorations in the Sociology of Law). Neuwied-Berlin: Luchterhand.

GELLNER, E. (1974) *Legitimation of Belief*. Cambridge: Cambridge University Press.

GELLNER, E. (1983) *Nations and Nationalism*. Oxford: Blackwell.

GENNARO, G. (1971) 'Potere e teoria sociale. Considerazioni intorno all' "eredità weberiana" della tipologia del potere legittimo' (Power and Social Theory. On the Weberian Typology of Legitimate Authority), *Sociologia*, 3: 127–90.

GILBERT, A. and WARD, P. (1984) 'Community Action by the Urban Poor: Democratic Involvement Community Self-Help or a Means of Social Control', *World Development*, 8: 769–82.

GINER, S. (1982) 'Political Economy, Legitimation and the State in Southern Europe', *The British Journal of Sociology*, 2: 172–99.

GINSBERG, M. (1981) *La giustizia nella società* (Justice within Society). Milano: Giuffrè.

GOLDSCHMIDT, D., SCHOFTHALER, T. and HOMANN, U. (1979) 'Die Soziologie in Wechselwirkung mit Bildungssystem,

Bildungspolitik und Erziehungswissenschaft' (The Establishment of Educational Sociology in the Federal Republic of Germany), *Kölner Zeitschrift für Soziologie und Sozialpsychologie*, 21: 294–323.

GOMEZ ORFANEL, G. (1977) 'Sociedad, educación y escuela: notas para un análisis de sus interrelaciones' (Society, Education, and School: Notes for an Analysis of Their Interrelationships), *Revista Española de la Opinión Publica*, 50: 143–70.

GOULDNER, A.W. (1970) *The Coming Crisis of Western Sociology*. New York and London: Basic Books.

GOZZI, G. (ed.) (1980) *Le trasformazioni dello Stato. Tendenze del dibattito in Germania e in USA* (The Transformations of the State. Current Debates in Germany and the USA). Firenze: La Nuova Italia.

GRAFSTEIN, R. (1981a) 'The Failure of Weber's Conception of Legitimacy: Its Causes and Implications', *Journal of Politics*, 2: 456–72.

GRAFSTEIN, R. (1981b) 'The Problem of Choosing Your Alternatives: A Revision of the Public Choice Theory of Constitutions', *Social Science Quarterly*, 2: 199–212.

GROSSI, G. (ed.) (1983) *Comunicare politica. Propaganda, immagine e progetto nelle pratiche comunicative della sinistra* (Communicating Politics. Propaganda, Image and Project in the Communicative Practice of the Left). Milano: Angeli.

GRUENWALD, E. (1934) *Das Problem der Soziologie des Wissens* (The Problem of the Sociology of Knowledge). Wien-Leipzig: W. Braumueller.

GUIZZARDI, G. (1976) 'The Rural Civilization: Structure of an "Ideology for Consent"', *Social Compass*, 2–3: 197–220.

GUIZZARDI, G. and PACE, E. (1981) *Grande idéologie et vie quotidienne dans la restructuration du champ religieux catholique*. Actes de la XVIe Conférence Internationale de Sociologie des Religions. Lille. 57–81.

GUMPERZ, J. and HYMES, D. (eds) (1962) *Directions in Sociolinguistics*. New York: Holt.

GUSFIELD, J. (1967) 'Moral Passage: The Symbolic Process in Public Designation of Deviance', *Social Problems*, 15: 175–88.

HABERMAS, J. (1962) *Strukturwandel der Öffentlichkeit* (The Structural Transformation of the Public Sphere). Neuwied: Luchterhand.

HABERMAS, J. and LUHMANN, N. (1971) *Theorie der Gesellschaft oder Sozialtechnologie. Was leistet die Systemforschung*? (Social

Theory or Social Technology. The Possibilities of Systems Theory). Frankfurt: Suhrkamp.

HABERMAS, J. (1973a) 'Wahrheitstheorien' (Theories of truth) pp. 211–65 in H. Fahrenbach (ed.) *Wirklichkeit und Reflexion: Walter Schulz zum 60. Geburtstag* (Reality and Reflection: for Walter Schulz's Sixtieth Birthday). Pfüllingen: Neske.

HABERMAS, J. (1973b) 'Was heisst heute Krise?' (What Does Crisis Mean Today?), *Merkur*, 4–5.

HABERMAS, J. (1976a) *Legitimation Crisis*. London: Heinemann.

HABERMAS, J. (1976b) *Zur Rekonstrucktion des historischen Materialismus* (On the Reconstruction of the Historical Materialism). Frankfurt: Suhrkamp.

HABERMAS, J. (1979) *Communication and the Evolution of Society*. Boston: Beacon Press.

HABERMAS, J. (1980) *Agire comunicativo e logica delle scienze sociali* (Communicative Action and Logic of the Social Sciences). Bologna: Il Mulino.

HABERMAS, J. (ed.) (1982) 'Einleitung' (Introduction), in: *Stichworte zur geistigen Situation der Zeit* (Keywords on the Spiritual Situation of our Time). Frankfurt: Suhrkamp.

HABERMAS, J. (1985) *The Theory of Communicative Action*. Boston: Beacon Press.

HADIYYA, A. (1984) 'Power and Legitimacy in Developing Countries', *Journal of the Social Sciences*, 3: 107–32.

HALEVY, E. (1965) *The Era of Tirannies*. New York: Doubleday.

HALL, J.H. (1981) *Diagnoses of Our Time. Six Views of Our Social Condition*. London: Heinemann.

HAMILTON, P. (1974) *Knowledge and Social Structure. An Introduction to the Classical Argument in the Sociology of Knowledge*. London and Boston: Routledge and Kegan Paul.

HAMMOUDI, A. (1980) 'Sainteté, pouvoir et société: Tamgrout aux XVIIe et XVIIIe siècles', *Annales*, 3–4: 615–41.

HAMPSON, N. (1974) *The Life and Opinions of Maximilien Robespierre*. London: Duckworth.

HANFLING, O. (1981) *Logical Positivism*. New York: Columbia University Press.

HARE, R.M. (1952) *The Language of Morals*. London: Oxford University Press.

HARE, R.M. (1969) 'The Lawful Government' in P. Laslett and W.G. Runciman (eds), *Philosophy, Politics and Society*. Oxford: Oxford University Press.

HECKMANN, H.D. (1981) *Was ist Wahrheit?* (What's the Truth?). Heidelberg: C. Winter Universität Verlag.

HELD, D. and THOMPSON, J.B. (eds) (1981) *Habermas. Critical Debates*. London: Macmillan.

HELD, D. et al. (eds) (1983) *States and Societies*. Oxford: Martin Robertson.

HEMPEL, C.G. (1966) *Aspects of Scientific Explanation and Other Essays in the Philisophy of Science*. New York and London: The Free Press–Collier Macmillan.

HERBST, P.G. (1976) *Alternatives to Hierarchies*. Dordrecht-Leiden: Martinus Nijhoff.

HINDESS, B. (1983) *Parliamentary Democracy and Socialist Politics*. London: Routledge and Kegan Paul.

HIRSCHMAN, A.O. (1970) *Exit, Voice and Loyalty*. Cambridge, MA: Harvard University Press.

HUDSON, R.B. (1978) 'Emerging Pressures on Public Policies for the Aging', *Society*, 5: 30–33.

HURRELMAN, H. (ed.) (1976) *Sozialisation und Lebenslauf* (Socialization and the Life-Cycle). Reinbek: Rowohlt.

ISAMBERT, F. (1979) *Rite et efficacité symbolique. Essai d'anthropologie sociologique*. Paris: Cerf.

IZZO, A. (ed.) (1970) *Il condizionamento sociale del pensiero* (The Social Determination of Thought). Torino: Loescher.

IZZO, A. (1978) *Il concetto di ideologia* (The Concept of Ideology). Milano: ISEDI.

JACOBELLI, A.M. (1985) 'Una riflessione filosofica sul problema della legittimazione' (Philosophical Considerations on the Problem of Legitimation), *La Critica Sociologica*, 73: 102–13.

JÄNICKE, M. (ed.) (1973) *Herrschaft und Krise* (Domination and Crisis). Opladen: Westdeutscher Verlag.

JANOWITZ, M. (1975) 'Sociological Theory and Social Control', *American Journal of Sociology*, 1: 82–108.

JANOWITZ, M. (1977) 'From Institutional to Occupational: The Need for Conceptual Continuity', *Armed Forces and Society*, 1: 51–54.

JASINKA-KANIA, A. (1983) 'Rationalization and Legitimation Crisis: The Relevance of Marxian and Weberian Works for an Explanation of the Political Order's Legitimacy Crisis in Poland', *Poland Sociology*, 2: 157–64.

JENCKS, C. (ed.) (1977) *Rationality, Education and the Social Organization of Knowledge*. London: Routledge and Kegan Paul.

JENNINGS, M.K. and NIEMI, R.G. (1974) *The Political Character of Adolescence*. Princeton: Princeton University Press.

JOHNSON, H.M. (ed.) (1979) *Religious Change and Continuity*. Washington: Jossey-Bass.

JORGENSEN, B. (1982) 'Defending the Terrorists: Queen's Counsel before the Courts of Northern Ireland', *Journal of Law and Society*. 1: 115–26.

KALBERG, S. (1980) 'Max Weber's Types of Rationality: Cornerstones for the Analysis of Rationalization Processes in History', *American Journal of Sociology*, 86: 1145–79.

KANT, I. (1959) *The Critique of Practical Reason and Other Works in the Theory of Ethics*. London: Longmans.

KATEB, G. (1979) 'On the "Legitimation Crisis"', *Social Research*, 4: 695–727.

KELLY, G.A. (1983) 'Faith, Freedom and Disenchantment: Politics and the American Religious Consciousness' in M. Douglas and S. Tipton (eds) *Religion and America: Spirituality in a Secular Age*. Boston: Beacon Press.

KELMAN, H.C. (1976) 'Some Reflections on Authority, Corruption, and Punishment: The Social-Psychological Context of Watergate', *Psychiatry*, 4: 303–17.

KOEHN, P. and HAYES, L.D. (1978) 'Student Politics in Traditional Monarchies: A Comparative Analysis of Ethiopia and Nepal', *Journal of Asian and African Studies*, 1–2: 33–49.

KOFELE-KALE, N. (1978) 'The Problem of Instrumental Leadership in Contemporary African Political Systems', *Journal of Asian and African Studies*, 1–2: 80–94.

KOKOSALAKIS, N. (1985) 'Legitimation Power and Religion in Modern Society', *Sociological Analysis*, 4: 367–76.

KREPLIN, K.W. (1981) 'Environmental Regulation as Legitimation: The Symbolic Politics of Air Pollution Control', *Humboldt Journal of Social Relations*, 2: 11–47.

KUHN, T. (1962) *The Structure of Scientific Revolutions*. Chicago: The University of Chicago Press.

La forza della riconciliazione (The Power of Reconciliation) (1984). Bologna: EDB.

LAKATOS, I. (1963–4) 'Proofs and Refutations', *British Journal for the Philosophy of Science*, XIV: 1–25, 120–39, 221–43, 296–342.

LAKATOS, I. and MUSGRAVE, A. (eds) (1974) *Criticism and the Growth of Knowledge*. Cambridge: Cambridge University Press.

LALLI, P. (1983) 'D'autres médecines: le paradoxe dans le quotidien', *Cahiers Internationaux de Sociologie*, LXXIV: 165–8.

LANDES, R.G. (1976) 'The Use of Role Theory in Political Socialization Research', *International Journal of Comparative Sociology*, 1–2: 59–72.

LANE, C. (1981) *The Rites of Rulers*. Cambridge: Cambridge University Press.

LANGTON, K.P. (1969) *Political Socialization*. New York: Oxford University Press.

LASLETT, P. and RUNCIMAN, W.G. (eds) (1962) *Philosophy, Politics and Society*. Oxford: Blackwell.

LEACH, E. (1966) 'The Legitimacy of Solomon. Some Structural Aspects of Old Testament History', *Archives Européennes de Sociologie*, 1: 58–101.

LENSKI, G. (1978) 'Marxist Experiments in Destratification: An Appraisal', *Social Forces*, 2: 364–83.

LEONARDI, F. (1984) 'I modelli evolutivi' (Evolutionary Models), *Sociologia e Ricerca Sociale*, 13: 193–241.

LESLIE, D.W. (1975) 'Legitimizing University Governance: Theory and Practice', *Higher Education*, 2: 233–46.

LESSNOFF, M. (1971) 'John Rawls' Theory of Justice', *Political Studies*, 19 (1): 63–80.

LEV, D.S. (1978) 'Judicial Authority and the Struggle for an Indonesian Rechtsstaat', *Law and Society Review*, 1: 37–71.

LE VAN-LEMESLE, L. (1983) 'L'économie politique à la conquête d'une légitimité 1896–1937' (Political Economy Fights for Legitimacy, 1896–1937), *Actes de la recherche en sciences sociales*, 47–48: 113–17.

LEVI, L. (1976) 'Legittimità' in N. Bobbio and N. Matteucci (eds) *Dizionario di politica* (Dictionary of Politics). Torino: UTET.

LEVY, M.J., Jr. (1952) *The Structure of Society*. Princeton: Princeton University Press.

LINDSTROM, L. (1982) 'Leftamap Kastom: The Political History of Tradition on Tanna, Vanuatu', *Mankind*, 4: 316–29.

LINGUET, S.N.H. (1767) *Théorie des loix civiles, ou principes fondamentaux de la société*. London, 2 vols.

LINGUET, S.N.H. (1770) *Lettres sur la théorie des loix civiles*. Amsterdam.

LINGUET, S.N.H. (1778) 'Tableau de l'état politique actuel du globe' in his *Mélanges de politique et de littérature, extrait des annales*.

LINZ, J.J. and STEPAN, A. (eds) (1978) *The Breakdown of Democratic Regimes*. Baltimore: Johns Hopkins University Press.

LIPSET, S.M. (1960) *Political Man. The Social Bases of Politics*. New York: Doubleday.

LIPSET, S.M., and SCHNEIDER, W. (1983) *The Confidence Gap: Business, Labor and Government in the Public Mind.* New York: The Free Press.

LLERA RAMO, F.J. (1984) 'El sistema de partidos vasco: distancia ideologica y legitimación politica' (The Basque Political Party System: Ideological Distance and Political Legitimation), *Revista Española de Investigaciones Sociologicas*, 28: 171–206.

LOMBARDO, M.G. (1984) 'Il senso etico della teoresi funzionalista' (The Ethical Meaning of the Functionalist Theories), *Fenomenologia e società*, January–March: 21–43.

LORENTZEN, L.J. (1980) 'Evangelical Life Style Concerns Expressed in Political Action', *Sociological Analysis*, 2: 144–54.

LÖWENTHAL, R. (1979) 'Political Legitimacy and Cultural Change in West and East', *Social Research*, 3: 401–35.

LUCKMANN, T. (1970) 'The Small Life-Worlds of Modern Man', *Social Research*, 37(4): 580–96.

LUCKMANN, T. (1967) *The Invisible Religion.* New York: Macmillan.

LUCKMANN, T. (1972) 'La costituzione del linguaggio nel mondo della vita quotidiana' (The Constitution of Language in the Life-World), *Rassegna Italiana di Sociologia*, 1: 61–77.

LUHMANN, N. (1965) *Grundrechte als Institution* (Constitutional Law as an Institution), Berlin: Duncker & Humbolt.

LUHMANN, N. (1971) 'Zweck-Herrschaft-System: Grundbegriffe und Praemissen Max Webers' (Purpose-Authority-System: Max Weber's Basic Concepts and Premisses) pp. 90–112 in N. Luhmann, *Politische Planung* (Political Planning). Opladen: Westdeutscher Verlag.

LUHMANN, N. (1977a) *Funktion der Religion* (The Function of Religion). Frankfurt: Suhrkamp.

LUHMANN, N. (1977b) 'Il fenomeno della coscienza morale e l'autodeterminazione della personalità' (The Phenomenon of Moral Conscience and the Ethical Self-determination of Personality) *Giornale di Teologia*, 100: 151–77.

LUHMANN, N. (1978) 'Soziologie der Moral' (The Sociology of Morality) pp. 8–116 in N. Luhmann and S.P. Pfuerstner (eds) *Theorietechnik und Moral.* Frankfurt: Suhrkamp.

LUHMANN, N. (1979) *Trust and Power: Two Works by N. Luhmann.* Chichester: Wiley.

LUHMANN, N. (1980, 1981) *Gesellschaft und Semantik* (Social Structure and Semantics). Frankfurt: Suhrkamp, (2 vols).

LUHMANN, N. (1981a) *Ausdifferenzierung des Rechts* (The Differentiation of Law). Frankfurt: Suhrkamp.

LUHMANN, N. (1981b) *Politische Theorie im Wohlfahrtstaat* (Political Theory and the Welfare-State). München-Wien.

LUHMANN, N. (1981c) 'Selbstlegitimation des Staates'. (The Self-Legitimation of the State), *Archiv für Rechts-und Sozialphilosophie*. 15: 65–83.

LUHMANN, N. (1981d) *Soziologische Aufklärung. Aufsätze zur Soziologie von Politik und Verwaltung* (Sociological Enlightenment. Essays in the Sociology of Policy and Administration). Wiesbaden: Westdeutscher Verlag.

LUHMANN, N. (1982) *The Differentiation of Society*. New York: Columbia University Press.

LUHMANN, N. (1983) *Legitimation durch Verfahren* (Legitimation through Procedure). Frankfurt: Suhrkamp.

LUHMANN, N. (1984a) *Soziale Systeme: Grundrisse einer allgemeinen Theorie* (Social System: Foundations of a General Theory). Frankfurt: Suhrkamp.

LUHMANN, N. (1984b) 'Die Theorie der Ordnung und die natürliche Rechte' (The Theory of Order and Natural Rights), *Rechtshistorisches Journal*, 3: 133–49.

LUHMANN, N. (1984c) 'I fondamenti sociali della morale' (The Social Foundations of Morality) pp. 9–20 in *Etica e politica. Riflessioni sulla crisi del rapporto fra società e morale*. Milano: Angeli.

LUHMANN, N. (1985) *A Sociological Theory of Law*. London: Routledge and Kegan Paul.

LUKES, S. (1974) *Power: A Radical View*. London: Macmillan.

LYMAN, S.M. (1975) 'Legitimacy and Consensus in Lipset's America: From Washington to Watergate', *Social Research*, 4: 729–59.

LYON, L. (1977) 'A Re-Examination of the Reform Index and Community Power', *Journal of the Community Development Society*, 1: 86–97.

MACHADO, M.B. (1979) 'Ciencia Politica e Socialização Politica nos Estados Unidos' (Political Science and Political Socialization in the United States), *Dados*, 22: 65–73.

MACHADO, M.B. (1980) 'Ideologia, Socialização politica e Dominação' (Ideology, Political Socialization, and Domination), *Dados*, 2: 131–49.

MACIOTI, M.I. (ed.) (1987) *I nuovi culti* (The New Cults). Roma: Ianua.

MADELLA, A. (1984) 'La formazione dei concetti: una rassegna delle teorie psicologiche e socio-antropologiche' (Concept Formation. A Review of Psychological and Socio-Anthropological Theories), *Sociologia e Ricerca Sociale*, 13: 45–68.

MAFFESOLI, M. (1979a) *La violence totalitaire – Essai d'anthropologie politique*. Paris: PUF.

MAFFESOLI, M. (1979b) *La conquête du présent*. Paris: PUF.

MAFFESOLI, M. (1982) *L'ombre de Dionysos*. Paris: Editions des Méridiens.

MAFFESOLI, M. (1985) *La Connaissance ordinaire. Prècis de sociologie compréhensive*. Paris: Librairie des Méridiens.

MANNHEIM, K. (1956) *Idéologie et utopie*. Paris: Editions Marcel Rivière.

MARCUSE, H. (1964) *One Dimensional Man. Studies in the Ideology of Advanced Industrial Society*. Boston: Beacon Press.

MARCUSE, H. (1965) *Kultur und Gesellschaft* (Culture and Society). Frankfurt: Suhrkamp.

MARLETTI, P. (1984) *Media e Politica* (Media and Politics). Milano: Angeli.

MARRADI, A. (1984) 'Teoria: una tipologia dei significanti' (Theory: a Typology of Meanings), *Sociologia e Ricerca Sociale*, 13: 157–81.

MARSH, A. (1977) *Protest and Political Consciousness*. London: Sage Publications.

MARSHALL, S.E. (1979) 'Islamic Revival in the Maghreb: The Utility of Tradition for Modernizing Elites', *Studies in Comparative International Development*, 2: 95–108.

MARSLAND, D. (1984) 'Public Opinion and the Welfare State: Some Problems in the Interpretation of Facts', *Sociology*, 1: 83–87.

MARX, K. (1946) *Capital*. London: Allen & Unwin.

MASCILLI MIGLIORINI, E. (1974) *La strategia del consenso* (The Strategy of Consent). Milano: Rizzoli.

MASTER, R.D. (1984) 'Ostracism, Voice, and Exit: The Biology of Social Participation', *Social Science Information/Information sur les Sciences Sociales*, 6: 877–93.

MAYNTZ, R. (ed.) (1980) *Implementation politischer Programme. Empirische Forschungsberichte* (The Implementation of Policy. Empirical Reports). Königstein/Ts: Athenäum.

MAZZOLENI, G. (1979) 'Il potere politico dei mass media' (The Political Power of Mass Media), *Problemi dell'Informazione*, 1: 51–77.

McCOMBS, H.E. and SHAW, D.L. (eds) (1977) *The Emergence of*

American Political Issues: The Agenda Setting Functions. West: St. Paul.

McQUAIL, D. (1983) *Mass Communication Theory. An Introduction*. Beverly Hills: Sage Publications.

MERELMAN, R.M. (1971) *Political Socialization and Educational Climates. A Study of Two School Districts*. New York: Rinehart and Winston.

MEYER, T. (1983) 'Grundlagen einer neuen Theorie der westlichen Industriegesellschaft: Fred Hirschs die Sozialen Grenzen des Wachstums' (Foundation of a New Theory of Western Industrial Society: Fred Hirsch's Social Limits to Growth), *Zeitschrift für Soziologie*, 1: 74–85.

MIDRE, G. (1985) 'Fra tilbud om arbeid til systemlegitimering' (Rehabilitation Policy and Practice), *Tidsskrift for samfunnsforskning*, 1-2: 200–22.

MISSIKA, J. and WOLTON, D. (1983) *La Folle du logis. La télévision dans les sociétés démocratiques*. Paris: Gallimard.

MITZMAN, A. (1971) *The Iron Cage: an Historical Interpretation of Max Weber*. New York: The Universal Library.

MIYOSHI, M. (1983) 'Against the Native Grain: Reading the Japanese Novel in America', unpublished paper.

MOL, H. (1976) *Identity and the Sacred. A Sketch for a New Social-scientific Theory of Religion*. Oxford: Basil Blackwell.

MOLES, A. (1982) *Labyrinthes du vécu*. Paris: Librairie des Méridiens.

MOLES, A. (1984) *La vie en contrebande*. Paris: Librairie des Méridiens.

MOLOTCH, H. and LESTER, M. (1974) 'News as Purposive Behavior', *American Sociological Review*, 39.

MOMMSEN, W. (1965) 'Max Weber's Political Sociology and His Philosophy of World History', *International Social Science Journal*, 1: 23–45.

MONGARDINI, C. (1969) *Ideologia e Società* (Ideology and Society). Roma: Bulzoni.

MONGARDINI, C. (1982) 'The Conditions of Consensus', *Revue Internationale de Sociologie*, 1–3: 12–29.

MONGARDINI, C. (1983) 'Legittimazione, consenso ed élites nell'Italia contemporanea: verso una nuova analisi dei processi politici' (Legitimation, Consent and Elites in Contemporary Italy. Toward a New Analysis of the Political Processes), *Sociologia del Diritto*, 1: 47–60.

MOODIE, T.D. (1975) 'The Dutch Reformed Churches as Vehicles of Political Legitimation in South Africa', *Social Dynamics*, 2: 158–66.

MORCELLINI, M. (ed.) (1986) *Lo spettacolo del consumo* (Consumption-Spectacle). Milano: Angeli.

MORIN, E. (1977, 1979) *La méthode*. 2 vols. Paris: Seuil.

MORIN, E. (1983) *De la nature de l'URSS*. Paris: Fayard.

MOSCA, G. (1972) *A Short History of Political Philosophy*. New York: Crowell.

MOWRER, O.H. (1960) *Learning Theory and the Symbolic Processes*. New York: Wiley.

MUELLER, G. (1979) 'The Notion of Rationality in the Work of Max Weber', *European Journal of Sociology*, 20: 149–71.

MUHLMANN, W.E. (1952) 'Aspekte einer Soziologie der Macht' (Aspects of a Sociology of Power), *Archiv für Rechts-und Sozialphilosophie*, 1: 84–113.

MÜLLER, G., RÖDEL, U., SABEL, Ch., STILLE, F., VOGT, W. (1978) *Ökonomische Krisentendenzen im gegenwärtigen Kapitalismus* (Economic Crisis — Trends in Contemporary Capitalism). Frankfurt: Campus.

MULLER, J.C. (1978) 'Ritual Legitimacy and Demography among the Rukuba (Plateau State, Nigeria)', *Revue canadienne des études africaines*, 1: 61–81.

MUNCH, R. (1976) *Legitimität und politische Macht* (Legitimacy and Political Power). Opladen: Westdeutscher Verlag.

MUNIZ, J.N. (1978) 'Cultura y crisis en el capitalismo avanzado. Anotaciones en torno a Daniel Bell' (Culture and Crisis in Advanced Capitalism: Annotations on Daniel Bell), *Revista Española de Investigaciones Sociologicas*, 1: 283–92.

NAMER, G. (1980) 'Die dreifache Legitimation. Ein Modell für eine Soziologie des Wissens' (Triple Legitimation. A Model for the Sociology of Knowledge), *Kölner Zeitschrift für Sozialpsychologie*, 22: 191–205.

NAMER, G. (1982) 'La triple légitimation: un modèle pour la sociologie de la connaissance', *Recherches sociologiques*, 1–2: 167–70.

NEGROTTI, M. (1984) 'I modelli di simulazione' (Simulation Models), *Sociologia e Ricerca Sociale*, 13: 183–91.

NIZARD, L. (1980) 'Les dynamiques contradictoires en oeuvre dans l'administration française: un essai d'explication théorique', *Revue française d'administration publique*, 15: 571–91.

NONET, P. and SELZNICK, P. (1978) *Law and Society in Transition: Towards Responsive Law*. New York: Farrar, Strauss & Giroux.

NOOIJ, A.T.J. (1977) 'Protest and Political Participation in Agriculture', *The Netherlands Journal of Sociology/Sociologia Neerlandica*, 1: 21–33.

NURMI, H. (1978) 'On Economic Theories of Political Institutions', *Munich Social Science Review*, 1: 7–24.

O'CONNOR, J. (1973a) 'Summary of the Fiscal Crisis of the State', *Kapitalstate*, 1: 79–83.

O'CONNOR, J. (1973b) *The Fiscal Crisis of the State*. New York: St Martin's Press.

O'CONNOR, T.H. (1979) 'The Irish in Boston', *The Urban and Social Change Review*, 2: 19–23.

OFFE, C. (1972a) 'Advanced Capitalism and the Welfare State', *Politics and Society*, 4: 479–88.

OFFE, C. (1972b) *Strukturprobleme des kapitalistischen Staates. Aufsätze zur politischen Soziologie* (Structural Problems of the Capitalistic States. Essays in the Sociology of Politics). Frankfurt: Suhrkamp.

OFFE, C. (1975) *Berufsbildungsreform. Eine Fallstudie über Reformpolitik* (The Reform of Vocational Training. A Case Study on Reform Policies). Frankfurt: Suhrkamp.

OFFE, C. (1977) *Lo stato nel capitalismo maturo*. (The State in Mature Capitalism). Milano: ETAS.

OFFE, C. (1983) 'Political Legitimation through Majority Rule?', *Social Research*, 4: 709–56.

OHAMA, J. (1953) *Pouvoir politique et pouvoir spirituel*. Paris: Rivière.

ÖHLINGER, T. (ed.) (1982) *Methodik der Gesetzgebung. Legistische Richtlinen in Theorie und Praxis* (Methodology of Law-Giving. Directions). Wien.

O'NEILL, J. (1977) 'Language and the Legitimation Problem', *Sociology*, 2: 351–58.

OPPENHEIMER, F. (1975) *The State*. Montreal: Black Rose.

ORUM, A.M. (1976) 'On the Explanation of Political Socialization and Political Change', *Youth and Society*, 2: 147–74.

PADOVANI, G. (1976) 'Esistono società senza un potere politico autoritario?' (Are there Societies without an Authoritarian Political Power?), *Studi di Sociologia*, 4: 377–86.

PAGLIANO, G. (ed.) (1985) *Letteratura e legittimazione* (Literature and Legitimation). Parma: Pratiche Editrice.

PAPAGIANNIS, G.J., BICKEL, L.N. and FULLER, R.H. (1983) 'The Social Creation of School Dropouts: Accomplishing the Reproduction of an Underclass', *Youth and Society*, 3: 363–92.

PARSONS, T. (1964) 'Evolutionary Universals in Society', *American Sociological Review*, 9.

PARSONS, T. (1969) *Politics and Social Structure*. New York: The Free Press.

PASQUINELLI, A. (1964) *Nuovi principi di epistemologia* (New Principles of Epistemology). Milano: Feltrinelli.

PASSERIN D'ENTREVES, A. (1970) *Obbedienza e resistenza in una società democratica* (Obedience and Resistance in a Democratic Society). Milano: Comunità.

PECCEI, A. (1984) 'Il mondo di domani' (The World of Tomorrow), in *Verso il Duemila* (Towards 2000). Bari: Laterza.

PELLICANI, L. (1976) 'La sociologia di Ortega y Gasset' (The Sociology of Ortega y Gasset), *Rivista di Sociologia*, 1: 61–106.

PELLICANI, L. (1983) 'La legittimazione del potere nella città secolare' (The Legitimation of Power in the Secular City), *Mondoperaio*, 10: 129.

PETRAS, J. (1980) 'Nicaragua: The Transition to a New Society', *Contemporary Marxism*, 2: 92–106.

PETRYSZAK, N.G. (1980) 'Sociological Theory and Human Nature', *Pacific Sociological Review*, 2: 131–50.

PHAYER, J.M. (1978) 'Politics and Popular Religion: The Cult of the Cross in France, 1815–1840', *Journal of Social History*, 3: 346–65.

PIKE, K.L. (1966) *Language in Relation to a Unified Theory of the Structure of Human Behavior*. The Hague: Mouton.

POGGI, G. (1978) 'Niklas Luhmann's Neo-functionalist Approach: an Elementary Presentation', *La Critica Sociologica*, 45–46: 31–46.

POPE, W., COHEN, J. and HAZELRIGG, L.E. (1975) 'On the Divergence of Weber and Durkheim: a Critique of Parsons' Convergence Thesis', *American Sociological Review*, 40: 229–41.

POPPER, K.R. (1969) *Conjectures and Refutations*. London: Routledge and Kegan Paul.

POPPER, K.R. (1972) *Objective Knowledge. An Evolutionary Approach*. Oxford: Oxford University Press.

POPPER, K. (1981) *La quête inachevée*. Paris: Calmann-Lévy.

POPPER, K. (1982) *La logique de la découverte scientifique*. Paris: Payot.

PORTINARO, P.P. (1981) 'Max Weber e Carl Schmitt' (Max Weber and Carl Schmitt), *Sociologia del Diritto*, 1: 155–82.

POULAT, E. (1974) 'L'Eglise romaine, le pouvoir et le savoir', *Archives de Sciences Sociales des Religions*, 37: 5–21.

POULAT, E. (1986) *L'Eglise c'est un monde. L'Ecclésiosphère*. Paris: Les éditions du Cerf.

PRANDI, C. (ed.) (1984) *Le società nei simboli religiosi* (Society in Religious Symbols). Milano: Angeli.

PRAITE, R. (1983) 'Multicultural Education: Four Normative Arguments', *Educational Theory*, 1: 21–32.

PUSEY, M. (1980) 'The Legitimation of State Education Systems', *The Australian and New Zealand Journal of Sociology*, 2: 45–52.

PUTNAM, H. (1978) *Meaning and the Moral Sciences*. London: Routledge and Kegan Paul.

QUINE, W.V.O. (1960) *Word and Object*. Cambridge: MIT Press.

QUINE, W.V.O. (1963) *From a Logical Point of View*. Cambridge MA: Harvard University Press.

QUINE, W.V.O. (1976) *The Ways of Paradox and Other Essays*. New York: Harvard University Press.

RAO, K.R. and MURTHY, K.R. 'A Note on Public Office, Legitimacy and Flow of Political Power in Village India', *Sociological Bulletin*, 2: 205–209.

RAWLS, J. (1962) 'Justice as Fairness', pp. 132–57 in P. Laslett and W.G. Runciman (eds) *Philosophy, Politics and Society*. Oxford: Blackwell (2nd series).

RAWLS, J. (1967) 'Distributive Justice', pp. 58–82 in P. Laslett & W.G. Runciman (eds.) *Philosophy, Politics and Society*. Oxford: Blackwell (3rd series).

RAWLS, J. (1971) *A Theory of Justice*. Cambridge (MA): University Press.

REHBINDER, M. and SCHELSKY, H. (eds) (1975) *Zur Effektivität des Rechts* (The Efficacy of Law). Düsseldorf.

REMMLING, G.W. (ed.) (1973) *Towards the Sociology of Knowledge. Origin and Development of a Sociological Thought Style*. London: Routledge and Kegan Paul.

RENAN, E. (1859) *Essais de morale et de critique*. Paris: Calmann-Lévy (7th edn).

RENSHON, S.A. (ed.) (1977) *Handbook of Political Socialization. Theory and Research*. New York: Free Press.

RESCHER, N. (1973) *The Coherence Theory of Truth*. Oxford: Oxford University Press.

RESTA, E. (1984) *L'ambiguo diritto* (The Ambiguity of Law). Milano: Angeli.

RIVETTI BARBO, F. (1961) *L'antinomia del mentitore nel pensiero contemporaneo. Da Peirce a Tarski* (The Antinomy of the Liar in Contemporary Thought from Peirce to Tarski). Milano: Vita e Pensiero.

RIVIERE, C. (1982) 'A quoi servent les rites séculiers?' *Social Compass*, 4: 369–86.

ROBERTSON, R. (1978) *Meaning and Change*. Oxford: Basil Blackwell.

RODRIGUEZ-CABELLO, E.L. (1982) 'Desencanto, crisis de autoridad y nacionalismo en la evolución politica del País Vasco' (Disillusion, Crisis of Authority, and Nationalism in the Political Evolution of the Basque Country), *Revista Internacional de Sociologia*, 41: 101–18.

RONGE, V. and SCHMIEG, G. (eds) (1971) *Politische Planung in Theorie und Praxis* (The Theory and Practice of Political Planning). München: Piper.

RONGE, V. and SCHMIEG, G. (eds) (1973) *Restriktionen politische Planung* (The Limits of Political Planning). Frankfurt: Fischer Athenäum.

RONGE, V. (1974) 'The Politicization of Administration in Advanced Capitalist Societies', *Political Studies*, 1: 89–93.

RONGE, V. (1977) *Forschungspolitik als Strukturpolitik* (The Politics of Research as Structural Policy). München: Piper.

ROOTES, C.A. (1980) 'Student Radicalism: Politics of Moral Protest and Legitimation Problems of the Modern Capitalist State', *Theory and Society*, 3: 473–502.

ROSITI, F. (1982) *Mercati di cultura* (Culture Markets). Bari: De Donato.

ROSSETTI, C.G. (1980) 'La politica della violenza e la crisi della legittimità razionale dello Stato' (The Politics of Violence and the Crisis of the Rational Legitimacy of the State), *Studi di Sociologia*, 3: 253–68.

RUFFINI, E. (1976) *Il principio maggioritario* (The Majority Principle). Milano: Adelphi.

RUGGIE, J.G. (1983) 'Human Rights and the Future International Community', *Daedalus*, 4: 93–110.

RUSCONI, G.E. (1982) ' "Discorso" e decisione. Il tentativo di

Habermas di fondare una razionalità politica' ("Discourse" and Decision. Habermas's Attempt to Found a Political Rationality) in M. Bovero (ed.) *Ricerche politiche. Saggi su Kelsen, Horkheimer, Habermas, Luhmann, Foucault, Rawls*. Milano: Il Saggiatore.

RUSCONI, G.E. (1984) *Scambio, minaccia, decisione. Elementi di sociologia politica* (Exchange, Threat, Decision. Elements of Political Sociology). Bologna: Il Mulino.

RUSSELL, B. (1948) *Human Knowledge. Its Scope and Limits*. London: Allen and Unwin.

RUSSELL, B. (1969) *The Authority and the Individual*. London: Allen and Unwin.

RYAN, A. (1976) *The Philosophy of the Social Sciences*. London and Basingstoke: Macmillan.

RYFFEL, H. (1969) *Grundprobleme der Rechts-und Staatphilosophie. Philosophische Anthropologie des Politischen* (Basic Issues in the Philosophy of Law and in the Philosophy of the State. A Philosophical Anthropology of the Political). Neuwied: Luchterhand.

RYFFEL, H. (1974) *Rechtssoziologie* (Sociology of Law). Neuwied: Luchterhand.

SABATIER, P. and WANDESFORDE-SMITH, G. (1979) 'Major Sources of Environmental Politics, 1974–77: The Maturing of a Literature', *The Policy Studies Journal*, 3: 592–604.

SACKS, H. (1970) *On the Overall Structural Organization of Conversation*. Irvine (CA): University of California Press.

SACKS, H., SCHEGLOFF, E. and JEFFERSON, G.J. (1974) 'A Simplest Systematics for the Organization of Turn-Taking for Conversation', *Language*, 696–735.

SANCHEZ CANO, J. (1976) 'Estudios sociales de Ferdinand Tönnies: Los problemas de legitimidad en el estado moderno' (The Social Research of Ferdinand Tönnies: Problems of Legitimacy in the Modern State), *Revista de Estudios Sociales*, 17–18: 251–58.

SAWER, M. (1978–79) 'The Politics of Historiography: Russian Socialism and the Question of the Asiatic Mode of Production 1906–1931', *Critique*, 10–11: 15–35.

SCAMUZZI, S. (1975) 'Per una sociologia della storia italiana: legittimazione e politica 1861–1974' (For a Sociology of Italian History: Legitimation and Politics 1861–1974), *Quaderni di Sociologia*, 1–2: 149–54.

SCAMUZZI, S. (1982) 'Luhmann: i rischi del potere nelle società avanzate' (Luhmann: The Risks of Power in Advanced Societies) in M. Bovero (ed.) *Ricerche politiche. Saggi su Kelsen, Horkheimer, Habermas, Luhmann, Foucault, Rawls*. Milano: Il Saggiatore.

SCARPELLI, F. (1982) 'Il sindacato maggiormente rappresentativo: modelli giuridici in crisi' (The Most Representative Trade Union: Legal Models in Crisis), *Sociologia del Diritto*, 1: 157–63.

SCHAFF, A. (1954) *Zu einigen Fragen der marxistischen und idealistichen Theorie der Wahrheit* (On Some Questions Inherent in the Marxist and Idealist Theory of Truth). Berlin: Dietz Verlag.

SCHATTSCHNEIDER, E.E. (1975) *The Semi-Sovereign People*. Hinsdale: Druden.

SCHEGLOFF, E. and SACKS, H. (1973) 'Opening up Closing' *Semiotica*, VIII: 289–327.

SCHLESINGER, P. (1981) ' "Terrorism", the Media, and the Liberal-Democratic State: A Critique of the Orthodoxy', *Social Research*, 1: 74–99.

SCHMITT, C. (1928) *Verfassungslehre* (Constitutional Theory). München-Leipzig: Duncker & Humblot.

SCHMITT, C. (1972) *Le categorie del 'politico'* (The Categories of the 'Political'). Bologna: Il Mulino.

SCHNAIBERG, A. (1982) 'Did You Ever Meet a Payroll? Contradictions in the Structure of the Appropriate Technology Movement', *Humboldt Journal of Social Relations*, 2: 38–62.

SCHOPENHAUER, A. (1966) *Le monde comme volonté et comme représentation*. Paris: PUF.

SCHROYER, T. (1975) 'The Re-Politicization of the Relations of Production: An Interpretation of Jürgen Habermas's Analytic Theory of Late Capitalist Development', *New German Critique*, 5: 107–28.

SCHUMPETER, J. (1961) *Capitalism, Socialism and Democracy*. London: Allen and Unwin.

SCHÜTZ, A. (1964) *Collected Papers*. 2 vols. The Hague: Martinus Nijhoff.

SCHWARTZ, R. and MILLER, J. (1964–65) 'Legal Evolution and Societal Complexity', *The American Journal of Sociology*, 70: 159–69.

SCOTT, D.M. (1978) *From Office to Profession: the New England Ministry, 1750–1850*. Philadelphia: University of Pennsylvania Press.

SEARLE, J. (1958) 'Proper Names', *Mind*, LXVII (266): 166–73.

SEARLE, J. (1969) *Speech Acts. An Essay in the Philosophy of Language*. London: Cambridge University Press.

SEGRE, S. (1981) 'Fondamenti giusnaturalistici della democrazia secondo Max Weber' (Natural Right Foundation of Democracy in Max Weber), *Sociologia del Diritto*, 1.

SELZNICK, P. (1961) 'Sociology and Natural Law', *Natural Law Forum*, VI.

SELZNICK, P. (1963) 'Legal Institutions and Social Control', *Vanderbild Law Review*, 17.

SELZNICK, P. (1969) *Law, Society and Industrial Justice*. New York: Russel Sage Foundation.

SERVICE, E.R. (1971) *Origins of the State and Civilization. The Process of Cultural Evolution*. New York: W.W. Norton.

SHERNOCK, S.K. (1984) 'Continuous Violent Conflict as a System of Authority', *Sociological Inquiry*, 3: 301–29.

SHILS, E. (1975) *Center and Periphery*. Chicago: Chicago University Press.

SHOEMAKER, P.J. (1984) 'Media Treatment of Deviant Political Groups', *Journalism Quarterly*, 1: 66–75.

SIMMEL, G. (1912) *Mélanges de philosophie relativiste*. Paris: Félix Alcan.

SIMON, H.A. (1958) *Administrative Behaviour*. New York: Macmillan.

SKIRBEKK, G. (ed.) (1980) *Wahrheitstheorien* (Theories of Truth). Frankfurt: Suhrkamp.

SKORUPSKI, J. (1976) *Symbol and Theory. A Philosophical Study of Theories of Religion in Social Anthropology*. Cambridge: Cambridge University Press.

SMUCKER, J. (1976) 'Reformist Themes in the Canadian Labour Congress', *Sociological Focus*, 2: 159–73.

SOHR, F. (1983) 'Innovation and Ideology in Adult Education: American and Italian Working Class Experiences', *The Insurgent Sociologist*, 4: 91–96.

SORGI, G. (1983) *Potere fra paura e legittimità* (Power between Fear and Legitimacy). Milano: Giuffrè.

SOROKIN, P. (1937) *Social and Cultural Dynamics*. New York: American Book Co., 1937–1941; London: Peter Owen, 1957.

SPENCER, H. (1902) *The Principles of Sociology*. 3 vols. London: Williams & Norgate. Vol. 2

SPENCER, M.E. (1970) 'Weber on Legitimate Norms and Authority', *British Journal of Sociology*, 2: 123–34.

SPENCER, R. (ed.) (1969) *Forms of Symbolic Action*. Washington: Washington University Press.

SPERBER, D. (1974) *Le symbolisme en général*. Paris: Hermann.

STANLEY, M. (1973) 'The Structures of Doubt: Reflections on Moral Intelligibility as a Problem in the Sociology of Knowledge', in G. Remmling (ed.) *Towards the Sociology of Knowledge. Origin and Development of a Sociological Thought Style*. London: Routledge and Kegan Paul.

STANYER, J. (1976) 'Irresistible Forces: The Pressures for a Science of Politics', *Political Studies*, 3: 237–52.

STARK, W. (1958) *The Sociology of Knowledge*. London: Humanities Press.

STAROBINSKI, J. (1982) *Montaigne en mouvement*. Paris: Gallimard.

STATERA, G. (1967) *Logica, linguaggio e sociologia. Studio su Otto Neurath* (Logics, Language and Sociology. A Study on Otto Neurath). Torino: Taylor.

STATERA, G. (ed.) (1982) *Consenso e conflitto nella società contemporanea* (Consensus and Conflict in Contemporary Society). Milano: Angeli.

STONE, G. (1975) *Cummulative Effects of the Media*. New York: Syracuse University Press.

STUART HUGHES, H. (1974) *Consciousness and Society*. London: Paladin.

TARANTINO, A. (ed.) (1980) *Legalità, legittimità e mutamento costituzionale* (Legality, Legitimacy and Constitutional Change). Milano: Giuffrè.

TARSKI, A. (1943–44) 'The Semantic Conception of Truth', *Philosophy and Phenomenological Research*, IV.

TARSKI, A. (1944) 'The Semantic Conception of the Truth and the Foundation of Semantics', *Philosophy and Phenomenological Research*, IV.

TAWNEY, R.H. (1964) *Equality*. London: Allen and Unwin.

TAYLOR-GOOBY, P. (1981) 'The State, Class Ideology and Social Policy', *Journal of Social Policy*, 4: 433–51.

TAYLOR-GOOBY, P. (1983) 'Legitimation Deficit, Public Opinion and the Welfare State', *Sociology*, 2: 165–84.

TEUBNER, G. (1983) 'Substantive and Reflexive. Elements in Modern Law', *Law and Society Review*, 17: 239–86.

TOMEO, V. (1981) *Il diritto come struttura del conflitto* (Law as the Structure of Conflict). Milano: Angeli.

TOULMIN, S.E. (1958) *Uses of Argument*. Cambridge: Cambridge University Press.

TREVES, R. (ed.) (1985) *Diritto e legittimazione* (Law and Legitimation). Milano: Angeli.

TUCHMAN, G. (1978) 'Professionalism as an Agent of Legitimation', *Journal of Communication*, 2: 106–13.

TUGENDATH, E. (1960) 'Tarskis semantische Definition der Wahrheit und ihre Stellung innerhalb der Geschichte des Wahrheitsproblems im logischen Positivismus' (Tarksi's Semantic Definition of Truth and Its Place in the History of the Problem of Truth within Logical Positivism), *Philosophische Rundschau*, 8: 213.

TULUMELLO, A. (1984) 'Il funzionalismo radicale di Luhmann: introduzione a un "intervista"' (Luhmann's Radical Functionalism: Introduction to an Interview), *Segno*, 48–9: 15–21, 25–33.

TURK, H. (1979) 'Imageries of Social Control: On the Publicized Birth and Early Life of Proposition 13', *Urban Life*, 3: 335–58.

TURNER, B.S. (1982) 'Nietzsche, Weber and the Devaluation of Politics: The Problem of State Legitimacy', *The Sociological Review*, 3: 367–91.

TYACK, D.B. (1976) 'Ways of Seeing: An Essay on the History of Compulsory Schooling', *Harvard Educational Review*, 355–89.

URSOM, J.O. (ed.) (1962) *How to Do Things with Words*. Oxford: The Clarendon Press.

USBERTI, G. (1978) *Logica, verità e paradosso* (Logics, Truth and Paradox). Milano: Feltrinelli.

USEEM, B. and USEEM, M. (1979) 'Government Legitimacy and Political Stability', *Social Forces*, 3: 840–52.

VAN DIJK, T.A. (1976) *Text and Context*. London: Longman.

VAN DIJK, T.A. (1980) 'The Semantics and Pragmatics of Functional Coherence in Discourse', *Versus*, 26/27: 49–65.

VAN DIJK, T.A. (1981) *Studies in the Pragmatics of Discourse*. The Hague: Mouton.

VARAS, A. (1982) 'Fuerzas armadas y gobierno militar: corporativización y politización castrense' (Armed Forces and Military Government: Military Corporatism and Politicization), *Revista Mexicana de Sociologia*, 2: 397–411.

VERGARA, P. (1982) 'Las transformaciones del Estado chileno bajo el regimen militar' (Transformations of the Chilean State under the Military Regime), *Revista Mexicana de Sociologia*, 2: 413–52.

VIDICH, A.J. (1975) 'Political Legitimacy in Bureaucratic Society: an Analysis of Watergate', *Social Research*, 4: 778–811.

VOBRUBA, G. (1978) 'Staatseingriff und Ökonomiefunktion: Der

Sozialstaat als Problem fur sich selbst' (State Intervention and the Economic Function: The Social Welfare State as a Problem for Itself), *Zeitschrift für Soziologie*, 2: 130–56.

WATZLAVICK, P., BEAVIN, J.H. and JACKSON, D.D. (1967) *Pragmatics of Human Communication*. New York: W.W. Norton.

WEBER, M. (1922) 'Die drei Reinentypen der legitimen Herrschaft' (The Three Pure Types of Legitimate Authority), *Preussische Jahrbücher*, 177.

WEBER, M. (1924) *Gesammelte Aufsätze sur Soziologie und Sozialpolitik* (Collected Essays on Sociology and Social Policy). Tübingen: Mohr.

WEBER, M. (1947) *Wirtschaft und Gesellschaft* (Economy and Society). Tübingen: Mohr.

WEBER, M. (1959) *Le savant et le politique*. Paris: Plon.

WEBER, M. (1964) *L'éthique protestante et l'esprit due capitalisme*. Paris: Plon.

WEBER, M. (1965) *Essais sur la théorie de la science*. Paris: Plon.

WEBER, M. (1968) *Economy and Society*. Berkeley: University of California Press.

WEBER, M. (1971) *Economie et Société*. Paris: Plon.

WEBER, M. (1982) *La ville*. Paris: Aubier Montaigne.

WEINGART, P. (1983) 'Verwissenschaftlichung der Gesellschaft-Politisierung der Wissenschaft' (Scientification of Society-Politicization of Science), *Zeitschrift für Soziologie*, 3: 225–41.

WEINSTEIN, M.A. (1975) 'Mass Society and the Crisis of Public Responsibility', *The Midwest Quarterly*, 1: 39–57.

WELCH, C.E., Jr. (1977) 'Warrior, Rebel, Guerrilla, and Putschist', *Journal of Asiatic and African Studies*, 1–4: 82–98.

WESSON, R.G. (1976) 'The Ideological Compass', *Quarterly Journal of Ideology*, 1: 10–15.

WHORF, B.L. (1956) *Language, Thought and Reality*. Cambridge (MA): MIT Press.

WICKHAM, A. (1980) 'Engendering Social Policy in the EEC', *m/f*, 4: 5–19.

WILLIAME, R. (1973) *Les fondements phénoménologiques de la sociologie compréhensive*. La Haye: Martinus Nijhoff.

WINCKELMANN, J. (1952) *Legitimität und Legalität in Max Webers Herrschaftssoziologie* (Legitimacy and Legality in Max Weber's Sociology of Authority). Tübingen: Mohr.

WINKLER, J. (1984) 'On the Structural Change in Voluntary Organisations: The Case of the "German Sport Association"

("DSB")', *International Review for the Sociology of Sport*, 1: 31–46.
WISMAN, J.D. (1979) 'Legitimation, Ideology-Critique, and Economics', *Social Research*, XLVI: 291–320.
WITTGENSTEIN, L. (1953) *Philosophical Investigations*. New York: Macmillan.
WITTGENSTEIN, L. (1969) *On Certainty*. Oxford: Basil Blackwell.
WOLF, J. (1981) *The Social Production of Art*. New York: St Martin's Press.
WOLFE, A. (1977) *The Limits of Legitimacy. Political Contradictions of Contemporary Capitalism*. New York: Free Press–Macmillan.
WOLFE, R.H., BARRINGTON MOORE Jr. and MARCUSE, H. (1965) *A Critique of Pure Tolerance*. Boston: Beacon Press.
WORRINGER, W. (1978) *Abstraction et 'Einfühlung'*. Paris: Klincksieck.
WRIGHT, L. (1973) 'Functions', *Philosophical Review*, 82: 139–68.
WRIGHT, L. (1976) *Teleological Explanation*. Berkeley–Los Angeles–London: University of California Press.
WRIGHT MILLS, C. (1963) *Power, Politics and People*. New York: Oxford University Press.
WRONG, D.H. (1968) 'Social Problems in Defining Social Power', *American Journal of Sociology*, 6: 673–81.
WUTHNOW, R. et al. (1984) *Cultural Analysis*. London: Routledge and Kegan Paul.
YANKELOVICH, D. (1975) 'The Status of Ressentiment in America', *Social Research*, 42, 4: 760–77.
YOUNG, M. (1956) 'The Meaning of the Coronation', *Sociological Review*, 1–2.
YOUNG, M.F.D. (ed.) (1971) *Knowledge and Control. New Directions for the Sociology of Education*. London: Collier-Macmillan.
ZANOTTI, A. (1982) 'Partiti politici della sinistra e nuovi soggetti politici' (Left-Wing Political Parties and New Political Subjects), *Revue Internationale de Sociologie*, 1–3: 286–99.
ZELENY, M. (ed.) (1980) *Autopoiesis. Dissipative Structures and Spontaneous Social Order*. Boulder: Westview Press.
ZELENY, M. (ed.) (1981) *Autopoiesis. A Theory of Living Organization*. New York: North Holland.
ZELENY, M. and PIERRE, N. (1976) 'Simulation of Self-Renewing Systems', pp. 150–65 in Jantsch and Waddington, *Evolution and Consciousness*. Addison: Wesley.

CURRENT SOCIOLOGY
La sociologie contemporaine

Information for Contributors

Each issue of this unique journal is devoted to a comprehensive Trend Report on a topic of interest to the international community of sociologists. Authors review current trends and tendencies in all areas of sociological work — theories, methods, concepts, substantive research and national or regional developments. The aim is to review new developments, to discuss controversies, and to provide extensive bibliographies. From time to time, Commentaries on Trend Reports are published in subsequent issues of the journal.

If you would like to propose a Trend Report, please send the Editor an outline or prospectus of the proposed issue and a brief *curriculum vitae*. A style sheet and detailed notes for the guidance of authors are available. Contributions may be written in English or French.

Correspondence concerning Trend Reports should be addressed to the Editor: James A. Beckford, Department of Sociology & Social Policy, University of Durham, Durham DH1 3JT, England.

All subscription enquiries should be addressed to the Publisher:

SAGE Publications
28 Banner Street, London EC1Y 8QE

International Sociological Association/ISA

CURRENT SOCIOLOGY

Association Internationale de Sociologie/La sociologie contemporaine

Volume 35
Number 3
Winter 1987

Street Foods: Testing Assumptions about Informal Sector Activity by Women and Men

Irene Tinker

PART 1
Introduction

PART 2
Invisible Workers

PART 3
Invisible Entrepreneurs

PART 4
Street Foods

PART 5
Seeing the Real World

SAGE Publications

Published three times a year by
SAGE Publications
London, Newbury Park, Beverly Hills, New Delhi
under the auspices of the International Sociological Association/ISA.
Subscription and advertising details available from
SAGE Publications Ltd, 28 Banner Street, London EC1Y 8QE, UK.
Institutions £47/$70.50; Individuals £22/$33
Second class postage paid at Westwood, NJ 07675.
Air freight and mailing in the USA by PSCA, 40 Carver Avenue,
Westwood, NJ 07675.

ISSN 0011-3921
Printed by J.W. Arrowsmith Ltd, Bristol, UK

Current Sociology is regularly listed in *Current Contents* and abstracted in *Sociological Abstracts*.

Volume 35 Number 3 Winter 1987

Street Foods: Testing Assumptions about Informal Sector Activity by Women and Men

Irene Tinker

PART 1
Introduction

PART 2
Invisible Workers

PART 3
Invisible Entrepreneurs

PART 4
Street Foods

PART 5
Seeing the Real World

Contents

STREET FOODS: TESTING ASSUMPTIONS ABOUT INFORMAL SECTOR ACTIVITY BY WOMEN AND MEN

Irene Tinker

Preface, v
About the Author, viii

PART 1
INTRODUCTION, 1

PART 2
INVISIBLE WORKERS, 5
Theoretical Assumptions, 5
Cultural Assumptions, 7
Collecting Statistics on Women's Work, 9
Conclusion, 17

PART 3
INVISIBLE ENTREPRENEURS, 18
Women Market Traders, 19
Informal Sector, 27
Donor Agencies and Microenterprise, 38
Conclusion, 50

PART 4
STREET FOODS, 51
EPOC's Street Foods Project, 52
Issues, 62

PART 5
SEEING THE REAL WORLD, 69
Linkages, 69
Environmental Issues, 70
Values and Motivations, 71
Conclusion, 72

Résumé, 75

Bibliography, 81

Preface

In our complex world there is need to concentrate on a few questions at a time; there is also the temptation to dig ever deeper into limited issues and forget the broader scene. In this monograph I have taken pieces of research from a wide range of disciplines in order to create the world of the street food vendor. As a political scientist I am therefore particularly grateful to the International Sociological Association for publishing this work. Obviously, if we are to understand reality we must be open to ideas from many perspectives; we must particularly avoid distorting what we see by the theories and assumptions which guide our research.

Because women had been rendered invisible by the economic development community as a result of stereotypes which blinded these planners to the reality of women's economic activities, the women in development movement came into being. Our goal has been, first, to fill in the gaps left in a description of economic life that leaves out half the human race. Secondly, we wish to use these data to alter, enhance or otherwise change development programming so that the benefits of donor assistance reach women as well as men.

This was the motivation behind the Street Foods project. In the face of negative evaluations of many well intended income-generated projects for poor women, the question was asked: what are poor women doing now to earn an income? Hence a look at street food vendors, but not women alone. We did not wish to commit the same crime of leaving out the other half of humanity. Thus street foods is a study of a sector, of who does what to make and sell foods on the streets of seven provincial towns in Asia and Africa. Similar projects in Latin America are in progress.

The study was conceived by the Equity Policy Center, a non-profit research and policy group which I set up in 1977. Funding for the first round of studies in the Philippines, Indonesia, Bangladesh and Senegal came from the Office of Women in Development at the US Agency for International Development. Many people throughout the agency, both in Washington and in the field, helped move the project from idea to completion, and I cannot possibly thank them all. However, Paula Goddard, as acting director of the WID office during negotiations, gave the project her time and advice, without which the project might never have been funded. As project officer, Jean

Ellickson brought with her a detailed knowledge of Bangladesh; John Hourihan inherited the project and ably supported it.

The second round of studies was supported by the Ford Foundation with grants directly to our collaborators in Nigeria, Egypt and Thailand. My thanks go particularly to Tom Kessinger and Ann Sutoro of the Jakarta office, John Gerhart in Cairo, Deborah Prindle in Lagos, and Kathleen McKee in New York.

A third round of studies, which have been stimulated by our findings and our design, are being undertaken by centres in Jamaica, Peru and India. It is our hope that this monograph will encourage additional work in this field; we would be pleased to send more detailed research designs to those interested. We would be grateful for copies of research findings relating to street food sellers, whatever the design or objectives.

At EPOC, many interns as well as staff worked on the project from its inception in September 1981. Pamela Hunte prepared an annotated review of the literature which laid the groundwork for this monograph. EPOC country directors conducted their pathbreaking research with the assistance of local staff: Jill Posner in Ziguinchor, Senegal; Naomi Owens in Manikganj, Bangladesh; Barbara Chapman in Bogor, Indonesia; and Gerald Barth with his wife Mei-Jean Kuo in Iloilo, the Philippines. Monique Cohen joined EPOC as project director in 1983 and produced a series of significant reports and papers based on the four country studies.

Our collaborators for the second round of studies took our basic research design and added questions of particular local significance. Olufemi Kujore and Tola Pearce, professors at the University of Ife, recently renamed the Obafemi Awolowo University, were concerned with food safety and nutrition. Sarah Loza, director of a group of Egyptian scholars called SPAAC (Social Planning, Analysis and Administration Consultants), wishing to promote a continuing interest in assisting street food sellers, linked the study both with the local administration and Minia University. Amara Pongsapich as deputy director of CUSRI (Chulalongkorn University Social Research Institute) provided oversight to the local staff which was led by Napat Sirisambhand. EPOC consultants assisted our collaborators: Lillian Trager in Ile-Ife, Nigeria; and Cristina Szanton in Chonburi, Thailand.

The idea of writing a Trend Report came from a French colleague, Andrée Michel. Jim Beckford, editor of *Current Sociology*, encouraged the idea. They both have my heartfelt thanks. Above all, and last only because it is difficult to know how to convey the depth of my appreciation for all his support, criticism and companionship throughout this project, I must thank my colleague and husband, Millidge Walker.

About the Author

Irene Tinker, holds an AB magna cum laude from Harvard University and a doctorate from the London School of Economics; to gather material for her thesis on India, she drove there through the Middle East and returned to London by car from Mombasa. She has taught at the University of California/Berkeley, Howard University, and the University of the District of Columbia. Currently, she is a visiting professor in the School of International Service of the American University in Washington, DC.

In 1978 she founded the Equity Policy Center to promote development policies and programmes which involve and benefit poor women and men. Previously she was the first director of the International Office of the American Association for the Advancement of Science and was Assistant Director of ACTION for policy and planning over such voluntary programmes as Peace Corps and VISTA. An activist as well as scholar, she also founded the International Center for Research on Women and co-founded the Wellesley Center for Research on Women. She was the US representative on the Board of the UN International Research and Training Institute for the Advancement of Women.

Her published works include articles and books which range from government in India and Indonesia to women's lobby groups in Washington. Recent work focuses on such development issues as microenterprise, energy, appropriate technology, population, and education.

The Equity Policy Center is at 4818 Drummond Avenue, Chevy Chase, MD 20815, USA.

PART 1
Introduction

Street foods are ubiquitous on urban streets. Yet, like most economic activity outside the modern sector, street food vending has until recently been attacked as exploitative, or dismissed as traditional, by economic development theorists. According to these various paradigms, vending would disappear in the future society. Municipal authorities also consider vendors, who clog downtown areas with their unsightly and unsanitary stalls, as reminders of underdevelopment. No wonder such officials have frequently decided to hurry history along by conducting periodic raids to clear the streets.

Given these negative assumptions, development planners have tended to categorize street vending as transitional and peripheral. Municipal authorities often declare vendors illegal. As a result, questions on their numbers or activities were simply not included in national censuses or collected for labour force participation surveys. Without data, planners have simply ignored the economic importance of street foods and similar activities of the urban informal sector, both as employment for the growing workforce and as supplier of critical urban services.

Inaccurate or incomplete data on the economic activities of women and men in rural areas of the developing world have also misled planners and contributed to the failure of many development projects. Debates over what constitutes 'work' have grown in intensity as statistics become the basis not only of plans but of regulations and taxes. Not only is work in agriculture counted differently in different countries, but home production and its marketing are seldom considered work. Such undercounting renders most women in rural areas invisible as workers. This realization, and the resultant dismissal of women as economic actors by development planners, fostered the creation and growth of the women in development community in the early 1970s (Tinker, 1983).

In response, a growing number of women in development scholars began first to document the actual work which women do in near-subsistence economies to support their families, and then to attack statistical definitions which excluded women's work. Data show not only that women work more hours per day than men, but that development has frequently increased their workload while lessening their access to resources of the family or community. Studies also underscore how essential women's income is to poor landless families.

As interest in urban informal sector activities begins to grow among both scholars and practitioners of the development community, it is essential that new data do not once again ignore or diminish the role of women. For this reason, in 1980, the Equity Policy Center, a non-profit research and policy group in Washington, DC, initiated a multi-country study of Street Foods to identify who makes, sells and eats prepared food on the streets of provincial towns. Results of this study establish both the importance of the sector to urban employment and services and the significant role which women play in the sector. Further, the study underscores the importance of urban–rural linkages in supplying the vendors, and suggests that street foods are a growing rural phenomenon. There is also evidence that 'invisible street foods' — meals prepared on contract — may be of even greater importance for income and food to urban dwellers. Finally, the statistical and definitional debates which began with reference to the rural area have equal application in urban areas.

Data from the Street Foods project build upon findings from a growing number of urban employment studies and projects which have begun to question the theoretical descriptions of the informal sector. Early studies tended to focus on small manufacturing and to emphasize the interrelationships between the informal and formal sectors. Underlying the conclusions in most such studies are implicit assumptions about the nature of management and the desirability of growth. Because studies were based on enterprises, consideration was seldom given to unpaid work done by household members. This methodology, and the selection of manufacturing as a focus, have tended to underestimate the participation of women in the informal sector. Alternatively, studies were done solely on women, such as market women or domestic workers, without collecting comparable data on men pursuing the same occupation.

Support for micro-level income activities became a focus for donor agencies in the mid-1970s as development programming turned from capital-intensive infrastructure and manufacturing emphases towards the provision of basic human needs. Poverty was perceived as the underlying problem affecting improved health, education or production. Programmes were designed to provide credit, training in book-keeping and accounting and other services, usually through a group or co-operative. Assumptions about incentives, group dynamics, growth and products permeate such planning. Particularly inflexible seemed to be the assumptions tying women to the production of sewn articles and handicrafts.

Evaluations of these various new income-generating activities have questioned their effectiveness. It seemed useful to gather data on actual income activities of the poor, and to use such information to inform new activities. EPOC designed the Street Foods project in order to gather data on a specific economic activity within the informal sector in order to discover the division of labour, if any, within the household with regard to the various tasks of buying, processing and cooking the foods sold; the amount, distribution and use of income so derived; and the importance of street foods in the diet of the customers. The resulting data challenge many of the assumptions identified above, and also indicate where more research is clearly needed.

Policy recommendations arising from this project call upon governments to recognize and support street food sellers, not disparage and harass them. Indeed, what is called for is a policy shift as significant as that which took place over the past decade with regard to slum dwellers. Such settlements were seen in the 1950s and 1960s as a temporary blight on the urban scene, one best removed by military or police effort. Today there are many schemes for slum upgrading and for the provision of sites and services for low-cost, self-built homes. Planners and administrators have faced the reality of urban housing; they must now do the same with regard to the urban informal sector.

The reality of street foods in face of its theoretic demise illustrates the dangers of imposing theoretical constructs on data rather than using data to refine or challenge the theory. The purpose of this monograph is, first, to utilize the data from the street foods study and other micro-level research to question current theoretical assumptions about the informal sector in general and about women's economic participation in particular. Secondly, the monograph will indicate how these theoretical insights, in turn, challenge assumptions made by development planners and so affect the design of development programmes and projects, particularly those relating to women's economic activities, micro-enterprises, and urban–rural linkages.

The monograph, following this introduction, consists of four sections and a bibliography. The first section on *Invisible Workers* reviews the evolutionary concepts of work in classic theories of development; relates these concepts to current statistical methods which have produced a skewed picture of economic activities of women and men in subsistence and informal sectors in both rural and urban areas; and reviews recent literature which establishes a data base on women's work in rural areas and thus reduces the invisibility of women's economic contributions to family and nation.

The second section on *Invisible Entrepreneurs* turns to the debate on the informal sector and further explores the reasons why the various economic activities now lumped under the indistinct term informal sector have for so long been left out of national accounts. This discussion draws on both the theoretical and substantive arguments as to the definition and importance of the sector. Two types of entrepreneurial activity where women predominate, as market traders and as home-based workers, are set within the wider debate. The growing interest of donor agencies and voluntary organizations in microenterprise resulted in another data source which is also reviewed. Their recommendations for ways of assisting the microentrepreneur are reviewed and analysed.

The pathbreaking Street Foods project, which looked at who makes, sells and eats foods sold on the street, is presented in the third section. For the first time, both the supply and demand of a single commodity offered in the informal sector has been studied in depth in order to ascertain both the magnitude of the sector and its importance to urban functioning. Concepts and methodology are briefly reviewed, and the seven country studies described. Much significant data are summarized which discuss the characteristics of vendors, the amount of family labour, income and its use, consumption patterns and governmental attitudes. Recommended interventions which might improve income or enhance the food are also presented.

The final section considers how findings from the Street Foods project challenge or support issues concerning the informal sector. The discussion then turns to the impact of these new data on development planning in order to show not only the relationship of theory to practice but how practice can inform theory. The necessity of disaggregating data by sex is underscored; only by looking at the actual work and lives of the poor can the design of development assistance programmes improve. But figures alone do not explain the feminization of poverty; new research is needed into the power relationship within the family. Overall, the monograph concludes that current theories seem unable to absorb new research; the challenge is to construct a new theory that more accurately reflects reality.

PART 2
Invisible Workers

The invisibility of male and female street food sellers in national accounts and development planning illustrates the inadequacies of much available statistical data on employment. Problems with these data only begin with their various definitions of *work*: how data are collected, by whom, from whom and when also influence answers. Underlying this issue are theoretical and cultural assumptions which affect not only what is studied, but what questions are asked and whether obviously incorrect answers are accepted. But while theoretical assumptions influence whether categories of economic activities are considered work, cultural assumptions about women's activities prejudice not only the inclusion of domestic activity as work, but the counting of unpaid productive work when done by women.

THEORETICAL ASSUMPTIONS

While theories are useful to organize and analyse disparate data, they also establish priorities and assign values to what is observed, and in this way mould and interpret reality. The recognition of the influence of *themata* in the history of physical science has permitted the revaluing of earlier scientific 'truths' (Holton, 1973). Similarly, economic theories may simultaneously illumine forces and motives; they may also obfuscate reality from other points of view.

Economists of both the liberal and Marxist perspectives have, by their definition of work, influenced both government policies and scholarly research for the past 50 years. During the great depression of the 1930s, governments began to collect statistics on who was employed or unemployed, in order to fashion recovery programmes. Work was defined as remunerated labour, in cash or in kind, which therefore adds to the national accounts. In this manner, housework and most subsistence activities were implicitly classified as non-productive because they were assumed to be for household consumption only (Beneria, 1982; Dixon-Mueller, 1985).

The International Labour Organization has gradually broadened the definition of work through a series of conferences. By 1982, the definition of economic activity included 'all production and processing of primary products, whether for the market, for barter, or for own consumption' (as quoted in Dixon-Mueller, 1985: 92).

When economists turned to development issues after World War II they were preoccupied with growth. Both neo-classical and neo-Marxist economists accept a progression of historic forms of world economy which lead inexorably from one to another. Their mutual focus on the modern/capitalist stage of economic development led them to dismiss, and often disparage, activities or modes of production associated with lower stages of development which were, in due course, expected to disappear.

According to liberal development theory, less developed countries will move from traditional systems through transitional to modern, as capital and technology are poured into their economies, enabling them to take off (Rostow, 1960). Traditional subsistence economies are obsolete, and in most places are already in transition to a monetized economy within which workers produce specialized crops and implements, selling their products in the market and buying for their own needs. Since the subsistence sector will gradually disappear as countries modernize, there is no point in collecting statistics on such activities other than agriculture, since they are deemed of marginal economic importance. By such definitions survival activities such as collecting firewood, fetching water or processing food are not considered work because they do not add to the national product.

Such theorists further argue that agricultural systems in subsistence societies are inefficient since lands are not cultivated full-time. Rural areas, therefore, hold a surplus of labour available to work in the new industries which the development planners propose to build (Lewis, J. and Kallab, 1986). Emphasis for planners should be on providing sufficient jobs in the modern urban sector for all workers. More recently the idea of agricultural-led growth has attracted support; both agriculture and rural industry are to expand and modernize, creating new employment in rural areas (Mellor, 1986).

Little is said in modernization theory about women, except to deplore the fact that women often mistakenly cling to outmoded traditional values. Rather, these theorists expected women to welcome the modernization process. The move away from subsistence or peasant agriculture would reduce the drudgery of their lives while the move towards modern egalitarian democratic societies would free them from authoritarian patriarchal family dominance (Jaquette, 1982).

For Marxists, too, peasant agriculture and household production are elements of non-wage labour in pre-capitalist systems which will be transformed into wage labour as the world capitalist system increases its power. The persistence of pre-capitalist modes of production in capitalist societies has more recently led to the recognition that such a transitional stage may be of long duration, and needs to be analysed in terms of the different stages of articulation between non-capitalist and capitalist modes of production (Simon and Ruccio, 1986; Long, 1984). Unlike liberal theory, the household production is recognized as an essential part of the reproduction of the labour force. But since such product is used, not exchanged, surplus is not created and so no accumulation occurs, and no growth (Hyden, 1980).

Because neither major development theory considered non-capitalist activities worth studying, both scholars and planners tended to focus on where a society was going, not where it was coming from. One did not study firewood, one studied rural electrification; one did not study subsistence agriculture or home-based production, one studied industrialization. As a result there was relatively little research before the 1970s in non-modern sector activities of either men or women. Definitions of productive work were reinforced by cultural assumptions, unchallenged by data.

CULTURAL ASSUMPTIONS

Subsistence requires a variety of activities for survival, of which production is only one. Men and women divide these activities in different societies in different ways (Benedict, 1934; Mead, 1955). Economic development has been identified with shifts in this sexual division of labour (Boserup, 1970; Illich, 1982), an issue further explored in the following section.

Historians note the parallel growth of private property and the seclusion of women (Sullerot, 1971; Boulding, 1976). Such restrictions on the mobility of women naturally reduced, though they did not stop, their market activities: children could be sent out to sell cooked food; neighbours could come to buy crafts (Simmons, 1975). Such activity is culturally invisible, though, because status accrues to families wealthy enough so that their women do not need to work (Abdullah and Zeidenstein, 1979). But it is work in the field that is particularly visible and so is reduced whenever possible. Time-use statistics collected by class in Bangladesh clearly show this trend of subsistence farmers reducing women's work as their income rises; it also shows that very poor women work the least, presumably because they cannot find employment and have little food to process or cook (Farouk, 1980; Tinker and Raynolds, 1982). It is these poverty-stricken women who compete for the road construction jobs provided through the Food-for-Work programmes (Marum, 1981); even traditional Islam accepts public work for women when it is necessary for survival.

That there is status attached to leisure is confirmed in an international comparison of time-budget studies which look at market activities, household work/home production, and leisure/sleep in developing, developed and planned economies (Evenson, 1983). Both men and women in developing countries have more leisure than men and women in the other economies, though men have considerably more leisure than women. However, only in developed economies do women have more leisure than men, a fact being rapidly eroded in the United States where some 40 percent of all women are now in the labour force, and where surveys show that husbands of working wives contribute only about 1 hour more of work to the household than husbands of non-working wives.

Liberal economic development theory grew out of the post-World War II experiences with the reconstruction of Europe. While women had had to take over many industrial and service jobs during the war years, economic and political leaders in Europe and North America assumed that women would return to the household as soldiers came home. Such middle-class male assumptions of the domestic role of women permeate development theory, which was in turn taught to the current leaders of many developing countries. Reality among the poor remained backward, traditional; the future would be an urban middle-class society where women did not work outside the household.

In planned economies, women are expected to do market work as much as men, but continue to handle the bulk of the household work. The result is that women in these societies have the least leisure of men or women in any other society (Evenson, 1983). At least their work is recognized as such, unlike that done by poor women in developing countries whose work is dismissed as trivial and is therefore uncounted in census figures.

In sum, it is clear that the exclusionary definition of work in the post-World War II era, as statistical collection expanded rapidly, greatly influenced what types of economic activity were studied. These studies in turn reinforced those assumptions on which they were based: that work outside the modern sector was peripheral and that women, on the whole, did not work.

COLLECTING STATISTICS ON WOMEN'S WORK

Given these theoretical and cultural assumptions about the definition of work outside the modern formal sector where most women function, it is not surprising that most of the early writing by women in development scholars focused on documenting women's actual economic activities (Tinker and Bo Bramsen, 1976; Wellesley, 1977; Jahan and Papenek, 1979; Dauber and Cain, 1979; Lewis, B., 1981). The women's movement and the UN Decade for Women legitimized the study of women for the first time, and a plethora of theses and dissertations by anthropologists and demographers added depth to the growing literature produced by evaluations of development projects and planning priorities.

The three world conferences which marked the UN Decade for Women: the 1975 UN World Conference for International Women's Year in Mexico City, the 1980 World Conference for the Decade of Women in Copenhagen, and the 1985 UN World Conference to Review and Appraise the Achievements of the United Nations Decade for Women in Nairobi, required country reports documenting basic facts about women's lives: health, education and employment. While such data are compiled for conference use, the secretariat also issues reports which utilize these data and combine them with other information available within and outside the United Nations system. For example, the background document issued by the secretariat for the Nairobi conference, entitled *World Survey on the Role of Women in Development*, goes beyond the earlier discussions on women in agriculture or employed by multinationals, to examine women in money and finance, trade, science and technology, and energy conservation (UN, 1984d). Unfortunately many such significant preparatory studies and surveys, both those published by the conference secretariat and those undertaken by UN specialized agencies, are not widely distributed. For example, among the important UN studies published as part of the preparations for Copenhagen were an evaluation of UN development programmes for rural women (UNDP, 1980) and a review of UN studies on women

(UN/BAW, 1980); and for Nairobi were studies of women in food production (FAO, 1984), and in the labour force (ILO, 1985a, b); and an evaluation of how the specialized agencies are integrating women (UNDP, 1985).

In addition to official documents, the interest spawned by the conferences encouraged non-governmental organizations to sponsor seminars preceding the official events in order to emphasize topics thought to be insufficiently explored in official documentation: on development for Mexico (Tinker and Bo Bramsen, 1976); on women's health for Copenhagen (Blair, 1980); and on third world perspectives (DAWN, 1985) and law for Nairobi (Schuler, 1986). In addition, panels, debates and discussions about women's condition worldwide were scheduled at the non-governmental meetings which ran parallel to the official governmental conferences, and encouraged more substantive interchange than the highly political world meetings. Reports of events at these dual conferences reflect both their substantive and their political nature (Tinker, 1981a; O'Barr et al., 1986; Tinker and Jaquette 1987).

Independently funded statistical studies and reports have provided a cross-checking of government data. The results are much-improved statistical data (ILO, 1985a; INSTRAW, 1985; Seagar and Olson, 1986; Sivard, 1985; US Bureau of the Census, 1985) and enhanced discussion of how to compile social indicators on women (UN, 1984a, b, c).

Changes in the priorities for the collecting of statistical data on work have progressed over the decade in a manner which parallels the changing emphases on women among development scholars and activists. Throughout the period, the primary concern has been on women's economic activities. Early development programmes, if they included women at all, saw women solely in their role as mothers: maternal and child health programmes or family planning programmes (Germain, 1976/77). The assumption has been that if women are proved to be valuable contributors to the gross national product, then development programmes will be designed to reach, include and benefit them as well as men (Jahan and Papanek, 1979; Charlton, 1984). Thus the gathering of statistics on women's work became a major preoccupation of women concerned with international development.

During the decade, the focus was first on women in near-subsistence societies, beginning with an analysis of the time which they spent in market — especially agricultural — and domestic survival activities. A more theoretical approach was to consider division of labour within rural households. Recognition of the feminization of poverty led to a concern for stimulating income-generating activities; efforts by donor agencies to set up such activities spawned investigations into small and micro-enterprise. Each of these areas of interest will be briefly reviewed in order to set the study of street foods in the progression of women in development studies.

Economic Activities of Rural Women

Since the bulk of the population in the developing countries live in rural areas where they support themselves as subsistence farmers or agricultural labourers, the first effort was to describe the lives of rural women around the world (Zeidenstein, 1979). Many early studies were funded by population agencies to help them understand why rural women were not adopting contraceptives. As the extent of women's work became evident, the economic value of children in societies with minimal investment in their training also became obvious (Reining, 1977).

Time-use studies, compiled in a wide variety of countries (White, 1976; McSweeney, 1979; Birdsall, 1980; Hart, 1980; Acharya and Bennett, 1981; FAO, 1983; Kumar, 1984), document women's long work-day in near-subsistence societies: market and domestic production account for between 10 and 12 hours for adult women compared to between 6 and 8 hours for adult men (Tinker, 1984). Data collected by observation allow the observer to utilize her own categories when classifying observed activities, and then to test out these categories with the respondents and so avoid problems of definition and cultural obfuscation; but this is time-consuming. Further, the researchers themselves alter the situation in some respects by intruding themselves in the lives of the respondents. On the other hand, survey techniques rely on the understanding and truthfulness of the respondent, while assuming that questioner and respondent share the same value system; one-time surveys also lack means for verification of replies. Anecdotes recount how a husband will reply that his wife does not work even though she is at that moment weeding the farm; or how a fifteen-year-old boy will be listed as head of household even though his mother earns the total family income.

Both methodological perspectives and empirical results are presented in an important collection of Rural Household Studies in Asia (Binswanger et al., 1980). The comparative use and advantages of observation, recall and surveys have been widely discussed, and combinations of them tested (Jain et al., 1979b; Zeidenstein, 1979; Anker, 1980; Acharya and Bennett, 1981; Miralao, 1982; Dixon-Mueller, 1985). Concern about how much time such studies consume in the lives of poor women has led to exploration of participatory research where respondents design studies and collect data, and then are remunerated or rewarded for their time either individually or collectively (Islam, 1982; Cecelski, 1984; Dasgupta and Maiti, 1986).

Data sets on time use are usually divided into productive or market work and family maintenance or survival activities. Yet even productive work in agriculture, which typically includes planting, weeding, harvesting and caring for livestock, often disappears in farm and population censuses (Dixon, 1982). Dixon-Mueller thoroughly analyses the reasons why women continue to be undernumerated as agricultural labourers, which primarily revolve around the confusion over unpaid family work; she compares different approaches to data collection and shows the disparities among various survey results (1985).

The female farming systems of Africa have been studied in depth by anthropologists (Guyer, 1978; Pala-Okeyo, 1980; Henn, 1986) and sociologists (Tadessa, 1982; Fortmann, 1985; Blumberg, 1986). Data have convinced major donor agencies that since women in sub-Saharan Africa grow some 80 percent of the food, and provide about half all agricultural labour in the region, they must figure in programmes designed to increase agricultural productivity (Dey, 1984; Palmer, 1985; Burfisher and Horenstein, 1985; Muzaale and Leonard, 1985; FAO, 1986).

Research on the agricultural activities of women in Asia indicates not only their continuing importance as unpaid family labour, but their growing employment as paid agricultural labour (Agarwal, 1984; Kandiyoti, 1985). Anthropologists have also documented the criticality of women's income to support poor households (Stoler, 1977; Mencher, 1987). Despite regional variations it is estimated that between 40 and 45 percent of agricultural labour is done by women (FAO, 1986).

In Latin America, FAO statistics show a lower agricultural participation rate, at less than 20 percent, than elsewhere in the world; in contrast the Caribbean participation is recorded as the highest at 54 percent (FAO, 1986). Social scientists continue to question these data, as they point out the importance of women's work in the agricultural sector which suggests a much higher participation rate (Deere and

Leon de Leal, 1980; Jaquette, 1983; Spindel et al., 1984; Flora, 1985; Wilson, 1985).

After 10 years of research into women's productive activities in agriculture, most development agencies accept the fact of women's agricultural work, although the implications of women's roles to project design are not always apparent to planners (Ahmad, 1984; Monson and Kalb, 1985). However, farm work seldom accounts for even half the long day of female subsistence farmers. A second major task of women is to prepare food crops first for storage and later for eating. They build storage huts for cereals and legumes; then carry the crops from the fields to the huts or home. They spend long hours threshing, winnowing and pounding grain, or equally long hours fermenting, shredding and drying cassava or preparing yams and tapioca for cooking. Yet these time-consuming activities are almost never included in labour force statistics, despite the fact that the recent changes in the ILO definitions for recording labour force participation would include all such processing of primary products whether or not they would be consumed at home.

In addition to food storage, processing and preparation, women are generally responsible for providing the fuel and water necessary for cooking the food (FAO, 1979). Depending on the geography, climate, environment and population density, these essential survival tasks take from 1 to 6 or even more hours per day (Cecelski, 1984; Dixon-Mueller, 1985). As pasture lands are taken over for food crops, women must also scavenge for fodder to feed their animals. A recent study in three villages in Uttar Pradesh, India, indicates that women spend 2.5 times as much human energy collecting fuel and fodder as they spend on agricultural production (Agarwal, 1984). Time is clearly a major constraint for poor rural women (Tinker, 1984) and must be considered if agricultural production is to be increased; examples of studies supporting these data include South and Southeast Asia (Reddy, 1980; Islam et al., 1984), Korea (Tinker and Cho, 1981), China (Croll, 1982), Peru (Alcantara et al., 1985), Senegal (Sow, 1986), and Ghana (Ardayfia, 1986).

The provision of processed fuel and water are of themselves considered productive activities in modern societies since they are provided by the commercial sector. As urban centres of the developing countries are integrated into the world economy they increasingly use so-called commercial fuels: fossil fuels and electricity. However, the drastic rise in prices of these fuels as a result of the oil crisis of 1973 has reversed this trend. The growing shortage of firewood in urban areas has led to a rapid increase in the commercialization of both wood and charcoal in Asia (Alam et al., 1985), Africa (Burne, 1985) and Latin America (Evans, 1984). While much of this new activity involves long-distance transport and is in the hands of men, short-distance head-carrying of twigs and branches is typically a women's job and an important source of income for the urban poor (Sebstad, 1982). Even in rural areas, firewood and charcoal are sold in increasing amounts (Kumar, 1984). Water is generally a free good in rural areas whether the end-use is human consumption or irrigation; but in urban areas water is often carried by handcart or over the shoulder into crowded squatter settlements and sold, usually by men.

Given the current methods of data collection of informal sector activities, a point discussed at length below, it is not clear just how much even these market sales of fuel or water are recorded statistically. Certainly these survival activities when done for household consumption do not become part of national accounts. There are efforts being made, however, to develop methods of giving value to the variety of unpaid domestic work (Goldschmidt-Clermont, 1982). Since the final document of the 1985 UN Conference in Nairobi, *Forward Looking Strategies*, calls for the inclusion of household work in national accounts in paragraph 120, more emphasis both on substance and methodology can be anticipated (UN 1985).

Technology and the Sexual Division of Labour

The sexual division of labour throughout history has been the focus for many studies of the changing roles of women. Ester Boserup analysed the impact of technology on women's agricultural activities; because technology has tended to go to men, the advent of the plough caused the shift from the slash-and-burn female farming system to a sedentary male farming system (Boserup, 1970). This pattern of supplying technology to men has continued as development programmes institute new methods and machinery (Tinker, 1981b). Too often such new technologies undercut women's traditional income activities such as making beer, puffed rice, or pottery for sale or pounding rice for a part of the product, and so rob them of income-producing activities (Dauber and Cain, 1979; Scott and Carr, 1985).

At the same time, new agricultural technologies have tended to increase women's work: larger fields or more fertilizers can increase the amount of time women must spend weeding; new cash crops are often grown on the closest and best soils, requiring women to walk further to the fields where they grow food (Henn, 1986). In comparing the impact of technological change in agriculture on women of various classes in Asia and Africa, Bina Agarwal finds that while women are less well-off than the men of their culture and class, there is a marked contrast between the two continents: in Asia the impact on women is in the same direction as that on men, in Africa men of a household might be better off while women of the same household would be worse off (Agarwal, 1984).

In poor households, women work on neighbours' fields as agricultural labourers. Elsewhere, men migrate to find employment, leaving the woman with all the agricultural tasks. As women begin to take on economic activities that historically have been done by men, men do not take over any of women's work. Ivan Illich (1982) calls this the move from the *reign of vernacular gender* to the *regime of economic sex*, whereby women move from a relatively egalitarian division of labour to a vastly unfair and exploitative one.

Poverty and Women

The lack of statistical evidence of women's economic activities, then, has led to a worsening of their lives as technologies meant to increase the productivity of subsistence households have had a negative impact on women in those households. The uneven distribution of rewards within the household had led to a theoretical discussion on the persistence of patriarchy (Rosaldo and Lamphere, 1974; Kandiyoti, 1985). Control and distribution of income within the family is the subject of several recent conferences and publications (Guyer, 1980; Ben-Porath, 1982; Bruce, 1987). Recognition that various family members within the household may have different needs or priorities has led to a debate over the nature of the household and whether it is co-operative, conflictual or authoritarian (Sen, 1983). The idea of pooling income which is a basis of the new household economics (Ben-Porath, 1982) is widely challenged, especially among Africanists where the question is whether the household is even a unit; they speak of 'hearth-holds' within the polygamous family (Guyer and Peters, 1984).

If women within households have benefited less than men in those households, women-headed households have seldom benefited at all. These households include widows, divorced and deserted women and the never-married. Because women in the last two categories often dissemble, women-headed households are undercounted (Yousef and Hetler, 1984). Recent data reflect this family disorganization; countries reporting over 30 percent of women household heads are Botswana with 45 percent and Jamaica with 33.8 percent. Other countries with over 20 percent women-headed households include: Malawi, Sudan, Ghana, Rwanda, El Salvador, Panama, Peru, Guyana, Venezuela and Hong Kong (US Bureau of the Census, 1985).

Throughout the world, women-headed households are the most poor; as the estimates of their numbers grow to over one-third worldwide, there is a growing concern about this feminization of poverty (Tinker and Bo Bramsen, 1976; Buvinic et al., 1983). As noted above, women in poor households are also increasingly poor, and often lack access to family income, not only for themselves, but to provide food for their families (Palmer, 1985). It became increasingly obvious to the development community that poor women needed money to survive, and that income of the woman was more likely to benefit the family than income of the man (Guyer, 1980; Bruce, 1987). Further, as a result of the UN Decade for Women (Tinker and Jaquette, 1987) there was growing pressure on donor agencies to fund women's projects.

The result was a spate of 'income-generating' projects for women throughout the world. At first most such projects were replicas of welfare-oriented efforts sponsored by elite women's organizations and church groups to assist poor women. Given the middle-class outlook of such groups, it is not surprising that these early efforts to provide income for women focused on sewing and crocheting. Too often these efforts provided pin-money, not income; they were seldom economically viable without the support of the sponsoring organization to provide raw materials and/or to buy the finished product. Teaching lace-making to Christian converts in India increased their income, but at the same time it undermined the traditional sexual division of labour by making them the primary household earners while turning their husbands from productive work (Mies, 1982). Subsequent disenchantment with these types of income-generating activities spurred both evaluations of such projects and research into actual income activities which poor women engaged in on their own.

CONCLUSION

This section has presented the reasons for the statistical invisibility of women in economic activity which has resulted in their increasing impoverishment in modernizing countries. The efforts of women in development scholars to document women's work in agriculture, and to argue for considering domestic production as economic activity, have been reviewed. Such efforts were primarily aimed at changing the way statistical data were used to record women's work in order to influence development programmes and priorities by requiring that consideration be given to the differential impact which development has on women and men. However, as the criticality of women's income to family survival became evident, women scholars and development practitioners increasingly focused on ways to provide income directly to women.

PART 3
Invisible Entrepreneurs

Traditional entrepreneurs have tended to be as invisible to labour statistics as have been subsistence workers. Development theories assumed that all these activities would be recast into large-scale specialized commercial enterprises. For years it was left to anthropologists to study traditional markets or to document home production in either rural or urban areas as part of the quaint but disappearing culture.

Economists began to look more closely at these activities only when it became painfully obvious that modern sector employment could not begin to employ the rapidly increasing labour force in developing countries. Development economics has assumed since its inception that there is a direction of change from traditional through transitional to modern. Since the discipline of economics has focused its inquiry on the workings of the formal sector, little attention was paid to economic activities which seemed destined to extinction. Nor was there much question in their minds that the broad principles of economics were universal.

This view had been questioned early in the century by economists writing on colonialism in Southeast Asia, who questioned the direct applicability of western economic principles to these plural societies due to different views concerning the values and motivations of the distinct and self-contained groups which made up these plural societies (Furnivall, 1939). Writing about 'pretake-off' Indonesia, anthropologist Geertz recognized the interplay of culture and economics in the move of the bazaar economy towards more sustained growth, and argued against assuming a uniformity of economic transformation. He writes that the 'total, system-wide conception of change involved in this sort of analysis is implicit in the dichotomous typological terms it seems inevitably to invoke: *gemeinschaft* vs. *gesellschaft*; tradition vs. modern, folk vs. urban' (Geertz, 1963: 144).

Yet it was once more a dichotomous typology that was introduced by the ILO in the early 1970s as it began an ambitious research programme into the informal sector (ILO, 1972). In the ensuing decade the use of this terminology has plagued the discussion and muddied the debate (Richardson, 1984; Moser, 1984); in the meantime, the concept of formal vs. informal sectors has been so ingrained into the literature that its use cannot be ignored.

The controversy concerning informal sector activity arises only as contemporary scholars try to fit it into preconceived theories of economics and of development, or include such data into national accounts. In this respect the documentation of urban and rural microenterprise runs into the same obstacles as did subsistence and farm activity described in the previous section. Here, too, the sexual division of labour has broken down sufficiently to allow women to engage in male activities; but men do not usually assist in housework or child-care responsibilities. As a result, women's occupational choices are more constrained than men's, a fundamental truth which escapes the economists' value system and causes many women to make 'irrational' choices according to the economic law of self-interest.

Over the past decade three different strands of inquiry have contributed to our knowledge of microentrepreneurs in developing countries: studies of women market traders, the debate over defining the urban informal sector, and empirical data collected for donor agencies wishing to assist small and micro enterprises. Too often, studies from one strand do not inform the others. This has been particularly true of the studies, usually by women, of women market traders. To underscore the interrelatedness of these data and their importance to the Street Foods project, I will briefly review significant findings and debates within these three substantive areas, contrasting their objectives and methods.

WOMEN MARKET TRADERS

The existence of women traders was noted in early missionary diaries of West Africa: 'Not less than a hundred of the King of Katunga's ladies . . . arrived here lately with loads of trona and country cloth, which they barter for salt, and various articles of European manufacture, particularly beads' (Richard and John Lander in 1833, as quoted in Sudarkasa, 1973: 35). Anthropologists were intrigued, and began documenting their role in the 1920s. Considered unique, these women were studied as an isolated phenomenon, their roles explained by their culture. Not until Ester Boserup (1970) related the existence of market women to female farming systems was the relationship of women traders to agriculture and technology explored;

she saw economic development undermining market women just as it was undermining the independent role of women farmers.

During the 1970s, interest in women in development on the one hand, and in microenterprise in urban and rural settings on the other, broadened the inquiry and engaged not only anthropologists but also economists, demographers, sociologists and political scientists. Their techniques emphasized surveys rather than long-term observation. Over the decade there has been an increasing predilection to design studies which include both micro- and macro-methodologies. This approach sets detailed micro-information into societal context, cross-checking the data sets obtained by different methodologies and so improving our understanding. In this section I will review only those micro-studies which focus on women market traders, leaving the broader studies to the subsequent sections (Anker et al., 1982).

As interest in women's economic activities in developing countries exploded in the early 1970s, increasing attention was paid to studies of the market women of West Africa (Gugler and Flanagan, 1978). Their trading acumen was world-famous; in Ghana and Nigeria they handled over 90 percent of food retailing (Robertson, 1987). Here, for many feminists, were the models for economically independent women (Tinker and Bo Bramsen, 1976). Indeed, a leading male anthropologist was moved to ask:

> Who is more modern, more western, more developed: a barefoot and illiterate Yoruba market woman who daily risks her security and her capital in vigorous individual competition with others like herself; or a Smith College graduate who spends her days ferrying her husband to the Westport railroad station and her children to ballet classes? (Mintz, 1971: 267–8)

Stories of their political influence in pre-colonial Ghana, and in colonial Nigeria and Cameroon, seemed only to confirm their status (Wipper, 1972, 1982; Okonjo, 1983).

Early studies in West Africa presented a cultural system characterized by a clear-cut sexual division of labour. Women's market activity grew out of their right to sell the surplus agricultural goods which they grew. In one instance, among the Yoruba with their urbanized settlement pattern, women had reduced their work on the farms and had for centuries been significant traders of the products their husbands grew (Sudarkasa, 1973). While most women traded locally, there are accounts of long-distance trading by both women and men throughout the region. The advent of colonialism increased the demand for both agricultural produce and goods brought in from

North Africa. Peaceful conditions allowed women traders to move freely throughout the region. But when colonialism created a new market which required literacy and accounting, the women were bypassed. Lebanese traders soon filled this vacuum in much of West Africa, creating a dual market system (White, 1982).

Separate budgets meant that women with few or no children could often accumulate savings which were their own to control. Such women often chose to repay their brideprice and become independent of both husband and father. Further, in some tribes, wealthy women could buy their own brides whose children were considered as belonging to the female-husbands' lineage (Uchendu, 1964). Such data made West African women appear truly equal in the eyes of feminists of the North.

While this cultural right to sell surplus existed among agricultural tribes throughout the continent, the lack of a market rendered such rights less important in East and Southern Africa until the colonial period. British colonial authorities in these areas of white settlement encouraged male migration to mines and cities, while at the same time prohibiting them from bringing wives and families (Hansen, 1987). This artificial household separation created an urban demand for prepared foods and traditional beer, which women continue to supply throughout this region (Nelson, N., 1979; Blumberg, 1981). After World War II the policy changed, and women were allowed into towns; but wages for men were too low to support their households and so most women responded by engaging in trade among Africans only, since it was still not legal for them to provision Europeans (Horn, 1987).

Independent Africa

The fate of market women in post-independent Africa has varied in response to the political and economic policies of the country's rulers. Kwame Nkrumah supported the Ghanaian market women, turning over to the more wealthy women import rights taken from foreigners. More typically, traders within one family group dealt in the same commodity in different markets, accumulating sufficient capital to move up from farm produce and prepared foods 'to higher status commodities like fish, provisions, hardware and eventually textiles' (Greenstreet, 1981: 17). However, subsequent regimes detained a few prominent trading women. Continuing to blame the shortage of foreign exchange on the women's trading activities, the government declared in 1976 that women traders would be restricted to dealing in perishable commodities. Attacks continued to be made against market women by the government, and in 1979 the large Makola market was demolished (Petritsch, 1981; Bay, 1982). Suspicion of traders persists despite the current requirement that all traders register; they are frequently accused of tax-dodging and so not contributing to national development (Greenstreet, 1981).

In Guinea the market women supported Sekou Touré in return for social policies improving women's legal rights and access to education (Little, 1973). Given the poor economic conditions of the country at the time of his death, the market women were not rich enough to prompt reaction. In Nigeria the tradition of market women is so strong that it has carried over into the middle class and become a family strategy. Men in the civil service not only set up their wives in trade, as is traditional, they also invest in the trade and use their contacts to increase its value, often retiring to join their wives in the business (Nwapa, 1981). This involvement of the elite in trading seems to have protected market women from direct attack as in Ghana.

Women in the markets in Abidjan or Dakar have been expanding since independence, particularly in the selling of fish and agricultural produce, and in marketing cloth (Le Cour Grandmaison, 1969; Lewis, 1976). These cloth traders are the most prosperous; continued trade links among the French-speaking countries have encouraged the flow of goods locally and internationally, so that the cloth sold in Abidjan may be batiked in Mali or fashioned in Dakar. Despite the complexity of such trade, most women continued keeping accounts in their heads in their own numeracy systems (Posner, 1983).

Most market women in these countries and elsewhere in Africa have neither such national nor international connections. In Zimbabwe they trade in agricultural produce they grow themselves on urban or periurban plots or buy at wholesale markets specializing in prepared foods and other household goods in order to feed and clothe their families and educate their children (Horn, 1987). Dried or smoked fish is a major trading commodity in Zambia (Jules-Rosette, 1982) as well as along the coast of West Africa. In Senegal, women purchase the catch from men, including their husbands, then dry the fish over fires on the beach (Le Cour Grandmaison, 1969; Vercruijsse, 1983). Networks of trading women move this product deep into the deserts.

Women work because they must, in order to fulfil their traditional responsibilities under a system of separate work and separate budgets, responsibilities that are harder to perform in a cash economy (Huston, 1978; Schuster, 1972). Their numbers have grown as both population and urbanization have increased; today it is estimated that 60 percent of food retailing in sub-Saharan Africa is in the hands of women (Blumberg, 1981).

Unfortunately, the influence of modernization is undercutting the position of women market traders in Africa in two ways: within the family, and within the economy. The adoption of western middle-class family patterns by the educated elite has made those women more dependent on their husbands both culturally and economically. Western laws reduce customary rights to land or family support of widows or divorcees and their children. Laws on monogamy obliterate rights of second wives while enforcement condones the practice. And the model is seeping down into the poor classes, bringing about the 'growing phenomena of the patriarchal household' (Robertson, 1987: 29). Hansen records the response among older women traders in Zambia to this 'gender hierarchy within the household' (Hansen, 1987: 21). They distance themselves from husband and kin, investing their resources in their children and also trying to save funds to support themselves alone as they age. Such strategies apparently do not work in Zaire where a women's earnings may be claimed by her husband's kin on his death if he has given her the usual symbolic sum when she began her trade (Wilson, 1982).

While such self-sufficiency reflects earlier interpretations of the independence of market women, other studies are revising our understanding of the role of African women in the household (Pellow, 1978; Afonja, 1981). The brideprice was paid by the man for rights to the women's labour and body. Only pregnant and lactating women were free of their husband's demands. As family planners soon realized, women had no control over their bodies or their fertility (Tinker et al., 1974). Economic independence may be a necessary, but it is not a sufficient, requirement for equality.

Economic development is tending to undercut the importance of women traders. The impact of male cash-cropping on their time was discussed above; most such produce is destined for the export market and tends to pass through quite different channels than the female-dominated internal market (Mintz, 1971). Price controls on agricultural produce affect women's profits (Posner, 1983). Licences and regulations favour the literate. Patriarchal husbands demand a share of profits. Required school attendance reduces a trader's supply of free family labour. Robertson comments that these constraints 'together have served over time to diminish the scale of women's trade . . . [and to] induce inefficiency in the distributive system, for which women are often blamed' (Robertson, 1987: 33).

Alternatives for illiterate urban women are few (Shields, 1980) resulting in an involution of the sector and lowering income. Yet women cannot survive without cash in the modern economy. Even among Muslim women in Nigeria who cannot physically participate in the market the need for cash pushes them into trading activities: they prepare food which their children sell in the markets (Simmons, 1975), a phenomenon not restricted to Africa. What we know about these invisible rural and urban small-scale enterprises will be discussed below.

Asia and Latin America

So much focus has been given to the market women of West Africa that women traders in Asia and Latin America are often overlooked. Boserup linked women food traders with female farming systems (Boserup, 1970), perhaps because that was where the studies had been done. Contemporary studies of Asia and Latin America show that women are active as visible market traders virtually everywhere, but their numbers are constrained in societies where Islamic cultural influences are strong. Even from seclusion, women participate in market trade, albeit invisibly: they prepare foods and other items at home but must have them sold in the market by children or male relatives (Schildkrout, 1982).

Even today, specific studies of market women outside Africa are comparatively few (Jellinek, 1977; Szanton, 1972; Edwards, 1980; Peluso, 1984; Bunster and Chaney, 1985; Picasso, 1986; Taylor et al., 1986). Two studies of women vendors in India describe the organizing activities more than their trading (Sebstad, 1982; Azad, 1985). Data on their activities are drawn from broader anthropological studies in time use (see Part 1) or in total market activity (Dewey, 1962; Hackenburg and Barth, 1984; Mintz, 1971); from demographic interest in women's work (Da Vanzo and Lee, 1983); from studies of women's status (Papenek, 1976); or from research into the informal sector (Moser, 1980, 1981, 1984; Arizpe, 1977; Jain et al., 1979a; Singh and de Souza, 1980).

Among the rice-growing societies of Southeast Asia women have historically played a particularly strong role in markets. Under traditional value systems, status flowed to priests and warriors, occupations reserved for men. When the colonial powers needed business acumen they brought in Chinese or Indians to provide needed middlemen services for their international trade. Because this system was in place for so many years, these foreign traders were able to penetrate into the countryside, so that most provincial markets reflected ethnic trading. Thus, while women predominate in local markets in much of the region, long-distance trade was never open to women.

In Java, indigenous women and men traded agricultural produce and traditional handicrafts while the Chinese provided links between these markets and urban areas (Dewey, 1962). The expulsion of Chinese from rural areas in 1959 seems to have had minimal impact on the types of trade in which women engage on Java; they continue to be circuit traders, or to sell produce and prepared food, cooking needs or crafts (Peluso, 1984). Women in cities continue to trade in foods and batiks, but an interesting class differential appears. Batik trading is an acceptable middle-class activity, often done out of suburban homes (Papenek, 1982). Food sellers are usually poor by comparison, though one foodstall entrepreneur, who also ran a boarding house for ice cream peddlers, accumulated considerable cash (Jellinek, 1977).

Women predominate in the markets of Thailand and the Philippines, dominating small-scale trade, much of which they produce themselves. Cristina Szanton's study of a market place in a fishing town on Panay Island shows how women sell that portion of the day's catch due their fisher husbands. Underscoring the impact of large-scale commercialization on this activity, she indicates that three-quarters of the fish catch is sent directly to Manila, either fresh or dried, leaving only one-quarter for local trade (Szanton, 1972). There is ample historic recording of women traders in Vietnam (Hoskins, 1975) but little current knowledge.

In South Asia the visibility of women in trade diminishes from south to north as the cultural residues of purdah grow stronger. A study of traders in Hyderabad, India, found that 50 percent of the small retailers were women, but most were from the southern part of the state (Singh, 1980). Three times as many women work in petty commerce in Madras as in New Delhi (Singh and de Souza, 1980). It is extreme poverty that pushes these women to sell on the streets of New Delhi; one study found one-quarter of them sole supporters of their families (Singh, 1980). Most of these women come from low castes; women from upper castes prefer invisible jobs such as those in home-based industry, even if the remuneration is less. In the Himalayan foothills, conservative religion has less influence on women's status than it does on the plains; the brewing and selling of a traditional liquor has been an historical occupation among Magar women in western Nepal. As among the beer makers in Africa, they have had to fight to keep their markets in the face of imported liquor (Molnar, 1982).

In areas strongly influenced by Islam the number of visible women traders falls, even within countries. On Java there are fewer women vendors in Bogor where the Muslims are more orthodox than in Jogjakarta (Chapman, 1984); in Northern Nigeria, Muslim women stay in seclusion and sell through intermediaries (Simmons, 1975). Only destitute Muslim women work in public in Bangladesh (Owens and Hussain, 1984). Nonetheless, many women contribute to market activities from the seclusion of their homes throughout South and West Asia.

In Latin America women are the preponderant vendors in the Caribbean and Central America, although studies specifically on market women are quite few. In Hispanic culture areas women play a significant market role in those societies where indigenous influences have remained strong, and where women in rural areas continue to grow and sell agricultural surplus and prepared foods. The typical connection between growing and selling agricultural surplus was observed in Nicaragua (Hagen, 1974). However, the high level of urbanization in much of Latin America requires more complicated urban–rural linkages; as a result, most of the market women in major cities buy produce from middlemen in Bogota (Moser, 1980), Lima (Bunster and Chaney, 1985) and Mexico City (Arizpe, 1977).

In the Caribbean, market women distribute, as well as market, agricultural produce in Haiti and Jamaica (Mintz, 1971; Edwards, 1980). Further, the higglers of Jamaica carry on an extensive inter-island trade, chugging from island to island trading fresh produce, canned and household goods and local crafts. A recent survey in Kingston shows that 84 percent of higglers are women; imported goods in the markets were primarily garments and footwear (Taylor et al., 1986).

Comment

Data show that women market traders provide a significant service by supplying foodstuffs for poor urban dwellers in most developing countries. Recent studies indicate that income from such economic activity varies, but tends to be lower than that for trading open to men. Most explain the variation by constraints on women due to their household responsibilities. Women work to feed and clothe themselves and their children and, if possible, to pay the children's school fees. Men's income is seldom completely donated to the household. Yet even among the free unions of the poor in Ecuador, 88 percent receive some financial assistance from their men (Moser, 1981). Thus even where there is no tradition of separate budgets, as in much of Africa, women work so that they can fulfil what they see as their responsibilities to their children. Particularly where formal marriage is rare, or where polygamy is accepted, poor women find they must rely on their own incomes, on their children, or on female networks for their survival. This trend conflicts with the countervailing pressure towards the domestication of women as they move into the middle class (Young and Moser, 1981).

Most women find employment in traditional women's work which is seen as an extension of the domestic sphere. Until now this economic niche has been reserved for women. Caroline Moser is concerned that this protection may be breaking down; she points to the growing trend for men in Guayaquil to take over the selling of foods which their wives prepare at home, and which previously they would have sold. 'Where this occurs, women's work is unwaged . . . an example of the structured division of labor in the household' (Moser, 1981: 26). Discussion of such fundamental issues of women's power within both family and society become inevitable if the issue of women's economic rights is to get beyond ethnographic description.

INFORMAL SECTOR

The debate concerning the characteristics and significance of small-scale employment outside the modern organized sector has had profound implications both for the academic and the development communities. Data produced in response to the growing interest in urban employment around the world fundamentally challenged contemporary development theories and so added to the momentum of those seeking a new development construct. Case studies of existing microenterprise showed how the working poor survive, and opened up new areas for development programming. Further, the predominance of women employed in the informal sector has captured the attention of male scholars and activists who had previously paid little attention to the growing literature on women in development.

Historical Debate

The debate over the definition and existence of the informal sector is usually traced to the adoption by the ILO of its World Employment Programme in 1969, and the subsequent recognition that it was proving impossible to expand the modern industrial sector fast enough to provide employment to the growing numbers of workers in developing countries. Thus ILO funded a series of urban studies to collect information on the informal sector which, for the purposes of its inquiry, was characterized by: (a) ease of entry; (b) reliance on indigenous resources; (c) family ownership of enterprises; (d) small scale of operation; (e) labour-intensive with adapted technology; (f) skills acquired outside formal schools; (g) unregulated and competitive markets (ILO, 1972).

At one level it was this definition that intrigued scholars, encouraging them to rush out and collect their own data in order to uphold, or question, these various characteristics. But it is unlikely that the debate would have engaged the attention of so many scholars and development experts had it not signalled the need for new theories or assumptions to replace the more limited ones then in vogue. For donor agencies the opening up of the informal sector provided a new avenue for channelling projects designed to assist the poor; this point is further discussed in the next section. For scholars the ILO approach indicated plainly that they believed the informal sector was a permanent and viable part of urban economy in developing countries. This concept threw down the gauntlet before development theorists, both liberal and Marxist, by confronting them with the challenge of incorporating these activities within their overall theoretical framework which, in both cases, had seen this sector as transitional. Further, recognizing the existence of the sector required a new definition of work to be formulated for use in collecting unemployment data; indeed, for ILO the issue was no longer *unemployment*, since it is obvious that most poor must work to survive, but what *type* of employment.

ILO's interest in funding informal sector studies was to obtain policy recommendations which would lead to greater employment opportunities for the urban poor. If the informal sector is simply small-scale enterprise, then an infusion of resources to the sector should result in its growth. But if the informal sector serves as the urban counterpart to subsistence agriculture, then it would remain inefficient unless structurally altered. Support for such a dependent sector would be synonymous with providing welfare; such efforts might assist an individual or group to obtain greater income, but there would be no investment or growth. Such questions needed to be addressed before programmes could be initiated.

However, it was the underlying theoretical issues which energized scholars around the world to weigh into the debate. Before the oil crisis of 1973 the industrialized countries were becoming ostentatiously wealthy; in most developing countries the rich were getting richer, the poor poorer. Donor nations were willing to consider changes in development priorities to provide basic human needs to the poor; but the demands by the developing countries in the United Nations for a New International Economic Order, with its focus on the restructuring of world trade, were turned aside by the United States. Many third world leaders considered the basic needs approach as unproductive welfare guaranteed to continue dependency. Into this provocative debate was inserted the issue of the informal sector. No wonder that many scholars interpreted the ILO approach as palliative, and argued that petty commodity workers exist at the will of, and are exploited by, large capitalists. To them the informal sector debate was seen as just another face of the same idol.

Drawn by the charged atmosphere, scholars from all persuasions began to investigate unrecorded urban economic activity to find out who was employed in what activities, whether the sector was evolutionary or involutionary, and whether the work was temporary or permanent; benign or exploitative; dualistic or a continuum; a refuge for the most disadvantaged or opportunity for the adventurous. 'Fundamentally', writes Bromley in the introduction to a landmark collection on the topic which he edited,

> these debates are between liberal, neo-classical evolutionary views that policies can be formulated to bring the 'benefits of development' to the poor, and radical, neo-Marxist views which often lead to the conclusion that only sharp (and often — some would say necessarily — violent) change can improve the situation of the poor in Third World Countries (Bromley, 1978: 1037).

After a decade of debate, and the publication of hundreds of commentaries and case studies, the complexity of actual economic activities which exist in addition to modern industrial and governmental employment has been well documented. Informal sector studies have focused on hawkers and vendors (Arizpe, 1977; McGee and Yeung, 1977; Bromley, 1978; Bunster, 1983), mobile shops (Prakash, 1972), betelnut sellers (Walsh, 1982), small-scale manufacturing (Gerry, 1978), domestic servants (Bunster and Chaney, 1985), garbage scavengers (Birkbeck, 1978), small grocery shops (Tokman, 1978), putting out systems in the North (Goddard, 1981; Allen, 1981) and South (Jain et al., 1979b; Singh and Kelles-Viitanen, 1987), decentralized European industry (Engellau and Sjoberg, 1984) and the bartering of services to avoid taxes (Berndt and Ferman, 1976), non-registered firms (Vargas Llosa, 1987), and house construction (Earthscan, 1981, UNCHS, 1984). Mentioned but unstudied as part of this ill-defined sector are gambling and crime; the ILO did commission one study in its Women, Work, and Development series on prostitution (Phongpaichit, 1982). Faced with this plethora of information, most writers are attempting to analyse economic activity in a particular city or a country rather than discussing abstract theoretical constructs. Detail has swamped theory.

A recent issue of the *Regional Development Dialogue* masterfully surveys the literature from both the mainstream (Richardson, 1984) and Marxist (Moser, 1984) viewpoints, and summarizes the state of the art. Essentially, everyone accepts that the informal sector is here to stay even though there is as yet no agreed definition of this elusive informal sector concept except to say that it is heterogeneous and difficult to define. The sector not only provides employment, but also essential commodities and services for rich and poor alike in cities everywhere, in developed, developing and centrally planned economies (Mathur and Moser, 1984). Particularly dependent on these services and goods provided by the informal sector are the urban poor who could not otherwise afford them (Schmink, 1986).

Current Issues

Now that the existence of the sector is accepted in all of its diversity, most scholars interested in the field have been conducting empirical studies, trying to refine categories and descriptors in order to make the study of the sector more accessible. Five sets of issues can be identified as most important: (1) the extent and nature of the relationships between the formal and informal sectors; (2) analysis of activities within the informal sector; (3) the differential problems of women working in the informal sector; (4) rural microenterprise; and (5) relationships between city size and the informal sector. Let me review these five current issues briefly, and relate them to development strategies.

In the earlier debates the prominence given the formal/informal dualism tended to create a dichotomy between these sectors which obfuscated their interconnections and interdependencies. Those favouring the dualist approach saw the informal sector populated with independent entrepreneurs whose difference from the formal sector was one of scale and access to resources; their policy prescription was to offer credit and management and training to these fledgling businesses and to encourage closer linkages with the formal sector through subcontracting and concession sales. Those favouring the petty commodity approach believed that the formal sector industries exploited the informal sector workers, and that greater autonomy was preferable (Moser, 1978).

The idea of exploitative relationships remains a major theme, especially among those scholars who see the distinction between the sectors as a classifying device for labour utilization (Mazumdar, 1975; Banerjee, 1981). Labour in the formal sector is protected or organized; labour in the informal sector is not, and therefore is open to greater exploitation. There are limits to the maintenance of the labour elite, however; wage levels and fringe benefits may be raised through governmental or trade union pressure to a point that industries may 'informalize' part or all of their production in order to maintain their profits. This phenomenon is not only a feature in Asia (Singh and Kelles-Viitanen, 1987) Uruguay (Prates, 1986), and Mexico (Beneria and Roldan, 1987), but it has also been occurring in Europe during the current recessionary period (Engellau and Sjoberg, 1984).

In many countries of South America the explosive growth of the informal sector is explained by the mire of governmental regulations required for registering and doing business there. In Lima much of urban transport and construction, in addition to small and even medium-sized industry, is considered informal. More typically, larger industries contract or put out parts of the production process to home-based workers. Such a system was widespread throughout the world in the nineteenth century. In this century, due both to changes in production and to the opposition of labour unions who see such work as a way of circumventing labour contracts, home-work had largely disappeared in the developed countries before the recent decentralizing trend. But not entirely; not in Italy (Goddard, 1981) or Britain, of which Allen (1981) writes: 'It may be that one of the reasons that homeworking was thought to have disappeared, is that it is done by women. . . . Another reason is undoubtedly that it does not fit the generally accepted view that home and work were separated in the process of industrialization'.

Despite the persistence of sewing and knitting home-based work in developed countries, the major concern of feminists there is the decentralizing tendencies implicit in recent technological changes, particularly in the fields of microprocessing and telecommunications (SPRU, 1982; Hartmann et al., 1986). In the United States the growth of home-based clerical workers — typists, medical and legal transcribers, data entry clerks, bookkeepers, and word processors — has raised the question whether legislation might be needed to protect them (US Congress, 1986).

In developing countries, where the line between home-crafts and modern home-based work is blurred, home-based work has continued to be a major economic activity. Generally artisans and handicraft workers — men printing bedspreads or women folk-painters — were seen as self-employed while women sewing blouses or rolling beedi cigarettes on contract were home-based out workers of the industries. The large-scale urban surveys which were part of the ILO series frequently missed these activities because they tended to focus on visible enterprises: those in the open air or in shacks. Such identification misses the wide variety of home-based economic activities, particularly those that engage women. This type of contracting out is of growing significance, and is clearly distinct from subcontracting to an informal sector firm. Recent studies of women in home-based production in Asia continue to make the distinction between own-account work and that done on contract. Their findings suggest that while the incidence of home-based work is increasing, the autonomy of the workers is decreasing (Singh and Kelles-Viitanen, 1987). Ela Bhatt, founder of the Self-Employed Women's Association in India, suggests a form of out-reach unionization would be the best protection for workers on contract (Bhatt, 1987); independent home-workers need their own organizations (Jumari, 1987; Noponen, 1987). The overall view is that the poor women who work in home-based occupations are paid subminimum wages and given no health or retirement benefits. On the other hand, the women are enabled to earn money while staying at home, and 'attach values other than purely economic ones to their home-based work' (Singh and Kelles-Viitanen, 1987: 14). For example, high caste Hindu women seek work in the privacy of their homes and may accept lower wages for this accommodation (Banerjee, 1981).

The complexity of the relationship between the large industry and the home-based worker reflects similar complexities in other subsectors with other types of relationships. Summing up the literature written on this topic, Richardson notes that there is widespread agreement that prosperity in the two sectors go hand in hand; but there is also the contradictory view that as employment in the formal sector falls, that in the informal sector increases, particularly with the entry of marginal workers, especially women. 'One of the problems in interpreting the IFS/FS links is that so many of the research studies have examined the IFS in isolation from the rest of the economy' (Richardson, 1984: 13).

A second major task being undertaken by researchers in the field is that of analysing and categorizing the informal sector. Besides studies which focus on a particular subsector such as small manufacturing, there are now studies of specific products such as plastic processing in Bombay and Pune (Kirloskar Consultants, 1985). EPOC's Street Foods studies looked across the informal food sector, considering not only the sellers of food, but the producers and consumers as well.

Taking a different approach, many authors have begun to divide the sector by the economic prospects of the enterprise. House (1984: 291) has divided the informal sector of Nairobi into two distinct groups: dynamic entrepreneurs and the community of the poor, 'a relatively stagnant group engaged in menial employment with subsistence returns to their efforts', characteristics which resemble early definitions of the whole informal sector. However, between these two types House identified a 'third group who are in a stage of transition and who display some of the characteristics of each of the polar groups' (House, 1984: 291). He found that at least 35 percent of his sample should be classed among the poor, many of whom he assumes will return to the rural areas to eke out an existence. It is of note that he did not include hawkers and petty traders in his survey; their numbers would have increased the membership of the community of the poor. While House retains dualist terminology for emphasis, he is in fact describing a continuum. In contrast, McCormick (1986) makes this continuum the basis of her study by assigning each a degree of formality. This indicator is derived from scores assigned for site, relationship to civil authority, technology, skill levels of workers, and management.

Recognizing this same division between those enterprises which are relatively prosperous and those on the margin, the DGAP sees the difference in terms of skills and access to resources, and so refers to this community of the poor as 'pre-entrepreneurial'. By this they mean people who are inexperienced but are in business because they have no other alternative way to survive (Ashe, 1985a).

Other writers equate this division with class. Bremen lists three divisions within the informal sector, in addition to the labour elite in the formal sector: small bourgeoisie, under-proletariat, and the very poor who are, in his interpretation, the undesirable criminal element (Romatet, 1983). This unsympathetic characterization of the poor is not verbalized in most other writings; rather the criminal element is ignored and the very poor are identified as being predominantly women heads of households. A recent example are Portes et al. (1986), writing about Uruguay. They stress that their findings not only clearly indicate a major difference between the owners and the workers of informal sector businesses, particularly in terms of income, but also in terms of individual characteristics.

> [I]nformal labor and small entrepreneurship are not determined by differential skills alone but are also associated strongly with certain ascriptive traits. This result is also in line with those of recent surveys, conducted elsewhere, which identify race and sex as major discriminating factors between informal workers and both informal employers and formal employees.... In the racially homogeneous Uruguayan labor market, it is sex which most clearly differentiates between these employment situations. The gender effect, in this case, goes beyond employment position to influence levels of remuneration within each directly (Portes et al., 1986: 739).

The third current issue, then, concerns the differential roles and aspirations of women working in the informal sector, for the division of the informal sector into successful entrepreneurs and an underclass which primarily consists of women adds a new dimension to the debate about whether, and how, donors should assist the sector. If one argues that as long as the sector is dependent, and therefore exploited by the formal sector, donor assistance will flow upwards and the poor will remain poor, then only structural change will assist the needy. If, however, individuals move up the economic scale and become dynamic entrepreneurs, then assistance to the sector is in order. But when the community of the poor is identified as women with children, whose double day barely allows survival, this description of the sector seems one-dimensional, and requires further elaboration.

This sexual differentiation, with women heads of households clustering at the poor end of the scale, was overlooked in many earlier studies, especially those by ILO, because they were concerned with employment enhancement and so concentrated on small manufacturing. Generally, data were collected only from visible enterprises, those operating in the open or in temporary physical structures. Women working in homes were obviously ignored under such circumstances. Further, there was a tendency to consider women, along with youth and elderly, as secondary earners. Thus, even when identifying a community of the poor, House did not bother to disaggregate his data by sex (1984).

By ignoring the critical importance to women and their families of the jobs in the informal sector, and therefore also ignoring the different reasons women have both for migrating and for often preferring informal-sector jobs, many of the hypotheses are undermined. For example, women may migrate, not because of the pull of jobs or the push of land pressure, but because their access to land through a husband has been changed by his taking a second wife, or by his death. Women often find formal-sector jobs difficult to combine with a job as household head due to rigid work schedules or distance to the work site. The limitations posed by household work, low skill levels and discrimination combine to perpetuate the growing feminization of poverty.

The final two current issues relate to spatial issues regarding where the informal sector enterprises are concentrated. These concerns are a response to the concentration of research on the informal sector in major metropolitan areas. The first question is whether the characteristic of the sector or of its workers is distinctly urban, or is it also a rural phenomenon? The second question is whether there is, by percentage, more or less informality in smaller towns as compared to larger agglomerations.

The problem of defining work in rural areas was discussed above in relation to on- and off-farm activities which related to survival. There it was noted that many categories of work escape numeration, that women's farmwork is frequently overlooked, but that new definitions of work are beginning to result in improved statistics. Research on market women also reveals economic activities which have tended to slip through national accounts. Homebased work is found as often in rural areas as in cities. It is surprising, given the fact that agriculture-led development is currently the dominant theme at the World Bank and other development agencies, that rural industry has been so little studied and so seldom included in the informal sector debate.

Historically, most rural crafts were part-time activities done when the demand for agricultural labour was low. Studies of rural time use indicate a wide range of such enterprises (Binswanger et al., 1980). ILO's Rural Employment Policies Branch funded a series of studies comparable to the informal studies series, but with a specific focus on 'poverty alleviation through increased employment opportunities and basic-needs satisfaction' (ILO, 1985c: 1). These studies analyse the determinants of poverty, assess agrarian reforms, analyse rural labour markets and explore the sexual division of labour. Indeed, much of the data on homebased work was funded through that section. But the studies do not interlink with, nor inform, those on the informal sector, or vice-versa.

There is one set of studies specifically on rural industry — those directed by Carl Leidholm from Michigan State University. The first set document the importance of rural industries in Africa. For example, in Sierra Leone, 78 percent of all industry in that country in 1974 was located in villages with less that 2000 inhabitants (Leidholm and Chuta, 1976). Data showed, however, that village enterprises were more likely to operate part-time than those in larger centres, and that there was significant seasonal variation in all small-scale industries. Only some 10 percent of these enterprises were in towns over 20,000 people. Data on the workers showed the average firm size was 1.8 persons. Among the industries surveyed — tailoring, blacksmithing, carpentry, baking, goldsmithing, and repairing of watches, radios, and shoes — women's contribution was small. Only in dyeing did women play an important role, contributing 16 percent of total labour — this underscores the fact of sex-segregated economic activities, particularly in Africa. In subsequent studies in Egypt, Leidholm found a much greater participation of women in rural industry by including the dairy industry, which is a totally female activity even to the marketing of surplus from rural areas in Cairo (de Treville, 1982).

The difficulties of studying rural industry are probably greater than those encountered in cities. One of the basic problems is the lack of agreed definition on what is rural. In most countries, census-takers have agreed to base their urban data on population density rather than geographic boundaries. By default, everything else is rural. But what of towns? At what point are they urban? Answers to these questions affect distribution of governmental programmes and funding in many countries, so that one finds different ministries using different definitions. The sparseness of current literature has meant that the critical debate on scope and definitions has not occurred, so that data are difficult to access or compare. Yet there seems little interest among the informal-sector scholars in looking at rural industry. Rather, this sector has been left to development organizations who focus on appropriate technology, food processing and handicrafts. Because there is no scholarly interest in documenting this area, such groups tend to have no institutional memory either for their own understanding or for theorists to utilize.

In contrast, the informal-sector scholars are now entranced with the issue of relating this activity to city size. ILO has listed it as a major area for future research (ILO, 1984a). The UN Center for Regional Development has initiated a research project on the functioning of the informal sector in small and intermediate-sized cities (Mathur and Moser, 1984). Since the definition of rural is indistinct, in that it clearly encompasses small urban places, there is an overlap of concern between those interested in rural industry and those focusing on industry in small towns. As this new line of spatial distribution of small-scale industry and the informal sector proceeds, it is to be hoped that the two groups of scholars exchange information and paradigms.

Questions to be addressed include whether the size of the informal sector increases or decreases with modernization. Do the types of employment change? Do the characteristics of workers in the informal sector change? To what extent will investment in this sector at the level of smaller cities inhibit migration to the metropolis? Is the sector more or less dynamic in smaller towns? Is the proportion of women among the community of the poor lower in smaller towns?

In sum, the early debates over the existence of the informal sector, over the dualistic division of urban economy and over the theoretical positions as to whether assistance to the sector could help its workers, or whether it merely prolonged the agony of the poor, have been swamped by the proliferation of data collected by a myriad of studies during the past 15 years. The sector has been declared a permanent feature of the economy, but its description and functioning are not sufficiently understood to become the basis of a new theory.

DONOR AGENCIES AND MICROENTERPRISE

The third strand of inquiry that has contributed to our knowledge of microentrepreneurs resulted from growing interest by donor agencies in working directly with the poor. Indeed, the 'discovery' of the informal sector came at a propitious time for the donor community. The ambiguous results of earlier development strategies which appeared to increase income disparities in most developing countries had resulted in a paradigm shift toward basic human needs, and a programmatic shift towards the poor.

Because the predominant focus of national and international donor groups has been the rural areas, there was little information on the realities of life in urban slums. The few urban programmes in existence at the beginning of the 1970s were concentrated on housing issues; but even here the major impetus for solving this problem came with the UN Conference on Habitat in 1976. When authors write about urban biases in development programmes they are discussing the bias towards the urban elite. In fact, in terms of community-level programmes, development was, and continues to be, characterized by a rural bias.

Not surprisingly, the major donor agencies incorporated the informal sector concept of the poor entrepreneur into their existing programmatic structure. Non-farm entrepreneurial activities which would bring income to the rural poor were introduced into major assistance programmes in areas that ranged from appropriate technology to population to integrated rural development. On the other hand, the small urban settlement programmes in the World Bank and Canada's International Development Research Centre initiated research into broad questions of urban existence, including income-earning activities (McGreevey, 1980; McGee and Yeung, 1977; Mohan, 1984). It was the local charitable and voluntary organizations that began or increased assistance programmes among the urban poor; the increased interest among the donor community expanded their funding base and brought them into the debate concerning the best ways to help the poor help themselves.

Rural Experience

During the 1950s and 1960s development agencies assumed that rural and community development programmes would provide infrastructure and resources to rural areas, and so stimulate agricultural productivity and raise farmers' incomes. Such programmes were necessarily under the supervision of appropriate government ministries which often displaced local traders by distributing agricultural inputs through government-controlled co-operatives. Marketing boards, set up by colonial regimes to provide a guaranteed price to the farmer, became the major purchaser of agricultural export crops, often at below world market prices in order to subsidize national development plans. In addition, since many newly independent countries favoured socialism, large-scale projects such as harbours and dams, and in some cases regional development schemes, were placed under public control. Private enterprise was identified with transnational corporations or moneylenders, both an anathema for most leaders of the developing countries at that time.

Yet these were the activities that had led to the growing income disparities in developing countries which had triggered the call for greater attention to basic needs. Clearly, new models were needed. Generally, there was a ratcheting down of rural programmes: tertiary irrigation streams not major dams, appropriate technologies not state of the art, labour- not capital-intensive. From our perspective of learning about microentrepreneurs, two significant concepts emerge from this reorientation which have universal applicability: one relating to the formation and functioning of groups, the other to product identification and marketing.

Bracketing a discussion of groups with that of entrepreneurs may seem strange, since entrepreneurs are portrayed as the essence of individualism. However, even large-scale entrepreneurs have trade organizations which provide them with contacts and information. For microentrepreneurs such support groups are clearly more essential. Historically the guild or caste provided such support. Today, with population pressures pushing people out of traditional employment patterns, whether these displaced people stay in rural areas or migrate to urban centres, new support mechanisms must be created. Familial relationships, real or fictive, and cultural/religious identifications serve as the basis for support groups, particularly in towns (Papenek, 1976; Lomnitz, 1977; Gugler and Flanagan, 1978). Indigenous support groups, however, cannot provide the infusion of resources available through intermediary organizations.

Development agencies have tended to favour geographic units as the basis for co-operatives which were, until recently, the grouping of preference, particularly for those relating to farming. The rhetoric of co-operatives fits in with the emphasis on the poor: co-ops are run by the local people and are perceived as egalitarian. Yet real-life experience of co-ops in Asia had been disastrous, for even in the tiniest village there is political hierarchy and social stratification (Tinker and Raynolds, 1982; ILO, 1984b). It should have come as no surprise that the man with the largest lands got the most loans, or that the leadership of co-ops mirrored village political control in terms of caste, class, religion or sex. Usually only the household head can belong to a co-op; cash distributions from produce go to the member irrespective of who does the work (Charlton, 1984). Thus men received the increased income from women's dairying in India (Jain et al., 1979a) or from coffee-growing in Kenya (Tinker, 1976).

A second type of group activity utilized for development programmes, and which is village-based, is that of obligatory work groups. Seen as an attempt to recapture traditional communal activities, such work groups have been used by most local authorities to build roads, construct irrigation ditches and build schools. Worthy projects, without doubt, but ones which place differential burdens on the poor and result often in differential utility. Landless households cannot benefit from irrigation; women-headed households often cannot supply labour for long-term projects, and may be expected to pay for a substitute. In Kenya today, a variant of these often coercive work groups has arisen. Perhaps because so many men migrate to the cities, women's groups seem uniquely charged with raising money to fund needed community facilities such as a school or a clinic. These groups are frequently called upon to supply entertainment and food for visiting bureaucrats, an activity of possible political, but certainly not economic, utility to them. Because of the demands on a woman's time, poorer women are excluded from these groups, which do have the potential of providing individual income as well (Muzaale and Leonard, 1985; McCormack, 1986).

A third type of group activity which had also become discredited is the effort by intermediary organizations to assist poor rural women to earn money by making handicrafts. Whether such programmes were set up by the government, as in Egypt, or by religious organizations or voluntary groups, they were based on the assumption that these women did not work, and so had time to devote to this activity. In most cases the poor women were first formed into groups for ease of training them in new activities. The crafts introduced were based on presumed skills of housewives: crocheting, sewing or batiking; the completed tablecloths, mats, or dresses were meant for middle-class consumption. Too often these activities were not economically viable: there was a limited market, quality was poor, and neither management nor distribution were included as a cost. Frequently, when the patron withdrew, the enterprise collapsed.

Such efforts were correctly seen as welfare, not enterprise, by the development community. Perhaps the major error in most such activities was to key the product to middle-class consumption, whether for the elite, for tourists, or the export market. Such markets are quickly saturated and increasingly competitive. Yet the assumptions of progress and modernization are so pervasive that the donor community tended at first to ignore both the traditional products and the indigenous markets.

The conclusions drawn from these unsuccessful models are clear. First, if the objective of forming a group is to facilitate reaching and assisting the poor, then members of such groups should be from similar socioeconomic backgrounds, and of a single sex. Further, such groupings should be recognized as mechanisms to help the individual, not the community. While meetings of these small groups can be used for literacy training and general information on nutrition, family planning, or health, the primary function should always take precedence. Other types of organizations can be set up in conjunction with the intermediary agencies to respond to other types of needs such as representing vendors in negotiations with the government. Similarly, these small functional groups should be distinguished from community organizations which reward participation in such intangible ways as status, satisfaction or political clout.

Secondly, the activities in which these microentrepreneurs engage should be ones that they understand, and for which they have the skills. The demand for their service or products should have a broad base so that the market is not quickly saturated. Thus the economic activities of such entrepreneurs are more likely to be attractive to the poor than to the elite or to foreigners.

Affinity Groups

A new model for organizing the poor has been evolving which meets these requirements. Variously called affinity or solidarity groups, their major reason for existence is to offer credit at reasonable terms to microentrepreneurs. The concept has been so quickly and widely adopted that it is difficult to trace its origin. Its traditional roots are in the revolving savings/credit associations which are still found throughout the developing world. Each member of a typical traditional savings group would put the same amount into a kitty every week; by turns, each member received the entire kitty, either by lot or by predetermined order. The advantage of such an association was that each individual member could save a considerable amount in order to buy furniture or jewellery, or pay school fees; trying to save at home might result in another family member begging for or appropriating the money.

The contemporary affinity group builds on the savings concept, and on the cohesiveness of group members. Its major new attribute is the infusion of loans from outside the community to be used for microenterprise only. The idea seems to have emerged as a result of the high degree of experimentation by both local and international non-governmental organizations in Bangladesh right after its independence in 1971. In face of the stark poverty and growing landlessness in that new country, the need to help the poor earn money was overwhelming. Every activist group, from those espousing revolution to those distributing birth control pills, began turning out jute bags and mats, and saturating the market. The more astute organizations began to encourage members to use their tiny profits from jute sales to invest in their own enterprises: husking rice, selling *pan*, raising a goat or pig (Tinker and Raynolds, 1982).

The Grameen Bank is often credited with the idea of simply giving loans for such activities. A description of its method of organizing borrowing groups will illustrate the model (ILO, 1984b). Organizers go into villages and talk to the landless about the availability of low-interest loans. In 1983 the total cost of a loan was 13 percent per year as compared with a local moneylender rate of 10 percent per week! Individuals interested in receiving a loan must first form their own group of five to ten members, all landless, from a single village, and of the same sex; they may not be related. The group must begin their own group savings account into which each member pays one *taka* during each required weekly meeting. This account grows through a tax on every loan; up to 50 percent of the fund is available for borrowing by members on terms they fix themselves. Loans from this fund may be used for social and medical needs, unlike the bank loans which must be used for productive purposes. In addition, each borrower must pay into an emergency fund which functions as insurance against illness or death. And all members must learn to sign their names.

Loans are made to one or two individual members in turn, with the group standing surety for the loan, acting in place of collateral. Since other members cannot receive a loan until the outstanding loans are repaid, there is tremendous social pressure to repay on time. Repayment rates worldwide for these petty loans are in the 90 percent ratio, far higher than any other type of loan. Loans must be for activities which will produce an income, so that the profitability of an enterprise is discussed by the group and sanctioned by the advisor. Generally, however, the choice of economic activity is left up to the individual.

This is the basic model. Most groups add other activities. The Grameen Bank itself uses its organization to funnel advice and information to its members. Since 40 percent of all borrowing groups are women, advice on nutrition and child-rearing is common. The organization encourages its members to sign a pledge against paying or receiving a dowry. Many groups have started literacy classes or calisthenics for its members. Groups from a single village are combined into centres; one such centre invested in a tubewell with which to water farmers' fields in return for a share in the harvest. In Kenya a women's group bought a boat. However, such group investment is the exception.

Urban Programmes

As interest grew among donor agencies in assisting the urban informal sector, several agencies sent out teams to assess existing urban programmes which had already been working with the informal sector entrepreneurs for some time in order to 'document what the real world had to teach us' (Farbman, 1981: vi). The sum of experience collected sees the informal sector through a different prism from the scholars. On the whole the findings add detail about the characteristics of the microentrepreneurs, and describe efforts to help enterprises of various sizes. More fundamentally, these assessments reveal a basic value cleavage in approach between the more traditional voluntary organizations which are wedded to humanitarian aid, and the economic-oriented donors more concerned with profit and growth. This difference of viewpoint and values obviously affected the outcome of evaluations so that the same programme which might be a success in the eyes of one observer would be insufficient in another's (Bear et al., 1982; Tendler, 1983).

These differences should not be seen as mutually exclusive, however, for both groups have tried to incorporate the dual concerns of equity and self-sufficiency in their programming. The voluntary community, aware of the enormity of the task of helping the world's poor, has been looking for ways to help the poor help themselves; microenterprise seems an obvious solution. On the other hand, the donor community was at the time going through a period of self-guilt for its role in helping the rich in the developing countries; its economists were taking a new look at ways to support small-scale, if not microenterprise. But as two major donors, the World Bank and USAID, shifted from focus on basic human needs and the poor in the 1970s to private enterprise in the 1980s, the assessments shifted as well. In the new lexicon, private enterprise meant growth. For enterprises to receive loans they must create new employment. New funding flowed to larger-scale enterprises, leaving the field of urban poor to the private intermediary organizations (McCormick, 1986).

This shift may perhaps be seen most clearly in the reports of the PISCES project which conducted the first and most comprehensive assessment in 1979 to find out the best way 'of assisting the smallest economic activities of the urban poor' (Farbman, 1981). By 1985, PISCES director Michael Farbman had recast his description of the project to reflect new priorities; he emphasizes that the project had 'shed light on strategies and approaches for promoting what is, arguably, numerically the largest component of the private sector in nearly all developing countries' (Ashe, 1985a: Foreword).

The difference between these two approaches was made clear in the first major assessment of 20 on-going projects in 16 countries of Asia, Africa and Latin America, done under the aegis of the PISCES project of USAID. As the first in its field, the analysis and terminology provided the framework for subsequent evaluations. The majority of these existing urban projects had originated with local private voluntary organizations; their funding, however, came from an array of public and private donor agencies. In addition, governmental offices set up to assist small enterprise, and several private banks which offered special loan programmes for small enterprise, were also reviewed.

The focus of all these evaluations was on the clients: who they were, what their skills were and how to help them. Two distinct types of beneficiaries were identified: pre-entrepreneurial and entrepreneurial. Those classed as pre-entrepreneurial were usually recent migrants who lacked the 'street smarts' which allowed the urban native to operate a micro-business. They were usually illiterate, and lacking in entrepreneurial skills (Ashe, 1985a). These conclusions would seem to be too particularly based on research in Kenya, where recent migration has been particularly high and where there is no strong tradition of women market traders. Being from rural areas does not necessarily correlate with lack of trading skills, as Singh and de Souza found in their study of major Indian cities (1980). Nonetheless, these categories are important, since knowing who are the intended beneficiaries, and what are their needs, strongly influences project design.

Overall, but clustered in the pre-entrepreneurial group, the overwhelming majority of clientele served by these projects was women. The National Council of Churches of Kenya (NCCK) reported that 76 percent of participants in its programmes in Nairobi and 6 secondary cities were women, and that they supported, on the average, 6.5 dependents (O'Regan and Hellinger, 1981). In the Philippines three-quarters of the beneficiaries in 4 different credit and support programmes assessed were women (Brown, 1981). Working Women's Forum was set up in Madras, India, to facilitate the flow of credit from national banks to women microentrepreneurs; their income is essential to the support of their households which consist typically of 8 to 10 people (Brown, 1981). In the slums of Bangalore, India, and San Salvadore, El Salvador, the supported enterprises were almost all run by women; men were seen by the project leader in Bangalore as 'drunkards, [or] irresponsible' (Brown, 1981: 362), while in San Salvador 'men and teenage boys tend to seek more prestigious employment in factories, markets, or other commercial establishments' (Fraser and Tucker, 1981: 168).

These findings are important, for women are often defined out of informal sector studies either by focusing on manufacturing enterprises or by assuming that all family enterprises are headed by men and that women are part-time family workers. Clearly the scope of the inquiry and its assumptions anticipate many of the findings. In other words, the same trend towards making women farmers invisible is at work in this sector as well. Gender is obviously a critical variable that needs to be incorporated into and analysed for all future studies of urban employment.

The intermediary organizations serving the urban poor adjusted their programmes to their clientele; few such organizations attempted to serve more than one level of beneficiary (Smith and Tippitt, 1982). Most of those concerned with the pre-entrepreneurial women and men basically propound a multifaceted community development approach. While their programmes for microentrepreneurs have become an important new strategy, these efforts generally remain embedded within other goals (Beardsley, 1982). For example, social workers employed by the NCCK must recommend individuals for participation in the Small Business Scheme; and the impact of such schemes is measured in improved household consumption or the payment of school fees as much as in profit (Ashe, 1985a: 68). Costs for these more complex programmes were necessarily higher, and results more difficult to assess. How much of the social overhead costs should be applied to costs of granting a loan, for example?

Almost all organizations involved in this multifaceted approach are private associations, often religiously based. Most have been doing charitable work for some years, and so bring with them attitudes and approaches that stress family survival rather than enterprise self-sufficiency. Their loan programmes, for example, have low payback rates, since many clients seem to treat them as gifts. These organizations continue to assume that 'those at the lower end of the spectrum have less need for capital and more need for how to make more productive use of their resources and manage better the cash that they have' (Lassen, 1984). Given the experience of the Grameen Bank, one wonders how much this approach is informed by the intermediary organization itself, and how much by the needs of the poor.

Entrepreneurial clients, while distinct from pre-entrepreneurial because they were already engaged in some sort of enterprise, do not form a homogeneous group. They range in size along a continuum from the single hawker selling peanuts from her basket to small industries turning out non-electric machinery. Generally the manufacturing enterprises had more employees and more income than the smaller service enterprises. A recent survey in Jordan found that 43 percent of the microenterprises, defined as having fewer than five employees, are engaged in industrial activity; the number of workers in all microenterprises is evenly distributed between paid and unpaid, and averages 2.18 per enterprise (Weidemann et al., 1987). The entrepreneurs themselves are not young men waiting for formal-sector jobs; rather they are older women and men who see their firm as a long-term economic activity. Their educational levels tend to be low, and the skills those learned as apprentices or in the home (Blayney and Otero, 1985). In most countries microenterprises operate outside governmental regulations which are usually set up with larger enterprises in mind, and can therefore be considered extra-legal if not actually illegal. As a result all microenterprises are open to varying degrees of harassment or bribery, though those actually on the street suffer the most.

Organizations working with these existing entrepreneurs offer credit as their major intervention. Indeed, credit was seen by most of the beneficiaries as their outstanding need, and is often the carrot used to pull them into the programmes; other expressed needs tended to be more specific to the type and size of the enterprise, but include access to raw materials, improved business practices, and marketing assistance. Credit is also perceived as the simplest to administer (Ashe, 1985a). However, the smaller the loan, the higher is the percentage it is likely to be of administration costs. Therefore, the intermediary organizations have been searching for low-cost methods of securing and collecting loans; many have adopted the affinity group model. It seems to work best among people with little history of entrepreneurship; in contrast, in the Philippines 'reliance on group credit and group responsibility . . . was almost completely debunked'; staff complained that organizing groups took time away from its central objective of giving credit (Brown, 1981: 332).

The goal of most of the intermediary organizations was to help the microentrepreneurs become self-sufficient. Their programmes often included accounting and business skills, high-cost efforts which do not seem to be particularly appropriate. Forming and supporting affinity groups also takes staff time. Thus most intermediary groups operate their programmes at a loss, and so must rely on donor support themselves; on the other hand, most donors would like to see both the intermediary organization and the microentrepreneur become self-sustaining. A point of debate is interest rates. Project reports indicate that even prime rate is low compared to moneylenders' rates, and that most microentrepreneurs are willing to pay more for credit than is charged by the highly subsidized loan programmes of most voluntary organizations (Smith and Tippitt, 1982).

Banks in some countries are being encouraged or required to lend to microentrepreneurs. The Philippines Commercial and Industrial Bank Money Shops are set up in any market where there are at least 400 potential individual clients (Brown, 1981). The Banco Popular y de Desarrollo Comunal in Costa Rica in one year loaned an average of \$247 to 83 solidarity groups with 447 members (63 percent male and 37 percent female) (Ashe et al., 1985). In several Indian cities the Bank of Baroda maintains special branches solely to make loans of less than \$2000 (Brown, 1981). The Badan Kredit Kecamatan in Central Java has 486 village mini-banks which made close to 300,000 loans totalling $15 million in one year. Most loans support petty trading; 60 percent of the beneficiaries are women. Originally the scheme was both urban and rural. But the character reference system that works so well in rural areas where recipients of loans must be sponsored by their village head did not work in cities. As a result, defaults were high, and the urban programmes were dropped (Lilly, 1984). The banks offered only loans, often at a few points above prime interest rates, in order to operate profitably (Smith and Tippitt 1982). On the whole, beneficiaries of banks are the larger entrepreneurs.

So the debate focuses in on the poor versus the larger entrepreneurs, on equity versus self-sufficiency (Hunt, 1983). Where should scarce resources be used? Right now the pressure is on the side of growth. Economists argue that only those programmes which can be scaled up should be supported. Loans which stabilize a small enterprise, or improve the quality of life of the entrepreneur, are not acceptable. Some complain that neither the leaders of the intermediary organizations nor the microentrepreneurs have a commercial orientation, although this may be changing (Hunt, 1985a). Certainly they are right if this means an overriding preoccupation with profit.

Indeed, an element of subsistence societies often praised by observers is their support system, which shares the wealth and so prevents the weak from destitution, a 'moral economy' (Scott, 1976); migrants often perpetuate this mutual assistance concept through their urban networks (Lomnitz, 1977). While this sense of responsibility for each other has been undermined by modernization in much of the world, many Africans still look with suspicion on the accumulation of wealth. Historically, the richer men of a village gained status, and in some tribes a title, by holding elaborate parties which effectively redistributed wealth; male savings associations often save in order to sponsor a drinking spree. In Kenya today women's groups not only work together, but tend to hold profits in a group savings account or to buy household goods as a unit, so that even if they use them individually they are protected from appropriation by their husbands (van Ryzin-Havens and Kobia, 1987). What seems at odds with western economic values may in fact be wise survival strategies.

What is clear from the debate is that as long as microentrepreneurial projects must be subsidized, they will only reach a miniscule part of the urban poor entrepreneurs. One way to reach greater numbers is through training. An artisan programme in the then Upper Volta was designed to upgrade existing craftsmen. In Kenya over 270 village polytechnics have been set up to teach such vocational skills as carpentry, masonry and tailoring. About three-quarters of the students are male. Nearly 80 percent of the graduates are employed, although only one-third set up their own enterprises. Among these new entrepreneurs the balance between men and women is nearly equal.

While these two African programmes reach to the poorest strata of society, the two training programmes in India tended to recruit from educated unemployed. The National Association of Educated Self-Employed Youth (NAESEY) in Madras 'appears to be the best system for developing new entrepreneurs that this study has been able to identify' (Brown, 1981: 360). Essentially NAESEY is a network of microentrepreneurs who collaborate to provide functions or services of a much larger organization. The first enterprises set up by its originator, Loyola Joseph, were tea kiosks, which operate like franchises. The kiosk operators must follow high cleanliness standards and charge similar prices; they are given a loan to buy the kiosk. All their basic commodities — tea, coffee, milk, biscuits — are bought from other NAESEY entrepreneurs. Loan repayments are collected by apprenticed NAESEY members. The income from a well-run kiosk approaches that of a middle-level civil servant (Brown, 1981).

Donors and scholars, then, both identify a community of the poor where survival, not profit, is the dominant goal. But even in the slums, and certainly counted as informal sector, are micro-and small entrepreneurs whose income surpasses that received by many in the formal sector. The goals and values of the clients must be understood before either programmes are designed or theories constructed. The goals and values of the intermediary organizations, and of the scholars, must also be assessed when trying to bring order out of a very complex universe (Hunt, 1985b).

Cognizant of the tendency of observers to assume that they and their clients hold identical values, PISCES project co-ordinator Jeffrey Ashe cautions us all in his prologue to the final report:

> We discredit what our clients are already doing and advise them to become what we want them to be: bigger, more collective, more formal, whatever. And we often end up managing sophisticated businesses the clients do not have the skills to manage themselves, marketing their goods through channels only we have access

> to, and providing them with training and orientation they never requested. We intensively assist a few, when we could use the same resources to assist many more (1985a: ii).

CONCLUSION

Three strands of inquiry have contributed to current knowledge about hitherto invisible entrepreneurs: women market traders, the informal sector and projects to assist the urban poor. Each perspective lends its own coloration to the debate: while a remarkable consensus on the basic issues and problems exists, there is little agreement as to the policy and programmatic implications of the data. All three sets of studies find wide class and income disparity among entrepreneurs active in the towns and cities of developing countries. Occupying the tiniest microenterprise strata, all identify a growing community of poor, largely populated by women and their children. But there is disagreement as to whether and how to help these poor women, particularly whether they are or can learn to be successful entrepreneurs.

There is even more disagreement over what it means to be a successful entrepreneur. Is sustainability a sufficient goal, or must a successful enterprise increase its productivity and profits, and employ more labourers? Why is investment in human capital not counted as success? And why must an urban business grow when a farmer can easily get loans to increase productivity but not size?

All three strands of inquiry deal implicitly with the informal sector, but almost no-one is concerned any more about drawing lines between informal and formal. The issue of place is of concern only to the scholars: market women know no boundaries between village, town or city; intermediate organizations run programmes wherever there are poor who want to become entrepreneurs. Among all groups there is a growing predilection to describe the real world of microentrepreneurs, assessing vertical ties to similar activities in the formal sector, seeking out rural linkages and noting horizontal relationships with other informal-sector enterprises rather than focusing on problems of exploitation and dependency between the sectors. Such was the intent of the Street Food project undertaken by the Equity Policy Center, which is described in the next section.

PART 4
Street Foods

The Street Foods project which the Equity Policy Center (EPOC) began in 1983 was designed specifically to collect information to answer the question: how do urban women earn money to support themselves and their families? Given the many unsatisfactory efforts of donor agencies and intermediary organizations to assist groups of women to produce income, we at EPOC wanted to find out what poor women were actually doing by themselves, or with the help of members of their family. Or were they helping their husbands, and if so, were they paid, or unpaid labour? What are the characteristics of the women and men street food sellers? How much money does an enterprise earn; who controls the use of that money, and for what purposes is the money used?

Street foods were selected because they are one of the most visible activities in the informal sector. Studies of market women traders often included prepared foods in the list of things these women sold. With few exceptions (see Moser, 1980), similar activities of men were not recorded, so that it is impossible to ascertain how large a share of the trade women controlled. Rather than study all activities of women traders, and try to compare them with activities of men traders, we decided to select a single sector and identify the role which women and men played within it.

A second set of questions revolved around the trade itself. Since the street food trade is one of the most visible activities of the informal sector, it is usually one of the most harassed by local officials. Therefore it was important to find out what regulations exist to control either their place of sale, or the foods they sell. Is their existence legal or illegal? Are they harassed, and by whom? What is the magnitude of the trade and its backward and forward linkages? What are other constraints of those selling street foods?

The final area of inquiry concerned possible ways of helping the vendors. Was credit their primary need, as it seemed to be for most informal-sector activities? Would credit help enterprises to grow? Was the sector viable or a dying institution? What did the vendors themselves perceive as their major problems?

Such a study would document, for the first time, both the demand and supply within a single sector. It would identify the work done by women and men, adding to our knowledge of the real work and putting additional pressure on the commissions who define work for national accounting purposes. Our findings would help clarify the needs of microentrepreneurs, particularly those considered to be part of the community of the poor. Above all, by presenting sex-disaggregated data for all the issues addressed, the Street Foods project would illustrate how critical such an approach is to understanding the reality of life, especially among the urban poor.

EPOC'S STREET FOODS PROJECT

The data presented here represent findings from a seven-country study which took place in two stages. The first round of countries studied during 1982–4, included Ziguinchor, Senegal; Manikganj, Bangladesh; Bogor, Indonesia; and Iloilo, the Philippines. The second round, in Ile-Ife, Nigeria; Minia, Egypt; and Chonburi, Thailand, were undertaken during 1984–6. These countries were selected where there was local interest and support, both from scholars and government; permits are necessary to conduct research if either the funds or the researchers are foreign. Negotiating for funds, identifying possible collaborators, getting governmental agreement, putting the research team together and selecting a town for the study site, these activities often take longer than conducting the research itself.

The basic study design was the same in all seven towns, but because the findings of the first round focused on the issues and problems, the second round of studies was able to add additional inquiries of particular local interest. In each country a variety of provincial towns were visited before one was selected; among other criteria it had to be small enough so that the entire urban area could be mapped and a full census taken of all sellers of foods on the street. Street foods include, by our definition, any food that can be eaten without further processing and is sold on the street, from pushcarts or baskets or balance poles, or from stalls or shops having fewer than four permanent walls.

Having completed the census the next step was to categorize the sellers by types of food: sweets, snacks, breakfast foods, light meals; and location: in fixed positions outside a cinema, near a school, in the market, or mobile vendors making fixed rounds. Using these categories a random sample of enterprises was selected for in-depth interviewing two or three times over the course of a year to measure seasonal variation. Details were asked about the vendors themselves, their families and the enterprise. A smaller sample of vendors was selected from those selling one of the five most-sold items for closer observation, both at the point of sale and at home. This sample was chosen to reflect women's contributions to the making or selling of these particular street foods. Data from this smaller sample, particularly regarding costs and profits, were used as a check against the broader survey instrument results. At each stage of the study the differences between the activities of women and men were carefully noted, to see whether the foods they sold, the places and times they worked, the implements they used or the organizations to which they belonged, were sex-specific.

Besides studying the microentrepreneurs themselves, and the economics of their street food enterprises, we were also concerned with the demand for, as well as the safety and nutritional value of, street foods. A random sample of customers was selected for interviewing to find out who eats street foods, and how often. In addition, in three countries a household survey of food consumption patterns was undertaken in order to find out how important street foods are to the diet of the general public. In the first round of countries an effort was made to judge nutritional values. The consensus was so clear that street foods provided an important part of total food consumption, particularly for the urban poor, that this issue was dropped from later study. In all countries the cleanliness habits of makers, whether at home or on the street, and of the sellers, were closely observed. In addition, during the first round studies, samples of the foods were analysed for bacterial contamination. The consistency of results from these tests, and the complications of initiating this activity, caused it to be dropped from the second round studies.

Since EPOC is a policy institute, the final step of the study was to design, in consultation with local research groups and intermediary organizations, possible interventions to improve the income of the vendors and/or the quality of the food. To enhance the possibilities of these recommended interventions being adopted, EPOC staff worked closely with local government officials throughout the research period. In some countries this consultation with scholars, activists and government officials was formalized by creating an advisory committee, either in the provincial town or in the capital, or both. In all cases, at the completion of the project, seminars were presented in both the town and the capital city to present the findings and discuss the interventions with as broad a range of interested local citizens and donor representatives as possible.

Data reported in the rest of this chapter are not individually cited. EPOC country directors were responsible for the their final reports and for presenting the report or a summary in the local language. Their final reports, listed in full in the bibliography, were authored by Jill Posner for Ziguinchor, Senegal; Naomi Owens and Naseem Hussain for Manikganj, Bangladesh; Barbara Chapman for Bogor, Indonesia; and Gerald Barth with his wife Mei-Jean Kuo for Iloilo, the Philippines. Much of the original analysis on the first four countries was done by EPOC project director Monique Cohen.

For the second round studies our collaborators undertook the research, with some consultation, and completed the final reports. Olufemi Kujore and Tola Pearce presented the final data for Ile-Ife, Nigeria, in a series of overlapping papers which are separately cited in the bibliography; a final report will combine them all. Sarah Loza authored the study of Minia, Egypt. Cristina Szanton and Napat Sirisambhand completed the study on Chonburi, Thailand.

Street Food Entrepreneurs

Data on who became street food entrepreneurs challenge earlier assumptions that workers in the informal sector are young migrants waiting for jobs in the formal sector. Further, although these data challenge inferences in informal sector literature that women entrepreneurs are generally to be found among the community of the poor, they nonetheless lend support to assumptions that the majority of women engaged in such activities are likely to make less money than men because of time and structural constraints. Further, they challenge the repeated assumptions about the marginal importance of women's income to their families' survival; in fact a woman's income is crucial to feed and clothe her children and pay their school fees. But these data do confirm the critical influences which sociocultural attitudes and practices have on women's work, a factor which contributes to the tremendous variation among male and female entrepreneurs and enterprises within the informal sector in different countries.

Table 1 presents basic data on the seven countries studied as to population size, number of enterprises selling street foods in the high season, and the percentage of enterprises outside the major commercial

TABLE 1
Street food enterprises by city

City	Urban population	Enterprises (high season)	Population per enterprise	Percentage outside commercial area
Manikganj, Bangladesh	37,996	550	69	8
Chonburi, Thailand	46,000	1,370	34	36
Ziguinchor, Senegal	86,295	1,534	56	59
Ile-Ife, Nigeria	135,000	2,603	52	87*
Minia, Egypt	200,000	784	255	52
Iloilo, Philippines	244,827	5,100	48	74
Bogor, Indonesia	248,000	17,760	14	85

*Twenty-three percent of foods are sold in completely residential areas; 64 percent in mixed residential and smaller commercial areas.

centres. Minia excepted, these data support the intuitive assumption that the number of street food enterprises increases with, and faster than, the increase in city size. A possible explanation for the exception of Minia lies in the types of food eaten as a regular diet and that eaten on the street. In most countries the traditional foods eaten at home take a long time to make, so that busy housewives or working women will avoid this effort by feeding their families street foods. However, in Egypt the basic diet of cheese and bread is served cold, so that meals require a minimum of preparation. On the other hand, the favourite street foods in Minia, sold by fully one-third of the vendors, are bean-based *foul* or *tamia*, both of which take considerable time to prepare.

The location of street sellers is important. Assumptions are made, when hearing the term street foods, that these vendors who sell from moving or parked carts congest the downtown streets. In fact, except in Manikganj, the predominant street food sellers plied their wares outside the main commercial areas. This is consistent with where most small eating establishments are found in any country: in the neighbourhoods where the families are. The fact that in tropical areas the vendors do not invest in permanent buildings should not be surprising; nor could most vendors afford such costs. This fact is important when considering urban plans and services.

In all countries the truly mobile vendor is in the minority. Most carts are pushed to the same location each day and removed at night. Some vendors have two regular positions: school and cinema, for example.

Even women selling from baskets carried on their heads tend to squat in the same place every day: in front of the court, next to the bus station, or outside the market place. There are some really mobile vendors: bicycle carts are used to pedal breads or sate or ices; shoulder balance poles allow a tiny stool to be carried on one end to balance the sweets or tea on the other. Such vendors follow a regular route every day. These mobile vendors accounted for perhaps a quarter of all sellers in Ife, 18 percent in Chonburi and 10 percent in Ziguinchor.

Seasonality is a major feature in Ziguinchor, where many vendors return to their family farms to assist in planting or harvest. Thus the total of vendors fell to less than half, from 1534 in the dry season to 748 in the rainy season. The fall was less precipitous in Chonburi, where the 1370 dry season vendors was reduced to 948 in the rainy season. In Bogor the total number of vendors dropped only by 5 percent in the prime agricultural season, perhaps reflecting the high population densities in rural Java. In Bangladesh the major variant was Ramadan rather than agricultural labour demands. During this Islamic month of fasting the number of vendor enterprises fell 45 percent, to 303. This holiday did not seem to affect other Islamic countries as much.

TABLE 2
Street food entrepreneurs by age and sex

City	Median age	Operators (%)			Women's involvement (%)
		Women	Men	Couples	
Manikganj, Bangladesh	32	1	99	—	37
Chonburi, Thailand	36	78	22	—	78
Ziguinchor, Senegal	35	77	23	—	77
Ile-Ife, Nigeria	34	94	6	—	94
Minia, Egypt	35	11	89	—	23
Iloilo, Philippines	41	63	10	27	90
Bogor, Indonesia	35	16	60	24	40

Table 2 indicates that the average vendor is middle-aged; this shows a consistency across cultures. In contrast, women's various roles in the making and selling vary by country, due to cultural and religious factors. In Ile-Ife and Iloilo women account for some 90 percent of all street food vendors; in Ile-Ife the women work alone, while in Iloilo a successful vendor may be joined by her husband. In Ziguinchor and Chonburi women form over three-quarters of the vendors; in both countries, as in Ile-Ife, women and men sell separate types of food and never work together. The lowest figures for women selling alone were 1 percent in Manikganj, 11 percent in Minia and 14 percent in Bogor, Indonesia; however, in these countries many wives made the foods their husbands sold, so that women worked worked in 23 percent of all enterprises in Minia, 37 percent in Manikganj and 40 percent in Bogor. These figures, even for vending alone, are higher than many found for the informal sector, many of which focused on more complex enterprises (Sethuraman, 1981). These data argue for more careful research design which is sensitive to who makes decisions in couple-run enterprises and will include family labour.

Education also varies across the sample. Illiteracy is presumed to characterize vendors, and this is indeed the case in the two African countries: 80 percent of those in Ziguinchor and 60 percent of those in Ile-Ife. It is also true among the women vendors in the more traditional Islamic countries studied: 93 percent in Minia and all in Manikganj were illiterate. However, in Manikganj the male vendors had considerable schooling with only 32 percent illiterate, 26 percent with between 6 and 10 years of school and another 6 percent with vocational school training. In Minia 47 percent of the men had had some schooling: 17 percent had graduated from secondary school. In Southeast Asia both women and men had more education. In Iloilo, in contrast, the average education among the vendors was 8 years in school; while 47 percent had 6 years or less, a third had completed high school and 20 percent had some university education. Since Iloilo is a university town, it is perhaps less surprising that some of the students who worked their way through college assisting street food vendors find that their income in this occupation is higher than most low-level governmental posts.

TABLE 3
Migration patterns of street food sellers

City	Birthplace				
	City	Near village	Region	Country	Foreign
Manikganj, Bangladesh	35	45	20	—	—
Chonburi, Thailand	36	—	30	34	—
Ziguinchor, Senegal	39	—	34	11	16
Ile-Ife, Nigeria	55	—	39	6	—
Minia, Egypt	55	13	29	—	—
Iloilo, Philippines	46	—	47	7	—
Bogor, Indonesia	23	22	55	—	—

Street food vendors are not recent migrants in any of the cities studied. Even among those who were not born in the town, most had lived there over 10 years. Several interesting facts stand out from the data on migration. First, increased rural poverty does not require migration. Many of those vendors born in rural areas near the city continue to live there, and commute daily to work in the city. This applies to all the villagers coming from near Manikganj; one-third of the vendors in Bogor live in villages, which means some of the migration has been to villages. Some of this anomaly is the result of municipal boundaries. For example, Manikganj municipality, where 55 percent of the vendors live is divided by residents into the town, where 39 percent live, and the 16 percent in rural suburbs that are not villages. A visitor could not distinguish between suburbs and village. Both the municipalities of Ziguinchor and Iloilo encompass farmland; in Senegal these farms provide alternative income for many vendors, but in the Philippines they seem mainly to supply ingredients. In Ile-Ife, 7 percent of the vendors maintained a farm which provided them with additional support.

In contrast, in Minia, only 3 percent of the vendors currently live in the rural area, so there has been in-migration from these areas to that city. However, 28 percent of the vendors in Minia commute from other urban areas in Minia Governorate while 29 percent listed their birthplace as urban areas in Minia or Upper Egypt. This means that of the current city vendors living in the city, 80 percent were born in the city, another 5 percent came from other urban areas, and 15 percent came from the rural areas.

The pattern of migration into Bogor clearly reflects changes in the countryside, and in this regard seems to fit the expected pattern of accelerating rural migration. Of the migrants, 14 percent came over 15 years ago, 45 percent during the 1970s and 41 percent in the first 3 years of the 1980s. The surge of migrants coincides with the introduction of the green revolution in rice cultivation, a system which requires fewer farm labourers. In Bogor, more women vendors (61 percent) than men (42 percent) were local in origin. This is the reverse of Chonburi where 80 percent of the men, in contrast with only 33 percent of the women, were native-born.

Street vending is a permanent occupation for many. We find that 20 percent of the vendors in Ziguinchor have sold the same product in the same place for over 20 years! Twenty-three percent of the establishments in Manikganj were founded before liberation 12 years earlier. In Chonburi the median age of an enterprise was 7.2 years.

Street food vendors, then, do not fit the pattern of recent migrants from rural areas seeking short-term employment. In the less urbanized countries many vendors have not migrated; rather they are landless or underemployed villagers who may happen to live near or within municipal boundaries. In the most urbanized country of Egypt, vendors are urban-born. While data suggest a high failure rate in the early years of an enterprise, a phenomenon found worldwide, it is also clear that many vendors make the street food trade a life's work.

The Street Food Trade

Street food vendors do not keep written records, but most have very clear memories of outlays and income. However, few are willing to confide such details to interviewers. Our data on income are the result of estimating daily costs and observing daily sales. These data were cross-checked during the in-depth studies of individual vendors. Overall statistics indicate that street food sellers make a reasonable income compared to other alternatives available in the cities, but there is wide variation between countries and within the occupation.

In Iloilo average profits are above the minimum daily wage; in Bogor they are higher than the wage for construction workers. In Manikganj incomes are more than twice the wage of an unskilled agricultural worker, more than that of a mason, and about the equivalent of a carpenter. Women vendors in Ziguinchor make more than housemaids. The Chonburi study shows a daily income range from 90 to 504 baht, with the lower end enough to support a family of four or five persons. However, averages mask poverty. In Ile-Ife the data were collected during the recession; data reveal about half the vendors making meagre profits, with only a quarter making a good income.

Income derived is essential to household survival. In Ziguinchor, 59 percent of the women vendors are the sole support of their families, which have an average size of 9.5 people! Women vendors in Minia provide the main sources of income in 55 percent of the survey, but men do so 70 percent of the time. In Chonburi, 20 percent of the women provided the main source of income for their families while another 21 percent of the women vendors, who were unmarried, contribute to their families' income. The women of Ile-Ife say they never share their incomes with husbands, a fact partially explained by data showing that 16 percent were not yet married; of those married, over half live in a polygamous union; and the modal family size is five to seven children. Still, in the poor economic situation of Nigeria at the time, one-third of the women had additional sources of income, the majority in other businesses.

In all countries the woman's income is used for household expenditures and for school fees. Typically, in Thailand, men supply the house, women the food. Due to Islamic strictures, men in Senegal are expected to provide the basic staple; in our sample 84 percent of the men bought a large bag of rice each month for family consumption. Women's daily expenditures on food over the month equalled that of the cost of the staple, but in their minds they were just supplying sauce for the rice; their major expenditures are for clothes and school fees. School fees were the reason given by many Iloilo women vendors for returning to work.

The street food trade is hard work. Overall, more than three-quarters of vendors are one-person enterprises, although they may have unpaid family help at home; the largest such enterprises were found in Africa; 95 percent in Ziguinchor, 84 percent in Ile-Ife, Nigeria. Unpaid family labour is also present at the point of sale: spouses, usually, but also children and parents. In general, about 10 percent of enterprises hire paid employees to help with the selling, though this figure is 25 percent in Iloilo. The average number of persons per enterprise is 1.7 both in Mania and in Manikganj, but most of the additional labour is unpaid family help.

Home help is used in processing and preparing foods: in Iloilo three-quarters of vendors sold products they or their families made; the figure is 80 percent for Egypt, perhaps an exaggerated finding since sellers of industrially made drinks and snacks were excluded from the survey questionnaire. In contrast, the trade in Manikganj is dominated by middle men (57 percent) who primarily sell products made by village women, such as puffed rice or canacur, a rice and pulse snack; only 35 percent are producer/sellers. Such a situation may reflect the involution of petty trade under high population pressure; and/or it may reflect cultural traditions of purdah.

In both Ziguinchor and Minia the foods that women sold took longer to prepare, somewhere between 2 and 3 hours; men tend to spend less time in preparation, about 1 hour. In both countries this allows men to sell on the street for longer periods. This tendency, and the fact that most women must also tend the house, means that women often sell for fewer hours; as a result, women working alone seemed in all countries to make less than men alone, except in Bogor where women often sell medicinal beverages which are highly profitable. Where couples work together, as in Iloilo and Bogor, the income was the highest.

This mix of processing and selling makes it difficult to classify the street food trade by using the usual economic categories of trading, manufacturing or service enterprises. In fact, street food entrepreneurs do all of these activities. Perhaps because of this mix, it seems likely that the street food trade will be a permanent feature of the urban environment.

Demand for Street Foods

Household survey data in four towns indicate a high demand for street foods by households in all income categories. In Bogor the average household spent 25 percent of the daily food budget on street foods; the figure is 30 percent in Iloilo: 20 percent is eaten away and another 10 percent is brought home to eat. In Chonburi the average household expenditure on street foods is 47 percent, with a slightly higher percentage of the budget being spent by the poorest income group. In fact in Thailand, where multiple dishes are the traditional diet, 70 percent of the households in Chonburi do not cook food for every meal and thus depend on street foods, eaten on site or brought home. Thirteen percent of those surveyed *never* cook at home: many are government employees who were transferred to town and have left their wives and families elsewhere. Households where the wife works away spend somewhat more for street foods than those households where the wife stays home. One of the busiest times of day is late afternoon as working wives pick up their families' evening meals; the vendors call them 'plastic bag housewives'.

In Ile-Ife 83 percent of all households surveyed buy breakfast between 4 and 7 days a week. However, a variation exists between different residential areas as to the percentage of household food budgets that go for street foods: in central Ife, and in the mixed residential/commercial area, over half the budget is spent on prepared foods; near campus or in the older residential area families spend only a third of their budget on street foods. Of particular interest is the opinion of the householders surveyed that they have increased their consumption of street foods. The report concludes:

TABLE 4
Occupations of street food customers: sex (percentages)

City	White-collar	Informal sector	Wage labour	Students/children	Housewives[a]	Other[b]	Percentage male
Manikganj, Bangladesh	19	40	3	12	1	24[c]	98
Chonburi, Thailand	20	38	10	15	10	7	38
Ziguinchor, Senegal	18	10	6	35	17	14	55
Ile-Ife, Nigeria	11	38[d]		46	—	5	n.a.
Iloilo, Philippines	21	47[d]		16	12	4	51
Bogor, Indonesia	14	37[d]		33	12	4	n.a.

[a]Housewives means unemployed women.
[b]Other includes unemployed men.
[c]Includes 22 percent farmers.
[d]Combines informal sector and wage-earners.

> it would appear that many people are reacting to the economic recession in Nigeria, and the difficulty of obtaining foodstuffs and cooking materials, by patronizing street sellers who prepare in bulk, thus enabling the food to be cheaper, because of the economies of scale. Thus eko [corn pudding] and stew may be substituted for home cooked rice, dodo or yam, all of which are increasingly costing more (Pearce, 1984: 26).

In order to regularize and regulate vendors selling on campus, the University of Ife has developed a *bukateria* system; the university supplies buka (stalls) with water and electricity for a nominal rent to vendors who have completed a course on nutrition and sanitation run by Olufemi Kujore of the nursing department. Indeed, it was Kujore's interest in extending this certification to vendors in the city that led to the collaborative effort to study the sector in that town. This approach for enhancing the safety of street foods is one that deserves emulation.

Customer surveys were conducted at the point of sale to determine who buys street foods. In four of the six countries with comparable data the greatest number of customers are informal-sector workers and casual wage labourers such as construction workers, masons and carpenters. Most of these labourers work outside the formal sector, so that it can be said that two-fifths of the customers of the vendors are their peers. Another fifth come from white-collar professions.

Students are important customers in all countries. They predominate in Ziguinchor and Ile-Ife, and constitute one-third of the buyers in Bogor. The Chonburi survey underrepresents the importance of street foods in the diet of children because their sale is regulated by governmental policy. This requires the school or university to select a particular vendor to supply food on the school campus. Other vendors must wait outside the school or university enclosure after school. Our figures do not include on-campus sales.

Data from Bangladesh underscore the pervasiveness of purdah; 98 percent of the 436 customers were male. Actually of the 10 female customers, only one was a housewife, but we have reported 1 percent of the sample to indicate that single woman. The other nine women included a school-teacher, four students, three wage labourers and a beggar.

ISSUES

The importance of street foods as income and food for the urban dweller has been clearly documented above. The equal importance of the sector to the municipality is also clear. In previous analyses of the economic implications of the data we have estimated that the proportion of the labour force directly or indirectly active in the street food trade ranges from a low of 6 percent in Manikganj to over 25 percent in Bogor. Aggregate yearly sales, expressed in 1985 US dollars, contributed two million US dollars to the economy of the small district town of Manikganj and an amazing sixty-seven million US dollars to the booming city of Bogor (Tinker et al., 1985). The point here is not the exact economic contribution, but its magnitude.

Municipal governments cannot afford to disrupt as important a sector as street foods, yet harassment is a more typical response than assistance. In EPOC's policy conclusions we argue that governments should legitimize the sector and support it with services and credit (Tinker et al., 1985). Three issue areas are particularly pertinent to our argument of putting reality before theory: harassment, food safety and credit.

Harassment of street vendors is so common, worldwide, that incidents are no longer news; but the effects are seldom studied. However, as the street foods study in Ile-Ife was nearing completion the new military government of Nigeria reactivated an old ordinance in July 1984 which forbids structures to be built close to major roads. According to the original inventory of street food sellers, 33 percent sold from buka (stalls) along the street and another 30 percent sold along the roadside. Thus the 'road clearance' operation, during which all buka were demolished, affected nearly 70 percent of all vendors. Local researchers interviewed the displaced vendors who relocated elsewhere. These vendors had to keep working since none of them had alternative sources of income. Over 50 percent were in their 40s, indicating continued pressure to support children. Before demolition, 75 percent of the enterprises that moved had employed assistants; after the move only 25 percent did. They found that over 90 percent of the street food sellers were making less than half the income they made before they were forcibly moved, while the rest were making even less (Kujore et al., 1986). What these facts tell us is that only the more successful vendors, those for whom street food selling was their only income source, continued vending in face of government harassment.

The insecurity engendered by the threat of government harassment was cited in the EPOC study as the major problem facing vendors. In Iloilo a vendors' association had been formed in an effort to reduce confrontations with the police. In return for self-policing to ensure the vendors did not sell in front of any store which objected, did not occupy more than half the pavement and kept their surroundings clean, the police reduced their harassment. At the final EPOC seminar the mayor and the head of the association, both of whom attended, agreed to meet and discuss other mechanisms to improve both the situation of the vendors and the appearance of downtown. In Manikganj a local social service group began, for the first time, to try to help organize the vendors. They met with the town and district officials during the EPOC seminar to discuss some way to legitimize the vendors by the bus stop and along the main road leading into the court area.

Harassment is primarily a problem of the pavement and roadside vendors. Most cities have long-term arrangements for vendors in or near market areas; regular taxes are charged in these areas and water is usually provided. Problems arise because of crowding. Vendors spill over into the lanes near the market, obstructing traffic. Government response is often to build new markets so far away from the customers that neither seller nor buyer will use them (Bromley, 1978).

Harassment is often justified with the argument that street foods are dangerous to eat. Our studies indicate that foods eaten soon after cooking are generally safe; contamination comes from unclean hands and plates, and from dust. Requiring food to be covered, as it is in Thailand, could reduce much contamination quickly. More important, the provision of clean water, in which to wash hands and dishes, would dramatically improve the safety of street foods. In Ile-Ife only 8 percent of the street food enterprises had access to running water. Other water sources were questionable: 69 percent of the vendors used shallow-well water; 3 percent used streams; 12 percent bought from a water vendor; a few used rain water!

Governments try to control street vending by requiring licences, yet too often the procedures are so time-consuming that few vendors apply. For example, in Egypt a food vendor most submit a series of certificates indicating good health, no criminal record, approval of the location from the local police station and health approval of utensils; also vendors need two photos and a birth certificate, and they must pay a fee. Even so, most of the favourite street foods are not allowed to be sold by vendors. Despite these regulations, two-thirds of the vendors in Minia held health certificates. In contrast, another law requires stationary vendors to pay for the space they occupy, but such permission is seldom granted.

Creating mini-markets in congested commercial areas along side streets or in open areas ought to become high priority for municipal planners. Clean water should be available to seller and customer alike, along with simple stools and trash receptacles. Those enterprises located in residential neighbourhoods should also be provided with basic water and sewerage facilities. The right to a space in a mini-market, and to water privileges, would be contingent on registration. Procedures should be simple, and the fee low. Since most vendors already pay some sort of fee or tax, this requirement would not seem too onerous. Access to prize spots near cinemas or on school grounds could be granted only after the vendor has passed a course on sanitation and nutrition. Such procedures would enhance the income of the vendors, improve the safety of the foods sold, improve the traffic flow and appearance of downtown areas and still allow an important part of the urban food system to function well.

Organizing vendors into associations would make the administering of the mini-markets easier. Such organizations also provide a convenient channel for the provision of other services. Health insurance seemed to be a major concern for these microentrepreneurs whose business relies on them alone. The provision of day care is often mentioned in those countries where young women are vendors. Our data show how culture-specific that issue is: mothers with children are typical in Nigeria and Peru (Picasso, 1986), but not elsewhere.

Credit is assumed by donor agencies to be the primary need of all microentrepreneurs. Efforts by intermediary organizations funded by donor groups and designed to reach the smallest enterprises were discussed in the preceding section. Credit was made available to such enterprises on the assumption that they would grow. The only new loan programme which reached microentrepreneurs in the towns studied was in Iloilo, where three vendors utilized low-cost bank loans. This low demand indicates both a traditional antipathy by vendors to borrowing and a lack of interest in expanding the business.

Vendors were asked where the capital came from to start their business. Almost all started with monies from their own savings or from relatives: 91 percent in Ile-Ife, 80 percent in Manikganj and 65 percent in Iloilo. Friends gave no-interest loans in another 10 percent of the cases in Manikganj and Ile-Ife. Only in Iloilo were moneylenders a significant source of starting capital; 18 percent borrowed. Another method of starting up without their own funds is to get an advance from the producer or a distributing company such as Coca Cola. Fifteen percent of the vendors in Iloilo began this way; 5 percent in Manikganj. Daily credit for foods to be prepared and sold that day was also common: 44 percent of vendors in Minia used this type of credit. No interest was charged on these foodstuffs, but many vendors thought that their costs would be reduced if they could buy in greater quantities.

Vendors did occasionally have to borrow, usually as a result of illness or for weddings, deaths, etc. Moneylender rates are extremely high, from 5 to 40 percent per month. Most vendors are rightly fearful of getting involved in such loans; yet alternative sources of low-interest credit for emergencies, as opposed to credit for the enterprise, are nonexistent. It was for this reason that the Grameen Bank required the affinity groups to set up emergency funds unrelated to economic activities; this fund may be loaned to members by vote of the members themselves.

Given the close connection between home and work site, it is not surprising that household and enterprise finances are frequently inseparable. Dipping into operating and investment capital when family emergencies arise is not uncommon; indeed illness of the seller can mean the end of the enterprise. This tendency to mix personal and business money often limits the ability of street food establishments to accumulate capital for further investment. It also makes lenders very nervous about loans; yet it is likely to be the personal needs for money that destabilize the business. The issue cannot be conveniently split.

While vendors would have liked some credit to improve inventories, few seem eager to expand. Even enterprises with considerable profit do not seem to want to undertake the sort of problems which arise when a family-run firm grows bigger. In a follow-up study in Iloilo to see if any street food vendors crossed the gap and became restaurant owners, not a single case was found of this type of scaling up (Barth and Kuo, 1984). There are many new difficulties involved in hiring employees, such as meeting a payroll, keeping accounts and providing space. Growth might necessitate finding larger quarters to make or sell, where before the house was used for one or both functions. Prepared foods must be sold quickly, or else they must be refrigerated or packaged, both of which mean additional investment. The risk of operating without a licence is also greater to larger enterprises. Further, government regulations are also more likely to be enforced on the slightly larger firms.

Instead of expanding the family enterprise into a different type of entity, investment by street food operators took other directions. The most common investment was in the education of children. Enterprises with sufficient income tend either to expand laterally or to move into other types of activity such as transport or the selling of groceries and other non-perishable foods. Some 19 percent of the firms in Iloilo sold at more than one location. In most cases such expansion was treated like a new firm run by another family member. Thus expansion is on an amoeba model, one of replication, rather than on the hierarchical model of a pyramid.

Findings from the street foods study illustrate the importance of primary research to find out how the urban poor actually support themselves. Equally critical is the necessity of disaggregating data by sex, so that the different roles and constraints of women and men are identified. As kin networks become increasingly fragile, the power relationships between women and men become critical in the distribution of income, whether earned by the woman or man. Invisibility disappears when theory is not allowed to triumph over reality.

PART 5
Seeing the Real World

The Street Foods study has added considerable data to the growing knowledge base about the poor in developing countries today. These data frequently have challenged the current wisdom about how countries develop economically. These straws of knowledge, added to the many other studies referred to in the sections on 'Invisible workers' and 'Invisible entrepreneurs', may help bring down the old, worn, plastered-over theories of development, so that a more equitable one can be constructed on a more realistic base.

Three problem areas, not yet explored, need to be added to this new base. They are complex concerns, still in need of much study. The following discussion is meant to set an agenda for further research on the linkages of the street food trade to national food systems; environmental issues of microenterprises; and the differential values and motivations of women and men microentrepreneurs.

LINKAGES

Street foods in urban settings was the topic of EPOC research; this aspect has been emphasized in the previous section. While the data suggest that street foods increase faster than city size, additional case studies are needed. As cities become larger, schoolchildren must increasingly eat at school while university students spill over from dormitories and also eat on the street. The pattern of having universities or schools select and train specific vendors to sell to students is one that deserves replication.

Visible street foods appear to be only part of the prepared-food sector in cities. Invisible street foods may turn out to be of equal importance. We observed, but did not study, the delivery of lunches and snacks to office workers. Usually this food was contracted for on a regular basis. Frequently the food was cooked in the basement or yard of the building; but it was also brought from home. The Annapurnas of Bombay provide a similar service for the textile workers: they deliver the noon meal to the factory. In addition, the workers come to the women's home for their evening meal (Savara, 1981). Wealthy working women in Bangkok send their maids to pick up the evening meal at a special kitchen; the meal is carried home in a stacked tiffin box, then heated in a microwave oven. In a Philippine barrio, one woman cooks regular meals for her neighbour who works as a laundress in town. Community kitchens in Lima's squatter settlements provide free meals to the families of volunteer cooks, and sometimes sell to families of working women who cannot participate. Clerks working in downtown Lima, where restaurants are expensive, contract to eat lunch in a woman's home. All of these activities are invisible, both statistically and to scholars; all are an essential part of the food system in urban areas.

Rural–urban linkages are of growing importance as planners focus on agriculture-led development. Rondinelli stresses the need to investigate 'how the economies of cities and towns in rural regions can be strengthened to provide off-farm employment and the services and markets essential to commercial farming' (1986: 256). A better understanding of the linkages within the food system can contribute to this knowledge. Street foods data showed that many rural residents made street foods at home and sold them in town. There were further indications of rural women selling prepared food to shops or vendors in town for resale, such as canacur in Manikganj which was primarily resold by middlemen. Sticky rice steamed in banana leaves was found to be a favourite sweet snack in Bogor. Our research design did not trace this sweet back to its village makers; we know nothing about the importance of this enterprise to the producer.

Similarly, data on the magnitude of the street food trade documented the importance of this sector as a market for locally grown agricultural produce. Our data sufficiently impressed the Governor of the region in which Iloilo is located that he recommended changes in the new rain-fed agricultural programme that was being developed (Tinker et al., 1985). The most successful street food enterprises in Iloilo were run by couples; while the wife tended the selling, the husband drove their truck to rural areas to buy produce directly. Organizations of vendors could increase their profits by developing or strengthening such linkages.

ENVIRONMENTAL ISSUES

A high percentage of street foods are made at home, either by the seller or by unpaid family assistance. Working at home, of course, solves the problems of childcare. Urban slums are often less clean than rural villages; both suffer from poor water supply and sewage disposal. Cleanliness is of greater concern for food handlers than it is for other occupations in the informal sector. Thus the general problem of increased crowding and decreased services in the urban slums of the developing world (Sethuraman, 1985) is particularly acute for street food producers and sellers.

Community centres where food could be cooked may be intellectually attractive, but realistically both the cost of construction and the problem of land make this a long-term dream in most countries. On the other hand, where such centres exist, or could be constructed, vendors could at least be trained in improved products and safe handling. Such a centre has been set up in a 'Pueblo Jovenes' outside Lima, where women make traditional cookies and cakes for sale downtown. Perhaps more promising is the use of local school buildings after hours. Multiuse buildings should be the goal in all slum upgrading schemes

VALUES AND MOTIVATIONS

Despite studies on the economic viability of microentrepreneurs, some economists continue to insist such activity is not truly an enterprise. According to ILO's Sethuraman:

> those entering such small-scale activities in urban areas are motivated mainly by employment and income rather than profit. Since the entrants to this sector are generally poor, ill-educated, ill-trained and often migrants, it is clear that they are neither capitalists seeking profitable investment outlets nor entrepreneurs . . . [T]he urban informal sector must be viewed as consisting of mainly small scale *units* (1981: 189)

In contrast, programmers for donor agencies classify microentrepreneurs as business people, not among the community of the poor. These classifications relate to the basic values held by different groups, and hence the type of support programme which should be introduced. The ILO approach emphasizes employment creation by having entrepreneurs invest profits back into the enterprise in order to expand. For them the highest value is the profit motive (Bear et al., 1982; Richardson, 1984).

Donors and intermediary organizations are willing to accept improved health, better housing, more children in school, even new clothes, as appropriate development goals. Consumption itself has a multiplier effect (Sethuraman, 1985) while an improved quality of life reduces the need for spending by government or organization on the health and welfare of the poor. If one must talk in economic equations, surely better cost–benefit analyses are in order.

On the other hand, many urban poor seem to retain values of responsibility for kin or community which may be called more moral than the single-minded pursuit of profits. Not only are there support networks to spread income, there is often a relationship between customer and seller that binds them to each other. In Ziguinchor, sellers of the breakfast porridge monie sold at a loss when millet prices rose precipitously, rather than lose valued daily customers. Is this unlike the loss-leaders frequent in retail shops in developed countries?

At the root of the problem is whether microenterprises can exist without subsidies and protection (Sethuraman, 1985). So complex are current systems of taxes and rebates, of incentives and special exceptions, that many formal sector industries are highly subsidized. Once again, what is needed are realistic assessments of who subsidizes whom.

The emphasis on economic values has contributed to the breakdown of the family support system in many countries. Data presented in this monograph show that employed women microentrepreneurs make less than their male counterparts. One explanation was that women spent longer on food processing, and so had less time to sell. They spent this time because they had little access to improved technology for processing the food. But women often had to work shorter hours because they had household tasks to accomplish. From around the world comes discouraging information about increased poverty and marginality of women (Heyzer, 1984; Young and Moser, 1981; Pellow, 1978). However, it is clear that income is not equivalent to status for women (Jain et al., 1979a). Scholars see the solution in the persistence of patriarchy (Bourque and Warren, 1981) and the inability of development programmes to address the 'underlying cause of female subordination–unequal gender relationships' (Rogers, 1983: 39).

CONCLUSION

The invisibility of women's work in a world which overvalues work, and the unpaid economic activity of women in a world which overvalues profit, help explain why women were for so long ignored by development theorists and practitioners alike. Over the past decade and a half the women in development community has documented women's work and shown why this work has been ignored in national accounts.

As the importance of women's economic contributions to household survival were acknowledged, programmes were set up to assist women in earning income. Because these programmes were not widely successful, EPOC undertook a study of microentrepreneurs in order to ascertain what poor women and men were doing to earn money in urban areas. Once more, the importance of women's income to family survival has been documented. But so has women's increasing disadvantage in the game of economic survival.

Basic to any new theory of development and change must be a recognition that other values exist besides those which exalt the profit motive and the unconstrained individual. The old encrusted development theories have fallen of their own inability to explain reality; at least part of their problem was the fact that they did not address the differential needs and problems of women and men, and so produced approaches to life that were inexcusably inequitable.

Revue française de sociologie

publiée avec le concours de
L'INSTITUT DE RECHERCHE SUR LES SOCIÉTÉS CONTEMPORAINES
CENTRE NATIONAL DE LA RECHERCHE SCIENTIFIQUE

59-61, rue Pouchet, 75849 Paris Cedex 17 — Tél. : 40 25 11 87 ou 88

OCTOBRE-DÉCEMBRE 1987, XXVIII-4 ISBN 2-222-96469-5

Sur la formulation des questions d'enquête
Un premier inventaire Jean-Paul GRÉMY

La participation aux associations
et le pouvoir municipal Richard BALME

NOTE DE RECHERCHE

Rupture et transition pour
les pensionnaires d'un centre
d'hébergement pour femmes battues Marcel DRULHE

NOTE CRITIQUE

L'apport de Gérard De Gré
à la sociologie de la connaissance
aux Etats-Unis François CHAZEL

LES LIVRES

Abonnements :

L'ordre et le paiement sont à adresser **directement** à :
Centrale des Revues, CDR
11, rue Gossin, 92543 Montrouge Cedex — Tél. : (1) 46.56.52.66
CCP La Source 33-368-61 CDR-Gauthier-Villars
Les abonnements sont annuels et partent du premier numéro de l'année en cours.

Tarif 1988 : L'abonnement (4 numéros) France .... 265 F
Etranger .... 312 F

Vente au numéro :

Par correspondance : Presses du CNRS, 20-22, rue Saint-Amand, 75015 Paris. Tél. : (1) 45.33.16.00 — Télex : 200 356 F.

A la librairie du CNRS, 295, rue Saint-Jacques, 75005 Paris. Tél. : (1) 43.26.56.11.

Tarif 1988 : Le numéro .... 84 F

Résumé: La 'Cuisine de la rue'

La 'cuisine de la rue'* est un type spécifique d'activité relevant de la microentreprise, et que l'on trouve dans toutes les villes du monde. Dirigé par les femmes dans de nombreux pays, ce service constitue une partie essentielle des chaines alimentaires urbaines dans les pays en voie de développement. Néanmoins, le commerce de la cuisine de la rue est illégal dans la plupart des pays; il est considéré par les leaders nationaux comme peu agréable à voir, insalubre, et dépassé. L'emploi dans le commerce de la cuisine de la rue n'est pas enregistré dans les calculs nationaux, comme cela arrive pour la plupart des secteurs irréguliers. Cependant, dans certaines villes, la cuisine de la rue pourvoit en fait des emplois à un dixième de la population, alors qu'elle entre pour 20% dans l'alimentation moyenne. Ces données et d'autres informations proviennent d'une étude réalisée sur sept pays et entreprise par l'Equity Policy Center (EPOC) de Chevy Chase, MD, USA, dont l'auteur en est le fondateur et le directeur.

Cette monographie débute par la recherche de raisons pour lesquelles les cuisinières de la rue et d'autres occupations similaires, dans les zones rurales aussi bien que dans les zones urbaines, sont classés dans un secteur d'activités de subsistance ou irrégulières, et sont rendus de ce fait statistiquement invisibles. En réalité on peut voir les femmes et les hommes travaillant manifestement dans les champs, allant chercher de l'eau et du bois pour le feu ou vendant des articles sur les trottoirs et les aires de marché à travers le monde.

Le problème surgit quand les recherches théoriques l'orientent de telle façon que les faits rassemblés masquent la réalité. La monographie suggère que c'est ce qui est arrivé au concept de travail, particulièrement tel qu'on l'a utilisé dans les pays en voie de développement. En accordant le même prix au travail qu'aux activités de secteur moderne, le travail effectué tant par les femmes que les hommes dans les sociétés pauvres, à l'intérieur et à l'extérieur des petites fermes et dans le secteur urbain irrégulier, a été au pire méconnu au mieux sous estimé. A cause d'informations inexactes les programmes d'assistance au développement ont fréquemment échoué dans les objectifs à atteindre.

Pendant la dernière décade, il y a eu une augmentation monumentale du nombre de subventions consacrées à des activités de travail invisible, pour leurs installations rurales et urbaines, réalisées par les chercheurs et par les practiciens du développement. Compte tenu que ces diverses branches de recherche s'informent rarement mutuellement, la monographie constate où en sont les choses à travers des domaines très différents mais qui néanmoins ont tous à voir avec la cuisine de la rue.

Dans la deuxième partie sur les 'travailleurs invisibles', le problème de définir le travail pour inclure les activités économiques en dehors du secteur moderne est analysé, et les efforts en cours pour élargir cette définition sont répertoriés. Un aperçu des études est présenté, documentant sur les activités économiques des femmes dans les sociétés pauvres. Les informations sur l'emploi du temps indiquent que la journée de travail d'une femme en secteur rural va de 10 à 12 heures, alors qu'elle va de 6 à 8 heures pour un homme. On cherche à savoir comment la fin de la ségrégation sexuelle dans le travail a augmenté le travail des femmes et réduit celui des hommes. L'augmentation de la pauvreté chez les femmes est liée à des hypothèses sur le soutien familial qui, de nos jours, peut fort bien ne pas venir.

La troisième partie a pour sujet: 'les entrepreneurs invisibles' parmi les pauvres des cités. Trois étapes de la recherche ont contribué à notre connaissance actuelle dans ce domaine. Les marchandes ont fort bien été étudiées en Afrique de l'ouest et il y a une information croissante sur les pays sud sahariens africains. Le rôle que jouent les femmes africains en tant que marchandes est à la fois requis et soutenu par la ségrégation sexuelle du travail dans ces sociétés. Aussi bien la politique gouvernementale que les systèmes compétitifs de livraison alimentaire nuisent au travail de ces marchandes, alors qu'au sein de la famille, les tendances vers les valeurs de classe moyenne poussent les femmes à la dépendance envers leurs maris. Un compte rendu de recherche moins abondant sur les marchandes en Asie et en Amérique Latine a été présenté et leurs rôles et leurs problèmes sont comparés à ceux des marchandes africaines.

Le débat des années 1970 sur le secteur illégal est repris. Comme le secteur de subsistence, les vendeurs de rue et les petits artisans ont toujours fait partie intégrante de la scène urbaine; ils ne déparaissaient qu'au niveau des statistiques. Leur existence continue à confondre les théoristes du développement économique de tendance aussi bien libérale que marxiste. Les tentatives pour réinterpréter les premières théories contribuent à expliquer pourquoi ce débat suscita tant de passions. On connaît le consensus actuel: le secteur est permanent, comme souvent est aussi la caractéristique dynamique de l'économie urbaine qui se compose d'un large éventail d'entreprises.

Les problèmes actuels sont alors identifiés et discutés. Les relations entre les secteurs légaux et illégaux continuent de faire l'objet d'un désaccord; soit-il bénin ou abusif? Une exploration du travail à domicile, qui est un phénomène grandissant dans les pays développés comme dans les pays en voie de développement, ajoute une dimension nouvelle au débat. Cette constatation que le secteur irrégulier est loin d'être homogène, a encouragé des études séparées sur différents types d'activités et sur les femmes ou les hommes qui travaillent à ces occupations. Le rapport conclue fréquemment à une gradation d'entreprises avec des entrepreneurs dynamiques d'un côté et une communauté pauvre d'un autre. Finalement, étant donné que la plupart des premières études sur le secteur irrégulier furent basées sur le secteur urbain, il fallait considérer les différences parmi des activités similaires pour des villes de tailles différentes et dans les zones rurales.

Une recherche sur les microentreprises parmi les pauvres en secteur urbain a fait le point sur la répartition et l'analyse des projets d'assistance déjà en place. Les organisations intermédiares qui mènent à bien ces programmes rapportent que la majorité écrasante de leur clientèle est féminine. Parmi les microentrepreneurs on peut distinguer plusieurs niveaux basés sur l'adresse, la taille de l'entreprise et la motivation. La plupart des organisations travaillent à un seul niveau. Un clivage des valeurs et des buts est observé entre le type humanitaire d'organisation intermédiaire qui tend à travailler avec le niveau le plus pauvre et ceux multipliés par le monde des affaires qui met l'accent sur le profit et la croissance qui travaillent avec les entrepreneurs les plus accomplis. Cette perspective affecte les types de programmes soutenus de même que la façon dont les crédits sont distribués et la manière dont le remboursement est effectué.

La quatrième partie a trait aux conclusions du projet de l'EPOC, *Street Food*, qui a recherché qui fabrique, vend et mange la nourriture vendue dans les rues de sept villes de provinces dans des pays en voie de développement. Les vendeurs de nourriture dans la rue se considèrent comme des employés permanents dans cette activité; ils ont tendance à être des hommes et des femmes d'un certain âge et sont rarement de nouveaux émigrants. L'implication des femmes dans la fabrication et la vente varie selon le pays suivant des raisons culturelles ou religieuses. Au Nigeria et aux Philippines les femmes représentent quelques 90% de tous les vendeurs de rue. Au Nigeria les femmes travaillent seules, alors qu'aux Philippines une vendeuse qui réussit peut être aidée par son mari. Au Sénégal et en Thaïlande les femmes représentent plus des trois-quarts des vendeurs. Dans ces deux pays, comme au Nigeria, les femmes et les hommes rendent des types de nourriture différents et ne travaillent jamais ensemble. Les plus basses proportions de femmes vendant seules étaient de 1% au Bangladesh, 11% en Egypte et 14% à l'ouest de Java, Indonésie. Néanmoins, dans tous ces pays-là, de nombreuses femmes préparaient les plats que leurs maris vendaient, de sorte que la participation des femmes dans les entreprises atteignait un total de 23% en Egypte, 37% au Bangladesh et 40% en Indonésie.

Le revenu du commerce de la cuisine de la rue dépassait légèrement le salaire d'ouvriers qualifiés. Pour une majorité des vendeurs, la vente de nourriture est leur seule ou principale source de revenu. Là où les femmes dirigent le secteur, leurs revenus sont élevés, mais partout ailleurs les revenus des femmes sont plus bas que ceux des hommes. C'est, néanmoins, une source essentielle de soutien pour la famille; au Sénégal dans 59% des cas les marchandes étaient le seul ou principal soutien dans leur famille, alors qu'au Bangladesh toutes les cinq étaient le seul soutien pour leur famille. L'importance du commerce semble augmenter avec l'accroissement de la taille des villes et atteindre entre 6 et 25% de la totalité de l'emploi dans les villes étudiées.

Environ un quart du budget alimentaire du ménage est dépensé dans la cuisine de la rue en Indonésie et aux Philippines. Les clients des restaurants de rue viennent de toutes le souches, mais les premiers clients sont d'autres microentrepreneurs et les pauvres des villes. Dans la plupart des pays les écoliers sont des clients importants. En général, la nourriture vendue est à la fois nutritive et saine.

Le problème majeur pour les vendeurs de rue est le harcèlement provenant du gouvernement. Des groupes intermédiaires essaient d'assister les vendeurs à former leurs propres organisations, particulièrement à entreprendre des démarches pour être reconnus par le gouvernement et bénéficier de ses services. Les autres buts de ces groupes incluent la mise en place de fonds de secours ou d'assurance maladie, là où il y a des vendeurs ayant des enfants en bas âges, on a institué des crèches qui fonctionnent la journée.

Les crédits sont utilisés avec parcimonie même lorsqu'ils sont accessibles à bas taux d'intérêt, car les propriétaires d'entreprises reconnaissent que l'expansion du commerce est difficile et risquée. L'extension prend la tournure d'une reproduction latérale ou d'une source améliorée des matières premières. Les profits des petites entreprises sont investis dans l'éducation scolaire de leurs enfants. Les entreprises aux revenus suffisants tendent à évoluer vers d'autres types d'activités tels que le transport ou la vente de produits d'épicerie et autres denrées non périssables.

Les conclusions de l'étude sur la cuisine de la rue illustrent l'importance des recherches préalables pour trouver comment les pauvres arrivent à s'en sortir dans les villes. Il est pareillement vital de répartir l'information par sexe, afin que les rôles et les contraintes des femmes et des hommes soient identifiées. Etant donné que les liens familiaux deviennent de plus en plus fragiles, les puissantes relations entre les femmes et les hommes deviennent critiques quant à la distribution du revenu selon qu'il est perçu par une femme ou par un homme. Quand on ne laisse pas la théorie triompher de la réalité, l'invisible disparaît.

*[*Note du traducteur:* 'cuisine de la rue'. Il n'existe pas d'expression en français pour traduire 'street food'. Il semble que 'cuisine de la rue' traduise alors exactement l'idée dont il s'agit: des plats cuisinés, faits, vendus et consommés dans la rue.]

Bibliography

ABDULLAH, T. and S. ZEIDENSTEIN (1979), 'Women's reality: critical issues for program design', in S. Zeidenstein (ed.).

ACHARYA, Mina and Lynn BENNETT (1981), *The Rural Women of Nepal: an Aggregate Analysis and Summary of Eight Village Studies*, Khatmandu, Center for Economic Development and Administration, Tribhuvan U., Book 9, Volume II. A truly groundbreaking series of studies on the activities and world views of women in eight villages in eight different parts of the country. Four studies conducted by Nepali and four by American scholars.

AFONJA, Simi (1981), 'Changing modes of production and the sexual division of labor among the Yoruba', *Signs*, 7 (2): 299–313.

AGARWAL, Anil (1984), 'Beyond pretty trees and tigers: the role of ecological destruction in the emerging patterns of poverty and people's protests', Fifth Vikram Sarabhai Memorial Lecture. New Delhi: Indian Council of Social Science Research.

AGARWAL, Bina (1984), *Women and Technological Change: Asian and African Experience*, New Delhi: Institute of Economic Growth.

AHMAD, Zubeida (1984), 'Rural women and their work: dependence and alternatives for change', *International Labour Review*, 123 (1) (Jan.–Feb.): 71–86. Author was director of the ILO's Programme on Rural Women and initiated many of the studies quoted in this monograph.

ALAM, Manzoor, Joy DUNKERLEY, K.N. GOPI and William RAMSAY with Elizabeth DAVIS (1985), *Fuelwood in Urban Markets: A Case Study of Hyderabad*. New Delhi: Concept.

ALCANTARA, Elsa, Manuela de la PENA, Martha ABUHADBA and Dorina FLORES (1985), *Crisis de Energia Rural y Trabajo Feminino en Tres Areas Ecologicas del Peru*. Geneva: ILO Programa Mundial del Empleo.

ALLEN, Sheila (1981), 'Invisible threads', *IDS Bulletin*, 12 (3): 41.

ANKER, Richard (1980), *Research on Women's Roles and Demographic Change; survey questionnaires for households, women, men and communities with background explanations*. Geneva: ILO.

ANKER, R., M. BUVINIC and N. YOUSSEF (eds) (1982), *Women's*

Roles and Population Trends in the Third World. London: Croom Helm.

ARDAYFIA, Elizabeth (1986), *The Rural Energy Crisis in Ghana: Its Implications for Women's Work and Household Survival*. Geneva: ILO World Employment Programme.

ARIZPE, Lourdes (1977), 'Women in the informal labor sector: the case of Mexico', *Signs*, 3 (1) (Autumn): 25–37.

ASHBY, Jaqueline (1985), 'Women and agricultural technology in Latin America and the Caribbean', *Women and Agriculture, and Rural Development in Latin America*. Cali, Colombia: CIAT.

ASHE, Jeffrey (1981), 'Synthesis and overall findings', referring to the PISCES Studies; in Farbman.

ASHE, Jeffrey (ed.) (1985a), *The PISCES II Experience: Volume I: Local Efforts in Micro-Enterprise Development*. Washington, DC: Agency for International Development. The second phase of this pathbreaking project; four pilot projects were set up to offer credit and other assistance to the poorest group of the informal sector. For phase 1 see Farbman, 1981.

ASHE, Jeffrey (ed.) (1985b), *The PISCES II Experience: Volume II: Case Studies from Dominican Republic, Costa Rica, Kenya, and Egypt*. Washington, DC: Agency for International Development.

ASHE, Jeffrey (1985c), 'Assisting the survival economy: the micro-enterprise and solidarity group projects of the Domincan Development Foundation', in Ashe, 1985b.

ASHE, Jeffrey, with Nancy MORITZ de MORALES, Angela ULIBARU, Marjorie LILLY (1985), 'Making a living: micro-businesses and the Banco Popular y de Desarrollo Comunal, San José, Costa Rica', in Ashe, 1985b.

AZAD, Nandini (1985), 'The Working Women's Forum', in Shimwaayi Muntemba (ed.), *Rural Development and Women: Lessons from the Field*. Geneva: ILO.

BABB, Florence E. (1982), 'Economic crisis and the assault on marketers in Peru', (Working Paper 06) Working Papers on Women in International Development, Michigan State University. A case study of the provincial city of Huaraz where the Peruvian government is taking action againt the small-scale marketers, blaming them for the rise in food prices. Babb argues that these marketers in fact keep prices down while providing a service to consumers.

BABB, Florence E. (1982), 'Marketers as producers: the "hidden" labor process of workers in petty commerce'. Paper presented at the annual meeting of the American Anthropological Association, Washington, DC, 6 December. 21 pp.

BANERJEE, Nirmala (1981), 'The weakest link', *IDS Bulletin* 12 (3).

BARTH, Gerald A. (1983), *Street Foods: Informal Sector Food Preparation and Marketing in the Philippines*. Washington, DC: Equity Policy Center.

BARTH, Gerald A. and Mei-Jean KUO (1984), *Crossing the Gap between Microeconomic Activities and Small-Scale Food Catering Establishments*. Washington, DC: Equity Policy Center.

BATES, Robert H. (1983), *The Regulation of Rural Markets in Africa*. AID Evaluation Special Study No. 14. Washington, DC: US Agency for International Development. 42 pp. An evaluation study on how rural markets are controlled and regulated by the governments of African nations to benefit non-farm sectors and urban consumers.

BAY, Edna (ed.) (1982), *Women and Work in Africa*. Boulder, CO: Westview. An excellent collection of studies documenting the decline in female productivity as a result of policies initiated under colonialism and continued today.

BEAR, Marshall, Henry JACKELEN, Michael TILLER with Doug HILL (1982), 'Microenterprise in the urban informal sector: case studies from Brazil and the Philippines'. ATI working paper. Washington, DC: Appropriate Technology International.

BEARDSLEY, John R. (1982), 'Program for investment in the small capital enterprise sector: PISCES Phase II'. Report on the second in a series of PISCES workshops, June 21–22 1982. Washington, DC. Cambridge, MA: Acción International/AITEC.

BEN-PORATH, Yoram, (ed.) (1982), *Income Distribution and the Family*, supplement to *Population and Development Review*, Vol. 8.

BENEDICT, Ruth (1934), *Patterns of Culture*. Cambridge, MA: Riverside Press.

BENERIA, Lourdes (ed.) (1982), *Women and Development: The Sexual Division of Labor in Rural Societies*, New York: Praeger, for ILO World Employment Programme. Valuable volume which presents case studies on women working in a variety of occupations, plus essays interpreting the trends. Her own chapter, 'Accounting for women's work', argues for counting both the use value and the exchange value of work.

BENERIA, Lourdes and Martha ROLDAN (1987), *The Crossroads of Class and Gender: Industrial Homework, Subcontracting, and*

Household Dynamics in Mexico City. Chicago, IL: University of Chicago Press.

BERNDT, Louise and Louis FERMAN (1976), 'Irregular economy: cash flow in the informal sector'. Report for the Center for Metropolitan Problems, National Institute of Mental Health, Washington, DC.

BHATT, Ela (1987), 'The invisibility of home-based work: the case of piece rate workers in India', in Singh and Kelles-Viitanen (1987). Author is charismatic founder of the SEWA, the Self-Employed Women of Ahmendabad. In this article she outlines the need for a National Commission of Self-Employed Women, which was subsequently set up by the Indian Government.

BIENEFELD, Manfred (1981), 'The informal sector and women's oppression', *IDS Bulletin*, 12 (3).

BINSWANGER, Hans P., Robert E. EVENSON, Cecilia A. FLORENCIO and Benjamin N.F. WHITE (eds) (1980), *Rural Household Studies in Asia*. Singapore: Singapore University Press. Important collection of empirical studies and discussions of methodological problems.

BIRDSALL, Nancy (1980), 'Measuring time use and nonmarket exchange', in W.P. McGreevey (ed.), *Third-World Poverty*. Lexington, MA: Lexington Books.

BIRKBECK, Chris (1978), 'Self-employed proletarians in an informal factory: the case of Cali's garbage dump', *World Development*, 6 (9–10).

BLAIR, Patricia (1980), *Health Needs of the World's Poor Women*. Chevy Chase, MD: Equity Policy Center (EPOC).

BLAYNEY, Robert and Maria OTERO (1985), 'Small and micro-enterprises: contributions to development and future directions for AID's support'. Report for the Employment and Enterprise Development Division. Washington, DC: USAID.

BLUMBERG, Rae Lesser (1979), 'Rural women in development: veil of invisibility, world of work', *International Journal of Intercultural Relations*, 3: 447–72.

BLUMBERG, Rae Lesser (1981), 'Females, farming and food: rural development and women's participation in agricultural production systems', in Barbara Lewis, 1981. Shows that work alone does not enhance women's status. Excellent bibliography.

BLUMBERG, Rae Lesser (1986), 'Gender stratification and economic development, paradigm and praxis at the intersection of social structure, human lives, and the African food crisis'.

Presented at the American Sociological Association; to appear in M.W. Riley, B. Hess and B. Huber (eds), *Social Structure and Human Lives*, 1988: Beverly Hills, CA: Sage.

BOSERUP, Ester (1970), *Women's Role in Economic Development*. London: George Allen & Unwin. Classic presentation of the impact of modernization and technology on women's work.

BOULDING, Elise (1976), *The Underside of History*. Boulder, CO: Westview Press. A tour de force review of history from a woman's perspective.

BOURQUE, Susan C. and Kay Barbara WARREN (1981), *Women of the Andes: Patriarchy and Social Change in Two Peruvian Towns*. Ann Arbor, MI: University of Michigan Press.

BROMLEY, Ray (1978), 'Introduction — the urban informal sector: why is it worth discussing?' and 'Organization, regulation and exploitation in the so-called "urban informal sector": the street traders of Cali, Colombia', in Ray Bromley, (ed.), *The Urban Informal Sector: Critical Perspectives, World Development* 6 (9–10) and republished separately by Pergamon. Basic primer for the informal sector debates.

BROMLEY, Ray (1982), 'From Calvary to white elephant: case of urban renewal and marketing reform in Cali, Colombia'. Centre for Development Studies, University College of Swansea.

BROMLEY, R. and C. GERRY (eds) (1979), *Casual Work and Poverty in Third World Cities*. New York: Wiley.

BROWN, Jason (1981), 'Case studies: Philippines and India', in Farbman, 1981.

BRUCE, Judith (ed.) (1987), *A Home Divided: Women and Income in the Third World*. Stanford, CA: Stanford University Press. An important series of studies which begin to penetrate the fog surrounding the income acquisition and control within the household.

BUNSTER, B. Ximena (1983), 'Market sellers in Lima, Peru: talking about work', in Buvinic et al., 1983.

BUNSTER, B. Ximena and Elsa CHANEY (photographs by Ellan Young) (1985), *Sellers and Servants: Working Women in Lima, Peru*. New York: Praeger. Portraits in words and pictures of domestic servants and street vendors set into the context of poverty and opportunity in Lima.

BURFISHER, Mary E. and Nadine R. HORENSTEIN (1985), *Sex Roles in the Nigerian Tiv Farm Household*. W. Hartford, CN: Kumarian Press.

BURNE, Simon (1985), 'Charcoal stove developments in Kenya: the present and the future'. London: Intermediate Technology Group working paper.

BUVINIC, Mayra, Margaret A. LYCETTE and William P. McGREEVEY (eds) (1983), *Woman and Poverty in the Third World.* Baltimore: Johns Hopkins University Press. Interdisciplinary collections of essays documenting women's poverty and women's economic contributions to poor households.

CARTER, Jean and J. MENDS-COLE (1982), *Liberian Women and their Role in Food Production and their Educational and Legal Status*. Liberia: USAID with the Government of Liberia.

CECELSKI, Elizabeth (1984), *The Rural Energy Crisis, Women's Work and Family Welfare: Perspectives and Approaches to Action*. Geneva: ILO Working Paper, World Employment Programme. Important discussion of the interrelationships between women's time and household fuel procurement and use.

CHAPMAN, Barbara (1984), *Streetfoods in Indonesia: Vendors in the Urban Food Supply*. Chevy Chase, MD: Equity Policy Center.

CHARLTON, Sue Ellen M. (1984), *Women in Third World Development*. Boulder, CO: Westview. Concise textbook which presents the issue thoroughly.

COHEN, Monique (1984a), *The Urban Street Food Trade: Implications for Policy*. Chevy Chase, MD: Equity Policy Center.

COHEN, Monique (1984b), 'The urban street food trade'. Draft Report submitted to USAID. Chevy Chase, MD: EPOC.

COHEN, Monique, H.C. BORRKFIELD and J.C. ENGLISH (1977), 'Functional diversity at the base of the urban system', *Journal of Tropical Geography*, 45: 12–25.

CROLL, Elizabeth (1982), 'The sexual division of labor in rural China', in Beneria, 1982.

DASGUPTA, Subhachari and Asok MAITI (1986), *The Rural Energy Crisis, Poverty and Women's Roles in Five Indian Villages*. Geneva, ILO. Based on people's participation in research.

DAUBER, Roslyn and Melinda L. CAIN (eds) (1979), *Women and Technological Change in Developing Countries*. Boulder, CO: Westview Press. Important collection of commentary and case studies by major women in development scholars.

DA VANZO, Julie and Donald Lye Poh LEE (1983), 'The compatibility of child care with market and nonmarket activities: preliminary evidence from Malaysia', in M. Buvinic et al., 1983.

DAWN (Development Alternatives with Women for a New Era)

(1985), *Development, Crises, and Alternative Visions: Third World Women's Perspectives*. DAWN, c/o Institute of Social Studies Trust, SMM Theatre Crafts Building, 5 Deen Dayal Upadhyay Marg, New Delhi 110 002.

DEERE, Carmen Diana and Magdalena LEON de LEAL, (1980), *Women in Agriculture: Peasant Production and Proletarianization in Three Andean Regions*. Geneva: ILO World Employment Programme Working Paper 10/13. These data are summarized in 'Peasant production, proletarianization, and the sexual division of labor in the Andes', in Beneria, 1982. Documents women's farm and household work.

de SOTO, Hernando (1985), 'Legacy of mercantilism stymies market creativity in Peru', *Wall Street Journal*, 4 January 1985.

de TREVILLE, Diana (1982), *Food Production and Distribution: Rural Marketing Systems in Egypt*. Cairo: The Ford Foundation. Provides data on women's work in the dairy industry.

DEWEY, Alice (1962), *Peasant Marketing in Java*. New York: Free Press of Glencoe.

DEY, Jennie (1984), *Women in Food Production and Food Security in Africa*. Rome: FAO.

DIXON, Ruth (1982), 'Women in agriculture: counting the labor force in developing countries', *Population and Development Review*, 8 (3): 539–66.

DIXON-MUELLER, Ruth (1985), *Women's Work in Third World Agriculture*. Geneva, ILO. Definitive study explaining under-counting of women farmers.

DJAMIJA, Jasleen (1984), 'Income-generating activities for rural women in Africa: some successes and failures'. In *Rural Development and Women in Africa*. ILO: Geneva.

EARTHSCAN (1981), 'Press Briefing Document No. 35' London: International Institute for Environment and Development. A primer on urban problems, readable, with tables but no bibliography.

EDWARDS, Melvin R. (1980), *Jamaican Higglers: their Significance and Potential*. Centre for Development Studies Monograph 7. Swansea, UK: University College of Swansea. A thorough investigation of higglers which traces their historical roots, discusses the differences between country higglers, stallholders and itinerants, and places his observations into existing literature.

EL-SANABARY, Nagat M. (ed.) (1983), *Women and Work in the Third World: The Impact of Industrialization and Global*

Economic Interdependence. Berkeley, CA: Center for the Study and Advancement of Women.

ENGELLAU, Patrik and Claes SJOBERG (1984), *The Informal Sector and the Memo Movement: Ideology Hand in Hand with Necessity*. Stockholm: Aspen Institute Nordic Countries Office. Summarizes reasons for the growing informal sector in Europe.

EPSTEIN, T.S. and R.A. WATTS, (eds) (1981), *The Endless Day*. New York: Pergamon. Details on the lives of Asian rural women, written by young Asian women scholars who lived for extended periods of time in villages and acted as liaison with local extension workers in order to involve rural women in development programmes.

ETIENNE, Mona and Eleanor LEACOCK (eds) (1980), *Women and Colonialization: Anthropological Perspectives*. New York: Praeger. A compelling set of papers concerning the effects of colonial intrusion on women's roles among Indians in North and South America, Africans of Kenya and Ivory Coast, and indigenous groups in Australia and on two Pacific islands.

EVANS, Margaret I. (1984), *Firewood versus Alternatives: Domestic Fuel in Mexico*. Oxford: Commonwealth Forestry Institute Occasional Paper 23.

EVENSON, Robert E. (1983), 'The allocation of women's time: an international comparison', *Behavior Science Research*, 17 (3/4): 196–215.

FARBMAN, Michael (ed.) (1981) *The PISCES Studies: Assisting the Smallest Economic Activities of the Urban Poor*. Washington, DC: US Agency for International Development. A superb report and assessment of projects designed to assist microentrepreneurs in the urban slums of Asia, Africa and Latin America.

FAROUK, A. (1980), *Time Use of Rural Women: A Six-Village Survey in Bangladesh*. Dhaka: Bureau of Economic Research, Dhaka University.

FISSEHA, Yacob and Omar DAVIES (1981), *The Small-Scale Manufacturing Enterprises in Jamaica: Socioeconomic Characteristics and Constraints*. East Lansing, MI: Michigan State University Working Paper 16.

FLORA, Cornelia B. (1985), 'Women and Agriculture', *Agriculture and Human Values*, special issue on women and agriculture, 2 (1) (Winter): 5–12. Excellent introduction to the issue that any women's work in agriculture is undervalued or ignored.

FOLBRE, Nancy (1984), 'Household production in the Philippines: a non-neoclassical approach', *Economic Development and Cultural Change*, 32 (2): 303–30. Shows the relevance of the bargaining power approach in understanding household production and household decisions in the Philippines.

FOOD AND AGRICULTURE ORGANIZATION (FAO) (1979), *Women in Food Production, Food Handling and Nutrition*. Rome: FAO Food and Nutrition Paper 8.

FAO (1983), *Time Allocation Survey: A Tool for Anthropologists, Economists and Nutritionists*, Rome: Food Policy and Nutrition Division, November.

FAO (1984), *Women in Food Production*, a report of an experts' consultation held in Rome in December 1983. Rome: FAO.

FAO (1986), *Population and the Labour Force in Rural Economies*. Rome: Economic and Social Development Paper 59.

FORTMANN, Louise (1985), 'Seasonal dimensions of rural social organization', *Journal of Development Studies*, 21 (3): 377–89.

FRASER, Peter H. and William R. TUCKER (1981), 'Case studies: Latin America', in Farbman, 1981.

FURNIVALL, J.S. (1939), *Netherlands India: A Study of Plural Economy*, Cambridge: Cambridge University Press.

GEERTZ, Clifford (1963), *Peddlers and Princes: Social Development and Economic Change in Two Indonesian Towns*. Chicago: Chicago University Press.

GEERTZ, Hildred (1961), *The Javanese Family*. New York: Free Press.

GERMAIN, Adrienne (1976/77), 'Poor rural women; a policy perspective', *Journal of International Affairs*, 30 (2): 161–72. Important analysis of the deteriorating position of rural women in developing countries, with suggestions for programmatic change. Author was able to put her ideas into practice as officer of the Ford Foundation.

GERRY, Chris (1978), 'Petty production and capitalist production in Dakar: the crisis of the self-employed', *World Development*, 6 (9–10).

GIBB, Arthur Jr (1982), *Employment Generation and the Small Business Sector in the Regions of the Philippines: A Survey Report*. Philippines: USAID.

GLAVANIS, Kathy R.G. and Pandeli M. GLAVANIS (1983), *The Sociology of Agrarian Relations in the Middle East: The Persistence of Household Production*, Trend Report of *Current Sociology*, 31 (2).

GODDARD, Victoria (1981), 'The leather trade in the bassi of Naples', *IDS Bulletin*, 12 (3).

GOLDSCHMIDT-CLERMONT, Luisella (1982), *Unpaid Work in the Household*, Geneva: ILO.

GREENSTREET, Miranda (1981), 'When education is unequal', *IDS Bulletin*, 12 (3).

GUGLER, Josef and William G. FLANAGAN (1978), *Urbanization and Social Change in West Africa*. Cambridge: Cambridge University Press.

GUYER, Jane (1978) *Women's Work in the Food Economy of the Cocoa Belt: A Comparison*. Brookline, MA: Boston University African Studies Center, working paper 7. Insightful research in Cameroon and Ghana.

GUYER, Jane (1980), *Household Budgets and Women's Income*. Brookline, MA: Boston University African Studies Center, working paper 28.

GUYER, Jane I. and Pauline E. PETERS (1984), *Conceptualizing the Household: Issues of Theory, Method and Application*, report of a workshop held at Harvard University, November 1984. Charlottesville, VA: Teleprint Publishing. Efforts to push economists to abandon their tendencies to treat the household as a unit.

HACKENBERG, Beverly and Gerald BARTH (1984), 'Growth of the bazaar economy and its significance for women's employment: trends of the 1970s in Davao City, Philippines', in Gavin Jones (ed.), *Women in the Urban and Industrial Workforce: South and Southeast Asia*. Canberra: The Australian National University. Distributed by the University of Hawaii Press, Honolulu. Both the article and the volume exemplify the growing interest in considering women's problems separately from men's.

HAGEN, Margaret (1974), *Notes on the Public Markets and Marketing System of Managua, Nicaragua*. Managua: Instituto Centroamericano de Administracion de Empreses.

HANSEN, Karen Tranberg (1987), 'Urban women and work in Africa: a Zambian case', *Transafrica Forum*, 4 (3).

HART, Gillian (1980), 'Patterns of household labour allocation in a Javanese village', in Binswanger et al., 1980.

HARTMANN, Heidi, Robert KRAUT and Louise TILLY (1986), *Computer Chips and Paper Clips*. Washington, DC: National Academic Press. Report by the Panel on Technology and Women's Employment of the National Research Council. A definitive study of the impact of technological change on women's employment in the USA.

HAZELL, Peter B.R. and Ailsa ROELL (1983), 'Rural growth linkages: household expenditure patterns in Malaysia and Nigeria'. Research Report No. 41. Washington, DC: IFPRI.

HELLINGER, Douglas and Fred O'REGAN (1985), 'Introduction to Africa case studies', in Ashe, 1985a, Vol. II.

HELLINGER, Douglas, Fred O'REGAN, Stephen HELLINGER and Blane LEWIS, (1985), 'The small business scheme of the National Council of Churches of Kenya', in Ashe, 1985b, Vol. II.

HENN, Jeanne Koopman (1986), 'Intra-household dynamics and state policies as constraints on food production: results of a 1985 agroeconomic survey in Cameroon'. Gainsville, FL: Conference on Gender Issues in Farming Systems Research and Extension, University of Florida.

HERSCHOVITZ, Linda (1985), 'The fruits of ambivalence: China's urban individual economy', *Pacific Affairs*, 58 (3), 23 pp. The individual economy is not growing quickly (from 150,000 to 3 million in the past 6 years) because of social prejudice against the self-employed. The problem which the government now faces is how to encourage entrepreneurs and simultaneously control their activities without scaring them off.

HEYZER, Noeleen (1984), 'Towards a framework of analysis', *IDS Bulletin*, 12 (3).

HOFMANN, Michael (1986), 'The informal sector in an intermediate city: a case in Egypt', *Economic Development and Cultural Change*, 34 (2). Notes difference in size and type of enterprise in a city and the surrounding rural areas; sees limited absorption for future unemployed.

HOLTON, Gerald (1973), *Thematic Origins of Scientific Thought: Kepler to Einstein*. Cambridge, MA: Harvard University Press.

HORN, Nancy E. (1987), 'Urban food provisioning and the role of market women in Harare, Zimbabwe'. Paper presented at the meetings of the Association for Women in Development, 15 April, Washington, DC.

HOSKINS, Marilyn (1975), 'Vietnamese women: their roles and their options', in Dana Rapheal (ed), *Being Female: Reproduction, Power, and Change*, World Anthropology Series. The Hague: Mouton.

HOUSE, William J. (1984), 'Nairobi's informal sector: dynamic entrepreneurs or surplus labor?' *Economic Development and*

Cultural Change, 32 (2): 277–302. House examines the results of a 1977 survey of Nairobi's informal sector, and concludes that it is not as exploitative as some scholars say. He paints an optimistic picture of this informal sector, since the rural income forgone would not have been as much as its urban alternative.

HUNT, Robert W. (1983), 'The evaluation of small-scale enterprise programs and projects: issues in business and community development', AID Evaluation Special Study No. 13. Washington, DC: US Agency for International Development, 52 pp.

HUNT, Robert W. (1985a), 'Searching for benefits'. AID Evaluation Special Study No. 28. Washington, DC: US Agency for International Development.

HUNT, Robert W. (1985b), 'Private voluntary organizations and the promotion of small-scale enterprise'. AID Evaluation Special Study No. 27. Washington, DC: US Agency for International Development, 47 pp. An examination of the role of international PVOs in small enterprise development which concludes that PVOs are helpful for the type of entrepreneurial activity required in the majority of development settings, mainly because of their 'staying power' and motivated staff willing to work with the poor and to accept small salaries.

HUSTON, Perdita (1978), *Message for the Village*. New York: The Epoch B Foundation. Interviews with village women about their problems and their view of change.

HYDEN, Goran (1980), *Beyond Ujamaa in Tanzania*, Los Angeles: University of California Press. A longtime observer produces a flawed report by utilizing only a male perspective.

ILLICH, Ivan (1982), *Gender*. New York: Pantheon. In a long, provocative essay, Illich argues that economic contraction is a prerequisite for peace between the sexes. Interpreted as a justification of returning to the sexual division of labour; most women disparage the book.

INTERNATIONAL LABOUR OFFICE (ILO) (1972), *Employment, Incomes and Equality: A Strategy for Increasing Productive Employment in Kenya*. Geneva: ILO. The baseline descriptors for assessing informal sector.

ILO (1984a), *Urbanisation, Informal Sector and Employment: A Progress Report on Research, Advisory Services and Technical Cooperation*. Geneva: ILO.

ILO (1984b), *Group-Based Savings and Credit for the Rural Poor*. Geneva: ILO. Papers presented at a seminar in Bangladesh by individuals involved in group-based savings in South and Southeast Asian countries.

ILO (1985a), *Women at Work*, 1 (85) entitled 'Women in a changing world: a decade of action', a special issue summarizing world trends of employment opportunity. Geneva: ILO.

ILO (1985b), *Resources, Power, and Women*. Proceedings of workshops in Asia and Africa which assess income-earning activities for rural women. Case studies for these meetings were edited by S. Muntemba, 1985. Geneva: ILO.

ILO (1985c), *The Challenge of Rural Poverty*. Geneva: ILO. A review of research and technical co-operation carried out by the Rural Employment Policies Branch concerning agrarian institutions and rural employment.

INTERNATIONAL RESEARCH AND TRAINING INSTITUTE FOR THE ADVANCEMENT OF WOMEN (INSTRAW) (1986), Expert Group Meeting on Measurement of Women's Income and Their Participation in the Informal Sector.

INSTRAW and United Nations Research and Training Institute for the Advancement of Women (1985), *Women in Economic Activity: A Global Statistical Survey (1950–2000)*. Bibliography; appendices on unemployment, male–female wages. Useful collection of data.

ISLAM, M. Nural, Richard MORSE and M. Hadi SOESASTRO (1984), *Rural Energy to Meet Development Needs: Asian Village Approaches*. Boulder, CO: Westview Press. Pathbreaking book which combines results of studies with discussion on various methodologies used to gather data on the lives of rural women and men, particularly participatory and action research. While the focus of this collection is on rural fuelwood use in Bangladesh, Philippines, Indonesia, Thailand and India, information collected includes time-use as well as an analysis of why many new household energy technologies failed.

ISLAM, Shamina (1982), *Exploring the Other Half: Field Research with Rural Women in Bangladesh*. Dhaka, Women for Women: House 67, Road 4, Dhanmondi Residential Area, Dhaka 5.

JAHAN, Rounaq and Hanna PAPANEK (eds) (1979), *Women and Development: Perspectives from South and Southeast Asia*. Dhaka: Bangladesh Institute of Law and International Affairs. Papers presented at a seminar in Dhaka, March 1977, delineating the issues of policy, programming, research and methodology as they relate to women in Asia.

JAIN, Devaki, with Nalini SINGH and Malini CHAND (1979a), *Women's Quest for Power*. Bombay: Vikas Publishing House. An assessment of women's activities designed to provide income or preserve security, from a Gandhian viewpoint.

JAIN, Devaki, N. SINGH and M. CHAND (1979b), 'Women's work: methodological issues', in Jahan and Papanek, 1979.

JAQUETTE, Jane (1982), 'Women and modernization theory: a decade of feminist criticism', *World Politics*, 34 (2). Excellent summary of various approaches by women scholars to development theory.

JACQUETTE, Jane (1983), 'The impact of modernization on women in Latin American agriculture', in Spindel et al., 1984.

JELLINEK, Lea (1977), 'The life of a Jakarta street trader', in J. Abu-Lughod and R. Rays (eds), *Third World Urbanization*. New York: Methuen. Anthropological study of a female street foods vendor, her relations with husbands and police and her struggle to survive.

JONES, Gavin (ed.) (1984), *Women in the Urban and Industrial Workforce: Southeast and East Asia*. Canberra: Australian National University. An important collection of studies on urban working women, their lives and their families, which deserves wider readership. Distributed by the University of Hawaii Press.

JULES-ROSETTE, Bennetta (1982), 'Women's work in the informal sector: a Zambian case study', Working Paper 3, East Lansing, Michigan State University.

JUMARI, Usha (1987), 'The future of home-based production', in Singh and Kelles-Viitanen, 1987.

KANDIYOTI, Deniz (1985), *Women in Rural Production Systems: Problems and Policies*. Paris: UNESCO.

KILBY, Peter and David D'ZMURA (1984), *Searching for Benefits*. Washington DC: Office of Private and Voluntary Co-operation.

KIRLOSKAR CONSULTANTS (1985), 'Technology adaptation in plastic processing industry in the informal sector: a case study of India'. Urbanization, informal sector and employment working paper, World Employment Program, ILO, Geneva.

KUJORE, Olufemi O. (1985), 'Street foods and street food vendors in Ile-Ife, Nigeria'. Ile-Ife, Nigeria: Department of Nursing, University of Ife, and Chevy Chase, MD: Equity Policy Center. Summary of findings of a study undertaken by university faculty with EPOC consultation.

KUJORE, Olufemi O., Tola O. PEARCE and V. AINA AGBOH

(1986), 'Effects of road clearance on the street foods enterprise in Ile-Ife'. Ile-Ife, Nigeria: University of Ife. Continuation of the street foods project begun in consultation with the Equity Policy Center.

KUMAR, T.M. Vinod (1984), 'Integrated rural development planning and energy priorities: participatory surveys in India micro regions', in Islam et al., 1984.

KUSTERER, Ken (1985), 'Her work, his leisure: the exploitation of surplus value on the domestic mode of production'. Paper read at the Society for the Study of Social Problems, Washington, DC, in August. Discusses problems of evaluating household work and setting them within a Marxist analysis.

LASSEN, Cheryl A. (1984). 'A systems approach for the design and evaluation of PVO small enterprise development projects'. Report of a working group of PVO and donor representatives. Washington, DC: Partners for Productivity.

LE COUR GRANDMAISON, Colette (1969), 'Activités économiques des femmes Dakaroises', *Africa*, 39. An exemplary study in an area neglected by French scholars.

LEIDHOLM, Carl (1973), *Research on Employment in the Rural Nonfarm Sector in Africa*. East Lansing, MI: Michigan State University. Outline of objectives and problems to be addressed in long-term study.

LEIDHOLM, Carl and Enyinna CHUTA (1976), *The Economics of Rural and Urban Small-Scale Industries in Sierra Leone*. African Rural Economy Paper 14. East Lansing, MI: Michigan State University. An early study in the series; one that establishes the importance of small-scale industries outside major urban areas.

LEWIS, Barbara (1976), 'The limitations of group action among entrepreneurs: the market women of Abidjan, Ivory Coast', in N. Hafkin and E. Bay (eds), *Women in Africa: Studies in Social and Economic Change*. Stanford, CA: Stanford University Press. A careful observer of contemporary market women.

LEWIS, Barbara, (ed.) (1981), *Invisible Farmers: Women and the Crisis in Agriculture*, Washington, DC: Office of Women in Development, Agency for International Development. An important collection prepared for the World Conference on Agrarian Reform and Rural Development, Rome, 1979. Papers address issues of agricultural work in developing countries and the United States; also included are chapters on extension, land rights, social forestry, off-farm jobs, education and women's organizations.

LEWIS, John P. and Valeriana KALLAB (eds) (1986), *Development Strategies Reconsidered*. New Brunswick NJ: Transaction Books for the Overseas Development Council, Washington, DC. Useful and concise update and analysis of mainstream development theory and practice.

LILLY, Marjorie (1984), 'Assisting the smallest economic activities of the urban poor'. A Report on the third in a series of PISCES Workshops, Washington, DC. Cambridge, MA: ACCION International/AITEC.

LITTLE, Kenneth, (1973), *African Women in Towns: An Aspect of Africa's Social Revolution*. Cambridge: Cambridge University Press. An early book presenting data on women in urban areas which goes far beyond the stereotype of market traders to look at many aspects of life in towns.

LOMNITZ, Larissa (1977), *Networks and Marginality: Life in a Mexican Shantytown*. New York: Academic Press. An exposition of a multitude of networks which help the poor to survive.

LONG, Norman (ed.) (1984), *Family and Work in Rural Societies: Perspectives on non-wage labour*, London: Tavistock. Focus is on persistence of traditional patterns of household production in capitalist economies.

LOZA, Sarah (1985), *Street Foods and Beverages in Minia City*. Final report of the SPAAC/EPOC study of street foods in Egypt.

MARUM, Elizabeth (1981), *Evaluation of CARE's Women's Development Program*. Dhaka: CARE, Women's Development Program.

MATHUR, Om Prakash and Caroline O.N. MOSER (1984), 'The urban informal sector: an agenda for research', *Regional Development Dialogue*, 5 (3): ix–xxi. More research is called for on the relationships of city size to the informal sector, and on the informal sector in centrally planned economies.

MAZUMDAR, D. (1975), *The Urban Informal Sector*. Washington, DC: World Bank Staff Paper 211.

McCORMACK, Jeanne, Martin WALSH and Candance NELSON (1986), *Women's Group Enterprises: A Study of the Structure of Opportunity on the Kenya Coast*. Boston, MA: World Education, Inc. A report of Tototo Home Industries and its work with 45 village groups. Focus is on group enterprises to which women contribute for presumed long-term return. Based on group activity for community betterment, there seems some problem with distribution of profits. Having income does not seem to affect women's status in Kenya.

McCORMICK, Dorothy (1986), 'Small manufacturing enterprise in Nairobi'. Department of Economics working paper. Nairobi: University of Nairobi.

McGEE, T.G. and Y.M. YEUNG (1977), *Hawkers in Southeast Asian Cities: Planning for the Bazaar Economy*. Ottawa: International Development Research Centre. Early classic which encouraged IDRC to work in urban areas.

McGREEVEY, Paul W. (ed.) (1980), *Third World Poverty*. Lexington, MA: D.C. Heath & Co., Lexington Books.

McSWEENEY, Brenda (1979), 'Collection and analysis of data on rural women's time use', in Zeidenstein, 1979.

MEAD, Margaret, (ed.) (1955), *Cultural Patterns and Technical Change*. New York: Mentor, The New American Library.

MELLOR, John (1986), 'Agriculture on the road to industrialization', in Lewis and Kallab, 1986.

MENCHER, Joan P. (1987), 'Women's work and poverty: women's contribution to household maintenance in two regions of South India', in Bruce, 1987.

MERRICK, Thomas and Marianne SCHMINCK (1983), 'Households headed by women and urban poverty in Brazil', in Buvinic et al., 1983.

MIES, Maria (1982), 'The dynamics of the sexual division of labor and integration of rural women into the world market', in BENERIA (ed.), 1982.

MINTZ, Sidney (1971), 'Men, women, and trade', *Comparative Studies in Society and History*, 13 (3): 247–69. Useful assessment of market traders.

MIRALAO, Virginia A. (1982), 'Methodological issues in the collection and analysis of women's time-use data'. Kuala Lumpur: Asian and Pacific Development Centre, Integration of Women in Development Programme, Occasional paper 3.

MOHAN, Rakesh (1984), *An Anatomy of the Distribution of Urban Income: Two Cities in Colombia*. Washington, DC: World Bank Working Paper 650. Part of a major World Bank study of Colombia's urban problems.

MOLNAR, Augusta (1982), 'Women and politics: the case of the Kham Magar of Western Nepal', *American Ethnologist*, 9 (3).

MONSON, Jamie and Marion KALB (eds) (1985), *Women as Food*

Producers in Developing Countries. Los Angeles, CA: co-published by University of California Los Angeles African Studies Center, African Studies Association, and UEF International.

MOSER, Caroline (1980), 'Why the poor remain poor: the experience of Bogota market traders in the 1970s', *Journal of Interamerican Studies and World Affairs*, 22(3): 365–87. An anthropologist's view of economic power and differentiation within the informal sector in Bogota slums. Large-scale sellers maximize profits; small-scale sellers operate at such a low level that expansion is impossible.

MOSER, Caroline (1981), 'Surviving in the suburbios', *IDS Bulletin*, 12 (3): 19–29. Analysis of the function and importance of women's work in the survival strategies among low-income households in Guayaquil, Ecuador.

MOSER, Caroline (1984), 'The informal sector reworked: viability and vulnerability in urban development', *Regional Development Dialogue*, 5 (3): 135–78. Insisting on the interrelationships between concepts, methodologies and policy recommendations, Moser weaves a discussion of these topics into a review of selected informal sector studies. While clearly preferring the petty commodity production to the dualist approach, and anthropological methods to broad surveys, she contrasts and analyses the differing results obtained by various approaches and methodologies.

MOSER, Caroline and J. MARSIE-HAZEN (1984), *A Survey of Empirical Studies in Industrial and Manufacturing Activities in the Informal Sector in the Developing Countries*. London: Development Planning Unit.

MUNTEMBA, Shimwaayi (ed.) (1985), *Rural Development and Women: Lessons from the Field*, 2 Vols. Geneva: ILO. Studies of specific projects designed to improve rural women's income in Asia and Africa, written by women from those areas.

MUZAALE, Patrick J. and David K. LEONARD (1985), 'Kenya's experience with women's groups in agricultural extension: strategies for accelerating improvements in food production and nutritional awareness in Africa', *Agricultural Administration*, 19: 13–28. Finds that the poorest women cannot afford to contribute labour to workgroups.

NELSON, Joan M. (1979), *Access to Power*. Princeton, NJ: Princeton University Press.

NELSON, Nici (1979), 'How women and men get by: the sexual

division of labour in the informal sector of a Nairobi squatter settlement', in R. Bromley and C. Gerry (eds), *Casual Work and Poverty in Third World Cities*. New York: John Wiley and Sons.

NELSON, Nici (ed.) (1981), *African Women in the Development Process*. London: Frank Cass.

NOPONEN, Helzi (1987), 'Organizing women petty traders and home-based producers: a case study of Working Women's Forum, India', in Singh and Kelles-Viitanen, 1987.

NWAPA, Flora (1981), *One is Enough*. Enugu, Nigeria: Tana Press. A charming and insightful tale by Nigeria's first female novelist.

O'BARR, Jean (ed.) (1982), *Perspectives on Power: Women in Africa, Asia, and Latin America*. Durham, NC: Duke University Press.

O'BARR, Jean et al. (1986), 'Reflections on Forum '85 in Nairobi, Kenya: voices from the International Women's Studies Community', *SIGNS*, Spring 11 (3). A collection of commentaries from around the world.

OKONJO, Kamene (1983), 'Sex roles in Nigerian politics', in Oppong, 1983.

OPPONG, Christine (ed.) (1983), *Female and Male in West Africa*. London: Allen and Unwin. Chapters by women and men from North and South dealing with changes in the informal relationships between women and men as a result of modernization.

O'REGAN, Fred M. and Douglas A. HELLINGER (1981), 'Case studies: Africa', in Farbman, 1981.

OWENS, Naomi and Naseem HUSSAIN (1984), *Street Foods in Bangladesh*. Chevy Chase, MD: Equity Policy Center. Part of EPOC's series of studies; this was done in the small administrative centre of Manikganj.

PALA-OKEYO, Achola (1980), 'Daughters of the lakes and rivers: colonialization and land rights of Luo women', in M. Etienne and Eleanor Leacock (eds), *Women and Colonization*. New York: Praeger.

PALMER, Ingrid (1985), *The Nemow Case*, W. Hartford, CN, Kumarian Press. A classic study of the negative impacts of largescale development projects on women, in this case a resettlement scheme in Kenya.

PAPANEK, Hanna (1976), 'Women in cities: problems and perspectives', in Tinker and Bo Bramson 1976.

PAPANEK, Hanna (1982), 'Men can't handle money but women can be trusted: earning and spending in an Indonesian city'. Paper for conference, Colombia University, on *Women and Income.* Findings from survey of middle-class women in Jakarta in 1973–4 shows that 43.3 percent of the women who earned money are self-employed/housewives commercializing domestic skills. Women holding jobs outside the homes differ from these self-employed. Ethnicity/culture shows some variance in employment patterns. Husbands gave conditional approval of job-holding: if it did not interfere with family responsibilities.

PEARCE, Tola Olu (1984), 'The place of street foods in the urban diet: a survey of Ile-Ife, Nigeria'. Paper at Africa Studies Association meetings, Los Angeles, October. Available from Department of Sociology/Anthropology, University of Ife, Ile-Ife, Nigeria, and Chevy Chase, MD: Equity Policy Center.

PELLOW, Deborah (1978), 'Work and autonomy: women in Accra', *American Ethnologist*, 5 (4): 770–85.

PELUSO, Nancy (1984), 'Occupational mobility and the economic role of rural women'. Population Studies Report Series 39. Jogyakarta, Indonesia: Gadja Mada University.

PETRITSCH, Machtild (1981), 'Women and development in Ghana'. Paper prepared for an Expert Group Meeting on Women and the International Development Strategy. Vienna: UN Social and Humanitarian Affairs Division.

PHONGPAICHIT, Pasuk (1982), *From Peasant Girls to Bangkok Masseuses*. Geneva, ILO: Women, Work and Development, 2. Disturbing study of prostitution and how the wages of these women support their families in northeast Thailand. Based on interviews of the girls and of their families in the rural areas. Author suggests low agricultural prices and sex tours exacerbate the trade.

PICASSO, Estrella (1986), 'Las Alimentadoras de Pueblo: vendedoras ambulantes de alimentos preparados'. Grupo de Trabajo: Servicios Urbanos y Mujeres de Bajos Ingresos — SUMBI. Lima, Peru: SUMBI.

PORTES, A., S. BLITZER and J. CURTIS (1986), 'The urban informal sector in Uruguay: its internal structure, characteristics, and effects', *World Development*, 14 (6).

POSNER, Jill (1983), 'The development of numerical cognition: cross-cultural perspectives', in H. Ginsburg (ed.), *The Development of Mathematical Thinking*. New York: Academic Press.

POSNER, Jill (1984), *Street Foods in Senegal*. Chevy Chase, MD:

Equity Policy Center. One of EPOC's series of studies, this one done in the provincial town of Ziguinchor.

PRAKASH, Aditya (1972), 'Rehri — the mobile shop of India', *Ekistics*, 34: 204.

PRATES, Suzana (1986), 'Reproduction, production and women's labour activities in the home', in *Women in Development: Perspectives from the Nairobi Conference*. Ottawa: International Development Research Centre (IDRC), Manuscript Report.

REDDY, Amulya K.N. (1980), *Rural Energy Consumption Patterns: A Field Study*. Bangalore, India: Application of Science and Technology to Rural Areas (ASTRA), Indian Institute of Science.

REINING, Priscilla et al. (1977), *Village Women: Their Changing Lives and Fertility*. Washington, DC: American Association for the Advancement of Science. An attempt to link status with fertility in Kenya, Mexico, and the Philippines.

RICHARDSON, Harry W. (1984), 'The role of the urban informal sector: an overview'. *Regional Development Dialogue*, 5 (3): 3–40. A superb review of recent literature organized as authors relate to the continuing debates about the informal sector: definition; size; links with the formal sector; income; skills and training; longevity; and the importance of the sector in cities of varying sizes. After underscoring the importance of the informal sector, he concludes with a series of policy recommendations.

ROBERTSON, Claire (1987), 'Food distribution and gender in Africa', *Transafrica Forum*, 4 (3).

ROGERS, Susan G. (1983), 'Efforts toward women's development in Tanzania: gender rhetoric vs. gender realties', *Women and Politics*, 2 (4).

ROMATET, Emmanuel (1983), 'Calcutta's informal sector: theory and reality', *Economic and Political Weekly*, 18 (50). Reviews theory and then tests it against studies of various small enterprises: tailoring, tanneries, plastics, and slim industries in a basti of Howrah. Argues for more associations to exert pressure on the formal sector.

RONDINELLI, Dennis (1986), 'The urban transition and agricultural development: implications for international assistance policy', *Development and Change*, 17: 231–63.

RONDINELLI, Dennis and K. RUDDLE (1978), *Urbanization and Rural Development*. New York: Praeger.

ROSALDO, Michelle Zimbalist and Louise LAMPHERE (eds) (1974), *Women, Culture, and Society*, Stanford: Stanford

University Press. Significant collection of essays, especially those exploring the dual private/public nature of women's lives.
ROSTOW, W.W. (1960), *The Stages of Economic Growth: A Non-Communist Manifesto*, Cambridge: Cambridge University Press.
ROTBLAT, Howard (1974), 'Social organization and development in an Iranian provincial bazaar', *Economic Development and Cultural Change*, 23: 292–305.
SAVARA, Mira (1981), 'Organizing the Annapurna', *IDS Bulletin*, 12 (3).
SCHILDKROUT, Enid (1983), 'Dependence and autonomy: the economic activities of secluded Hausa women in Kano', in Oppong (ed.), 1983.
SCHMINK, Marianne (1986), 'Women in the urban economy of Latin America', in M. Schmink et al., (eds), *Learning About Women and Urban Services in Latin America and the Caribbean*. New York: The Population Council.
SCHMINK, Marianne, Judith BRUCE and Marilyn KOHN (eds) (1986), *Learning about Women and Urban Services in Latin America and the Caribbean*, New York: The Population Council. Pathbreaking collection reviewing urban women's special concerns about housing, food and services.
SCHULER, Margaret (1986), *Empowerment and the Law: Strategies of Third World Women*. Washington, DC: OEF International, 1815 H St. NW, 20005. Short essays by women around the world clearly show the relationship between law and development.
SCHUSTER, Ilsa (1972), 'Marginal lives: conflict and contradiction in the politicisation of female traders in Lusaka, Zambia', in Bay, 1972.
SCIENCE POLICY RESEARCH UNIT (SPRU) (1982), *Micro-electronics and Women's Employment in Britain*. Brighton: University of Sussex.
SCOTT, Gloria L. and Marilyn CARR (1985), *The Impact of Technology Choice on Rural Women in Bangladesh: Problems and Opportunities*, World Bank Staff Working Paper 731. Washington, DC: The World Bank.
SCOTT, James C. (1976), *The Moral Economy of the Peasant: Rebellion and Subsistence in Southeast Asia*. New Haven: Yale University Press.
SEAGAR, Joni and Ann OLSON (1986), *Women in the World: an International Atlas*. New York: Simon & Schuster. Covers basic data, then adds feminist issues including sex for sale, patriarchy

and abortion. Excellent graphics.

SEBSTAD, Jennifer (1982), *Struggle and Development Among Self-employed Women: A Report on the Self-employed Women's Association, Ahmedabad, India*. Washington, DC: US Agency for Development.

SEN, Amartya (1983), 'Economics and the family', *Asian Development Review*, 1 (2): 14–26. A leading economist looks at differential treatment of women in the family.

SETHURAMAN, S.V. (ed.) (1981), *The Urban Informal Sector in Developing Countries: Employment, Poverty and Environment*. Geneva: ILO. A significant volume in which the editor summarizes the findings of a series of ILO-funded studies assessing the links between employment promotion in the urban informal sector and improvement of the urban physical environment. Nine case studies are included from Africa, Asia and Latin America.

SETHURAMAN, S.V. (1985), 'Informal sector in Indonesia: an assessment of policies', Technical Report 2. Geneva: ILO.

SHIELDS, Nwanganaga (1980), *Women in the Urban Labor Markets of Africa: The Case of Tanzania*. World Bank Staff Working Paper No. 380, 131 pp. A review of recent shifts in the pattern of female migration and of the jobs they find in the cities. It explores reasons why there are very few women in the formal sector of the urban economy even though they make up 50 percent of the urban work age population.

SIMMONS, Emmy B. (1975), 'The small-scale rural food-processing industry in Northern Nigeria', *Food Research Institute Studies*, 14 (2): 147–61. Early study documenting that women in seclusion engage in economic activities.

SIMON, Lawrence H. and David F. RUCCIO (1986), 'Methodological aspects of Marxian approach to development: an analysis of the modes of production school', in Wilber, 1986.

SINGH, Andrea Menefee (1980), 'Women in the marketplace: hawkers and street peddlers'. Paper presented at the annual meeting of the Indian Sociological Society, Meerut, UP, 1–3 November.

SINGH, Andrea Menefee and Alfred de SOUZA (1980), *The Urban Poor: Slum and Pavement Dwellers in Major Cities of India*. New Delhi: Manohar Publishers.

SINGH, Andrea Menefee and Anita KELLES-VIITANEN (1987), *Invisible Hands: Women in Home-Based Production*. New Delhi: Sage. An important collection of a dozen studies on a long-neglected topic. This volume reports on studies, primarily by Asian scholars, of both traditional and modern home production in India, Bangladesh and Sri Lanka.

SIVARD, Ruth Leger (1985), *Women . . . a World Survey*. World Priorities, Box 25140, Washington, DC 20007, USA. Prepared for the UN Women's Conference, Nairobi, 1985. Basic information on work, education, health and laws.

SMITH, C. and Bruce TIPPITT (1982). *Study of Problems Related to Scaling Up Micro-Enterprise Assistance Programs: Phase I*. Boston: Trade and Development International Corporation.

SOW, Fatou (1986), *Les femmes et les projets d'énergie au Sénégal: impact sur le travail féminin et le bien-être familial*. Geneva, ILO: Programme Mondial de L'Emploi.

SPINDEL, Cheywa, Jane JAQUETTE and Mabel CORDINI (1984), *A Mulher Rural e Mudancas no Processo de Producao Agricola*. San José: Costa Rica, Instituto Interamerican de Cooperacao para a Agriculture (IICA). Papers in Spanish and Portuguese presented at a seminar on 'The Changing Roles of Women and Men in Modernizing Agriculture', Säo Paulo, Brazil, September 1983, organized by the Equity Policy Center with Fundacao Carlos Chagas.

STOLER, Ann (1977), 'Class structure and female autonomy in rural Java', in Wellesley Editorial Committee, 1977. Data indicate that the poorer the family the more important is the woman's income to its survival.

SUDARKASA, Niara (aka Gloria MARSHALL) (1973), *Where Women Work: A Study of Yoruba Women in the Marketplace and in the Home*. Ann Arbor, MI: Museum of Anthropology, University of Michigan, Anthropological paper 53.

SULLEROT, Evelyne (1971), *Women, Society, and Change*. New York: McGraw-Hill, World University Library. Explains her view of the origins of female subordination.

SZANTON, Cristina (1972), *A Right to Survive: Subsistence Marketing in a Lowland Philippine Town*. University Park and London: Pennsylvania State University Press.

SZANTON, Cristina and Napat SIRISAMBHAND (1986), *Thailand's Street Vending: The Urban Informal Sector and Traditional Fast Foods*. Report on joint CUSRI (Chulalongkorn University Social Research Institute) EPOC study project completed in Chonburi. Chevy Chase, MD: EPOC.

TADESSA, Zenebeworke (1982), 'The impact of land reform on

women: the case of Ethiopia', in Beneria, 1982.

TAYLOR, Alicia, Donna McFARLANE and Elsie LeFRANC (1986), 'The higglers of Kingston', in M. Schmink et al., 1986.

TEILHET-WALDORF, S. and W.H. WALDORF (1983), 'Earnings of self-employed in an informal sector: a case study of Bangkok'. *Economic Development and Cultural Change*. 31 (3). Important study which disaggregates data by gender.

TENDLER, Judith (1983), *Ventures in the Informal Sector, and How They Worked Out in Brazil*. Evaluation Special Study 12. Washington, DC: US Agency for International Development.

TIMBERG, Thomas and C.V. AIYAR (1984), 'Informal credit markets in India', *Economic Development & Cultural Change*, 33 (1).

TINKER, Irene (1981a) 'A feminist view of Copenhagen', *SIGNS*, 6 (3). This article sparked a series of letters to the editor, some of which were published in *SIGNS* 6 (4) and 7 (3), and responded to in 8 (2). At issue was the realistic scope of women's issues.

TINKER, Irene (1981b) 'New technologies for food-related activities: an equity strategy', in Dauber and Cain, 1981. A plea to technologies to relieve the long working day of women in near-subsistence societies.

TINKER, Irene (1983), 'Women in Development', in I. Tinker (ed.), *Women in Washington: Advocates for Public Policy*. Beverly Hills, CA: Sage. History of passing and implementing the Percy amendment.

TINKER, Irene (1984), *The Real Rural Energy Crisis*. Chevy Chase, MD: Equity Policy Center. Also published in the series *Human Energetics*, Vol. 11. New Delhi: Wiley Eastern for the Energy Research Group of the International Development Research Centre, Ottawa, Canada. Neither new cookstoves nor the planting of trees have worked as strategies to address the growing desertification in many parts of the world. Argues that the wrong questions were addressed, that the solutions were not set into the context of the time-consuming drudgery which characterizes women's lives in subsistence economies.

TINKER, Irene (1976), 'The adverse impact of development on women'. In I. Tinker and M. Bo Bramsen (eds), *Women and World Development*, New York: Praeger for Overseas Development Council, Washington, DC. Published in Spanish as *Las Mujeres en el Mundo de Hoy*. Buenos Aires: Editorial Faterna, 1981. Commission papers and workshop reports of an international seminar held prior to the International Women's Year Conference in Mexico, June 1975. Lays the base for the women in development movement.

TINKER, Irene and Hyoung CHO (1981), 'Women's participation in community development in Korea', in Man-Gap Lee (ed.), *Toward a New Community Life: Reports of International Research Seminar on the Saemaul Movement*. Seoul, Seoul National University Institute of Saemaul Undong Studies. How government-sponsored women's clubs allowed women to organize outside the household, and the important consequences.

TINKER, Irene and Monique COHEN (1985), 'Street foods as a source of income for women', *Ekistics*, 310 (Jan./Feb.). Results of the Street Foods project which focus on women; part of a special issue on women in honour of the end of the UN Decade for Women.

TINKER, I., W. COUSINS, P. REINING and W. SCHWIDLER (1974), *Culture and Population Change*. Washington, DC: American Association for the Advancement of Science. Report of the Advisory Committee on Cultural Factors in Population Programs for presentation at the World Conference on Population, Bucharest. State of the art summary.

TINKER, Irene and Jane JAQUETTE (1987), 'UN Decade for Women: its impact and legacy', *World Development*, 15 (3) (March). An analysis of the politics of UN conferences and how women utilized three conferences and a decade to infuse women's concerns in the UN agenda.

TINKER, Irene with Laura T. RAYNOLDS (1982), *Integrating Family Planning and Women's Enhancement Activities: Theory and Practice*. Chevy Chase, MD: Equity Policy Center. A review of income-generating activities in Egypt and Bangladesh, set in a worldwide review.

TINKER, Irene with Monique COHEN and Coralie TURBITT (1985), *Utilizing the Street Food Trade in Development Programming*. Chevy Chase, MD: Equity Policy Center. Final report of the first round of country studies which emphasizes how the research findings might be incorporated into programmes from rain-fed agriculture to credit.

TOKMAN, Victor E. (1978), 'An exploration into the nature of informal–formal sector relationships', *World Development*, 6 (9–10).

TRAGER, Lillian (forthcoming), 'A re-examination of the urban informal sector in West Africa', *Canadian Journal of African Studies*. Finds less exploitation of informal sector enterprises in Africa than in Latin America. Emphasizes backward linkages to rural producers.

UCHENDU, Victor (1964), *The Iqbo of Southeast Nigeria*. New York: Holt Rinehart and Winston.

UNITED NATIONS (UN) (1984a), *World Survey on the Role of Women in Development*. Report of the Secretary-General to the World Conference to Review and Appraise the Achievements of the United Nations Decade for Women: Equality, Development and Peace. A/CONF.116/4. Picture of women's status based on reports from all UN member countries.

UN (1984b), *Compiling Social Indicators on the Situation of Women*. New York: Statistical Office, F.32, DIESA.

UN (1984c), *Handbook of Household Surveys*. New York: Statistical Office, F.31, DIESA.

UN (1984d), *Improving Concepts and Methods for Statistics and Indicators on the Situation of Women*. New York: Statistical Office, F.33, DIESA.

UN (1984e), *World Survey on the Role of Women in Development: Report of the Secretary-General*. World Conference to Review and Appraise the Achievements of the UN Decade for Women, A/CONF.116/4, December.

UN (1985), *Forward Looking Strategies*... World Conference to Review and Appraise the Achievements of the United Nations Decade for Women: Equality, Development and Peace, A/CONF.116/12.Rev.1. Major political document for the conference, July.

UNITED NATIONS BRANCH FOR THE ADVANCEMENT OF WOMEN (UN/BAW) (1980), 'Review of Recent United Nations System Studies on the Effective Mobilization of Women in Development'. Vienna, IESA/BAW/WP.1, February.

UNITED NATIONS CENTRE FOR HUMAN SETTLEMENTS (Habitat) (1984), *Small-scale Building Materials Production in the Context of the Informal Economy*. Nairobi: UNCHS Habitat.

UNITED NATIONS DEVELOPMENT PROGRAMME (UNDP) (1980), *Rural Women's Participation in Development*. Evaluation Study No. 3. New York. An insightful review of concepts; regional views on major themes of the 1980 Mid-Decade Conference on Women: health, employment, and education; and four country case studies: Rwanda, Syria, Indonesia and Haiti. A staff paper under the direction of Ulla Olin.

UNDP (1985), *Women's Participation in Development: an Inter-organizational Assessment*, Evaluation Study No. 13. New York. Updating of the 1980 Study No. 3, which increased scope to all women and included programmes of other specialized agencies more explicitly. Democratic Yemen is the alternative case study for the West Asia region. Exists in a long and short form (which contains only the findings from the case studies).

US AGENCY FOR INTERNATIONAL DEVELOPMENT (1985), *Report on the Workshop on Private Voluntary Organizations and Small-Scale Enterprise Development*. AID Program Evaluation Discussion Paper No. 22. 17 pp. Workshop held 31 October to 2 November 1983, in Washington, DC.

US BUREAU OF THE CENSUS (1985), *Women of the World*, series: four regional areas with interpretation and a summary of data on 120 developing countries. Published for the Office of Women in Development, USAID. Basic data on population, distribution, marital status, fertility, work and education. Superintendent of Documents, US Government Printing Office, Washington DC 20402, USA.

US CONGRESS, HOUSE OF REPRESENTATIVES (1986), 'Pros and cons of home-based clerical work'. Hearings before the Committee on Government Operations. Washington, DC.: Government Printing Office.

UNIVERSITY OF MINNESOTA (1983), *Sex/Gender Division of Labor: Feminist Perspectives*. Selected papers from conference, with implicit comparisons of US historical trends to current changes in developing countries today. Challenges the assumption that women are economically marginal because of their biological roles.

VAN RYZIN-HAVENS, Lani and Ruth KOBIA (1987), *The Trickle Up Program in Kenya: An Evaluation Report*. Nairobi: the Ford Foundation.

VARGAS LLOSA, Mario (1987), 'In defense of the black market', *New York Times Magazine Section*, 22 February.

VERCRUIJSSE, Emile (1983), 'Fishmongers, big dealers and fishermen: cooperation and conflict between the sexes in Ghanaian canoe fishing', in Oppong (ed.), 1983.

VINING, Daniel R. (1985), 'The growth of core regions in the third world', *Scientific American*, 252 (4), April.

WALKER, S. Tjip (1987), *Making Agricultural Extension Work with*

Women: The Efforts of the MIDENO Project in Cameroon. Chevy Chase, MD: EPOC. Analysis and history of an exemplary extension service.

WALSH, A.C. (1982), *Street Vending in Port Moresby 1982*. A Report to the National Capital District Interim Commission. Dept of Geography, University of Papua, New Guinea.

WEIDEMANN, Wesley, C., George PULVER, Laurene SEMENZE and Diana de TREVILLE (1987), *Small Business Development Project, Phase I, Jordan*. Washington, DC: ARIES Project, Robert Nathan Associates.

WELLESLEY EDITORIAL COMMITTEE (1977), *Women and National Development: The Complexities of Change*. Special issue of *SIGNS*, 3 (1).

WHITE, Benjamin (1976), 'Population, involution and employment in rural Java', *Development and Change*, 7: 267–90.

WHITE, E. Frances (1982), 'Women, work, and ethnicity: the Sierre Leone case', in Bay, 1982.

WHITE, Sylvia (1985), 'African women as small-scale entrepreneurs: their impact on employment creation', in Monson and Kalb, 1985.

WILBUR, Charles K. (ed.) (1986), *The Methodological Foundations of Development Economics*, special issue of *World Development*, 14 (2). Presents current thinking of liberal, dependency and Marxist schools of thought.

WILSON, Fiona (1985), 'Women and agricultural change in Latin America: some concepts guiding research', *World Development*, 13 (9): 1071–35.

WILSON, Francille Rusan (1982), 'Reinventing the past and circumscribing the future: *Authenticité* and the negative image of women's work in Zaire', in Bay, 1982.

WIPPER, Audrey (ed.) (1972), *The Roles of African Women: Past, Present and Future*, special issue of the *Canadian Journal of African Studies*, 6 (2). A landmark collection of essays which has provided the base for much of the subsequent research.

WIPPER, Audrey (1982), 'Riot and rebellion among African women: three examples of women's political clout', in Jean O'Barr (ed.), *Perspectives on Power*. Durham: Duke University Press.

WONG, Luke S.K (1971), 'The Aplichau squatter area', in *Asian Urbanization*, Hong Kong: University Press.

YOUNG, Kate and Caroline MOSER (eds) (1981), *Women and the Informal Sector*. Brighton, England: Institute of Development Studies, University of Sussex *Bulletin*, 12 (3). An important collection of case studies and analytical essays which document the critical role women play in a variety of informal-sector activities. The editors' final essay draws a comparison between the informal sector and women's unpaid housework, while being oppressed by society or their husbands, or both.

YOUSEF, Nadia H. and Carol B. HETLER (1984), *Rural Households Headed by Women: A Priority Concern for Development*. Geneva, ILO World Employment Programme Working Paper 10/31. Summary of current fragmentary knowledge of topic; suggested research agenda.

ZEIDENSTEIN, Sondra (ed.) (1979), *Learning About Rural Women*, special issue of *Studies in Family Planning*, 10 (11). Series of short articles summarizing state of the art at the time, including time-use budgets.

Gender, delinquency, and the Great Depression: A test of power-control theory
Bill McCarthy and *John Hagan*

Labour surplus and local labour markets in the Nova Scotia fish processing industry
Gene Barrett and *Richard Apostle*

State constructed industrial relations and the social reproduction of production: the case of the Canadian IDIA
Bob Russell

A comparison of the mobility structures of francophones and anglophones in Québec: 1954, 1964, 1974
François Béland

T.F. McIlwraith and Anthropology at the University of Toronto 1925–63
John Barker

Class voting and class consciousness in Canada
Jon Pammett

REVIEW ESSAY
New introductory sociology textbooks
J. Graham Morgan

PHILOSOPHY AND SOCIAL CRITICISM

International Quarterly Journal

11:2 (Winter 86) Jürgen Habermas:
"The New Obscurity: The Crisis of the Welfare State and the Exhaustion of Utopian Energies"

11:3 (Summer 86) Jacques Taminiaux:
"Phenomenology and the Problem of Action"

11:4 (Fall 86) Cornelius Castoriadis:
"The Nature and Value of Equality"

Volume 12 (1987)
Agnes Heller: "Hannah Arendt on the 'Vita Contemplativa'"

Ferenc Feher: "Freedom and the 'Social Question'; Hannah Arendt's Theory of the French Revolution"

Special Issue on Foucault

David M. Rasmussen, Editor
Subscription Rates $15 Student / $20 Individual/ $55 Institutions / $3.95 Single Issues / $5.95 Double Issues / Send check or money order to Philosophy & Social Criticism, Department of Philosophy, Boston College, Chestnut Hill, MA 02167 USA

CURRENT SOCIOLOGY
La sociologie contemporaine

Information for Contributors

Each issue of this unique journal is devoted to a comprehensive Trend Report on a topic of interest to the international community of sociologists. Authors review current trends and tendencies in all areas of sociological work — theories, methods, concepts, substantive research and national or regional developments. The aim is to review new developments, to discuss controversies, and to provide extensive bibliographies. From time to time, Commentaries on Trend Reports are published in subsequent issues of the journal.

If you would like to propose a Trend Report, please send the Editor an outline or prospectus of the proposed issue and a brief *curriculum vitae*. A style sheet and detailed notes for the guidance of authors are available. Contributions may be written in English or French.

Correspondence concerning Trend Reports should be addressed to the Editor: James A. Beckford, Department of Sociology & Social Policy, University of Durham, Durham DH1 3JT, England.

All subscription enquiries should be addressed to the Publisher:

SAGE Publications
28 Banner Street, London EC1Y 8QE

THE SHAPING OF SOCIAL ORGANIZATION

Social Rule System Theory with Applications

TOM R. BURNS &

HELENA FLAM

The Shaping of Social Organization introduces a new theory — social rule system theory — and applies it to the analysis of major institutions of modern social life. The book presents social rule system theory as a framework with which to investigate these institutions. It clarifies the principles behind their formation, maintenance and transformation.

The book draws on a wide range of case studies: from artificial insemination to energy forecasting and administration. It provides insights into wage negotiation systems, the emergence of informal rule systems, and the multiple sources of social and structural incoherence in modern societies. It advances a distinctive approach to the study of actor-structure dynamics, placing itself in a scholarly tradition developed by major thinkers such as Weber, Giddens and Harre.

December 1986 • 384 pages
Cloth (8039-8027-2)

SAGE Publications Ltd
28 Banner Street, London EC1Y 8QE
SAGE Publications Inc
2111 West Hillcrest Drive, Newbury Park, CA 91320, USA